The Hamlyn All-Colour Dictionary

Harold E. Priestley M.A., M.Ed., Ph.D.

Hamlyn

London · New York · Sydney · Toronto

First edition 1975
Second impression 1976
Published by
The Hamlyn Publishing Group Limited
London · New York · Sydney · Toronto
Astronaut House, Feltham, Middlesex, England
© Copyright The Hamlyn Publishing Group Limited 1975
ISBN 0 600 31744 7
Printed in Spain by Mateu-Cromo

How to use this book

How often do you use a dictionary? I'm sure that whenever you do you rarely feel it is worth while to study it for more than a few minutes. You probably use one simply to find the meaning of a word, or to help solve a crossword puzzle. This is a great pity, because words are fascinating things and are very important in our lives; we use them to let people know what we are thinking, and to show what we are feeling.

This dictionary has therefore been written with more than one idea in mind. The most important of course is to give the meanings of words. This book contains well over 5,000 main words, or head-words as they are called, with their meanings. Some of the words such as **act**, **bear**, **go**, **cross**, **frame** and so on, have so many meanings that they could only all be given in a very large book of many volumes, but this dictionary gives those most often met with, and they are numbered 1, 2, 3, 4 . . .

Words, like different parts of machines, are made to work for us, and the second use of a dictionary is to show how they can be put to work as moving parts of the machine called language. The simplest way of doing this is to put them into sentences which show how they are used. Some of the sentences in this book I have made up myself; some are quotations from great writers, especially from Shakespeare, who was the greatest sentence-constructor of all time. In all of them the words are working hard, describing things you see, things that are done, events of everyday life, giving scraps of information you may not have known before.

In these pages the headword is printed in **bold** type and it is followed by the same word in brackets, divided into parts or syllables. Sometimes two words may look alike, whereas in fact they are not pronounced in the same way at all, and have different meanings. In such cases stress marks are shown to help you; for example, **conduct** (cón-duct) and **conduct** (con-dúct) are two separate words with two separate meanings. Instructions are also given as to how to pronounce certain words, where there might be doubt as to how to do so. When the word is used as part of a sentence to show its meaning, it is printed in *italics*. Look, for instance, at the first word in the book, **abandon**, and see how this is done.

Some words have others made from them. **Electric**, for instance, is the root for **electrical**, **electricity**, **electrify** and **electrocute**. These are also in **bold** type and many have sentences to show their meaning. Thus the dictionary, though having over 5,000 headwords, gives the meanings of many more. When, however, a word connected with another has itself more than two meanings, it is made into a headword. Thus, **family** has five meanings, **familiar** has four meanings and has another word, **familiarity**, made from it, so both **family** and **familiar** are given as headwords.

Many words have beginnings, or prefixes, which alter their meanings. **Appear**, for instance, means 'to show itself'; **disappear** means the opposite; **reappear** means 'to show itself again'. **Un-** is a simple prefix meaning 'not', and so **unequal**, **unjust**, **unlike**, **unable** etc. all come under the same headword because they are so easy to understand. Where the meaning of a word beginning with **un-** is not so clear (**uncanny**, **uncouth**) it is treated as a separate headword.

The English language also contains many word-endings, called suffixes, and these change the meaning of the word. Take, for instance, **-able** (**adorable**), **-al** (**mechanical**), **-ion** (**confusion**). There are many others which are used in the same way to create new words.

A good game would be to take a simple word such as **care**, and see how many words you can make from it. Another useful game is to take a common word such as **head** or **shoot**, write down as many meanings of the word as you can think of, and then compare your answer with the entry in the dictionary.

There are many thousands more words in our language than appear here, but a study of what is in this book will teach you to understand, spell and use correctly those that you meet in everyday reading and conversation.

H. E. Priestley

abandon (a-ban-don) 1. leave for ever: The captain was the last to *abandon* ship. 2. give up: The attempt to rescue the climbers was *abandoned*.

able (a-ble) having strength, knowledge, skill or power: I am *able* to pay for this bicycle. – Strong men are *able* to lift heavy weights. **ability** the physical or mental power to do something: Has he the *ability* to pass the examination?

aboard (a-board) on or on to a ship or plane: 'You are now *aboard* the steamship *Alexander*,' said the captain.

aborigine (ab-o-rig-i-ne) one of a race of people living in a country from the earliest times. *Aborigines* have lived in Australia for at least 20,000 years.

about (a-bout) 1. around, everywhere, here and there: Don't leave litter *about*. – Stop rushing *about*! 2. almost: I've had just *about* enough of your rudeness! 3. a little more or a little less: This book has *about* a hundred pages. 5. around: When I reached the playground there was nobody *about*. 6. the other way: '*About* turn' means turn and face the other way.

above (a-bove) 1. overhead: He was surprised by a sudden cry from *above*. 2. higher than: The water rose *above* my waist. 3. greater in number, price than: The poor boy can't count *above* ten.

abroad (a-broad) 1. near and far: The news of the theft soon spread *abroad*. 2. to or in another country: We are going *abroad* for our holidays.

abrupt (a-brupt) 1. sudden: I came to an *abrupt* stop. 2. *abruptly* speaking in haste or without good manners: He answered *abruptly*, 'No!'

absence (ab-sence) 1. time spent away: Please look after my dog in my *absence*. 2. being without something or somebody: The trial could not be held because of the *absence* of the chief witness. **absent** away, not present: Why were you *absent* from school this morning?

absorb (ab-sorb) soak up, take up: Blotting paper *absorbs* ink. – Stamp collecting *absorbs* all my spare time. **absorbent** able to soak up: A sponge is *absorbent*.

absurd (ab-surd) foolish: He told me an *absurd* story about a dog that talked.

accept (ac-cept) 1. consent to receive: Though your payment is late, I *accept* it. 2. answer 'yes' to: I am delighted to *accept* your kind invitation. **acceptable** welcome, would be gratefully received: The gift of a piano is very *acceptable*.

accident (ac-ci-dent) something which happens and has not been expected: This morning's fog caused a number of *accidents* on the road. – Our meeting in the street was a lucky accident. **accidental** by *accident*: Our meeting was quite *accidental*.

accompany (ac-com-pa-ny) *accompanies, accompanied, accompanying* 1. go with: Our teacher will *accompany* us to the zoo. 2. play music with: If I sing, will you *accompany* me on the piano?

accordion (ac-cor-dion) a musical instrument which has bellows, and keys that look like piano keys.

account (ac-count) 1. explain or tell what has happened, give reasons: Nobody on the plane could *account* for the missing passenger. 2. A statement of money paid and received: The treasurer of our club keeps an *account* of all its funds. 3. explanation, report or description: You must give an *account* of all your movements. **on account of** because of: Our school has been closed *on account of* the bus strike.

accuracy (ac-cu-ra-cy) being correct, having no mistakes: Complete *accuracy* is needed in all these accounts. **accurate** correct, free from mistakes: Every answer must be *accurate*.

accuse (ac-cuse) say that somebody has done wrong: Why do you *accuse* my brother? He has been wrongly *accused*.

accustom (ac-cus-tom) become or make used to: I am not *accustomed* to cold weather but by taking walks I am *accustoming* myself to it.

ace 1. a card showing only one heart, diamond, spade or club: When I turned up the cards I found that I had all four *aces*. 2. a person who shows great skill, a champion: The motorcycling *ace* was the first to arrive at the winning post.

ache 1. be in lasting pain: I have walked until my feet *ache*. 2. a pain that lasts: Can anybody please cure me of this terrible tooth*ache*? (back*ache*, ear*ache*).

achieve (a-chieve) 1. get something done: Nothing is ever *achieved* without effort. 2. do something successfully, obtain by trying: The young commander has *achieved* much fame.

acid (ac-id) 1. sour: This lemonade is too *acid*; it needs more sugar. 2. a substance which burns or tastes sour: The *acid* burnt a hole in his coat.

acorn (a-corn) the seed of an oak tree.

acquaint (ac-quaint) make known to: Please *acquaint* us with what is to be done in this matter.—We are well *acquainted* though we are not friends. **acquaintance** a friend, friendship: Dr Brown is an *acquaintance* of mine.—'Should auld (old) *acquaintance* be forgot?' (Robert Burns)

acquire (ac-quire) obtain for oneself: If I could only *acquire* a good yacht I would sail round the world.

acre (a-cre) 4,840 square yards of land: 'For sale, large house with four bedrooms and one *acre* of garden.'

acrobat (ac-ro-bat) a person who can do clever tricks with his body: The *acrobats* at the circus walked the tightrope and performed on the trapeze.

across (a-cross) 1. from side to side: Here is a bridge *across* the river. 2. on or to the other side of: My uncle lives *across* the road.—Can you swim *across* this stream?

act 1. anything you do: Walking, running, writing and playing are all *acts*. **action** a single act: You will be sorry for your *actions*. – To help a blind man across the road is an *act* of kindness. 2. The main division of a play: Macbeth is killed in the last *act* of Shakespeare's play. 3. Take part in some kind of entertainment: I love *acting* more than anything else. 4. do, behave: Our lives are in danger; we must *act* quickly and *act* like men. **actor, actress** a person who takes part in plays. **active** always doing things. **activity** a hobby or occupation: In this club there are all kinds of *activities*.

acute (a-cute) 1. sharp, pointed: An *acute* angle is less than a right angle. 2. keen: A bloodhound has an *acute* sense of smell as well as *acute* hearing.

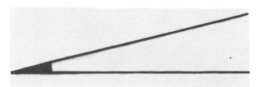

add join or put one thing or number with another: We *add* two to three to get five. – Don't *add* the sugar until the water boils. **addition** adding or something added: The grocer did a quick *addition*. – My baby brother is a welcome *addition* to our family.

address (ad-dress) 1. say something: The chairman stood to *address* the meeting. 2. direct to the attention of: Please *address* all complaints to the manager. 3. a speech or talk to an audience: Today's *address* will be on the dangers of smoking. 4. the place to which one's letters should be sent: My home *address* is 31 Field Road.

adenoids (ad-e-noids) growths at the back of the nose and in the throat which sometimes prevent breathing through the nose.

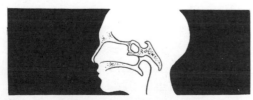

adhesive (ad-hes-ive) sticky: Gum is an *adhesive* substance. **adhesive tape** tape which is sticky on one side and is used for fastening parcels and bandages.

adjust (ad-just) change something to make it right: My bill has been wrongly added; will you please *adjust* it.

admiral (ad-mi-ral) a naval officer who commands warships: The *admiral* gave the order for the battle to begin.

admire (ad-mire) 1. think of a person with respect and wonder: Who can help *admiring* a champion athlete? 2. like and enjoy: Everybody *admired* the view from the top of the mountain. **admiration** respect, wonder, pleasure: We are filled with *admiration* for your courage.

admit (ad-mit) 1. let in: No dogs will be *admitted*. 2. confess: An honest man always *admits* his mistakes. **admission** being let in: All tickets show the price of *admission*.

adopt (a-dopt) 1. take the child from another family as a member of one's own family: We have *adopted* this little girl. She is our *adopted* daughter. 2. take an idea or a custom: Many foreigners living in England have *adopted* English manners.

adore (a-dore) 1. love and respect: My little brother *adores* his mother. **adorable** worthy of being *adored*: My kitten is an *adorable* little creature.

adult (a-dult) 1. a grown-up person: In ten years I shall be an *adult*. 2. grown-up ways: When you are older we hope you will behave in an *adult* manner.

advance (ad-vance) 1. move forward, go ahead: '*Advance*, men,' called the captain. 2. raise or rise: Shopkeepers are *advancing* their prices. 3. money paid before it need be paid: Unless I get an *advance* on my wages my money will not last the week.

advantage (ad-van-tage) something which helps: The long arms of the boxer are a great *advantage* to him. **take advantage of** profit by: You should *take advantage of* my advice.

adventure (ad-ven-ture) an exciting experience: Every boy longs for some kind of *adventure*.

advertise (ad-ver-tise) make something known to people by means of newspapers, posters, handbills, television or radio: If you want to sell your tennis racket, why not *advertise* it? **advértisement** a way of telling people: We have put an *advertisement* in the evening paper.

advice (ad-vice–rhymes with *ice*) opinions of one person as to what another person should do: If you follow the doctor's *advice* you will get well.

advise (ad-vise–rhymes with *size*) 1. offer an opinion: The motor mechanic *advises* a complete repair. 2. inform the public: A poster has appeared *advising* people of a water shortage.

aero (ae-ro) having to do with air or aircraft.

affair (af-fair) 1. something which happens: The visit of the Prime Minister was an important *affair*. 2. business of any kind: I put my *affairs* in order before leaving the country.

affect (af-fect) change, make a difference to: The sudden cold weather has *affected* his health.

affection (af-fec-tion) love: I will always think of you with great *affection*. **affectionate** loving: This letter is signed 'Your *affectionate* sister'.

afford (af-ford) have enough money or time for something: How much can you *afford* to spend on a radio?

afraid (a-fraid) feeling fear, frightened: 'Who's *afraid* of the big, bad wolf?'

after (af-ter) behind, following: 'They all ran *after* the farmer's wife.'–Spring is welcome *after* the cold days of winter. **afternoon** the time between noon and evening. **afterwards** at a later time: We will have dinner and go to the dance *afterwards*.

again (a-gain) one more time, another time: The headmaster cannot see you now, so please come *again*.–The policeman rang the doorbell *again* and *again*.

against (a-gainst) 1. touching: Don't lean *against* that post; it is not safe. 2. not agreeing with: He joined the army *against* his father's wishes. 3. in an opposite direction to: It is hard to run *against* the wind.

age 1. number of years a person has lived: Children may join this club at the *age* of eleven. 2. a time or period in history: Stone *Age* people used stone for making tools. 3. a time in one's life: When I was your *age* I could ride a bicycle. 4. grow old: Grandfather has *aged* this year; his hair has turned quite white.

agent (a-gent) 1. a person who manages the business of other persons for them: My brother is an *agent* for a timber company. **agency** a firm working as an *agent*: A travel *agency* arranges journeys and holidays. 2. a spy: This week an enemy *agent* has been arrested.

agitate (a-gi-tate) make trouble, cause anxiety: If you *agitate* the crowd there may be shooting. **agitator** someone who stirs up others to cause trouble: All the fighting was caused by *agitators*.

ago (a-go) in the past, time which has gone by: The meal was cooked an hour *ago*.—Long, long *ago* there lived a wicked witch.

agony (ag-o-ny) great pain: The little dog hurt its paw and howled in *agony*.

agree (a-gree) 1. say yes to: He *agreed* to sing in the choir. 2. have similar opinions: The workmen all *agreed* on the wages they wanted. 3. be equal to the same: We have added up the numbers and our answers *agree*. **agreeable** giving pleasure: This violin has an agreeable sound. **agreement** a promise or an arrangement: All the countries made an *agreement* not to go to war.

agriculture (ag-ri-cul-ture) growing crops for food and rearing animals on farms: How many people in this country make a living by *agriculture*? **agricultural** having to do with *agriculture*: The people of Great Britain buy many *agricultural* products from other countries.

ah an expression of happiness, sudden surprise, pity, sorrow or gladness: *Ah*, there you are!—*Ah*, you've made a big mistake.

ahead (a-head) 1. forward: 'Full steam *ahead*!' called the captain. 2. in front: Can you see clearly the way *ahead*? 3. before: The train arrived *ahead* of time.

aid 1. help: If you need him he will come to your *aid*.—We are collecting in *aid* of the homeless. 2. something which helps: My mother wears a *hearing aid*. **first aid** treatment given to the sick and injured before the doctor arrives: After the accident the ambulance men gave *first aid*.

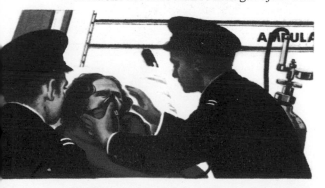

ail 1. be in trouble in body or mind: What *ails* you when you won't eat your dinner?—The children of these poor people are always *ailing*. **ailment** an illness: No doctor can cure every *ailment*.

aim 1. point, the act of pointing: He *aimed* at the target.—He took *aim* and fired. 2. intend: My sister *aims* to become a nurse. 3. a purpose: My brother's *aim* is to become a doctor.

air 1. a mixture of gases that surrounds the earth: Birds fly through the *air*.—Open the windows and let in the fresh *air*. 2. expose to fresh *air*: Mother *airs* the beds before she makes them.

aisle (rhymes with *mile*) a passageway between rows of seats: The bride walked up the *aisle* to the altar.

ajar (a-jar) open a little way: It is very cold in this room; there must be a door *ajar* somewhere.

alarm (a-larm) 1. a signal to warn of danger: If you hear footsteps, sound the *alarm*. 2. something which gives an *alarm*: The burglar *alarm* rang in the jewellery store.—Every morning the *alarm* clock sounds at seven. 3. to frighten: I was *alarmed* to hear the whistle.

alas (a-las) a word used mostly in stories to show sadness or pity: *Alas*, my dear brother is dead!

album (al-bum) a book with blank pages on which one can write or stick pictures and stamps: Will you please sign your name in my *album*?

alcohol (al-co-hol) a colourless, intoxicating liquid found in brandy, whisky, wine and beer: To drink too much *alcohol* makes one intoxicated or drunk. **alcoholic** containing *alcohol*; a person who cannot stop taking *alcoholic* drinks is often drunk.

alderman (al-der-man) *aldermen* a member of a town council who is elected by the other members.

ale a light-coloured beer.

alert (a-lert) quick to notice or understand things: It is the duty of a detective to be on the *alert* at all times.

algebra (al-ge-bra) a form of mathematics in which letters are used for numbers: When x equals 1, $2x$ equals 2.

alias (a-li-as) name taken by a person in addition to his own: This man's real name is John Smith but his *aliases* include Tim Brown and Bob Scott.

alibi (a-li-bi, rhymes with *sky*) evidence that one was in another place when a crime was committed: I have an *alibi*, sir. I was abroad at the time of the robbery.

alien (a-li-en) a person who lives in a foreign country without the rights of local citizens: A German living in England is an *alien*.

alike (a-like) very much the same, similar: The twins are as much *alike* as two peas in a pod.

alive (a-live) living, not dead: When we took the dog out of the river it was still *alive*.

all every bit of, the whole of, every one of: *All* my life I have wanted to ride a horse. – *All* my thoughts are of you. – What is good for one is usually good for *all*.

alley (al-ley) 1. a narrow roadway, usually between buildings: The back doors of these houses open on to an *alley*. 2. a smooth, enclosed pathway for bowling, a bowling *alley*.

alligator (al-li-ga-tor) a large, broad-snouted reptile related to the crocodile which lives in lakes and rivers in America and China.

allow (al-low) 1. permit, let: No dogs are *allowed* here. – *Allow* me to carry your bag! 2. agree to give: My father *allows* me ten pence a day to spend on fares. **allowance** a fixed amount of money granted: Family *allowances* are being raised this year; each family is to be *allowed* more money by the government.

ally (al-ly) *allies*, *allied*, *allying* join with another by making an agreement or treaty: In 1939 Great Britain and France were *allied* countries; they were *allies*. **alliance** an agreement made between two countries to help each other against a common enemy.

almighty (al-might-y) having all power, powerful: '*Almighty*, victorious, Thy great Name we praise' (from a well-known hymn).

almond (al-mond, pronounced *ah-mond*) The stone of the fruit of the *almond* tree used in making cakes and sweets.

almost (al-most) nearly: We have *almost* enough money to buy a new car.

alone (a-lone) 1. by oneself, without others being present: This carpenter lives *alone* in the wood. 2. only, by itself: Sunshine *alone* will not make plants grow; they need water too.—Leave that dog *alone*; he bites.

along (a-long) 1. from one end to the other, or part of the way: Let's take a stroll *along* the road. 2. onwards: 'Pass *along* the bus please,' called the conductor. 3. with (a person): I'm going to the fair; will you come *along*?

aloud (a-loud) loud enough to be heard easily: The drowning man called *aloud* for help.

alphabet (al-pha-bet) all the letters used in any language, put into a certain order: The English *alphabet*, sometimes called the ABC, has twenty-six letters. **alphabetical** in the order of the *alphabet*: Please arrange these names in *alphabetical order*.

already (al-read-y) by or before this time: When we left the house the clock had *already* struck five.

alsatian (al-sa-tian) a large dog which looks like a wolf, whose ancestors came from Alsace in France.

also (al-so) too, in addition: A good secretary must be able to write shorthand and *also* to spell correctly.

altar (al-tar) a table in a church where a priest performs the ceremony of Holy Communion: The vicar knelt at the *altar* to pray.

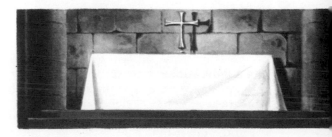

alter (al-ter) change, make different: If this suit does not fit you the tailor will *alter* it.— This list is full of mistakes; the numbers must be *altered*.

although (al-though) even if, though: *Although* his clothes are shabby, he is a very proud man.

altitude (al-ti-tude) height, distance above the earth or above sea level: We are now flying at a very high *altitude*.

altogether (al-to-geth-er) fully, entirely: This answer is not *altogether* correct; there is a number missing.

aluminium (a-lu-min-i-um) a dull, silver-coloured metal that is very light in weight. Parts of aircraft and cooking utensils are made of *aluminium*.

always (al-ways) at all times: *Always* think before you speak.

am one form of the word *be*, used with I; I *am* a pupil at a comprehensive school, and I *am* in the third form.

amateur (am-a-teur) a person who makes, or studies, anything for pleasure and not profit: This is the work of an *amateur* photographer.

amaze (a-maze) to surprise: I was amazed by the story in last week's magazine. **amazement** being surprised: He looked in *amazement* at the unexpected visitor.

ambassador (am-bas-sa-dor) an official of the highest rank sent by the government of one country to live in another country so as to keep contact with its government.

ambulance (am-bu-lance) a car built specially for carrying sick and injured people: The *ambulance* arrived within five minutes of the accident.

ambush (am-bush) a surprise attack from an enemy who has been in hiding: The invading army marched into an *ambush* and many men were killed.

amen (a-men) a word said at the end of a prayer meaning 'So be it.'

ammonia (am-mo-ni-a) a colourless gas with a sharp, strong smell: The fumes from the *ammonia* brought tears to his eyes.

ammunition (am-mu-ni-tion) gunpowder, shells, bullets and all other explosives used for shooting from guns and cannon: The French army surrendered for want of *ammunition*.

among (a-mong) 1. with many other things or people: I found this letter *among* his papers. 2. to each person or between all persons: The old man shared his land *among* his sons. **amongst** surrounded by: One boy amongst all others was especially talented.

amount (a-mount) 1. add up to or become: My gas bill *amounts* to more than usual this month. 2. total or whole quantity: The thief took with him a large *amount* of money.

ample (am-ple) more than enough: There is *ample* refreshment for all who come to the hotel. **amply** sufficiently: You will be *amply* rewarded for all you have done for me.

amputate (am-pu-tate) cut off (part of the body): The poisoned finger must be *amputated*. **amputation** a cutting off: This afternoon the surgeon has performed three *amputations*.

amuse (a-muse) entertain, make laugh or smile: The comedian *amused* the whole audience with his stories. **amusement** something which entertains: The cinema and television are favourite *amusements*.—To everyone's *amusement* the actor's wig fell off.

analyze (an-a-lyze) separate something into its parts to find out what it is made of: When the substance was *analyzed*, sulphur and charcoal were found. **analysis** an examination made by separating into parts: The *analysis* showed that the powder contained poison.

ancestor (an-ces-tor) a person who came before others in a family. Our fathers, mothers, grandparents and all before them are our *ancestors*.

anchor (an-chor) 1. a heavy metal hook on an iron chain used to hold a ship in place: When we drop *anchor*, it digs into the sea bottom and prevents the boat from moving; when we weigh *anchor* we pull it up again. 2. fasten in place with an *anchor*: The fishermen *anchor* their boats in the bay. 3. fix or fasten: The flagpole was *anchored* to the roof with bolts.

ancient (an-cient) of times long ago: People of *ancient* Britain lived in huts and dressed in skins.—Singing carols at Christmas is an *ancient* custom.

and 1. a word used to join words *and* groups of words: I put on my hat *and* left the room. 2. added to: Two *and* two make four.

angel (an-gel) 1. a messenger of God who comes from heaven: 'The *angel* of the Lord came down' (Christmas hymn). 2. a charming person or child: Isn't he a little *angel*!—Be an *angel* and bring my knitting.

anger (an-ger) bad temper, fury, displeasure: When he saw the ruins of his house he was filled with *anger*. **angry** showing resentment, feeling *anger*: 'Now the *angry* lion roars' (Shakespeare). **angrily** in an *angry* manner: The prisoner looked *angrily* about him.

angle (an-gle) a point where two lines meet, or the space between two lines meeting at a point: A triangle has three *angles*.—Here the two streets met at an *angle*.

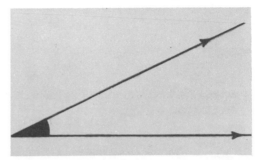

animal (an-i-mal) a living thing that can feel and move about. All birds, fishes and insects belong to the *animal* kingdom. A dog is a four-footed *animal*.

ankle (an-kle) the joint between the leg and the foot: The goalkeeper sprained his *ankle* and was carried off the field.

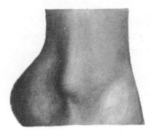

anniversary (an-ni-ver-sa-ry) a date of the year on which something important happened in an earlier year: October 21st is the *anniversary* of the Battle of Trafalgar.

annoy (an-noy) irritate, cause trouble to, make angry: I hope my singing is not *annoying* you. **annoyance** something which irritates, being irritated: I found to my great *annoyance* that I had no postage stamps.

annual (an-nu-al) 1. coming once a year: Christmas Day is an *annual* holiday. 2. by the year: The *annual* rent of this house is far too high. 3. a plant that lives for one year or less: Nasturtiums and dahlias are *annuals*. **annually** once a year: I pay my subscription for this magazine *annually*.

anorak (an-o-rak) a warm, waterproof jacket with a hood.

another (an-o-ther) 1. one more: Sing *another* song, please. 2. a different: That shirt is dirty; put *another* one on.

answer (an-swer) 1. a reply: A prize will be given for the correct *answer* to all ten questions. 2. go to see what is wanted or who is calling: Who will *answer* the doorbell? 3. be suitable: We have no hammer, but this large stone will *answer* our purpose.

antarctic (ant-arc-tic) near the South Pole: Penguins live in the *Antarctic*.

antelope (an-te-lope) an animal very much like a deer.

anthem (an-them) a song, usually a sacred one sung by a choir: The congregation remained seated while the *anthem* was sung.

anti (an-ti) against. Many words begin with this prefix: *anti*-freeze protects water in the car radiator, *anti*dotes are taken against the effects of poison, *anti*septics prevent the spread of germs by killing them.

antique (an-tique) something made long ago which is valuable because of its age: Here is a shop which sells nothing but *antiques*.

anxiety (anx-i-e-ty) *anxieties* fear of what may happen: I await your reply to my letter with great *anxiety*. **anxious** in some fear as to what may happen: Are you really so *anxious* about your health?

any (an-y) 1. no special or particular one: Pick *any* card you like. 2. not even one or a little: We don't want *any* milk today, thank you. 3. some: Did the doctor give you *any* pills? **anybody** any person: Is *anybody* there? **anyhow** in any way: The cell was locked and he couldn't get out *anyhow*. **anyone** any person: *Anyone* can go in without paying. **anything** something, one thing: Can you do *anything* about this broken window? No, I can't do *anything*. **anyway** no matter what happens: I don't think I can open the window, but I'll try *anyway*. **anywhere** in any place: I am looking for my watch but I can't find it *anywhere*.

apart (a-part) 1. away, off to one side: The teacher took him *apart* and spoke to him quietly. 2. one from the other: These twins are so much alike that you can't tell them apart. 3. to pieces: The officer took the gun *apart* to clean it. 4. distant: The two houses are at least a mile *apart*. **apartment** a room or group of rooms in a larger building forming a separate home: We have rented an *apartment* at the seaside.

ape 1. an animal that belongs to the monkey family. 2. imitate, copy: The man refuses to *ape* the manners of the rich.

apologize (a-pol-o-gize) admit making a mistake or doing wrong and say that one is sorry: You must *apologize* to your mother for being rude. **apology** words saying that one is sorry: 'Please accept our sincere *apologies*' (from a business letter).

apostle (a-pos-tle) a messenger, especially one of the twelve men chosen by Jesus Christ to spread his teaching: The *apostle* preached the gospel in many lands.

apparel (ap-par-el) clothes, dresses, suits: In the shop window was a notice, 'Women's *apparel* sold here.'

appeal (ap-peal) 1. ask, plead: We are *appealing* for money to rebuild our church. 2. the act of pleading: Our *appeal* is sure to succeed. 3. take a case to a higher court: The prisoner's lawyer asked permission to *appeal*. 4. attract, seem pleasant: The idea of a holiday in Spain *appeals* to me.

appear (ap-pear) 1. be seen, show itself: The football team did not *appear* until it was time for the game to start. 2. seem or look: This hole *appears* to have been made by moths. **appearance** the way a person or a thing looks: A coat of paint would improve the chair's *appearance*.

appetite (ap-pe-tite) a desire for food and drink: After a long walk you should have a good *appetite*. **appetizing** good to eat, looking or smelling delicious: From the kitchen came the *appetizing* smell of roast pork.

applaud (ap-plaud) clap the hands to show pleasure at the end of a speech or song: The orchestra was *applauded* for ten minutes. **applause** clapping and demonstration of approval after a performance.

apple (ap-ple) a round fruit that grows on a tree and is red, yellow or green.

apply (ap-ply) 1. put on: As this is a nasty cut, we will *apply* a plaster. 2. have to do with: The order to stay in school does not *apply* to those who finished their work. 3. ask to be given: All British citizens may *apply* for passports. **appliance** instrument that can be used for a special purpose: A new *appliance* has been invented for opening cans and bottles. **application** request: Entry forms for this examination may be had on *application* at the Town Hall.

appoint (ap-point) select, choose: This meeting is being held to *appoint* a new secretary. **appointment** an agreement to meet, a position: 1. I have an *appointment* with the dentist. 2. I am applying for the *appointment* of chief clerk.

apprentice (ap-pren-tice) a youth who has agreed to serve a master for a number of years in return for learning a trade.

approach (ap-proach) 1. come near: 'DANGEROUS CROSSROADS. *APPROACH* WITH CAUTION' (public notice). 2. the act of coming nearer: Most old people fear the *approach* of winter. 3. a way or road to a place: All the *approaches* to this camp are patrolled by guard dogs.

approve (ap-prove) give consent: All his actions have been *approved* by the chairman. **approval** satisfaction, agreement: When I explained what I had done the chief inspector expressed his *approval*.

apricot (ap-ri-cot) a pinkish-yellow fruit resembling a peach.

April (A-pril) the fourth month of the year.

apron (a-pron) an article of clothing worn over a dress to keep it clean: You should always wear an *apron* when you wash dishes.

aqua, aque (a-qua-) having to do with water.

arc part of the line which makes a circle.

arcade (ar-cade) a number of arches on columns making a covered way in which there may be shops; a covered way with shops.

arch 1. part of a building or wall curved like the arc of a circle. *Arches* may be round, pointed or shaped like horseshoes. 2. shape like an *arch*, curve upwards: The kitten *arches* its back when it is angry.

archbishop (arch-bish-op) a bishop of the highest rank: The *Archbishop* of Canterbury crowned Elizabeth II Queen of England in Westminster Abbey.

archer (arch-er) a person who shoots with bow and arrows. **archery** a pastime or sport in which one shoots with the bow.

architect (ar-chi-tect) someone who designs buildings and makes sure that the builders carry out his plans.

arctic (arc-tic) the most northerly part of the world nearest the North Pole.

are one form of the word *be*, used with *we*, *you* or *they*: We *are* your sons, you *are* our parents and they *are* our grandparents.

area (a-re-a) the size in any kind of measurement (square feet, square metres etc.) of a flat or curved space: Do you know how to find the *area* of a circle?

arena (a-re-na) a space, usually a circle, with seats all round, in which the Romans held games and fights, and where today bullfights are sometimes held.

argue (ar-gue) present reasons for or against a thing: If you wish to buy the house, why *argue* about the price? **argument** a discussion or debate: Why all this *argument*?

arise (a-rise) 1. get up: She *arose* early to water the flowers. 2. result: We have promised to meet whenever a difficulty *arises*.

arithmetic (a-rith-me-tic) the study of using numbers: In *arithmetic* we learn to add, subtract, multiply and divide.

ark the large boat which Noah built to save his family and the world's animals from the Great Flood. The story is told in the Bible—Genesis, chapters 6 to 9.

arm 1. take up weapons or *arms* to make war: Every country *arms* itself in self-defence. 2. one of the two upper limbs of a person: He held the parcel under his right *arm*. 3. a part at the side or end of a seat to support a person's *arm*: Who broke the *arm* of this chair?

around (a-round) 1. along all sides: It took ten minutes to walk *around* the school. 2. to another side of: Walk *around* the corner and tell me what you see. 3. about or near: It is dangerous to play *around* the fire. 4. in a circle: The dog ran *around* and *around*. 5. about a certain time: I'll meet you *around* nine o'clock. 6. In all directions: Look *around* you and see the wonderful view.

arrange (ar-range) 1. put into some order: We will *arrange* these books in alphabetical order of authors' names. 2. make plans: Everything has been *arranged* for the wedding. **arrangement** putting in order: My sister won the prize for flower *arrangement*.

arrears (ar-rears) money owing which has not been paid, or work which has not been done: The poor woman was in *arrears* with her rent.

arrest (ar-rest) 1. seize by authority of the law: The police have *arrested* a man; they have made an *arrest*. 2. stop: By the swift action of the driver, the train was *arrested* before it reached the barrier.

arrive (ar-rive) come, get to a place: I expect the train to *arrive* at six this evening. **arrival** the act of arriving: All is ready for the *arrival* of the mayor.

arrow (ar-row) 1. a pointed stick shot from a bow: The archer shot his *arrow* into the air. 2. a sign pointing in a certain direction: Follow the *arrows* and you are sure to arrive at the zoo.

arsenic (ar-sen-ic) 1. a substance used for making glass and in dyeing. 2. a white substance which is a deadly poison.

art 1. drawing, painting, sculpture: My brother teaches *art* in a college. 2. music, ballet, poetry, literature and the creation of anything that is beautiful: A hall has been built for concerts, plays and exhibitions of all the *arts*.

artery (ar-te-ry) *arteries* one of the tubes which carry blood from the heart to other parts of the body. **arterial** (of a road) specially made to carry traffic between large towns.

article (ar-ti-cle) 1. a thing, a separate part: In the shop were shoes, overcoats and other *articles* of clothing. 2. a piece of writing in a newspaper, magazine or book.

articulated (ar-tic-u-la-ted) having separate parts joined together. **articulated lorry** a tractor with a separate truck or wagon attached, designed so as to turn more easily.

artificial (ar-ti-fi-cial) not found in nature but made by man: How clever of you to make such beautiful *artificial* flowers.

artist (ar-tist) 1. a person who draws, paints pictures, makes models or statues. 2. a person who is very good at some art such as music and the writing of poems, novels or plays.

asbestos (as-bes-tos) a grey substance which does not catch fire. It can be made into garments and other articles which are fireproof.

ascend (a-scend) go up or come up: At the end of the valley the road began to *ascend*. **ascent** going or coming up: Sir Edmund Hillary and Tenzing were the first men to make the *ascent* of Mount Everest.

ash 1. the powdery remains of a thing that has been burnt: Please do not drop cigarette *ash* on the carpet. 2. a tree with silver-grey bark and hard wood. **'The Ashes'** a trophy gained by the cricket team winning a series of Test Matches between England and Australia.

ashamed (a-shamed) feeling unhappy because of having done wrong or having failed in some way: Please forgive me; I am very *ashamed* of myself.

ashore (a-shore) 1. to the shore: The ship was driven *ashore* by strong winds. 2. on land: The sailors stayed *ashore* for seven days.

aside (a-side) to one side, apart: He was tired of reading and laid his book *aside*.– Every week I put ten pence *aside* to buy records.

ask 1. call for something: The beggar *asked* me for money. 2. call for an answer: Don't *ask* silly questions. 3. invite: Have you been *asked* to the wedding?

asleep (a-sleep) 1. sleeping: Don't make a noise while the baby is *asleep*. 2. numb: I have been lying on my arm and it is *asleep*.

asphalt (as-phalt) a dark, sticky substance like tar. *Asphalt* is mixed with small pieces of stone to pave roads.

aspirin (as-pirin) a medicine that helps to relieve pain: I have a headache: please give me an *aspirin* tablet.

ass 1. a long-eared animal resembling a small horse, a donkey: Along came the woodcutter, riding on an *ass*. 2. A silly, stupid person: Be quiet and don't make an *ass* of yourself.

assassin (as-sass-in) a person who is paid to murder another person.

assemble (as-sem-ble) 1. come together: The children *assemble* each morning for prayers. 2. collect, put together: The workmen *assemble* the parts of a car. **assembly** a meeting: Morning *assembly* at school is at nine o'clock.

assign (as-sign) give work to be done: Our teacher will *assign* us our tasks for the day. **assignment** a piece of work: My own *assignment* is to count the banknotes.

assist (as-sist) give assistance or help: I cannot *assist* you in finding the lost property. **assistance** help: I can give you *assistance*. **assistant** a helper: My brother is chief *assistant* to the manager.

associate (as-so-ci-ate) 1. be in the company of somebody: You have been told not to *associate* with strangers. 2. think of two or more things (or persons) in connection: Everybody *associates* chips with fish. 3. a person who joins with another in some activity: Here is the list of my business *associates*. **association** a number of persons who join together in the same activity: Are you a member of the Automobile *Association*? **association football** a football game in which nobody but the goalkeeper may touch the ball with the hands.

asthma (asth-ma) an illness affecting the chest which makes breathing very difficult.

astonish (as-ton-ish) amaze, fill with surprise: We are quite *astonished* to see you looking so well. **astonishment** surprise, amazement: When the king saw the beggar girl dressed in fine clothes he could not hide his *astonishment*.

astro- (as-tro-) having to do with the stars. **astronomy** the study of the stars. **astrology** the telling of fortunes by the stars. **astronaut** a traveller in space.

asylum (a-sy-lum) 1. a place to which people go who for any reason are unable to look after themselves. 2. protection given by a country to a foreigner who has fled from his own country: Great Britain has given *asylum* to many people from other lands.

at 1. a place where or a time when things are done: Meet me *at* the bus stop *at* six. 2. in the direction of: Don't you dare throw stones *at* my dog!

ate past tense of the word *eat*: The puppy *ate* the bone.

athlete (ath-lete) a person who is good at some sport: He plays football, sprints and does the high jump; he is a great *athlete*. **athletic** strong, well-built and active; concerned with sports: He is an *athletic* young man and belongs to our *athletic* club. **athletics** games and sports needing physical fitness. What is your favourite form of *athletics*?

atlas (at-las) a book of maps.

atmosphere (at-mo-sphere) the air and gases which surround the earth: The rocket rose swiftly out of the earth's *atmosphere*.

atom (a-tom) the smallest particle of which anything is made up: Water is composed of *atoms* of hydrogen and oxygen. **atom bomb** one of the most powerful bombs ever made. **atomic pile** a great power station used for the making of electricity.

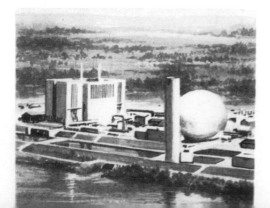

attach (at-tach) fasten or join: Please *attach* labels to your luggage. **attachment** 1. something fastened or used with: This sewing machine has several *attachments* so that it can do different kinds of work. 2. affection for someone.

attack (at-tack) 1. make a violent attempt to hurt a person or capture a place: We *attacked* the enemy fort by night. – A gang of roughs *attacked* the old man. 2. an attempt made against a person or a place: The fort will only be captured by making a bold *attack*.

attempt (at-tempt) 1. try to do something: You will break your leg if you *attempt* to jump from such a height. 2. a try, an effort: He hit the bullseye at the very first *attempt*.

attend (at-tend) 1. go to, be present at: The Queen *attended* the memorial service. 2. go with: Good luck *attend* you on your journey. **attend to** keep one's mind on, look after, serve: He will not learn if he does not *attend to* his lessons. – Are you being *attended to*, madam? **attendance** being present, or the number present: A doctor is in *attendance* at all hours. – There was a good *attendance* at the concert.

attention (at-ten-tion) notice: My *attention* was drawn to a figure moving in the darkness. – Please pay *attention* to me! **at attention** standing straight and still: The men stood *at attention* when the roll was called.

attic (at-tic) the room just under the roof of a house: We have made our *attic* into a bedroom.

attitude (at-ti-tude) what one thinks or feels about somebody or something: I do not like your insolent *attitude* towards your teacher.

attract (at-tract) draw or pull towards, get the attention of: A magnet *attracts* iron and steel.—This star singer is sure to *attract* a large audience. **attraction** pulling towards, a person who has power to *attract*: The new goalkeeper is a great *attraction*. **attractive** pleasant, noticed by all: What an *attractive* girl she is!

auction (auc-tion) a public sale at which goods are sold to the person who offers the highest price. **auctioneer** a person who sells goods by *auction*: 'Sold for ninety pounds,' called the *auctioneer*.

audible (au-di-ble) loud enough to be heard: Your voice is not *audible* over the telephone; speak more *audibly* please.

August (Au-gust) the eighth month of the year.

aunt the sister of one's father or mother. *Aunts* by marriage are the wives of the brothers of your father and mother.

author (au-thor) 1. the writer of a book, story, play or essay: Dickens is my favourite *author*. 2. the person who started something: We must find the *author* of this mischief and punish him.

authority (au-thor-i-ty) *authorities* 1. the power and right to give orders, and make others obey: The master had *authority* over the class. 2. a book or person who can give information: A good dictionary is the best *authority* on the spelling of words. 3. the person or persons in charge: All attacks of scarlet fever must be reported to the *authorities* (or the Health *Authority*).

autobiography (au-to-bi-og-ra-phy) *autobiographies* the story of a person's life written by himself or herself.

autograph (au-to-graph) the signature of a person: May I have your *autograph*, please?

automatic (au-to-ma-tic) 1. working by itself, mechanical: We used an *automatic* pump to clear the water from the pond. 2. done without thought: Breathing and the beating of the heart are *automatic*. 3. a small pistol: Turning round quickly, the enemy agent drew his *automatic*.

automobile (au-to-mo-bile) a car, bus or van that moves under its own power.

autumn (au-tumn) the third season of the year, coming between summer and winter.

avalanche (av-a-lanche) 1. a great mass of snow, ice or earth which slides down the side of a mountain: *Avalanches* come in spring when the snow is melting, sometimes burying whole villages. 2. a large amount: The speaker was met by an *avalanche* of protest.

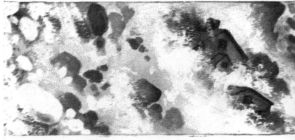

avenue (av-e-nue) 1. roadway with trees on both sides. 2. a street: My address is 4 Greenways *Avenue*. 3. a way, direction: We looked everywhere, but there was no *avenue* of escape.

average (av-e-rage) 1. the result when several quantities are added and the total divided by the number of quantities: In his last three matches the batsman scored 50, 72 and 127, *average*: 83. 2. usual, normal: To be a good engineer a man needs more than *average* ability.

avoid (a-void) keep or get away from: They kept in the shadow of the wall to *avoid* being seen.

await (a-wait) wait for: We *await* your reply. – Nothing but trouble *awaits* him.

awake (a-wake) *awakes, awoke, awaking* not asleep: The baby is *awake* and crying to be fed. **awaken** wake up a person: He was *awakened* suddenly by a loud cry.

award (a-ward) 1. give as a prize: An English scientist has been *awarded* the Nobel prize. 2. something, such as a medal, given as a prize: My mother received the highest *award* for baking.

aware (a-ware) conscious, able to notice things: Are you *aware* that you have taken my seat?

away (a-way) 1. to or at another place: Take *away* those dirty boots! – The swimming baths are only a mile *away*. 2. on and on, all the time: There he was, blowing *away* on his trumpet. 3. go to nothing: In a week the snow will all have melted *away*.

awe respect and wonder, sometimes with fear: The thought of climbing the high mountain filled them with *awe*. **awful** very bad: An *awful* accident has happened on the railway. – What *awful* writing; do it again! **awfully** very or very much: I'm *awfully* sorry.

awhile (a-while) for a short time, for a while: Lie down here and rest *awhile*.

awkward (awk-ward) 1. clumsy, not having much skill in movement: I feel so *awkward* in these new shoes. 2. not very safe or very convenient: Drive carefully; this is an *awkward* bend in the road. – Wednesday is an *awkward* day for shopping.

axe a tool with a sharp edge and a long handle: We need an *axe* to cut down this tree.

axle (ax-le) a bar on which the wheels of a vehicle are fastened and on which they turn.

B

babble (bab-ble) 1. talk like a baby in words not easy to understand: Why don't you stop *babbling* and speak clearly? 2. murmur, of a stream or brook: 'I *babble* over pebbles' (Tennyson, *The Brook*).

baboon (ba-boon) a large monkey which has a face like that of a dog.

baby (ba-by) *babies* a very young child: The *baby* was asleep in its mother's arms.

bachelor (bach-e-lor) 1. a man who has not been married: He is 35 and is still a *bachelor*. 2. a man or woman who has taken the first degree in a university: My sister is a *Bachelor* of Arts and my brother is a *Bachelor* of Science.

back 1. the rear side of the body: He jumped on to the horse's *back*. – I have strained my *back* through lifting heavy parcels. 2. the part of anything that is opposite the front: Please use the *back* door. 3. go or make go *back* part first: We have *backed* the car out of the garage. 4. a football player who helps to keep the ball away from his side's goal. 5. return: Give me *back* my freedom. 6. support with money or other help: If I want to buy this house my uncle will *back* me. **background** that part of a picture, a scene or a design which is behind all the rest, in the distance: The blue vase looked beautiful against the light grey *background*. **backwards** towards the back or rear. **backward** slow to learn: Why are you *backward* with your arithmetic?

bacon (ba-con) meat from the back and sides of a pig, preserved with salt: We have eggs and *bacon* for breakfast every morning.

bacteria (bac-te-ri-a) the simplest living beings, too small to be seen without a microscope: Some *bacteria* cause diseases.

bad 1. not good, evil, wicked: It is *bad* to take things which are not yours. 2. unlucky: 'That's just too *bad*!' he said, looking at his torn clothes. 3. severe: We have had a *bad* winter and there have been many *bad* colds about. 4. not of good quality, rotten: Every egg we bought was *bad*.

badge something worn to show that a person belongs to a certain class or group of people: The traffic warden wears a *badge*.—I have passed the examination for the gardener's *badge*.

badger (badg-er) a small grey animal which lives in holes in the ground and comes out at night.

badminton (bad-min-ton) a game played with rackets and shuttlecocks.

baffle (baff-le) 1. puzzle: His questions *baffled* me completely. 2. stop, prevent: The burglars were *baffled* when the alarm rang.

bag 1. a sack or container made of paper, cloth, leather, string or plastic: The grocer put the loaf into a paper *bag*.—'I did dream of money-*bags* tonight' (Shylock in Shakespeare's *Merchant of Venice*). 2. suitcase: Porter! Please take my *bags* to the taxi. **baggage** suitcases: My *baggage* was quickly put on the train. **bagpipe** a musical instrument played by blowing air into a bag and pressing it out through pipes.

bagatelle (bag-a-telle) a game like billiards played by striking a ball into holes at the end of the table farthest from the player.

bail (sometimes spelt **bale**) 1. scoop: The boat will sink if we don't *bail* out the water. 2. the two small pieces of wood laid across the stumps in cricket. 3. pay money, or the money paid to free a prisoner until the day he is to be tried.

bait 1. food or something looking like food to tempt fish or animals so that they can be caught: Worms and maggots are used as *bait* on the fisherman's hook. 2. use *bait* for catching something: The fisherman *baited* his hook with a fly.

bake 1. cook in an oven: Please *bake* a chocolate cake for my birthday. 2. harden by heat or become hard through heat: The sun has *baked* the earth hard. **baker** a person who makes bread and cakes. **bakery** a place where *baking* is done.

balance (bal-ance) 1. an instrument for weighing. 2. keep the weight or amount equal on both sides: The acrobat carries a long pole to *balance* himself on the tightrope. 3. power to keep steady or upright: He lost his *balance* and fell into the pond.

balcony (bal-co-ny) *balconies* a raised platform standing high up on the wall of a building: We had a fine view of the procession from the *balcony* of the Town Hall.

bald 1. having no hair or very little hair: More men than women go *bald* when they grow older. 2. without trees or bushes: High above the forest ran a range of mountains, their summits *bald* and bare.

bale (see **bail**) a large bundle of material packed for sending to another place: The men at the dock were loading *bales* of cotton. **bale out** to jump with a parachute out of an aircraft which can no longer fly.

ball 1. an object which is round and may be solid or hollow: We live on a great *ball* called the earth. – She is winding the wool into a *ball*. 2. a game played with a *ball*: We sent the children out to play *ball*. 3. a party where there is dancing: Cinderella danced with the prince at the *ball*.

ballast (bal-last) anything heavy which is carried in a ship to keep it steady and to stop it turning over.

ballet (bal-let – pronounced *bal-lay*) an entertainment which consists of dancing and music which usually tells a story.

balloon (bal-loon) 1. a bag filled with hot air or with a gas lighter than air, which makes it rise into the air when set free. 2. a small coloured bag of rubber which extends when filled with air and is used in children's games.

ballot (bal-lot) 1. a piece of paper given out in elections on which to mark the names of the people one wants to elect. 2. the act of marking the paper: This evening we will *ballot* for a new chairman. **ballot-box** the box in which ballot papers are put after voting.

balm a sweet-smelling ointment used to ease pain. **balmy** (of the weather) soft, gentle and warm: How pleasant are the *balmy* breezes of June!

balustrade (bal-us-trade) a row of short, upright posts which support a railing: He stood on the balcony with both hands on the *balustrade*.

bamboo 1. a tall, tropical or semi-tropical plant with long hollow stalks. 2. the stick of the *bamboo* plant, used to support other plants in the garden.

banana (ba-na-na) a fruit which is long and shaped like a finger: *Bananas* grow in warm climates.

band 1. a strip of cloth or other material: Her dress is trimmed with a *band* of black velvet. 2. a long narrow stripe different in colour from the background: This envelope has a black *band* all round the edge. 3. a group of persons, musicians, robbers or pirates. 4. come together in a group: Let us *band* ourselves together to fight for our rights. **bandage** a narrow strip of cloth for binding a wound: The cut was bleeding and a *bandage* had to be applied.

bandit (ban-dit) a robber, often one of an armed band which attacks travellers: Keep your rifles loaded, there are *bandits* in this valley.

bang 1. a loud, sudden noise: The door was closed with a *bang*. 2. make a loud sudden noise: Don't *bang* the door please. 3. a hard knock or blow: I fell to the ground and *banged* my elbow.

bangle (bang-le) a band of metal or other material worn as an ornament round the wrist or ankle.

banish (ban-ish) punish by sending away: 'O *banish* me, my lord, but kill me not' (Shakespeare, *Othello*).

banister (ban-is-ter) a handrail that runs down the open side of a staircase to prevent a person falling off: It is dangerous to slide down the *banisters*.

banjo (ban-jo) a musical instrument with strings which are plucked with the fingers.

bank 1. a long pile or heap: The workmen built a *bank* of earth to keep out the flood. 2. the land along the sides of a river, stream, lake or canal. 3. a company which keeps money for others; the building in which those employed by such a company work: I have ten pounds in the *bank*. – The merchant went to the *bank* to ask for a loan. 4. a box of some kind to keep money, sometimes shaped like a pig: How much have you in your piggy-*bank*? **banker** a man whose business is to manage a bank. **banknote** a piece of paper issued by a bank and used as money. **bankrupt** unable to pay one's debts so that one's goods have to be sold.

banner (ban-ner) a flag or a large sheet bearing words and carried on long poles: *Banners* are carried by those who walk in processions.

banquet (ban-quet) a meal, usually costly, provided on some special event: Every year in November the Lord Mayor holds a *banquet*.

banter (ban-ter) 1. joke with or tease a person: The audience laughed and began to *banter* with the comedian. 2. playful talk, merry teasing: It is time to stop all your *banter* and begin serious work.

baptize (bap-tize) 1. dip a person in water or pour water over him to make him a member of a Christian church. 2. give a name to a person in church: I baptize you Sarah Jane. **baptism** the act of *baptizing* a person.

bar 1. a long, solid piece of metal: The thief came out armed with an iron *bar*. 2. a piece: We need a new *bar* of soap. 3. a bank of sand across the mouth of a river: We took a pilot on board to guide the ship past the *bar*. 4. anything that stands in a person's way: A person's colour should never be a *bar* to success. 5. a line running up and down on written music dividing it into beats, or the number of beats: Most march tunes have four beats in a *bar*. 6. a railing in a court-room behind which the prisoner stands: The judge addressed the prisoner at the *bar*. 7. keep out: You have been *barred* from the team because of bad conduct. 8. a counter where drinks and meals are served: Quick lunches may be had at this *bar*.

barb a short, sharp point which curves backwards from the main shaft: Crochet hooks and fish-hooks are *barbed*. **barbed wire** wire with points sticking out used on fences.

barbarian (bar-ba-ri-an) a person who is savage, uncivilized. **barbarous** cruel and savage: In some countries *barbarous* punishments are given to those who break the law.

barbecue (bar-be-cue) 1. a feast in the open air in which meat is roasted over a fire: On the last day of our holiday a *barbecue* was held on the beach. 2. to roast an animal whole.

barber (bar-ber) a person, usually a man, whose trade is to shave and cut the hair of his customers.

bare 1. without covering, without clothing: We stood with *bare* heads. – The outline of the mountain was bleak and *bare*. 2. empty: 'When she got there, the cupboard was *bare*' (Old Mother Hubbard). 3. show, uncover: The savage animal stood with *bared* teeth. **barely** hardly, scarcely: You have *barely* enough time to catch the bus. **barefoot** without shoes or stockings. **bareheaded** with no cap or hat.

bargain (bar-gain) 1. an agreement to buy, sell or exchange: I'll give you five pence for your knife. Is it a *bargain*? 2. something bought cheaply: Two apples for the price of one is a very good *bargain*. 3. try to agree about price: The price is three pounds and I refuse to *bargain*.

barge a large flat-bottomed boat for carrying goods on rivers or canals and round coasts.

bark 1. a loud, harsh cry made by a dog. 2. make a short, loud sound like a dog: 'Halt!' *barked* the sergeant. 3. the rough outside covering of the trunk and branches of a tree.

barley (bar-ley) a plant which looks like grass and is grown for its seed, also called *barley*: *Barley* is used for drinks such as *barley-water* and lemon *barley*. Beer and whisky are made from *barley*.

barn a large building in which hay and corn are stored, and in which farm animals may be kept. **barnyard** the enclosed space around a barn: The farmer's wife was feeding the chickens in the *barnyard*.

barometer (ba-rom-e-ter) an instrument which measures the pressure of the atmosphere: A *barometer* often has a dial or clock which tells us what kind of weather we may expect.

barracks (bar-racks) large buildings built for soldiers to live in.

barrel (bar-rel) 1. a large wooden vessel with curved sides used to store liquids such as beer, vinegar and oil. 2. the tube of a gun or pistol out of which the bullet is fired.

barricade (bar-ri-cade) 1. a number of objects, such as tree trunks, carts, and buses placed across a street or in front of a building to defend it. 2. put up a *barricade*: We *barricaded* ourselves in at the end of the alley.

barrier (bar-ri-er) a fence, a desert, a range of mountains; anything which stops progress: The first *barrier* we met was a wide river.

barrow (bar-row) a small cart pushed or pulled by hand: Most *barrows* have two wheels but a wheel*barrow* has only one.

barter (bar-ter) exchange goods without using money: The islanders are willing to *barter* cocoa, oil, copper and other goods for machinery.

base 1. the bottom part of anything, the part on which all other parts stand: A triangle stands on its *base*.—The *base* of this pillar is of granite. 2. protected area where an army is stationed and where they keep their stores. **base camp** a camp climbers use as a headquarters: On 14th July we set up the last *base camp* before going to the summit. **baseball** an American game played by two teams on a field with four *bases*. 3. build: Our business is *based* on honest trade. **basement** the lowest part of a building which is often below ground level.

bashful (bash-ful) shy, easily frightened: Come out of that dark corner, you *bashful* little boy!

basin 1. a dish, wide at the top, of metal or pottery: The *basin* was chipped and began to leak. **wash-basin** a bowl fixed to a wall or floor and fitted up with taps and a pipe for water to drain away. 2. the area drained by one river: The *basin* of the Thames provides much of London's water.

basket (bas-ket) a container made of twigs, grasses or thin strips of wool woven together: The customers at the supermarket carry their shopping in wire *baskets*. **basketball** a game played with a large round ball by two teams, each trying to throw it through a *basket* on a pole.

bass (rhymes with *case*) 1. the lowest part in music: If you sing the treble part I'll sing the *bass*. 2. very low in pitch: My father has a deep *bass* voice. 3. a man who sings *bass*.

bat 1. a wooden stick used in games for hitting a ball. 2. use a *bat*: The captain came to the wicket when it was his turn to *bat*. 3. an animal like a mouse which has wings and flies at night.

batch a quantity or a number of things or persons coming at one time: The first *batch* of loaves was taken out of the oven.– A new *batch* of prisoners has arrived at the camp.

bath 1. wash the body, a washing of the whole body: Mother *baths* the baby every morning and I have a hot *bath* before going to bed. 2. water for a *bath*: I'll have a *bath* ready for you when you come home. 3. a container for water and other liquids: The chemist put the piece of copper into a *bath* of acid. 4. a building where *baths* may be taken: Are we going to the swimming *baths* this morning? **bathroom** a room with a bath, also sometimes with washbasin and lavatory.

bathe 1. enter water: It is fun to *bathe* in the sea. **bathing hut** a small building on the beach in which clothes can be changed for *bathing*. **bathing suit** a short, light garment worn for *bathing*. 2. put water on: That wound needs *bathing* with hot water.

baton 1. a short, thin stick used by the conductor of a band, choir or orchestra to beat time. 2. a short, thick stick used by a policeman. 3. a short stick carried by a field-marshal.

battalion (bat-tal-ion) part of an army. A *battalion* is made up of several companies. Three or more *battalions* make a regiment.

batter (bat-ter) 1. a mixture of flour, eggs, milk, sugar, and butter beaten together and used for cooking: Who likes *batter* pudding? 2. strike hard and often, beat out of shape: The police had to *batter* down the door. They found the old man wearing a *battered* hat.

battery (bat-ter-y) *batteries* 1. a device for making electricity: The *battery* of a car makes the lights burn and helps to start the motor. 2. a group of guns in an army or on a ship: On a signal from the admiral every gun in the *battery* was fired. 3. a large number of cages in which hens are kept for the production of eggs.

battle (bat-tle) 1. a fight between two armies: Napoleon was defeated at the *Battle* of Waterloo. 2. struggle: We shall certainly win the *battle* against crime.– The ship *battled* bravely against the storm. **battlefield** a place where a battle takes place or has taken place. **battleship** one of the largest ships of war carrying thousands of men.

bawl cry out loudly: 'Help! Help!' *bawled* the frightened boy.

bay 1. a broad expanse of water partly surrounded by land. 2. reddish brown (of horses): The sergeant was riding a magnificent *bay*. 3. bark or howl (of a hound): We could tell from the *baying* of hounds that the hunt was near. **bay window** a window built out from a room with glass on three sides.

bayonet (bay-o-net) a dagger used for slashing, thrusting and stabbing, which can be fixed on to the barrel of a rifle.

bazaar (ba-zaar) 1. a sale of goods to raise money for charity given to a church or some other organization: This week we are holding a *bazaar* for the benefit of the homeless. 2. a marketplace, or street of shops in an eastern country.

be *am, is, are, was, were, been, being* 1. exist: There *is* a mouse in the kitchen. 2. With other words parts of **be** show how things and persons *are* and what they do: I *am* sorry, I *was* not listening. *Is* it raining? If not, I *am* going to school but I may *be* late.

beach 1. the seashore, covered with sand or pebbles: We love to see the children playing on the *beach*. 2. push or pull a boat on to the shore: We brought the boat in and *beached* her.

beacon (bea-con) 1. a fire lit on the top of a hill as a signal: A distant *beacon* warned the ship's captain that there were rocks ahead. 2. a high post carrying a flashing lamp where there is a street crossing.

bead 1. a small ball of wood, glass or metal with a hole through it for thread or string: In the shop window there were long strings of brightly-coloured *beads*. 2. a drop: The grass glistened with *beads* of dew.

beagle (bea-gle) a small hound with short legs, used for hunting.

beak the strong, hard part of a bird's mouth: The thrush picked up the worm in its *beak*.

beaker (bea-ker) 1. a large cup without a handle, for drinking. 2. a glass vessel used for experiments in chemistry.

beam 1. a strong, heavy piece of wood: The carpenter laid down long, wooden *beams* on which he nailed the floor boards. 2. a ray of light or of electricity: We saw the enemy plane in the *beam* of the searchlight. 3. smile: Watch him *beam* when he sees what we have for dinner

bean a plant which bears seeds in long pods. The seeds, and sometimes the pods are eaten.

bear *bears, bore, borne, bearing* 1. a large, heavy animal with thick fur and large claws: Polar *bears*, black *bears* and grizzly *bears* are dangerous animals. 2. produce: This tree *bears* the very finest plums. 3. carry: The *bearers bore* the coffin to the side of the grave. 4. endure: He had to *bear* the pain of a sprained ankle. 5. support: Don't go on the ice; it is too thin to *bear* your weight. **bearer** one who carries: The cheque I took to the bank said 'Pay *bearer* £2.50p'. **bearings** direction in which a place lies: The forest was so thick that the party lost their *bearings*.

beard hair on the cheeks and chin: I met a man with a long, white *beard*.

beast 1. an animal with four feet: Don't torment my dog; leave the poor *beast* alone. 2. a person who behaves badly. **beastly** bad, nasty: I have a *beastly* cold.

beat 1. hit again and again: Listen to the rain *beating* on the window. 2. mix well with a fork or other utensil: You should *beat* the cream until it becomes stiff. 3. defeat: The champion was *beaten* at the winning post. 4. a repeated throbbing sound: I can hear the *beating* of my own heart. 5. a regular stroke: In this march there are four *beats* in a bar. 6. the route which a sentry or a policeman walks regularly. **beater** a person or a tool that beats: Mother uses an egg *beater*. **beating** a thrashing with the hand or a stick.

beauty (beau-ty) *beauties* 1. everything which gives pleasure to those who see or hear: 'A thing of *beauty* is a joy for ever' (John Keats). 2. a lovely person or thing, giving pleasure and joy: Look at this rose; isn't it a *beauty*! **beautiful** lovely, pretty: In front of the palace there was a *beautiful* garden. **beautify** to make *beautiful*. They are beautifying the city with trees.

beaver (bea-ver) an animal with fur that lives in ponds and streams. *Beavers* have sharp teeth. They bite into the trunks and branches of trees to make dams across rivers.

because (be-cause) for the reason that: The poor boy could not go to school *because* he had no shoes.

beckon (beck-on) signal by a movement of the hand, arm or head: The sergeant *beckoned* us to follow him.

become (be-come) *becomes, became, becoming* come or grow to be: One day he hopes to *become* a doctor. **become of** to happen to: 'Whatever will *become* of me?' said the little mouse.

bed 1. a piece of furniture on which to sleep. **bedding** blankets, sheets, quilts: After the little boy had been sick, all the *bedding* had to be washed. **bedroom** the room in which the beds stand. 2. a small piece of ground on which there are plants: Every garden should have a flower-bed but yours is a *bed* of nettles. 3. the bottom of a body of water: The *bed* of the river is sandy.

bee a small insect which makes honey. **beehive** a box of wood or straw specially made for *bees* to live in.

beech a tree with a smooth bark and hard wood which bears small nuts.

beef the flesh of a cow, ox or bull, used as meat: On Sundays we have roast *beef* for lunch.

been past tense of the word *be*: It has *been* a lovely day today.—Have you *been* eating my sweets?

beer an alcoholic drink made with malt and hops.

beet a plant with a large red or white root. Red *beet*root may be boiled and eaten in salad; white *beet* is used to make sugar.

beetle (bee-tle) an insect which has hairy forewings, useless for flying.

before (be-fore) 1. earlier than: We all arrived *before* the clock struck six. 2. in front of, in the presence of: Your name comes *before* mine on the list.—Why have they brought me *before* a judge? 3. at some time past: I have seen this film *before*. **beforehand** at some time before a certain thing happened: If you are going abroad, please make all the arrangements *beforehand*.

beg ask for something—food, money, help: Have mercy, I *beg* you.—We are so poor we have to *beg* for our bread. **beggar** a person who *begs* or belongs to a group of people who *beg*: The king fell in love with the *beggar* maid.

begin (be-gin) *begins, began, begun, beginning* start: What time does the concert *begin*? **beginning** start: This is the *beginning* of our journey. **beginner** a person who is *beginning* to learn something: I shall not win, I am only a *beginner*.

behave (be-have) act correctly, with good manners, be polite: The class *behaved* well at the museum.—The firemen *behaved* gallantly. **behaviour** the way one *behaves* or acts: The young hero was praised for his gallant *behaviour*.

behind (be-hind) 1. at or to the back of: Quick! Hide *behind* the door. 2. late: The milkman is *behind* with his deliveries this morning.

behold (be-hold) *beholds, beheld, beholding* look at or see (used by poets and in the Bible):

'My heart leaps up when I *behold*
A rainbow in the sky' (Wordsworth).

being (be-ing) 1. existence: The world came into *being* millions of years ago. 2. a living thing: Men, women and children are all human *beings*.

belch 1. throw out flame or smoke: Smoke from the *belching* furnaces darkened the sky. 2. bring gas up from the stomach through the mouth.

belfry (bel-fry) *belfries* a room in which bells are placed, usually high up in a church tower.

belief (be-lief) anything we feel sure is true: I have a firm *belief* in his honesty. **believe** be sure that something is true: It was once *believed* that the world was flat.

bell 1. a vessel like a cup, made of metal. Most *bells* have a 'tongue' inside which strikes the metal and makes a ringing sound. 2. any device for making a ringing sound: The door*bell* rang, but nobody was there.

bellow (bel-low) 1. make a loud noise like a bull: The wounded animal *bellowed* with rage. 2. a loud roar or cry like that of a large animal: The hunters heard a *bellow* from the depths of the forest.

belly (bel-ly) *bellies* the lower front part of the body: They fastened the sling under the horse's *belly* and hoisted it aboard the ship. **belly-landing** when a plane cannot use its landing wheels and has to slide to a stop along the ground.

belong (be-long) 1. be owned by: This bicycle *belongs* to me. 2. have as a right or proper place: All your toys *belong* in this cupboard. 3. be a member of: Do you *belong* to the school choir? **belongings** the things one owns: He keeps all his *belongings* in a tin trunk.

beloved (be-loved or be-lov-ed) 1. loved: He died, *beloved* of all who knew him. 2. a dearly loved thing or person: Every night she takes her *beloved* doll to bed.

below (be-low) 1. under, lower than: It is against the rules of boxing to hit *below* the belt. 2. at the bottom of a page or farther on in the book: Please sign your name *below*. – See *below* for further instructions.

belt 1. a flexible band or strip of cloth, leather etc., worn round the waist: His trousers were held up by a red *belt*. 2. Any wide strip of land: Nobody is allowed to build houses on the green *belt* round the city.

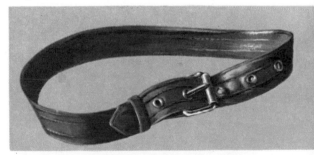

bench 1. a long wooden or stone seat: There is room for six people on this *bench*. 2. the table on which a carpenter or shoemaker works.

bend *bends, bent, bending* 1. curve or make something curve: Don't *bend* that stick too much or it will break. – Drive carefully, there is a *bend* in the road. 2. stoop: He *bent* down to pick up the pin.

beneath (be-neath) under, below: We sheltered from the rain *beneath* the arch.

benefit 1. help, do good to: A long holiday will *benefit* the whole family. **benefit by** be helped by: The town will *benefit by* the new market. 2. gain, profit, kindness: The hall has the *benefit* of a good stage. – From him we have had many great *benefits*. 3. a performance to raise money for a charity or for a person: The concert is for the *benefit* of local charities.

beret (be-ret, pronounced *be-ray*) a soft round cap of cloth or other material: The *beret* is now worn by British soldiers.

berry (ber-ry) *berries* a small fruit with seeds which usually grows on a bush.

berth a bed usually fixed to a wall or the floor. On a ship there are often two *berths*, one above the other.

beside (be-side) at the side of, close to:
There came a big spider
And sat down *beside* her
    (*Miss Muffet*, Nursery rhyme).
besides in addition to, as well as: There were two boys in the orchard *besides* me.

bet 1. risk money on one's own forecast of the result of a race, a match or an election: I'm *betting* that Arsenal will win today. 2. an agreement to pay something if one is wrong: You made a *bet* with me and I won. **betting shop** a shop into which people can go to make (or lay) *bets*.

betray (be-tray) 1. act with deceit towards, give away the secrets of others: Judas *betrayed* Jesus with a kiss. 2. show something that one wants to hide: The face of the accused boy *betrayed* his guilt. **betrayal** the act of betraying: Judas' deed was a sad *betrayal*.

better (bet-ter) one form of the word good: I feel *better* today, thank you. – If you go into the next shop you will get a *better* bargain.

between (be-tween) 1. from one place or time to another: There are ten yards *between* the two posts. 2. keeping apart: Do you see the barbed wire fence *between* those two gardens? 3. share: The old man divided the sweets *between* the two boys.

bevel (be-vel) a surface which slopes, such as a picture frame.

beverage (bev-er-age) any kind of drink: tea, lemonade, coffee: Look down the list of *beverages* and order what you would like.

beware (be-ware) be watchful; take care: *Beware* of the dog.

beyond (be-yond) 1. at or to the other side of, farther than: The spies had fled *beyond* the frontier and they were well *beyond* our reach.

bib 1. a piece of cloth fastened under a child's chin to stop food from spoiling its clothes. 2. the part of an apron which covers the chest.

Bible (Bi-ble) the sacred writings of the Christian and Jewish religions: Every morning our teacher reads us a few verses from the *Bible*.

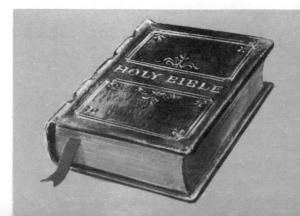

biceps (bi-ceps) a large muscle on the front of the upper arm: My brother is strong; when he bends his arm the *biceps* are round and hard.

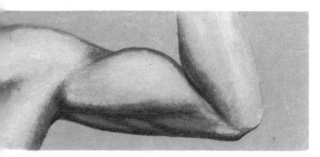

bicycle (bi-cy-cle) a machine with two wheels, for riding on, made to go by pressing with the feet on pedals: Do you go to work by bus or on your *bicycle*?

bid *bids, bade, bidden, bidding* 1. offer money: I *bid* £10 for that guitar. 2. the amount offered: Harry's *bid* was the highest. 3. order or command: A good servant always does as he is *bid* (or *bidden*). 4. invite: I am *bidding* all my friends to my wedding. 5. say or tell: She wept when we *bade* farewell.

big 1. large: A *big* lorry stood opposite the shop door. 2. very important: He is a *big* man in the wool trade.

bikini (bi-ki-ni) a very brief, two-piece bathing suit for girls.

bill 1. the beak of a bird: The duck had a large worm in its *bill*. 2. a statement in writing saying how much money one owes: Father asked the waitress for the *bill*. 3. a proposal for a law, to be discussed in Parliament: The House of Commons discussed the *bill* for raising pensions.

billet (bil-let) 1. lodge soldiers or other people in private houses by order of the government: During the war I was *billeted* with a family in Rugby. 2. a temporary home: Private Smith had a good *billet* with the blacksmith and his wife.

billiards (bill-iards) a game for two people played with long sticks called cues and ivory balls, on an oblong table covered with cloth.

billow (bil-low) 1. a large wave: The ship was tossing like a cork on the huge *billows*. 2. rise and move like a wave: Black smoke *billowed* from the burning haystack.

billygoat a male goat.

bin a large container for storing coal, corn, flour or bread: Put the broken pieces of the vase into the dust*bin*.

bind *binds, bound, binding* 1. tie or fasten: We *bound* his arms behind him. – The reaper *bound* the sheaves. 2. fasten a strip of tape or cloth along and over the edge of: Will you please *bind* the sleeve of my coat with leather. 3. fasten sheets of paper into a cover or book: I have written all these poems and I am going to have them *bound*. **binding** the cover of a book: The books will look handsome in a *binding* of red leather. 4. tie round or put a bandage on: The Good Samaritan *bound* up the poor man's wounds. 5. be forced to agree to do something: I am *bound* to appear in court tomorrow. 6. be sure to: This book is by Mark Twain; it's *bound* to be good.

biography (bi-og-ra-phy) the story of a person's life written by another: The *biography* of Dr Johnson was written by James Boswell.

biplane (bi-plane) a plane with two pairs of wings, one pair above the other. There are very few *biplanes* in use today.

birch 1. a tree with smooth bark. 2. a bundle of *birch* rods tied together, once used for punishing boys.

bird a creature with wings and covered with feathers. Some kinds of *birds*, such as the penguin, are not able to fly.

birth 1. being born, beginning of life: My little brother weighed seven pounds at *birth*. 2. descent: Some people are of noble *birth*, others are of humble *birth*. **birthday** the day of one's *birth* or the anniversary of that day: On 27th May I shall celebrate my *birthday*.

biscuit (bis-cuit) a small, dry piece of bread or cake made from dough rolled flat and baked. There are chocolate *biscuits*, cheese *biscuits* and many other kinds, sweet and savoury.

bisect (bi-sect) divide into two parts, usually equal: A right angle when *bisected* makes two acute angles.

bishop (bish-op) a clergyman who is head of a number of churches in a diocese or district.

bison (bi-son) a wild ox, the American buffalo: Herds of *bison* once roamed the prairie.

bit 1. a small piece: Please give me a *bit* of your bar of chocolate.—I shall do all the work, *bit* by *bit*. 2. a small metal bar which forms part of a horse's bridle. 3. a tool which fits into another tool called a brace and is used for boring holes.

bitch a female dog, wolf or fox.

bite *bites*, *bit*, *bitten*, *biting* 1. cut into something with the teeth: He *bit* off a large piece of cake.—Does your dog *bite*? 2. a piece *bitten* off or broken off: Don't keep all the chocolate; give this little boy a *bite*. 3. the act of biting: He ate it all in one big *bite*. 4. sting: If you go near the stream you'll be *bitten* by the gnats. 5. an injury caused by being *bitten* or stung: The *bite* on his arm became very swollen.

bitter (bit-ter) 1. with a harsh, disagreeable taste: The medicine was almost too *bitter* to swallow. 2. very cold and fierce: A *bitter* wind was blowing over the marshes. 3. angry, disappointed, sorrowful: The friendship ended in a *bitter* quarrel.—He was very *bitter* at not being chosen for the team.

black 1. the darkest colour known; the opposite of white: The highwayman rode off on his *black* mare. 2. dark: It was a *black* night, with pouring rain. **blackguard** an evil, dishonest person. **blackleg** a name given by workpeople on strike to those who refuse to join them. **blackmail** taking money from people by threatening to reveal things they wish to keep secret. **black sheep** a lazy wasteful person, a disgrace to friends or family. **blacksmith** a man who repairs and makes things out of iron.

bladder (blad-der) 1. a bag inside the body in which urine or waste liquid collects. 2. the rubber or plastic bag inside a football which is blown up through a tube.

blade 1. the flat part of a knife, axe or chisel which cuts: I need a new *blade* in my razor. 2. the flat part of a cricket bat or propeller. 3. a long, narrow leaf: She tickled my nose with a *blade* of grass.

blame 1. believe or say that someone is in the wrong, accuse: Don't *blame* others for your own mistakes. 2. responsibility for having failed or done wrong: The driver accepted the *blame* for the accident. **to blame** in the wrong, responsible for: Who is *to blame* for starting the fire?

blank 1. an empty space (on paper): Please fill in the *blanks* with your name and address. 2. unmarked, not written on or printed on: You must use up all the *blank* pages before you get a new exercise book. 3. without interest or expression: When I asked for my passport I was met with a *blank* stare. 4. having forgotten: In the examination his mind suddenly went *blank*. 5. a cartridge with no bullet: We fired a number of *blanks* to scare the birds.

blanket (blan-ket) 1. a thick cover used on a bed: On cold winter nights we put extra *blankets* on our beds. 2. to cover as with a *blanket*: Thick snow *blanketed* the ground.

blast 1. a strong, sudden rush of wind: The door was blown open by a cold *blast* of air. 2. a sound made by the blowing of a trumpet or horn: The contest was heralded by a bugle *blast*. 3. blow up, destroy: His hopes of victory were suddenly *blasted*.

blaze 1. bright flame or fire: I poured oil on the ashes and they burst into a *blaze*. 2. burst into flame, burn brightly: The firemen turned their hoses on the *blazing* building. 3. shine brightly: The garden *blazed* with tulips of all colours. **blazer** an informal jacket worn for sporting activities, sometimes in the colours or carrying the badge of a school or club: My father wears the *blazer* of the Royal Marines.

bleach 1. make or become white: We hung the clothes in the sun to *bleach*. 2. a preparation to make clothes, hair, baths white: Please go to the chemist for a bottle of *bleach*.

bleak cold and bare, swept by winds: The rescue party had to cross the *bleak* moor.

blear make faint or dim to the sight: Our vision was *bleared* by the heavy rain.

bleat 1. the cry of a sheep, lamb, goat or calf. 2. make a cry like that of a sheep.

bleed *bleeds*, *bled*, *bleeding* lose blood from wounds: 'If you prick us, do we not *bleed*?' (Shakespeare, *The Merchant of Venice*).

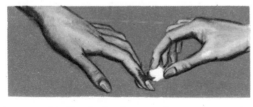

bleep a high-pitched sound sent out by radio, earth satellites, or spacecraft.

blend 1. mix together: All our wines are skilfully *blended*. 2. go well together: How beautifully the colours of the curtains *blend* with the wallpaper! 3. mixture: Our *blend* of tea is of the highest quality.

bless 1. ask or hope that God may protect: 'God bless us every one!' (*A Christmas Carol*, Dickens). 2. make holy: The priest *blessed* the bread at the altar. 3. call God holy, praise God: 'We *bless* Thy holy Name.' **blessed** fortunate, gifted with: He was *blessed* with excellent health. **blessing** a favour given by God; a happy result: Let us ask a *blessing* on this food. – What a *blessing* that your life was saved!

blind 1. unable to see: Let us help this *blind* man to cross the road. 2. make *blind*: Two men were *blinded* by the explosion in the pit. **blind to** unable or not willing to understand: The boy's mother is *blind to* all his faults. **blind turning** a turning in the road, dangerous because one cannot see what is coming. **blind alley** an alley that has no way out; a job in which there is no chance of promotion. **blindfold** cover the eyes; with the eyes covered by a bandage: He was taken, *blindfold*, into the dark room. 3. a cover for a window which can be raised or lowered: Please lower the *blind*; it is getting dark.

blink 1. open and shut the eyes quickly: The sun is so strong it makes me *blink*. 2. shine unsteadily, often in the dark: At last we saw the lights *blinking* through the trees.

bliss perfect happiness: A day on the beach: what *bliss*! **blissful** full of happiness, delightful.

blister (blister) 1. a small swelling under the skin, filled with liquid: I have walked and walked until I have *blisters* on both feet. 2. make or get blisters on: He cannot work hard with his hands because they *blister* easily. 3. a similar swelling on metal or painted wood: I had barely finished painting the door when the intense heat caused a large *blister*.

blitz a word from the German meaning a sudden attack, usually by a large force of aircraft.

blizzard (bliz-zard) a severe storm with snow driven by a fierce wind: The climbers found a small cave where they could shelter from the *blizzard*.

block 1. a piece of wood or stone used for building: The pyramids of Egypt are built of great *blocks* of stone. 2. a large piece of wood on which a person rests his neck for execution: Charles I of England was executed on the *block*. 3. stand in the way of, stop: 'NOTICE. ROAD *BLOCKED* BY ICE'. 4. a building or large group of buildings joined together: The houses were all torn down to make room for a new office *block*. 5. (in cricket) stop a ball with the bat to prevent it hitting the wicket. **blockage** something stopping the flow or movement, usually in a pipe or drain.

blood 1. the red liquid flowing through the veins and arteries of the body. **bloodhound** a large dog which can trace people or game by following their scent. **bloodthirsty** eager to kill and taking pleasure in killing. **blood donor** a person who allows his blood to be taken for transfusion into the veins of other people.

bloom 1. to flower or open into flower: Violets and primroses *bloom* in spring. 2. a flower: The gardener brought in a bunch of beautiful *blooms*. 3. to flourish, be beautiful: The girl was *blooming* with happiness at her engagement party.

blot *blots, blotted, blotting* 1. a mark caused by ink spilt or dropped on paper: There are too many *blots* on this page. 2. make a mark by dropping ink or crossing out words: I could not read the letter because too many words had been *blotted*. **blotter** a book containing sheets of *blotting paper*; a piece of wood on which *blotting paper* has been fixed. **blotting paper** soft paper used to soak up ink.

blouse a shirt worn mainly by women, tucked into a skirt or trousers at the waist: She surprised everybody by going to the wedding in a *blouse* and skirt.

blow *blows, blew, blown, blowing* 1. (of air or wind) drive, force, move, flow: A gentle breeze was *blowing*. 2. move by blowing: The captain could not prevent the ship being *blown* on to the rocks. 3. a hard stroke: He was knocked unconscious by a *blow* on the head. 4. a shock or dreadful happening: The loss of my position as a foreman was a great *blow*. **blow up** damage or destroy by causing an explosion: We could not cross the river because the bridge had been *blown up*. **blow over** to pass away: They all hid until the trouble had *blown over*.

blubber (blub-ber) 1. weep noisily or say something between sobs: 'Stop *blubbering*,' said father, 'and eat your dinner.' 2. the fat of whales, walruses and other sea animals: *Blubber* is used for making oil.

bluff 1. make others afraid by pretending to be strong or clever: You were not sent here to collect the money; you can't *bluff* me. 2. talk intended to mislead others: Take no notice of his *bluffing*, he is a coward.

blunder (blun-der) 1. make a mistake. 2. a mistake: Whatever can have caused him to make such a *blunder*! 3. move here and there in a clumsy way: The old man *blundered* into a deep ditch.

blunt 1. with no point or sharp edge: Nobody can shave with a *blunt* razor or carve with a *blunt* knife. 2. make *blunt*: He *blunted* his knife by trying to cut stone with it. 3. honest, speaking plainly: I'm a *blunt* person, and I'll tell you the truth.

blush 1. turn red in the face from shame or confusion: 'I'm sorry I copied, sir,' he replied, *blushing*. 2. a redness of the face caused by shame or shyness.

bluster (blus-ter) 1. blow strongly and violently: There is a *blustering* wind tonight. 2. talk noisily and with threats: Why does he *bluster* so? It's time somebody put an end to all his *bluster*.

boar a male pig: They hunted the wild *boar* in the forest.

board 1. a long, flat, thin piece of wood: We need more *boards* to lay this floor. 2. a flat piece of wood for a special purpose: We have all kinds of *boards* in stock, chess-*boards*, draught*boards*, diving-*boards* and notice-*boards*. 3. meals supplied and paid for, usually by the week: Mrs Jones charges a small amount a week for *board* and lodging. 4. live at another person's house, paying for food: We all *board* at Mrs Jones's. 5. get on to a ship or train: We *boarded* the vessel at five o'clock. 6. persons appointed to take charge of a business or other activity: There is a leak in our gas supply, please phone the Gas *Board*. **on board** on or in a ship, train or aeroplane: Before he blew the whistle he made sure that everybody was *on board*.

boast 1. praise the things one does or talk too much about the things one has: Every time we meet he *boasts* about his strength. 2. something to talk proudly about: It is my *boast* that I have never been late for work. **boastful** continually *boasting*: How we dislike *boastful* people!

boat a small vessel for travelling on water, using oars, by steam or with a motor.

bob *bobs, bobbed, bobbing* 1. move up and down: The boat was *bobbing* on the waves like a cork. 2. a style of haircut for women and children.

bobbin (bob-bin) a small roller on which thread is wound.

bobsleigh (bob-sleigh) a racing sledge carrying two people, with two pairs of runners, used in tobogganing: There are *bobsleigh* events in the winter Olympic Games.

bodice (bod-ice) the upper part of a woman's dress, fitting the body.

body (bod-y) *bodies* 1. a whole person or animal, not including the mind: This old woman may be weak in *body*, but she is sound in mind. 2. the trunk of the human *body*: He had three wounds in the legs and one in the *body*. 3. a dead person or animal, a corpse: 'Bring the *body* into the chapel' (Shakespeare, *Hamlet*). 4. a large quantity of matter, a number of people: Lake Windermere is a large *body* of water. – A *body* of strikers stood in front of the factory gates. **bodily** as a whole, without taking a thing apart: The house was moved *bodily* farther up the street. **bodyguard** a man who goes about with a person to protect him from harm.

bog a marsh or swamp: A number of peasants were digging peat from the *bog*. **boggy** soft, wet, swampy, marshy: At the bottom of the slope the ground became *boggy*.

boisterous (bois-ter-ous) rough, loud, violent: The *boisterous* wind blew down all our fences. – He could not make his voice heard over the noise of the *boisterous* crowd.

bolt 1. a metal bar which fastens a door or window: Every night we make the door secure with a *bolt* and lock. 2. a metal pin on which a nut can be screwed. 3. fasten with a *bolt*: The chassis of the car is *bolted* to the frame. 4. a shaft of lightning (often called a *thunderbolt*). 5. run away in alarm or fright: As soon as the boys saw the farmer coming, they *bolted*. 6. swallow quickly: Eat slowly; it is bad for you to *bolt* your food.

bomb 1. a hollow container filled with explosive material: Some *bombs* explode when dropped from planes, others, called delayed action *bombs*, explode only after several hours. 2. drop *bombs* on: The planes *bombed* the fort and destroyed it. **bomber** a plane made specially for dropping *bombs*.

bond 1. an agreement to pay money in return for a loan. Every *bond* usually states a time for payment and how much interest is to be paid. 2. something which brings people close together: My sister and I are united by *bonds* of affection. 3. anything that binds a person: The prisoners were brought to the castle in *bonds*. **bondage** slavery: Many years ago this tribe was sold into *bondage*.

bone 1. one of many parts which make up the skeleton of a person or an animal: We cut off the meat and gave the *bones* to the dog. – 'The knee *bone*'s connected to the thigh *bone*' (popular song). 2. take the bones out of: Please *bone* the fish before I take it home. **bony** full of bones: This piece of fish is so *bony* that I can't eat it.

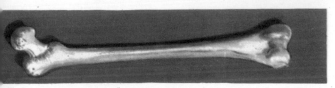

bonfire (bon-fire) a large fire in an open space: On Guy Fawkes night the sky was red with the glow of *bonfires*.

bonnet (bon-net) 1. a close-fitting covering for the head, often tied under the chin: Put the baby's *bonnet* on and take her for a walk. 2. the metal covering over the front part of a motor-car: He raised the *bonnet* and inspected the engine.

bonny or **bonnie** (bon-ny, bon-nie) 1. handsome, pretty, healthy: 'My *bonnie* is over the ocean' (old song).

bonus (bo-nus) A payment of money in addition to what is usually paid: I was surprised to get such a large *bonus* from the firm last Christmas.

boo 1. an expression of dislike, sometimes used to animals: '*Boo*,' said the little boy to the goose. 2. use such an expression: The audience *booed* the comedian until he left the stage.

book 1. written, printed or blank sheets of paper fastened together in a cover: I am reading a *book* about horses. 2. give or receive an order for seats at a theatre or concert: Please *book* me three seats for the pantomime. 3. write down somebody's name, especially that of a footballer who has committed a foul or other offence. **booklet** a thin *book*. **bookmaker** (or **bookie**) a person who takes people's bets at horse races or in a shop.

boom 1. a long, deep sound: Far away we heard the *boom* of a gun. 2. prosper, become rich: Towns near the new oilfield are *booming*. – The wool trade is *booming* this year. 3. a quick increase in prices giving profits: Yesterday there was a sudden *boom* in copper.

boomerang (boo-me-rang) a bent, or curved piece of hard wood which when thrown returns to the person who throws it. *Boomerangs* are used by Australian natives.

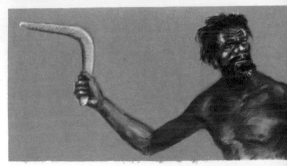

boost 1. lift or raise by pushing from behind or below: How can I climb this wall unless you give me a *boost*? 2. raise, increase: The scarcity of bananas has *boosted* the price.

boot 1. a heavy shoe reaching above the ankle. High *boots* may reach to the knee. 2. a place for baggage usually at the rear of a motor car.

booth 1. a small room or compartment for a telephone or for voting: You will find the telephone *booth* at the end of the street. 2. a stall for the sale of goods in a street market.

border (bor-der) 1. a side, edge or margin: My white handkerchief has a blue *border*. – There is a *border* of flowers round the lawn. 2. a dividing line or boundary between lands: The spy escaped over the *border* to his own country.

bore 1. pierce, make a narrow, deep hole, drill: The carpenter *bored* two holes in the door. 2. tire people with talking too much: How that man *bores* me with his stories! 3. a dull tiresome person: He's very kind, but oh, what a *bore* he is!

born 1. one form of the word *bear*, having come into the world by birth: I was *born* on 21st January. 2. having some great talent or fault: He is a *born* artist as well as a *born* liar.

borne past tense of the word *bear*, endured: I have *borne* your impudence as long as I can.

borrow (bor-row) take a thing, promising to give it back at a later time to its owner: May I *borrow* your bicycle for an hour?

boss 1. an employer, a person who sees that other persons do their work: I went to the *boss* and asked him if I could be absent tomorrow. 2. order others to do things: Stop *bossing* me about.

both the two: He has an apple and an orange, and he will eat them *both.—Both* John and his sister have dark hair.

bother (both-er) 1. annoy, cause trouble: He has lost his watch, but it doesn't seem to *bother* him.—Don't *bother* your teacher. 2. take the trouble: Nobody ever *bothers* to read the instructions. 3. worry, trouble: I had no *bother* at all with your dog.

bottle (bot-tle) a container, usually of glass, with a narrow neck: Who threw that ink-*bottle* across the classroom? 2. put into *bottles* to store: The wine is ready now and it's time we *bottled* it. **bottleneck** a narrow strip of road where traffic often has to wait to get through: If you go along these side roads you will avoid the *bottleneck.*

bottom (bot-tom) 1. the lowest part: There's a hole in the *bottom* of this bucket. 2. lowest: You will find the dictionary on the *bottom* shelf. 3. bed of a lake, sea, river: I threw in the stone and it sank to the *bottom.* 4. seat of a chair or the part of the body that sits on it: That chair *bottom* wants mending.

bough (rhymes with *now*) a large branch growing from the trunk of a tree:
'Merrily, merrily, shall I live now
Under the blossom that hangs on the
bough (Shakespeare, *A Midsummer Night's Dream*).

bought one form of the word *buy*: Yesterday I *bought* a new raincoat.

bounce 1. spring back after hitting a wall or a floor: A rubber ball *bounces* when it is dropped. 2. make a thing *bounce*: If you *bounce* the ball I'll catch it. 3. jump up and down: Don't *bounce* on that bed or you'll break the springs.

bound 1. going in the direction of: 'We're *bound* for the Rio Grande' (sea shanty). 2. be limited by, next to: London is *bounded* by six counties. 3. spring, jump, leap: He was over the fence in one *bound.*— The dog came *bounding* towards its master. 4. one form of the word *bind*: Our family Bible is *bound* in leather. 4. a dividing line or limit: If you cross the road you will be out of *bounds.*

boundary (bound-a-ry) 1. a dividing line or border: A fence marks the *boundary* between my garden and his. 2. in cricket, hitting the ball to the *boundary* of the field, scoring 4 or 6.

bouquet (bou-quet, pronounced *bo-kay*) a bunch of flowers: The bride carried a *bouquet* of roses and carnations.

bow (rhymes with *so*) 1. a knot made with one or more loops: She wore a *bow* of pink ribbon in her hair. 2. a strip of wood, curved by a string stretched between its ends, used for shooting arrows: Every archer had his *bow* ready. 3. a slender stick with horse hair stretched from end to end, used to play a violin or other musical instrument which has strings. **bow-tie** a necktie fastened with a bow. **bow-legged** with legs curved outwards at the knees.

bow (rhymes with *now*) 1. bend down, stoop to express greeting, shame or surrender: The chauffeur *bowed* politely as we approached the car. – We will never *bow* to false gods. 2. the front part of a boat: From the *bows* they were able to see the white cliffs of Dover. 3. the action of bending down: The audience applauded and the conductor made a deep *bow*.

bowel (bow-el) 1. part of the digestive system of the body. 2. inward parts: Precious metals lie buried in the *bowels* of the earth.

bowl 1. a hollow dish: In our cupboard we have a sugar-*bowl* and a salad *bowl*. 2. the contents of a *bowl*: Goldilocks ate up Baby Bear's *bowl* of porridge. 3. send a ball to a person who is batting in the game of cricket. **bowling green** the area of short grass on which the game of *bowls* is played. **bowling alley** see **alley**.

bowler 1. the person *bowling* the ball to the one who is batting. 2. a hard rounded hat, usually black.

box 1. a container, usually of wood, cardboard, metal or plastic: I keep my toys in a wooden *box*. 2. what a *box* holds: I offered him a chocolate and he ate the whole *box*. 3. a small compartment for a few people, separated from all others in a theatre: We watched the play from a *box* near the stage. 4. fight with the fists: I learnt to *box* in the gym. **boxer** a boy or a man who boxes; a dog related to the bull-dog with a smooth coat.

boy a child who will one day be a man: When I was a *boy* I played all kinds of games. **boyish** like a *boy*: Stop your *boyish* games and start work.

boycott (boy-cott) join with others in having nothing to do with a person or a group of persons; refuse to accept the products of another country. (From the name of Captain *Boycott* who was treated in this way in Ireland in 1880.)

brace 1. an appliance used to hold tight or give support: The wall of this house is not safe; we must put a *brace* on it. 2. straps worn over the shoulders to support the trousers. 3. a tool which holds another tool called a bit and which can be turned to make holes. 4. strengthen, make firm: He expected bad news and *braced* himself to meet it.

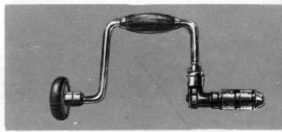

bracelet (brace-let) a band of metal or other material worn as an ornament about the wrist.

bracket (brack-et) 1. a support of wood or metal for a shelf, a lamp or other article on a wall. 2. one of two marks ( ) used in writing or in print to enclose words or figures.

brag *brags*, *bragged*, *bragging* boast, talk too much about oneself, the things one has or what one can do: Why is he always *bragging* about his money?

braid divide into parts and plait: When your hair is long enough we will *braid* it. 2. hair, silk etc. woven into a plait or band, sometimes used for the edge or trimming of cloth or a garment: The admiral's uniform is trimmed with gold *braid*.

brain a mass of soft grey matter inside the skull of a human being or an animal: We think with our *brains* and our *brains* control the movements of our bodies. **brainwashing** a method of forcing a person to give up his own beliefs and accept those which are pressed on him. **brainwave** a sudden bright idea.

brake a device used to make vehicles slow down or stop: When the car is running we use the foot-*brake*, but when it is standing still we put on the hand-*brake*.

bramble a bush which carries long prickly shoots and bears blackberries.

bran the outer covering of grains, sometimes separated from the grain before it is ground: *Bran* is fed to poultry and horses.—Wholemeal bread has *bran* in it.

branch 1. a limb of a tree which grows from the trunk or from another *branch*. Leaves grow on *branches* in summer. 2. a division of a river, road, railway, mountain range, a family or an organization: The Ministry of Transport has decided to close the *branch* line.—I belong to the junior *branch* of a distinguished family.

brand 1. mark with a hot iron: In olden days criminals were *branded*. 2. the mark which is *branded* on: We can tell by the *brand* that these steers do not belong to this ranch. 3. a trade name of a particular product: How do you like this new *brand* of coffee?

brandy (bran-dy) a strong alcoholic drink usually made from grapes. *Brandy* in small quantities is used as a medicine but too much *brandy* makes one intoxicated.

brass a bright yellow metal which is a mixture of copper and zinc: The thieves took all our money as well as a pair of *brass* candlesticks.

brave 1. not afraid to face danger or pain: The *brave* boy rushed into the burning room. 2. face, meet: To reach home we must *brave* the dangers of the forest. 3. an American Indian warrior: The chief drew up his *braves* for the last attack. **bravely** with courage: Though the storm was raging the party *bravely* struggled on. **bravery** courage: The Victoria Cross and the George Cross are given only for acts of great *bravery*.

bray 1. the cry of a donkey; the loud sound of a trumpet. 2. make a loud, harsh cry or sound: 'The kettledrum and trumpet thus *bray* out' (Shakespeare, *Hamlet*).

bread 1. a food made with flour and yeast, mixed, kneaded and baked in an oven. 2. food: 'Give us this day our daily *bread*' (*The Lord's Prayer*). **breadwinner** the person who works to support a family.

break *breaks, broke, broken* 1. smash or be smashed: Who *broke* this chair?—We were pulling the cart and the rope *broke*. 2. make useless: He wound his watch too far and *broke* it. 3. crush, abandon: I wish I could *break* the habit of smoking. 4. interrupt: We *broke* our journey at the next inn. 5. change in some way: John's voice *broke* when he was 14. 6. an interval: There will now be a *break* for lunch. 7. a new start: I think that after all his bad luck he deserves a *break*. **breakfast** the first meal of the day which *breaks* the long fast of the night before.

breast chest; the upper front part of the human body or an animal's body: 'You must cut this flesh from off his *breast*' (Shakespeare, *The Merchant of Venice*).

breath 1. air taken into and sent out of the lungs: Take a deep *breath* before you dive in. 2. movement of air: The day was hot with hardly a *breath* of air. **breathless** or out of *breath*, panting, breathing hard and quickly through running or violent exercise.

breathe 1. take air into the lungs and send it out again: The smoke from this factory is poisoning the air we *breathe*. 2. tell (a secret): If I tell you, promise not to *breathe* a word to anyone.

breeches (breech-es) short trousers fitting round the waist and just below the knees: The man wore red *breeches*, yellow stockings and shoes with silver buckles.

breed *breeds*, *bred*, *breeding* 1. keep for producing young: How long has your brother been *breeding* rabbits? 2. a kind or variety of animals: He started his farm with the finest *breed* of sheep. 3. produce young, multiply: Flies *breed* quickly. 4. cause: Flies and dirt *breed* diseases.

breeze a gentle wind: The Union Jack is fluttering in the *breeze*.

brew 1. make by boiling and fermenting or by scalding: Beer is *brewed* from hops and malt.—Is the tea *brewed* yet? 2. bring about, form: The sky is dark and a storm is clearly *brewing*.

briar or **brier** (bri-ar) a plant with sharp thorns along its stem: Wild roses are *briars* and standard roses are grown on *briars*.

bribe 1. money, favours or gifts made to a person to get him to do something which may be wrong or dishonest: The officers were put in prison because they had accepted *bribes*. 2. give a *bribe* to: The man who saw the robbery had been *bribed* to keep silent. **bribery** the giving or taking of bribes.

brick 1. a piece of clay shaped and baked hard, used in building: 'This little pig built his house of *bricks*' (nursery story). 2. anything shaped like a *brick*: Please buy me a *brick* of ice cream. 3. a building toy: Children love playing with *bricks*.

bride a woman newly married or about to be married: The *bride* wore a long dress of white silk. **bridegroom** a man newly married or about to be married: The *bridegroom* took the ring and placed it on the *bride's* finger. **bridesmaid** a young woman or girl who attends the *bride* at the wedding.

bridge 1. a structure built over a river, road or railway for people and vehicles to cross: London *Bridge* is one of the most famous *bridges* in the world. 2. a platform across the deck of a ship which is used by the captain and officers: The captain gave his orders from the *bridge*. 3. a game played with cards. 4. a thin piece of wood used to support the strings of a violin or other stringed instrument.

bridle (bri-dle) the part of a horse's harness that fits over the head and includes the bit, the straps and reins.

brief 1. short: Please write me a *brief* note when you reach home. 2. shorts or underpants without legs. 3. a short summary or a plan of action given in advance to the crew of an aircraft or to anybody going on a mission.

brigade (bri-gade) 1. part of an army consisting of several regiments: The whole *brigade* moved into battle formation. 2. a group of people organized for special work: The Fire *Brigade* was called out three times in a single night.

brigand (brig-and) a member of a gang of robbers, a bandit.

bright 1. shining, giving light: The moon is very bright tonight. 2. cheerful and happy: How I love to see all your *bright* faces! 3. very clever: I am giving this prize to the *brightest* boy in the class. **brighten** make bright: We will *brighten* up this room with a fresh coat of paint.

brilliant (bril-liant) 1. very bright, sparkling: The pilgrims were dazzled by a *brilliant* white light. 2. very clever: This *brilliant* boy has won a scholarship to university. **brilliance** great brightness: The diamond is valuable because of its great *brilliance*.

brim 1. the part of a hat which turns outwards at the bottom of the crown: The tramp wore a dirty old hat with a torn *brim*. 2. the top edge of a cup, bowl or glass: The company filled their glasses to the *brim*.

brine water containing a great deal of salt: The butcher pickled the pork in a tub of *brine*.

bring *brings, brought, bringing* come with something, carry or lead: *Bring* your coat if you think it will rain. – 'The wise may *bring* their learning' (hymn). 2. cause: April showers *bring* May flowers (old rhyme).

brisk active, quick, lively: We went for a *brisk* walk. – Trade is *brisk* this morning.

bristle (bris-tle) one of the short stiff hairs in brushes or in the coats of some animals.

broad large, wide across: This river is too *broad* for us to swim.

broadcast (broad-cast) send out in all directions as in sowing seed; spread news, especially by radio: The Queen is to *broadcast* on Christmas Day.

bronco (bron-co) a wild or half-tamed horse used in western North America: Every good cowboy should be able to ride a *bronco*.

bronze a yellowish metal made by melting copper and tin together: The sculptor has made a *bronze* statue of our leader.

brooch an ornament for the dress which has a pin at the back to make it fast.

brood 1. all the young birds hatched at the same time in a single nest: The hen had a *brood* of 12 chicks. 2. a popular expression for a mother's children: Here comes Mrs Grimes with her *brood*. 3. think sadly about one's troubles: All day long the poor man *brooded* about the loss of his son.

brook a small stream: 'He went to the *brook* where he shot a little duck' (nursery rhyme).

broom 1. a stiff brush with a long handle: Take the *broom* and sweep the garden path. 2. a shrub with yellow flowers which grows on sandy soil. **broomstick** the handle of a *broom*: 'Up flew the wicked witch on her magic *broomstick*' (fairy tale).

broth the water in which meat or fish has been boiled. This is thickened with vegetables and served as soup.

brother (broth-er) the son of the same parents as another person: This boy and girl are *brother* and sister; they have the same mother and father. **brotherhood** a group of men who consider themselves as dear to each other as *brothers*. **brother-in-law** the husband of one's sister or the *brother* of one's husband or wife.

brought past tense of the word *bring*: 'He hath *brought* many captives back to Rome' (Shakespeare, *Julius Caesar*).

brow 1. eyebrow; the arch of hair above the eye: Her hair is fair, but her *brows* are dark. 2. forehead: 'His *brow* is wet with honest sweat' (Longfellow, *The Village Blacksmith*).

bruise 1. an injury to one's body caused by a blow or bump which turns the skin a dark colour but does not break it: When we rescued him he was covered with *bruises*. 2. cause a *bruise*: If you fall off your bicycle you might *bruise* your leg.

brunette (bru-nette) a girl or woman whose eyes and hair are dark.

brush 1. a tool with stiff hairs or bristles. There are tooth*brushes*, nail*brushes*, hair-*brushes*, scrubbing *brushes* and many other kinds of *brushes*. 2. clean with a *brush*: When we *brush* our clothes, we *brush* off the dirt. 3. rub against when passing: 'Stop!' I cried as he *brushed* rudely past me.

brute 1. a savage, cruel or unkind person: 'Leave me alone, you *brute*,' she cried. 2. animal (not including man): Stop teasing that dog: leave the poor *brute* alone. **brutal** cruel, savage: His *brutal* conduct brought him a long prison sentence.

bubble (bub-ble) 1. a ball of liquid containing air or gas which floats in the air and on liquids: As the diver sank in the water they saw the *bubbles* rise to the top.–'I'm for ever blowing *bubbles*' (old song). 2. form *bubbles*: When the water *bubbled* I turned the gas off.

buck 1. a male deer, goat, hare or rabbit. 2. jump with arched back and all four feet off the ground: The cowboy mounted the bronco but it *bucked* and threw him.

bucket (buck-et) a vessel of wood, metal, canvas or plastic with a handle for carrying coal, water, milk etc.

buckle (buck-le) 1. a fastener of metal, bone or plastic with a spike which goes through a hole in a belt or strap. 2. fasten with a buckle: 'One, two, *buckle* my shoe' (old rhyme). 3. crumple up because of a heavy weight or strain: The front of the car *buckled* with the force of the collision.

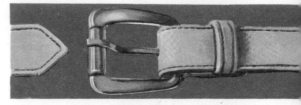

bud *buds, budded, budding* 1. a leaf or flower before it unfolds: It is spring and the rose bushes are full of *buds*. 2. form *buds*: The trees are beginning to *bud*; they are in *bud*.

budgerigar (bud-ge-ri-gar) or **budgie** a small Australian bird of the parrot family: I have taught my *budgie* to talk.

budget (bud-get) a written document showing how much money was received and spent last year, and how much it is believed will be received and spent next year: Today the Chancellor of the Exchequer will present his *budget* to Parliament.

buffalo (buf-fa-lo) a term used to describe the bison of North America, the distinct Cape Buffalo of Africa, and the Wild and Water Buffalo of Asia.

buffer (buf-fer) two rods on springs put on vehicles to lessen the blow when they stop or touch each other.

buffet (buf-fet) 1. knock against: Our frail boat was *buffeted* by the winds and waves. 2. a blow. 3. a number of blows: After a severe *buffeting* the challenger was knocked to the floor. 4. (pronounced *boo-fay*) a counter or table where food and drink may be bought and consumed: We had a hasty meal at the railway station *buffet*.

buffoon (buf-foon) a jester, a clown or a person who behaves like one: He should spend less time playing the *buffoon* and more time on his work.

bugle (bu-gle) a small brass horn used by soldiers, sailors, boy scouts: The troop was called together by the sound of the *bugle*. **bugler** a person who blows a *bugle*.

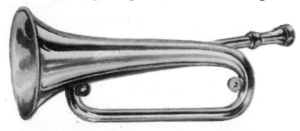

build make by putting together many parts: We need to *build* a factory to employ all these people. – My brother is *building* a stereo receiver. **building** a house or other construction of stone, bricks, wood, concrete etc. **builder** a person who constructs or helps to construct *buildings*.

bulb 1. a thick root, often round, which may be fit to eat: Some plants grow from seeds, others from *bulbs*. 2. a hollow shaped object of glass: The *bulb* of a thermometer contains mercury. An electric *bulb* gives light.

bulge 1. swell outwards: My Christmas stocking is *bulging* with good things. 2. a swelling: The chestnuts made a great *bulge* in his pocket.

bull the male of an animal, especially of the ox family, the elephant, rhinoceros etc: The hunter suddenly found himself faced by a huge *bull* elephant.

bullet (bul-let) a shaped piece of lead that is fired from a gun or revolver.

bulletin (bul-le-tin) a short statement of news, put out for the information of the public: 'No further *bulletins* concerning the duke's illness will be issued' (from a newspaper).

bully (bul-ly) *bullies, bullied, bullying* 1. a blustering, boastful person who terrifies or hurts those who may be weaker. 2. use one's strength to frighten, rob or hurt others: Today the school *bully* was thrashed by a smaller boy. He will never *bully* anyone again.

bump 1. a swelling on the body caused by a knock or blow: After the baby fell she had a *bump* on her head. 2. hit, strike or knock against something else: The drunken man *bumped* into a lamp post. – Slow down or you'll *bump* the car in front. **bumpy** full of raised places and hollows: What a *bumpy* road this is! **bumper** a bar in front and behind a motor vehicle put there to lessen the damage which might be done by a collision.

bun a small, sweet roll or cake, often containing currants: At Easter we always eat hot cross *buns* (hot *buns* with a cross marked on them).

bunch a number of things growing or held together, a cluster: Out of his pocket he drew a *bunch* of keys. – He bought his mother a pretty *bunch* of violets.

bundle (bun-dle) 1. a number of things bound, tied or fastened together: Please tie these old clothes into a *bundle* and sell them. 2. wrap, bind or put together: We *bundled* all the oddments into an old sack. 3. send somebody quickly and rudely: Before he was aware of what was happening, he was *bundled* into a big black van.

bungalow (bun-ga-low) a house with only one storey: By the side of the old cottage we have built a new *bungalow*.

bungle (bun-gle) do a piece of work badly: This workman *bungles* every job he does. **bungler** a person who is continually making mistakes.

bunk a narrow bed, usually fixed to a wall or the floor: We shall save space if we build two *bunks*, one above the other.

bunting (bun-ting) brightly coloured cloth used to make flags and decorations: When the Queen visited our town the streets were hung with flags and *bunting*.

buoy (pronounced *boy*) 1. a floating object used to mark a channel and to guide ships. 2. a floating object used to keep a person from sinking: His life was saved by clinging to the *buoy*.

bur or **burr** a rough part of a plant which contains seeds. A *bur* sticks to the clothes and to the coats of animals.

burden (bur-den) 1. a load: He was carrying a heavy *burden* on his back. 2. something that must be borne: This country carries a heavy *burden* of taxation. 3. the weight of cargo a ship can carry: Our ship's *burden* is 3,000 tons.

bureau (bu-reau) *bureaux* or *bureaus* 1. a writing desk with drawers. 2. a branch or department of government which deals with one activity: Farmers consult the Weather *Bureau*, tourists the Tourist *Bureau* and every city should have an Information *Bureau*. **bureaucracy** a government of paid officials called **bureaucrats**, who go by the rules and against whom there is often no remedy for unfair treatment.

burglar (bur-glar) a person who breaks into a building to steal: We should all make our houses secure against *burglars*. **burglary** robbery from buildings: The prisoner was given six months in gaol for *burglary*.

burn *burns, burned, burnt, burning* 1. use for light or heat: This lamp *burns* oil and our stove *burns* gas. 2. be on fire: When we arrived the fire was *burning* merrily. 3. hurt by fire: Many of the survivors were badly *burned*. 4. make *burn*, set on fire: The gardener piled up the dead leaves and *burnt* them. 5. an injury or mark made by something hot: The hot iron made a nasty *burn* on my hand. 6. sting: Too much mustard will *burn* your tongue.

burrow (bur-row) 1. dig a hole in the ground: Rabbits, badgers and moles *burrow*. 2. a nest or home made in the ground by a *burrowing* animal: This field is full of rabbit *burrows*.

burst 1. break apart, explode: We were late because of a *burst* tyre. – Shells were *bursting* all round us. 2. rush suddenly: All at once the children *burst* into the room. 3. start suddenly: The birds in the wood *burst* into song.

bury (bur-y) *buries, buried, burying* 1. put under the ground: We *buried* our dead leader on top of a mountain. 2. cover up, hide: You will find the gold *buried* under a pile of sacks. **burial** the act or ceremony of *burying*: 'Give him *burial* in his father's grave' (Shakespeare, *Titus Andronicus*).

bus a public vehicle with a long body and seats for passengers: Every morning I take the *bus* to school. **bus stop** the place where passengers get on and off the *bus*.

busby (bus-by) a tall fur hat worn by certain regiments in the British Army.

bush 1. a low plant with a hard stem and many branches rising from the ground: Roses, blackcurrants and gooseberries grow on *bushes*. 2. a stretch of land covered with *bushes* and small trees, chiefly in Australia and New Zealand. **bushy** thick with bushes or with hair: The track led us over a *bushy* plateau. – The man who met us had a long *bushy* beard.

business (bus-i-ncss) 1. buying and selling: I am a teacher but my brother is in *business*. 2. a firm consisting of one or more people: My father is the head of a shoe *business* and has a factory. 3. one's duty; what one has to do: It is your *business* to be at school in time. – Mind your own *business*.

busy (bus-y) 1. active, fully occupied: Don't disturb me; I'm *busy*. 2. full of activity and work: The shops are *busy* this morning.

butcher (butch-er) a man who keeps a shop in which he cuts up meat and sells it to the public.

butter (but-ter) 1. the cream from milk which when beaten or churned becomes a soft, light yellow solid: Don't spread too much *butter* on your bread. 2. certain substances like *butter*, such as cocoa *butter* and peanut *butter*. 3. spread *butter* on: You must *butter* your own bread. **buttermilk** the liquid left after the *butter* has been made from the cream. **butterscotch** a sweet made by boiling *butter* and sugar together.

button (but-ton) 1. a knob or disc of brass, pearl, bone or plastic which acts as a fastening or a decoration on clothing: Please sew a *button* on my trousers. – The coster's dress is decorated with thousands of pearl *buttons*. 2. fasten with *buttons*: It's a cold morning, so *button* your coat. 3. a small object which looks like a *button* and which is pressed to make something work: The doctor pressed the *button* and rang the doorbell. **buttonhole** the hole in clothing through which a *button* goes.

buy *buys*, *bought*, *buying* acquire something by paying money: 'She went to the tailor to *buy* him a coat' (Old Mother Hubbard). **buyer** a person who *buys* a thing, or who *buys* goods to be sold in a large store: We have not yet found a *buyer* for our piano. – My sister is a *buyer* for a London supermarket.

buzz 1. a low humming sound like that of bees: We heard the continual *buzz* of many voices. 2. make a *buzzing* noise: The wasps *buzzed* all around us.

by 1. at the side of, near: Come and sit *by* me. 2. through the use of or the doing of: Miners have to work *by* the light of lamps. – We went to London *by* train. – The house was built *by* my grandfather. 3. along: We shall go on foot *by* the shortest route. 4. as soon as; not later than: I should be ready to see you *by* five o'clock. 5. past: The express train roared *by*. – We were friends in days gone *by*. **by and by** later on: I will meet you *by and by*. **bygone** in past time: In *bygone* days men wore armour in battle. **bypass** a road that goes round a town: If you drive along the *bypass* you will miss the busy streets. **bystander** a person standing near: Several *bystanders* were injured in the explosion.

C

cab 1. a taxi*cab* or taxi: There are not many buses so it would be quicker to call a *cab*. 2. the covered part of a locomotive or lorry, where the driver sits: The driver leant out of his *cab* while the passengers boarded the train.

cabaret (ca-ba-ret, pronounced *cabaray*) an entertainment provided in a restaurant or night-club while guests are dining.

cabin (ca-bin) 1. a small house or hut: Robinson Crusoe built himself a *cabin* to sleep in. 2. a small room in a ship: For this cruise we have taken a *cabin* with two bunks. 3. the enclosed place in an aircraft designed for crew, passengers or cargo.

cabinet (cab-i-net) 1. a piece of furniture consisting of shelves, drawers or places for holding things of value, letters, pottery, etc: I keep all my antiques in a special *cabinet*. **filing cabinet** a case in which letters and other documents are kept in order. 2. a piece of furniture which holds a radio, record player or television. 3. the body of ministers which governs a country: The British *Cabinet* (capital C) is led by the Prime Minister.

cable (ca-ble) 1. a thick, strong rope, often made of several wires twisted together: The crew made the ship fast to the dock with thick *cables*. 2. a similar rope of twisted wire used for conducting electricity: The street had to be dug up before the damaged *cable* could be repaired. 3. send a message by *cable*. **cablegram** (or **cable**) a message sent by *cable*. **cable railway** a railway on which cars are hauled by a moving *cable*.

cadet (ca-det) a young person who is being trained to become an officer in the army, navy, air force or police. *cadet* corps (pronounced *core*) a group of persons being trained for one of these services.

café (ca-fé, pronounced *cafay*) a room or building where refreshments or meals are served: After the theatre we went into a *café* for a meal. **cafeteria** a restaurant where people serve themselves from a long counter.

cage an enclosed space like a box made with wires or bars in which birds or animals are kept: Everybody ran when the lion escaped from his *cage*.

calculate (cal-cu-late) find out by working with numbers: Before we make a journey round the world we must *calculate* how much it will cost. **calculation** the result of *calculating*: according to my *calculation* it will cost more than we can afford.

calendar (cal-en-dar) a list of the days, weeks and months in any year showing the number of each day in every month and the most important days in the year: Please look on the *calendar* and find the date of Easter Monday this year.

calf *calves* 1. the young of a cow and of certain other animals: The little *calf* could stand as soon as it was born.—At dawn the hunters passed a herd of elephants with their *calves*. 2. the fleshy, muscular part of the leg between knee and ankle.

callous (cal-lous) without pity, caring nothing for the suffering of others: It was *callous* of him to let the poor animal starve.

calm 1. (of the weather) quiet, with no wind: Jesus spoke to the sea and it became *calm*. 2. not excited: The whole crew kept *calm* as the boats were lowered. 3. make or become *calm*: The nurse tried to *calm* the sick child. 4. a time when everything is peaceful and quiet: The *calm* of the country is welcome after a busy day in town.

calorie (cal-o-rie) an amount of heat, an amount of energy supplied by food: An ounce of white bread supplies 69 *calories*.—People who are fat should reduce the number of *calories* they consume each day.

camel (cam-el) an animal with a long neck and either one or two humps on its back. *Camels* are used as beasts of burden, for carrying people and goods over deserts.

camera (cam-e-ra) a machine for taking photographs: When we go on holiday we always take a *camera*. **cameraman** a person who works a *camera* in a film studio or a television studio.

camouflage (cam-ou-flage) 1. a way of disguising men, guns, ships etc. so that an enemy cannot see them. Soldiers *camouflage* their guns by covering them with branches. Their uniforms are *camouflaged* by green and brown patches. 2. the means used to make anything hard to see: The spots of the leopard are a natural *camouflage* in the forest.

camp a group of tents, caravans or other simple buildings where people can live, usually for a short time: You will find the scouts' *camp* on the edge of the wood. 2. live in a *camp* or in a tent for a time: We *camped* for the night by a little stream. **camper** a person who lives for a time in a tent, caravan etc: This field is for *campers* only.

campaign (cam-paign) 1. a plan of action to defeat an enemy, to get money or for any other purpose: Our firm is starting an important advertising *campaign* for our new toothpaste. – The Germans were defeated in a well-planned *campaign* by the Allies. 2. take part in a plan to achieve some purpose or other: The Liberal Party is *campaigning* to get its candidates elected to Parliament.

camphor (cam-phor) a white, strong-smelling substance used in medicine and for making celluloid. Small *camphor* balls are put into drawers and wardrobes to keep moths out of clothes.

can 1. know how to, have the strength, the ability or the right to do a thing: I *can* both see and hear. – *Can* you play the piano? 2. a metal container for oil, fruit, fruit juices, vegetables, fish etc: For their evening meal the explorers opened a *can* of soup. 3. put into a *can* and seal so that no air can get in: *Can* you understand this old joke? In Canada they grow apples. They eat what they *can*, and what they can't eat they *can*.

canal (ca-nal) a channel dug by man either for boats or for taking water to fields where crops are growing. **canal boat** a boat specially made to carry loads from place to place by *canal*.

canary (ca-na-ry) a small bird, usually yellow, which sings sweetly. *Canaries* are kept in cages as pets.

cancel (can-cel) 1. cross out, draw a line through: If you copy the answers, your examination paper will be *cancelled*. 2. make a mark on postage stamps to show that they have been used. 3. state that something decided on will not be done or take place: I have *cancelled* my order for a television set. – Because of rain the football match has been *cancelled*.

cancer (can-cer) a tumour on or in the body which grows and may cause death.

candidate (can-di-date) 1. a person who is being put forward or is putting himself forward for a certain position: Mr Jones has offered himself as a *candidate* for the City Council. 2. a person taking an examination: 'All *candidates* should be in the examination room by 9 a.m.'

candle (can-dle) a stick of wax with a wick or string through it. When the wick is lit it slowly burns up the wax to give light: 'How far that little *candle* throws its beams' (Shakespeare, *Merchant of Venice*). **candlestick** a holder for a *candle*: On the mantelpiece were two brass *candlesticks*.

cannabis (can-na-bis) a drug made from parts of the Indian hemp plant.

cannibal (can-ni-bal) a person who eats human flesh. *Cannibals* are now only found among primitive peoples in remote parts of the world.

cannon (can-non) a large gun fixed to the ground or on wheels. In olden days *cannon* fired heavy balls of iron or stone. Modern *cannon* (or *cannons*) fire shells.

canoe

canoe (ca-noe) a light boat which is propelled by hand-paddles.

canopy (can-o-py) *canopies* a covering of cloth or other material fixed on a frame or held over a person by hand: The Queen sat under a *canopy* to watch the tournament.

canteen (can-teen) 1. a place to which soldiers, factory workers, schoolchildren etc. can go to buy and eat food. 2. a box or chest of silver or cutlery: The couple received a *canteen* of cutlery as a wedding present.

canvas (can-vas) strong, coarse cloth used for tents, sails, bags or coverings: This summer we spent three weeks under *canvas* (in camp).–All my best pictures have been painted in oil colours on *canvas*.

canvass (can-vass) go from door to door asking for votes, subscriptions, orders for goods etc: I am *canvassing* for the Labour Party. Will you promise to vote for our candidate? **canvasser** a person who canvasses: A notice outside this house reads, 'No circulars, no hawkers, no *canvassers*'.

canyon (can-yon) a very deep valley with steep sides, through which a stream or river may flow. The Grand *Canyon* of Colorado is one of the most spectacular sights in the United States.

cap 1. a small soft covering worn on the head: Some *caps* have peaks or small brims in front to shade the eyes. 2. a small cover for such things as bottles, jars, car radiators etc. 3. small pieces of thin paper which hold gunpowder for use in toys: The little boy's pistol is harmless: it only fires *caps*. 4. a special headdress: My sister wears a nurse's *cap*, my brother has a football *cap* and my father wears the *cap* and gown of his university. 5. put a *cap* or cover on, award a *cap* to a scholar, footballer etc: The raspberry jam we made has gone cold; shall we *cap* it?–England's great centre forward has been *capped* twenty times.

capable (ca-pa-ble) able, having knowledge, strength or skill to do a thing well: This work is poor, you are *capable* of doing better. **capably** well, skilfully: This work has been *capably* done.

capacity (ca-pac-i-ty) 1. the power to hold or contain: The Rovers' Football ground has a *capacity* of 50,000, and sometimes it is full to *capacity*. 2. the power to do: You have the *capacity* for achieving great things.

capital (cap-i-tal) 1. the city where the government of a country is carried on: London is the *capital* of England. Paris, Rome and Madrid are other *capital* cities. 2. (of letters of the alphabet) large and formed differently from small letters: We begin every sentence with a *capital* letter. 3. money or property which can be used in business: If you have not enough *capital* you must borrow it. 4. excellent: '*Capital*!' he replied when I told him of my plan. **capitalist** a person who has *capital* and uses it in business.

capitulate (ca-pit-u-late) give in, surrender: After the final attack the enemy was forced to *capitulate*.

capsize (cap-size) (of a boat or ship) turn over or make turn: If you rock the boat, it will *capsize*.

capsule (cap-sule) 1. a small case for seeds in a flower. 2. a tiny container of medicine taken like a pill, which dissolves in the body: The doctor has told me to swallow one *capsule* every four hours. 3. the compartment of a rocket in which the astronauts live.

captain (cap-tain) 1. a leader: Nobody knows who is the *captain* of the rebels.–The strength of a football or cricket team depends largely on its *captain*. 2. a commanding officer in the army or navy. 3. the person in charge of a ship: The *captain* was the last to leave the sinking liner.

capture (cap-ture) 1. make a prisoner of, take or seize: We *captured* 1,000 men and all the enemy's guns. 2. the act of *capturing* or being caught: A large reward is offered for the *capture* of the thief. **captive** a prisoner: In the campaign the army took thousands of enemy *captives*. **captivity** being held *captive*: Wild birds should not be kept in *captivity*.

car 1. a vehicle moving along the road under its own power, an automobile: My brother had taken the *car* so I went to work by bus. 2. the coach of a railway train: Shall we go to the dining *car* now?

caramel (car-a-mel) 1. a kind of soft toffee: May I have four ounces of *caramels*, please? 2. burnt sugar used for flavouring: The little boy ate a large helping of *caramel* pudding.

caravan (car-a-van) 1. a company of people going together for safety through desert country: We were saved from death by a *caravan* of pilgrims and camels. 2. a covered cart or wagon used by people to live in: This summer we are spending our holiday in a caravan.–
  'I wish I lived in a *caravan*
  With a horse to ride, like a gipsy man'
  (R. L. Stevenson).

carcass (car-cass) the dead body of an animal: The butcher cut up the *carcass* into joints to sell to his customers.

card 1. a piece of thick paper, blank or printed, used for brief messages: Why didn't you send me a Christmas (birthday, Easter) *card* this year? 2. one of the 52 *cards* used for games such as whist or poker: Would you like a game of *cards*? **cardboard** a thick, stiff paper used for making boxes etc.

cardigan (car-di-gan) a knitted woollen jacket buttoning up the front: Put on your *cardigan* today; it's very cold.

care 1. like: Would you *care* for a cup of tea? 2. be interested in: I don't *care* what you say about me but I do *care* what other people think. 3. look after: We are sending a doctor to *care* for the refugees. 4. attention, thought: 'His work needs much more *care*' (school report). 5. sorrow, anxiety: This poor woman is worn down by all her *cares*. **careful** paying attention, being watchful: Be *careful* how you walk down this muddy lane. **careless** thoughtless, paying little or no attention: He left all the lights burning: how *careless* of him. **caretaker** a person who is paid to look after a building.

career (ca-reer) a method of earning a living for which one has to be trained: While you are at school you should prepare for a worthwhile *career*.

cargo (car-go) *cargoes* goods carried by ship or plane: The vessel docked at Liverpool with a *cargo* of cotton.

carnival (car-ni-val) a time when people make merry and feast, with processions, dancing etc: The streets are decorated with flags and bunting for the great Spring *Carnival*.

carpenter (car-pen-ter) a workman who makes anything, especially parts of buildings and furniture, from wood: The *carpenter* came today to lay a new floor in our dining-room.

carpet (car-pet) 1. thick material of wool, hair or man-made fibre for covering floors: He walked in dirty boots all over our clean *carpet*. 2. a covering of grass, leaves, ferns etc. 3. cover smoothly, as with a *carpet*: The woodland glades were *carpeted* with wild flowers.

carriage (car-riage) 1. a vehicle for carrying people, usually with four wheels, pulled by horses: Motorcars have now taken the place of horse-drawn *carriages*. 2. a compartment of a railway train: You will find the first-class *carriages* in front, sir. 3. manner of holding the head and body: He has the *carriage* of a soldier.

carry (car-ry) 1. move from one place to another: '*Carry* your bag, sir?' said the porter. 2. keep, possess: Our store always *carries* a good stock of electrical appliances. 3. win, pass by voting: With a swift attack our army *carried* the fort. – The motion to raise money for the hospital was *carried*. 4. hold the head and body in a certain manner: Our visitor was tall and thin and *carried* himself very awkwardly. **carry on** continue doing something: This firm *carries on* its business all the year.

cart 1. a two-wheeled vehicle for carrying loads: Once there were butchers' *carts*, farmers' *carts* and many others, but now most things are carried by vans and lorries. 2. take or carry away in a *cart*: The dustmen have *carted* away all the rubbish.

carton (car-ton) a box of stiff paper or cardboard: Will you please hand me that *carton* of dried figs?

cartridge (car-tridge) a case of metal or cardboard which holds explosives: He took with him his rifle and twenty *cartridges*.

carve 1. cut a design on or cut into shape: We *carved* our initials in the bark of the tree. – This statue has been *carved* out of stone. 2. cut meat into pieces: Our host began to *carve* the huge leg of mutton. **carver** a person who *carves* things; a knife used at table for *carving* meat.

case 1. a box, carton or container: The books were brought in a large packing-*case*. – Has anybody seen my spectacle-*case*, my jewel-*case*, my suit-*case*, my dressing-*case*, or my pillow-*case*? 2. a condition, how things are, a state of health: In *case* of accident, call the police. – The doctor was called to deal with a severe *case* of measles. 3. a matter to be settled by law: If he does not pay we shall take the *case* to court. **casing** a covering, wrapping or frame: This electric wire has a plastic *casing*. – The window-*casing* has rotted and needs replacing.

cash 1. money, in coins or notes: I cannot pay you in *cash*, would you please take a cheque? 2. give or get cash for: You can *cash* this postal order at any post office. **cashier** a person who looks after money in a bank or a large store.

casket (cas-ket) a small box for holding valuable things: The duchess kept her jewellery in a silver *casket*.

cassock (cas-sock) a long garment worn by some priests, or singers in church choirs: All our choirboys wear the *cassock* and surplice.

cast 1. throw: Fishermen *cast* their nets: the Roman soldiers *cast* lots for Christ's clothing. – I am *casting* my vote for the best candidate. 2. pour into a mould to make a shape: This statue was *cast* in bronze. **cast iron** iron which has been shaped in this way. 3. the group of actors in a play or film: We shall choose the *cast* for the school play tomorrow. **cast-offs** clothing which the owner does not wish to wear again.

castle (cas-tle) 1. a large building or group of buildings once used as a fort and dwelling-place: The duke's *castle* stood on a high hill and was defended by walls and strong towers. 2. a large house or mansion. 3. one of the pieces in a game of chess, the upper part shaped like the tower of a *castle*.

casual (cas-u-al) happening by chance, not thought of before: I learnt of her success through a *casual* meeting, and a *casual* remark. **casualty** a person injured by accident or in battle: The enemy suffered many *casualties*.

cat 1. a small animal with a coat of fur, kept as a pet and to catch mice. 2. an animal of the *cat* family which includes tigers, lions, panthers and leopards. 3. (short for *cat-o-nine-tails*) a whip with nine knotted lashes once used to flog soldiers, sailors and prisoners. **cat's eye** a small reflector placed in the middle of the road to guide motorists in the dark.

catalogue (cat-a-logue) 1. a book or list of names, or of names of articles describing them and telling how much they cost: Before we went into the sale we bought a *catalogue*. 2. make a list: All the books in this library have now been *catalogued*.

catamaran (cat-a-ma-ran) a small craft made up of two hulls fastened side by side.

catapult (cat-a-pult) 1. a device for throwing large stones or small pellets: Giant *catapults* were used in ancient times to break down the walls of castles and cities.– My brother made a *catapult* with a forked stick and a piece of elastic. 2. a device which launches planes from the deck of an aircraft carrier.

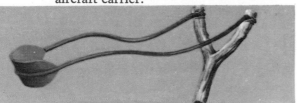

cataract (cat-a-ract) 1. a waterfall which drops from a great height: The roar of the *cataract* could be heard miles away. 2. a growth on the eye which prevents people from seeing well: This old man is to have an operation to cure the *cataract* in his left eye.

catch *catches, caught, catching* 1. take and hold on to something which moves: Watch the goalkeeper *catch* the ball with both hands.–Our cat *caught* three mice today. 2. surprise, discover: Don't let me *catch* you stealing apples! 3. become ill: Last week I *caught* cold and now I have *caught* influenza. 4. become entangled with, prevented from moving: Oh dear, I've *caught* my trousers on a nail! 5. something which fastens: Put the *catch* on the door as you go out. 6. a trick to deceive: He said the small knife was worth more than the large one, but I knew there was a *catch* somewhere. **catch fire** begin to burn: The plane dived to the ground and *caught fire*. **catch up** to follow and become level with: Run along; I'll soon *catch up* with you.

cater (ca-ter) provide anything people require, such as food or entertainment: This magazine *caters* for all who enjoy adventure stories. **caterer** a person or firm supplying and sometimes serving food and drink for a party or entertainment.

caterpillar (cat-er-pil-lar) 1. a small insect which later develops into a moth or butterfly. 2. a tractor which runs by means of a steel belt working on two or more wheels, enabling it to haul heavy loads over hard or soft ground.

cathedral (ca-the-dral) the chief church in the district controlled by a bishop: Many people visit the *cathedral* to see the bishop's throne.

Catholic (cath-olic) 1. a person who belongs to the Roman *Catholic* Church, led by the Pope. 2. (small c) universal, involving all: Their taste in music was *catholic*.

cattle (cat-tle) cows, bulls, calves and steers: Every evening in winter the farmer brings in the *cattle* from the fields.

cauliflower (cau-li-flower) a cultivated plant which has in the centre a mass of solid white flowers: The *cauliflower* is eaten as a vegetable.

cause produce, make happen: We do not know what *caused* the accident.–Sun and rain *cause* the flowers to grow. 2. reason, that which makes a thing happen: Lack of good food was the *cause* of his illness. 3. a thing which people believe in and are working for: We fight in the *cause* of freedom and our *cause* is worthwhile.

caution (cau-tion) 1. care, being on the alert: At the road junction stood a sign 'PROCEED WITH *CAUTION*'. 2. warn: The referee *cautioned* the player to avoid foul play. 3. a warning: The traffic warden gave me a friendly *caution* against parking on the double line. **cautious** careful: Please be very *cautious* when going down the steep staircase.

cavalry (cav-al-ry) soldiers who fight on horseback: The British *cavalry* charged, breaking the enemy line. **cavalier** a soldier on horseback who fought for King Charles I in the English Civil War.

cave a hollow place underground or in the side of a cliff: We found the treasure hidden in a deep *cave*. **cave in** to fall or sink, give way: We had barely left the tunnel when the roof *caved in*. **cavity** an empty or hollow space: 'That *cavity* in your tooth must be filled,' said the dentist.

cease stop, come to an end, finish:
'When the wind blows the cradle will rock.
When the wind *ceases* the cradle will fall' (nursery rhyme).

ceiling (ceil-ing) 1. the overhead surface inside a room: The bedroom walls have paper on them but the *ceiling* is painted. 2. the highest distance an aircraft can go: Our new plane has a *ceiling* of many thousand metres.

celebrate (cel-e-brate) 1. do something to show that a day or a happening is important: We *celebrate* birthdays, wedding anniversaries, Christmas, Easter and Guy Fawkes Day among others. 2. honour and think well of: We *celebrate* the names of all our national heroes. – Dickens was a *celebrated* novelist. **celebration** an occasion when some person or special event is *celebrated*: Did you attend the victory *celebrations* yesterday?

cell 1. a small room in a prison or monastery: Every morning the prisoners were taken from their *cells* for exercise. 2. One of many separate spaces or parts: There are hundreds of *cells* in a honeycomb. – The bodies of men and animals are made up of *cells*. 3. a device which makes electricity and which is part of a battery.

cellar (cel-lar) a room under the ground used for storing things: Our house is heated by a boiler in the *cellar*.

celluloid (cel-lu-loid) a plastic material used for making combs, buttons, film for cameras and many other articles. *Celluloid* is very useful but easily catches fire.

cement (ce-ment) 1. a substance made by burning lime and clay which is soft when mixed with water, but then becomes very hard. *Cement* is used for building, making roads and laying floors. 2. any material that sets hard, fills holes or sticks things together: We mended the broken vase with china *cement*. 3. join firmly together, stick: The ornament was broken and we had to *cement* the parts together.

cemetery (cem-e-ter-y) *cemeteries* a burial ground or graveyard not part of a church: My friend is the caretaker of a military *cemetery*.

censor (cen-sor) an official who examines books, letters, plays, films etc. to make sure that anything not thought suitable is left out: The play was so severely cut by the *censor* that it was not worth presenting.

census (cen-sus) a counting of all the people living anywhere: In our town, according to the last *census* there were 53,000 people.

centigrade (cen-ti-grade) a scale on the thermometer showing 100 degrees between the freezing point and the boiling point of water: A comfortable temperature for a room is about 20 degrees *centigrade*.

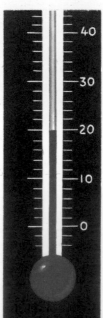

centipede (cen-ti-pede) a long active animal like an insect whose body has many sections, each with a single pair of legs: When we turned up the stone a number of *centipedes* scurried off.

centre (cen-tre) 1. the middle point: Please put a dot at the *centre* of this circle. 2. an important place to which people go: There are many *centres* for winter sports in Switzerland. 3. keep in the *centre*: *Centre* yourself in the front row. **centre forward** and **centre half** (back) two important positions in a football team. **central** middle or chief: You cannot always be the *central* attraction. – That is the *central* point of any argument.

century (cen-tu-ry) *centuries* 1. one hundred years: Few people live a *century*. 2. a hundred runs scored by one man in a game of cricket: We all applauded when the captain scored a *century*.

cereal (ce-re-al) any kind of grain used for food: Wheat, rye and rice are all common *cereals*.

certain (cer-tain) sure; of which there is no doubt: I am *certain* he will come. 2. a special person or thing, but not named: 'A *certain* man went down from Jerusalem to Jericho' (Parable of the Good Samaritan). **certainly** without doubt: Am I wanted by the police? *Certainly* not. – I shall *certainly* complain to the Chief Constable.

certificate (cer-tif-i-cate) a printed or written statement which can be produced as evidence that a certain thing is true: If you want to enter college, you must send your birth *certificate*.

chain 1. many links or rings fastened together to make an unbroken line: 'No *chain* is stronger than its weakest link, (proverb). 2. a number of things or events connected together in some way: From the air a long *chain* of mountains could be seen. – My present sorry state is the result of a long *chain* of misfortunes. 3. make fast with a *chain*: If you don't *chain* your dog to the gate he will run away.

chalk 1. soft white powdery material made from limestone: The teacher took a stick of *chalk* and began to write on the blackboard. 2. write, draw or mark with *chalk*: I wish I could find out who has *chalked* all over my fence.

challenge (chal-lenge) 1. invitation to fight, run a race, or enter a contest: I took it as a *challenge* to have to learn reasonable French in a year. 2. make or send out a *challenge*: The Black Knight *challenged* anybody to fight him. **challenger** the person who makes the *challenge*.

chamber (cham-ber) 1. a private room, especially a bedroom: Sleeping Beauty was found in a *chamber* of the royal palace. 2. a large room where parliament or a town council meets: The House of Commons is the lower *chamber* of the British parliament. 3. a committee which exists for a special purpose: In our town the *Chamber* of Commerce looks after the interests of traders and shopkeepers. 4. the part of a rifle or gun in which the cartridge or shell is placed before firing.

chamois (cham-ois, pronounced *shamwah*) a goatlike antelope which lives in mountainous regions of Europe and southwestern Russia. A **chamois** (pronounced *shammy*) **leather** is a piece of soft leather used for cleaning windows.

champion (cham-pi-on) 1. the person who wins or takes first place in a game or contest: For years my son has been unbeaten *champion* on the tennis court. **championship** the position of a *champion*: He has gained the table tennis *championship* of all England.

chance 1. accident, something that had not been expected: I met my cousin by *chance* at the zoo. 2. an opportunity: You may never have such a *chance* again. 3. happen by *chance*: If I *chance* to meet him I will pass on your message.

chandelier (chan-de-lier) a support for lights hanging from the ceiling. A *chandelier* has several branches, each of which holds a light.

change 1. put in place of: Have you *changed* your shirt this morning? 2. make different, become different: The ship could not enter the harbour until the wind *changed*.– Since the operation he has been a *changed* man. 3. a difference, something put in place: Please note our *change* of address. 4. money in coins of small value: 'Please count your *change* before leaving' (notice in a shop). **changeable** likely to *change*, often *changing*: What *changeable* weather we have had this month!

channel (chan-nel) 1. a stretch of water joining two seas: The English *Channel* lies between the North Sea and the Atlantic Ocean. 2. a line of deeper water in a river or harbour: The *channel* is marked by a line of buoys.

chapel (chap-el) 1. a place used for worship, usually smaller than a parish church, or a small place for prayer inside a church: Near the church door there are two tiny *chapels*.–His school has its own private *chapel*. 2. a place of worship used by some Christians who do not belong to the Church of England: In our village there are Methodist and Congregational *chapels*. **chaplain** a priest or clergyman who takes services in a *chapel*: My eldest brother is a *chaplain* in the Royal Air Force.

character (char-ac-ter) 1. the things in a person's disposition that make him different from others: The archbishop is a man of noble *character*. 2. all the good qualities which make for excellence in a person: For this important work we need a man of *character*. 3. a person who is noted for what he has done or for some special *characteristic* of behaviour: The money has been given by a prominent local *character*.–What an odd *character* the old sailor is. 4. a person in a book or play: Of all Dickens's *characters* I like David Copperfield best.

charcoal (char-coal) a black substance made by burning wood slowly until it is black. *Charcoal* is used by artists for sketching, and to burn in stoves to produce heat: My grandmother used an iron which burned *charcoal*.

charge 1. accuse: 'You are *charged* with burglary,' said the judge. 'I deny the *charge*,' replied the prisoner. 2. ask as a price for: What would you *charge* for mowing my lawn? 3. put on a note or make a record of something to be paid later: Please *charge* this sum to my account. 4. rush forward, attack: '*Charge*!' commanded the general. 5. load, fill: The soldiers *charged* their rifles as the enemy advanced. 6. something one is *charged* with. 7. the price asked for: The *charge* has recently been increased. 8. the amount of powder put into a gun or used to make an explosion: The miners blew up a rock with a *charge* of dynamite. 9. work given as a duty: You are now in *charge* of the works. **charger** the horse on which a knight in olden times rode to war.

charity (char-i-ty) *charities* 1. help given to the poor and sick: Today we are holding a concert for *charity*. 2. a society organized to give help: At Christmas time all the *charities* ask people to contribute money. 3. kindness, willingness to forgive: The world would be a sad place if there were no *charity*. **charitable** kind, generous and forgiving.

charm 1. power to give pleasure: The mistress of the house is a person of great *charm*. 2. something believed to have magic power: 'Take this *charm*,' said the fairy 'and nothing can hurt you.' 3. please, give pleasure: We were *charmed* by the wonderful scenery. 4. use magic on, protect: This man says he can *charm* snakes.–He must lead a *charmed* life.

chart 1. a sheet of paper on which a list or diagram gives information on weather, prices, or temperature: On the wall is a *chart* giving the times when the trains leave. 2. a map used by sailors to show where rocks and lighthouses are. 3. put on a *chart*: make a map of: The explorer *charted* all the lands he discovered.

chase 1. run after in order to capture or drive away: I was *chased* into a corner and could run no further. 2. act of *chasing*, pursuit: The thief was caught after a long *chase* by the police.

chassis (chas-sis, pronounced *shassi*) the framework on which a motorcar, or the parts of a radio are mounted: The car was sent back to the factory because of a fault in the *chassis*.

check 1. compare: Would you *check* this bill please? It has been wrongly calculated. 2. hold back or stop: The traffic jam *checked* our progress for an hour.— My speed was *checked* by the strong wind. 3. a pattern of lines making squares of different colours: This cloth is very good, sir. Would you like the plain or the *check*?

cheek 1. the two sides of the face below the eyes: The baby has round, rosy *cheeks*. 2. impudence: He had the *cheek* to ask me to lend him money.

cheer 1. shout encouragement: Let's *cheer* our team to victory, boys! 2. make glad, give comfort or happiness: Your letters have *cheered* me up greatly. **cheerful** happy or bringing happiness: A sunny day makes us all *cheerful*. **cheery** lively and gay: He greets everybody with a *cheery* smile. 3. a shout of joy or encouragement: The captain called for three *cheers*.

cheese 1. solid food made by separating the thick part of milk and shaping it into a cake: Cream *cheese*, Cheddar *cheese*, Stilton *cheese* and many other kinds are eaten in England.

chemist (chem-ist) 1. a scientist who studies how substances are made up and how they change when put with other substances. 2. a person who sells medicines, drugs, and toilet articles, as well as preparing the medicines which the doctor prescribes. **chemistry** the study of how substances are made up and how they behave when put together, heated, cooled etc.

cheque (pronounced *check*) a written order to a bank to pay money to the person who presents it: Will you please pay these *cheques* into my bank account?

cherish (cher-ish) 1. look after a person or a thing with care: We *cherished* the old lady until the day she died. 2. hold on to a belief or a hope: I have always *cherished* the hope of going to Australia.

chess a game for two players played on a black and white check board of 64 squares with 16 pieces. **chessboard, chessmen** the board and pieces used in the game of chess.

chest 1. a large box with a lid and sometimes drawers, used to store tools, linen, clothes, or jewellery. **chest of drawers** a piece of furniture consisting of drawers fitted into a frame. 2. the upper front part of the body: The general wore three rows of medals on his *chest*.

chestnut (chest-nut) 1. a tree with a smooth, reddish-brown nut. 2. the nut of the *chestnut* tree: Do you like roasted *chestnuts*? 3. the wood of the *chestnut* tree. 4. reddish brown: the race was won by a beautiful *chestnut* mare.

chew crush, cut and grind into tiny pieces with the teeth: You should always *chew* your food well before swallowing it.

chicken (chick-en) a young fowl bred for its meat and its eggs. **chick** a small *chicken*: The white hen has just hatched 12 *chicks*. **chickenpox** an illness in which a person breaks out in many small red spots.

chief 1. a leader, a person placed over others: The Indian *chief* summoned his brave warriors to the council of the tribe.— What do you wish me to do next, *chief*? 2. most important, placed over others: London is the *chief* city in England.—The *Chief* Constable led the search for the missing boy. **chiefly** mainly: My work is concerned *chiefly* with the young cadets.

child *children* a boy or girl who has not yet grown up: a son or daughter: This *child* is only three years old. He is the youngest of my *children*.

chill 1. make cold or become cold: The bottle of wine was put on ice to *chill* it. 2. an illness caused by cold: He caught a *chill* through getting his feet wet. 3. coldness: There is quite a *chill* in the air this morning. **chilly** cool or rather cold. **chilblain** a painful swelling on hand or foot, caused by cold.

chime 1. series of notes sounded on bells: The *chimes* echoed on the frosty air. 2. the bells giving these notes: We ring the *chimes* on Christmas Eve. 3. ring, show the time by ringing: The church clock *chimed* the hour of twelve. 4. interrupt people who are talking: 'I like that,' he *chimed* in.

chimney (chim-ney) a structure like a long tube built into a house to draw the fumes from a fire up and out of the building. **chimney-pot** a pipe of earthenware or metal fixed to the top of a chimney. **chimney-sweep** the person who comes with a large brush to clear the soot out of the *chimney*.

chin the lowest part of the face, below the mouth: The old man had a long beard on his *chin*.

china (chi-na) 1. white clay which has been baked, glazed and made into cups, saucers, plates, and dishes. 2. dishes made out of *china*: We put out the best *china* when the vicar came to tea.

chink a narrow crack, split or opening through which one may peep or through which the wind blows: 'Pyramus and Thisbe . . . did talk through the *chink* of a wall' (Shakespeare, *A Midsummer Night's Dream*).

chip 1. a small piece broken or cut off: We gathered *chips* (of wood) to start a fire. 2. a thin strip of wood used for making baskets. 3. a finger of fried potato cut from a slice and fried with others: Who's having fish and *chips* for supper? 4. cut or break pieces off.

chiropodist (chi-rop-o-dist) a person who looks after the feet of other people and treats their complaints.

chirp make light, short, sharp sounds: Sparrows *chirp* during the day and crickets at night.

chisel (chis-el) 1. a tool with a sharp steel edge at one end. Carpenters use *chisels* to shape wood and to trim stone. 2. trim or cut with a *chisel*: If you *chisel* a piece off the edge of the door, you will make it fit better.

chloroform (chlo-ro-form) a thin colourless liquid which easily turns to vapour. The vapour of *chloroform* can be used to make a person unconscious before an operation.

chocolate (choc-o-late) 1. a substance made by grinding the seeds of the cacao tree. *Chocolate* can be drunk mixed with hot milk and sugar or made into small blocks or bars for eating. 2. the colour of *chocolate*, dark brown. **choc-ice** ice cream coated with *chocolate*.

choice 1. something chosen or picked: Here are a dozen pens; now make your *choice*. 2. the right or chance to choose: You have no *choice* in the matter; you will join the navy. 3. the very best: '*Choice* pears, lady, buy my *choice* pears!' he called.

choir 1. a number of people who sing together: I am a member of the school *choir*. 2. the part of a church where the church *choir* is situated.

choke 1. be unable to breathe because the throat is blocked: Don't gulp your soup; you'll *choke*. 2. spoil by filling up: Our garden is *choked* with weeds, and the drains are *choked* with rubbish. 3. stop somebody breathing because of fumes or pressure on the throat: Though almost *choked* by smoke he succeeded in pulling the child out of the fire.

choose *chooses, chose, chosen, choosing* pick or select a thing one wants to do: Why do you *choose* the smallest piece of cake? – My brother has *chosen* to be a doctor.

chop 1. cut by striking with a knife or axe: Please *chop* down this tree and then *chop* the wood into small sticks. 2. a slice of meat with the bone in it: I'll have a pork *chop* if there are no mutton *chops* left. **chopsticks** the two sticks used by the Chinese for eating.

chord three or more notes of music played together in harmony.

chore a small duty which one does, usually in the home: I wash up, I sweep the floor, I clean the silver and so do all the household *chores*.

chorus (cho-rus) 1. music for a choir or a large number of singers: The choir sang the Hallelujah *Chorus*. 2. the part of a song which comes after the verse and is sung by everybody.

Christian (Christ-ian) a follower of Jesus Christ who believes in His teachings. **Christianity** the teachings of Christ. **Christian name** the name given to a person at birth which comes before the surname. **christen** give a *Christian* name to a person when baptized in a church. **Christmas** 25th December, the anniversary of the birth of Jesus Christ.

chromium (chro-mium) a bright substance which shines like silver and is used for plating taps, car fittings, and also used for making pigments in photography.

chrysanthemum (chrys-an-the-mum) a garden flower with small petals which blooms in autumn and early winter.

chubby (chub-by) round and plump: The small boy was *chubby* rather than fat.

chuckle (chuck-le) 1. a low, quiet laugh: A *chuckle* ran through the class when the blackboard collapsed. 2. laugh softly and quietly: I will tell you a story that will make you *chuckle*.

chunk a large piece: Please put a few *chunks* of coal on the fire.

church 1. a building to which Christians go for public worship: 'He goes on Sunday to the *church*' (Longfellow, *The Village Blacksmith*). 2. a body of Christians who worship in the same way: The Christian *Church* includes the Catholic *Church*, the *Church* of England, the Methodist *Church* and many others. **churchyard** the ground around the *church*.

churn 1. a tub in which cream is shaken to make butter. 2. shake and beat cream in butter-making.

cigar (ci-gar) tobacco leaves made into a tight roll for smoking: Sir Winston Churchill was hardly ever seen without his *cigar*. **cigarette** shreds of tobacco rolled in a piece of thin paper for smoking.

cinder (cin-der) a small piece of coal, or other material partly burned: Every morning we sweep up the *cinders* and clean the grate.—Oh dear, my chocolate cake has been burnt to a *cinder*!

cipher (ci-pher) 1. the figure 0 which represents nought. 2. a method of writing in code so that it can be understood only by those who know the code: Sir, we have just received this message in *cipher*.

circle (cir-cle) 1. a perfectly round line on which every point is the same distance from the centre. 2. a number of people who meet to do things together: In our club we have a music *circle*, a ladies' *circle* and a hobbies *circle*. 3. move in a *circle*: Our plane had to *circle* round the airport for two hours before landing.

circular (cir-cu-lar) 1. round, the shape of a *circle*: The woodman was cutting up the logs with a *circular* saw. 2. a letter or notice sent out to many people: A *circular* was left in our letter-box telling us of the carpet sale. **circulate** go round or send round: Blood *circulates* in the human body.—News is *circulated* by means of newspapers, radio and television. **circulation** sending round, the number sent round: This evening newspaper has a *circulation* of 25,000 copies.

circumference (cir-cum-fer-ence) the outer boundary: Do you know how to find the *circumference* of a circle?

circumstance (cir-cum-stance) a state or condition, a group or set of facts: This family needs help; they are in desperate *circumstances*.—Please describe the *circumstances* under which this accident happened.

circus (cir-cus) 1. a show in which clowns, performing animals and acrobats take part. 2. a place, originally circular, where many streets meet: Nobody should visit London without seeing Piccadilly *Circus*.

cistern (cis-tern) a water tank from which pipes run to taps: Every house should have *cisterns* for supplying hot and cold water.

city (cit-y) a large town whose people are given special rights to govern themselves: Among the largest *cities* in the world are Tokyo, New York, London and Paris. **citizen** a person belonging to a *city* or a country who has the right to vote and take part in its government: I am proud of being a British *citizen*.

civilization (ci-vi-li-za-tion) 1. the development of a people from a primitive to an advanced society. The advantages of art, science, education and government: The *civilization* of mankind has taken thousands of years. 2. the way in which a nation or race lives and thinks: European *civilization* has influenced much of the world. 3. a nation or part of the world at a certain point in its history: We are now studying the ancient *civilizations* of Egypt and Sumer. **civilize** train and educate people to a higher level of behaviour and culture.

claim 1. demand something as a right: Does anybody *claim* this pencil?—I *claim* your protection. 2. say that something is true: He *claimed* that he held the record for weight lifting. 3. take up time or attention: This is a hard task: it will *claim* all your perseverance. 4. a right: His *claim* to the crown was accepted.

clamber (clam-ber) climb with difficulty, using hands and feet: He had to *clamber* up the steep roof to reach the chimney.

clamp 1. an appliance for holding things together: First we glued the boards, then we put a *clamp* on them. 2. a heap of potatoes stored for the winter under straw, earth and rubbish. 3. to fasten with *clamps*.

clank 1. a loud sound as of metals banging together: We heard the *clank* as the car struck the stone wall. 2. make a *clank*: 'Nearer and nearer came the spectre, *clanking* its chains' (from a ghost story).

clash 1. make a loud, harsh noise: The musicians *clashed* their cymbals as the king rode by. 2. a loud, harsh noise: The battle began with the *clash* of arms. 3. disagree, conflict in opinion: Our beliefs *clash* and we cannot agree about anything. – The colour of her skirt *clashed* badly with her coat.

clasp 1. a device, usually of metal, for fastening things together: Will you please fasten the *clasp* of my dress? 2. fasten with a *clasp*. 3. hold tightly: In this game you form a circle and *clasp* hands.

class 1. a group of persons taught together: I have joined a *class* to study German. 2. a group of things which are of the same kind: Our grocer divides his eggs into three *classes*, large, medium and small. 3. put into a *class* or group: I would *class* him among the greatest men alive today. **classroom** a room in which a *class* of students is taught.

clatter (clat-ter) 1. a loud rattling noise as if hard objects are being knocked together: We were awakened by the *clatter* of horse's hoofs. 2. make a *clatter*: All the plates and dishes *clattered* to the floor.

claw 1. a sharp nail, usually curved, on the foot of an animal: I still have the mark of the cat's *claws* on my leg. 2. tear, scratch, pull as if with *claws*: He was badly *clawed* by a tiger.

clay a kind of earth which is soft and sticky when wet and becomes hard when dry: Tiles, bricks and many kinds of pottery are made of *clay*.

clean 1. free from dirt, smoke or anything impure: All people should be able to breathe *clean* air, drink *clean* water and wear *clean* clothing. 2. free from wrong-doing or anything impure. 3. skilful: He scored six runs with a *clean* hit. 4. remove dirt from, make *clean*: I must *clean* my shoes and have my suit *cleaned*. **cleaner** a person or anything which *cleans*: Our window-*cleaner* comes once a fortnight. – I need a bottle of carpet *cleaner*.

clear 1. easy to see through, bright: The water was so *clear* that the bottom of the lake could easily be seen. – The sun shone in a *clear* sky. 2. easy to understand: Two and two make four. Is that *clear*? 3. easy to see or hear: She spoke in a loud, *clear* voice. 4. free oneself from anything which is in the way: Please *clear* the table. – Before I could sing I had to *clear* my throat. 5. away, not touching: 'Stand *clear* of the doors, please!'

clergyman a Christian minister qualified to take religious services.

clerk (pronounced *clark*) 1. a person who works in an office, such as a bank, copying statements and keeping accounts: My father is an insurance *clerk* and my brother is a railway *clerk*. 2. an important officer who looks after the business affairs of a government or a large company: Every town has its Town *Clerk*.

clever (clev-er) quick to learn, skilful, smart: I give in; you are far too *clever* for me. – This picture was painted by an extremely *clever* artist.

click 1. make a sharp, short sound: The key *clicked* in the lock, and we were trapped. 2. a sharp, short sound: One *click* of the latch and he was gone.

cliff the face or front of a high, steep rock: 'DANGER! Visitors are warned not to approach the edge of the *cliff*.' (public notice)

climate (cli-mate) the general weather conditions of a region: My doctor says that the English *climate* is too cold and wet for me.

climb 1. go up, grow up: The plane *climbed* quickly above the clouds. – The ivy has *climbed* as high as the roof. 2. an ascent by climbing: We reached the summit after a difficult *climb*.

cling *clings, clung, clinging* hold tightly to: *Cling* to me and you won't fall – I can't, the snow is *clinging* to my shoes.

clinic (clin-ic) a place where medical treatment is given: Go to the *clinic* and ask the doctor to examine you.

clip 1. a wire or metal device for holding tightly: My letters are blowing away; bring me a paper *clip*. 2. an ornament which *clips* on a garment: She wore a dress with a gold *clip*. 3. fasten with a *clip*: The clerk *clipped* the papers together. 4. cut or cut off with scissors or shears: The dog's hair has been *clipped* unevenly. 5. punch a hole: The bus conductor *clipped* my ticket. **clippers** a tool with small knives in it like scissors, for cutting hair.

cloak a loose outer garment, usually without sleeves: The villain strode on to the stage in a long black *cloak*. **cloakroom** a place where hats and coats may be left; a lavatory.

clock an instrument by which one can tell the hour of the day or night: I have a *clock* which hangs on the wall and a watch which I wear on my wrist.

close (rhymes with *dose*) 1. near a place or person: Our house is *close* to the church. – Come and sit *close* to me. 2. near in time: It is now *close* to eight o'clock. 3. dear: He is one of my *closest* friends. 4. nearly equal: The race ended in a *close* finish. 5. short of fresh air, difficult to breathe: Please open a window; it is far too *close* in here. 6. strict, very careful: The patient was kept under *close* watch for three weeks. **closely** well, strictly: See that this man is *closely* guarded.

close (rhymes with *those*) 1. shut: *Close* your eyes and go to sleep. 2. bring or come to an end: We shall *close* the shop at six o'clock. 3. end: He will come back at the *close* of the day.

cloth 1. material made by weaving threads of wool, silk, hair, flax, cotton or other fibre: You will need several metres of *cloth* for this dress. 2. a piece of *cloth*: Bring me a floor-*cloth* and a dish-*cloth*; I have spilt the tea on the table-*cloth*.

clothe dress: I saw an archer *clothed* in green. **clothes** articles of dress or coverings: I need new *clothes* for the wedding. – Have you enough *clothes* on the bed? **clothing** clothes: We wear heavier *clothing* in winter than in summer.

cloud 1. a large body of vapour or ice particles floating in the sky: Black *clouds* often bring rain. 2. smoke or dust or a collection of insects floating in the air: The sky was darkened by a *cloud* of locusts. 3. become dark or dim as if by a *cloud*: Before we reached home the sky had *clouded* over. – Her eyes were *clouded* with tears. **cloudy** filled with *clouds*, not clear: The mud would not settle and the water was still *cloudy*. **cloudless** having no clouds: The sun shone in a *cloudless* sky.

clown a man who performs in a circus, paints his face, dresses comically and does amusing tricks: *Clowns* are great favourites with children.

club 1. group of persons who have joined together either to help each other or to follow some sport or pastime: In our village there is a football *club*, a tennis *club* and a cricket *club*. 2. one of the four sets of cards in a pack: I put down the ace of *clubs* and won the game. 3. a stick with a metal head used in playing golf. 4. a heavy wooden stick, thick at one end, used as a weapon: Our little band was attacked by savages armed with *clubs*. 5. hit with a stick or other weapon: The hunters *clubbed* the animal with their rifles.

clue an idea, a happening or something left behind which helps to solve a problem: A pair of spectacles was the only *clue* to this murder. – 'Who did this?' roared the sergeant. 'I haven't a *clue*, sir.'

clumsy (clum-sy) 1. awkward, not having much skill in movement: Are you one of those *clumsy* people who walk into lamp-posts? 2. something not easy to use, poorly made: A pocket-knife is a *clumsy* tool for opening a tin.

cluster (clus-ter) 1. a number of things of the same kind growing or held together: I'll have that *cluster* of grapes, please. 2. come together in a *cluster*: *Cluster* round me, children, and I'll tell you a story.

clutch 1. seize with hands or claws, hold tightly: A drowning man will *clutch* at a straw (proverb). 2. mastery: 'Ah!' said the wicked witch, 'now I have you in my *clutches*!' 3. a device that joins two working parts of a machine, putting the machine in or out of action: The *clutch* of a car connects the engine with the wheels.

coach 1. a closed carriage with four wheels, pulled by horses: Mail *coaches* used to carry letters, stage *coaches* carried people and a state *coach* carries the queen to important ceremonies. 2. a railway carriage. 3. a bus which travels long distances. 4. a teacher who has only one or two pupils: I have private *coaches* for French and mathematics. 5. teach a small number: Our football team is being *coached* by a famous player.

coal 1. a black mineral sold in chunks and burned to give heat. 2. a piece of wood or *coal* which is burning: The dog stood on a live *coal*. **coalfield** a district where *coal* is dug from under the ground.

coarse 1. rough, not fine or smooth to the touch: We mixed the cement with *coarse* sand.—He wore a jacket of *coarse* cloth. 2. vulgar, common: Nobody likes his *coarse* manners.

coast 1. land lying along the side of water: We live in a cottage on the *coast* of Cornwall. 2. move without effort: I love *coasting* downhill on a bicycle.

coat 1. an outer garment with sleeves: It's cold today so put on your thick *coat*. 2. anything that covers: This door needs another *coat* of paint. 3. the hair or fur of an animal: 'I love little pussy, her *coat* is so warm' (nursery rhyme). 4. cover: The picture-frame is *coated* with dust.—Take this sugar-*coated* pill.

coax persuade somebody to do or say something by being kind and patient: I had to *coax* him into lending me his transistor radio.

cobbler (cob-bler) a man who mends shoes: Now that most shoes are mended by machinery there are very few *cobblers* left.

cock 1. the male of the farmyard fowl and of many other kinds of birds. 'Who killed *cock* robin?' (nursery rhyme). 2. turn upwards: The little dog *cocked* up its ears. **cocksure** so confident that one boasts about one's strength or cleverness.

cocoa (co-coa) powdered chocolate mixed with milk and water and usually taken as a hot, sweet drink.

coconut (co-co-nut) the large brown fruit of the coco palm tree. The outside is a very hard shell, and the inside a layer of white nut, while the centre is a white, milky juice.

cocoon (co-coon) the silky case or covering made by a caterpillar to protect itself during the winter before it changes into a moth or butterfly.

cod (also **codfish**) a large fish caught in the northern seas. **Cod-liver oil** the oil from the liver of the *cod*, used in medicine as a source of vitamins A and D.

code 1. a system of signs or secret writing used for sending messages. The Morse *code* is made up of dots and dashes.—I will send you a letter in our private *code*. 2. a rule or set of rules or laws by which people live: A scout should have a strict *code* of honour.

co-education (co-ed-u-ca-tion) education of boys and girls in the same school and in the same class.

coffee a drink made with the roasted and ground seeds of the *coffee* plant: Will you have cream in your *coffee*?

coffin (cof-fin) a box or case in which the dead body of a person is placed for burial: 'Stand back, and let the *coffin* pass' (Shakespeare, *Richard III*).

coil 1. to wind into rings one above the other: The snake *coiled* itself round my legs and I fell. 2. a continuous ring or spiral made by winding round and round: I need a *coil* of wire to connect the electricity in our new bathroom.

coin 1. a piece of metal money: In my pocket I have two gold *coins* and two silver *coins*. 2. make *coins* from metal: Money is *coined* at the Royal Mint. 3. make up new words or phrases: The word 'aerodrome' was *coined* from the two Greek words 'aero', the air, and 'dromos', a course or ground, to mean a place from which aeroplanes could fly.

coincide (co-in-cide) 1. fit; agree in every way: The two circles *coincide*.—My opinion exactly *coincides* with yours. 2. happen at the same time: We can never meet because our holidays do not *coincide*. **coincidence** something which agrees with another, just by chance: We both like chocolate pudding! What a *coincidence*!

cold 1. not warm or hot: There's a *cold* wind today.—How I hate *cold* porridge! 2. an illness of the nose and throat making one cough and sneeze: 'Harry cannot come to school as he is in bed with a *cold*.' 3. unkind, not friendly: I don't mean to be *cold* to people I don't know well, I'm just shy.

collapse (col-lapse) fall in, come tumbling down: Before we could reach the burning house, all four walls *collapsed*.

collar (col-lar) a band, or that part of a garment which is worn round the neck: I would like a fur *collar* on this coat. 2. a band of metal joining two pipes.

colleague (col-league) one of a group of persons working together: I can't tell you the price, but I will ask my *colleague*, Ann Taylor.

collect (col-lect) 1. bring together, gather together, come together: We are *collecting* money for charity.—A crowd soon *collected* to see the famous film star. 2. gather together and keep: Do you *collect* foreign stamps? **collection** a group of things or people, a sum of money *collected*: Have you seen my *collection* of matchboxes?—We will send the *collection* to the blind.

college (col-lege) a place where people can study subjects to a higher level than in school: My sister is at the local *college* studying to be a teacher.

collide (col-lide) come together with great force: The two lorries *collided* head on. **collision** when two things *collide*: Twenty people were killed in the *collision* on the railway.

colonel (colo-nel, pronounced *kernel*) an officer in the army who commands a regiment.

colony (col-o-ny) *colonies* 1. a country or state founded by people who have left their own country: People from England, France and Spain founded *colonies* in North America. 2. people from one country who live together in a small part of another country: In London there are small Italian and Greek *colonies*. 3. a number of animals or plants living or growing together: Have you seen the *colony* of wasps at the bottom of the garden? **colonial** having to do with *colonies*: England was once a great *colonial* power.

colour (col-our) 1. how the light from the things we see strikes the eye: Green is the *colour* of grass and blue is the *colour* of the sky. 2. put *colour* on: I have *coloured* the walls of my study green. **colours** ribbon, dress, badge or flag: We are all proud of our school *colours*. – The cavalry charged with *colours* flying. **colour-blind** not able to tell the difference between certain *colours*. **colourless** without *colour*: Water is a *colourless* liquid.

colt a young male horse under the age of about five years.

column (col-umn) 1. a tall pillar or post used as a support in buildings: The roof was supported by five white *columns*. 2. a long line or row: I spend my life adding up *columns* of figures. – A *column* of soldiers marched down the road.

comb a piece of metal, plastic etc., with teeth for straightening hair or wool: My hair is tidy because I always carry a *comb*. 2. a structure of wax made by bees for storing honey. 3. straighten by using a *comb*: Wool has to be *combed* before it can be spun. 4. search everywhere: The police *combed* the entire district to find the thief.

combat (com-bat) 1. fight, struggle. **single combat** a fight between two persons: David and Goliath met in *single combat*. 2. to fight: The doctors are doing all they can to *combat* disease.

combine (com-bine) join or put together: We must *combine* to destroy this pest. – I find it hard to *combine* business with pleasure. **combination** two or more things put together: He was ruined by a *combination* of folly and bad luck.

come 1. move forward: *Come* this way, please. 2. happen, occur: Christmas *comes* but once a year. 3. reach: The water *came* up to my neck. 4. become: My tie has *come* undone. 5. amount to: Your grocery bill *comes* to less than usual this week. **coming** to happen soon: I am a candidate in the *coming* election.

comedy (com-e-dy) *comedies* A play or film which ends happily, contains very little sadness and is sometimes humorous. **comedian** an actor who makes people laugh, an amusing person: Who is your favourite television *comedian*?

comet (com-et) a bright body orbiting the sun and trailing a tail of light: Halley's *comet* can be seen on earth every 76 years.

comfort (com-fort) 1. soothe or cheer: 'God hath *comforted* his people' (the Bible). 2. being at ease, having what one wants: It would be lovely to live in *comfort* and have everything one wants! **comfortable** giving *comfort* or being in *comfort*: What a *comfortable* chair this is! Are you *comfortable* in it?

comic (com-ic) 1. Funny, humorous: Sing one of your *comic* songs, please! – Isn't he a *comic*! 2. a paper for children containing stories illustrated with numerous pictures. **comical** amusing, humorous: He entertained the party with a number of *comical* tricks.

comma a punctuation mark which shows a slight break in a sentence. **inverted commas** marks (' ') which show the beginning and end of speeches.

command (com-mand) 1. order: The general *commanded* his men to lay down their arms. 2. an order: If you obey my *commands*, all will be well. **in command** in charge: The captain is *in command* of the ship. **commander** a person in charge, a naval officer ranking below a captain.

commence (com-mence) begin: The battle *commenced* at dawn.

commerce (com-merce) trade, buying and selling goods: *Commerce* between our two countries is increasing. **commercial** having to do with *commerce*: We expect a *commercial* traveller to visit our shop today.

commit 1. perform, do: Is it known who has *committed* the murder? 2. give up, put into the care of: I am *committing* all my business affairs to you. **committee** a small body of people appointed to do a certain piece of work: We should appoint a *committee* to raise money for the charity.

common (com-mon) 1. usual, frequent, often occurring: The daisy is a *common* flower in England. 2. belonging to all, shared: This field is *common* land. **in common** shared by two or more persons: The twins have everything *in common*. **House of Commons** the body elected by the people of Great Britain and Northern Ireland as one part of Parliament. **Commonwealth** all the peoples of the world connected with Britain and once part of the British Empire.

communicate (com-mu-ni-cate) pass on or exchange news, feelings etc.; make known: *Communicate* with me by post when you reach Brighton. **communication** news sent from place to place: Have you had any *communication* from your uncle yet?

community (com-mu-ni-ty) *communities* people living together in a town, country, village, or settlement: Our little *community* runs its own *community* centre.— The Commonwealth is a *community* of millions of people.

company (com-pa-ny) *companies* 1. being with others: I have always been fond of your *company*. 2. persons who have joined together in business: A new *company* has been formed for the manufacture of toys. 3. people who take part in a play or entertainment: 'Is all our *company* here?' (Shakespeare, *A Midsummer Night's Dream*). 4. a unit of soldiers commanded by a captain. 5. the name of a business firm: W. S. and *Co.* (abbreviation of *company*) **companion** a friend, one who keeps *company* with another: My dog is my faithful *companion*. **companionship** association of companions.

compare (com-pare) examine things to find out how they are alike and how they differ: When we had done our sums we *compared* answers. **comparison** likeness or difference: *Comparisons* between countries are often meaningless.

compass (com-pass) an instrument with a needle which points north, used for showing direction. All the points of the *compass* are marked on its dial. **pair of compasses** an instrument for drawing circles and measuring distances.

compete (com-pete) take part in any contest: I should love to be able to *compete* in the Olympic Games. **competition** a contest: Are you taking part in the chess *competition*?—Yes, I shall be in *competition* with the champion. **competitor** one who competes: How many *competitors* has the United States in the Olympic Games this year?

complain (com-plain) say that something is wrong: My friends feel they must *complain* about the noise their neighbours make. **complaint** a statement that something is not right, an illness: You should write the details of your *complaint* on this form.— Mumps and measles are fairly serious *complaints*.

complexion (com-ple-xion) appearance, natural colour of the skin, hair, eyes etc. If you want to improve your *complexion*, use this cream.

complicate (com-pli-cate) make more diffi-cult: If you tell the family you will only *complicate* matters. **complicated** made up of many parts: A transistor set is a *complicated* machine. **complication** the result of *complicating*: When the new accounts came in we discovered further *complications*.

compliment (com-pli-ment) 1. an expression of praise: You have paid me a great *compliment*. 2. a greeting: '*Compliments* of the Season' (from a Christmas card). 3. to praise, congratulate: I *compliment* you on your skill in riding.

compose (com-pose) 1. make up, arrange, put together: I have *composed* a poem. – Gunpowder is *composed* of sulphur, charcoal and saltpetre. 2. become or make calm: *Compose* yourself; don't get so excited! **composition** something put together, the parts of which it is made: This overture is a fine *composition*. – What is the *composition* of air, of bread, of water?

comprehensive (com-pre-hen-sive) taking everything in: He has a *comprehensive* grasp of electrical work. **comprehensive school** a school which replaces separate grammar and secondary modern schools.

computer (com-pu-ter) an electronic machine able to program information and, questioned on it, produce the correct answer.

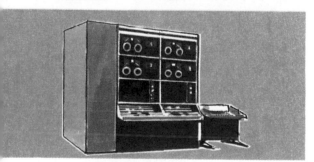

conceal (con-ceal) hide, keep secret: Be careful, several stones *conceal* snakes. – I cannot *conceal* my horror.

conceit (con-ceit) exaggerated pride in one-self: Don't be too full of *conceit*. **conceited** vain, proud.

concern (con-cern) 1. have to do with, have an effect on: The escape of John's rabbit *concerns* us all. 2. be unhappy, make un-happy or anxious: I am very *concerned* about his illness. 3. have to do with: This letter *concerns* nobody but the chief clerk. 4. something one is very interested in: My main *concern* is that you should be happy. 5. a business or firm: It is a large *concern* producing books and magazines.

concert (con-cert) a musical entertainment: Will you be singing or playing in tonight's *concert*?

condition (con-di-tion) 1. state of affairs, business, health, repair: Weather *conditions* are perfect for swimming. 2. some-thing needed before something else is possible: Strict training is one of the *conditions* for joining the club. **on condition that** only if: You can go out *on condition that* you are home for tea.

conduct (cón-duct) behaviour, the way one acts: He was given a medal for good *conduct*.

conduct (con-dúct) 1. guide, lead: '*Conduct* me to the king' (Shakespeare, *King John*). 2. take charge of: Tonight's service will be *conducted* by the bishop. 3. direct and lead a choir, orchestra or band: At this performance the composer himself will *conduct*.

conductor (con-duc-tor) 1. the leader of a choir, band or orchestra: Every singer must watch the *conductor*. 2. a person in charge of passengers on a bus, train or other vehicle who collects fares and issues tickets: Please do not leave until the *conductor* rings the bell. 3. a substance that allows heat or electricity to pass through it: One of the best *conductors* of electricity is copper.

cone 1. a solid figure with a circular base and which comes to a point at the top. 2. the pod of an evergreen tree containing the seeds: The ground beneath the pine was strewn with *cones*. 3. the hollow wafer which is filled with a portion of ice-cream.

confer (con-fér) 1. give or grant: The Russian novelist has had many honours *conferred* on him. 2. meet and discuss: We are here to *confer* on the question of cruelty to animals. **conference** a meeting for discussion: This week we are attending a *conference* on teaching methods.

confess (con-fess) 1. admit that one has done wrong or is at fault: I must *confess* that I cannot do arithmetic. 2. tell one's sins to a priest. **confession** a statement admitting that one is at fault: The guilty man has at last signed a *confession*.

confide (con-fide) 1. tell something to somebody knowing it will be kept secret, trust a person: You are the only one in whom I can *confide*. **confidential** secret, private: What I am telling you now is strictly *confidential*. **confidence** faith in oneself or others: I have every *confidence* in my power to win. **confident** having faith in oneself or others.

confuse (con-fuse) 1. mix up, jumble: All your questions *confuse* me. 2. mistake one for another: A colour-blind person *confuses* green with red. **confusion** disorder: When we entered the house we found everything in *confusion*.

congratulate (con-grat-u-late) say that one is pleased about a person's good fortune or success: You played a good game; we all *congratulate* you.—I *congratulated* the boy on escaping unhurt.

congregate (con-gre-gate) meet together: I propose that we *congregate* at the entrance to the park. **congregation** all those, except for the minister and the choir, attending a church service.

conjurer or **conjuror** (con-ju-rer) one who practises magic and entertains people with clever tricks: We all clapped when the *conjurer* brought a rabbit out of a hat.

connect (con-nect) 1. join or put together, be joined: Now we must *connect* the radiogram with the electricity supply.— I am *connected* with a firm which sells cars. 2. think of different things as being related: We always *connect* glove with hand, shoe with foot and bread with butter. **connection** (or **connexion**) a going with or being *connected*: Water was escaping from the pipes because of a loose *connection*.—This firm has no *connection* with any other in the town.

conquer (con-quer) 1. overcome: It is not easy to *conquer* bad habits. 2. take possession of by force: William of Normandy *conquered* England. **conquest** the act of *conquering*: Because of his *conquest* of England William became king.

conscious (con-scious) awake, able to notice what is going on: I was fully *conscious* all through the operation.

consent (con-sent) 1. agree, permit: My father will never *consent* to our marriage. 2. permission: When he knows how responsible I am, I feel sure your father will gladly give his *consent*.

conserve (con-serve) keep, save, preserve: He has won his heat, now he must *conserve* his strength for the final race. **conservation** official preservation of natural resources: A committee is considering the *conservation* of our rivers and forests. **conservative** having a tendency to preserve existing conditions, institutions etc. **Conservative** (capital C) one of the political parties in Great Britain.

consider (con-sid-er) 1. think about: We are *considering* a holiday in France this summer. 2. bear in mind: Don't play the accordion with the doors open; *consider* the feelings of others. 3. what one thinks of a thing or a person: Everybody *considers* him a good footballer, but I don't *consider* it wise to put him in the first team. **considerable** very large: This car must have cost a *considerable* amount of money.

consist (con-sist) be made up of: A day *consists* of 24 hours. – The programme *consisted* of songs and piano music.

consonant (con-so-nant) any letter of the alphabet except a, e, i, o and u.

constable (con-sta-ble) a policeman: The light was seen by the *constable* on his beat. – The Chief *Constable* is the head of the police force of this city.

constellation (con-stel-la-tion) a group of stars first named by people in ancient times. The Great Bear is a *constellation* which can be seen in winter in the Northern Hemisphere.

constitution (con-sti-tu-tion) 1. the rules by which a group, a town, or a country is governed: According to the *constitution* of our club, all members must attend the meetings. 2. the bodily structure or make-up of a person: Nobody who has a weak *constitution* should do hard physical work.

construct (con-struct) build, put together, make: Robinson Crusoe *constructed* a shelter for himself. **construction** a building, something made or built: The *construction* of the bridge has taken a whole year.

consult (con-sult) 1. get information or advice from: I feel ill and must *consult* my doctor. 2. join together to think about something: Before we strike, we must *consult* with our union members.

consume (con-sume) 1. use up, eat, drink up: We have *consumed* all our food. – This stove *consumes* a gallon of oil a day. 2. destroy: The whole factory was *consumed* by fire.

consumption (con-sump-tion) 1. the amount *consumed*: The *consumption* of meat has increased this year. 2. a disease which destroys part of the body.

contact (con-tact) 1. touch: Suddenly my head came into *contact* with the post. – We are old friends, so don't let us lose *contact*. 2. connection (or connexion) for electric current: If you break *contact*, the light will go out. 3. get in touch with: Please *contact* this office for more information.

contagious (con-ta-gious) spreading through touch (of a disease): Measles and chickenpox are *contagious* diseases.

contain (con-tain) hold within itself: This bag *contains* a hundred marbles. 2. be equal to. 3. keep one's feelings under control: When he insulted me I could hardly *contain* myself (or *contain* my rage). **container** a box, bottle, barrel etc. purposely made to *contain* things: Shampoo can be bought in plastic *containers*.

content (con-tént) 1. satisfied with things as they are: Are you *content* with your present wages? 2. satisfy, make *content*: We shall have to *content* ourselves with our poor climate.

contents (cón-tents) what is *contained* in a vessel, a *container*, a book etc.: On the first page you will find a list of *contents*. – The thief tore off the lid and *gazed* at the *contents* of the box.

contest (con-tést) 1. fight, argue, try to win: Will he be *contesting* a seat in Parliament this year? 2. fight, struggle: The favourite won after a hard *cóntest* of ten rounds.

continent (con-ti-nent) 1. One of the chief land masses of the world: Give the names of all the *continents*. 2. Europe without Great Britain: My business often takes me to the *Continent*. **continental** belonging to, or similar to what is on the *Continent*: We are all in favour of *continental* wines, and *continental* cookery.

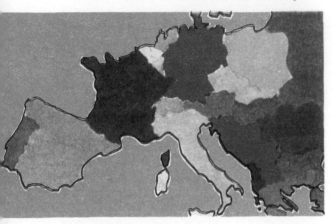

continue (con-tin-ue) 1. go on being or doing, proceed: He *continued* writing until the candle went out. – I hope the weather will *continue* fine tomorrow. 2. start again where something has been left off: This story will be *continued* in our next week's issue. **continual, continuous** going on all the time: I am tired of the *continual* roar of the machinery.

contract (cón-tract) an agreement to supply goods or do work at a fixed price: According to the *contract*, the builder must have completed this house within six months.

contract (con-tráct) 1. agree by making a *contract*: He has *contracted* to build the house for a relatively small sum. 2. make, or become, smaller: Metals *contract* as they become colder. – When we speak we *contract* 'do not' into 'don't'.

contrary (con-tra-ry) 1. opposite, against: Driving on the right hand side of the road is *contrary* to the law in England. 2. (usually pronounced *contrairy*) stubborn, refusing to give in to others: 'Mary, Mary, quite *contrary*, how does your garden grow? (nursery rhyme)

contribute (con-trib-ute) 1. give money, help: Who will *contribute* food and clothing in aid of the homeless? 2. be a cause of: Love of money *contributed* to his downfall. **contribution** something given: The smallest *contributions* are thankfully received.

control (con-trol) 1. power to order, or keep back: The conductor has perfect *control* over the orchestra. 2. a device that helps to operate a machine: To pilot an aeroplane you must know how to handle the *controls*. 3. manage, direct: The teacher can no longer *control* the class. 4. keep back: When my cat died I could not *control* my tears. 5. make more or less, regulate: This handle *controls* the supply of oil to the stove.

convenient (con-ven-i-ent) handy, suitable: What a *convenient* kitchen you have; everything is in a *convenient* place.

convent (con-vent) 1. a society of women known as nuns, living in a place apart from others and devoting their lives to the service of God. 2. the building in which nuns live. 3. a school where children are taught by nuns.

convention (con-ven-tion) a meeting of members of a society for a special purpose: Next week the Liberal Party holds its annual *convention*.

conversation (con-ver-sa-tion) talk between two or more people: We had an interesting *conversation* about our hobbies.

convict (con-víct) declare in a court of law that somebody has committed an offence: I have never been *convicted* of dangerous driving.

convict (cón-vict) a person found guilty of a crime and serving a prison sentence as a punishment.

cook 1. prepare food by heating in some way: We can *cook* food by boiling, baking, frying or roasting. 2. a person who *cooks*: My mother is a wonderful *cook*. – Did you see the *cook* in his tall white cap? **cooker** a stove on which food is *cooked*.

cool 1. between warm and cold: Is your soup *cool* enough yet? 2. calm, not afraid: Keep *cool*; it's only a door creaking. 3. not very friendly or interested: His speech was good but he had a *cool* reception. 4. make or become *cool*: The factory is *cooled* by electric fans. – Has my porridge *cooled* yet?

coop 1. a small cage, usually for poultry: Every morning I clean out the chicken-*coops*. 2. be forced to stay in a place: How I hate to be *cooped* up in this tiny house!

cooperate (co-op-er-ate) work together: We are both doing the same kind of work. Why don't we *cooperate*? **cooperation** working together: With *cooperation* we shall achieve good results. **co-op** a shop owned by a *cooperative* society, an organization for buying and selling run by its own members.

copper (cop-per) 1. a reddish brown metal: *Copper* is one of the best conductors of electricity, and electric flex is made from it. 2. *copper*-coloured.

copy (cop-y) 1. a piece of art, a paper, a letter etc. made exactly like another: I thought I had bought a masterpiece, but alas, it was only a *copy*. – Have you a *copy* of yesterday's daily paper? 2. make a *copy* of: Now *copy* this poem from the blackboard. 3. take answers for examination questions from another person's work: All these answers are wrong, but they are all alike. Who's been *copying*?

coral (co-ral) a hard substance built on the sea bed from the shells of small creatures: I have bought you a necklace made of pink (red, white) *coral*.

cord 1. a length of thick string or thin rope: The parcel has been tied with thick *cord*. 2. part of the body which is like a *cord*: From the spinal *cord*, nerves go to every part of the human body. – The vocal *cords* in the throat make it possible for us to speak.

core 1. the hard, centre part of apples, pears and some other fruit: He ate the apple and threw away the *core*.

cork 1. the bark of the *cork* tree: *Cork* is used to make lifejackets, stoppers for bottles and many other things. 2. put in the *cork* or stopper: If the bottle is not firmly *corked* the wine may be spilt. **corkscrew** an instrument with a metal spiral used for drawing out *corks*.

corn 1. the seed of any grain, plant or cereal: On our way south we passed fields of ripening *corn*. 2. a hard painful growth of skin on the foot.

corner (cor-ner) 1. a point where two lines, surfaces, edges, streets etc. meet: 'Little Jack Horner sat in a *corner*' (nursery rhyme). – You can get sweets at the shop at the *corner* (or the *corner* shop). 2. a hiding place or secret place: When we searched the house we found money in all kinds of odd *corners*. 3. in association football a kick from the *corner* of the field towards the goal of the opposing side. 4. put into a position from which it is impossible to get out: They came towards me from all sides and I found myself *cornered*.

cornet (cor-net) 1. a musical instrument like a trumpet with three keys. 2. a biscuit shaped like a cone which holds ice cream.

coronation (co-ro-na-tion) the ceremony of crowning a king, queen or emperor.

corporal (cor-por-al) a soldier in the army, ranking below a sergeant.

corpse a dead body, usually of a man, woman or child.

correct (cor-rect) 1. true, right: Your answer is *correct*.—Is this the *correct* way to play the game? 2. proper, showing good manners or taste: It is not *correct* to eat peas with your knife. 3. put or make right: Please sir, will you *correct* my spelling? **correction** something done to put right a mistake: I have had to make several *corrections* on your drawing.

correspond (cor-res-pond) 1. be in agreement with, be right for: This house *corresponds* exactly with my needs. 2. be alike, be equal to: The duties of a president *correspond* in many ways to those of a king. 3. communicate: I *correspond* regularly with my friend in Australia. **correspondent** one with whom a person communicates, a person who is employed by a newspaper or magazine to send reports regularly: Here is a message from our *correspondent* in Hong Kong.

corridor (cor-ri-dor) a passage connecting various parts of a building, compartments of a railway train etc.: The train was so crowded that there was no standing room even in the *corridor*.

cost 1. be worth: How much does this hat *cost*, please? 2. end in loss: Careless work could *cost* you your job. 3. price paid for: The *cost* of this house has risen a great deal in the past week. 4. what has to be paid to achieve or obtain something: The climbers will reach the summit whatever the *cost*.

costume (cos-tume) 1. dress or clothes made in a certain style: The kilt is the national *costume* of the Scotsman.—We have made all our own *costumes* for the school play.

cottage (cot-tage) a small house, usually in the country: The workers on this farm live in a row of *cottages*.

cotton (cot-ton) 1. a soft, white fluff which grows round the seeds of the *cotton* plant: *Cotton* is made into thread which is spun and woven into cloth. 2. made from *cotton*: I feel cool in this *cotton* shirt. **cotton wool** *cotton* from the plant cleaned and used for pads and bandages.

couch a piece of furniture for seating two or more people, usually with a back and armrests: When we have visitors I often have to sleep on the *couch* at night.

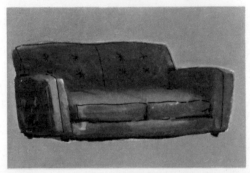

cough (pronounced *coff*) 1. send out air from the lungs through the throat with a sudden sharp sound: The smoke in the room made her *cough*. 2. an illness which makes one *cough*: Send for the doctor, please, I have a terrible *cough*.

council (coun-cil) a group of persons chosen by others to make rules or carry out plans: The Town *Council* meets each week in the Council Chamber. **councillor** a member of a *council*, usually a town *council*.

count 1. recite numbers one after the other: Harry can *count* up to 100. 2. include or be included when *counting* things or people: Make a list of the boys' names but don't *count* any over 10 years old. 3. think, consider: *Count* yourself lucky that you were not drowned! 4. rely, depend: May we *count* on you to join the procession? 5. be valuable: In the last mile of the race, every second *counts*. 6. addition: In the final *count* of votes our candidate was well ahead. **counter** the long table or bench in a shop behind which the assistant stands to serve the customer.

counterfeit (coun-ter-feit) 1. made in imitation, not genuine: This money is *counterfeit*; nobody will accept it. 2. to make *counterfeit*, especially of money: The men who *counterfeited* the notes are now in prison.

country (coun-try) *countries* 1. land lived in by a nation, the land in which one was born: England is my native *country*. 2. any kind of land: The *country* across which we passed was overgrown with prickly bushes. 3. land with large open spaces mainly used for farming, and away from towns: I love the fresh air of the *country*.

county (coun-ty) a division of Great Britain: Yorkshire is the largest *county* in England.

couple (cou-ple) 1. two persons or things: The animals went into Noah's ark in *couples*. – We are now an engaged *couple*, but soon we shall be a married *couple*. 2. fasten, join, connect two things: The luggage compartment was *coupled* to the train.

courage (cour-age) bravery: The fireman received a medal for his *courage*. **courageous** possessing or showing *courage*: His medal was won by a *courageous* act.

courier (cou-ri-er) 1. a messenger carrying important news. 2. a person employed to arrange all the details of a journey: The *courier* booked all our hotels, looked after our tickets and accompanied us on our holiday.

course 1. a movement forward: the *course* of this river lies through beautiful scenery. – I shall ask many questions in the *course* of my enquiries. 2. a ground: We play golf on golf *courses* and horses run on race*courses*. 3. a route, a way or direction to be taken: The aeroplane went off *course* and landed in France. 4. a series of classes, talks, lectures, medical treatments etc.: I have just started a *course* in cookery. 5. one of many parts of a meal: Will you have soup or grapefruit as your first *course*, sir? **of course** certainly: Will you pay me for this? *Of course* I will.

court 1. the place where law cases are heard and decided: If you do not pay me I shall have to take you to *court*. 2. the place where a great ruler lives, as well as the people who live there or go there on special occasions: The Royal *Court* is now in residence at Buckingham Palace. 3. a space marked out for games: The tennis championships are played on the *courts* at Wimbledon. 4. an open space wholly or partly enclosed by walls or buildings: Several children were playing in the *court*. 5. try to gain the affection of a woman in the hope of marrying her: The Prince *courted* Cinderella because of her charm and beauty. 6. take risks carelessly: Children who cross the road without looking are *courting* danger. **courtier** a person who attends the *court* of a king or sovereign. **court-martial** a special *court* for trying members of the armed forces by military law.

courteous (cour-te-ous) polite, kind, showing good manners: Always be *courteous* to the old and infirm. **courtesy** politeness: This shop assistant is well liked because of her *courtesy*.

cousin (cou-sin) the son or daughter of one's aunt or uncle.

cow 1. an animal kept on a farm to supply milk; the female of the bull or ox. 2. the female of the seal, elephant and some other animals. **cowboy** a man who rides a horse and looks after large herds of cattle in some parts of the United States. **cowshed** or **cowhouse** a building in which *cows* are kept and where they are milked.

coy shy or pretending to be shy: 'Don't be so *coy*!' said the handsome stranger.

crack 1. a long thin line where something is split but not broken off: One should never drink from a glass which has *cracks* in it. 2. a sudden sharp sound: The horses galloped off at the first *crack* of the whip. 3. excellent, very clever: He is a *crack* shot, as well as a *crack* footballer. 4. make something *crack* or break: Will you please *crack* this nut for me? 5. (of a voice) to become harsh: The speaker was shouting so loudly that his voice began to *crack*.

crackle (crack-le) 1. a cracking sound: We heard the *crackle* of dry twigs. 2. make a cracking sound: The dry twigs *crackled* as we walked. **crackling** the crisp skin of pork that has been well roasted.

cradle (cra-dle) a small bed or cot on rockers: The baby was asleep in its small wooden *cradle*.

craft 1. work requiring some skill or art: When I was young I learnt the *craft* of a silversmith. 2. a boat or small ship: *Craft* of all shapes and sizes were on the lake. 3. cheating, cunning, trickery: My purse was taken from me by *craft*. **craftsman** one who does skilled work. **crafty** full of *craft* or cunning: Watch him; he's as *crafty* as a monkey!

cram 1. fill a thing as full as possible: He quickly *crammed* the clothes into a suitcase. 2. fill one's memory with facts for an examination.

cramp a sudden pain in a muscle often caused by cold or overwork: Two members of the football team had to retire from the field because of *cramp*.

crane 1. a large wading bird. 2. a machine for lifting heavy weights: All along the quay there is a row of *cranes*. 3. stretch (the neck): The little girl had to *crane* her neck to see over the crowd.

crank 1. a bar shaped like an L used to set a machine in motion: If you can't start the engine any other way, use the *crank*. 2. make a machine go with a *crank*: He had to *crank* up the engine. 3. a person with strange habits and ideas: He won't sleep on a bed or sit on a chair; what a *crank* he is!

crash 1. fall down making a loud noise: The tray full of dishes *crashed* to the floor. 2. be wrecked: The plane *crashed* on take-off. 3. a fall, blow, explosion or collision; the noise made by it: The whole building collapsed with a loud *crash*.—In the *crash* on the motorway both drivers were hurt.

crate a large container of basketwork or wood: A *crate* of apples has just been delivered.

crater (cra-ter) the mouth or hole at the top of a volcano: Fire and molten rocks were suddenly flung from the *crater*.

crawl 1. move slowly, pulling the body along the ground: The worm *crawled* across the path. 2. move on hands and knees: My baby brother *crawls* but he cannot yet walk. 3. go very slowly: The traffic was so heavy that the cars were *crawling*. 4. be covered with: The doorstep was *crawling* with insects. 5. a stroke in swimming which gives great speed.

crayon (cray-on) a stick or pencil of coloured chalk, charcoal or wax: This morning we will draw in *crayon* (or with *crayons*).

crazy (cra-zy) 1. foolish, insane: It was *crazy* of you to give away your watch. 2. excited about something: I'm *crazy* about his latest film.

creak 1. a harsh squeaking sound: The wooden floor *creaked* under his feet. 2. make a squeaking sound: In the darkness he heard the *creak* of a door being opened.

cream 1. the fatty part of milk which rises to the top and is made into butter. 2. a substance or a food resembling *cream*: ice *cream*, shaving *cream*, shoe *cream*, furniture *cream* etc. 3. the best part: Only the *cream* of the forces take part in the military tattoo.

crease 1. line made on paper or cloth by pressing: *Don't you admire the* crease *in my trousers?* 2. (in cricket) the white line which marks the position batsmen and bowlers should take. 3. mark or wrinkle by folding: *This cloth easily* creases.

create (cre-ate) cause to be, produce: *This inventor has* created *a new machine.–Her marriage* created *quite a sensation.* **creation** something created: *Hamlet was one of Shakespeare's greatest* creations. **creature** an animal or human being.

credit (cred-it) 1. approval, recognition: *I wrote the song but the singer took the* credit. 2. the amount of money one has in the bank: *Your account shows a* credit *for once.* 3. something added to; a good reputation: *You are a* credit *to your school.* 4. believe, trust: *He ran away from school? It's hard to* credit *it.*

creek a narrow stream of water or inlet: *Let us go for a swim in the* creek.

creep crept, creeping 1. move quietly with the body close to the ground: *The cat* crept *silently towards the bird.* 2. grow along the ground or up walls: *See how the ivy* creeps *along the walls of this church.* 3. move slowly: *Our car could only* creep *through London because of the traffic.*

crest 1. a small bunch or tuft of feathers on a bird's head. 2. the top of a hill or of a large wave: *The white* crests *dashed themselves against the sea wall.* 3. a decoration, once resembling feathers on a hat or a helmet, or shown on a coat of arms: *The Royal Arms has for its* crest *a crowned lion.*

crew 1. a group of persons in charge of running a ship or aircraft: *Every large aircraft has an* aircrew *which flies it, and a ground* crew *which services it.* 2. any group of people working together on a task: *We hired a* crew *to clear the streets of snow.*

crib a bed with rails to prevent a child from falling out.

cricket (crick-et) 1. an outdoor game played in summer with eleven players on each side. 2. a small brown insect like a grasshopper which jumps and makes a chirping sound by rubbing its legs together.

crime an evil act punishable by law. **criminal** a person who commits a crime: *The* criminal *was sent to prison for stealing the paintings.*

crimson (crim-son) deep red: *I like your* crimson *scarf.*

crinkle (crin-kle) 1. a tiny wrinkle in paper, cloth or other material: *Before she could wear the dress all the* crinkles *had to be ironed out.* **crinkly** with crinkles or very curly.

cripple (crip-ple) 1. a person unable to walk properly: *My brother is a* cripple *and can only walk on crutches.* 2. make weak or injure: *The miner was* crippled *for life by an explosion.–The old lady is* crippled *with rheumatism.*

crisp 1. hard and dry, easy to break: *We like our chips to be* crisp. 2. cool, fresh: *A walk in the* crisp *morning air will do you good.*

critic (crit-ic) a person skilled in judging the merits of something artistic, and who writes reviews about new books, plays or music: *His new play has been highly praised by the* critics. **criticize** point out the good and bad parts of something, find fault with: *I have finished building the shed; will you* criticize *my work?* **criticism** a statement criticizing something: *I was glad to have your* criticism *of my book.*

critical 1. finding fault, likely to find fault: My employer is very *critical*. 2. dangerous: The patient is in a *critical* condition.

croak 1. a low, hoarse sound: All night long the frogs were *croaking*. 2. make a *croaking* sound.

crochet (cro-chet, pronounced *croa-shay*) a kind of needlework done by making loops and pulling the thread through with a hook.

crocodile (croc-o-dile) a large reptile with four legs, a long body, and powerful jaws and tail which lives in tropical waters and marshes.

crook 1. a stick or staff used by a shepherd. 2. a bend or curve: The car came round the *crook* in the road. 3. a dishonest person: The accused man was one of a gang of *crooks*. 4. bend: 'Come here,' he said *crooking* his finger. **crooked** not straight, not honest: Look in the mirror, your hat is *crooked*.—Don't buy from him, he is well known for his *crooked* tricks.

crop 1. the amount of corn, hay, or fruit that has been produced: The wheat *crop* is excellent this year. 2. a pouch-like enlargement of a bird's throat in which its food is partly digested. 3. a thick growth: You'll recognize him by his *crop* of black hair. 4. bite off: The grass had been *cropped* short by the cattle. 5. cut short: The horse's tail had been *cropped*. 6. appear unexpectedly: All sorts of questions *cropped* up.

cross 1. a mark made by drawing one line across the middle of another. 2. a medal shaped like a *cross*: The Victoria *Cross* is given for valour.—The *Cross* of St George is on the Union Jack. 3. a stake or post with another fixed across it: Christ died on the *Cross*. 4. a mixture of breeds: A mule is a *cross* between a horse and a donkey. 5. go, or place across: Don't *cross* your legs!—'Why does a chicken *cross* the road?' (a riddle). 6. go against, oppose, get in somebody's way: Don't *cross* me or I shall lose my temper! 7. pass in a

journey or in the post: Our letters must have *crossed*. 8. in a bad temper: Dear me, how *cross* you are!

crouch sink down, bending the knees and body: At last we found him, *crouching* behind the hedge.

crow 1. a large black bird: The *crows* are eating the farmer's corn. 2. make a shrill cry: Every morning we hear the cock *crow*. 3. a shrill cry: The cock's *crow* awakens us. 4. cry out happily: Listen to the baby *crowing*! 5. boast: You may have won the race, but that's nothing to *crow* about.

crowd 1. many people close together: There was a large *crowd* outside Buckingham Palace. 2. push close together: 'Please don't *crowd* into the bus,' called the conductor.—The room is *overcrowded* with furniture.

crown 1. a head-dress worn by kings, queens and some nobles: The royal *crown* of England contains many jewels. 2. the power of a king, queen or emperor: 'I thrice presented him a kingly *crown*' (Shakespeare, *Julius Caesar*). 3. a wreath put on the head: The fairy queen wore a *crown* of roses. 4. the top of the head or of a hat: Jack fell down and broke his *crown* (nursery rhyme). 5. to put on a *crown*: English monarchs are *crowned* by the Archbishop of Canterbury. 6. reward: At last my efforts have been *crowned* with success.

crucify (cru-ci-fy) put to death by fastening a person to a cross by his hands and feet.

crude 1. raw, just as it is taken from the earth or harvested: We obtain *crude* oil from the North Sea and *crude* sugar from the sugar-cane. 2. rough, not complete: The huts of the natives are rather *crude*.

cruel (cru-el) taking pleasure in the pain and suffering of others: It is *cruel* to beat an animal. **cruelty** *cruel* treatment: There are laws to punish *cruelty* to children.

cruise 1. travel from place to place: We *cruised* for three days in search of the enemy. 2. a voyage, usually by boat: This year we are taking a *cruise* round the world. **cruiser** a fast warship, a fast boat: There were two cabin *cruisers* in the harbour.

crumb 1. a small piece of bread, cake, or biscuit: After the meal we threw the *crumbs* to the birds. 2. a small amount: All we could get from him were a few *crumbs* of information. **crumble** break or fall into very small pieces: You should *crumble* the bread before sprinkling it on the dish. – The walls of this house are *crumbling*.

crumple crush into small creases: If you don't pack your things neatly they will *crumple*.

crunch 1. crush noisily with the teeth: The dog was *crunching* a bone. 2. make a *crunching* sound: The snow *crunched* under our feet.

crusade (cru-sade) 1. one of the wars made long ago by Christians to take the Holy Land from the Muslims. King Richard I of England went on the Third *Crusade*. 2. any struggle for a worthwhile cause or idea: Our *crusade* is to obtain good homes for everybody. **crusader** a person who went on a *crusade* or who takes up a good cause.

crush 1. squeeze out of shape or break: 'FRAGILE–DO NOT CRUSH' (on a parcel for posting). 2. become full of creases, lose shape: When we received the flowers they were all *crushed*. 3. defeat completely: In a single battle the enemy was *crushed*. 4. a crowd of people pushed or pressed together: We could not reach the doors because of the *crush*.

crust 1. the surface of a loaf or a pie, baked hard: The beggar asked for a *crust* of bread. 2. a hard covering, a hard surface: There was a thin *crust* of ice on the pond.

crutch a long stick or staff to support a lame person. A *crutch* has a broad piece which fits under the armpit.

cry *cries, cried, crying* 1. shout: 'Look out,' he *cried* as he threw the ball to me. 2. shed tears: Why is Sally *crying*? 3. a loud call, scream or shout: He gave a *cry* of pain. 4. a fit of weeping: You'll feel better after a good *cry*.

crystal (crys-tal) 1. a substance like glass which is clear and shines: She wore a brooch of tiny *crystals*. – *Crystals* of snow are formed in many beautiful shapes. 2. made of clear shining glass: On the table were four *crystal* vases.

cub 1. a young lion, bear, fox, wolf etc. 2. a junior scout between the ages of 8 and 11.

cube a solid figure which has six square sides all of equal size: The basin was full of sugar *cubes*.

cucumber (cu-cum-ber) a creeping plant which bears a long green fruit (also called a *cucumber*), eaten as a vegetable and in salads.

cud that part of the food which the cow, ox, and other animals which have two stomachs bring up from the first stomach to be chewed again.

cuddle (cud-dle) hug, hold lovingly in the arms: I don't like being *cuddled* myself, but I love to *cuddle* my doll.

cue 1. a long straight wooden rod, thin at one end and tipped with a leather pad: Billiard players use *cues* to strike the ball. 2. the last part of one actor's speech which shows the next actor when to begin his own speech: I missed the *cue* which meant we had to repeat the scene. 3. a hint on how to behave: Take your *cue* from me; watch what I do and copy me exactly.

cuff 1. the band around the bottom of a sleeve of a shirt or coat, fastening round the wrist. **cufflink** a link for fastening a *cuff*. 2. a blow, give a blow with the hand or fist: He gave me a painful *cuff* on the face.

cultivate (cul-ti-vate) 1. prepare land for sowing and help crops to grow: On our journey we passed miles of *cultivated* land. 2. try to bring something into being: I am doing my best to *cultivate* his friendship. **cultivation** the act of *cultivating*. **cultivator** a machine for *cultivating* the land.

cunning (cun-ning) 1. sly, clever at deceiving others: The fox is a *cunning* animal. 2. slyness, craft: All our *cunning* was needed to catch the canary.

cup 1. a small container with a handle, used with a saucer for drinking. 2. what a *cup* holds, a *cupful*: How I would like a *cup* of tea! 3. a vessel of some metal (gold, silver etc.) given as a prize: Who's going to win the football *cup* this season? 4. form a shape like a *cup*: He *cupped* his hands and drank from the pool. **cupboard** a piece of furniture or small room with shelves and drawers (so-called because it was once used for *cups*). **cup tie, cup final** stages in the competition in some sport in which a *cup* is won.

curator (cu-ra-tor) an official in charge of a museum or art gallery.

curb 1. keep in check, control: Can't you *curb* your impatience? 2. a strap of leather which passes under the jaw of a horse, used as a means of control.

curd the thick, soft part of sour milk. **curdle** (of milk) to sour so that the *curds* become separated.

cure 1. make well after an illness: I can *cure* you if you will do what I order. 2. treat substances like food, leather and tobacco, so as to preserve them: When I was a boy we used to *cure* our own bacon. 3. something one does or takes to become well: Your best *cure* would be a good rest.

curfew (cur-few) 1. ringing of a bell in the evening telling people to cover their fires and put out lights. 2. in modern times, under martial law, a signal to all people to remain indoors: A *curfew* was imposed at 8 p.m. and only lifted at 7 a.m.

curious (cu-ri-ous) 1. eager to learn, to find out: I have always been *curious* about the mechanism of old clocks.—Why is he so *curious* about our affairs? 2. strange, hard to understand: He asks such *curious* questions: What a *curious* creature he is! **curiosity** a desire to learn an unusual thing: I'm full of *curiosity* about this letter.

currant (cur-rant) a small, sweet dried grape grown mostly in California and Greece: Please put plenty of *currants* into the cake.

current (cur-rent) 1. water, air, gas etc. flowing in a stream: He swam too far out and was carried away by the *current*.—A *current* of hot air blew through the corridor. 2. the flow of electricity through a wire: All the lights went out when the *current* failed. 3. in use today: Can you lend me the *current* number of the magazine?

curse 1. a request that somebody be punished, injured or destroyed: 'Bless them that *curse* you' (New Testament). 2. a cause of damage: Grey squirrels are a *curse* on this farm. 3. use bad language, swear.

curtain (cur-tain) 1. a hanging piece of cloth in front of a window or door: Please draw the *curtains* and keep out the draught. 2. a hanging screen of heavy cloth to hide a stage from the audience: The *curtain* rose on the first act of the play.

curve 1. a line that changes direction gradually: he rubbed out the angle and drew a gentle *curve*. 2. bend in a *curve*: The road *curved* round the foot of the mountain.

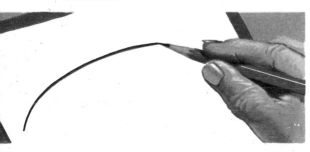

cushion (cush-ion) 1. a small bag filled with feathers, air, sponge rubber or other soft material to sit or kneel on: On the chair was a *cushion* of many colours. 2. to supply with *cushions*: The train was fitted out with *cushioned* seats.

custody (cus-to-dy) 1. care: When her father died she was put into her aunt's *custody*. 2. care of the police: He was caught in the act of stealing and handed into *custody*.

custom (cus-tom) 1. a way of behaving which people consider and accept as correct: It is the *custom* for everybody to stand when the National Anthem is sung. 2. something done by a person or a group over a long period of time: It is my *custom* to take a walk before breakfast. 3. always buying from the same person, shop or firm: You have given us your *custom* for the last twenty years. 4. taxes due to a government when foreign goods are brought into a country: Did you have to pay *customs* duties on this Swiss watch? 5. the government department for collecting taxes: It took us two hours to get through *customs*. **customary** usually done: I will take my *customary* walk this morning. **customer** a person giving his *custom* to a firm or shop. 'We offer special low prices to our regular *customers*' (notice in a shop window).

cut 1. divide into pieces, make an opening with a sharp instrument: The butcher *cut* the meat into joints.—My father *cut* himself while shaving. 2. make shorter by *cutting*: The lawn needs *cutting*. 3. a way to go: Take the short *cut* and you will soon be there. 4. purposely avoid speaking to a person: I said good morning to him but he deliberately *cut* me. 5. smaller by taking out or away: This scene (of a play) is too long; it will have to be *cut*. **cutlet** a piece of meat *cut* from a larger joint for cooking. **cutlery** knives, forks, spoons, scissors etc.

cutting (cut-ting) 1. something cut from a newspaper or magazine. 2. part of a plant cut off and re-planted to take root. 3. a way or road dug by removing part of a hill: Children must not play on the banks of the railway *cutting*.

cyclone (cy-clone) a violent storm during which the wind blows round and round.

cygnet (cyg-net) a young swan.

cylinder (cyl-in-der) a long object, circular at both ends. Hollow, metal *cylinders* are used in engines as part of the means of providing power.

cymbal (cym-bal) one of a pair of round brass plates used as a musical instrument. *Cymbals* are struck against each other to make a clashing sound.

D

dab 1. touch, put on gently: He *dabbed* the wound with a pad of damp cottonwool. 2. a very small quantity *dabbed* on: The clown had a *dab* of red paint on his nose.

dagger (dag-ger) a short pointed knife with two edges used as a weapon: The unfortunate man had been stabbed with a *dagger*.

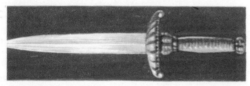

dairy (dai-ry) *dairies* 1. a place, room or building where milk and cream are made into butter and cheese: All our butter comes direct from the *dairy*. 2. a shop or company which sells milk, butter, cheese etc: Mother sent me to the *dairy* for half a pint of cream.

dam 1. a barrier, wall or bank to stop water flowing or to make a pond, reservoir etc.: A large *dam* has been built to supply water to the farmers. 2. stop water flowing with a *dam* or bank: You will be able to cross the stream where it has been *dammed*.

damage (dam-age) 1. harm or injury that spoils something: The storm has done great *damage* to the crops. 2. money paid to somebody for injuries done: The victim was awarded *damages* by the judge. 3. injure or harm, resulting in spoiling something: All the houses had been *damaged* by the flood.

damp moderately wet, moist: You'll catch cold if you sit on *damp* grass. 2. make *damp*: Before clothes are ironed they should be *damped* (or *dampened*).

dance 1. move with the feet or body, usually in time to music: After supper we shall *dance* on the lawn. 2. move quickly:

Beside the lake, beneath the trees,
Fluttering and *dancing* in the breeze.
(Wordsworth, *The Daffodils*)

3. a number of movements done in time with music: May I have the next *dance*, please? 4. a party mainly for *dancing*: Are you going to the *dance* tonight?

danger (dan-ger) 1. a chance that harm or injury will happen: *DANGER – NARROW BRIDGE* (warning sign for motorists). – If you go by that road your life may be in *danger*. 2. a possible cause of harm or injury: He's a careless driver and a *danger* to others. **dangerous** a possible cause of danger: Drive carefully; there is a *dangerous* bend ahead.

dare 1. have enough courage to do something: *Dare* you jump off that high wall? 2. challenge a person to do something: He *dared* me to climb the apple tree. **daring** bold: This is the most *daring* robbery I know of.

dark 1. without or with very little light: He found himself in a *dark* and dangerous alley. 2. approaching black in colour: I like your *dark* green coat. 3. secret, hidden: If I tell you, will you keep it *dark*? 4. sad, gloomy, without hope: Why do you always look on the *dark* side? 5. absence of light: Try to come home before *dark*. **darken** make *dark* or become *dark*: The sky *darkened* and it began to rain. **darkness** being *dark*: We found the building in complete *darkness*.

darn 1. mend clothes by crossing and weaving threads to fill up a hole. Mother, my socks need *darning*. 2. a place where a thing has been *darned*: You can't go out with that *darn* in your sock!

dart 1. move, spring, run, suddenly and swiftly: A rabbit *darted* out of its burrow. 2. a running or springing movement. 3. a small weapon with a sharp point thrown at a board in the game of *darts*

date 1. the time (day, month, year or period) when something happened or existed: The *date* of the battle of Hastings was 1066. 2. a meeting: I am sorry I can't meet you tomorrow but I have another *date*. 3. put a *date* on: My letter to you was *dated* 3rd May. **out of date** no longer used or usable. **up-to-date** the very latest in use: Our firm uses the most *up-to-date* methods. 4. the small sweet fruit of the *date* palm which grows in North Africa and South-east Asia.

daughter (daugh-ter) a female child of her parents: We wish to announce the birth of a *daughter*. **daughter-in-law** the wife of one's son.

day 1. the light period between the rising and setting of the sun: The watchman works all night and sleeps during the *day*. 2. the period between one midnight and the next—twenty-four hours: Let me have your answer in two *days* from now. 3. a period of time: In my young *days* there was no such thing as television. **daybreak** dawn. **daydreams** pleasant thoughts when the mind wanders. **daylight** the light of the sun. **daily** happening or coming every day: Has anybody seen the *daily* paper?

daze not knowing what to do, not thinking clearly: He was lying on the ground in a *daze* (in a *dazed* condition).

dazzle (daz-zle) make it difficult for somebody to see, act or think clearly: He was *dazzled* by the headlights of the approaching car.—Your brilliant speech has completely *dazzled* us all.

dead 1. no longer living: How long have your grandparents been *dead*? The ground was covered with *dead* leaves.—On 11th November Great Britain mourns its war *dead*. 2. no longer in use: We tried to telephone but the line was *dead*. **deaden** make fainter or decrease: The doctor gave her a pill to *deaden* the pain. **deadly** tending to cause death: This poisoned dart is a *deadly* weapon. **deadlock** when two sides cannot agree: The dispute between the firm and the trade union has reached a *deadlock*.

deaf 1. unable to hear: Beethoven, the great composer, wrote his most brilliant compositions when he was completely *deaf*. 2. unwilling to listen: The judge was *deaf* to every appeal for mercy. **deaf-aid** a small appliance used to improve the hearing. **deafen** make so much noise that others cannot hear. **deafness** being *deaf*: *Deafness* is a great handicap.

deal 1. a quantity, amount: A great *deal* of money has been spent this Christmas. 2. a bargain, agreement: I have the money and you have the goods, so let's make a *deal*. 3. give out: Who *dealt* the cards last? Whose *deal* is it now? 4. trade, do business: We *deal* only in the best quality goods. 5. have to do with: This book *deals* with hunting in Africa.—How do you *deal* with a case of armed robbery? **dealer** one who buys and sells: A general *dealer deals* in all kinds of goods.

dear 1. loved: They are *dear* friends of mine. 2. (used when beginning a letter): '*Dear* Sir . . .' 3. high in price, charging high prices: Beef is very *dear* this month. 4. used to show surprise or annoyance: Oh *dear*! I've lost my gloves again. **dearly** greatly, at a great cost: We love her *dearly*.

death 1. the end of life: The flood caused many *deaths*.—His *death* was a great blow to his friends. **deathbed** the bed on which ones dies. **deathtrap** a situation which may cause *death*: This road is too narrow for heavy traffic. It is a *deathtrap*.

debate (de-bate) 1. a discussion, especially in a meeting of people: After a long *debate* a new chairman was chosen. 2. discuss or argue about something: The City Council *debated* the question of road repairs.

decay (de-cay) 1. go bad: The smell came from a heap of *decayed* vegetables. 2. rotting: How can we stop tooth *decay*?

deceive (de-ceive) mislead; make a person believe something which is false: The Bible tells us how Jacob *deceived* his father. **deceit** deceiving: Now tell me the truth; I am not used to *deceit*. **deceitful** full of *deceit*: Nobody can trust a *deceitful* person.

December (De-cem-ber) the twelfth month of the year.

decent (de-cent) 1. respectable: You need a pair of *decent* shoes. – He comes from a *decent* family. 2. in good taste: If you come with us you must behave with *decent* manners. 3. good, satisfactory: At last I have a good job and a *decent* salary. 4. kind, likeable: That's very *decent* of you! **decency** good manners: You might have had the *decency* to tell me you were going away.

decide (de-cide) 1. settle a question: Shall I stay or go away? It's not easy to *decide*. 2. judge in a dispute: The judge *decided* in favour of the injured person. **decision** the act or result of *deciding*: I have reached a *decision* which cannot be changed.

decimal (dec-i-mal) having to do with tens or tenths. **decimal system** money or weights reckoned in tens. **decimal fraction** part of a whole number written in this way after a *decimal* point. **decimalization** the changing of money, weights, measurements etc. into the *decimal* system.

declare (de-clare) 1. make known to all: The result of the poll was *declared* at midnight. – The two sides have *declared* an armistice. 2. make a statement about goods brought into the country, one's income etc.: 'Have you anything to *declare*?' asked the customs officer. 3. (in cricket) close an innings before all the side has batted. **declaration** something *declared*: Immediately after the *declaration* of war, the army attacked.

decline (de-cline) 1. refuse, say no to: My offer of help was *declined* with thanks. 2. fail in strength or in amount: The patient slowly *declined* in health. 3. a falling in strength, amount etc.: The *decline* in the cost of vegetables has helped us through the winter.

decorate (dec-or-ate) 1. make more gay, pretty or beautiful: Let's *decorate* the Christmas tree. 2. paint (a building), put wallpaper etc. on the inside walls: The rooms of our headquarters have been newly *decorated*. 3. reward a person with a medal: The brave firemen were *decorated* by the Chief Officer. **decoration** the painting of a building, the medal given to a person: I like the *decoration* of your dining-room. – Have you yet received your *decoration* for bravery? **decorator** a person who *decorates* houses and buildings for a living, especially their interiors.

decrease (de-crease) 1. become less or smaller: The amount of money I had in the bank has *decreased* by half. 2. lessening, growing smaller: There has been a gradual *decrease* in car accidents.

dedicate (ded-i-cate) 1. give up time or money for some special purpose: He has *dedicated* himself completely to writing spy stories. 2. print in a book that it has been written in honour of a person the author loves or respects. 3. declare that a building is for a certain purpose: This hospital was *dedicated* by the mayor to the service of children. **dedication** words used in *dedicating* a book, the act of *dedicating* a building: The service of *dedication* was held in the great hall.

deep 1. going far down: In some places the ocean is 8,000 metres *deep*. 2. low in sound: The preacher spoke in a *deep* voice. 3. dark in colour: Her shawl is a *deep* red. 4. coming from far down: Now take a *deep* breath. **deep-freeze** a refrigerator which keeps food very cold to preserve it for long periods.

defeat (de-feat) 1. overcome in contest or battle: Our football team was badly *defeated* in the final. 2. the act of *defeating* or being *defeated*: Our *defeat* ended all hopes of winning the cup.

defect (de-fect) 1. fault, want, lack, imperfection: He suffers from a bad speech *defect*. **defective** faulty, having *defects*: The motorist was fined because his brakes were *defective*.

defend (de-fend) 1. fight for, work for the defence of: We must all help to *defend* our country. 2. speak or write in support of: I am ready to *defend* my cause against whoever attacks me. **defendant** the person or persons against whom a charge is brought in a court of law: 'Not guilty, your Honour,' answered the *defendant*.

define (de-fine) 1. explain what something means: How would you *define* this word? 2. show or state very clearly: The tree was clearly *defined* against the horizon. – Before I start work would you please *define* my duties? **definite** clear, easy to see, exact: There is a very *definite* line marked on this map. – Where were you at 8 o'clock? Please be *definite*. **definition** the act of explaining, explanation: I don't agree with your *definition* of honesty.

defy (de-fy) 1. challenge the power of, resist: Nobody dared *defy* the cruel conqueror. 2. refuse to obey: You are sure to be punished if you *defy* the law. 3. be too difficult: The fort *defied* all our attempts at capture. **defiance** refusal to obey, resistance: The captain attacked in *defiance* of orders to remain at his post. **defiant** refusing to obey: I do not like your *defiant* manner.

degree (de-gree) 1. one 360th part of a complete turn: Ninety *degrees* make one right angle. 2. one unit in measuring temperature: 59 *degrees* on the Fahrenheit scale equals 15 *degrees* Centigrade. 3. a small amount, a small space of time: He is improving by *degrees*. – One day he will reach a high *degree* of skill. 4. a title given after a university course: I would like to work for the *degree* of Bachelor of Science.

dejected (de-jec-ted) sad, unhappy: He has been *dejected* ever since he failed the examination. **dejection** a state of sadness: He remains at home, unable to conquer his *dejection*.

deliberate (de-lib-er-ate) 1. done on purpose: Your delay was *deliberate* defiance of authority. 2. slow, careful: The headmaster's speech was plain and *deliberate*. 3. think about, talk about: Before we elected our candidate we *deliberated* for hours. **deliberation** careful thought and discussion: Nobody should take such a serious step without long *deliberation*.

delicate (del-i-cate) soft, tender: I cannot bear the hot sun because of my *delicate* skin. 2. fine, cleverly made: The goldsmith showed us a ring of the most *delicate* workmanship. 3. easily made ill or broken: The old lady is in *delicate* health. 4. easily able to detect changes: In this hospital we have the most *delicate* instruments. **delicacy** exotic and delicious food given to invalids or as a special treat. **delicatessen** a shop selling exotic foods, chiefly foreign; the foods sold in such a shop.

delicious (de-li-cious) pleasing and delightful in every way: This apple pie tastes *delicious*. – From the kitchen came the most *delicious* smell.

delight (de-light) great pleasure, enjoyment: To our great *delight*, the band played the Blue Danube Waltz. 2. give great pleasure, take pleasure: How *delighted* we are to see you again. – The boy *delights* in teasing his small sister. **delightful** giving pleasure: We had a *delightful* journey down the river.

delinquent (de-lin-quent) doing wrong, a person doing wrong: The police wish there were fewer young *delinquents*. **delinquency** wrongdoing: Juvenile *delinquency* is a great problem these days.

demand (de-mand) 1. ask for: When we reached the main gate the guard *demanded* to see our passports. 2. need: This work *demands* the very greatest skill. 3. something *demanded*, asked: I haven't enough money to meet all your *demands*. 4. a wish to have or get: The *demand* for turkeys is greater than ever this Christmas.

democracy (de-moc-ra-cy) *democracies* 1. a government in which all adult citizens take part, usually by electing members to their parliaments. 2. a country which has this kind of government: Great Britain is one of the oldest *democracies* in the world. **democrat** a person who believes in *democracy* as the best form of government. **democratic** having to do with *democracy*: There are many nations which do not have a *democratic* form of government.

demolish (de-mol-ish) pull down, destroy: The house was *demolished* by fire. **demolition** pulling down, destroying: All the buildings in these streets are awaiting *demolition*.

demonstrate (dem-on-strate) 1. show to others: A traveller has called to *demonstrate* how the new sewing machine operates. 2. proclaim opinions in public: Today thousands of people will *demonstrate* against the government's new Act. **demonstration** any kind of showing: Would you like me to give a *demonstration* of this new sewing machine? – They will attend a *demonstration* in Hyde Park.

dense 1. close together, not easily seen through: We were soon moving through a *dense* crowd of people. – *Dense* smoke billowed from the burning building. 2. stupid, not clever: Can't you do this puzzle? You must be *dense*.

dentist (den-tist) a person who takes out, fills and cares for people's teeth. **dental** having to do with teeth: We are trying our best to find ways to prevent *dental* decay. **dentifrice** tooth-powder or tooth paste. **denture** a plate of artificial teeth which fits on to the gums.

deny (de-ny) *denies, denied, denying* 1. declare that something is not true: We *deny* all rumours that this shop is to close. 2. say 'no' to a request: He *denied* an interview to the local newspaper.

deodorant (de-o-dor-ant) a substance that destroys odours, often sprayed in a room or on the body.

depart (de-part) go away, leave: The train *departs* at 10.30. **departure** the act of going away: I have postponed my *departure* until tomorrow.

department (de-part-ment) a division of an organization, a government, a business or a country: The *department* of French at this university has an excellent reputation.

depend (de-pend) 1. need: I earn my own spending money but I *depend* on my parents for everything else. 2. trust, rely: Can I *depend* on you to vote for me? **dependent** depending on: As long as he is out of work he is *dependent* on his parents. **dependant** someone who depends on another for support or favour.

deport (de-port) 1. send a person by force out of a country: This foreigner, who was suspected of spying, has been *deported*. 2. behave oneself in a certain way: You should learn to *deport* yourself as a gentleman. **deportation** the sending of undesirable persons out of a country. **deportment** behaviour, the way of acting: You need a few lessons in *deportment*.

deposit (de-pos-it) 1. put, lay, place: Paul *deposited* the kitten on my lap. 2. store to keep safe: I have *deposited* the deeds of my house in the bank. 3. money paid in part payment for an article one is buying: We will deliver the goods on payment of a 10 per cent *deposit*. 4. matter, earth, precious stones etc., laid down by floods and other natural happenings: Valuable *deposits* of oil and gas have been found in the North Sea. – The fire in the kitchen left a thick *deposit* of soot on everything.

depress (de-press) 1. push or pull down: If you *depress* the lever the engine will start. 2. make sad: I was *depressed* to have to leave the party so early.

depression (de-pres-sion) 1. sadness, being depressed: I am overcome by *depression* whenever I receive bad news. 2. a hollow or a place where a surface has sunk: The car bumped over a *depression* in the road. 3. a lessening of air pressure in the atmosphere which usually brings clouds and rain: 'A deep *depression* is moving eastwards over the Irish Sea' (weather report).

deprive (de-prive) take away from somebody: The absence of news *deprived* us of hope. – What would you do if you were *deprived* of books?

depth 1. distance from top to bottom: What is the *depth* of the river at this point? 2. the deepest, worst, lowest or most distant: He lives in the *depth* of the country and cannot be visited in the *depth* of winter. **depth-charge** a bomb thrown into the sea to be used against enemy submarines.

deputy (de-pu-ty) *deputies* a person chosen to act for or represent somebody else: The manager cannot attend the meeting but will send his *deputy*.

descend (de-scend) 1. go or come down: The path *descended* into a deep valley. – If you try to *descend* the stairs too quickly you may fall. 2. the children and grandchildren of: I am *descended* from a distinguished family. 3. be handed down from one generation to another: The ownership of this land *descended* to me from my father. 4. attack: A band of Indians suddenly *descended* on the wagon train. **descent** going down, being handed down, attack: The climber was injured during the *descent*. **descendant** one who is *descended* from: Most of our kings and queens are *descendants* of William the Conqueror.

describe (de-scribe) 1. say what something or somebody is like: Please *describe* the man you saw in the street. 2. mark or draw (in geometry): We will *describe* a circle round this square. **description** a statement about what something or somebody is like: A *description* of the wanted man was handed in at the police station.

desert (de-sért) go, run away from: He told me he had *deserted* from the navy. – When we reached the town it was quite *deserted*. 2. leave without money or help: This poor woman has been *deserted* by her husband. **deserter** one who has *deserted* from the army, navy, air force etc. **desertion** leaving, abandoning.

desert (dés-ert) a large area of land without water or trees, with very few inhabitants: A caravan of camels crossed the *desert*.

deserve (de-serve) merit something: For his gallant rescue of the child the fireman *deserves* a medal. – You *deserve* to be punished.

design (de-sign) 1. drawing, plan or pattern: We like the *design* you have produced for the new children's playground. – The artist had drawn a complicated *design* of triangles. 2. to make *designs* for: I have *designed* a wonderful machine for bending iron bars.

desire (de-sire) 1. a great longing for: I told him of my *desire* to visit Greece. 2. long for: What do you most *desire* in life, money, happiness or fame? **desirable** to be *desired*: 'This *desirable* residence for sale' (notice outside a house). **desirous** wishing to be or have: Our country is *desirous* of trading with yours.

despair (des-pair) 1. having lost all hope: When I think of how I have failed I am driven to *despair*. 2. lose or give up all hope: We have heard nothing of our friends for months, and *despair* of their safety; we even *despair* of their lives.

desperate (des-per-ate) in despair, ready to do anything, dangerous: This is my last *desperate* act against *desperate* criminals.

despise (des-pise) think badly of, feel contempt for: He *despised* the accumulation of riches.

destine (des-tine) to be set apart for some work: I was *destined* to be a sailor. **destiny** a power which is believed to decide a person's future: Whatever dangers I meet, it is my *destiny* to survive them. **destination** the place to which somebody is going: We shall pass through Paris but our final *destination* is London.

destroy (des-troy) ruin, bring to nothing, break to pieces: Don't *destroy* your books; you may need them later. – The rain has completely *destroyed* the harvest this year. **destruction** *destroying*, being *destroyed*: A lighted cigarette caused the *destruction* of the house by fire. **destructive** causing *destruction*, fond of *destroying*: I hate *destructive* criticism. – This *destructive* child has broken all her toys.

detail (de-tail) 1. a small part, a small fact: The plan he drew me was correct in every *detail*. 2. give a special task to: I have been *detailed* to guard the railway line.

detain (de-tain) keep back, make to wait: James was late, because he was *detained* at the office. **detention** being *detained*, being kept late at school: His *detention* in prison lasted a week. – This boy has been put in *detention* for being late.

detect (de-tect) find something out: A fault has been *detected* in the steering of your car. **detection** discovery: We need more police to help in the *detection* of crime. **detective** a person whose work is to find and arrest criminals: A squad of *detectives* was sent to discover the jewel thieves.

deter (de-ter) hinder or discourage somebody from an action: I hope my advice will *deter* you from attempting the impossible. **deterrent** something which may *deter*: It was hoped that the hydrogen bomb would be the final *deterrent* (i.e. that it would stop nations from making war).

detergent (de-ter-gent) a substance which cleans, removes dirt: Today we have many things besides soap which act as *detergents*.

determine (de-ter-mine) 1. decide on: I have *determined* to take a course in science. 2. be the fact which decides: The state of the ground will *determine* whether or not the match can be played. **determination** the power to decide and carry out: Anne's *determination* to become an actress was exceptional.

detonate (de-to-nate) explode with a great noise: The bomb was taken to the marshes and *detonated*. **detonator** that part of a bomb which causes it to explode.

develop (de-vel-op) 1. grow or cause to grow: Harry has *developed* into a first-class pianist. – He is exercising to *develop* his finger muscles. 2. treat a photographic film with chemicals so that a picture can be made from it.

device (de-vice) 1. something made to carry out a special purpose: A new *device* has recently been invented for slicing bacon. – A nuclear *device* has been exploded in the Pacific Ocean. 2. a plan or scheme: 'I have a *device* to make all well' (Shakespeare, *A Midsummer Night's Dream*).

devil (de-vil) 1. an evil spirit which does wicked things. 2. (in the Bible) Satan, the chief of all evil spirits. 3. a cruel, wicked person. 4. a poor, unfortunate person.

devote (de-vote) give up one's time, energy etc. to one thing: His whole life has been *devoted* to healing the sick. 2. be mainly concerned with: This society is *devoted* to the study of geography. **devoted** loving, loyal: We are all *devoted* subjects of the Queen. **devotion** being *devoted* to, having great love for.

devour (de-vour) 1. eat greedily: 'Some evil beast hath *devoured* him' (*The Book of Genesis*). 2. read, look at, hear, listen with great attention: He *devoured* the story of the missing fortune. 3. destroy: The whole factory was *devoured* by fire.

dew the drops of water which form on grass in the evening and on chilly mornings: The morning *dew* shone on the grass.

diagram (di-a-gram) a drawing or plan which explains how a building, a piece of machinery etc. is to be built or made: The engineer produced the *diagram* of his new invention.

dial (di-al) a flat surface on which numbers or letters and sometimes pointers show the time, weight, temperature, gas or electricity consumed. Clocks, radio sets, gas and electricity meters and telephones all have *dials*.

dialect (di-a-lect) a way of speaking used in one part of a country: Last night we heard a radio play in the Yorkshire *dialect*.

diamond (di-a-mond) 1. a precious stone used in jewellery, which sparkles brightly: She wore a *diamond* ring. 2. one of the four suits in a pack of cards. **diamond wedding** the sixtieth anniversary of a wedding. **rough diamond** a kind-hearted person with rough manners.

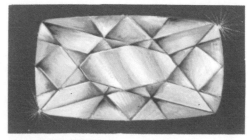

diary (di-a-ry) *diaries* a written record of what a person does or thinks each day: I have kept a *diary* for the last ten years.

diarist a person who keeps a diary: The most famous *diarist* in England was Samuel Pepys.

dictate (dic-tate) 1. say words aloud so that another person may write them down: The manager *dictated* a letter to his secretary. 2. give orders to others: You need not *dictate* to me; I already know what to do. **dictation** saying words aloud, to be written down, or to be recorded by a machine: She wrote at my *dictation*. **dictator** a powerful ruler who must be obeyed: Parliament was dismissed and the Prime Minister became the *dictator* of the country. **dictaphone** a machine used in an office which records words for a typist to copy later.

dictionary (dic-tion-ary) a book which gives the meanings of words in one language or translations of words from one language into another: I often have to consult my *dictionary* when writing letters.—May I borrow your French–English *dictionary* please? **diction** the way a person speaks, chooses and pronounces words.

die 1. cease to live, come to the end of life: Flowers, plants, animals and human beings all die in time.—One may *die* of hunger, of thirst, through illness, in battle, as well as through many other causes. 2. a block of metal with a design on it for making coins, medals, and stamping designs on paper and other materials.

diet (di-et) the food we usually eat: Most people live on a mixed *diet* of meat, fruit and vegetables. 2. the food one may be limited to eating: Don't tempt me with cream or sweets; I'm on a *diet*.

differ (dif-fer) 1. be unlike in any way: My brother and I *differ* both in appearance and opinions. **difference** the way in which people or things *differ* from each other: Sarah doesn't know the *difference* between a sheep and a goat. **different** *differing* one from another: We are twins but we wear clothes of *different* colours.

difficult (dif-fi-cult) 1. hard, not easy: I have been set a very *difficult* sum for homework. 2. hard to please: He won't do this, he won't do that; he's just being *difficult*. **difficulty** something *difficult*: If you have *difficulty* (or are in *difficulties*) with your French, I will help you.

digest (di-gest) 1. (of food) change or be changed inside the body: He is an invalid and can only *digest* liquid foods. 2. take into the mind so that it can be remembered and used: I *digested* everything in this book in a week. **digestion** the power or act of *digesting*: I have a good *digestion* and can eat anything.

diligent (dil-i-gent) taking care and making efforts in what one does: He has always been a *diligent* student. **diligently** in a *diligent* manner: I will work *diligently* if you employ me. **diligence** effort, continued steady work.

dim 1. faint, weak, not bright, not easy to see: We saw the *dim* outline of a ship through the fog. 2. not able to see clearly: The old man's eyes are *dim* with age. 3. make or grow *dim*: The lights in the theatre began to *dim* as the curtain rose.

dimension (di-men-sion) measurement, length, width, depth, height or area: Please write down the *dimensions* of this field. **three dimensional** (of a picture) giving the appearance of depth as well as height and breadth, like a view of the actual thing.

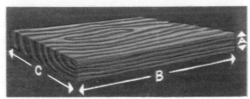

diminish (di-min-ish) become smaller or less: In this severe winter our supplies of food are swiftly *diminishing*.

dine have dinner: Come early please, we *dine* at seven o'clock. **dining-room** the room in which one *dines*.

dinghy (din-ghy) *dinghies* 1. a small boat. 2. a boat made of rubber or some material that can be expanded and filled with air, used by people in an aircraft when forced down over water.

dingy (din-gy) looking dirty, dark: What a *dingy* old suit you are wearing.—We were led into a small, *dingy* room.

dinner the main or chief meal of the day: We have *dinner* at one o'clock, but some people have *dinner* in the evening. 2. a party at which people dine, a banquet: Are you coming to the golf club *dinner* this evening?

diocese (di-o-cese) the district under the care of a bishop: There are over a hundred churches in this *diocese*.

dip 1. put into and take out again: To wash this garment, *dip* it in warm soapy water.— I can't *dip* my hand into my pocket (give you money) every time you ask me. 2. go or bring down: Always *dip* your headlights in the dark. 3. a quick bathe: Shall we go for a *dip* in the sea?

diphtheria (diph-the-ri-a) a serious disease of the throat: *Diphtheria* is infectious and when it breaks out the authorities should be notified.

direct (di-rect) 1. straight, not turning to one side or the other: By this road you can go *direct* to Bristol. 2. show the way: Could you please *direct* me to the station? 3. address a letter or parcel: You have opened a letter which was *directed* to me. 4. order: The policeman *directed* the crowd to keep clear of the building. 5. turn: We will now *direct* our attention to the figures on the blackboard. **directly** quickly, straight: I'll be home *directly*. We are now steering *directly* for the shore. **director** a person who *directs* or manages the affairs of a business or other organization: The Board of *Directors* will meet this afternoon.

direction (di-rec-tion) 1. the way in which a person or thing is going: If you want to reach Buckingham Palace, you are going in the wrong *direction*. 2. instructions, information: The *directions* for use are printed on the packet. 3. management, control: In future you will work under the *direction* of the Chief Clerk.

disable (dis-a-ble) injure, make unable to do things: Since the motor accident this man has been completely *disabled*.

disagree (dis-a-gree) 1. fail to agree, have different opinions: They are good friends, but even friends sometimes *disagree*.—We have both done the sum but our answers *disagree*. 2. not be good for: I do not like the seaside, the air and the food *disagree* with me. **disagreeable** not pleasant: Which do you hate most, the *disagreeable* weather or our *disagreeable* companions?

disappear (dis-ap-pear) go away, go out of sight: The sun *disappeared* below the horizon, and the stars came out. **disappearance** vanishing, going out of sight, loss: I can't understand the *disappearance* of my watch.

disappoint (dis-ap-point) 1. fail to do what has been promised or what one wishes: I'd like to trust you but you have *disappointed* me too many times. **disappointment** being *disappointed*: At three o'clock rain stopped play. What a *disappointment*!

disarm (dis-arm) 1. take weapons away: The enemy forces were captured and *disarmed*. 2. (of nations) to cut down the size of their armies, navies and air forces: The fear of attack prevents a nation from *disarming*. **disarmament** the act of *disarming*: During the last fifty years there have been many proposals for *disarmament*.

disaster (dis-as-ter) any sudden great misfortune that happens to a person or a number of people: His father's accident was a great *disaster*. **disastrous** causing *disaster*: This year there occurred one of the most *disastrous* earthquakes in history.

discharge (dis-charge) 1. give out, send out: The ship's cargo was *discharged* the day after she docked. 2. fire (a weapon): At the signal the archers *discharged* their arrows. 3. dismiss, send away from work: After a week in hospital the patient was *discharged*.—Because of shortage of work, half the staff has had to be *discharged*. 4. do a duty, pay a debt. 5. carrying out, paying: Be strict in the *discharge* of your duties. 6. the act of giving out, firing or dismissing: The *discharge* of a rifle echoed over the moors.—After his *discharge* from the navy he found work as a cook.

disciple (dis-ci-ple) 1. one of the twelve men who first personally followed Jesus Christ. 2. a person who follows the teachings of another.

discipline (dis-cip-line) 1. training of the mind, body and the character to fit one for life: All who belong to the army live under military *discipline*. 2. control: The teacher cannot keep good *discipline*.

discontent (dis-con-tent) not being satisfied or content: If you told me the reason for your *discontent*, perhaps I could help you. **discontented** not satisfied, unhappy: I am *discontented* because I am never thanked for what I have done.

discontinue (dis-con-tin-ue) stop: Please *discontinue* the delivery of newspapers this week.

discourage (dis-cour-age) lose or take away hope or confidence: If you wish to take the examination don't let him *discourage* you. **discouragement** loss of hope: The loss of all his books was a great *discouragement* to him.

discover (dis-cov-er) find out: Columbus *discovered* America.—I have suddenly *discovered* that I can swim four strokes. **discovery** the act of *discovering*, something *discovered*: The *discovery* of America changed the world.—Captain Cook went on several long voyages of *discovery*.

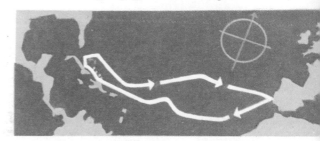

discus (dis-cus) a round plate of metal or stone thrown in athletic contests in ancient Greece and Rome. Throwing the *discus* is also an event in the modern Olympic Games.

discuss (dis-cuss) talk about, argue about, examine by talking: Before starting their journey they *discussed* their plans thoroughly. **discussion** talk, examination: Our *discussion* has lasted three hours and the subject is still under *discussion*.

disease (dis-ease) any illness of human beings, animals or plants: Mumps, measles, scarlet fever and chickenpox are well-known *diseases*. **diseased** suffering from *disease*.

disgrace (dis-grace) 1. shame, loss of the respect of others: There is no *disgrace* in hard work. 2. bring shame upon: My cousin has *disgraced* his family by his bad behaviour. **disgraceful** bringing or causing disgrace: What a *disgraceful* mess!

disguise (dis-guise) 1. do something to change the appearance, sound etc.; mislead or conceal who or what one is: Father entered the room *disguised* as Santa Claus. 2. things used and done to change appearance: She went to the ball in the *disguise* of a flower-girl.

disgust (dis-gust) 1. a feeling of strong dislike or anger: I could not hide my *disgust* at not being offered a part in the play. 2. cause *disgust*: His rude manners *disgust* all who meet him. **disgusting** causing dislike: What *disgusting* behaviour!

dish 1. a shallow container for holding food: Please bring the *dish* for the potatoes. 2. food brought in a *dish*: Take this *dish* of potatoes to the table. 3. something very good to eat: 'Wasn't that a dainty *dish* to set before a king' (nursery rhyme). **dish up** put into a *dish* to serve for dinner: Shall I *dish* up now, mother? **dishes** all the crockery: Who is going to wash the *dishes* today?

dishonest (dis-hon-est) not honest, prepared to cheat: I have written down a list of *dishonest* actions.–They are what we can expect from *dishonest* persons. **dishonesty** not being *honest*: I did not think he was capable of such *dishonesty*.

disinfect (dis-in-fect) keep free from germs so that disease does not spread: After the patient had recovered, the room had to be *disinfected*.

dismal sad, dark, gloomy, miserable: We found ourselves in a *dismal* cave.–We have had *dismal* weather all the summer.

dismiss (dis-miss) 1. send away: School will *dismiss* (or be *dismissed*) at noon today. 2. discharge from employment: Three secretaries have been *dismissed* this week. **dismissal** act of *dismissing*: His *dismissal* was a great blow to his family.

disobey (dis-o-bey) refuse to do what one is ordered to do: I do not agree with your commands but I cannot *disobey* you. **disobedience** refusal to obey: You will be punished for your *disobedience*. **disobedient** refusing to obey: Who is the most *disobedient* boy in school?

disorder (dis-or-der) absence of order, confusion: The thieves had left everything in *disorder*.–Police had to be called in to deal with the *disorder* among the crowd. **disorderly** with no order, in confusion: He found himself surrounded by a *disorderly* crowd of jeering men.

display (dis-play) 1. show: Every week we *display* different kinds of shoes in our shop window.–2. a show or exhibition: Last week I attended three *displays* of the latest fashions.

dispose (dis-pose) 1. get rid of: When we have eaten the chicken, how do we *dispose* of the bones? 2. set out or place in order: The toy soldiers were *disposed* in straight lines. 3. be willing to do something: I am not in the least *disposed* to help you. **disposal** getting rid of: The town council has made a new plan for the *disposal* of rubbish.

dispute (dis-pute) 1. challenge: He is a man whose honesty has never been in *dispute*. 2. argument, debate: We shall not sell this piece of land until the *dispute* about the price has been settled.

disqualify (dis-qua-li-fy) deprive of fitness or right: Any competitor who arrives late will be *disqualified*.

dissolve 1. fade from sight when put into a liquid and become part of it: Salt, sugar and many other substances *dissolve* in water. 2. put a solid into a liquid so that it dissolves: 'Directions: *dissolve* two tablets in water and take after meals' (on a medicine bottle).

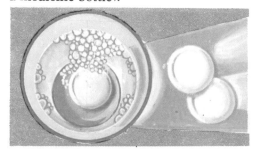

distance (dis-tance) 1. amount of space between two points: The *distance* between our houses is longer by road than if we go through the fields. 2. a place farther away: We heard a faint cry in the *distance*. **distant** far away in space, time, or relationship: All this happened in the *distant* past to a *distant* cousin of mine.

distinct (dis-tinct) 1. plain, clear, easily seen or heard: In the shadow we saw the *distinct* figure of a man. 2. different, not like, apart: I can see two *distinct* shapes.— Keep these yellow pencils *distinct* from the red ones. **distinction** difference, a mark of honour which makes a person different from others: The Victoria Cross and the George Cross are the two highest awards for gallantry.

distinguish (dis-tin-guish) 1. recognize the difference between: Can you *distinguish* red from green? 2. make oneself famous or well known: He has *distinguished* himself by acts of bravery. **distinguished** famous: All the most *distinguished* doctors were present at the conference.

distract (dis-tract) draw attention away: I am adding up figures, so please don't *distract* me with your questions! **distracted** confused, anxious: Mary was *distracted* with worries. **distraction** anxiety amounting almost to madness, passion: 'Darling,' he said, 'I love you to *distraction*.'

distress (dis-tress) 1. pain, sorrow, suffering: The blind man is in *distress* because of the loss of his dog. 2. danger: The boatman sent up a rocket as a signal of *distress*. 3. cause *distress*: We are much *distressed* because of the death of our leader.

distribute (dis-trib-ute) 1. hand out, give out, send out: These circulars should be *distributed* the week before the meeting. 2. spread: The manure should be *distributed* evenly over the field. **distribution** giving, sending out or spreading: Will you be going to the *distribution* of prizes at the school?

district (dis-trict) 1. part of a country or town: We live in a farming *district*. 2. having to do with a *district*: The old lady needs the attentions of the *District* Nurse.

distrust (dis-trust) 1. doubt, have no trust in: I would lend you money if I did not *distrust* you. 2. want of trust: I have a great *distrust* of people who talk too much.

disturb (dis-turb) 1. break the quiet or peace, cause to worry: When Jane is asleep we try not to *disturb* her.—We were greatly *disturbed* by the bad news. 2. put out of the right order: Who's been *disturbing* the books on this shelf? **disturbance** something that disturbs, disorder: Did you see the *disturbance* in the street?

ditch a long narrow channel in the ground: There were *ditches* on both sides of the road to carry away the water.

divide (di-vide) 1. separate or be separated into parts: We *divided* the money between us. 2. cause to disagree: We were still *divided* on the question as to how much money should be paid. **division** the act of *dividing*, a part: We were present at the *division* of the money. **divisible** that which can be exactly divided: 81 is *divisible* by 9.

divine (di-vine) 1. from God, like God or like a god: 'I know him for a man *divine* and holy' (Shakespeare, *Measure for Measure*). 2. very good, excellent: We had *divine* weather during our holidays.

divorce (di-vorce) 1. end a marriage by law: Henry VIII *divorced* two of his six wives. 2. the ending of a marriage in this way: Our neighbour has obtained a *divorce* from her husband.

dizzy (diz-zy) a feeling of giddiness: May I sit down please? I feel *dizzy*. **dizziness** being *dizzy*: Do you suffer from *dizziness* after you have danced?

do *did, done* 1. perform an action: What are you *doing* with those books? 2. make, work at, carry out: Have you *done* your homework yet? No, I am still *doing* my arithmetic. 3. be good, satisfactory: I haven't a larger stick, so perhaps this will *do*. 4. cook: Do you like your meat well *done*? 5. used with words of action: *Do* you like chocolate? I *did* once, but I *don't* like it now.—*Did* you bake that cake?

dock 1. a platform or platforms built on a river or on the seashore where ships may be loaded, unloaded, or repaired. **dry dock** a *dock* from which water may be pumped out. **dockyard** an enclosed place where there are many *docks*. 2. (of a ship) to go, be brought or taken into a *dock*. 3. that part of a court of law where an accused person stands.

doctor (doc-tor) 1. a person who has received the highest degree of a university: The chairman of this committee is a *Doctor* of Law. 2. a person who has been trained in medicine and treats people who are ill: If your cold is so bad you should see the *doctor*. 3. treat for illness: We tried to *doctor* the little girl but she showed no improvement. 4. patch up, make something work: It is not a very good engine, but it could be *doctored* to make it work.

document (doc-u-ment) a written or printed paper giving evidence or proof: They landed with no *documents* to show their date of birth, marriage or to what country they belonged. **documentary** a film or television programme showing some special aspect of life.

dog an animal kept by man as a pet or to guard the house, work with the police, with shepherds etc.: Every year *dogs* of many breeds are shown at Crufts in London. **dogfight** a battle in which a number of aircraft take part. **dog-tired** tired out, exhausted.

doll a toy usually made in the likeness of a baby or a little girl.

dollar (dol-lar) a unit of money used in the United States, Canada, Australia, Mexico and other countries.

dome a rounded roof with a circular base: St Paul's Cathedral has a particularly handsome *dome*.

domestic (do-mes-tic) 1. having to do with the home and the family: My *domestic* duties are to wash the dishes and clean the windows. 2. Having to do with one's own country: Our newspaper has both *domestic* and foreign news. 2. (of animals) kept by man: Dogs, cats, horses, cows and sheep are all *domestic* animals.

dominate (dom-i-nate) 1. have control over: He is not strong enough to *dominate* everybody he meets. 2. overlook: The chief lived in a castle which *dominated* the whole valley below.

donkey (don-key) ass: The old man brings his *donkey* and cart to collect old iron.

doom 1. fate or destiny, death, ruin or some future evil: The captive did not know the *doom* that awaited him. 2. condemn: All my work is *doomed* to be forgotten. – The town has been *doomed* to destruction.

door 1. a movable barrier of wood or some other material designed to close up an entrance: When we reached the house we found all the *doors* locked. – The *door* of this cupboard does not fit properly. 2. a house (in a row): Does my brother live next *door* to you? No, he lives two *doors* away. **doorway** the opening leading into a room or a house: The old man was sitting in his chair in the *doorway*.

dope 1. a thick liquid used as varnish: Have you put the *dope* on the model plane yet? 2. a harmful drug. 3. give a drug: After the race it was found that one of the horses had been *doped*.

dormitory (dor-mi-to-ry) *dormitories* a room for sleeping, usually with many beds, most commonly found in a school or similar institution.

dose a quantity of medicine to be taken at one time: Repeat the *dose* every four hours (instructions on a medicine bottle).

dot 1. a small round mark made with pencil or pen: The Morse code is made up of *dots* and dashes. 2. mark with a *dot*: Don't forget to *dot* your i's. **dotted** sprinkled as if with *dots*: The fields were *dotted* with sheep and cattle.

double (dou-ble) 1. twice as much in weight, strength, quality, goodness, cost etc.: The price of food is *double* what it was ten years ago. 2. make or become *double*: Our shop has *doubled* its trade since we bought it. 3. fold in two: The sheet of paper must be *doubled* before you write on it.

doubt 1. be uncertain in opinion, distrust: I *doubt* the truth of his story. 2. uncertainty, absence of trust: Is there any *doubt* that we shall succeed? **doubtful** feeling or causing doubt: I am *doubtful* about going out this morning: the weather is *doubtful*. **doubtless** without doubt: You have *doubtless* heard the story of the Three Bears.

dough (pronounced *doe*) flour or meal mixed with water and made into paste for making bread, cake, pastry etc. **doughnut** a small cake of *dough* fried in deep fat, shaped like a ring or a ball.

dove a bird of the pigeon family: Noah opened the window of the ark and sent out a *dove*. 2. a symbol of peace: 'Be as wise as serpents and as harmless as *doves*' (The Gospel of St Matthew).

down 1. from higher to lower: He is going *down* the hill. – Who knocked this little boy *down*? – Sit *down*, please. 2. from an earlier to a later time: This watch was handed *down* from my grandfather. 3. bring, put, knock *down*: The strikers have *downed* tools this morning. **downcast** sad, depressed. **downfall** a heavy fall of rain, a fall from riches or power: His *downfall* was caused by gambling. **downward** from a higher to a lower place: We soon came to a *downward* path which led to the city. 4. the soft feathers of young birds, the soft hair on some plants or seeds, or other fine, soft hair.

doze 1. sleep lightly: The old man *dozes* in his chair after lunch. 2. a short, light sleep: He fell into a *doze*.

dozen (doz-en) twelve: Please deliver three *dozen* eggs this week.

draft 1. plan, sketch or outline: Have you made a *draft* of (or *drafted*) the speech you are to give tomorrow? 2. a small number of people taken from a larger body for some special work (especially members of the forces).

drain 1. a ditch or pipe for carrying away water or waste liquids: A long *drain* ran from the farm to the nearby stream. 2. something that uses up strength, time, money etc.: His expensive education was a severe *drain* on the family's finances. 3. make drier by allowing water or other liquids to flow away through a *drain*: If these marshes were *drained* the land could be used for farming.

drama (dra-ma) 1. a play for theatre, film or television: Don't miss the *drama* at the cinema tomorrow evening. 2. plays: For three years he has been studying *drama* at the evening institute. **dramatic** having to do with *drama*; excitement such as one might get in *drama*: This is one of the finest *dramatic* performances we have seen.—My parachute jump from the burning aeroplane was the most *dramatic* moment of my life. **dramatize** make a play of: We plan to *dramatize* the story of St George and the Dragon.

drape hang cloth, curtains etc. in folds round or over something: The statue was *draped* in a dustsheet. **draper** a person who sells cloth, linen and other materials for curtains, table-cloths or clothing. **drapery** goods sold by a *draper*.

draught (pronounced *draft*) 1. a strong current of air in an enclosed space: If you sit in a *draught* you may catch cold. **draughty** causing *draughts*: What a *draughty* room this is! 2. the depth of water needed to float a ship: To sail near this coast we need boats of shallow *draught*. 3. the amount one can drink at one time: Not many men can drink so much beer at one *draught*. **draughts** a game for two players, played with round pieces on a board of black and white squares.

dread 1. fear of something: She has always had a *dread* of spiders. 2. fear: I *dread* meeting that man again. **dreadful** causing *dread*, unpleasant: The recent earthquake has been a *dreadful* disaster.—What *dreadful* weather we have had this week!

dream 1. the things we seem to see and hear when we are asleep: Tell me about the *dream* you had last night. 2. have *dreams*; see and hear things in one's sleep: 'I did *dream* of money-bags tonight' (Shakespeare, *The Merchant of Venice*). 3. imagine: I often *dream* of what it would be like if I had lots of money.

dreary (drear-y) 1. dull, dark, gloomy: It was a *dreary* day in November. 2. long, uninteresting: I went home at the end of a *dreary* day's work.

dredge 1. a machine for making channels and ditches deeper. 2. clear a lake or stream with such a machine: The lake had to be *dredged* before the body was found. **dredger** a boat which carries a dredge.

drench wet something all over, soak through: The rain had *drenched* us to the skin and we had to change all our clothing.

drift 1. be carried along by air or water: The snow has *drifted* in front of our door.—The boat is *drifting* down the river. 2. something caused by *drifting*: We had to dig our way through the snow*drifts*.

drill 1. a tool or machine for making holes: I could soon fix this shelf if I had an electric *drill*. 2. make holes with a *drill*: Please *drill* three holes for the screws. 3. training or exercise, often by repeating over and over again: The cadets' *drill* looked very professional.—Now we will do a little *drill* in French grammar. 4. train or be trained: The men are *drilled* every day by the sergeant.

drip fall or let fall in drops: Rain was *dripping* from the trees. **dripping** fat melted out of meat which has been roasted: Please may I have some *dripping* on my bread?

drive *drove, driven* 1. make an animal or a person move by force: Once a week we *drive* the sheep to market. 2. operate a machine, an engine, bus or car; direct and guide a plough or cart: I am learning to *drive.*–Then please *drive* with care. 3. travel in a vehicle: Last year we *drove* through France to Italy. 4. carry in a vehicle: *Drive* me to the station, please. 5. move with force: He *drove* a nail into the post. 6. compel, force: This noise is *driving* me mad. 7. a journey in a vehicle: Shall we go for a *drive* this morning? 8. a private road: The gate leading to the *drive* was locked. 9. a competition (usually with playing cards): There will be a whist *drive* this evening. **driver** a person who *drives*: My uncle is a taxi *driver*.

droop bend over because of tiredness or want: The flowers are *drooping* and need water.

drop 1. a very small quantity of a liquid that forms a tiny round ball as it falls: Take five *drops* in a tablespoonful of water (directions on a bottle of medicine). 2. something shaped like a *drop*: Do you like lemon *drops*? 3. movement from higher to lower: Is this your first *drop* by parachute? 4. fall or make fall: I *dropped* my hat in the road.–The aeroplane *dropped* from the sky. 5. become or make something come to an end: We have argued long enough, so please let the matter *drop*.

drown 1. to die or cause to die in water through not being able to breathe: He fell into the river and was *drowned*. 2. make a noise loud enough to prevent other sounds from being heard: He tried to speak but his voice was *drowned* by the boos of the crowd.

drowsy (drow-sy) sleepy, half-asleep: I always feel *drowsy* after a large meal.

drug 1. a substance used to prevent or cure a disease: Put labels on all *drugs* and keep them away from children. 2. a substance that causes sleep, or any kind of intoxication: Some *drugs* are habit-forming and may cause much harm. 3. give *drugs* to, especially to cause one to sleep: Jean had to be *drugged* to stop the pain. **druggist** a chemist, a person who sells drugs, medicines and toilet articles.

drunk 1. past tense of the word *drink*: Have you *drunk* all the milk yet? 2. be intoxicated through *drinking* liquids containing alcohol: I have often seen him *drink*, but I have never seen him *drunk*. 3. a person who is *drunk*: The constable brought two *drunks* into the station. **drunkard** a person who is often drunk.

due 1. to be paid, to come: When is your next payment *due*? 2. right, fair: When this is all over you will have your *due* reward. 3. money to be paid for membership: I could not attend the annual meeting because I had not paid my *dues*. **due to** caused by: The accident was *due to* a leaking petrol tank.

duel (du-el) 1. a fight between two persons with weapons, under agreed rules in the presence of other persons called seconds: He was badly wounded in a *duel*. 2. fight a *duel* or *duels*: *Duelling* is forbidden in most countries today.

duet (du-et) a piece of music specially written for two people to sing or play.

dull 1. not bright or clear: We stay indoors on *dull* days.—His coat was a *dull* brown colour. 2. slow to learn: He is not stupid, but just a little *dull*. 3. not interesting: I found this book so *dull* I could not finish it. 4. make or become *dull*: The patient must be given a drug to *dull* the pain.

dumb 1. unable to speak: Many deaf people are also *dumb*. 2. silent for a short time: When the lion faced him he felt *dumb* with terror. **dumb-bell** a short bar with weights at both ends used for exercising the muscles.

dunce someone who learns very slowly; a stupid person.

dungeon (dun-geon) a dark cell or room under the ground into which prisoners used to be thrown: He had existed for three months in a *dungeon* infested with rats.

duplicate (du-pli-cate) 1. make an exact copy of: I asked you to write another letter, but you have *duplicated* this one.—I am sending out a hundred *duplicated* copies of this circular. 2. one thing which is exactly like another: I have lost the key of my door; could you please lend me a *duplicate*? **duplicator** machine which produces exact copies of something written or printed.

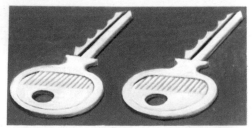

durable lasting a long time: I would like to buy a *durable* pair of shoes for heavy work. **duration** the time during which something exists: He was in the army for the *duration* of the war.

during (dur-ing) while something is going on or lasting: *During* the winter months the hours of daylight are short.—We always have a break for tea *during* the afternoon.

dusk the short time towards the end of daylight when the sky is becoming dark: He remained hidden all day and only emerged at *dusk*. **dusky** dark-coloured, dim.

duty (du-ty) *duties* 1. something one must do: I have *duties* to my parents, my teachers and my friends. 2. a tax on things exported from or imported into a country: I am afraid you will have to pay *duty* on these bottles of wine. **dutiful** doing one's *duty* well: There was never a more *dutiful* servant than Man Friday.

dwarf 1. a person, animal or plant much smaller than others of the same kind: Ten *dwarfs* perform in this circus.—This week we are having a sale of *dwarf* rose trees. 2. prevent from growing: Some plants are purposely *dwarfed* for use indoors. 3. make to appear small when put against other objects: Our little car was *dwarfed* by the huge wagons which it passed on the road.

dye make a different colour, usually by dipping in coloured liquid: Our curtains have been *dyed* blue. 2. material used for *dyeing*: May I have a packet of dark red *dye*?

dynamite (dy-na-mite) a substance specially made to explode with great force: The thieves burst open the safe with *dynamite*. 2. blow up with *dynamite*: We can hear the quarrymen *dynamiting* the rocks.

eager (ea-ger) keen, wanting to do, be or have: Why are you so *eager* to go to France? **eagerly** in an *eager* manner: I *eagerly* await your answer to my letter. **eagerness** very great desire: I can understand your *eagerness* to pass this examination.

ear 1. an organ of the body by which sounds are heard: My friend is deaf in both *ears*, so please speak louder. 2. power to hear and distinguish between sounds: Have you a good *ear* for music? 3. the part of a grain plant on which the seeds appear. **earphone** that part of a receiver placed over the *ear* by which one can hear sounds by telephone and radio.

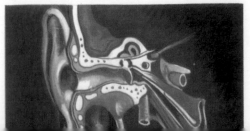

early (ear-ly) *earlier, earliest* 1. near to the beginning of a period of time: Meet me *early* this evening at the station. 2. before the usual time: I always arrive *early* at school. 3. one who does a thing in good time: 'The *early* bird catches the worm' (proverb).

earn gain or deserve, receive something in return for work: How much do you *earn* a week? **earnings** what one receives for work: I put most of my *earnings* into the bank.

earnest serious, determined to do or be: 'An *earnest* worker' (school report). **in earnest** in a serious manner: I am *in earnest* when I tell you not to smoke so much. **earnestly** in an *earnest* manner: We *earnestly* hope you will be present at our celebrations.

earth 1. the planet on which we live: The astronauts could see the *earth* from the moon. 2. ground: The balloon came to *earth* not far from the farm. 3. soil, dirt: Plant the roots carefully in the *earth*, and don't scatter *earth* on the path. **earthen** made of baked earth. **earthenware** jugs, jars and other pots made from baked *earth*. **earthworm** a worm that lives in the soil **earthquake** a sudden shaking of the *earth's* surface causing buildings to fall or be damaged: Two hundred people died in the recent *earthquake*.

east 1. the direction in which the sun rises: Three wise men came from the *east* to Bethlehem. 2. lands lying in this direction: Turkey and Egypt are in the Near *East*, China and Japan are in the Far *East*. 3. coming from the *east*: There is a cold *east* wind today. **easterly** to or from the *east*: Walk in an *easterly* direction and you will come to the house. **eastern** in the part lying in the east: Norfolk and Suffolk are counties in *eastern* England.

eccentric (ec-cen-tric) 1. behaving in a strange, unusual manner: We often laugh at *eccentric* people. 2. being or moving round a point which is not in the centre: All the planets move in *eccentric* orbits round the sun.

echo (ech-o) 1. sound which comes back, reflected from a wall, a rock etc.: Shout louder and listen for the *echo*. 2. send back an *echo*: The woods *echoed* with the sound of rifle fire.

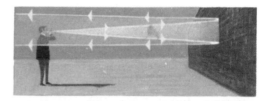

eclipse (e-clipse) 1. the hiding of sunlight from the earth when the moon passes in front of it. This is called a solar *eclipse* or an *eclipse* of the sun. 2. the complete or partial disappearance of the moon when the earth passes between it and the sun. This is called a lunar *eclipse* or an *eclipse* of the moon. 3. make something else seem poor, dull, small or unimportant: His wonderful violin playing *eclipsed* that of all other competitors.

ecology (e-col-o-gy) that part of science which deals with the habits of living beings and the effect on them of their surroundings: If we pollute the rivers with waste matter, and the air around us with poisonous fumes, we could disturb the earth's *ecology* and harm the human race.

economy (e-con-o-my) 1. saving, not wasting things, making the best use of what one has: It is false *economy* to buy cheap things which quickly wear out. **economize** make the best use of what one has: We have *economized* all the year so as to have a good holiday. **economics** the study of how goods and materials are made and distributed to all parts of the world.

edit (ed-it) prepare a book, a newspaper or film for publication or presentation. **editor** a person who does this or who is in charge of this work. **edition** the form in which a book or newspaper is published: You can now buy this book in a cheap *edition*.–Have you the latest *edition* of today's paper?

educate (ed-u-cate) teach, train: I was *educated* at the local school.–One must be well *educated* to become a lawyer. **education** instruction, training: Travelling is an excellent *education*.

effect (ef-fect) 1. result: Has this ointment had any *effect* on your sore finger? 2. how something is seen, felt or heard: Nobody liked the play, but the sound *effects* were very good. 3. cause: This medicine is sure to *effect* a cure. **effective** having an *effect*: Do you know an *effective* remedy for a sore throat?

efficient (ef-fi-cient) able to do things well: All our goods are produced by *efficient* craftsmen. **efficiency** being *efficient*: Her *efficiency* in running the office was quite outstanding.

effort (ef-fort) the use of physical or mental power, trying hard: He solved the puzzle with very little *effort*.–Please make every *effort* to come to the meeting.

eight the number (8) coming after 7 and before 9: Divide these *eight* boys into two groups of four. **eighteen** the number *18*, *eight* plus ten. **eighty** the number *80*, *eight* multiplied by ten or ten groups of *eight*: My grandfather is *80* years old today.

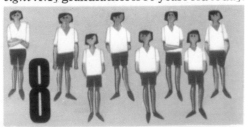

elaborate (e-lab-or-ate) worked or done very carefully: They made *elaborate* plans for their escape.–The leader produced an *elaborate* diagram of all the secret passages.

elbow (el-bow) 1. the joint where the upper and lower parts of the arm meet: He sat with his head in his hands and both *elbows* on the table. 2. that part of the sleeve of a coat which covers the *elbow*: Let me darn that big hole in the *elbow* of your jersey. 3. a joint which brings two pipes together at an angle. 4. force one's way with the *elbows*: He *elbowed* his way through the crowd.

elder (el-der) 1. older (of two people): Have you seen my *elder* brother John this morning? 2. an officer in some Christian churches: Our church is governed by a committee of *elders*. **elders** people who are older: He is a rude boy, and impudent to his *elders*. **elderly** becoming old: We have decided to pay regular visits to the *elderly* couple in our street. **eldest** the oldest of three or more people: When I give the prizes to these girls I will start with the *eldest*.

elect (e-lect) 1. choose: At this meeting we shall *elect* a new committee. 2. decide: I have *elected* not to stand for the post. **election** choosing, being *elected*: We are sorry that you are not standing for *election*. **elector** one who *elects*: We are making a register of *electors* in this town.

electric (e-lec-tric) worked by or having to do with *electricity*: Please switch on the *electric* light. **electrical** having to do with *electricity*: I work in a shop selling *electrical* supplies and I am an *electrical* engineer. **electrician** a person who works with *electrical* apparatus: Our light has gone out; please send for an *electrician*. **electricity** a force that gives light, heat and power and which can be sent or distributed through wires. **electrify** put *electricity* into: Don't touch that fence it is *electrified*. **electrocute** kill by means of *electricity*: The dog touched a live wire and was instantly *electrocuted*.

elegant (el-e-gant) handsome, graceful, well-dressed: We were received at the door by an *elegant* young man.

element (el-e-ment) 1. one of the simplest substances of which matter is composed and which cannot be split into others. Copper and zinc are *elements*: mixed together they make brass. 2. the simplest parts of anything: He has not yet learnt the *elements* of arithmetic. 3. the surroundings, occupation or hobby which make one feel happy: I'm in my *element* making model aeroplanes. **elementary** simple, in its very simplest form: This is an examination in *elementary* French. – 'Elementary, my dear Watson' (Conan Doyle, *The Adventures of Sherlock Holmes*).

elephant (el-e-phant) the largest four-footed animal now living. *Elephants* are found in Africa and Asia.

elevate (el-e-vate) lift up, raise, improve: An *elevated* railway may be seen over the tops of the houses. **elevation** height, altitude: The climbers reached snow at an *elevation* of several thousand metres. **elevator** a machine that lifts things on a belt with buckets; a building for lifting and storing grain.

eleven (e-lev-en) 11, the number between 10 and 12: 11 is an odd number and cannot be divided into equal parts. 2. a football, hockey or cricket team: I am the captain of our second *eleven*.

eliminate (e-lim-in-ate) get rid of, take or put away: Please *eliminate* all those words beginning with the letter A. – This man is the thief; all other suspects have been *eliminated* (from the list).

ellipse (el-lipse) an oval: Some *ellipses* are shaped like circles, others are long and narrow.

elocution (el-o-cu-tion) good speech, especially in public: If you want to be an actor, you must take lessons in *elocution*. **eloquence** speaking well, using words with great skill: The speaker's *eloquence* brought loud cheers from his audience.

embark (em-bark) go on board ship, take people or things on board: We *embark* for South America tomorrow. **embarkation** *embarking* or being *embarked*: Owing to severe storms our *embarkation* was postponed until the following day.

embarrass (em-bar-rass) make anxious, shy or uncomfortable: Don't ask so many *embarrassing* questions. **embarrassment** something which hinders or makes uncomfortable: Our chief *embarrassment* is the need for more money.

emblem (em-blem) a sign, something drawn, written or made which represents something else: The rose is the *emblem* of England, the leek is the *emblem* of Wales.

embroider (em-broi-der) decorate cloth with stitches of various colours and designs: I would like to buy this *embroidered* tablecloth please. **embroidery** stitching in colours and designs: This is the most beautiful hand-*embroidery* we have seen.

emerge (e-merge) 1. come out: When everybody had gone, he *emerged* from his hiding-place. 2. become known: Since this man was tried for housebreaking, new facts have *emerged* which may prove his innocence. **emergency** a sudden happening which makes it necessary to act quickly: In case of *emergency*, please call the Fire Brigade.

emigrate (e-mi-grate) leave one's own country to live in another: My brother *emigrated* to New Zealand ten years ago. **emigrant** a person who *emigrates*: Every year thousands of *emigrants* leave this country for Canada.

eminent (em-i-nent) famous, well-known, among the very best: An *eminent* artist was born in this town. **eminence** being famous, well-known, among the best: He achieved *eminence* because of the discoveries he made.

emotion (e-mo-tion) strong feeling, excitement of mind: Anger, love, fear and pleasure are among the chief *emotions*. **emotional** feeling strong *emotion*, causing deep *emotion* in others: The rebel leader made an *emotional* appeal for support.

emperor (em-per-or) the ruler of a number of countries: Alexander the Great was *emperor* of all the lands in the Near East. **empire** all the countries under the rule of one person or one country: The British *Empire* was one of the largest the world has ever known.

emphasis (em-pha-sis) stress laid on a word or anything else of importance: In this sentence the *emphasis* is on the word 'go'.– We lay special *emphasis* on speed and good service. **emphasize** lay stress on: She *emphasized* the value of foreign travel in her talk.

empty (emp-ty) 1. having nothing inside: The chocolate box was *empty* when I returned. 2. make or become *empty*: '*Empty* your pockets,' said the police inspector.

enchant (en-chant) 1. fill with joy and pleasure: Her singing *enchanted* us all. 2. (in fairytales) use magic on: The prince and princess met in an *enchanted* garden.

encourage (en-cour-age) help, inspire, give courage to: He was given a place in the first team and this *encouraged* him to continue his training. **encouragement** being given *courage* or help: I owe all my success to the *encouragement* of my father.

encyclopedia (en-cy-clo-pe-dia) a book or a number of books which give information about all branches of knowledge: In my *encyclopedia* I found a long description of life in Mexico.

endeavour (en-deav-our) 1. effort, attempt: He succeeded in his *endeavour* to break the record. 2. try, attempt: We are *endeavouring* to raise funds for the building of a new sports centre.

enemy (en-e-my) 1. a person who tries to harm another: He who was my friend is now my greatest *enemy*. 2. one army which is fighting another: We met the *enemy* in battle and defeated him. 3. anything which may harm: Foot and mouth disease is one of the farmer's greatest *enemies*.

energy (en-er-gy) 1. power to do things: The position of a chief of police requires a man of great *energy*. 2. Liveliness: He has so much *energy* he runs instead of walking. **energetic** full of energy: This *energetic* young man is sure to be promoted.

engage (en-gage) 1. employ for a short time: We had to *engage* a private detective. 2. promise or agree to marry. 3. be doing, busy with: The author is at present *engaged* on a life of Charles Dickens. **engagement** promise, agreement to marry, arrangement to be at a place or to meet somebody: Their *engagement* was announced at last night's party.–I'm sorry I can't come to the football match; I have another *engagement*. **engagement ring** ring worn by those who are *engaged* to be married.

engine (en-gine) a machine that produces power for driving other machinery: Today there are not many steam *engines* because most *engines* run on petrol or electricity. **engineer** a person who designs, repairs or looks after engines, builds bridges, railways or docks: I would like to be an electrical *engineer*.

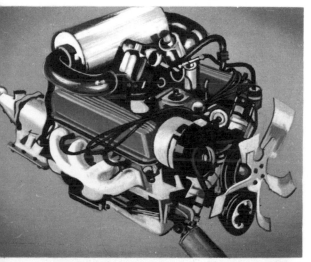

enjoy (en-joy) 1. get pleasure from, like: I have always *enjoyed* playing ball games. 2. have as an advantage or benefit: He has *enjoyed* good health all his life. **enjoyable** giving pleasure or happiness: We spent an *enjoyable* evening together. **enjoyment** pleasure or happiness: His chief *enjoyment* is the building of model railways.

enlighten (en-light-en) give information or knowledge: If you don't know the meaning of this law, let me *enlighten* you. **enlightenment** knowledge: We badly need *enlightenment* on questions of road safety.

enlist (en-list) 1. join or be taken into: It is five years since I *enlisted* in the Royal Air Force. – The government have been compelled to *enlist* more than a hundred skilled engineers. 2. get, obtain: May I *enlist* your help in our efforts to increase the number of playgrounds in our town?

enormous (e-nor-mous) huge, large, very great: We have spent an *enormous* amount of money building this swimming pool.

enough (e-nough) 1. as large, as many or as much as is needed: Have we *enough* bread to last until tomorrow? – Is he tall *enough* to join the police force? – Will this sum be *enough*?

enquire (en-quire) ask: I am *enquiring* about the fare to Rome by air. **enquiry** question, investigation: We have had several *enquiries* about the price of our house. – The government is ordering a full *enquiry* into the complaints.

entangle (en-tan-gle) 1. catch by a snare or among obstacles: He had not swum far before he became *entangled* in weeds. 2. get into difficulties: Through spending too much money he was soon *entangled* in debts. **entanglement** barbed wire or other material to prevent an enemy passing: The street was blocked by a barbed wire *entanglement*.

enter (en-ter) 1. come or go into: Slowly the procession *entered* the cathedral. 2. join: Do you hope to *enter* the teaching profession? 3. write (names etc.): Have all the sums owing to us been *entered* in the book? **entrance** door or gate for going in, act of going in: Please use the side *entrance*. – We had to force an *entrance* through the kitchen window. **entry** coming or going in, an item put in a book or on a list: On his *entry* into the room, all the lights were switched off. – If you are absent I must make an *entry* on the register.

enterprise (en-ter-prise) something done which needs special care or boldness: The climbing of Mount Everest was a difficult *enterprise*.

entertain (en-ter-tain) 1. receive as guests: We often *entertain* our friends to dinner. 2. interest or amuse in any way: I do conjuring tricks to *entertain* the children. **entertainment** a performance: The evening's *entertainment* was very amusing.

enthusiasm (en-thu-si-asm) great interest, eagerness: His songs were received with great *enthusiasm*. **enthusiastic** feeling eagerness or interest: I am not very *enthusiastic* about walking holidays.

entire (en-tire) whole, complete: I am in *entire* agreement with you. **entirely** wholly, completely: I have built the boat *entirely* on my own.

envelop (en-vél-op) wrap, cover: All day long the sun was *enveloped* in clouds. **envelope** (én-vel-ope) a paper cover especially made to hold letters and papers: We enclose an addressed *envelope* for your reply.

environment (en-vi-ron-ment) 1. surroundings, conditions under which one lives: A person's character may be affected for good or ill by early *environment*. 2. the land, water and air around us: We should not allow smoke from factories and fumes from petrol to pollute our *environment*. **environs** districts surrounding a town: Here is a map of Leeds and its *environs*.

envy (en-vy) 1. a feeling of unhappiness because others are richer, more intelligent, healthier, better looking etc.: I am filled with *envy* at her success. 2. a person or object which causes *envy*: His new speedboat was the *envy* of all who saw it. 3. feel *envy*: How we all *envy* him his new speedboat! **envious** full of *envy*: I am not *envious* of his skill in games.

epidemic (ep-i-dem-ic) a disease which spreads among many people at the same time: The school had to be closed during the *epidemic* of measles.

episode (ep-i-sode) an event or description of an event in a series of events: His long illness was an unfortunate *episode*. – Read the next *episode* of this thrilling story next week.

equip (e-quip) supply, provide with what is needed: The explorers were fully *equipped* for their dangerous journey. **equipment** things needed for a special purpose: Camping *equipment* is sold here.

erase (e-rase) rub out: This answer is wrong, you must *erase* it. **eraser** something, usually a piece of rubber used to *erase*: One end of this *eraser* is for pencil marks the other for typewriting errors.

erect (e-rect) 1. upright, standing on one end: He stood *erect* as the medal was pinned on his chest. 2. set up, build: A statue has been *erected* to the memory of Joan of Arc. – How long will it take to *erect* this theatre? **erection** setting up, something set up or built: The *erection* of the theatre will take six months.

errand (er-rand) a short journey to take, bring or convey a message: Harry is employed to run *errands*.

escape (es-cape) 1. slip away, free oneself: Nobody has ever *escaped* from this castle. 2. find a way out: The air is *escaping* from one of these tyres. 3. keep free from: We turned down a side street to *escape* the crowd. 4. act of getting free or finding a way out: That was a narrow *escape*. – There is an *escape* of gas where the two pipes join. 5. a means of *escape*: He saved his life by running down the fire-*escape*.

escort (es-cort) 1. a person, ship or aircraft accompanying others to give protection or prevent from escaping: The prisoner was brought to court under armed *escort*. 2. go with as *escort*: The convoy of merchant ships was *escorted* across the North Sea.

especial (es-pe-cial) great, main: I have an *especial* interest in this young boxer. **especially** very, particularly: James is *especially* keen on boxing.

essay (es-say) a short piece of writing, usually on one subject: The class was asked to write an *essay* on caring for pets.

essence (es-sence) 1. the most important part or quality of something: I can give you the *essence* of my speech in a few words: keep to the rules. 2. that part of a substance remaining when everything not needed has been removed: At the shop she bought a bottle of *essence* of peppermint. **essential** most important, necessary: A good knowledge of shorthand is *essential* to a secretary.

establish (es-tab-lish) set up, organize: Our firm was *established* a hundred years ago. **establishment** an organization (school, business, church, shop etc.): Who is the owner of this *establishment*?

esteem (es-teem) 1. think very well of, respect greatly: The bishop is highly *esteemed* by us all. 2. respect, high opinion of: If you are honest you will keep the *esteem* of your friends.

estimate (es-ti-mate) 1. judge, calculate size, thickness, value, weight, cost etc.: I *estimate* my debts to be lower this month. 2. a rough idea or calculation: According to my *estimates*, he could not arrive before dinner.

etc. (short for *et cetera*) and other things, and so on: The box was full of nails, screws, nuts, bolts, hooks *etc*.

eternal (e-ter-nal) lasting, or seeming to last for ever: 'The gift of God is *eternal* life' (Paul's epistle to the Romans, 6). – I'm so tired of this *eternal* toothache! **eternity** time that has no end or seems to have no end: It seemed an *eternity* before the rescue party arrived.

ether (e-ther) 1. a colourless liquid used to make people unconscious: When my tooth was taken out I was given *ether*. 2. the substance once believed to fill the space between stars, through which heat, light and electricity passed: The light and heat of the sun reach us through the *ether*.

evacuate (e-vac-u-ate) 1. leave a place, usually because of danger: When the firing became too intense, the army *evacuated* the town. 2. remove people from a place because of danger: After the earthquake, all those living in the city were *evacuated*. **evacuee** a person who has been *evacuated*.

evaporate (e-vap-o-rate) turn into vapour or steam: When the sun came out the water quickly *evaporated*.

even (e-ven) 1. level, flat: The surface of a bowling-green must be perfectly *even*. 2. regular, the same: This liquid must be kept at an *even* temperature. 3. a number which can be divided by 2: 2, 4, 6, 8 and 10 are all *even* numbers. 4. still, yet: You have played well, but you can play *even* better if you try. – You haven't *even* started your homework. **evenly** regularly: To make the grass grow, the fertilizer should be spread *evenly* over the lawn.

evening (eve-ning) that part of the day between sunset and bedtime: I will meet you tomorrow *evening* at about 7 o'clock. – Thank you for a pleasant *evening*.

event (e-vent) 1. anything that happens: Please make a list of the chief *events* of last year. 2. one of the competitions or races in a sports meeting: Will all competitors please line up for the first *event*. Why do you follow him *everywhere* he goes?

evidence (ev-i-dence) 1. anything that proves what happened: There is enough *evidence* to convict him of theft. 2. mark, trace: The state of the body showed every *evidence* of a struggle. **evident** plain, clear: Your fingers are brown, so it's *evident* that you smoke.

evil (e-vil) 1. bad, wicked, sinful: You are advised to keep away from *evil* company. 2. bad things, thoughts etc.: I hope you don't think *evil* of me. 3. unfortunate: This man has fallen on *evil* days. 4. wrongdoing: 'Depart from *evil* and do good!' (The epistle of Peter).

evolution (ev-o-lu-tion) 1. growth, development: The lecturer described the *evolution* of modern radio from the time of its discovery. 2. the belief that one form of life has descended from another simpler, more primitive form: We do not yet know every step in man's *evolution*.

exaggerate (ex-ag-ger-ate) describe something as better, larger, worse, louder etc., than it really is: He says the climb took ten hours, but I'm sure he's *exaggerating*. **exaggeration** giving such descriptions: Don't believe him, he's fond of *exaggeration*

example (ex-am-ple) 1. something which shows or illustrates: Give me an *example* of an animal which produces wool. 2. a person or object to be copied: We should set a good *example* to those younger than ourselves.

excavate (ex-cav-ate) dig, usually in order to find something: A complete Saxon village has been *excavated*. **excavation** digging: *Excavation* has proved that ancient peoples once lived here. **excavator** a machine or a person who digs.

exceed (ex-ceed) 1. be greater than: The amount of money I received *exceeded* my wildest hopes. 2. go faster than: Too many drivers *exceed* the speed limit (go faster than they are allowed). **exceedingly** very, extremely: Warm clothing should be worn in this *exceedingly* cold weather.

excel (ex-cel) do or be better than, do very well: He *excels* as a musician. – 'She *excels* each mortal thing' (Shakespeare, *Who is Sylvia?*). **excellent** very good: 'Has done *excellent* work this term' (school report). –

This is an *excellent* example of an early steam-engine.

except (ex-cept) but, leave out: Everybody comes to school in time *except* you. **exception** something not included: I have watered the whole garden with the *exception* of the rose-trees.

exchange (ex-change) 1. give back for something else: Would you *exchange* this radio for a better one please? 2. the act of *exchanging*: An *exchange* of prisoners was arranged between the two commanders. 3. a place where goods etc. are *exchanged*: In this town we have a Corn *Exchange* and a Wool *Exchange*, and our merchants deal on the Stock *Exchange* in London. **telephone exchange** the building where telephone lines are connected.

excite (ex-cite) stir up the feelings of: Please don't *excite* my brother; he is too ill. – Don't get *excited*! **excitement** being *excited*: When the first goal was scored the crowd went mad with *excitement*.

exclaim (ex-claim) cry out suddenly: 'Leave me alone!' he *exclaimed* angrily. **exclamation** a sudden short cry: He held up his enemy's sword with a fierce *exclamation* of triumph. **exclamation mark** a punctuation mark (!) put after an *exclamation* in writing or printing.

excursion (ex-cur-sion) a short journey or trip, usually taken for pleasure: There's a cheap *excursion* to the sea tomorrow. Are you going on an **excursion ticket**? (a special ticket at a cheap rate covering the journey there and back.)

excuse (ex-cuse) 1. forgive: '*Excuse* me,' he exclaimed when he trod on my toe. 2. set a person free from some duty, debt etc.: Because the class had done well, all were *excused* the last lesson. **excuse** a reason for one's conduct: What is your *excuse* for coming late this morning?

execute (ex-e-cute) 1. do, carry out: All repairs are carefully *executed*. 2. put to death, usually by cutting off the head: Two of Henry VIII's wives were *executed*. **execution** carrying out, putting to death: The *execution* of his plan was perfect.—This was once a place for public *executions*.

exercise (ex-er-cise) 1. something done again and again to make a person skilful: Swimming is a good *exercise* for the body and chess is a good *exercise* for the mind.—If you want to learn the piano you must do your five-finger *exercises*. 2. movements of troops, ships etc. to keep them alert and fit for battle: The Seventh Fleet is out on *exercise* this week. 3. take *exercise*: Now you may *exercise* your brains on this puzzle. 4. use: If you are to succeed you will need to *exercise* all your skill. **exercise book** a book used for *exercises* in any subject.

exert (ex-ert) 1. use: By *exerting* all our strength we managed to move the heavy log. 2. try (always used with *self*): Can't you *exert* yourself to rise early in the morning? **exertion** using strength, skill etc.: Thanks to our *exertions*, the heavy log was at last moved.

exhaust (ex-haust) 1. use up, tire out: At last our supplies of food were *exhausted*.—After the long race, the winner collapsed, *exhausted*. 2. the tube in the engine from which waste, petrol fumes etc. are sent out: When he started the engine, clouds of black smoke poured out from the *exhaust*. **exhaustion** being tired out, unable to move or go further: The rescue party arrived to find the climbers in a state of *exhaustion*.

exhibit (ex-hib-it) 1. show: Are you *exhibiting* this year in the flower show?—The centre forward *exhibited* his great skill by scoring two goals. 2. something shown: 'Please do not touch the *exhibits*' (notice in a museum). **exhibition** show: The mayor opened the *exhibition* of paintings this morning.—I have never seen such an *exhibition* of anger before.

exist (ex-ist) 1. be: Hospitals *exist* for the purpose of healing those who are ill. 2. continue to be or to live: How long can a person *exist* without water?—The earth has *existed* for millions of years. **existence** being, way of living: Nobody doubts the *existence* of electricity.—How I would like a quiet, peaceful *existence*!

exit (ex-it) 1. way out: There are ten *exits* from this theatre. 2. departure of an actor from the stage: 'They have their *exits* and their entrances' (Shakespeare, *As You Like It*).

exotic (ex-o-tic) of foreign character, exciting and unusual: Much as I love salmon, it is too *exotic* to have every day.

expect (ex-pect) think something will happen: I *expect* it will rain today.—Are you *expecting* a telegram from your brother? **expectation** what may be *expected*: The *expectation* of life is still longer for women than for men.—I have chopped all this wood in *expectation* of a good fire.

expedition (ex-pe-di-tion) a journey for a special purpose: We are going on an *expedition* to the North Pole. 2. people going on such a journey: All the members of the *expedition* returned safely.

expel (ex-pel) send, force or drive out: Why has this boy been *expelled* from school?

expense (ex-pense) cost or charge: At whose *expense* has this banquet been provided? **expend** spend: It's useless to *expend* any more energy in teaching this lazy girl. **expenditure** spending, amount spent: We must cut down our *expenditure* on luxuries.

experience (ex-pe-ri-ence) 1. obtaining knowledge by seeing and doing: We know by *experience* that the machine works well. – This work would suit a person of your *experience*. 2. something which happens to a person: My journey to Greece was a most interesting *experience*. 3. meet with, see, feel: He *experienced* great hardships climbing the mountain in winter.

experiment (ex-per-i-ment) 1. a test to discover what will happen: In this *experiment* you will see that the liquid turns red. 2. make such a test: It is dangerous to *experiment* with gunpowder.

explain (ex-plain) 1. tell the meaning of: Please *explain* how to do this puzzle. 2. account for, give reasons why: Can you *explain* why your clothes are covered in paint? **explanation** *explaining*: I don't think any *explanation* is needed.

explode (ex-plode) 1. burst with a loud noise: The firework *exploded* in a shower of lights. – Many houses were evacuated when the army *exploded* the bomb. **explosion** the loud noise caused by something *exploding*: The *explosion* could be heard in the next village. **explosive** a substance which may explode: A lorry containing *explosives* has overturned in the road.

explore (ex-plore) 1. travel through a new land to find out about it: David Livingstone *explored* large parts of central Africa. 2. examine a problem to try to solve it: We must *explore* every means of escape. **explorer** a person who travels in order to make discoveries: The *explorer* gave an account of his travels in Arabia. **exploration** *exploring*: The *exploration* of space has only just begun.

export (ex-port) 1. send goods to another country to be sold: This firm *exports* all the cars made here. 2. something sent out of a country to be sold: Our chief *exports* are figs, dates, lemons and oranges.

expose (ex-pose) 1. uncover, leave uncovered: It is dangerous to *expose* your body too long in the sun. 2. show, bring to everybody's notice: At last your crimes have been *exposed*. 3. allow light to enter a camera to make a photograph or film: This film has now been *exposed* and needs developing. **exposure** being *exposed*: The climber had died of *exposure* (to the weather). – The *exposure* of all the crimes he had committed surprised the world.

express (ex-press) 1. say or tell in words or by actions: How can I *express* my gratitude to you? 2. a train which goes very quickly: It takes less time to do this journey by **express** than by car. 3. a service for carrying goods: Please send the parcel by *express*. **expression** a way of saying something: This gift of flowers is a small *expression* of my gratitude. – He told me to buzz off. What an *expression*!

extend (ex-tend) 1. make longer: Our holidays are being *extended* by one week. – We could reach the roof if only we had an *extending* ladder. 2. stretch out: He *extended* his hand and I shook it. 3. reach: This road *extends* a long way into the forest. **extension** a part added on: The *extension* to our dining room cost a great deal of money. **extent** length or area: What is the *extent* of your garden?

extinguish (ex-tin-guish) put out (a fire): It took the fire brigade two hours before the fire was completely *extinguished*. **extinguisher** a device used to put out fires.

extract (ex-tract) 1. take out, press out, copy out from a book etc.: Can you *extract* this thorn from my finger? – Do you know how to *extract* the juice from a lemon? – I have *extracted* this paragraph from the original copy of the agreement. 2. something taken out, pressed out, copied out: The invalid is now well enough to take a little *extract* of beef. – The poet will read *extracts* from his own work. **extraction** taking out: The *extraction* of the tooth was very difficult.

extraordinary (ex-traor-di-nar-y) not usual, out of the ordinary: Your grasp of this difficult subject is *extraordinary*. **extraordinarily** extremely, very, surprisingly: '*Extraordinarily* good at French' (school report).

extravagance (ex-trav-a-gance) waste, spending too much (money, effort, time etc.): Owing to his *extravagance* we are all in debt. **extravagant** wasteful, spending more money than one ought to: With as much money as you have, you can afford to be *extravagant*.

extreme (ex-treme) 1. farthest: We live at the *extreme* end of the village. 2. very great: We could not move owing to the *extreme* cold. – The *extreme* heat made him thirsty. 3. belonging to either end: Heat and cold, love and hate, height and depth are *extremes*. **extremity** extreme point, end: Cold first affects the *extremities* of the body (hands, feet etc.). – At times we feel *extremities* of both joy and sorrow. **extremely** very: I was *extremely* glad to see you at church on Sunday.

F

fable (fa-ble) a short story, often with animals as characters. Every *fable* teaches a lesson. – What does the *fable* about the hare and the tortoise teach us? **fabulous** 1. absurd, not possible to believe; something heard of only in *fables*. 2. wonderful: What a *fabulous* painting!

fabric (fab-ric) cloth or other material which is woven, knitted or made of felt: Wool and cotton are natural *fabrics*; nylon is an artificial *fabric*, made by man.

fact something that is true; what has really happened: I cannot help you unless you tell me all the *facts*. – You were not at school today; I know it for a *fact*.

factor (fac-tor) 1. a whole number (except 1) by which a larger number can be divided: 2, 3, 4, 6, 8, and 12 are *factors* of 24. 2. a fact which helps towards a certain result: Skill, perseverance and economy are the *factors* which have helped to build this business.

factory (fac-to-ry) workshop, a building in which things are made: All our customers are invited to visit our *factory*.

faculty (fac-ul-ty) the power to do things: He has a great *faculty* for music. – Is he in possession of all his *faculties*? (Can he see, hear, speak, think, understand etc.)

fade 1. lose colour, become less bright: Take down those *faded* curtains. 2. grow dim, faint, go out of sight: As the daylight *faded*, all our hopes of rescue *faded* with it.

faint 1. not clear, not easy to hear or see: In the distance we heard a *faint* cry. – There was a *faint* trace of blood on his sleeve. 2. weak, exhausted: When the men were rescued they were *faint* with cold. 3. lose consciousness: When she heard the news she *fainted*. 4. losing consciousness: She fell down in a *faint*.

fair 1. just, honest: What we want is *fair* play and a *fair* share for all. 2. neither bad nor good, just average: He has a *fair* knowledge of German. 3. fine (of the weather): We hope the day will be *fair*. 4. light in colour, pale: I am dark, but my sister is *fair*. 5. beautiful: 'Mirror, mirror on the wall; who is the *fairest* of them all' (fairy tale). 6. a large market, often with shows and entertainments: At the *fair* there are roundabouts and swings. – Are you going to the Trade *Fair*?

fake 1. something which is said to be genuine but is not: The picture was said to have been painted by Rembrandt, but it was a *fake*. 2. imitate a picture, statue etc., or tell a story in order to deceive: This piece of furniture has been *faked* to make it look antique.

false 1. wrong, not true: I thought I heard the bell ring, but it was a *false* alarm. 2. lying: His story was completely *false*. 3. not loyal: Beware of *false* friends! 4. not real: Many elderly people now have *false* teeth. – I need more *false* hair for my doll's head. **falsehood** lie, lying: If he blames you he is guilty of *falsehood*.

falter (fal-ter) move, walk, act or speak with hesitation: At the end of the climb our steps began to *falter*. – 'I–I really don't know,' he *faltered*.

fame being known by all: Would you rather have *fame* or wealth? **famous** known by all: I would far rather be *famous* than wealthy.

familiar (fa-mil-i-ar) 1. well known: This is a very *familiar* tune. 2. knowing something well: Are you at all *familiar* with Dickens' novels? 3. knowing a person well: My bank manager and I are on very *familiar* terms; we are great friends. 4. friendly: It is not a good idea to be too *familiar* with dishonest people. **familiarity** being *familiar* with: Your *familiarity* with radio will be of great use to this firm.

family (fam-i-ly) 1. parents and children: All the members of my *family* are keen riders. 2. children: Do you belong to a large *family*? 3. all people descended from one person: His *family* has been in the wool trade for a hundred years. 4. a group of living beings related to each other: The grey squirrel belongs to the rat *family* and the tiger to the cat *family*. 5. having to do with a *family*: Is this your brother? I can see a *family* resemblance.

famine (fam-ine) 1. a shortage of food: This year there has been a poor harvest and thousands are dying of *famine*. 2. a shortage of other things: The lack of rainfall caused a water *famine*. – Many factories have had to close because of the cotton *famine*.

far *farther*, *farthest* 1. at a distance: Don't go *far* away. – Stand a little *farther* back. – Is it *far* along this road? 2. distant: Three kings came from a *far* country. – China and Japan are in the *Far* East. 3. more distant: Go to the *far* end of the room. – We will hang the picture on the *far* wall, opposite the fireplace.

farce 1. a play for acting, full of ridiculous events, specially written to make people laugh. 2. a series of events, so pointless as to seem laughable: Our meeting with the Board of Directors was a *farce*.

fare 1. money charged for making a journey: '*Fares* please!' called the conductor. 2. a person who rides in a hired vehicle: The taxi-driver had five *fares* in the first two hours. 3. food provided at table: You should stay at the Crown Hotel; the *fare* is marvellous. 4. make progress, get on: How have you *fared* with your music lessons lately? **farewell** (may you *fare* well) goodbye.

farm 1. a piece of land used for raising animals and growing food: We spent our holidays on a fruit *farm*. 2. use land for this purpose: My uncle *farms* cattle. **farmer** a person who owns or manages a *farm*. **farmyard** that part of a *farm* round which the buildings, farms and sheds stand.

fascinate (fas-ci-nate) charm, attract, hold the attention: We were *fascinated* by the graceful movements of the dancers. **fascination** power to interest or charm: The game of chess holds the greatest *fascination* for me.

fashion (fash-ion) 1. a way of doing something: Don't talk to me in that *fashion*! 2. a way of dressing which people like and admire: Did you go to the *fashion* display yesterday? 3. make: He *fashioned* the sword and spear with great skill. **fashionable** in *fashion*; worn by, visited by people: He considered the French Riviera a *fashionable* place to holiday.

fat 1. a white or yellowish substance found in meat, milk and the bodies of animals: 'Jack Sprat could eat no *fat*' (nursery rhyme) 2. having much flesh on the body: If you are too *fat*, you should eat less. **fatten** make fat: The farmer is *fattening* his pigs for Christmas. **fatty** with much *fat*: Do you like *fatty* bacon?

fate 1. a power which is thought to make things happen in a way that cannot be changed: It was our *fate* to meet. 2. death; what will happen in the end: The judge will decide your *fate*.—Prepare to meet your *fate*. **fatal** ending in death: 'The driver of the car sustained *fatal* injuries' (account of an accident). **fatality** an event which ends in death: There were many motoring *fatalities* during the summer holidays.

father (fath-er) 1. the male parent: My *father* works in a bank. 2. God: 'Our *Father*, Which art in heaven' (The Lord's Prayer). 3. a priest in a church: My parents were married by *Father* Brown. 4. names which represent time, Christmas etc.—*Father* Time, *Father* Christmas. **father-in-law** the *father* of one's wife or husband.

fatigue (fa-tigue) being very tired: The lost boy was found almost dead from cold and *fatigue*.

fault 1. something which is imperfect or wrong: This radio does not work because there is a *fault* in its construction. 2. responsibility for having done something: Whose *fault* is it that the radio does not work? **faulty** having a fault or faults: I have found a *faulty* connection between these two wires. **faultless** having no *faults*: This examination paper gets full marks, it is absolutely *faultless*.

favour (fa-vour) 1. an act of kindness: Would you please do me a *favour* and post these letters? 2. approval: 'The king shows *favour* to a wise servant' (The Book of Proverbs). 3. a badge, ribbon or rosette: All the team's supporters wore yellow and red *favours*. 4. support, show *favour* to: A good judge *favours* neither side. 5. do things for: John will now *favour* us with some of his conjuring tricks. **favourable** approving, helpful: Is he *favourable* to our scheme? We must wait for a *favourable* moment to explain it. **favourite** one to whom *favour* is shown or believed able to win: Who is teacher's *favourite*?

fear 1. the feeling one has when danger may be near: He stood, gripped by *fear*, on the edge of the cliff. 2. be afraid of: 'Do not *fear* me,' said the giant. **fearful** terrible, having *fear*: Yesterday there were many *fearful* accidents on the motorway.—We are all *fearful* as to what may happen. **fearless** having no *fear*: He walked on, *fearless* of danger.

feat a difficult deed which needs skill: The making of a moon rocket is a brilliant *feat* of engineering.

feather (feath-er) one of the light coverings of a bird: The pillows on this bed are stuffed with *feathers*.

feature (fea-ture) 1. a part of the face. 2. The face: This young man has very sharp *features* (eyes, nose, chin etc.). 3. a part which is most noticed: What are going to be the main *features* of your speech? 4. bring to one's notice as being important: This week we are *featuring* the best bargains in swimsuits.

February (Feb-ru-ar-y) the second month of the year.

fee money paid for some service: What is your *fee* for twelve piano lessons?

feeble (fee-ble) weak: Help this *feeble* old man across the road.—He answered in a *feeble* voice.

feed 1. give food: Every morning I *feed* the horses. 2. food for animals: Is there enough chicken *feed* in the bin? 3. a pipe to carry fuel etc. to a machine: The car will go better if you clean out the petrol *feed*.

feel 1. learn about by touching and handling: The blind man *felt* his way along the street.—Just *feel* this pear; is it soft enough to eat? 2. notice through something touching: He suddenly *felt* someone gripping his arm. 3. be in a certain condition: Do you *feel* warm (cool, comfortable, strong, well) enough? 4. think: We *feel* that this work would be too hard for him. **feeler** one of two long arms like hairs, which an insect uses to *feel*, find food, find its way etc. **feeling** pain, pleasure, anger etc. which one *feels*: He left me with a *feeling* of great anxiety, but I tried not to show my *feelings*.

fellow (fel-low) 1. a man or boy: The poor *fellow* hurt his shoulder. 2. somebody belonging to the same group, class, nation etc.: I shall make a speech to all my *fellow*-citizens. **fellowship** a group of friends, friendly meeting and companionship: I enjoy the *fellowship* of cheerful people.

felt 1. the past tense of the word *feel*: Suddenly I *felt* cold. 2. wool or hair pressed hard to make thick cloth: How do you like my new *felt* hat?

female 1. a woman, girl or she-animal: When the Arab ship sank the only person rescued was a young *female* slave. 2. having to do with women and girls: Why do *female* factory workers get such low wages? **feminine** female: Women and girls belong to the *feminine* sex.

fence 1. a wall or barrier made of wooden sticks, metal or wire to keep animals apart or to keep people out: The farmer's field was surrounded by a high wooden *fence*. 2. surround by a *fence*: It would be a good thing if we *fenced* in this playground. 3. fight with long thin swords or blunt thin swords called foils: When do you have your *fencing* lessons?

fender (fen-der) 1. a metal guard in front of a fireplace. 2. a guard of metal or other material to lessen the shock when two vehicles collide.

ferment (fer-ment) change or be changed by the adding of such materials as yeast: Wine is made by *fermenting* the juice of grapes.

fern a plant with green feathery leaves which has no flowers.

ferro-concrete (fer-ro-con-crete) concrete which has inside it iron or steel bars to strengthen it and prevent it cracking under strain.

ferry (fer-ry) 1. a place from which a boat or aircraft may carry people across water: There is a boat waiting at the *ferry*. 2. the boat or aircraft which crosses: Are you waiting for the next *ferry*? 3. take people or goods across water by *ferry*: Our car is being *ferried* across the Channel to France.

fertile (fer-tile) 1. (of land) rich, producing good crops: Where is the most *fertile* soil to be found? 2. (of people) having many ideas: This poet has an extremely *fertile* imagination. 3. (of seeds, eggs etc.) these seeds are guaranteed to be 80 per cent *fertile* (80 out of 100 will produce plants). **fertilize** make *fertile*: This soil will not produce corn until it has been *fertilized*. **fertilizer** a substance used to *fertilize* soil. **fertility** being *fertile*: Has the *fertility* of this soil been tested yet?

festival (fes-ti-val) 1. time for feasting and rejoicing: *Christmas is the most important festival of the Christian year.* 2. a series of performances of music, drama etc., usually held once a year: *Last year he won the first prize for conducting at the music festival.* **festive** having to do with a feast: *The pantomime will be performed all through the festive season.* **festivity** merry-making, joyful happenings: *Many wedding festivities take place at Easter time.*

fetch 1. go and bring back: *Fetch my spectacles from the drawer please.* 2. sell for money: *This watch fetched a considerable sum at the auction.*

fete 1. festival or open air entertainment: *We are looking forward to the Hospital Fete (to raise money for the hospital).* 2. honour a person by giving a dinner or party: *When the hero returned home he was feted everywhere he went.*

fever (fe-ver) 1. a high temperature of the body caused by some illness or other: *Yesterday morning the patient developed a high fever (his temperature became very high).* 2. a disease belonging to a certain group in which high temperature occurs: *My brother is in hospital with scarlet fever.* 3. high excitement: *We waited for the postman in a fever of impatience.*

few not many: *only a few people have read these letters.* **quite a few, a good few** a number: *There are quite a few marbles in this box.*

fiancé a man to whom a woman is engaged to be married. **fiancée** a woman to whom a man is engaged to be married.

fibre (fi-bre) one of the thin hairs which make up wool, cotton and other materials: *When fibres are twisted and spun together they make threads.* **fibreglass** *fibres* of glass looking rather like cotton wool and used to prevent heat leaking out of rooms etc.

fickle (fick-le) never the same, always changing: *Good friends are never fickle.* – *'Oh fortune, all men call thee fickle'* (Shakespeare, *Romeo and Juliet*).

fiction (fic-tion) 1. something untrue: *I don't believe you; your whole story is a piece of fiction.* 2. imaginative writing consisting of stories which are invented: *The novels of Charles Dickens are works of fiction.*

fiddle (fid-dle) 1. a violin: *I can play the fiddle if you will dance.* 2. play the violin. **fiddler** a person who plays the violin. 3. dishonest act: *He was well known for fiddling the accounts.*

fidget (fid-get) 1. never stop moving: *All through the meal she was fidgeting.* 2. a person who *fidgets*: *Keep still, and don't be a fidget.*

field 1. a piece of land, usually with a wall or fence round it: *We watched the cows grazing in the field.* – *What is the area of a football field?* 2. an area bounded by the limits of sight or force: *This small star is quite outside the field of vision (it cannot be seen).* – *When I put down the magnet the magnetic field can be seen.* 3. a place where a battle has been fought; a *battlefield.* 4. (in cricket) stop a ball after it has been hit by the batsman: *'Well fielded!' said the captain.*

fierce savage, cruel, violent: *We found ourselves face to face with a fierce tiger.* – *Why don't you try to control your fierce temper?*

fifteen, fifty, see **five.**

fig a small fruit shaped like a pear which has small seeds and is soft and sweet inside. *Figs grow in warm countries. Most of the figs eaten in colder lands have been dried.*

fight 1. struggle against a person, animal, nation, country etc.: The two men were *fighting* with swords. – This country has no desire to *fight* any other. 2. a struggle: One day we shall win our *fight* for freedom. – Will you watch the *fight* for the world championship?

figure (fig-ure) 1. a sign that represents a number: The teacher drew a large *figure* 8 on the blackboard. 2. a shape in geometry: He drew three *figures*: a square, a triangle and a rectangle. 3. arithmetic: I have always been good at *figures*. 4. the shape of a living being: At last we saw a *figure* approaching in the distance. 4. the shape of the human body: I must diet to keep my slender *figure*. 5. a well-known or great person: Churchill was one of the greatest *figures* in this century. 6. work out, understand: He hasn't spoken to me all this week; I can't *figure* it out. 7. play a part: Falstaff *figures* in three of Shakespeare's plays.

fill 1. make full or become full: Please *fill* this glass with water. – Gradually the room *filled* with smoke. 2. hold a position and do all the work needed in it: I applied for the post but it had already been *filled*. – He *fills* the position of Mayor with great ability. 3. as much as is desired: 'You may eat your *fill* of this pie,' said the baker.

filly a female foal or colt: The big race was won by a four year old *filly*.

film 1. a thin coat or layer: Can you see the *film* of dust on this polished table? 2. material which has been rolled and is put into cameras to take pictures: The entire *film* has been exposed; I need a new one. 3. a motion picture: 'Showing now – one of the greatest *films* of all time' (notice outside a cinema). 4. take a motion picture: You can't go into the studio during *filming*.

filth 1. dirt which is very unpleasant: We found the floor of the room covered with *filth*. 2. things written or printed which are obscene: I'm surprised to find you reading that *filth*! **filthy** very dirty: Come and wash your hands; they're *filthy*.

fin 1. that part of a fish which is used when it swims. 2. anything shaped like a *fin*: We discovered the *fin* of a large bomb sticking out of the ground.

final (fi-nal) 1. last: I have just read the *final* chapter. – I would like to see the *final* match. – Will you be at the *final*? 3. the last edition of a newspaper: 'Late night *final*!' called the newsboy. **finalist** a person who has won all the rounds and plays in the *final*. **finally** lastly: *Finally*, this is my decision.

finance (fi-nance) 1. money: The *finances* of this company are in order. 2. having to do with money: We were short of funds and had to borrow from a *finance* company. **financial** of money: During the last year we have been in *financial* difficulties. **financially** with regard to money: Are you in a good state *financially*? **financier** a person who deals in money.

fine 1. a sum of money paid as a punishment: He had to pay a heavy *fine* for careless driving. 2. make a person pay a *fine*: 'You will be *fined*,' said the magistrate. 3. bright, clear: When the weather is *fine* we will go for a walk. 4. handsome, splendid, enjoyable: He is a *fine* young man. – You have a *fine* view from the top of the hill. 5. in very small pieces: He let the *fine* sand run between his fingers. 6. very narrow: Please get me a pencil with a *fine* point. 7. excellent: He is a very *fine* pianist.

finish (fin-ish) 1. bring to an end, come to an end: Have you *finished* playing football? – When does morning school *finish*? 2. the last part: How many competitors were still in the race at the *finish*? 3. a fine, smooth surface: This wood has a beautiful *finish*. 4. put a *finish* on, do well: The dress has been beautifully *finished*.

fir an evergreen tree which bears cones and has small sharp leaves like needles.

fire 1. burning, things burning: *Fire* is both a friend and an enemy to man. – Every morning I light the *fire*. – Several villages were destroyed by the forest *fire*. 2. shoot from a gun, catapult or bow: '*Fire!*' called the captain. – We took aim and *fired*. 3. shots from guns etc.: For five hours we were under *fire* (being shot at). **fireproof** that does not burn: Every stage should have a *fireproof* curtain. **firing-line** the front line (of trenches) most exposed to enemy *fire*.

firm 1. solid, not moving: At last we were walking on *firm* ground. 2. a group of persons who carry on a business: I am now working for a *firm* of furniture-removers. 3. not changing, steady, always the same: I have *firm* faith in your honesty. – Speak up in a strong, *firm* voice. **firmly** in a *firm* manner: We fixed the post *firmly* in the ground.

fish 1. an animal living in water, breathing through gills and having fins for swimming: One, two, three, four, five: once I caught a *fish* alive (nursery rhyme). 2. catch *fish*: Yesterday we went *fishing* in the lake. **fisherman** a man who earns his living by *fishing*. **fishery** an area of the sea where *fishing* is carried on.

fist the hand tightly closed: Don't shake your *fist* at me!

fit 1. right, suitable for: Is the water *fit* to drink? 2. in good health: To play good football one has to be very *fit*. 3. be the right size: Try this dress on and see if it will *fit* you. 4. put something on or in a special place: Will you please *fit* a new lock on this door. 5. a short attack: I had a sudden *fit* of coughing. 6. a sudden attack of a disease in which one falls and moves violently: We were standing in the queue when he was seized by a *fit*. **fitter** a person who in dressmaking cuts out and *fits* garments; a workman who *fits* together pipes or parts of machines.

five the number between 4 and 6: Every week I work *five* days. **fifteen** 5 added to 10 = *15*. **fifty** 5 multiplied by 10 = *50*: My father is *50* years old this week.

fizz make a hissing sound: Soda water *fizzes* as the bubbles rise to the top. **fizzle** make a soft *fizzing* sound. **fizzle out** come to an end without achieving anything: We started a fund to raise money for a sports field, but it *fizzled out*.

flabby (flab-by) soft, weak (of muscles): What *flabby* muscles you have; you need more exercise.

flag 1. a piece of cloth with a design on it to show the country or organization to which it belongs, or one used to give a signal: The Union Jack is the *flag* of Great Britain. – The Blue Peter is the *flag* which shows that a ship is about to leave port. 2. become weak: When I was running the last mile my strength began to *flag*. 3. give a signal by waving a *flag*: There was danger ahead and the signalman *flagged* down the train. **flagstone** a square or oblong piece of stone laid for people to walk on.

flake 1. a small, thin, flat piece: Snow*flakes* fall from the sky. 2. peel off in *flakes*: The paint is *flaking* off the front door.

flame 1. the part of a fire which blazes up: In ten minutes the whole building was in *flames*. 2. burn with a *flame*: He poured on paraffin oil and the fire *flamed* up. 3. (of the face) become red: His face *flamed* with fury.

flank 1. the soft part of the body between ribs and hip: He pressed his spurs into the horse's *flank*. 2. a position on the right or left side of a person or an army: Our right *flank* advanced and cut off the enemy's supplies. 3. be on the *flank* of: Our house is *flanked* on the one side by the station and on the other by the cinema.

flannel (flan-nel) 1. a soft woollen cloth: Hanging on the clothes-line was an old *flannel* nightdress. 2. a face cloth.

flap 1. wave up and down, move from side to side: The flags were *flapping* in the wind. – The bird *flapped* its wings and flew away. 2. a piece of cloth, wood, paper etc. that folds over, covering an opening: He raised the *flap* and went behind the counter. – You must seal the *flap* of the envelope before posting the letter.

flare 1. burn brightly and unsteadily, the flame rising and falling quickly: He blew the flame and it *flared* up in his face. 2. become angry: When I mentioned his sister he *flared* up at me. 3. a device for making a light which *flares*: the men in the boat lit a *flare* to guide the rescuers. 4. the side of a long skirt which spreads or widens gradually.

flash 1. a bright light that comes suddenly and then goes out: The car passed with a *flash* of its headlamps. 2. burst suddenly into light, then go dark again: The lightning *flashed*. 3. a thought that occurs suddenly: An idea *flashed* into my mind. 4. send a sudden light as a signal: The news of peace was *flashed* across the world by radio. **flashlight** a small electric torch which has a battery inside it; a device that gives a sudden *flash* to take photographs where there is not enough light.

flask a bottle with a narrow neck used in the laboratory or for holding wine or spirits.

flat 1. level: A vast area of *flat* land stretched before us. 2. at full length, spread out: I slipped and fell *flat* on my face. 3. (in music) below the true tone: Stop! You are singing a little *flat*. 4. dull, without interest: The party was *flat*, the conversation was *flat*, even the beer was *flat*. 5. a stretch of *flat* land: He was walking towards us across the mud *flats*. 6. a dwelling, usually part of a larger building:

We live in a council *flat* (a *flat* for which we pay rent to the council) **flatten** make *flat*: The whole city was *flattened* by the earthquake.

flatter (flat-ter) 1. compliment, praise too much: You must want something to *flatter* me like this! 2. show a thing or person looking better than they really do: The portrait *flatters* me. **flattery** praise which is not meant: We prefer the truth to *flattery*. **flatterer** a person who *flatters* us.

flavour (fla-vour) 1. taste: Which *flavour* do you like, lemon or raspberry? 2. give a flavour to: I am going to *flavour* this cake with vanilla essence. **flavouring** something which gives *flavour*: Too much *flavouring* can spoil a cake.

flaw something that spoils, makes a thing worth less: The vase is perfect except for a *flaw* on its rim. – There's a *flaw* in your argument. **flawless** perfect, without a single fault.

flax 1. a plant with a blue flower. 2. the thread which is made from the fibres taken from the *flax* plant. **flaxen** the colour of thread of *flax*: pale yellow.

flea a small, wingless insect that feeds on human or animal blood, and is able to leap a long way.

flee *fled*, *fleeing* run or hurry away from: 'Let us *flee*,' said the fly; 'Let us fly,' said the flea; so they flew through a flaw in the flue (an old rhyme).

fleece 1. the wool cut all in one piece from a sheep: Jason and his companions sailed out in search of the Golden *Fleece*. 2. swindle, strip of money: Don't make friends with gamblers or they will *fleece* you of your money.

fleet 1. a number of ships which sail together under the command of a single officer: This admiral commands the Mediterranean *Fleet*.—The fishing *fleet* sailed out into the North Sea. 2. aircraft or buses under one firm or working together: My brother runs a *fleet* of taxis. 3. moving quickly: What a *fleet* runner! **fleeting** passing quickly: Let us make the best use of the *fleeting* hours.

flesh 1. the soft part of the body covering the bones: 'I have more *flesh* than any other man' (Falstaff in *King Henry IV* – Shakespeare). 2. the body as contrasted with the spirit: 'The spirit is willing but the *flesh* is weak.'

flex 1. bend: He *flexed* his arm to show the size of his muscle. 2. wire which bends easily and is used for conducting electricity to lights. **flexible** bending easily: An acrobat has *flexible* joints.—The light bulb was hanging on a length of *flexible* wire.

flicker (flick-er) 1. burn unsteadily: The match *flickered*, and then went out. 2. a faint flash of light: At the end of the tunnel there was a *flicker* of light. 3. the smallest measure: There is still a *flicker* of hope that they will be rescued.

flight 1. flying movement through the air: 'The eye could not follow it in its *flight*' (Longfellow, *The Arrow and the Song*). 2. a journey by air: How long does the *flight* take from London to Rome? 3. a number of birds moving through the air: A *flight* of swallows has just passed over us. 4. a number of steps: A *flight* of steps led to the king's chamber. 5. running, flying, fleeing, driving away: You must seek safety in *flight*.—The enemy was quickly put to *flight*.

flinch draw back, move back quickly: Only cowards *flinch* from danger.—David faced Goliath without *flinching*.

fling *flung*, *flinging* 1. throw with great force: *Fling* your spears all together.—Suddenly the great gate was *flung* open. 2. move quickly and violently: I *flung* myself on him and hurled him to the ground. 3. a lively Scottish dance, the Highland *Fling*.

flip 1. throw something quickly: He *flipped* an ace on the table. 2. toss in the air by a movement of thumb and finger: The captain *flipped* the coin and it landed heads up.

flipper (flip-per) 1. the fin or foreleg of certain sea animals such as seals, penguins and turtles. 2. special footwear which look like *flippers* worn by frogmen.

flit fly quickly, dart: The birds are *flitting* from branch to branch.

float 1. rest on the surface of water or other liquid: Cork *floats* on water. 2. make float: We *floated* the little boat down the stream. 3. start a business: We are *floating* a new company and need your money. 4. Anything that *floats*: The nets and lines of fishermen are held up by *floats*. 5. money given to the treasurer of an organization to meet daily expenses. 6. a wagon or cart which is drawn in a procession: In the Lord Mayor's Show were a number of brightly decorated *floats*.

flog whip severely: Soldiers and sailors are no longer *flogged* for any offence.

flood 1. water flowing over a place that is usually dry: Thousands of people have lost their homes through the recent *floods* in India. 2. a large number of people: There was a *flood* of visitors at the zoo. 3. cover with water: It was impossible to plough the *flooded* fields. 4. arrive in great numbers: Requests for information have *flooded* in.

florist (flor-ist) a person who sells flowers and plants in a shop.

floss soft threads of silk before being spun, the fluffy part of the seeds. **candy floss** sugar spun into fine threads and eaten off the end of a short wooden stick.

flour wheat or other grain ground fine: *Flour* is used for making bread and cakes.

flourish 1. grow quickly and well, be healthy: These plants will *flourish* if you give them plenty of sunlight.–How are you today? *Flourishing!* 2. be alive at a certain time: Shakespeare *flourished* during the reign of Queen Elizabeth I. 3. an extra curve or decoration on a written letter: All his capital letters are written with a *flourish*. 4. a loud piece of music on trumpets, usually played at important ceremonies: '*Flourish*: drums and trumpets. Enter KING RICHARD' (stage directions to Shakespeare's *King Richard II*).

flow 1. move along as a river does: The Thames *flows* into the North Sea. 2. hang down: She was dressed in a *flowing* gown. 3. stream: We tried to stop the *flow* of blood.

flower 1. the blossom of a plant, the part that produces the seeds: Bring a bunch of *flowers* from the garden. 2. the best part of anything: In the war our country lost the *flower* of its youth. 3. produce *flowers*: When does the rose tree *flower*?

flu see **influenza**.

flue a tube or pipe which carries smoke out of a building by way of a chimney: The chimney-sweep came to clean the *flues*.

fluid (flu-id) 1. liquid: I have bought a bottle of brake *fluid* (liquid for the brake system of a car). 2. able to flow as liquids do: You can't use this oil for lubricating; it is not *fluid* enough. 3. easily changed: We can meet at any time: our plans for the day are *fluid*.

flush pour water over or through: We had to *flush* the drains because they were stopped up with dirt. 2. blush, become red in the face: He *flushed* with pride to hear he had won the song contest. 3. a rush of blood to the face. 4. level: He laid the concrete *flush* with the bottom of the door.

flute a musical wind instrument, like a recorder, consisting of a tube closed at one end, and with holes in the side which are stopped by the fingers.

flutter (flut-ter) 1. move or beat: We heard the *fluttering* of wings. 2. beat in an irregular way: I could feel my heart *fluttering* with excitement. 3. being excited: It's not serious, don't get into a *flutter*.

fly *flew, flown, flying* 1. move through the air with or without wings: It is autumn and the birds are *flying* south.–Shall we *fly* to Italy or go by train? 2. an insect with wings: Keep the *flies* away from the food. 3. go quickly: I shall be late for school; I must *fly*. 4. move in the air, be blown here and there: Pieces of paper *flew* about in the wind.

foal a young horse: A male *foal* is called a colt and a female *foal* is called a filly.

foam 1. a white liquid made up of tiny bubbles: *Foam* forms on the sea when it is rough and on streams that flow quickly. 2. make *foam*: The beer *foamed* when it was poured into the glass.

focus (fo-cus) 1. a point where rays of light or heat meet: 'Let me get you into *focus*,' said the photographer, 'so that the picture will be clear.' 2. the point at which people's interest is fixed: The *focus* of everybody's attention is the rise in the cost of living. 3. fix an instrument so that rays of light or heat come together: I have *focused* the camera on two trees in the distance. 4. keep one's attention on something: Let us *focus* all our energy on escaping from prison.

foe enemy, opponent: His *foes* had surrounded him completely and there was no escape.

foil 1. prevent another from carrying out his plans: '*Foiled* again!' roared the villain. 2. metal rolled very thin and used for several purposes: Please bring a roll of baking *foil* from the shop. 3. a very light sword with a button at the point, used for fencing.

fold 1. bend (paper, cloth etc.) so that two surfaces are next to each other: He *folded* the letter carefully and put it in his pocket. 2. that which can be *folded*: Our sitting-room has *folding* doors and the windows have *folding* shutters. 3. the place where a thing is folded: A Scotsman's kilt hangs in *folds* from the waist. 4. an enclosed place where sheep are kept. 5. to bring the sheep into such a place: Every night in winter the shepherd *folds* his sheep (he drives them into the *fold*). 6. cover, wrap: *Fold* the scarf round your neck so that you don't catch cold. **folder** a holder of paper or cardboard for keeping papers or drawings in.

foliage (fol-i-age) the leaves of trees and plants: What beautiful *foliage* this chestnut tree has!

folk 1. people. 2. having to do with the customs of part of a country: In our county we have our own *folk*-songs, *folk*-dances and *folk*-tales.

follow (fol-low) come, go or be after: I'll go first and you *follow*.—What number *follows* 24? 2. go along: *Follow* this path, and turn right at the church. 3. understand: Blue and yellow make green. Do you *follow*? 4. do what you are told: *Follow* the directions on the packet.—*Follow* my advice and you won't make mistakes. 5. work at a certain trade: All my family has *followed* the sea (been sailors or fishermen). 6. come as a result: If you work hard, success is sure to *follow*. **follower** a person who *follows* or supports: The filmstar has many *followers*. **following** people or things which *follow*: Christ had a great *following*.—You will enjoy the *following* story.

folly (fol-ly) foolishness, foolish actions: It would be *folly* to sell such a beautiful house!

fond 1. taking pleasure in: Are you *fond* of music? 2. loving: I am *fond* of all my nephews and nieces. **fondle** touch or stroke lovingly: Don't *fondle* the dog, he doesn't like it. **fondness** being *fond*: Your *fondness* for hot sauces surprises me.

font the basin in a church which holds water for the ceremony of baptism.

food something which can be eaten: Human beings and animals all need *food*.—Vegetarians eat only vegetable *foods*.

fool 1. a person without much sense, one who is stupid: He was a *fool* to give away all he possessed. 2. a clown who is paid to make people laugh, a jester. 3. a person who has been deceived or tricked: You made a *fool* of me! 4. behave like a *fool*: Stop *fooling* and get on with your work. 5. cheat: Don't pretend you can swim; you can't *fool* me. **foolish** not wise, without sense: It is *foolish* to cross a road without looking where you are going. **foolishness** being *foolish*.

foot *feet* 1. that part of the body below the leg, on which people and animals walk: The boy hurt his *foot* on a stone. 2. the lowest part: If you stand at the *foot* of the ladder I'll climb up.–On the third day we reached the *foot* of the mountain. 3. twelve inches: My brother is six *feet* tall. **footstep** the sound of a person walking: We could hear the *footsteps* crunch in the deep snow.

forbid (for-bid) *forbade, forbidden* not allowed: I *forbid* you to cross that bridge.– Smoking is *forbidden* in this theatre.

force 1. strength: Out in the stream we felt the full *force* of the current.–I can see the *force* of your arguments. 2. something that causes changes or movement: A satellite going round the earth resists the *force* of gravity. 3. a body of men employed for a certain purpose: The police *force* has been increased in strength.–The motor industry employs a large labour *force*. 4. the Army, the Navy and the Royal Air *Force* are called the armed *forces*. 5. power, action: A new law has just come into *force* to keep down prices. 6. use *force*: When we reached home we found that the locks had been *forced*. 7. make plants grow quickly: What colour is *forced* rhubarb?

ford 1. a place where a river is shallow enough to be crossed on foot by wading through water. 2. cross a river at a *ford*.

fore 1. the front: Will all passengers travelling to Southampton go to the *fore* part of the train. 2. well known: He has recently come to the *fore* as an opera singer. **forecast** an account of what will probably happen: Did you hear the weather *forecast* this morning? **forefathers** ancestors: My *forefathers* have lived here for hundreds of years. **foreman** a man who is in charge of or leads a number of others: The *foreman* reported that three machines were not working.– 'Not Guilty' announced the *foreman* of the jury. **foremost** the very first: Who is the *foremost* poet of our time? **foresee** see something which is going to happen: Bring your raincoat, I *foresee* a storm. **foresight** the ability to foresee: We would have been ruined but for your *foresight*. **forestall** prevent another person doing a thing by doing it first: I was going to clean this window but you *forestalled* me. **foretell** say that something is going to happen: Is it possible to *foretell* the future? **forethought** planning ahead, thinking of what may happen: Your *forethought* has saved the firm a large sum of money.

foreign (for-eign) in, from or belonging to another country: Firms which carry on *foreign* trade should employ some persons who speak *foreign* languages. **foreigner** a person belonging to a *foreign* country.

forest (for-est) land covered with trees: Bears can still be found in the *forests* of North America. **forester** a man who looks after a *forest* or an area where there are woods.

forfeit (for-feit) 1. lose or give up something as a result of doing wrong or not obeying rules: If he causes another accident he will have to *forfeit* his driving licence. 2. something *forfeited*: If you can't give the answer to this riddle you must pay a *forfeit*.

forge 1. a special fireplace where a blacksmith softens iron so that it can be hammered into shape. 2. a building in which metals are shaped and worked into articles of use. 3. shape something by heating and hammering: The ship lost its anchor and a new one had to be *forged*. 4. make a copy of another person's handwriting or printing in order to deceive: The shopkeeper refused to accept this note because it had been *forged*. – Did you *forge* my signature? **forger** a person who *forges* signatures, documents, notes for his own purposes. **forgery** *forging*: After a trial lasting three days the jury found him guilty of *forgery*.

forget (for-get) *forgot, forgotten* fail to remember: I'm afraid I've *forgotten* your name. – Don't *forget* to post the letter. **forgetful** often *forgetting*: He is the most *forgetful* person I know.

forgive (for-give) *forgave, forgiven* 1. pardon, say that you do not wish to punish: I have apologized to you; am I *forgiven*? 2. give up all claim: '*Forgive* us our debts, as we *forgive* our debtors' (*The Lord's Prayer*, Revised Version). **forgiveness** pardon, *forgiving*: I know I have done wrong and beg your *forgiveness*.

formula (for-mu-la) 1. symbols used for writing in science, chemistry and mathematics: What is the *formula* for water? 2. a number of directions for making or putting together: The *formula* has been stolen by an enemy agent.

fort or **fortress** (for-tress) a building, group of buildings or town made strong for defence against an enemy.

fortnight (fort-night) two weeks, 14 days: I shall be on holiday for the next *fortnight*.

fortune (for-tune) 1. chance, luck: Good *fortune* and bad *fortune* are the same to me. 2. money, property, wealth: 'My face is my *fortune*' (I possess nothing but my good looks). – He went abroad to seek his *fortune*. **fortunate** lucky: You were *fortunate* to find me at home.

forty the number *40*, coming between 39 and 41, 10 multiplied by 4: *Ali Baba and the* Forty *Thieves* is an old story from the East. **fortieth** next after the 39th; one of *40* equal parts: He has given one-*fortieth* of his fortune to charity.

fossil (fos-sil) an animal or plant which has been buried for millions of years and hardened like rock: Have you seen my collection of *fossils*?

foul 1. smelling or tasting bad, filthy: We opened the windows to let out the *foul* air. 2. evil, wicked: The use of *foul* language will be punished. 3. *foul* play, not according to the rules: '*Foul*!' roared the crowd as the goalkeeper fell. 5. (of weather) not fair: On the third day our ship ran into *foul* weather. 6. dirty or make filthy: You can be fined for allowing dogs to *foul* the pavements.

found start (a building, city, organization etc.): Rome was *founded* long before the birth of Christ. – With the money saved we *founded* a hospital. **foundation** the *founding* of a building etc., the basis of a belief: This year is the 50th anniversary of the *foundation* of our society. – There is no *foundation* for such a story. **foundations** the parts of a building which are below the ground and on which it is based. **founder** a person who *founds* or starts an organization, church etc.

foundry (found-ry) a place where metal is melted and moulded into various shapes.

fountain (foun-tain) a continual spring of water made to spurt up from a pipe or pipes and then allowed to drop back: In our park is an ornamental *fountain* and near it a drinking *fountain* which provides cool water.

four the number (4) between three and five: On my hand are *four* fingers and one thumb. **fourteen** (14) *four* added to ten (10); also **fourth** (4th) **fourteenth** (14th).

fox a small, wild animal resembling a dog. *Foxes* are very destructive and are hardly ever tamed.

fraction (frac-tion) 1. a part of something larger: 4 is a *fraction* of 12. 2. a part of a whole number: $\frac{1}{2}$ (one-half), $\frac{1}{4}$ (one-quarter) and $\frac{3}{4}$ (three-quarters) are all *fractions*.

fracture (frac-ture) 1. a break or crack: The leak was caused by a *fracture* in the water pipe. 2. break, crack: The cyclist fell off his machine and *fractured* his skull.

fragile (frag-ile) delicate, easily broken: A label on the parcel read 'FRAGILE – HANDLE CAREFULLY'. – All kinds of pottery are *fragile*.

fragment (frag-ment) a piece broken off, a small piece: All that was left of the plane were a few *fragments* of metal.

fragrance (fra-grance) a sweet, pleasant smell: Early spring always brings the fragrance of violets. **fragrant** sweet-smelling, pleasant: 'The fields are *fragrant* and the woods are green' (Shakespeare, *Titus Andronicus*).

frail fragile, easily broken, weak: Put down that china teapot; it is too *frail* for you to carry. – Have pity on a *frail* old man!

frame 1. the skeleton of a building, or an animal, which holds it together: The *frame* is already erected and the brick-layers are at work. 2. the wooden, metal or other border round a picture, door or window: 'It was only a beautiful picture in a beautiful golden *frame*' (old popular song). 3. put a *frame* round: When are you going to *frame* my photograph? 4. make a false charge against a person: I did not commit the theft; somebody has *framed* me. **framework** the skeleton on which a thing is constructed.

frank 1. open and honest in speech, saying what one thinks: Please give me your *frank* opinion. – To be quite *frank*, I'd rather not. 2. cancel the stamps on letters as they pass through the post office.

frantic (fran-tic) excited, wild with joy, rage or fear, frenzied: I have had no news of him for days and I am *frantic* with anxiety.

fraternal (fra-ter-nal) like a brother, brotherly: We send you our *fraternal* greetings. **fraternity** brotherhood, people who are joined together by similar interests or occupations: Do you belong to the medical *fraternity*? – My brother has joined a *fraternity* of monks. **fraternize** mix with people who are or have been enemies: The armed forces occupying this town are forbidden to *fraternize* with the inhabitants.

fraud 1. cheating, deceiving others: You are guilty of *fraud* and will be imprisoned for one month. 2. a person who cheats or deceives others: You told me it was real gold! You *fraud*! 3. a thing that deceives: This tooth paste is a *fraud*; my teeth are no whiter than before.

freak 1. unusual or odd: The plane was brought down by a *freak* wind. 2. an animal or person which is not like any others of the same kind: One of the kittens in the litter is a *freak*. It has one blue eye and one green eye.

freckle (freck-le) 1. a small light brown spot on a person's skin: My face has always been covered with *freckles*. 2. become covered with *freckles*: You have been in the sun only an hour and you're already *freckled*.

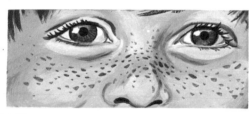

free 1. able to do as you please: I can do what I want, go where I want, say and think what I want; I am quite *free*. 2. without payment or cost: Take these packets of sweets; they are *free*. 3. not busy: Will you be *free* to join me at six this evening? 4. make *free*, set at liberty: He opened all the cages and *freed* the little birds. **freedom** being free: After a long time in prison he was given his *freedom*. **free-for-all** a fight in which anybody can join. **freelance** a person who does not work for any one employer on a salaried basis: My brother is a *freelance* journalist. **free trade** trade between countries *free* from customs and duties. **free-wheel** ride a bicycle down hill without pressing the pedals.

freeze *froze*, *frozen* 1. become or make so cold that a liquid or gas becomes solid: Winter is here and all the ponds are *frozen*. 2. preserve food by making it very cold: Meat from New Zealand arrives *frozen*. 3. feel cold: Please switch on the electric fire; I'm simply *frozen*. 4. a period of very cold weather: When will this terrible *freeze* end? 5. a period when wages or prices are not allowed to rise or fall. **freezer** a machine or a special room for *freezing* food.

freight 1. goods carried from one place to another: Does this ship carry *freight* as well as passengers? 2. money charged for carrying goods: 'Dear Sir: We will supply you with all the materials you need if you pay the *freight*' (or the *freight* charges). **freighter** a ship which carries goods.

frenzy (fren-zy) wild or violent excitement, fury: He dashed out of the room in a *frenzy*. – 'It's a knock-out!' roared the crowd in a *frenzy*. **frenzied** furious, excited: Please stop all this *frenzied* rushing around.

frequent (fré-quent) 1. happening often: There seems to be no reason for these *frequent* attacks of sickness. **frequent** (fre-quént) go often to: 'How I wish you wouldn't *frequent* prize-fights,' said his mother. **frequency** rapid occurrence: This district is noted for the *frequency* of thunderstorms. – My heart beats at a *frequency* of 72 beats a minute.

friction (fric-tion) 1. the rubbing of one thing against another: *Friction* causes things to become hot. – Oil is used to prevent *friction* heating and wearing away parts of machinery. 2. quarrelling between persons: There has always been *friction* between me and my cousins.

Friday (Fri-day) the sixth day of the week. Good *Friday*: the *Friday* before Easter, the anniversary of the crucifixion of Jesus.

friend 1. a person, not a relative, whom one knows well, likes and respects: 'He was my *friend*, faithful and just to me' (Shakespeare, *Julius Caesar*). 2. a person who helps other people or supports a cause: Will you join the *Friends* of our local hospital. **friendless** having no *friends*: Every night, *friendless* and alone, people sleep on benches in the park. **friendship** the feeling that exists between friends: Our *friendship* has lasted since we were boys.

fright 1. sudden fear: The long white cloak you are wearing gave me a *fright*. 2. a ridiculous looking person or thing: You look a *fright* wearing that red wig. **frighten** give a *fright* to: When he saw the angry lion he became very *frightened*. **frightful** not pleasant, awful: What *frightful* weather. – Don't talk to him, he's a *frightful* bore!

frigid (frig-id) 1. very cold: Greenland has a *frigid* climate. 2. not friendly, showing no sympathy: The audience gave the speaker a *frigid* reception.

frill a trimming on cloth gathered at one edge: The sleeve had a broad *frill* at the wrist. **frilled** having a *frill* or *frills*: She wore a *frilled* skirt.

fringe 1. an ornamental border of threads which hang loose: The curtain had a bright yellow *fringe*. 2. edge: He saw the fight from the *fringe* of the crowd. 3. the front part of the hair which falls over the forehead and is cut straight: Why don't you wear your hair in a *fringe*? 4. put a *fringe* on, act as a *fringe* to: Do you like my *fringed* curtains?—Our lawn is *fringed* with flowerbeds.

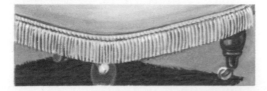

frisk 1. jump and run as if in play: The lambs are *frisking* in the meadow. 2. search a person for hidden weapons. **frisky** in a *frisking* manner, playful: Today I brought home a *frisky* little puppy.

fritter (frit-ter) 1. waste (time, money, energy etc.): He has *frittered* away his youth on useless ventures. 2. a small cake made of fried batter, sometimes containing fruit or jam: Who'd like another apple *fritter*?

frog 1. a small, cold-blooded animal living on land and in water: *Frogs* have long back legs and move by jumping. 2. a fastener like a long wooden or plastic button which is put through a loop to fasten coats, cloaks etc. **frogman** a person who swims under water, wearing a special rubber suit, and flippers on his feet.

frolic (frol-ic) 1. frisk playfully: We watched the kittens *frolic* on the lawn. 2. a merry joke, lively play: The news of his injury put an end to our *frolics*. **frolicsome** lively, wanting to play: What a *frolicsome* little creature!

front 1. the side which faces forwards: You've spilt egg down the *front* of your dress. 2. at the *front*: We have a fountain in the *front* garden. 3. where the fighting is: My son has been at the *front* all through the war. 4. the promenade by the sea or lake: Come for a walk along the *front*. **frontier** the part of a country which faces another country: All along the *frontier* there is a line of barbed wire entanglements.

frost 1. a state of the temperature which causes water to turn to ice: There is a hard *frost* this morning. 2. frozen vapour like a white powder which forms on very cold days: He scraped the *frost* off the top of the wall with his finger. 3. cover with *frost* or something looking like *frost*: Frost the cake lightly with icing sugar. 4. give a *frost*like surface: Most of the doors have panes of *frosted* glass. **frosty** very cold: I don't like this *frosty* weather. **frostbite** injury to a part of the body from *frost*: He had to abandon the polar expedition because of *frostbite*. His feet were badly *frostbitten*.

froth 1. foam, numbers of small bubbles on the top of a liquid: Don't put much detergent into the water; it makes too much *froth*.—Froth forms on beer when it is poured into a glass. 2. make *froth*: The mad dog charged, *frothing* at the mouth.

frown 1. wrinkle the forehead, to look displeased: Don't *frown*; it wasn't I who broke the lamp. 2. a *frowning* look: I could tell by his *frown* that he was angry.

fruit 1. that part of a tree or plant containing the seeds which is used by man or animals: *Fruits* such as apples, pears, oranges and plums can be eaten.–Do you like *fruit*? 2. result, reward: We hope all his efforts will bear *fruit*. **fruiterer** a person who sells fruit. **fruitful** bringing good results: Our appeal for more money has been very *fruitful*. **fruitless** bringing no results: Don't waste your time on *fruitless* schemes. **fruity** tasting like fruit: These sweets have a *fruity* flavour.

fry *fried* 1. cook or be cooked in boiling fat: I shall *fry* an egg for my breakfast.–Do you like *fried* fish? 2. the young of fishes, hatched in large numbers, a word sometimes applied to children: Come along, small *fry*, tea is ready.

fuel (fu-el) 1. material used for burning: Have you any coal or wood? We need more *fuel*.–'A poor man came in sight, gathering winter *fuel*' (Carol, *Good King Wenceslas*). 2. (often re*fuel*) supply with *fuel*, put *fuel* into the tank of an engine: Our plane stopped for two hours to re*fuel*.

fugitive (fu-gi-tive) a person running away or fleeing: I was a *fugitive* from a dangerous gang.

fulfil (ful-fil) do, carry out (a duty, a mission etc.): I have *fulfilled* all my promises to you.–My dangerous mission has now been *fulfilled*.

full 1. able to hold no more: The drawer is *full* of clothing. 2. complete; as fast, long, high etc. as possible: The car is going at *full* speed.–He drew himself up to his *full* height. **full-back** the football player nearest to the goalkeeper who helps to defend the goal. **fully** completely: The distance from here is *fully* half an hour's walk.

fumble (fum-ble) 1. feel clumsily with the hands: I was *fumbling* in the dark for my flashlight. 2. handle awkwardly: We lost the game of cricket because the captain *fumbled* the ball.

fume 1. smoke, gas or vapour which smells strong: Black *fumes* rose from the burning building. 2. give off *fumes*: Don't handle the coke until it has stopped *fuming*. 3. show anger or irritation: He was *fuming* about the broken window. **fumigate** treat a room, a building, a tree etc. with *fumes* to kill germs or pests.

fun 1. playfulness, amusement: We always have *fun* at the swimming pool. 2. something or some person causing *fun*: Throwing snowballs is great *fun*. **for fun** as a joke: I only did it *for fun*! **funny** causing *fun*, strange: How *funny* the clowns are.–There's nothing in my money-box. That's *funny*!

function (func-tion) 1. the special work of a person or thing: The *function* of a knife is to cut. 2. do what is expected of somebody or something: The brakes of the car have ceased to *function*. 3. a public event: How many *functions* did the Mayor attend last week?

fund 1. a supply of money for some special purpose: A *fund* has been started for the victims of the recent earthquake. 2. some quality of character or knowledge: You may have an endless *fund* of jokes but my *fund* of patience is exhausted.

funeral (fu-ner-al) 1. burying or burning a dead body and the service connected with it: All his relatives came to the *funeral*. 2. having to do with a *funeral*: The *funeral* procession entered the church.

fungus (fun-gus) *fungi* a plant that grows on other plants or on decaying matter: The mushroom is a *fungus* that can be eaten.

funnel (fun-nel) 1. a tube which opens at the top like a cone, down which liquids can be poured into a container. 2. the tube serving as an outlet for smoke in a ship or an engine.

fur 1. the soft hair which covers certain animals such as the fox, cat, beaver and rabbit. 2. the skin of an animal which has *fur*, used as a coat: My sister wore a fox *fur*. 3. the crust left inside a kettle through the boiling of water. **furred** (of a kettle) having *fur* inside it. **furrier** a tradesman who makes and sells *furs*. **furry** like *fur*: The coat was made of some kind of *furry* material.

furlough (fur-lough) a short holiday, especially for such people as soldiers, missionaries and people who live abroad: My uncle is home on a month's *furlough*.

furnace (fur-nace) a structure specially built to contain a fire: *Furnaces* are used to heat buildings, to produce metals etc.

furnish (fur-nish) 1. provide: We can *furnish* you with everything you require for fishing. 2. fit up a house with necessary appliances: I would like to see your study well *furnished*. **furnishings** all the things required to *furnish* a room, including curtains and pictures. **furniture** all those things which can be moved in a house—beds, tables, chairs etc., used to *furnish* a room or other space. **furnisher** a person who sells *furniture*: There are many house *furnishers* near here.

furrow (fur-row) 1. a long deep cut or ditch made in the ground by a plough. 2. a deep wrinkle on the face. 3. make wrinkles in: The old woman's forehead is *furrowed* with age.

further (fur-ther) 1. farther, to a greater distance: He went *further* and *further* into the tunnel. 2. more: Let me have *further* information about the goods you need. 3. help forward: Would this sum of money help to *further* your plans?

fury (fu-ry) 1. violent anger: When the king saw the ruins of his palace his *fury* knew no bounds. 2. frenzy, fierceness: He had to face the *fury* of the storm. **furious** full of *fury*, without control: Mother will be *furious* if we forget to buy the flowers.– The battle raged fast and *furious*.

fuse 1. the string or tube which carries the flame to set off an explosive charge: We had to run before the *fuse* burnt out and the bomb exploded. 2. a piece of metal which allows electricity to pass through it but melts if too much is passed, thus stopping the current. **fuse wire** special kinds of wire used for *fuses*.

fuselage (fu-se-lage) the body of an aircraft: The wings and tail must now be fitted on to the *fuselage*.

fusilier (fu-si-lier) a soldier who once carried a light musket: The British army has several regiments of *fusiliers*.

fuss 1. a useless display of anxiety: What a *fuss* he makes about nothing. 2. show worry: Don't *fuss*; we will soon put everything in order. 3. attention which may not be necessary: Why do you make such a *fuss* of your little dog? **fussy** in the habit of *fussing* or making a *fuss*: I like her, but she is far too *fussy*.

future (fu-ture) 1. time which will come after the present: In *future* we will write to you every week. 2. having to do with the *future*: What are your *future* plans?– May I introduce my *future* wife?

fuzz soft fluff or down. **fuzzy** covered with down, indistinct: Everything appears *fuzzy* without my spectacles.

gable (ga-ble) a three-cornered outside wall of a building enclosed by two sloping roofs and the line between their lowest points: The *gable* of the house we live in faces the street.

gag 1. something thrust into the mouth to prevent a person speaking. 2. put something into a person's mouth to prevent speech: He was bound and *gagged* and put into a dark room.

gaiety (gai-e-ty) cheerfulness, merry-making: Christmas is a time of *gaiety* for the children.

gain 1. get, obtain: To *gain* time we ran across the churchyard. 2. get nearer or reach: Run faster, they are *gaining* on us.–We shall never *gain* the top of the hill in time. 3. increase: You should eat more food if you wish to *gain* weight. 4. go ahead of the correct time: Will you please adjust my watch; it *gains* five minutes in a day. 5. something obtained, profits, winnings: I keep rabbits as a hobby and not for *gain*.– The thief had nowhere to store his ill-gotten *gains*.

gala (ga-la) an occasion of festivity and show: Are you going to the hospital *gala* (to raise money for the hospital)?– The last performance is to be a *gala* night.

galaxy (gal-ax-y) *galaxies* a large number of stars forming a light band in the sky but which cannot be seen separately: The earth is part of a *galaxy* called the Milky Way.

gale 1. a strong wind: They took shelter from the *gale* in a cave. 2. a sudden loud noise, usually cheerful: As soon as he entered the room there was a *gale* of laughter.

gallant (gal-lant) 1. brave: King Arthur and his *gallant* knights sat at the Round Table. 2. stately, good-looking: Many a *gallant* ship has sailed away and not returned. 3. polite to ladies: Who is the *gallant* young man in the blue suit?

gallery (gal-le-ry) *galleries* 1. a room in which pictures and other works of art are displayed: The exhibition at the National *Gallery* will end this week. 2. a platform extending from the inner walls of a church, theatre or hall: The cheapest seats in the theatre are in the *gallery*.– In the House of Commons there is a press *gallery* (for newspaper reporters). 3. a room specially set apart for shooting, a shooting-*gallery*.

gallon (gal-lon) a measurement of liquids; 1 *gallon* equals 4·5 litres. He stopped at the garage and bought two *gallons* of petrol.

gallop (gal-lop) 1. move very fast by leaps: He can ride his bicycle as fast as a horse can *gallop*. 2. the fastest speed a horse can go: The highwayman rode off at full *gallop*.

gallows (gal-lows) the wooden frame of uprights and cross pieces used for hanging criminals: The famous highwayman Dick Turpin ended his life on the *gallows*.

gamble (gam-ble) 1. play games for money: The four men were seated at a table *gambling* with cards. 2. lose money by *gambling*: He has *gambled* away a fortune. 3. a great risk: We may win or lose, it's all a *gamble*.

game 1. sport played according to rules: Football, tennis, rugby and cricket are all *games*. 2. materials for playing: We sell all kinds of *games* in this shop. 3. a contest in which people run, jump etc.: The Olympic *Games* are held every four years. 4. a cunning plan: You're making me pay twice over; I know your *game*. 5. wild animals that are hunted or shot: There is plenty of *game* on these moors. 6. brave, ready to go on fighting or working: This job will take a long time, but I'm *game* if you are.

gammon (gam-mon) the lower end of a side of bacon: How many rashers of *gammon* would you like?

gander (gan-der) a male goose: 'Goosey, goosey *gander*, whither (where) do you wander? (nursery rhyme).

gang 1. a group of persons working together: He passed a *gang* of navvies digging a hole in the road. 2. a group of criminals: The chief of police had tried for six months to break up the *gang*. **gangplank** a moveable way which can be placed against the side of a ship to allow passengers to come ashore. **gangster** a member of a group of criminals. **gangway** a passage between seats or walls along which people may walk.

gaol (pronounced *jail*) 1. a prison: The thief was sent to *gaol* for three months. 2. send a person to prison: Do you think he will be *gaoled*? **gaoler** a person who looks after prisoners.

gap 1. an opening: We can climb through the *gap* in the hedge. 2. an empty space, something not filled in: Can you fill the *gaps* in this puzzle?—I know a little French but there are many *gaps* in my knowledge.

gape 1. open the mouth wide; stare in surprise with the mouth open: He stood *gaping* at the huge elephant. 2. be wide open: There was a *gaping* hole in the roof.

garage (ga-rage) 1. a building in which cars are kept: I will buy the house if there is a *garage*. 2. an establishment where cars are stored and repaired: They took the car to the *garage* to have the oil changed.

garbage (gar-bage) scraps of uneaten food put aside for pigs and other animals to eat.

garden (gar-den) 1. a piece of ground on which flowers and vegetables are grown: In the kitchen *garden* vegetables are grown. 2. part of the name of a street: We have recently moved into a house in Newbury *Gardens*. 3. attend to a *garden*: I can't come for a walk today; I shall be *gardening* all afternoon. **gardener** a person who looks after a *garden*.

gargle (gar-gle) 1. wash the throat by holding liquid in the mouth and breathing through it: Every morning I *gargle* with cold water. 2. a substance used for *gargling*: Salt and water make a good *gargle*.

garland (gar-land) 1. flowers and leaves made into a circle or crown: The fairy queen wore a *garland*. 2. decorate with *garlands*: The winners of the races were *garlanded* with laurel wreaths.

garlic (gar-lic) a plant like an onion which has a very strong taste and smell.

garment (gar-ment) an article of clothing: 'May I then change these *garments*?' (Shakespeare, *Coriolanus*)

garnish (gar-nish) 1. decorate food for the table: The main course was meat *garnished* with green herbs. 2. something used to decorate food for the table: What shall we use as a *garnish* for this salad?

garret (gar-ret) a room on the top floor of a house under the sloping roof; an attic: Our *garret* is used for storing toys and other things we do not use.

garrison (gar-ri-son) 1. a force of soldiers stationed in a town or fort: The city was defended by a strong *garrison*. 2. station soldiers in a town or fort: Men of the East Anglian Regiment are *garrisoned* here.

garter (gar-ter) 1. a band worn round the leg for holding up stockings. 2. the badge of the highest order of English knighthood.

gas 1. any substance that is not solid or liquid: Air is a mixture of two *gases*, oxygen and nitrogen. 2. a *gas* used as a fuel: Is your house heated by *gas*? 3. *gas* or *gases* which are poisonous. 4. poison with *gas*: Soldiers in the First World War wore *gas*-masks to prevent themselves being *gassed*.

gash 1. a long, deep cut: The horse had a deep *gash* in its leg. 2. make a deep cut: He fell off the wall and *gashed* his arm.

gasp 1. breathe quickly as one does after running hard: When the boy was rescued from the water he was *gasping* for breath. 2. a short quick breath.

gate an opening that can be closed with a moveable barrier: After a long journey we arrived at the *gate* of the city.—I will meet you at the garden *gate*.

gather (gath-er) 1. put, come, or bring together: A crowd *gathered* round the scene of the accident.—He *gathered* up his belongings and went home. 2. pull into small folds and sew together: The blouse was *gathered* at the neck. 3. understand: I *gather* from what you say that you have spent holidays in Italy.

gauge (pronounced *gage*) 1. distance between the wheels of a vehicle: A railway of narrow *gauge* runs on lines that are near to each other. 2. an instrument for measuring: Every morning we inspect the rain *gauge*. 3. measure: How do you *gauge* the amount of water in this barrel?

gaunt 1. thin, lean (of a person): His illness had left him *gaunt* and pale. 2. bare, grim (of a place): *Gaunt* trees surrounded the castle.

gay 1. merry, cheerful: Let us be *gay* before we part. 2. making people cheerful: Dresses of *gay* colours filled the shop window.—The band played *gay* music. **gaily** in a *gay* manner: They walked along the road singing *gaily*.

gaze 1. look long and steadily:
    'I *gazed* and *gazed* but little thought
    What wealth to me the show had brought'
      (Wordsworth, *The Daffodils*).
2. a long steady look: Her *gaze* rested on a gaily-dressed doll.

gazette (ga-zette) 1. the name of certain newspapers: Have you seen this morning's *Gazette*? 2. an official journal published by the government containing lists of appointments and promotions, bankruptcies etc.

gear 1. a set of wheels working together to make a machine run: There are five *gears* on this car including the reverse *gear*. 2. machinery used for a special purpose: The pilot of the aircraft signalled that his landing *gear* was out of order. 3. everything one needs for a special purpose: Have you put all your fishing *gear* together? **in gear** with the *gears* adjusted so that the motor will turn the wheels and the vehicle can move.

gelatine (gel-a-tine) a substance added to water which makes jelly. *Gelatine* is made from the hoofs and bones of animals.

gelignite (gel-ig-nite) a substance made from various chemicals and used as an explosive: The rock was too hard to break and had to be blasted with *gelignite*.

gem a precious stone: The king wore a crown studded with *gems*.

gendarme (gen-darme) a member of the police force in France and some other countries: Luckily the *gendarme* spoke English and directed us to the station.

gender (gen-der) a grammatical means of grouping words: The word 'man' is masculine *gender*, 'girl' is feminine *gender* and 'table' is neuter *gender*.

general (gen-er-al) 1. affecting all people or things: It looks as if there may be a *general* strike (a strike of all workers).—When is the next *general* election? 2. rough, not in detail: We now have a *general* idea of what you require. 3. an army officer next in rank above a lieutenant-general and below a field-marshal.

generation (gen-er-a-tion) 1. one step in the descent of a family: This is a photograph of four *generations*—my great-grandmother, my grandmother, my mother and myself. 2. people born about the same time: All those under the age of 25 belong to the younger *generation*. 3. the average period between the ages of parents and children: How many *generations* have been born since the beginning of the twentieth century?

generator (gen-er-a-tor) a machine used for making steam, electric current etc.

generous (gen-er-ous) 1. willing to share with others: We need people who are *generous* both with money and time (willing to give time to help others). 2. plentiful: He took a *generous* helping of pudding.—What a *generous* gift you have made towards the building of new tennis courts. **generosity** being *generous*: We are grateful for your great *generosity*.

genial (ge-ni-al) 1. pleasant, kindly, warm: A *genial* atmosphere at work is essential. 2. mild (of the climate).

genius (gen-i-us) 1. someone who is outstandingly brilliant at some kind of work, art etc.: Mozart was a musical *genius*. 2. brilliance: Not everyone has the *genius* to paint masterpieces. 3. ability: It is possible to have a *genius* for mathematics without being a *genius*.

gentle (gen-tle) kind, mild, friendly, not violent: He is only a child; be *gentle* with him.—'I will be mild and *gentle* in my words' (Shakespeare, *Richard III*).

gentleman (gen-tle-man) *gentlemen* a man who acts honourably and considers other people in everything he does: Your brother is a perfect *gentleman*.

genuine (gen-u-ine) real, true: Are these diamonds *genuine* or imitation?—We heard of his death with *genuine* sorrow.

geography (ge-og-ra-phy) the study of the earth's surface, mountains, rivers, climate, population etc.: It is possible to travel throughout a country without knowing its *geography*.

geology (ge-ol-o-gy) the study of the earth's crust and its rocks: *Geology* has revealed that some mountains are millions of years old.

geometry (ge-om-e-try) that part of mathematics which deals with lines, angles, surfaces and solid bodies: What does *geometry* tell us about the area of a rectangle?

geranium (ge-ra-ni-um) a plant with either red, white or pink flowers which has a strong scent: *Geraniums* grow wild in Spain throughout the summer.

germ a small organism or microbe that can be seen only with a microscope. *Germs* may live in an animal's body and cause disease. **germicide** a preparation made to kill *germs*.

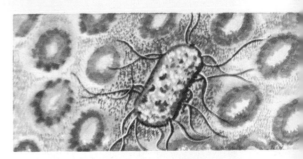

gesture (ges-ture) 1. a movement of the hand, head or other part of the body to show feelings, needs, ideas etc.: He made a *gesture* of disgust at the dirty water. 2. an action to express a feeling: Will you please contribute a small sum as a *gesture* of goodwill.

get 1. receive, be given: How much did you *get* for your watch?—I'm *getting* a bicycle for my birthday. 2. procure, have something done: You should *get* your hair cut. 3. go from one place to another: When did you *get* home?—Every morning I *get* up at seven o'clock. 4. bring, take or place: '*Get* me to the church on time' (song from *My Fair Lady*).—I can't *get* all my things into this box. 5. pass from one condition to another: Please don't *get* angry with me. 6. hear or understand: I didn't *get* the last sentence. 7. be ill with: He has *got* a bad cold.

geyser (gey-ser) 1. a hot spring which sends up water. 2. an apparatus for producing hot water, usually in a bathroom or kitchen.

ghost 1. the spirit of a dead person which haunts living people: 'I know him! Marley's *ghost*!' (Dickens, *A Christmas Carol*). 2. the very smallest: He hasn't the *ghost* of a chance. The **Holy Ghost** the Spirit of God; the third Person of the Trinity: 'Praise Father, Son and *Holy Ghost*' (*The Old Hundredth*).

giant (gi-ant) 1. a very large, strong man: The *giant* Goliath was killed in battle by David. 2. very large: This year I have grown several *giant* cabbages. **gigantic** very large: We went home with a *gigantic* appetite.

giddy (gid-dy) 1. feeling that everything is whirling round: Let me sit down please, I feel *giddy*. 2. too fond of pleasure: She's too *giddy* to work hard at her job.

gift 1. something given as a present: He gave me the most charming *gift* of flowers. 2. ability: He has a *gift* for music. 3. having to do with *gifts*: You will get what you want at the *gift* shop.

giggle (gig-gle) 1. laugh in a silly way: When we saw the clown we couldn't help *giggling*. 2. a short, light laugh: Her only answer was a *giggle*.

gild cover with a thin coating of gold: Please would you *gild* this picture-frame? **gilt** a thin coating of gold: This brooch is not gold; it's only *gilt*.

gill 1. the organ with which a fish breathes under water. 2. (pronounced *jill*) one-quarter of a pint of liquid.

gimlet (gim-let) a small tool used for making holes in wood.

gin 1. a trap for catching animals. 2. a drink containing alcohol, flavoured with juniper berries, orange peel etc. 3. a machine for separating cotton from its seeds.

ginger (gin-ger) 1. the root of the *ginger* plant: Root *ginger* is preserved and eaten; ground *ginger* is put into cakes. 2. looking or tasting like *ginger*, of a reddish-brown colour: Do you see the *ginger*-headed boy drinking *ginger*-beer? **gingerbread** cake or biscuit flavoured with *ginger*.

gipsy (gip-sy)–or **gypsy** *gipsies* someone belonging to a minority race who lives in a caravan and wanders about the country, earning a living by dealing in scrap-metal, basket-making, peg-making and other work of the same kind.
'I wish I lived in a caravan
With a horse to ride, like a *gipsy*-man.'
(Robert Louis Stevenson)

giraffe (gi-raffe) a tall, African animal with a very long neck, long front legs and dark spots on a yellow skin.

girdle (gir-dle) 1. a belt or cord worn round the waist. 2. anything that goes round anything else in a circle: 'I'll put a *girdle* round about the earth in forty minutes' (Puck, in Shakespeare's *A Midsummer Night's Dream*). 3. put a *girdle* round: Puck said he would *girdle* the earth.

girl a young woman, a female child, a daughter: The little *girl* swims very well for her age. **Girl Guide** a member of an organization for *girls* to develop health, character and home-making ability. **girlish** like a *girl*: She answered with a burst of *girlish* laughter. **girlhood** the time or state of being a *girl*: During my *girlhood* we wore our hair in long plaits.

give *gave, given* 1. make a present of: Every boy was *given* a bag of sweets. 2. hand over in exchange: What will you *give* me for this whistle? 3. provide: Cows *give* us milk and butter. 4. cause: I hope this work will not *give* you too much trouble. 5. perform an action: He *gave* a sigh and a groan before he *gave* the door a good push. 6. become less strong or firm: If you push hard enough the door will *give*. **give up** stop trying, lose hope: Don't ask me any more questions, I *give up*!

glacier (gla-cier) a mass of ice that moves very slowly down the side of a mountain.

glad 1. happy, pleased: How *glad* I am to see you at last. 2. giving happiness or pleasure: We celebrated the *glad* occasion with a party. **gladness** joyfulness, cheerfulness.

glamour (glam-our) power to charm or fascinate: I love the *glamour* of a royal procession. **glamorous** having the power to charm: Who is the most *glamorous* film star you know?

glance 1. look quickly: It was midnight when I *glanced* at my watch. 2. Slip or bounce off: The spear *glanced* harmlessly off his shield. 3. a quick look: Have a *glance* at this car and tell me what you think of it.

gland an organ of the body which takes substances from the blood and helps the body to keep healthy. Two *glands* in the human body are the saliva and sweat *glands*.

glare 1. a strong light: We were almost blinded by the *glare* of the approaching car's headlamps. 2. an angry look: He met me at the door with a fierce *glare*. 3. shine with a strong light: We walked all day in the *glaring* sun. 4. stare or glance fiercely or angrily: The two boys stood for a moment *glaring* at each other.

glass 1. a hard substance which can be seen through: Windows are made of *glass*.—Have you seen my *glass* scent-bottle anywhere? 2. certain things which are made of *glass*: Bring your magnifying *glass* and your field-*glasses*. 3. quantity or contents of a drinking *glass*: Will you have a *glass* of wine or a *glass* of beer? 4. spectacles: He needs to wear his *glasses* to read the newspaper. **glassware** articles made of *glass*.

glaze 1. cover with or put in glass: Many of the windows in this house need re*glazing* (*glazing* again). 2. cover with a shiny, glossy surface: This vase has been beautifully *glazed*.

gleam 1. a beam or flash of light: At last he saw a faint *gleam* from an upstairs window. 2. send out *gleams*: We could see the town-lights *gleaming* in the valley below. 3. a fragment, the slightest bit: We will work to rescue the trapped miners as long as there is a *gleam* of hope.

glee great joy, delight or pleasure: The arrival of the circus was received with *glee*.

glen a narrow valley with steep sides: Many armies have been ambushed in this *glen*.

glide move along continuously as without effort: Slowly our boat *glided* down the stream. **glider** an aeroplane that flies without an engine.

glimmer (glim-mer) 1. a faint gleam which comes and goes: Do you see the *glimmer* of light in the distance? 2. give a faint gleam: The moonlight *glimmered* through the trees. 3. a fragment (as in gleam).

glimpse a very quick look, an imperfect view: They caught a *glimpse* of the thief running round the corner.

glisten (glis-ten) shine brightly, sparkle: The queen's dress *glistened* with precious stones.

glitter (glit-ter) sparkle with quick flashes of light: The frost *glittered* in the morning sun.

globe 1. a large round object, especially one which shows a map of the world. 2. a round vessel or cover: We need a new *globe* for the electric light.

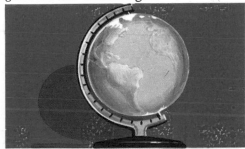

gloom 1. almost total darkness: The thick forest cast a *gloom* over the travellers' path. 2. despair, sadness, hopelessness: The thought of spending a year away from home filled him with *gloom*. **gloomy** dark, dismal, depressing: The rain poured down from a *gloomy* sky.—If our team plays badly the prospect for the future is a *gloomy* one.

glory (glo-ry) *glories* 1. honour and praise given to a person who has done something great: His bravery won him great *glory*. 2. great splendour: Here comes the king in all his *glory*. 3. be proud about something: The man *glories* in his power. **glorious** excellent, admirable in every way: What a *glorious* morning!—The soldiers were given a *glorious* welcome.

gloss a bright surface: I like my shoes to have a good *gloss*. **glossy** having a polished surface: Please print my photographs on *glossy* paper.

glove a covering for the hand with separate parts for each finger: Do you prefer *gloves* of wool or leather?

glow 1. shine with heat but without flame: I love sitting in front of a fire that *glows*. 2. show pleasure, pride, health: The children's faces *glowed* with joy. 3. gentle, dim light: During the strike we worked by the *glow* of an oil lamp. 4. an expression of emotion, pleasure, pride or embarrassment: He received the prize with a *glow* of delight.

glue 1. a sticky substance made to fasten things together: He used *glue* to mend the broken picture-frame. 2. stick things with *glue*: We must *glue* the two pieces of wood together.

glum sad, gloomy: I felt very *glum* after my failure to pass the examination.

glut 1. more than is needed: Why is there such a *glut* of apples in the shops this week? 2. give, have, supply, eat more than is needed: Don't *glut* the animals with too much food. **glutton** one who eats too much.

glycerine (glyc-er-ine) a clear, sweet liquid made from oils, used in medicine and explosives.

gnat (pronounced *nat*) a small insect that has two wings, feelers, and a sting.

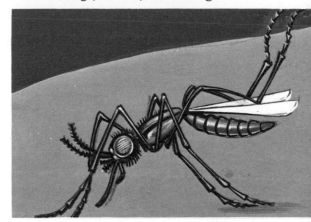

gnaw (pronounced *nor*) wear something down with constant biting as a dog with a bone: The mice have *gnawed* a hole in the sugar sack.

gnome (pronounced *nome*) a small elf or goblin, a make-believe being said to live under the ground, who guards treasure: Have you ever seen a *gnome* or do they only appear in fairy tales?

go *went*, *gone*, *going* 1. move from one place to another: Does this train *go* from London to Liverpool? 2. change: Don't let the meat *go* bad. 3. reach: Does this road *go* to the station? 4. leave: When did they *go*? 5. work: This car *goes* by electricity. 6. be put, find a place: Where does this table *go*?–Will all the books *go* in this box? 7. disappear, be used up: At last all his money was *gone*. 8. attend: Do you *go* to this school? 9. have certain words or music: How does the chorus *go*? 10. an attempt: Do have a *go*!

goal 1. in a football match, the space between the posts through which the ball has to pass in order to score: Our team spent most of their time defending the *goal*. 2. when the ball passes between the posts: '*Goal*' yelled the crowd as the ball went into the net. 3. what one hopes to be or to do: My *goal* is to become the manager of this firm. **goalkeeper** the football player whose task is to defend the *goal*.

goat a domestic animal with horns which gives milk.

gobble (gob-ble) 1. gulp, eat noisily and quickly: Don't *gobble* your food! 2. the cry, or to make the cry of a turkey-cock.

goblet (gob-let) a drinking glass with a stem and a base but no handle.

goblin (gob-lin) an ugly, mischievous elf or spirit supposed to harm human beings: We read about *goblins* in fairy tales.

god 1. (with a capital G) the maker and governor of the world and the whole universe: *God* said 'Let there be light.' 2. a being that is worshipped: The ancient Greeks had many *gods*. 3. a person or thing which people love, praise or value: Some make a *god* of money, others make *gods* of film stars and singers. **goddess** a female god. **godfather, godmother** (or **godparents**) persons who promise when a child is baptized to make sure it is brought up as a Christian. **godsend** a piece of unexpected good fortune. **godly** very religious.

goggles (gog-gles) spectacles with special thick rims and frames to protect the eyes from injury.

gold 1. a precious yellow metal used for making jewellery and coins: This ring is made of pure *gold*. 2. the colour of *gold*: The sun set in a blaze of *gold*. **golden** made of *gold*; the colour of *gold*: He placed in her hand a *golden* coin.–My cousin has long *golden* hair. **golden wedding** the 50th anniversary of a wedding. **goldfish** a small *golden*-coloured fish. **goldsmith** a craftsman who makes or sells articles of *gold*.

golf an outdoor game in which a small white ball is driven with a club, the object being to get it into a hole in as few strokes as possible. **golfer** a person who plays *golf*. **golf links** or **golf course** the specially prepared ground on which *golf* is played.

gong a piece of metal shaped like a saucer which gives out a sound when struck: At the sound of the *gong* the guests took their places at the dining table.

good *better*, *best* 1. satisfactory, doing what is needed: This is a *good* knife but the other one is *better*. 2. helpful: This medicine will be *good* for your cough. 3. satisfying: I could eat a *good* meal. 4. pleasant: We had a *good* time at the concert. 5. kind: It was *good* of the young man to carry my luggage. 6. well-behaved: My son is very *good*; he hardly ever cries. 7. a little more than: You will have to walk for a *good* three hours. 8. that which is *good*: Jesus went about doing *good*. 9. use: We tried a hammer, but it was no *good*. **goods** property, things owned: All the *goods* in this shop are for sale.

goodbye farewell (said by people on parting).

good-humoured always cheerful.

good-natured having a pleasant nature.

goodwill a feeling of friendliness to people:

To show my *goodwill* I am charging you less than the full price.

goose *geese* a large bird like a duck but with a longer neck: The eggs of *geese* and the flesh of the *goose* are delicious to eat.

gorge 1. a very narrow valley between high hills: A swift stream flows through the *gorge*. 2. eat greedily: The little boy *gorged* himself on chocolate cake.

gorgeous (gor-geous) magnificent; with beautiful colours: What a *gorgeous* dress this is!

gorilla (go-ril-la) the largest of the apes living on the ground.

gospel (gos-pel) 1. the teaching of Jesus Christ: Christ's disciples preached the *Gospel*. 2. one of the four books of the New Testament: Please read chapter 6 of the *Gospel* of St Matthew.

gossip (gos-sip) 1. talk about other people's private affairs: Has anybody been *gossipping* about me? 2. a person who is fond of *gossip*.

gouge (pronounced *gowge*) 1. a chisel with a sharp curved edge for making grooves in wood. 2. cut out with a *gouge*: If you make an inkstand you must *gouge* out a groove to hold the pen.

govern (go-vern) rule or control the affairs of a state: 'How should you *govern* any kingdom?' (Shakespeare, *Henry VI*, part 3). **government** the body of persons who *govern* a state: In Great Britain the Prime Minister is head of the *government*. **governor** a person who *governs* a province, or who manages with others the affairs of a school, society etc.

gown 1. a dress worn by a girl or a woman. 2. a loose, flowing outer garment worn by judges, members of universities etc.: All the masters and mistresses in our school wear *gowns* on Speech Day.

grab 1. grasp quickly, snatch: He *grabbed* a hockey-stick and ran on to the field. 2. a quick snatch: 'Stop thief!' I shouted, making a *grab* at the fleeing figure.

grace 1. a beautiful movement which pleases and attracts others: If you wish to act on the stage you must learn to move with *grace*. 2. a prayer of thanks for food: Before the meal the headmaster said *grace*. 3. the way of addressing a duke, a duchess or an archbishop: We are very glad Your *Grace* was able to attend our meeting. **graceful** full of *grace*, showing *grace*: The whole company joined together in a *graceful* dance.

gracious kind, showing pleasure, merciful: 'God save our *gracious* Queen' (the British National Anthem).

grade 1. rank: A sergeant is a *grade* higher than a corporal. 2. quality: We stock only the best *grade* of butter. 3. step (in a course of instruction): Work will be harder now that you have reached the third *grade*. 4. sort out into different qualities: These eggs have all been *graded*.

gradient a measure of the steepness of a slope: This hill has a *gradient* of one in ten.

gradual rising or falling in small amounts: Have you noticed the *gradual* rise in the cost of butter?

grain 1. the small hard seed of plants used for food: We saw field upon field of ripe *grain*. 2. a single seed of such a plant: A *grain* of mustard seed is very small. 3. a very small hard piece: The seashore is made up of millions of *grains* of sand. 4. the way in which the fibres of wood go: When wood is chopped, it is split along the *grain*. 5. the tiniest bit: Unless you show a *grain* of sense, you will not succeed.

gram or **gramme** a unit of weight in the metric system.

grammar (gram-mar) the study of words and how they make up a language: In this *grammar* lesson we will study the construction of sentences. **grammar school** an English secondary school in which Latin was once the chief subject taught. **grammatical** having to do with *grammar*: In the sentence 'We be tall but you be small' there are two *grammatical* mistakes.

gramophone (gram-o-phone) a machine which reproduces sound which has previously been recorded on records.

grand 1. splendid, large, most important: The best pianists always play on a *grand* piano.–The best place to see a match is from the *grand*stand. 2. magnificent, fine, enjoyable: There is a *grand* view from the top of the mountain. 3. very highly respected: He is a *grand* companion for a journey; a *grand* old man. **grandfather, grandmother, grandparents** the parents of one's father or mother. **grandson, grand-daughter, grand-children** etc. the children of sons and daughters.

granite (gran-ite) very hard rock used for buildings, monuments etc.

granule (gran-ule) a small grain. **granulated** in the form of small grains: May I have a spoonful of *granulated* sugar?

grant 1. allow, give: 'I will *grant* you three wishes,' said the fairy. 2. agree, admit to be true: I *grant* the truth of what he says; it can be taken for *granted*. 3. something given, usually money from a government or organization: He received a *grant* to continue his studies.

grape the black, brown or green berry or fruit that grows in bunches on a vine and which can be eaten: This wine is made from *grapes* grown in Italy. **grapevine** the plant on which *grapes* grow.

grapefruit a large acid-tasting fruit, with a juicy, edible pulp, and yellow skin.

graph a diagram ruled with lines which show how things are related to each other: This *graph* shows the room temperature during the day, and the other *graph* shows the rainfall throughout the year.

grapple (grap-ple) seize and struggle with: I *grappled* with the thief and pulled him to the ground.–He *grappled* with the difficult problem but could not solve it.

grasp 1. seize and hold firmly: He *grasped* the beam and held on until help arrived. 2. try to seize: 'A drowning man will *grasp* at a straw' (proverb). 3. understand: He showed me how to work out the problem but I could not *grasp* it. 4. firm hold: 'Ah,' said the villain, 'now I have you in my *grasp*!' 5. understanding: At last I have a good *grasp* of the method.

grass 1. a green plant with narrow leaves, growing close to the ground: The pastures are covered with rich *grass* for the cattle to graze. 2. other plants of the same kind with long narrow leaves: Reeds, bamboos and plants which bear grain are all *grasses*.

grasshopper an insect remarkable for its powers of leaping, and the chirping noise produced by the males.

grate 1. a frame of iron or steel for holding the fuel in a fireplace: Every morning Cinderella was made to clean out the *grate*. 2. rub against a rough piece of metal and break into small pieces: To make this dish, take a small piece of cheese and *grate* it carefully. 3. make a harsh sound by rubbing: This chalk *grates* when I write on the blackboard. **grater** a rough sheet of metal pierced with holes for *grating*: I cannot find the nutmeg-*grater*. **grating** a wooden or metal cover placed over an opening.

grateful (grate-ful) thankful, showing thanks: I should be most *grateful* for your help in this matter. **gratify** give pleasure, make *grateful*: We were all *gratified* by the result of the match.

gratitude thankfulness: He showed his *gratitude* by sending a large sum of money.

grave 1. a hole dug in the ground for burying a dead body: 'Duncan is in his *grave*' (Shakespeare, *Macbeth*). 2. solemn: 'I am afraid you have made a mistake,' he said, looking *grave*. 3. serious: You have made a *grave* mistake.

gravel (grav-el) large numbers of small stones mixed with sand, used to make paths and roads.

gravity (grav-i-ty) 1. the force which draws objects to the centre of the earth: Through the force of *gravity* earth satellites are kept in regular orbit, the earth keeps its distance from the sun and the moon from the earth. 2. (see *grave*) seriousness: Do you realize the *gravity* of your offence?

graze 1. eat grass in fields: All day long the cattle *graze*. 2. scrape in passing, rubbing off the skin or the surface: The boy *grazed* his knee on the railings. 3. a mark or a place where the surface is broken through *grazing*: Have you seen the ugly *graze* along the side of the car?

grease 1. oil or fat from plants, animals or any other source: The axle of the cart is squeaking and needs *grease*. 2. put on or apply *grease*: Will you please *grease* the hinges of the gate. **greasy** covered with *grease* or having too much *grease* in it: You should wipe your *greasy* fingers on the napkin.

great 1. much better than the average: King Solomon showed *great* wisdom. 2. Famous, very able, worthy of being remembered: Shakespeare is England's *greatest* dramatist, but who wrote the *greatest* novels? 3. very large: The whale is one of the *greatest* animals alive. 4. very enjoyable: It's going to be *great* fun at the sports tomorrow. 5. those relatives who are two generations removed: My *great*-uncle is my father's uncle. **greatness** importance, being *great*: 'Some men are born *great*, some achieve *greatness* and some have *greatness* thrust upon them' (Shakespeare, *Twelfth Night*).

greed a desire to have more of something than is necessary or good for one. **greedy** having *greed*: Misers are *greedy* for money.

greet receive with words expressing good wishes or friendship: I was *greeted* at the door by the owner of the house.–The postman *greets* everybody with a smile. **greeting** words spoken on meeting a person, or written expressing good wishes: We send *greetings* to all our friends at Christmas.

grenade (gre-nade) a small bomb either thrown, or fired from a rifle: Our company attacked the enemy trenches with hand-*grenades*.

grid 1. a system by which electricity is carried over the whole country by cables stretched between high pylons. 2. a network of lines on a map. 3. a grating.

grief deep sorrow: This misfortune has been a great *grief* to him. **grieve** cause *grief* to, be filled with *grief*: You have *grieved* me with your bad conduct. **grievance** something which causes one to *grieve*, or to be unhappy: We should like to hear all your *grievances*. **grievous** severe: The prisoner was accused of causing *grievous* bodily harm.

grill 1. cook by keeping directly under a flame or heat: Shall I *grill* the sausages? 2. a room in a restaurant in which *grilled* dishes are served. 3. question very closely for a long period: The prisoner was *grilled* for several hours. **grille** a barred gate enclosing a cell, a prison, a counter etc.

grim solemn, stern, severe: The boys climbed the mountain with *grim* determination.

grime dirt, coating the surface of an object: The ornaments were found to be covered with a layer of *grime*. **grimy** dirty, covered with *grime*: I must wash my *grimy* hands before dinner.

grind *ground* 1. crush into small pieces: The miller *grinds* the wheat into flour. 2. Sharpen by rubbing on stone: I cannot cut down the tree until my axe has been *ground*. **grinder** a thing or a person who *grinds*: The organ-*grinder grinds* out a tune. **grindstone** a circular stone turned on an axle on which tools are sharpened.

grip 1. grasp and hold firmly: You must *grip* the oars tightly when you row. 2. a tight hold: Don't lose your *grip* on the oar. 3. understanding: After three weeks' study he had a good *grip* of the subject. 4. something which *grips*: May I have a card of hair-*grips* please? 5. power, mastery: They remained all night in the *grip* of fear.

gristle whitish, tough tissue found in meat: The meat was too full of *gristle* to chew.

grit 1. minute particles of sand or stone: As they walked along the wind blew *grit* in their faces. 2. courage, pluck: The climbers showed their *grit* by holding on to the rock face.

grizzled (griz-zled) having grey hair: 'To the boy Caesar send this *grizzled* head' (Shakespeare, *Antony and Cleopatra*). **grizzly** a large, fierce grey bear living in North America.

groan 1. make a low sound, usually caused by pain: The injured passengers lay *groaning* in the darkness. 2. the low sound made by *groaning*: We heard their *groans* and set out to rescue them. 3. make a sound resembling a *groan*: The heavy machinery *groaned* to a halt.

grocer (gro-cer) a person who keeps a shop, selling tea, sugar, flour, spices, and other articles of household use. **grocery** the trade of a *grocer*: My parents have recently bought a *grocery* business. **groceries** all the things a *grocer* sells: Have you remembered to buy the *groceries* this week?

groom 1. a person who takes charge of horses. 2. a man who has just been married or is about to be married: We all drank the health of the bride*groom*. 3. feed, brush and care for a horse: This horse badly needs *grooming*. **well-groomed** well-dressed and of attractive appearance.

groove 1. a long hollow cut into the surface of metal or wood (see *gouge*). 2. the line cut into the surface of a gramophone record along which the needle slides to produce the sound.

grope feel one's way or search for things one cannot see: The lamp went out and the children were left *groping* in the dark.

ground 1. the surface of the earth, the soil: Lie on the *ground*!—I have planted the seeds in the *ground*. 2. land set apart for a special purpose: Large *grounds* surround the house.—We spent the afternoon on the cricket-*ground*. 3. reasons for saying or doing something: On what *grounds* does the witness base his evidence? 4. the surface on which a design has been drawn: Our flag consists of a blue cross on a white *ground*. 5. touch the bottom of the sea, touch or remain on the land: All the aircraft have been *grounded* because of high winds. 6. a fundamental knowledge: My son has had a good *grounding* in foreign languages. **groundless** without reason: Your fears of failure are quite *groundless*.

group 1. a number of persons or objects placed together: The children formed themselves in *groups* of six.—Can you tell me the names of the flowers in this *group*? 2. put or gather into *groups*: These shells are *grouped* according to their colour.

grouse 1. a wild bird which lives on moors and is shot for sport. 2. grumble or sulk.

grow *grew, grown, growing* 1. become larger, increase in size: Corn *grows* well in these fields.—My cousin is *growing* faster than I am. 2. cultivate; allow to grow: Last year we started to *grow* mushrooms in the cellar.—The old man has *grown* a beard. 3. change: It is *growing* dark.—As the boy *grows* older he also *grows* taller.

growl 1. make a deep fierce sound in the throat: Why does the dog *growl* when I pat it? 2. say something in a deep unpleasant voice: 'I don't care what you do!' he *growled*. 3. a fierce low sound; an angry exclamation: He answered with an angry *growl*.

grub 1. larva of certain insects. 2. dig something out of the ground: The men spent the morning *grubbing* around the field.

grudge 1. be unwilling to give or grant: I would go to London but I *grudge* paying the fare. 2. a feeling of dislike, jealousy or spite against a person: He bears me a *grudge* because he thinks I cheated.

gruesome (grue-some) making one shudder with horror: He told a *gruesome* story about medieval forms of torture.

gruff harsh and deep in sound: He suddenly heard a *gruff* voice behind him.

grumble (grum-ble) 1. complain and find fault in a bad-tempered way: He *grumbled* at the waiter because the meal was cold. 2. a complaint or complaints made in a bad temper: He takes all his *grumbles* to the minister.

guarantee (guar-an-tee) 1. a promise that something supplied will be satisfactory or that things will be done: We give you a *guarantee* that the train will arrive on time. 2. promise to do something should another person fail: I have *guaranteed* payment of this debt. 3. something offered to make sure that payment will be made: Banks often accept the deeds of property and insurance policies as *guarantees*.

guard 1. protect from danger or interference: Sentries were posted to *guard* the camp and two men *guarded* the prisoners. 2. take care to prevent: Do all you can to *guard* against losing your money. 3. a person or persons keeping watch: He slipped past the *guards* when they were not watching. 4. a person employed to look after a train, a lighthouse, a gaol, human life etc. 5. an object designed to protect people or objects from harm or damage: A fire-*guard* should always be used when children are in a room. **guardian** a person who is legally responsible for someone under age or not able to look after his property: When Mary's parents died her uncle became her *guardian*.

guerrilla (guer-ril-la) a person fighting for a cause who is not a member of a regular army: *Guerrillas* move quickly from place to place and may attack unexpectedly. **guerrilla war** a war carried on by people who are not members of regular armies.

guess 1. give an opinion based not on what one knows but on what one thinks may be true: I would *guess* your age to be about 20.–You're wrong; *guess* again! 2. an opinion formed in this way: How many marbles have I in my hand? You have three *guesses*.

guest 1. a person staying for a meal or for a period of time at another person's house: How many *guests* are invited to her wedding? 2. a person staying at an hotel, inn, or boarding house. **paying guest** a person staying at a private house and paying for board.

guide 1. a person who shows others the way: A *guide* had to be hired to take the expedition through the jungle. 2. a person who shows others round a building, exhibition etc. 3. anything that helps to influence actions: Always let your conscience be your *guide*. 4. a book or some reading matter to help one to find one's way: I bought a *guide* to the exhibition. 5. act as a *guide*: Who will *guide* us across the moor? **guidance** *guiding*, being *guided*: We are willing to accept your *guidance*.

guilt having done wrong and deserving to be punished: After being questioned the prisoner admitted his *guilt*. **guilty** to blame for wrong done: The jury brought in a verdict of *guilty*.

guitar (gui-tar) a musical instrument having six strings which are plucked with the fingers.

gulf a part of the sea partly surrounded by land: Much of the world's oil comes from the states around the Persian *Gulf*.

gull a large sea-bird with webbed feet: In winter the *gulls* fly over the land in search of food.

gullet (gul-let) the passage through which food passes from the mouth to the stomach: Harry found he had a fish-bone stuck fast in his *gullet*.

gully (gul-ly) 1. a small valley cut by rain-water: In the heavy storm the water poured down the *gully*. 2. a gutter specially made to carry water off a building: Every autumn we clean out the *gullies* for the winter.

gulp 1. swallow quickly and greedily: He *gulped* his food, and then ran off to catch the bus. 2. a single act of swallowing: He drank half a glass of water at one *gulp*.

gum 1. a sticky substance used mainly for sticking paper together: *Gum* does not stick as firmly as glue. 2. the flesh in the mouth covering the base of the teeth: When you brush your teeth you should not neglect your *gums*.

gun a weapon which may be small enough to fire bullets or large enough to fire shells and rockets: Muskets, rifles and cannons are *guns*. **gunman** a man who uses a *gun* to attack and rob people. **gunpowder** powder used to fire *guns* and to cause explosions. **gunner** a soldier in the artillery, a naval officer or a member of an air-crew in charge of *guns*.

gurgle (gur-gle) 1. a sound like that of bubbles rising through water: They sat, listening to the *gurgle* of the brook. 2. make a bubbling sound: At the sight of the doll the baby *gurgled* with pleasure.

gush 1. rush or burst out suddenly: Tears *gushed* from her eyes before I had a chance to explain what had happened. 2. a sudden flow or outburst: At last the prospectors were rewarded by a powerful *gush* of oil.

gust a sudden blast of wind: As he turned the corner a *gust* almost blew him off his feet.

gutter (gut-ter) a channel which carries away water: In autumn the *gutters* are often blocked with fallen leaves.

gymnasium (or **gym**) (gym-na-sium) a room which contains all kinds of apparatus for exercise and body-building: The master took us to the *gym* for rope-climbing.

gypsy see **gipsy**

habit (hab-it) 1. something which a person does often, and may find difficult to give up: I have formed the *habit* of rising early.—It is possible to cure the *habit* of smoking. 2. a dress worn for a special purpose: The monk stood before the altar wearing a brown *habit*.

hack cut or chop clumsily: We cleared a way through the wood by *hacking* at the branches. **hacksaw** a saw used for cutting metal. **hacking cough** a deep, harsh cough.

haggard (hag-gard) looking pale and worn as if from want, hunger, overwork or suffering: At the door of the hut appeared a woman with three lean and *haggard* children.

hail 1. salute or greet, welcome: The soldiers *hailed* him as their leader. 2. call: I shall *hail* a taxi. 3. originally come from: I live in London but I *hail* from Scotland. 4. frozen rain falling from the sky: The *hail* battered against the windowpane. 5. a shower of anything: A *hail* of blows fell on him as he passed through the crowd.—From the enemy lines came a *hail* of bullets. 6. fall as *hail* or like *hail*: Don't go out yet; it's *hailing*.

hair the natural covering of the human head and on the skins of some animals and plants: The young man has black *hair* but his father's *hair* is grey. **hairy** covered with *hair*.

half 1. one of two equal parts: *Half* of four is two; *half* of six is three. 2. up to, down or about *half*: This box is nearly *half* full. 3. partly: I must have been *half*-asleep. **half-brother, half-sister** a brother or sister by one parent only. **half-back** (in football or hockey) one who plays between the forwards and the backs. **half-time** the short space of time between the two *halves* of a game. **halfway** the distance: 'When they were *halfway* up the hill they were neither up nor down' (from *The Grand Old Duke of York*).

hall 1. space at the entrance of a building which opens on to various rooms: The front door opened and we entered a large *hall*. 2. a large building or room where public functions (concerts, meetings etc.) are held: We went to a concert at the Albert *Hall*. 3. a large medieval country house: The *Hall* was the centre of village life.

halt 1. a stop: The party came to a *halt* at the foot of the hill. 2. come to a stop: The party *halted* at the foot of the hill. 3. bring to a stop: The leader *halted* the party at the foot of the hill.

halter (halt-er) 1. a rope or strap put round the head of a horse so that it can be led. 2. a rope used for hanging a person: 'Enter Cade's followers with *halters* round their necks' (stage directions, Shakespeare, *Henry VI*, part 2).

ham the upper part of a pig's back leg: *Ham* is often eaten salted and smoked.—Do you like *ham* and eggs?

hamlet (ham-let) a small village or group of houses, often without a church: The woodcutter lived in a *hamlet* in the depth of the forest.

hammer (ham-mer) 1. a tool with a metal head for breaking things and driving in nails. 2. strike with a *hammer*: The sole has come off my shoe; will you please *hammer* it on for me? 3. strike: He *hammered* at the door with his fists.

hammock (ham-mock) a hanging bed or couch made of canvas or netting which may be swung by means of ropes at each end: In the garden is a *hammock* which swings from two trees.

hamster (ham-ster) a small, short-tailed animal; a rodent which is kept by children as a pet.

hand 1. the part of the body at the end of the arm, consisting of a palm, the thumb and four fingers: What are you holding in your *hand*? 2. someone who is employed to work with his *hands*: 120 *hands* work in this factory. 3. a pointer on a dial: The clock has an hour *hand* and a minute *hand*. 4. direction: On every *hand* the crowd yelled loudly. 5. a number of cards in a card game given to one person: There are three aces in his *hand*. 6. give, pass: Please *hand* me the hammer. **handy** skilful, easy to reach: Are you *handy* with your fists? Then have your boxing gloves *handy*.

handle (han-dle) 1. the part of a tool or utensil by which it may be held: Careful! The *handle* of the pan is hot. 2. hold or touch with the hands: Please do not *handle* the exhibits (notice in an exhibition). 3. control, manage: Hundreds of policemen were needed to *handle* the crowd. 4. buy and sell: We *handle* all kinds of sporting goods.

handsome (hand-some) 1. good-looking: A *handsome* young man came into the room. 2. generous: The hospital has received a *handsome* gift of two ambulances.

hang 1. attach something so that it is held only from above: His coat was *hanging* on the hook. 2. place something so that it *hangs*: *Hang* your coat on the hook. 3. be put to death or die by *hanging* with a rope round the neck: In olden days highwaymen were *hanged* for their crimes. **hanger** a frame on which clothes are *hung*.

happy (hap-py) pleased, content: Are you *happy* with your work?–We should be *happy* if you would come to dinner tomorrow. **happiness** being happy or pleased; gladness: The rain could not spoil our *happiness*.

harass (har-ass) 1. trouble, torment, worry: He felt *harassed* through lack of money. 2. attack again and again: We *harassed* the enemy until they were forced to retreat.

harbour (har-bour) 1. a stretch of water along the shore where ships may shelter: The ship has gone into *harbour* for repairs. 2. give shelter or refuge to: I refuse to *harbour* those who flee from justice. 3. keep in mind: For years he has *harboured* thoughts of revenge.

hard 1. firm, solid: the ground is frozen *hard* as iron. 2. difficult, not easy to understand: Is this sum too *hard* for you? 3. involving energy: He has worked *hard* all day. 4. full of unhappiness and suffering: The animals on the moor had a *hard* winter.–We are passing through *hard* times. 5. strict: You are serving a *hard* master. 6. with determination: We work *hard* and we play *hard*. 7. with force: He struck the iron *hard* with his hammer. **harden** make or become *hard*: If you leave the glue for ten minutes it will *harden*. **hardship** suffering: We have learnt to bear *hardship* with patience. **hardware** 1. metal goods such as nails, pans, kettles, locks etc. 2. the *hard* parts in a computer system.

hardy 1. strong and healthy: These *hardy* plants will live through the winter. 2. bold and daring: A few *hardy* volunteers entered the enemy lines.

harm 1. hurt, injury, damage: No *harm* will come to those who obey the rules. 2. hurt or injure: If you pat the dog he will not *harm* you. **harmful** causing *harm*: Too much exercise can be *harmful*. **harmless** doing no *harm*: When the detonator was removed the bomb became *harmless*.

harmonica (har-mon-i-ca) a mouth organ; an instrument which produces notes by blowing and sucking through small holes.

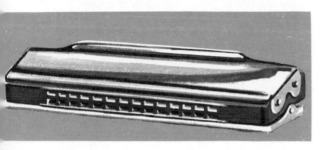

harmony (har-mo-ny) 1. notes sounded together to give a pleasing effect: The choir sang in four-part *harmony*. 2. colours put together to give a pleasing effect: There is a pleasant *harmony* of colours in this picture. 3. agreement between the tastes, feelings, opinions etc. of people: If we work in *harmony* we shall succeed. **harmonious** in *harmony*: We have arranged the furniture to produce a *harmonious* effect. **harmonize** make *harmony*, bring things into *harmony*: Do the curtains *harmonize* with the wallpaper design?

harness (har-ness) 1. the straps by which an animal is attached to a cart, plough or other vehicle: Take down the *harness* from the wall and put it on the horse. 2. put on *harness*: The horse has already been *harnessed* and is ready for work. 3. use rivers, tides, air currents etc. to serve human needs: Mankind has now *harnessed* the power within the atom.

harp a musical instrument consisting of strings on a frame, and played with the fingers. **harpist** a person who plays a *harp*. **harpsichord** a musical instrument resembling a piano, the strings of which are plucked by leather or quill points moved by keys.

harpoon (har-poon) 1. a spear with barbs that stick backwards from the point: *Harpoons* are fired from guns and used to catch whales and large fish. 2. strike with a *harpoon*.

harsh 1. rough and disagreeable to the eye, the ear, the touch or the taste: He answered in a *harsh* voice. 2. severe, cruel: Ten years in prison was a *harsh* punishment for the crime he had committed.

harvest (har-vest) 1. the time for taking in the crops: The *harvest* has been completed and the summer is over. 2. the amount of grain, hay etc. collected: If the weather stays fine we shall have a good *harvest*. 3. take in the crops: We shall be *harvesting* the wheat during the next two weeks. **harvester** a person or a machine that takes in the crops: The farmer has just bought a mechanical *harvester*.

hash meat chopped up and re-cooked: Today *hash* is being served. **make a hash of** do something very badly.

hatch 1. an opening in a door, wall or in a floor which can be closed and covered: We have a *hatch* between the kitchen and the dining-room. 2. cause young to break out of an egg: We hope the chickens will be *hatched* today. 3. (of eggs) break and allow the young to come out: Ten of the thirteen eggs have *hatched*. 4. make a plot or scheme: What surprise have you *hatched* today?

hatchet a small axe with a short handle: Take the *hatchet* and chop this wood for the fire.

hate 1. dislike very much: 'Your majesty hath no just cause to *hate* me' (Shakespeare, *Henry IV, part 2*). 2. **hatred** a great dislike: Do you still think of him with *hatred*?

haughty (haugh-ty) proud, showing one has a high opinion of oneself: The king received the messenger with a *haughty* stare.

haul 1. move by pulling: We *hauled* the logs to the bank of the river. 2. a good pull: One more *haul* and the great rock moved. 3. the amount taken through effort: A record *haul* of fish was brought in.

haunt 1. visit often after death as a spirit or ghost: The old house is said to be *haunted*. 2. return often to the thoughts: He is continually *haunted* by the fear of being robbed. 3. a place often visited: This lonely glen is one of his favourite *haunts*.

have had 1. possess, own: I have a pen and a pencil. 2. take: Do you *have* butter on your toast? 3. get: You will *have* your money back. 4. cause to be done: When are you *having* your shoes mended? 5. hold: Let's *have* a party this week. 6. meet with: He *had* great difficulty in climbing the stairs. 7. showing an action that is or is not yet past: I *have* finished reading the book.–I *haven't* drunk my coffee yet. 8. receive: We are *having* the Smiths to dinner this week. **have to** must: I *have to* feed the cat.

hawk 1. a large strong bird that eats other birds and animals. 2. go from house to house selling things: Have you seen a man *hawking* firewood? **hawker** a person who *hawks* things 'Hawkers not admitted on these premises' (notice outside a factory).

hazard (haz-ard) 1. a risk or danger: 'FIRE *HAZARD*. Do not throw down lighted cigarettes' (notice at the entrance to a wood). 2. risk: The fireman *hazarded* his life to save his comrade.

haze slight mist: *Haze* often occurs during the early morning. **hazy** rather misty, vague, confused in mind: When he received the news he was *hazy* about what to do next.

he a pronoun used instead of the name of a boy, man or male animal: Spot is a good dog; *he* never bites.

head 1. the part of the body above the neck which contains eyes, ears, nose and mouth: He fell asleep as soon as his *head* touched the pillow. 2. that side of a coin on which the head of the ruler appears: '*Heads*', called the captain as the coin was tossed. 3. ability: Have you a good *head* for figures? No, I have a good *head* for heights. 4. the part of an article which is like a *head*: He hit the nail on the *head*. 5. top: The name at the *head* of the page is that of a boy at the *head* of the class. 6. chief: The President is the *head* of state. 7. front: He walked at the *head* of the column. 8. a point of land jutting out into the sea: Have you ever been on Flamborough *Head*? 9. the place where a boil bursts: The *head* of the boil must be lanced. 10. be at the *head*: The procession was *headed* by the Mayor. **headmaster** the master in charge of a school. **headline** the top line on a newspaper sheet, usually in large print. **headway** progress: We shall not make much *headway* until the clouds have gone. **heading** the title or words at the top of a piece of written or printed matter. **headlong** head first: He tripped and fell *headlong* into the pit.

health the condition of the body or mind: Good *health* depends on good food and exercise. **healthy** in good *health*, bringing good *health*: To be *healthy* it helps to live in a *healthy* climate.

heap 1. a pile, a great quantity: Who put that *heap* of bricks in front of our garden gate? 2. pile up: The sand had been *heaped* against the wall.

hear 1. notice a sound with the ears: Did you *hear* what I said? 2. attend to, listen to: Now we will *hear* what you have to tell us. 3. learn about, have news: Have you *heard* from your sister in Australia? **hearing** the ability to *hear*: His *hearing* is not good.

hearse a carriage specially made to carry a coffin at a funeral: Twenty mourners followed the *hearse*.

heart 1. the muscular organ that pumps the blood throughout the body: As long as we live our *hearts* continue to beat. 2. the centre of feelings or emotions: We talk of people being hard-*hearted*, kind-*hearted*, soft-*hearted* or broken-*hearted*. 3. courage: I hadn't the *heart* to turn the beggar from the door. 4. the centre: The *heart* of the celery is the most delicious part.—They were lost in the *heart* of the jungle. 5. one of the four suits of playing-cards: Do you have the king of *hearts*? **by heart** from memory: Learn this poem *by heart*. **heart failure** when the *heart* suddenly ceases to beat. **hearty** strong, large, cheerful: He answered with a *hearty* laugh.

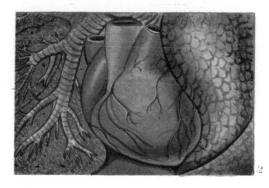

hearth 1. the floor of a fireplace: I have just swept the *hearth*. 2. the fireplace: We sat round the *hearth* and told ghost stories.

heat 1. being hot: 'Fear no more the *heat* o' the sun' (Shakespeare, *Cymbeline*). 2. feeling, emotion: The chairman spoke with great *heat* on the subject. 3. make hot: Have you *heated* the water for the bath? **heater** a device for *heating*.

heath a stretch of wild, flat, uncultivated land, often covered with small shrubs, coarse grass and heather: Macbeth saw three witches on the *heath*. **heather** a small plant with tiny white or purple flowers.

heave 1. lift with force: They *heaved* the large crate on to the cart. 2. lift and throw: He suddenly *heaved* a brick through the shopwindow. 3. utter: The poor woman *heaved* a sigh. 4. rising and falling regularly: Our ship rides on the *heaving* billows. 5. a pull, a throw: All together with a *heave*!

heavy (heav-y) 1. weighing a great deal: The porter will carry your *heavy* luggage.—I wear my *heavy* overcoat in cold weather. 2. very great: We flew through a *heavy* thunderstorm.

hedge 1. a line of small trees or bushes planted together to form a fence: We sat down in the shade of the *hedge*. 2. put a *hedge* round: They *hedged* the field to keep in the cattle. 3. prevent a person doing what he wishes: I feel *hedged* in by all these rules. **hedgehog** a small animal covered with spines that eats insects.

heed 1. listen, pay attention: He doesn't *heed* what people say to him. 2. attention: Pay *heed* to what I say. **heedless** paying no attention: They pressed on, *heedless* of danger.

heel 1. the back part of the foot: I have a blister on my *heel* through walking. 2. repair the *heel* of a sock or shoe: My shoes badly need *heeling*. 3. lean to one side: The boat *heeled* over without warning.

hefty (hef-ty) big, strong: We need three *hefty* men.—Give the rope a *hefty* pull!

heifer (heif-er) a young cow that has not had a calf.

height 1. the distance from bottom to top: What is the *height* of this door? 2. a high place: 'Come down, O maid, from yonder mountain *height*' (Tennyson). 3. the greatest: It would be the *height* of folly to go out when the storm is at its *height*.

heir a person who has the right to another's property when that person dies: I am my father's rightful *heir*.–Who is *heir* to the throne? **heiress** a woman who is *heir* to property. **heirloom** a valuable article handed down from one generation to another: This brooch is a valuable family *heirloom*.

helicopter (hel-i-cop-ter) an aircraft that flies by means of large blades which revolve above it: *Helicopters* can rise and land in very small spaces. **heliport** a place where *helicopters* can land passengers, refuel and fly off again.

hell 1. a place or state of punishment of the wicked after death; the opposite to heaven. 2. a state of great misery and suffering.

hello (hel-lo) a friendly greeting, a cry made to attract attention, a word used when one picks up a telephone receiver: *Hello, hello, who's there?*

helm the wheel used to steer a boat: We are safe with the captain at the *helm*. **helmsman** the man who steers the boat.

helmet (hel-met) a covering worn to protect the head: Every motorcyclist must wear a *helmet* in case of accident on the road.

help 1. do part of another person's work to make it easier: I will *help* you with your arithmetic. 2. serve food: Would you please *help* me to a little more meat.–*Help* yourself. 3. stop, prevent: I can't *help* catching a cold every winter. 4. assistance, aid: You wouldn't have done it without my *help*. 5. a person or thing which has *helped*: You have been a great *help* to me. **helpful** giving *help*: He was *helpful* in lending money. **helpless** without *help*, unable to *help* oneself: I would be *helpless* without my car.

hem 1. the edge of a piece of cloth, folded back and sewn: Please put up the *hem* on this skirt. 2. put up a *hem*: The dress was *hemmed* before ironing. **hemstitch** an ornamental stitch made by gathering threads together and tying them.

hemisphere (hem-i-sphere) half a sphere, ball or globe; half the earth: We divide the earth into the northern and southern *hemispheres*.

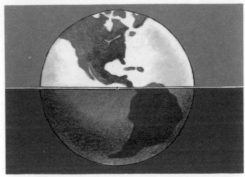

hen the female of the farmyard fowl: The *hens* have laid more eggs than usual today.

her 1. a word used instead of the name of a girl, woman or female animal: She loves music; play *her* a tune. 2. belonging to *her*: I know she is here; this is *her* coat. **hers** belonging to *her*: Is this coat *hers*? **herself**: She ought to be ashamed of *herself*.

herald 1. a person who, in olden days, carried messages from one ruler to another: 'Here comes the *herald* of the French' (Shakespeare, *Henry V*). 2. something which announces: The cuckoo is the *herald* of the spring. 3. announce: The call of the cuckoo *heralds* the coming of spring.

herb 1. a plant which withers during winter leaving only the root alive. 2. a plant whose leaves, flowers or roots are used for flavouring food, or for making medicines or scents. **herbal** having to do with *herbs*: My mother believes in *herbal* remedies. **herbalist** a person who grows or sells *herbs* and *herbal* preparations.

herd 1. a large number of cows, bison, deer and similar animals feeding or travelling together: A *herd* of buffalo approached the bank of the stream. 2. a person who looks after cattle and other animals: Here comes the *goatherd* with his flock. 3. gather animals together: When evening came the cows were *herded* into the farmyard.

here at or to this place: Stand *here*; come *here*!–*Here* we are! **hereabouts** near this place: Does Mr Jones live *hereabouts*? **hereafter** after this time: 'You shall know more *hereafter*' (Shakespeare, *Twelfth Night*).

hermit (her-mit) a person who lives alone, away from all others, to lead a religious or quiet life: Many early Christian saints were *hermits*. **hermitage** the dwelling-place of a *hermit*.

hero 1. a man or boy who has done some brave deed: The brave fireman was given a *hero*'s welcome. 2. the chief character in a story or play: Oliver Twist is the *hero* of a novel by Charles Dickens. **heroic** done by, like, or fit for a *hero*: We love to read of *heroic* deeds. **heroism** great valour, courage: The rescue from the burning building was an act of great *heroism*. **heroine** a female *hero*: Nurse Cavell was a *heroine* of the First World War.

herring (her-ring) a small fish caught in the sea and used for food.

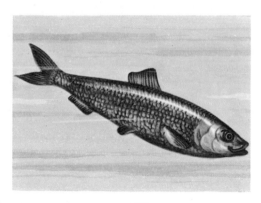

hesitate (hes-i-tate) doubt, stop for a short time as if not certain whether to go on: I've thought about joining the Scouts but I'm still *hesitating*.–He *hesitated* for a moment before flinging open the door. **hesitation** the act of *hesitating*: 'Not guilty,' he answered without the slightest *hesitation*.

hibernate (hi-ber-nate) sleep all through the winter, as some animals do: Bats and hedgehogs are animals which *hibernate*.

hiccup (hic-cup) or **hiccough** 1. a sudden stopping of the breath which sounds like a light cough: Do you know how to cure a *hiccup*? 2. make a *hiccup*: I've been *hiccupping* ever since breakfast.

hieroglyph (hi-er-o-glyph) a picture of an object representing a sound, word or part of a word: The writing of the ancient Egyptians was in *hieroglyphs*. **hieroglyphic** written in *hieroglyphs*: Can you read this *hieroglyphic* script?

high 1. having an extent upwards: This wall is too *high*. 2. excellent, chief: He is a man of very *high* reputation.–The case is to be tried in the *High* Court. 3. near the top of the scale in music: He can sing both *high* and low. 4. expensive, costing money or effort: I have paid a *high* price for my information. 5. going bad: When I bought this meat I didn't realize that it was already *high*. **high-fidelity** (of radio etc.) giving a sound as near as possible to the original (shortened to **hi-fi**). **highlands** country far above sea level. **high-pitched** sounding *high* up the musical scale: This song is too *high-pitched* (or pitched too *high*) for him to sing. **highroad, highway** a main road. **highwayman** a robber stopping travellers on the *highway*. **Highness** the title of honour given to royal persons.

hike 1. a long walk in the country: They went for a *hike* in the Lake District. 2. walk long distances: I *hiked* to the next town. **hiker** one who *hikes*: On the way he met a group of *hikers*.

hill 1. a place where the ground rises above the surrounding land: From the top of the *hill* we could see five towns. 2. a slope: 'Jack and Jill went up the *hill*' (nursery rhyme). 3. a heap of earth made by ants, moles etc. **hilly** having many *hills*: Derbyshire is a *hilly* county.

hilt the handle of a sword or dagger: He plunged the knife up to the *hilt* into the cushion.

him a boy, man or male animal: We are doing this to please *him*.–When did you last see *him*?–The dog is hungry, give *him* a bone. **himself** *him*: He washed *himself* before going out.

hind (of wheels, legs, parts etc.) the back: The horse is lame in the *hind* legs.—He gave it a pat on its *hind*quarters (the parts round the tail). **hindmost** farthest behind, nearest the back: We were *hindmost* in the queue.

hinder (hin-der) delay, get in the way of: Work on the road has been *hindered* by bad weather. **hindrance** something which delays: The shortage of bricks has been a *hindrance* to our plans for building the house.

hinge 1. a joint on which a door, a gate or a lid can be made to open or shut: They have oiled the *hinges* to stop the door squeaking. 2. depend: The success of our team *hinges* on the conduct of the players.

hint 1. suggest something without mentioning it directly: They *hinted* that it might be possible to borrow the money. 2. a piece of advice: Here is a *hint* for taking oil stains out of clothes.—All you need do is drop a *hint*, and I'll go.

hip the part of the body where the legs are joined to the trunk.

hippopotamus (hip-po-pot-a-mus) a large, plant-eating animal with a huge head, short legs and thick skin that lives in the rivers of Africa.

hire 1. obtain something or the help of somebody for a fee: The hall can be *hired* for the evening. 2. money paid for the use of goods or services: How much is the *hire* of this car for the day?

his belonging to him: Is this *his* bicycle? Is this bicycle *his*? No, it's mine.

hiss 1. make a sound like that of a long 'sss' or like steam rushing through a small opening: Steam *hissed* from the radiator and the engine stopped. 2. show dislike, or disapproval by making this sound: Every comedian has been *hissed* off the stage at some time. 3. a *hissing* sound: With a *hiss* the snake raised its head.

history 1. the story or record of what has happened in the past: Which period of *history* do you prefer, ancient or modern?—Have you studied the *history* of either this town, or this company? 2. a book or account of past events: This week a new *History* of England has appeared. 3. the story of a person or a thing: Last week I read 'The *History* of Mr Polly', by H. G. Wells.' **historian** a person who writes about *history*. **historic** important in *history*: The battle of Waterloo was an *historic* event. **historical** true, not imagined or in fiction: The characters in the novel were all *historical*.

hit 1. strike with force: The car *hit* a lamppost and rolled over. 2. find: At last I have *hit* on the true explanation. 3. score in cricket: The captain *hit* 50 runs. 4. wounded, damaged: Our firm has been hard *hit* by the recent strikes. 5. a blow: A violent *hit* on the chin knocked him out. 6. a successful performance: His song has been a great *hit*.

hitch 1. pull up: *Hitch* up your trousers! 2. fasten, tie or become tied: It was time to *hitch* the dog team to the sleigh. 3. a kind of knot used by sailors. 4. a short delay: There was a *hitch* in the proceedings when the best man misplaced the wedding ring. **hitch a lift,** stop motorists and ask for a lift. **hitch-hiker** a hiker who *hitches* lifts.

hive 1. a box specially made for bees to live in. 2. a number of busy people: The factory was a *hive* of industry.

hoard 1. a secret store: The miser's *hoard* of coins was found in a hole under the stairs. 2. store secretly: Do you know where your dog *hoards* his bones?

hoarding (hoard-ing) 1. a temporary wooden fence round a building which is being erected. 2. a board on which advertisements and notices are posted.

hoax 1. play a mischievous trick on somebody: He was *hoaxed* into going to the football stadium when there was no match. 2. a mischievous trick: Who played that *hoax* on him?

hobby (hob-by) something one does out of interest in spare time: Wine-making is his favourite *hobby*.

hoe 1. a tool for use in the garden: A *hoe* is used to loosen the soil and uproot weeds. 2. work with a *hoe*: Has he *hoed* the carrot-bed?

hoist 1. lift up, usually with ropes and pulleys: The grand piano had to be *hoisted* up and pushed through an open window. 2. a device for lifting things: The car was put on the *hoist* so that it could be inspected.

hold *held* 1. keep the body or part of it in one position: *Hold* out your hand. 2. take something and keep it for a while: Shall I *hold* your coat?—Don't *hold* him back if he wants to go. 3. contain: Will this wardrobe *hold* her dresses? 4. keep back: A diver needs to *hold* his breath for long periods. 5. organize, conduct: They are *holding* a meeting to decide on future action. 6. remain as it is or was: How long will this fine weather *hold*?—Will the rope *hold* for another five minutes? 7. fasten: The shelves are *held* together by screws. 8. occupy, be in possession of: He *holds* most of the land in this field. 9. the act of *holding*, grasp: He lost his *hold* and fell down the cliff. 10. something that gives a place to *hold* or grasp: There are very few *holds* on this side of the cliff. 11. the part of a ship where cargo is stored: The ship sailed home with a cargo of wheat in her *hold*. **holder** an article specially made to *hold* something: Has anybody seen my cigarette-*holder*?

holiday (hol-i-day) 1. a day when all work is suspended: Christmas Day and Boxing Day are national *holidays*. 2. a period when one does not go to work: I'm spending my *holiday* at Torquay this year.

hollow (hol-low) 1. with an empty space inside: A cricket ball is solid but a tennis-ball is *hollow*. 2. sounding as if it comes from something *hollow*: He answered in a *hollow* voice. 3. a little valley: The *hollow* was yellow with primroses. 4. make a *hollow* in: They *hollowed* out the ground to make a fishpond.

holster (hol-ster) a leather holder for a pistol or revolver, attached to a belt or saddle.

holy (ho-ly) 1. having to do with God or religion: Most Christians read the *Holy* Bible, attend *Holy* Communion and regard Jerusalem as the *Holy* City. 2. having given oneself up to religion: This *holy* man lives a *holy* life. 3. sacred: 'The place on which you stand is *holy* ground' (*The Book of Exodus*).

home 1. the place where one lives: My *home* is in the north of England. 2. a place where people or animals are cared for: The dogs' *home* is not far from the nursing *home*. 3. the place where an animal or plant lives and grows: India is the *home* of the tiger and the Indian elephant. 4. having to do with one's own country: The government supports *home* industries and hopes to increase *home* trade. 5. having to do with a house: The building societies are granting more *home* loans this year. 6. at or to one's *home* or one's own country: He has gone *home*.—'Though your lads are far away they dream of *home*' (from a song of the 1914–18 war). **homely** simple, making one think of *home*: his parents are *homely* people. **homeless** having no *home*. **homesick** sad at being away from *home*. **homeward** towards *home*: 'The ploughman *homeward* plods his weary way' (Gray's *Elegy*). **homework** the part of a lesson to be prepared outside school hours.

honest (hon-est) telling the truth, not cheating, fair: He is *honest* in all he does.– I will give you my *honest* opinion. **honesty** being *honest*: 'I know thou art full of love and *honesty*' (Shakespeare, *Othello*).

honey (hon-ey) the sweet, sticky liquid made by bees: Will you have *honey* or marmalade on your bread? **honeycomb** the small six-sided cells made of wax in which the bees store their *honey*. **honeymoon** the holiday taken by a newly married couple: We spent our *honeymoon* in Paris. **honeysuckle** a climbing plant with sweet-smelling flowers.

honour (hon-our) 1. respect, admire: '*Honour* thy father and thy mother' (The Ten Commandments). 2. pay respect: The dead soldier was *honoured* by a military funeral. 3. high respect: They held a dinner in *honour* of the President. 4. good character: He is a man of *honour*. 5. a polite title, especially of certain judges: Would your *Honour* please come this way? **honourable** deserving of *honour*: 'Brutus is an *honourable* man' (Shakespeare, *Julius Caesar*).

hook 1. a piece of metal or other material which is curved so that things can be caught and held on it: Each of these two curtains is hung by ten *hooks*. 2. fasten or catch with a *hook*: He sat all afternoon on the river bank but *hooked* only one fish. 3. shape like a *hook*: This walking stick has a *hooked* handle.

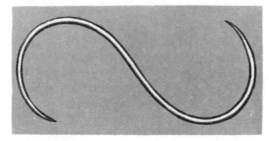

hooligan (hool-i-gan) a member of a gang of men or boys who makes trouble in streets and other public places.

hoop 1. a circular band of wood, wire or metal: A barrel is made of many pieces of curved wood secured by *hoops*.– The little boy was bowling his *hoop*. 2. a circular frame once used to make skirts stand out. 3. a circular ring over which paper has been stretched: The trainer held up a *hoop* and the dog jumped through it.

hoot 1. the cry made by an owl. 2. (of an owl) make a cry. 3. make a cry like that of an owl; make fun of, mock: The audience *hooted* so loudly that the speaker's words were drowned.

hope 1. a wish for something to happen, and a feeling that it will happen: We have every *hope* that the brooch will be found. 2. expect and wish: We *hope* to see you at our next annual meeting. **hopeful** believing that a thing will happen: Our team is *hopeful* of victory. **hopeless** having no *hope*, giving no reason to *hope*: All attempts at rescue are *hopeless*.

horizon (ho-ri-zon) the line where sky and earth or sea appear to meet: At last the sun rose over the eastern *horizon*. **horizontal** in line with or parallel to the *horizon*, level, flat: The lines on our exercise books are *horizontal*.

horn 1. a hard point or spike, sometimes curved, growing out of the heads of cattle and some other animals: 'There was a maiden all forlorn who milked a cow with a crumpled *horn*' (nursery rhyme, *The House that Jack Built*). 2. made of *horn*: My walking stick has a *horn* handle. 3. an instrument played by blowing, once made of *horn*, but now of metal: 'Little Boy Blue, come blow your *horn*' (nursery rhyme). **hornpipe** an English dance once danced by sailors to an instrument called a *hornpipe*.

horoscope (hor-o-scope) a diagram of the position of the stars at the time of a person's birth, believed to show that person's character and possible future.

horrible (hor-ri-ble) or **horrid** terrible: Last night I had a *horrible* dream. **horror** something that makes a person feel terrified: He looked with *horror* at the dreadful scene. **horrify** fill with *horror*: I was *horrified* when you told me you were going.

horse 1. a large, solid-hoofed animal employed to carry a rider or as a beast of burden: The *horse* is one of the most valuable domestic animals. 2. a frame or block on legs used for a special purpose: In the gym we have a vaulting-*horse*.

hose 1. a flexible tube through which water can be forced: I need a long *hose* to water my garden. 2. stockings or tights: 'Your *hose* should be ungartered (Shakespeare, *As You Like It*). **hosier** a person who sells men's socks, shirts, collars, underwear etc. **hosiery** articles sold by a *hosier*.

hospital (hos-pi-tal) a building where the sick and injured are given medical treatment: Last year he spent a fortnight in *hospital*.

hospitality (hos-pi-tal-i-ty) the generous reception and entertainment of guests: We have thoroughly enjoyed your kind *hospitality*. **hospitable** always ready and willing to offer *hospitality* to others.

host 1. a person who receives and entertains guests: Would you please act as *host* at our annual dinner? 2. a person who keeps an inn: Our *host* was a stout, jolly person who smoked a pipe. 3. a large number; an army: There is a *host* of difficulties to be overcome. **hostess** a woman who acts as a *host*. **air-hostess** a woman who sees to the comfort of passengers in an aeroplane.

hostage (host-age) a person taken by an enemy as a guarantee that an agreement will be kept: When no reply was received the bandits threatened to kill their *hostages*.

hostel (host-el) a building in which students, workmen being trained and others may live at a cheap rate: We went for a walking tour in Wales, staying in Youth *Hostels*.

hotel a building where people may have meals and stay the night: Could you please recommend a good *hotel* in this town?

hound 1. a dog with a very keen sense of smell, used for hunting, tracking and racing: The lost children were found with the help of blood*hounds*. 2. follow, worry and persecute: For three years the man was *hounded* by the secret police.

hour 1. sixty minutes; one 24th part of a day: He waited an *hour* at the bus-stop. 2. the time of day: 'Now is the *hour* when we must say goodbye' (song). 3. a period of time: You can contact the manager during office *hours*. **hourly** every *hour*; at any *hour*: The buses run *hourly* on this route.–We are expecting a reply *hourly*.

house 1. a building in which people live: We have bought a *house* in the country. 2. a building used for a special purpose: a cow-*house*, a ware*house*, a bake*house*, a store*house* etc. 3. a family: The British Royal Family belongs to the *House* of Windsor. 4. the audience in a theatre: All this week we have played to full *houses*. 5. have room for people or goods: Can we *house* ten families in these buildings?–Is the room large enough to *house* all your possessions? **household** everybody living in a *house*: The master called all the *household* together to tell them the good news. **housekeeper** a woman who is employed to manage the affairs of a *household*. **housewife** a woman who is head of a family, looks after the *house* and the welfare of the family.

hover (hov-er) stay in or near one place in the air: The hummingbird *hovered* in front of the hibiscus flower. **hovercraft** a vehicle which moves on a cushion of air and can travel over land or water.

howitzer (how-itz-er) a cannon with a short muzzle which fires shells high into the air, falling on the required place.

howl 1. a long loud cry: Do you hear the *howl* of the wolf? 2. make a long, loud cry: The wild wind *howls* across the moor. 3. cry with howling sounds: The speaker was *howled* down and could not be heard.

hub 1. the central part of a wheel into which the spokes fit. 2. a place of importance as being the centre of an industry etc.: Birmingham is the *hub* of the British hardware industry.

huddle crowd close together: The sheep *huddled* together for warmth.

hue colour: The *hue* of his complexion showed that he had spent much of his life in the open air.

hug 1. hold tightly in the arms: The little girl *hugged* her doll. 2. keep close: Our boat *hugged* the shore to avoid the swift currents. 3. a close embrace: She gave the little boy a big *hug*.

huge very large indeed: They were suddenly faced by a *huge* elephant.–This month we have several *huge* bills to pay.

hull 1. the covering of some fruits and seeds, especially peas and beans. 2. the body of a ship: At last the *hull* disappeared below the horizon. 3. take off the outer covering of: We must *hull* the peas before they can be cooked.

hum 1. make a sound like that of bees; sing with the lips closed: You will soon learn the tune if you *hum* it. 2. move about busily: On the morning of our departure the camp *hummed* with activity. 3. a *humming* noise: In the distance we heard the *hum* of men's voices.

human (hu-man) about people or like people: There was no other *human* being on the island. **humane** merciful, kind-hearted: We treat all animals by *humane* methods.–The Royal *Humane* Society was founded in 1774 to help to save people from drowning.

humble (hum-ble) 1. modest, not showing pride in oneself or what one does: He is *humble* enough to admit his mistakes. 2. of low rank: Born of *humble* parents, he became a famous scientist. 3. make a person *humble* or lower his opinion of himself: Our enemies have been *humbled*.

humid (hu-mid) damp (of a climate): It is easy to catch cold in this *humid* air. **humidity** dampness, amount of moisture in the air: The *humidity* of the atmosphere is greatest in the early morning.

humour (hu-mour) 1. power to cause amusement or be amused: You will see the *humour* in this story if you have a sense of *humour*. 2. temper, state of mind: Don't talk to him just now; he's in a bad *humour*. 3. agree with, give way to: If he is in a bad *humour* we'd better *humour* him. **humorous** having *humour*: There are many *humorous* programmes on television.

hump a round lump, a raised place: Some camels have one *hump*, others have two.

hunch 1. a hump. 2. a suspicion: I have a *hunch* that it may lead to success. 3. form a hump with one's back: He was sitting *hunched* over his desk. **hunchback** a person with a hump on his back.

hundred 10 times 10; the number next after 99: He counted up to *100* before turning round. – There were several *hundred* people in the stadium.

hunger (hun-ger) 1. the need for food: The man was faint from *hunger*. 2. a need or desire: Nothing could satisfy his *hunger* for adventure. 3. have a need or desire: 'Blessed are they who *hunger* and thirst after righteousness' (The Gospel of St Matthew). **hungry** needing food or some other satisfaction: The boy is *hungry*; give him a cake.—Some people are *hungry* for riches, others for fame.

hunt 1. chase wild animals either for food or for sport: Prehistoric man lived mainly by *hunting*. 2. seek for: I have *hunted* all day for my thimble. 3. a chase after a person or animal: We have found a clue and the *hunt* for the murderer has begun. 4. a search for something: Everybody joined in the *hunt* for the lost purse. **hunter** a person who *hunts*: Many native African tribes are skilful *hunters*. **huntsman** a man who has charge of the hounds during a *hunt*.

hurdle (hur-dle) 1. a frame of wood which can be moved from place to place to fence in animals. 2. a frame specially made to be jumped over during a certain kind of race: The British competitor knocked down the third *hurdle*. 3. a hindrance, a difficulty: If we can only get over the first few *hurdles* our export trade will begin to make profits.

hurl throw with great force: The hunter *hurled* his spear at the lion.—He *hurled* himself at the locked door.

hurricane (hur-ri-cane) a violent, tropical storm: Hundreds of houses have been destroyed in the recent *hurricane*.

hurry (hur-ry) 1. great haste: In his *hurry* to catch the train he forgot his overcoat.—Don't talk to me now, I'm in a *hurry*. 2 move with great haste: He *hurried* off to catch the bus.

hurt 1. cause injury or pain: He *hurt* his foot jumping over the fence. 2. damage: Will the sudden rain *hurt* the crops? 3. harm, injury: I am sorry; I intended no *hurt*. **hurtful** causing *hurt*: Smoking has been proved *hurtful* to health.

husband (hus-band) 1. a married man: Her *husband* is a fireman. 2. save, keep ready for use: You should *husband* your strength for the battle tomorrow.

hush 1. make quiet, became quiet: The bishop spoke to a *hushed* congregation. 2. a quietness, stillness: We took a walk in the *hush* of the evening. **hush money** money paid to a person to keep quiet.

husk the dry outer covering of some seeds: When we thresh wheat we separate the grain from the *husk*.

husky (hus-ky) 1. big and strong: A tall, *husky* fellow appeared in the doorway. 2. (of the voice) rough and hoarse: He spoke in a low, *husky* voice. 3. a dog used by Eskimos to draw sledges.

hustle 1. push roughly: The three men were *hustled* into the police van. 2. hurry: 'This way, men, and *hustle*!' cried the sergeant. 3. movement and activity: The parade ground was a scene of intense *hustle* and bustle.

hut a small building or shelter: The gardener lived in a *hut* in the woods.—We meet every Friday evening in the Scouts' *hut*. **hutch** a small box or cage in which rabbits are kept.

hydrant (hy-drant) a large water pipe, usually in the street, to which a hose can be fitted for cleaning, or in case of fire.

hydraulic (hy-drau-lic) worked by water power: At the mine there is a powerful *hydraulic* pump.

hydrogen (hy-dro-gen) a gas which has no colour, taste or smell and burns with a faint blue flame: Water is composed of two gases, *hydrogen* and oxygen. **hydrogen bomb** the most powerful bomb known, many times more powerful than the atom bomb.

hygiene (hy-giene) the science of healthy living: Part of our course is the study of *hygiene*.—To be healthy, one must obey the rules of *hygiene*. **hygienic** free from germs or anything that may cause disease.

hymn a song of praise to God or to a god: This *hymn* has six verses.—The ancient Greeks sang *hymns* to Apollo.

hyphen (hy-phen) a small stroke used to connect two words together: Mr Hartley-Smith has a *hyphen* in his name.

hypnotize (hyp-no-tize) put into a state of sleep in which a person's acts can be directed by someone else. **hypnotism** the science that makes a person fall asleep, or into a trance: Doctors sometimes use *hypnotism* as a means of curing their patients. **hypnotic** having to do with *hypnotism*. **hypnosis** deep *hypnotic* sleep produced by the *hypnotist*. **hypnotist** a person who practises *hypnotism*.

hypocrite (hyp-o-crite) a person who pretends to be better or more virtuous than he really is: 'The joy of the *hypocrite* (is) but for a moment' (The Book of Job). **hypocrisy** making oneself appear better or more virtuous than one really is.

hypodermic (hy-po-der-mic) characterized by the injection of medical treatment under the skin. **hypodermic needle** a needle used with a syringe to inject under the skin.

I the word used by the person speaking to mean himself or herself: *I* will meet you at the station if *I* can be there in time.

idea (i-dea) 1. knowledge: Have you any *idea* how much this ring cost me? 2. a plan: I like your *idea* for decorating this room. 3. opinion: Our *ideas* on education are very different.

ideal (i-deal) 1. perfect: This is *ideal* weather for a long walk. 2. what one would like to be or have: My *ideal* house would have a double garage and a spare room for the children.—He is my *ideal* actor. **ideally** in accordance with an *ideal*: *Ideally*, it should be possible for everyone to have a house of his own.

idiot (id-i-ot) 1. a person so feeble in mind as to need caring for by others. 2. an absent-minded or foolish person: He leaves everything lying about, he's such an *idiot*. **idiotic** foolish: He had the *idiotic* idea of building an aeroplane in his back garden.

idle (i-dle) 1. doing nothing, not working: Two hundred men are *idle* owing to the strike. 2. lazy: He is so *idle* that he would rather go cold than light the fire. 3. worthless: His mind is full of *idle* dreams.—You have been listening to *idle* gossip. 4. be *idle*: A number of young men were *idling* at the street corner. 5. (of an engine) run slowly: He allowed the engine to *idle* while he inspected it. **idler** a person who *idles*: The work is hard and we want no *idlers* here. **idleness** being *idle*: The prisoner spent two years in *idleness*.

idol 1. an image of a god: The people of this tribe worship *idols*. 2. a person very much loved or admired: He is the sportsman of the year and the *idol* of the crowd. **idolize** make an *idol* of, love very much: Mary and John *idolize* their grandson.

if 1. granted that, given that: *If* you ask me I shall come.—Call me *if* you need my help. 2. whether: Do you know *if* the buses are running? 3. though: I don't care *if* it snows.

ignorance (ig-no-rance) not knowing: His mistake was due to *ignorance*.—He was in complete *ignorance* of our visit. **ignorant** not knowing, lacking knowledge: I am quite *ignorant* of what you intend to do.—He is so *ignorant* he can't add two and two together. **ignore** take no notice of: Add up these columns but *ignore* the figures in the margin.—I spoke to him but he *ignored* me.

ill 1. not in good health: He has been *ill* for six weeks. 2. bad, harmful: I had the *ill* luck to miss the train. 3. badly: They were an *ill*-matched pair. 4. evil: We shall stick together through good or *ill*. **illness** being *ill*: I was absent from work owing to *illness*.

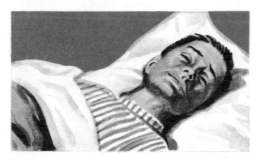

illegal (il-le-gal) against the law: It is *illegal* to park a car on a double yellow line.

illuminate (il-lu-mi-nate) 1. give light to: Most houses are *illuminated* by electricity. 2. decorate with bright lights of many colours: When the Queen visited the town the main streets were *illuminated*. 3. decorate lettering with designs and colours: This manuscript was *illuminated* by monks in the Middle Ages. **illumination** lighting, being lit or decorated: It is worth visiting Paris to see the *illuminations* at Christmas.

illusion (il-lu-sion) something seen or thought which does not exist or which is unreal or false: He is under the *illusion* that he owns a gold mine.—This line looks longer than the other, but it is an optical *illusion*.

illustrate (il-lus-trate) 1. decorate with pictures: The book is *illustrated* on every page. 2. explain: The lecturer *illustrated* his points with experiments and diagrams. **illustration** a picture, diagram, story etc. which explains: This dictionary contains many *illustrations* in colour.—I will tell you a story as an *illustration* of what I mean.

imagine (i-mag-ine) make a picture in the mind: Can you *imagine* what life would be like on a desert island?—He *imagines* that he is a wonderful singer. **imaginary** existing in the mind but not real: The equator is an *imaginary* line round the earth. **imagination** the power of *imagining*: The story of *Robinson Crusoe* was written entirely from the author's *imagination*. **imaginative** having a good *imagination*: Daniel Defoe was one of England's most *imaginative* writers.

imitate (im-i-tate) copy the behaviour or actions of others: Can you *imitate* the singing of birds?—Constable's paintings are well worth *imitating*.

imitation 1. copying: Now I will give an *imitation* of the roar of a lion. 2. not real: She was wearing a necklace of *imitation* pearls.

immediate (im-me-diate) 1. coming at once: Your complaint will receive *immediate* attention. 2. nearest: My cousin and his wife are our *immediate* neighbours. **immediately** at once: Go and fetch the doctor *immediately*.

immense (im-mense) extremely large, boundless, very great: The famine has already caused *immense* suffering. **immensely** enormously: He enjoyed himself *immensely* at the party.

immigrate (im-mi-grate) come from a foreign land into another country and settle there (the opposite of emigrate). **immigrant** a person coming from a foreign land to settle: During recent years many *immigrants* have arrived in Great Britain.

immortal (im-mor-tal) 1. living for ever: The gods of the ancient Greeks were believed to be *immortal*. 2. remembered for ever: The plays of Shakespeare and the music of Bach are *immortal*. **immortality** 1. the condition of being *immortal*. 2. fame or remembrance: Dickens achieved *immortality* through his writings.

impact (im-pact) 1. a collision: The car turned over on *impact*. 2. force, strength: The *impact* of the blow sent him reeling.

impassable (im-pass-a-ble) not possible to travel on or cross: The snow had made the roads *impassable*.–Before them lay an *impassable* jungle.

impatient (im-pa-tient) not patient or willing to wait: The children were *impatient* to open their Christmas parcels. **impatience** unwillingness to wait: He could not hide his *impatience* to hear what had happened.

imperfect (im-per-fect) having many faults or mistakes: We cannot pay full wages for *imperfect* work. **imperfection** a fault: The car had to be taken to the garage because of an *imperfection* in the steering.

imperial (im-pe-ri-al) having to do with an empire or emperor: Napoleon was head of the *Imperial* Court of France. **imperialism** a belief in the value of a large empire. **imperialist** a person who believes in extending an empire.

impersonate (im-per-son-ate) pretend (either in a play or in real life) to be somebody else: Who is *impersonating* Guy Fawkes?–He was imprisoned for a year for *impersonating* the bank manager.

impertinent (im-per-ti-nent) insolent, not showing respect: He was a very *impertinent* child. **impertinence** being insolent: He was punished for his *impertinence*.

implement (im-ple-ment) 1. a tool, an instrument: Men of the Stone Age worked with *implements* of flint and bone. 2. fulfil a promise or a contract: With the final payment, my agreement with him was fully *implemented*.

impolite (im-po-lite) not polite, not showing good manners: How *impolite* to pass in front of people without saying 'excuse me!' **impoliteness** being *impolite*.

import (im-port) 1. bring goods from a foreign country: All this wool has been *imported* from Australia. 2. goods brought in from another country: This has been a record year for *imports* from Canada.

important (im-por-tant) 1. meaning a great deal: When can we discuss the *important* question of road repairs? 2. having a position of power: The most *important* person in this town is the Mayor. **importance** being *important*: Fire prevention is a matter of the greatest *importance*.

impose 1. put on (a tax), put in force (a law): The government has *imposed* new taxes on property.–Owing to the recent riots a curfew has been *imposed* on the town. 2. take advantage of: I don't want to *impose* on you, but would you please witness my signature? **imposition** something *imposed*, a task given in school for some reason: The *imposition* of new taxes has shocked everybody.

impossible (im-pos-si-ble) not possible; that which cannot be done: It is *impossible* to climb that mountain.

impress (im-press) 1. mark or stamp by pressing something on: The shape of a cross was *impressed* on the soft clay. 2. fix in the mind: Let me *impress* on you the value of learning French. 3. produce an effect on the mind: All his boasting does not *impress* me in the least. **impression** the effect produced by *impressing* on materials or on persons: Robinson Crusoe saw the *impression* of a foot in the sand.– The minister's speech made a great *impression* on his audience.

imprison (im-pris-on) put or keep in prison: After a long chase he was caught and *imprisoned*. **imprisonment** being *imprisoned*: His *imprisonment* lasted nine months.

improve (im-prove) 1. become or make better: I would like to *improve* my French pronunciation.–It will only *improve* with practice. 2. make use of: 'How doth the little busy bee *improve* each shining hour' (Isaac Watts, *Divine Songs*). **improvement** getting better; something that makes another thing better: There is an *improvement* in the weather this morning.–The exercise is an *improvement* on the one you did last week.

impudent (im-pu-dent) rude, not polite, not showing respect: The *impudent* child took the gift without a word of thanks. **impudence** being *impudent*: He had the *impudence* to try and trip me up.

impure not pure or clean: They were all ill from drinking *impure* water. **impurity** something which makes *impure* or unclean: Several *impurities* have been found in this water.

in 1. showing a place: Look what I found *in* this drawer. 2. showing a movement or direction into: He ate the apple and threw the core *in* the fire. 3. showing time: He was taken prisoner *in* the war. 4. showing what is around: I don't want to go out *in* the rain; (*in* the dark; *in* the cold). 5. showing shape or position: We sat *in* three rows, then marched out *in* single file. 6. showing manner: Don't talk *in* such a loud voice. 7. here, at home: Is your mother *in*? 8. showing what one does: My brother is *in* the navy and my father is *in* banking. 9. (of a game) showing what one side or the other is doing: Which side is *in*?–He's been *in* two hours and scored 60 runs.

incense (in-cense) 1. a substance which when burnt gives off a sweet smell: *Incense* is burnt in some churches. 2. make angry: He was *incensed* when the bus set off and left him behind.

inch 1. a measure of length; one twelfth part of a foot. 2. a small amount of space: He made his way *inch* by *inch* along the narrow passage. 3. move very slowly: he *inched* his way along the wall.

inclination (in-cli-na-tion) 1. a slope, a nod: A gentle *inclination* led up to the house. 2. a desire: My *inclination* was to take the longer route.

incline (in-cline) 1. slope or slant: From this point the hill *inclined* steeply. 2. dispose or be disposed to (do something): I feel *inclined* to call the police. 3. a slope: It was risky making our way down the *incline*.

include (in-clude) count in or be counted in: This bill *includes* everything you have bought this week.—Am I *included* in the invitation? **inclusion** being *included*: The *inclusion* of the two boys brings the number to a hundred. **inclusive** including: The amount charged is *inclusive* of tax.

income (in-come) money received for work, goods etc.: How much is your annual *income*? **income tax** a tax based on a person's *income*.

incorrect (in-cor-rect) not correct, wrong: The newspaper printed an *incorrect* account of the trial.

increase (in-crease) 1. make or become greater or larger: I am *increasing* my contribution to the building fund.—Don't *increase* speed until the road is clear. 2. a growing greater: Last week we had an *increase* in wages.

incurable (in-cur-a-ble) that cannot be cured: The man is dying because his illness is *incurable*.

indecent (in-de-cent) vulgar, offending against good taste or behaviour.

indeed (in-deed) really: I was very glad *indeed* to see you.

independence (in-de-pen-dence) freedom, not being dependent: The money he has inherited has given him *independence*.—Most lands which once were British possessions have achieved their *independence*. **independent** not being controlled by others: He is a person of *independent* means; he has no need to work for a living.

index (in-dex) *indexes* or *indices* 1. a list at the end of a book which gives the names of subjects dealt with in alphabetical order and the pages on which they are to be found. 2. a list giving levels of wages and prices compared with an earlier date: The wage *index* shows an annual rise of 4 per cent. **index finger** the finger next to the thumb, with which we point. **card index** a number of cards in alphabetical order which show where information or objects are to be found.

indicate (in-di-cate) point out, show: An arrow *indicated* the way to the cloakroom. **indication** a sign, something to show: He gave no *indication* of his annoyance. **indicator** something which shows: The *indicator* showed that the car was gaining speed.

indigestion (in-di-ges-tion) difficulty in digesting food: He gets *indigestion* every time he eats cheese. **indigestible** hard or impossible to digest: His stomach is too weak to deal with *indigestible* solids.

indigo (in-di-go) a deep blue dye made from a plant of that name.

indirect (in-di-rect) 1. not straight, roundabout: When traffic is heavy on main roads it is often quicker to go by an *indirect* route. 2. not intended or aimed at: He cycles for the good of his health; breaking records is only an *indirect* result.

indistinct (in-dis-tinct) not clearly seen, heard or understood: Through the mist we saw the *indistinct* figure of a man.

individual (in-di-vid-ual) for or of one person only: This firm caters for *individual* tastes (every person is considered separately).—He has an *individual* way of addressing people (different from all others).

indoors (in-doors) inside or into a house or other building: You have been *indoors* all day and should go for a walk.—Where's father? You'll find him *indoors*.

industry (in-dus-try) 1. hard work: His *industry* was rewarded by an increase in salary. 2. a branch of trade or manufacture: The making of vehicles is one of Britain's greatest *industries*. 3. the manufactures of a district, a country, a continent, the world: Japanese *industries* have made great advances. **industrial** having to do with *industry*: We live in an *industrial* society.—Our factory is in the middle of a large *industrial* estate. **industrious** hard-working.

inexpensive (in-ex-pen-sive) not costing much: She bought attractive but *inexpensive* clothes.

infant (in-fant) 1. a child under the age of 7: How many *infants* are there in this school? 2. having to do with an *infant* or *infants*: 'Hark while *infant* voices sing' (part of a hymn). **infancy** the time when one is an *infant*: I remember my *infancy* well.

infantry (in-fant-ry) soldiers who march and fight on foot: The enemy was driven back by a furious *infantry* charge.

infect (in-fect) 1. pass disease germs: He was *infected* with typhoid through drinking *infected* milk. 2. pass on ideas or moods: Her melancholy has *infected* us all. **infection** a disease which has been passed on: It was many weeks before the *infection* could be checked. **infectious** spread by being carried through the atmosphere: Diphtheria, measles and many other diseases are *infectious*.

infiltrate (in-fil-trate) 1. pass through the lines of an enemy without being seen. 2. pass almost without being noticed into people's minds: In many lands newspapers are censored to stop certain ideas *infiltrating* into the minds of the people.

infirm (in-firm) weak in body or mind: The state helps to care for the old and *infirm*. **infirmary** a building in which people who are ill may be treated; a hospital. **infirmity** some kind of weakness: 'I have a strange *infirmity* which is nothing to those that know me' (Shakespeare, *Macbeth*).

inflame (in-flame) 1. become red, swollen and tender: This wound has become *inflamed*. 2. become angry, filled with rage: The crowd were *inflamed* with anger at his words. **inflammation** being *inflamed*, an *inflamed* place in the body: Pneumonia is accompanied by *inflammation* of the lungs.

inflate (in-flate) blow up, fill with air or gas: He took the pump and *inflated* the car tyres. **inflation** a rising of prices caused by undue expansion in money, or bank credit.

inflict (in-flict) cause suffering or pain to another person: I cannot *inflict* pain on dumb animals.

influence (in-flu-ence) 1. the power to alter or change the actions of others: The bishop used all his *influence* to end the quarrel. 2. have an effect on: The attractive packaging was bound to *influence* the housewives. **influential** having *influence*: We shall need the help of *influential* persons to raise the money.

inform (in-form) 1. give knowledge to: 'We beg to *inform* you that our store is now open.' 2. tell the police: He was caught because somebody *informed* against him. **information** something told: For further *information* please apply at the counter. **informative** containing much *information*: I have just read a very *informative* book about keeping bees. **informer** a person who gives evidence to the police against someone.

informal (in-for-mal) without special dress or ceremony: The Prime Minister paid an *informal* visit to France and held *informal* conversations about trade (conversations of which no records were kept).

inhabit (in-hab-it) live or dwell in: They found that the island was *inhabited* by cannibals. **inhabitant** a person or animal *inhabiting* a place: The only *inhabitants* were a race of cannibals.

inherit (in-he-rit) 1. receive property, rights, titles etc. from one's ancestors: My cousin has *inherited* all his father's land. 2. receive certain qualities of appearance and character from one's ancestors: He has *inherited* his mother's good looks and his father's intelligence. **inheritance** *inheriting*; the things and qualities one *inherits*: He has acquired his property by *inheritance*.

initial (in-i-tial) 1. the first: Today we are taking the *initial* steps to buy this land. 2. the first letter of a word or name: Please write your *initials* here. 3. put one's *initials* on: He *initialled* the contract at the foot of every page.

inject (in-ject) force a liquid into a part of a living body with a syringe: The patient was *injected* with penicillin. **injection** *injecting*; something *injected*: After an *injection* of morphia the patient fell into a deep sleep.

injure (in-jure) damage, hurt: My brother has been *injured* in a car crash. **injured** hurt, offended: He felt *injured* at not receiving an invitation to the wedding. **injurious** harmful, likely to cause *injury*: Too much smoking has been proved to be *injurious* to one's health. **injury** damage, an *injured* condition: He received an *injury* to his right arm.

inlet (in-let) a strip of water extending into the land from a larger body of water: We anchored in an *inlet* overhung by trees.

inn a public house supplying meals and beds for the night: Mary and Joseph found a lodging in a stable because there was no room at the *inn*.

inner (in-ner) inside: The tyre had to be changed because there was a puncture in the *inner* tube.

innings (in-nings) the time in some games when a team takes turns in batting: 240 runs were scored in an *innings* lasting 5 hours. 2. the time a single person is batting: In his first *innings* he scored 69 runs.

innocent (in-no-cent) 1. not guilty: He was *innocent* of the crime. 2. doing no harm: It was an *innocent* remark. 3. knowing nothing of evil: 'Murder not this *innocent* child' (Shakespeare, *Henry VI, part 3*). **innocence** being *innocent*: Is there any doubt about his *innocence*?

inoculate (in-oc-u-late) give an injection to a person to prevent disease: The doctor has *inoculated* everyone who has been in contact with the victim. **inoculation** being *inoculated*: All those going on this expedition must have an *inoculation* against yellow fever.

insane (in-sane) mad, senseless: His sufferings in the prison camp drove him *insane*. **insanity** being *insane*: Because of an attack of *insanity* the king could not be crowned.

insect (in-sect) a tiny animal with six legs, and a body made up of three parts: *Insects* include ants, bees, butterflies, grasshoppers and many other small creatures. **insecticide** a substance, often in powder form, for killing unwanted *insects*.

insert (in-sert) put in: He *inserted* the key in the lock and turned it.–A notice of the date of the election was *inserted* in the newspaper. **insertion** something put in: The *insertion* of the needle into his arm was quite painless.

inside (in-side) 1. the side that is in anything: The *inside* of the coat was lined with wool. 2. the stomach and bowels: I have a pain in my *inside*. 3. to, on or in the *inside*: It's cold; let's go *inside*.–Look *inside* the box.

insincere (in-sin-cere) not honest or sincere, not meaning what one says: An *insincere* person can never be trusted. **insincerity** being *insincere*.

insist (in-sist) say something or make a statement with great force: I must *insist* on your telling the truth.–Come home with me; I *insist*. **insistent** said with force: In spite of our *insistent* demands, nobody came to inspect the radio. **insistence** *insisting* on a request, fact or demand: Our complaints were attended to only after repeated *insistence*.

insolent insulting, offensive in manner: There is no need to be *insolent* when you are asked a question. **insolence** being *insolent*: He was dismissed for *insolence*.

inspect (in-spect) examine very carefully to see that everything is correct: Every morning the machinery is *inspected* for faults. **inspection** being *inspected*: Every Friday this factory is open for public *inspection*. **inspector** a person whose work is to *inspect*: This week our school has been visited by Her Majesty's *Inspectors*. **police inspector** a rank in the police force next above a sergeant.

inspire (in-spire) fill with hope, trust, enthusiasm or other good feelings: My conversation with your friend has *inspired* me to work harder. **inspiration** something that *inspires*, a sudden bright idea leading to action: Your encouragement gave me the *inspiration* to write a book.

install (in-stall) 1. put in, fix in place: We have just had a new hot water tank *installed*. 2. hold a ceremony to give a person an important office: The new Lord Mayor was *installed* yesterday. **installation** *installing*: The *installation* of the hot water tank took a whole day.

instalment (in-stal-ment) 1. part of a story which is to be continued in the next issue of a magazine. 2. part of a debt paid at fixed times: We are paying for our car in monthly *instalments*.

instance (in-stance) an example: There are many kinds of good deeds; let me give you an *instance*. **for instance** as an example: You could, *for instance*, help a blind man to cross the road.

instant (in-stant) 1. now: Tell him to come here this *instant*. 2. happening in a moment, at once: To swallow the capsule would cause *instant* death. 3. specially made to be prepared quickly: Have you seen the jar of *instant* coffee?

instead (in-stead) in place of: We could not get beef so we had lamb *instead*.

instep (in-step) the arched upper part of the foot between toes and ankle: I have a high *instep*.—You need a support for a fallen *instep*.

institution (in-sti-tu-tion) 1. a building used as a school or hospital: Today we are visiting an *institution* for old people. 2. custom; something which has been done for a long time: Slavery as an *institution* is illegal in Europe. 3. setting up or starting: Much good has been done through the *institution* of a Citizens' Advice Bureau.

instruct (in-struct) 1. teach: Who is *instructing* these boys in gymnastics? 2. command: I have been *instructed* to accompany you to the station. **instruction** teaching, directions: I am willing to pay well for *instruction* in playing the guitar.—He asked for *instructions* to reach the station. **instructor** a person who *instructs*: If you are in difficulties with your carpentry, ask the *instructor*.

instrument 1. a tool or apparatus: Special *instruments* are needed for breaking open this safe. 2. an *instrument* specially made to produce music: How many *instruments* does your cousin play? **instrumental** acting as a means of doing something: He has been *instrumental* in obtaining a house for a friend. **instrumentalist** a person who plays a musical *instrument*.

insulate (in-su-late) protect by special coverings from loss of heat or electricity: Our hot water tank is *insulated* with thick padding. **insulating tape** tape specially made to wrap round electric wire to prevent anything touching the wires.

insult (in-sult) 1. act or speak in a way that hurts or offends another person: He *insulted* the whole company by refusing to drink the health of the President. 2. an action or remark which *insults* others: They were all determined to bear his *insults* no longer.

intelligence (in-tel-li-gence) 1. power to understand and learn: Has he the *intelligence* to handle this machine? 2. news, knowledge: According to the latest *intelligence*, the enemy was planning an attack. **intelligent** having or showing *intelligence*: All I want is an *intelligent* answer to my question. **intelligible** that can be understood: I could not get an *intelligible* explanation of his actions.

intercept (in-ter-cept) take, catch or seize something between its departure and its arrival: He threw the ball to John but I *intercepted* it.—Ten enemy fighters were *intercepted* over the Channel.

interfere (in-ter-fere) show too much interest in other people's business: He was given a black eye because he *interfered* in the fight.—Please do not *interfere* with the switches. **interference** *interfering*: We cannot hear the radio clearly because of *interference* from foreign stations.

interior (in-te-ri-or) inside: We learnt about the country by exploring the *interior*.—Do you like the *interior* decorations of this house?

international (in-ter-na-tion-al) happening between nations: The lecturer spoke about *international* trade.—Esperanto is the best-known *international* language.

interpret (in-ter-pret) 1. explain, make clear: Could you please *interpret* this part of my Income Tax form? 2. show by performing, painting etc.: This pianist *interprets* the work of Chopin brilliantly. 3. translate: We do not understand what is said; would you please *interpret* for us? **interpretation** a meaning given by explanation or performance: She gave a magnificent *interpretation* of the character of Portia. **interpreter** a person who translates from another language: The United Nations employs many *interpreters* when speeches are relayed to the Assembly.

interrupt (in-ter-rupt) 1. make a break in: The harvest was *interrupted* by a heavy rainstorm. 2. break in on the work or conversation of other people: What was I talking about when you *interrupted* me? **interruption** the act of *interrupting*, a breaking in: A dispute about prices caused an *interruption* in the flow of trade.

interval (in-ter-val) 1. time between: There will be an *interval* of ten minutes between the acts. 2. space between: Observers were stationed along the route at frequent *intervals*.

interview (in-ter-view) 1. a meeting between an employer and a person applying for a post: The result of the *interview* was not known until the following day. 2. a meeting between an important person and a reporter who wishes to know his views: The Prime Minister has granted an *interview* to the reporter. 3. have an *interview* with: He has *interviewed* many interesting people.

intimate (in-ti-mate) 1. close and familiar: He has many *intimate* friends. 2. private: People do not often reveal their most *intimate* thoughts. 3. (of something one has studied) very well known: He has an *intimate* knowledge of astronomy. **intimacy** close friendship or knowledge of someone.

intoxicate (in-tox-i-cate) 1. make a person drunk: He was *intoxicated* and could not walk straight. 2. excite a person so that he cannot think clearly: *Intoxicated* with fury, the crowd rushed the gate. **intoxication** being *intoxicated*: The man was accused of driving a car in a state of *intoxication*.

introduce (in-tro-duce) 1. make persons known to each other: May I *introduce* my brother-in-law? 2. make use of for the first time: New machinery was *introduced* into the factory. 3. bring forward: A bill on housing has been *introduced* into the House of Commons. 4. insert: The doctor *introduced* a tube into the patient's throat.

introduction (in-tro-duc-tion) 1. introducing or being introduced: The *introduction* of new methods has caused a strike. 2. making persons known to each other: I would like an *introduction* to the Prime Minister. 3. the first chapter, paragraph or sentence of a book or a speech: By way of *introduction* let me tell you a story. **introductory** which *introduces*: Have you read the *introductory* chapter of the book?

invade (in-vade) enter another country as an enemy and try to take it by force of arms: William of Normandy *invaded* England in 1066. **invader** a person who *invades*: Extra forces were needed to repel the *invaders*. **invasion** *invading* or being *invaded*: All attempts at *invasion* have been defeated.— It was an *invasion* of our privacy.

invalid (in-va-lid) 1. a person who is weak through illness or injury: He has been an *invalid* for the last ten years. 2. having to do with an *invalid*: We shall have to borrow an *invalid* chair. 3. take people out of the forces because they are unfit: My uncle has been *invalided* out of the Royal Air Force. **invalid** (in-vál-id) of no force or value: Without your signature your cheque is *invalid*.

invent (in-vent) 1. make or plan something that has not existed before: The gramophone was *invented* by Thomas Alva Edison. 2. make up: He will *invent* any excuse to get himself out of trouble. **invention** *inventing*; something *invented*: Radio is one of the greatest *inventions* of modern times. **inventor** a person who *invents*: Tell me the name of the *inventor* of the hovercraft.

investigate (in-ves-ti-gate) examine, enquire into, find out about: The causes of the accident are being *investigated*. **investigator** a person who *investigates*: The police are being assisted by a private *investigator*. **investigation** an examination or enquiry: A complete *investigation* has been ordered into the disaster.

invite (in-vite) 1. ask somebody to attend or to do something: You are *invited* to the opening of the new library.–The public is *invited* to attend the meeting. 2. tempt, encourage: The warm sunshine *invites* us to relax in the garden. **inviting** tempting: How *inviting* the sea looks! **invitation** the act of *inviting*: something that *invites*: Thank you for the *invitation*.

iodine (i-o-dine) a dark brown substance obtained from seaweed, used as an antiseptic and germicide.

iron (i-ron) 1. a hard, heavy metal from which steel is made. 2. an article made of *iron*: In the hearth was a set of fire-*irons*. The prisoners were handcuffed and in *irons*. 3. a device for pressing cloth: He asked for an *iron* to press his trousers. 4. smooth cloth with an *iron*: Will you help me *iron* these shirts? 5. clear up a difficulty: After all the difficulties had been *ironed out* the contract was signed. 6. strong: To escape from this country one needs an *iron* will and nerves of *iron*. **iron curtain** a phrase first used by Sir Winston Churchill to denote the closed border between the West and the communist countries allied to Russia.

irregular (ir-reg-u-lar) 1. not straight or even: The coastline of Norway is one of the most *irregular* in the world. 2. against the rules: Your absence from roll-call this morning was highly *irregular*.

irritate (ir-ri-tate) 1. annoy, make angry: Don't *irritate* him with all your questions. 2. make sore: Walking in these shoes has *irritated* the inflammation in my foot. **irritation** *irritating* or being *irritated*: He could not hide his *irritation* when his past record was mentioned.

island (rhymes with *highland*) 1. a piece of land surrounded by water: Malta is an *island* in the Mediterranean. 2. a platform in a busy road for the safety of people: When the green light appeared we crossed to the *island*. 3. having to do with an *island*: How I long to go back to my *island* retreat! **isle** another word for an *island*: The *Isle* of Wight lies off the south coast of England.

issue (is-sue) 1. come out, go out, flow out, put out, publish: A little stream *issued* from the bare rock.–Food was *issued* to the starving people. 2. something that is published: Have you received this month's *issue* of the catalogue? 3. result: He will leave the country whatever the *issue* of the trial.

isthmus (isth-mus) a strip of land joining two larger bodies of land: The Panama Canal crosses the *Isthmus* of Panama.

item (i-tem) 1. a separate article on a list: The first *item* on our programme is a song from *The Pirates of Penzance*. 2. a piece of news: What is the most important *item* in this morning's paper?

ivy (i-vy) a climbing evergreen plant with shiny leaves: The walls of many old buildings are covered with *ivy*.

J

jack 1. a device for lifting heavy weights, especially cars and other vehicles: The lorry was raised off its back wheels by means of a hydraulic *jack*. 2. a small ball at which the players aim in the game of bowls. 3. the knave in a pack of playing cards, ranking between the ten and the queen. 4. a flag: The Union *Jack* is the flag of Great Britain. 5. raise a weight with a *jack*: The car had to be *jacked* up to change the tyre. **jackass** 1. a male ass. 2. a foolish person. **jackpot** the chief prize in a lottery and in some games.

jacket (jack-et) 1. a coat which reaches just below the hips. 2. outside covering: Do you like potatoes in their *jackets*?–The book had an illustrated paper *jacket*.

jag cut or tear unevenly. **jagged** uneven, with rough edges: In the distance we saw the *jagged* outline of the hills.

jam 1. crush, be crushed: The man's leg was *jammed* between two huge rocks. 2. become fixed so that a machine cannot work: The brakes *jammed* and the car would not move. 3. crowd tightly together: People were injured when the crowd *jammed* the exits.–He *jammed* his clothes into a suitcase and hurried out. 4. interfere with a radio programme broadcast from another station: The enemy forces found it impossible to *jam* the broadcasts from the capital. 5. many things or people crowded together: Owing to an overturned lorry there is a heavy traffic *jam* on the motorway. 6. an awkward or difficult situation: I owe more money than I can pay; can you help me out of this *jam*? 7. a preserve made by boiling fruit with sugar: Will you have *jam* or marmalade for breakfast?

jangle (jan-gle) a long loud clanging sound: We heard the *jangle* of the fire-engine's bell.

January (Jan-u-a-ry) the first month of the year.

jar 1. give unpleasant feelings: The jangling of the bell *jars* on my ears. 2. conflict with: These reds and yellows *jar* with each other. 3. a shock: He had a nasty *jar* when he fell from his motor-cycle. 4. a vessel with a wide opening at the top: The dustbin was full of empty jam-*jars*.

javelin (jave-lin) a long, light spear, thrown by hand in sports events.

jaw one of the two bones forming the frame of the mouth: The champion retired from the ring with a broken *jaw*.

jealous (jeal-ous) a feeling of resentment against another who is more successful, wealthier etc.: She has always been *jealous* of your good looks. **jealousy** being *jealous*: 'Love, thou know'st, is full of *jealousy*' (Shakespeare, *The Two Gentlemen of Verona*).

jeer 1. mock, cry out or laugh rudely: The crowd *jeered* when the player was sent off the field. 2. mockery, rude laughter: The speaker could not be heard because of the *jeers* of the audience.

jelly (jel-ly) *jellies* 1. a food made by boiling sugar and fruit juice which, when cool makes a soft, transparent substance: The cook brought in a dish of pineapple *jelly*. 2. a portion of this substance turned out of a mould on to a dish: The cook brought in a large pineapple *jelly*. 3. any substance resembling *jelly*. **jellyfish** a fish whose body resembles a soft, circular piece of *jelly*.

jerk 1. a sudden movement: He indicated the turning with a *jerk* of his head. 2. move quickly: Don't *jerk* the steering-wheel. **jerky** moving in *jerks*: After a while the horse broke into a slow, *jerky* trot.

jersey (jer-sey) 1. a woollen garment which covers the body down to the waist, and the arms: Slowly he pulled the *jersey* over his head. 2. a cow belonging to the breed which once came from *Jersey*, the largest of the Channel Islands.

jet 1. a stream of liquid or gas, coming from a small opening: *The fireman turned a jet of water on the burning building.* 2. a hard, black mineral which can be highly polished. **jet propulsion** power given to an aeroplane through an engine which sends out *jets* of gas. **jet aircraft** aircraft driven by *jet* engines.

jewel (jew-el) a precious stone such as a diamond or a pearl: *The princess wore a dress embroidered with jewels.* **jeweller** a person who makes or sells *jewels*. **jewellery** rings, brooches, pendants and other ornaments often set with *jewels*.

jingle (jin-gle) 1. a light ringing or tinkling sound: *We heard the distant jingle of bells.* 2. make such a sound: *He jingled the coins in his pocket.* 3. an attractive little rhyme which is easily remembered: *Have you heard the jingle, 'Coughs and sneezes bring diseases'?*

job 1. an employment: *He has found a job as a waiter.* 2. a task completed: *You've made a good job of polishing that table.* **jobber** a dealer on the Stock Exchange. **jobbing** doing whatever *jobs* are given: *Do you know where I can find a jobbing gardener?*

jockey (jock-ey) a person, usually a professional, who rides in horse races. **jockey for position** push or jostle others to get a better place.

join 1. put or fasten together, unite: *He tied a knot to join the two pieces of string.*— *Let's join together in a song.* 2. come together: *I will meet you where the two roads join.* 3. become a member: *Last week he joined the cricket club.* 4. a place where two things are put or fastened: *She mended the jug so that we could not see the join.* **joiner** a man specially trained to work with wood: *The joiner made us a beautiful, carved table.*

joint 1. a place where two things are joined together: *The carpenter taught his son how to make a half-lap joint.* 2. a piece of meat for cooking: *In came the cook carrying a large joint of beef.* 3. a place in the body where the bones come together: *The old man has rheumatism in his joints.*—*He fell, and put his knee out of joint.* 4. having to do with two or more people: *We hold this land in joint ownership.*

joke 1. something done or said to make people laugh: *Have you heard any new jokes lately?*—*I'm sorry, I only meant it as a joke.* 2. make *jokes*: *Stop joking and be serious for a moment.*

jot 1. make a short note of: *I'll jot the date down in my diary.* 2. the least bit: *I don't care a jot what he says.* **jotter** a book in which one scribbles rough notes. **jottings** rough notes.

journal (jour-nal) 1. a daily record of events: *He kept a journal for the last ten years of his life.* 2. a newspaper or magazine: *Have you seen this week's Pets' Journal?* **journalism** the work of writing or publishing newspapers. **journalist** a person who writes, edits or publishes *journals*.

journey (jour-ney) 1. a voyage from one place to another: *Will you go with me on this journey?* 2. time taken in making a journey: *We reached the camp after a journey of six weeks.* 3. make *journeys*: *I have journeyed through every country in Europe.*

joy 1. great pleasure, gladness: *We learned with joy that he had arrived safely.* 2. a person, thing or happening that causes *joy*: *What a joy this weather is!* **joyful** having or causing *joy*: *Have you heard the joyful news?* **joyless** having no *joy*, sad: *I have never met such a joyless person.* **joyous** full of *joy*, with *joy*: *A joyous crowd thronged the square.*

jubilee (ju-bi-lee) 1. the celebration of an anniversary: *In 1897 the country celebrated Queen Victoria's Diamond (60th) Jubilee.* 2. a period of gaiety and merry-making: *Let everybody join the jubilee.* **jubilation** joy and merrymaking.

judge 1. a person who gives the final decision in a court of law: Without hearing further evidence the *judge* dismissed the case. 2. a person who decides the result of a competition: The *judge* awarded the first prize to the fastest cyclist. 3. act as a *judge*: The entries were *judged* by the famous film star. 4. form an opinion: Not knowing all the facts, I am unable to *judge*. **judgment** (or **judgement**) a decision, wisdom: The *judgment* favoured neither side.– I admire your *judgment* in this matter.

judo the art of self-defence first practised in Japan: In *judo* strength counts far less than skill.

jug 1. a deep vessel or pitcher with a handle. 2. what a *jug* holds: He drank a whole *jug* of milk. 3. stew or boil in a *jug*: I shall *jug* the hare tomorrow.

juggle (jug-gle) 1. do tricks with balls, plates, hoops, or furniture etc., to entertain people: He can *juggle* with three balls at the same time. 2. deceive by trickery: The chief cashier was sent to prison for *juggling* the accounts. **juggler** a person who *juggles*: This *juggler* can do many astonishing tricks.

juice 1. the liquid part of fruit, vegetables or meat: If you were to drink the *juice* of an orange every morning, you would catch fewer colds. 2. the liquids in the body that help to digest food; the digestive *juices*. **juicy** full of *juice*: Would you like a ripe, *juicy* peach?

July the seventh month of the year.

jumble (jum-ble) 1. mix or be mixed up: The coins in his collection were all *jumbled* together in a drawer. 2. a mixture, confusion: My mind is a *jumble* of ideas. **jumble-sale** a sale of second-hand articles, usually to raise funds for an organization or for charity.

jump 1. leap, rise in the air by suddenly stretching the legs: 'The cow *jumped* over the moon' (nursery rhyme). 2. go over something by *jumping*: Can you *jump* this fence? 3. move with a sudden jerk: Don't shout; the noise makes me *jump*. 4. the act of *jumping*: He has already done ten parachute *jumps*. 5. a sudden jerk of the body: She gave a *jump* every time there was a flash of lightning. 6. a sudden rise: Have you noticed the *jump* in the price of fruit this week? **jumper** somebody or something that *jumps*; a garment pulled over the head, usually made of wool: She is knitting a brown *jumper* for me.

junction (junc-tion) 1. a place where roads or routes meet: A policeman directed traffic at the road *junction*. 2. a place where anything is joined: There is a fault at the *junction* of these electric cables.

June the sixth month of the year.

jungle (jun-gle) land in hot countries, covered by trees, bushes and creeping plants so close together that it is difficult to pass through: He was lost for months in the African *jungle*.

junior (ju-nior) a person younger or lower in rank than another: He is my *junior* by three years.

junk 1. a flat-bottomed Chinese boat. 2. old articles no longer used: The hut in the garden is crammed with old *junk*.

jury (ju-ry) *juries* 1. a body of people (twelve in Great Britain) chosen to listen to cases in court and then give a decision of guilty or not guilty. 2. a body of persons chosen to decide or award a prize in a competition: The piano competition was judged by an international *jury* of musicians.

just 1. very recently: They have *just* arrived. 2. exactly: It's *just* ten minutes since we left. 3. now: We're *just* going. 4. only: He's *just* a poor tramp. 5. giving a command: *Just* look at that! 6. barely: He's only *just* tall enough to reach the shelf. 7. fair: Your punishment will be *just*. 8. reasonable: He has been blamed without *just* cause.

justice (just-ice) 1. fair and reasonable treatment: I demand to be treated with *justice*. 2. lawfulness: I believe in the *justice* of my cause. 3. the decision of the law: In time he will be brought to *justice*. 4. a judge: A new Lord Chief *Justice* has been appointed. 5. a magistrate: He was tried before a *Justice* of the Peace.

jut stand out: The corner of the house *juts* into the street.

K

kaleidoscope (ka-lei-do-scope) 1. a tube in which there are many pieces of coloured glass. When a person looks through the eyepiece of the tube and turns it, the pieces fall into different positions and create colourful patterns. 2. a scene which is continually changing: Sunlight and moving clouds made a *kaleidoscope* of colour over the fields and woods.

kangaroo (kan-ga-roo) a marsupial animal with powerful hind-legs, that moves in long jumps and carries its young in a pouch, found in Australia and New Guinea.

keel the frame of wood or metal on which the hull of a boat is constructed.

keep *kept, keeping* 1. have in one's possession: I'm giving you this watch to *keep*. 2. observe, be true to: He never *keeps* a promise. 3. celebrate: We *keep* Christmas by going to church in the morning. 4. take care of: He is looking for somebody to *keep* house for him. 5. possess and look after: How many in this class *keep* white mice? 6. remain: *Keep* quiet! 7. hold: He was *kept* in prison for a week. 8. go on, continue doing something: *Keep* smiling! 9. remain good, fit to eat: How long will this fish *keep*? 10. food, lodging and attendance: How much a week do you pay for your *keep*? **keeper** a person who looks after something: He works as a game*keeper* and is goal*keeper* in our team. **keeping** care: I am leaving all my goods in your safe-*keeping*. **keepsake** something to *keep* and remember another person by: It's a *keepsake*; my uncle gave it to me.

keg a small barrel: The admiral divided a *keg* of rum among the crew.

kennel (ken-nel) a small hut in which a dog is kept. **kennels** a place where dogs may be left to be cared for: While we were on holiday we took our alsatian to the *kennels*.

kerb the edge of a path or pavement separating it from the road: He stood on the *kerb* waiting for the bus.

kernel (ker-nel) 1. that part of a seed inside any fruit. 2. the softer part inside the shell of a nut which can be eaten. 3. the most important part of a discussion or problem: The *kernel* of the matter is this: you did not arrive in time.

kettle (ket-tle) a metal container with a lid, spout and handle, in which to boil water: I can't make tea until the *kettle* boils.

key 1. a piece of metal designed for opening a door, winding up a clock, a machine etc.: 'Her father, he has locked the door, her mother keeps the *key*' (an old English song). 2. a list of answers to problems, or a translation from a foreign language: I can't translate this into English without first looking at the *key*. 3. that part of a machine or musical instrument pressed down by the finger: This piano can't be played; the *keys* are stiff. 4. a group of notes all related to each other and based on one of the notes in the musical scale: We will sing this song in the *Key* of F. 5. something which helps solve a puzzle, or which controls a region: The *key* to this question is the production of coal.— Gibraltar is no longer the *key* to the Mediterranean Sea. **keyboard** the rows of *keys* on a typewriter, a piano, organ, accordion etc. **keynote** the note on which a musical *key* is based. **keyhole** the hole into which a *key* is inserted. **keystone** the stone at the top of an arch which holds all the others in place.

kick 1. strike with the foot: He *kicked* the ball into the net. 2. dismiss: He played badly and was *kicked* out of the team. 3. (of a gun) jerk suddenly when fired. 4. the act or result of *kicking*: Give it a good *kick*.

kid 1. a young goat. 2. (slang) a child, a childish person. 3. (slang) deceive, play a joke on: You can't *kid* me!

kidnap (kid-nap) steal, carry away and hold as a prisoner: A prominent businessman has been *kidnapped* by bandits.

kidney (kid-ney) an organ of the body, one of a pair, which separates the waste matter from the blood and passes it out of the body as urine.

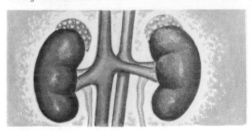

kill 1. put an end to the life of: He was *killed* in a motor accident. 2. the act of *killing*: He hunted all day with the pack and was present at the *kill*.

kiln an oven for burning lime, baking pottery etc.: He owns a number of brick *kilns* in this district.

kilo- (ki-lo) a unit of 1,000. **kilometre** a thousand metres. **kilogram** a thousand grams. **kilolitre** a thousand litres. **kilowatt** a thousand watts (in electricity).

kilt the short pleated skirt worn by some people in Scotland: The men of the Highland regiment went on parade in *kilts*.

kin people related to each other: Who is the next of *kin*? (nearest relative). **kinship** relationship by birth: *Kinship* is a strong bond between members of many families.

kind 1. a sort, variety or class: This is a different *kind* of apple from the one I had yesterday. 2. (of payment or gifts) not in money but in goods: Please bring your contributions in *kind* to our harvest festival. 3. showing thoughfulness and love for others: 'Is she *kind* as she is fair?' (song from *Two Gentlemen of Verona*, Shakespeare). **kindly** in a *kind* manner: The policeman spoke *kindly* to the little boy. **kindness** being *kind*: Thank you for your *kindness* to my son. **kind-hearted** *kind*: The *kind-hearted* man took the child home.

kindergarten (kin-der-gar-ten) a school for very young children: John plays at the *kindergarten* while his mother does the shopping.

kindle (kin-dle) 1. catch fire, start a fire burning: After much effort we *kindled* a flame from the damp wood. 2. bring forth: His speech *kindled* great enthusiasm among the audience.

kindred (kin-dred) 1. relationship by birth; all one's relatives: All my *kindred* live in the south of England. 2. springing from the same source: English, German, Dutch and Norwegian are *kindred* languages. **kindred spirit** a person with similar tastes to someone else.

king 1. a male ruler of a country: The first *King* of all England was Egbert. 2. a very important person in some business: This library was given by the great steel *king*, Andrew Carnegie. 3. the principal piece in a game of chess. 4. a playing card with the picture of a *king*'s head on it.

kingdom (king-dom) 1. a country ruled over by a king or queen. 'A horse! a horse! my *kingdom* for a horse!' (Shakespeare, *Richard III*). 2. one of the three great groups of the natural world: the animal, vegetable, and mineral *kingdoms*. **kingfisher** a small bird which catches fish in rivers and lakes.

kiosk (ki-osk) a small building for a special purpose such as selling newspapers, telephoning etc.: You can buy your morning paper at the *kiosk* outside the station.

kipper (kip-per) a herring which has been cleaned, salted and dried in the air or in smoke.

kit the equipment needed by a soldier, sailor, workman, or for some sport: Have you brought your riding *kit*?—He cannot build the shed without his tool-*kit*.

kitchen (kit-chen) the room in a house or building used for cooking: The cook was preparing dinner in the *kitchen*. **kitchen garden** a garden in which herbs and vegetables are grown for the *kitchen*.

kite 1. cloth or paper stretched out on a framework of wood which can be thrown into the air and flown at the end of a long string. 2. a bird belonging to the hawk family.

kitten (kit-ten) a baby cat: The *kitten* loves playing with a ball of wool.

knack (pronounced *nack*) cleverness, a clever way of doing something: Tying a sailor's knot is not difficult when you have learnt the *knack*.

knapsack (knap-sack, pronounced *napsack*) a bag of canvas or leather carried on the back and containing the things one needs on a walk, a march or in war: Napoleon said that every soldier carried a field-marshal's baton in his *knapsack*.

knave (pronounced *nave*) 1. a dishonest man: Only a foolish person trusts every *knave* he meets. 2. the card between 10 and queen in a pack of playing cards; the jack: He took the trick with the *knave* of diamonds. **knavery** dishonesty.

knead (pronounced *need*) mix or work over with the hands: The baker *kneads* dough for the oven; the masseur *kneads* our muscles to keep us fit.

knee (pronounced *nee*) 1. the joint which connects the upper and lower part of the leg: Peter has fallen and hurt his *knee*. 2. that part of a pair of trousers which covers the *knee*: His trousers were worn at the *knees*. **kneecap** the oval bone that protects the joint of the *knee*: He could not play in the match because of a fractured *kneecap*. **kneel** sink down on the *knees*, rest on the *knees*: Let us *kneel* in prayer.

knell (pronounced *nell*) the solemn sound of a bell, rung when a person has died.

knickerbockers (knick-er-bock-ers, pronounced *nickerbockers*) loose breeches gathered in at the knees.

knife (pronounced *nife*) knives a sharp metal blade fixed to a handle and used for cutting: There are table-*knives*, fish-*knives*, pocket-*knives*, as well as *knives* of many other kinds.

knight (pronounced *night*) 1. a brave man in the middle ages who commanded a body of soldiers: King Edward went to war with a large army and a thousand *knights*. 2. a nobleman in old legends: Have you read the stories of King Arthur and his *Knights* of the Round Table? 3. a man who has been honoured by the monarch for his services and has the title 'Sir' before his name. 4. a piece in the game of chess.

knit (pronounced *nit*) 1. form stitches, usually with wool, so that they join to make a garment: Are you *knitting* that jumper for me? 2. join together: He will not walk again until the broken bone in his leg has *knitted* firmly. **knitting** the action or the material made by *knitting*: While we watched television, grandma went on *knitting*.

knot (pronounced *not*) 1. a place where pieces of rope, string, etc., have been tied together: Can you undo the *knot* in my shoelace? 2. a piece of ribbon or material tied in a certain way: Can you tie a sailor's *knot*? 3. a hard part in wood where a branch has once grown from another branch or from the trunk of a tree: He found it very hard to plane down the *knots*. 4. a number of persons standing close together: A *knot* of spectators had gathered round the scene of the accident. 5. a measure of the speed of a ship: We were sailing westwards at 30 *knots*. 6. make a *knot* or *knots*, tie rope or string together with *knots*: The rope had been *knotted* in many places. **knotty** full of *knots*: He bought three boards of *knotty* pine at the woodyard.

know (pronounced *no*) *knew*, *known*, *knowing* 1. understand, to have learnt: Do you *know* how to open this door?–He *knows* two of Wordsworth's poems. 2. be acquainted with a person: I *knew* you when you were a little boy. 3. understand through experience: He has *known* both riches and fame. 4. be able to distinguish: He *knows* a good piece of leather from a poor one. **know of** be informed about: Do you *know of* any good books on gardening? **knowledge** understanding, being familiar with, aware of: A good *knowledge* of French is needed.–They left the camp without the leader's *knowledge*.

knuckle (knuck-le, pronounced *nuckle*) 1. a joint in the finger, or between the fingers and the hand: The teacher rapped on the table with his *knuckles*. 2. the joint between the foot and leg of an animal.

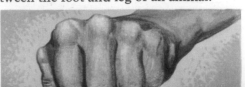

L

label (la-bel) 1. a small piece of paper, wood, cardboard, cloth, plastic or metal which can be attached to an article or substance giving information about it: The plant *labels* have all been attached. 2. fix on a *label*: Have you *labelled* your luggage yet?

laboratory (lab-or-a-to-ry) a room in which people do scientific experiments, especially in chemistry and physics.

labour (la-bour) 1. work: Road-making is hard *labour*. 2. those who work: More skilled *labour* is needed to make these goods. 3. a government department or political party having to do with workers: We have invited a minister in the last *Labour* government to address us. 4. try hard, work: He has *laboured* for years to make this company a success. 5. move with difficulty: The car is *labouring* badly on hills. **labourer** a worker: We employ 200 skilled and 300 unskilled *labourers*.

labyrinth (lab-y-rinth) a maze of roads, paths or passages from which it is very difficult to free oneself: We lost him in the *labyrinth* at Hampton Court.

lace 1. a fabric made of threads joined by knots and making many patterns, used for trimming dresses, covers and uniforms: The dress had a beautiful *lace* collar. 2. a piece of cord used to draw parts of an article of clothing together: Fasten your shoe*lace* or you may fall. 3. fasten by means of *laces*: We cannot use the football until it has been properly *laced*.

lacquer (lac-quer) 1. a varnish that dries quickly giving a hard, shiny surface: The doorhandle badly needs a coat of *lacquer*. 2. brush on *lacquer*: When are you going to *lacquer* your bicycle?

ladder (lad-der) 1. a set of steps that can be moved, consisting of two long pieces with crosspieces for the feet to rest on. 2. a place in a garment where a thread has broken leaving a tear: I can't go to the party with a *ladder* in my stocking.

ladle (la-dle) 1. a large spoon with a long handle: She used a *ladle* to serve the soup. 2. remove from one vessel to another with a *ladle*: She *ladled* the soup from the pan into the dish.

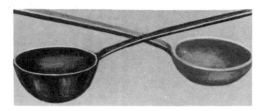

lady (la-dy) *ladies* 1. a woman. 2. a girl or woman with good manners. 3. a title: *Lady* Astor was the first woman Member of Parliament. **Our Lady** the Virgin Mary. **Lady-Chapel** a chapel in a church dedicated to the Virgin Mary. **ladybird** a reddish brown flying beetle with black spots on its wings.

lag 1. move slowly, fall behind: Don't *lag* behind or we shall miss the bus. 2. a space of time: There was a time-*lag* of ten seconds between the lightning-flash and the thunder. 3. wrap hot water pipes with material to protect them against frost.

lagoon (la-goon) a body of shallow water separated by low banks from the sea or connected with it by a narrow strait: The *lagoon* in which they took shelter was surrounded by high palm trees.

lair the den or resting place of a wild animal: They tracked the lion to its *lair*.

lake a large body of water surrounded by land: Windermere is the largest *lake* in England.

lamb 1. a young sheep: 'Mary had a little *lamb*' (nursery rhyme). 2. the flesh of the young sheep: We had *lamb* and green peas for dinner.

lame 1. crippled, injured: He is still *lame* from an injury on the football field. 2. sore, injured: My *lame* leg must be bandaged. 3. not satisfactory: He gave me a very *lame* excuse for being late.

lament (la-ment) 1. mourn, show great sorrow: 'I do *lament* the sickness of the king' (Shakespeare, *Richard III*). 2. an expression of sorrow in verse or song.

laminate (lam-i-nate) 1. separate or split into thin layers. 2. cover with thin metal plates. **laminated plastic** (or *hardboard*) sheets of closely pressed paper or board, covered with hard resin and made to shine.

lamp a device for giving light: The interior of the hut was lit by a single paraffin *lamp*. **lamplight** the light from a *lamp*.

lance 1. a long spear: In medieval times knights carried *lances* into battle. 2. pierce with a *lancet*: The doctor *lanced* the boil. **lancet** a small sharp instrument used by doctors and surgeons.

land 1. the solid part of the earth's surface: Less than one-third of the earth's surface is *land*; the rest is sea.—We are travelling to Rome by *land*. 2. a country: '*Land* of my fathers' is a Welsh national hymn. 3. come to *land* or bring to *land*: We *landed* at Southampton this morning.— He has just *landed* a large fish. **landlord, landlady** the man, woman or body of people who own property and let it for rent to others: Our *landlord* is responsible for all the outside painting of this house.

landing (land-ing) 1. coming or bringing to *land*: The aeroplane made a forced *landing*. 2. a platform at the top of or between two flights of stairs: You will find my office on the second *landing*.

lane 1. a narrow road: A country *lane* led to the edge of the moor. 2. the name of a street: I will see you at my office in Chancery *Lane*. 3. a route used by ships crossing the oceans. 4. a part of a road marked out for traffic: Traffic turning left please keep to the inside (or nearside) *lane*.

language (lan-guage) a means of communication by words, signs or symbols: French is the second *language* taught in English schools.–We communicate with the deaf and dumb in sign-*language*.

lantern (lan-tern) a case with transparent sides for enclosing a light and protecting it from the wind: A man walked along the dark road carrying a lighted *lantern*.

lap 1. the front part of a person's body from waist to knees, when seated: The little boy sat on his mother's *lap*. 2. once round a racecourse: He had to retire from the race in the third *lap*. 3. take up with the tongue: The cat *lapped* up the milk. 4. the sound of water moving: We could hear the waves *lapping* against the side of the boat.

lapel (la-pel) the front edge of a coat or jacket that folds back to make the collar: My new coat has black velvet *lapels*.

lapse 1. a slight failure: I am atraid I suffered from a *lapse* of memory. 2. an interval of time: I saw him again after a *lapse* of ten years. 3. neglect what is good: He has *lapsed* into idleness. 4. pass out of existence through failure to use: Your right to use this pathway *lapsed* two years ago.

larceny (lar-ce-ny) stealing, the wrongful taking away of another person's goods: He was charged with *larceny* and condemned to a year in prison.

lard the fat of pigs melted down and prepared for cooking.

larder (lard-er) a room or cupboard in which food is stored.

large of great size or amount: He won a *large* sum of money on the pools. **large-scale** thorough, covering a large area: *Large-scale* investigations are now taking place. **at large** free (of wild animals, criminals etc.): The convict who escaped from Dartmoor is still *at large*. **largely** to a *large* extent: His failure was *largely* due to bad luck.

larva (lar-va) *larvae* an insect immediately after it has come from the egg, and appears like a small worm. The best known of all *larvae* is the caterpillar.

lash 1. beat, strike with violence: The horse *lashed* out with his hind legs. 2. rouse: Mark Antony *lashed* his hearers to a fury against Brutus (*see* Shakespeare, *Julius Caesar*). 3. fasten tightly with rope: *Lash* the cases to the roof of the car. 4. that part of a whip which can be swung to give the stroke: The *lash* had nine knots in it. 5. the hairs on the edge of the eyelid, the eye*lash*.

lass a girl or young woman: 'On Richmond hill there lives a *lass*' (old English song).

lasso (las-so) (rhymes with *shoe*) 1. a long rope with a slip-knot and noose, used by cowboys for catching horses and cattle. 2. catch with a *lasso*.

last 1. final, after all others: I am the *last* to speak, my speech will be the *last*. 2. coming just before the present: Where were you *last* night? 3. the only one (ones) left: He shared his *last* sandwich with me.–One *last* hope remains. 4. be enough for: The boys had enough food to *last* four days. 5. A piece of iron or wood shaped like a foot on which shoes are made or stretched: My shoes are a little tight; would you please put them on the *last*?

latch 1. a device to hold a door or gate shut: He lifted the *latch* and entered. 2. a small lock: We dropped the *latch* (locked the door) for the night. 3. fasten with a *latch*: It's no good *latching* the stable door after the horse has gone.

late 1. after the time fixed or expected: Why were you *late* for school this morning? 2. near the end: These flowers bloom *late* in the year. 3. recent, that has just happened: He has been out of work since the *late* strike. 4. recently dead: This watch belonged to her *late* husband. **lately** recently: Have you seen your friend *lately*?

lath (rhymes with *path*) a thin strip of wood: We need a few more *laths* to repair the trellis.

lathe a machine in which a piece of wood or metal can be fixed and shaped by turning: His hobby is making candlesticks on a *lathe*.

lather (lath-er) 1. the mass of white foam which forms as, for instance, when soap is rubbed with water: When a horse is worked too hard *lather* forms at its mouth. 2. make and apply *lather*: Never try to shave until you have *lathered* your face well.

latitude (lat-i-tude) 1. the number of degrees north or south of the Equator: Buckingham is on the 52nd line of *latitude* north. 2. freedom to act or speak: The director gives him much *latitude* in arranging his working hours.

latter (lat-ter) 1. belonging to the later part of a certain period: We are now in the *latter* half of the 20th century. 2. the second of two: Of the two novels 'Barnaby Rudge' and 'Oliver Twist', I prefer the *latter*.

laugh 1. make sounds with the voice and movements of the face to show joy or merriment: The story made everybody *laugh*. 2. the act of *laughing*: We all had a good *laugh* when we heard the story. **laughter** *laughing*: From the next room came the sound of *laughter*.

launch 1. float a boat or ship: When the ship was *launched* a large crowd assembled. 2. start a scheme, an action or a project: A heavy attack was *launched* on the enemy. 3. a small motor-driven boat which carries passengers on short journeys: They were taken down the river by motor-*launch*.

laundry (laun-dry) *laundries* 1. a place where clothes are washed and ironed: Have my shirts come back from the *laundry* yet? 2. clothes or linen to be washed and ironed: Has the *laundry* come back yet? **launder** wash and iron. **launderette** a place to which people may take their clothes and have them washed in a machine while they wait.

lava (la-va) molten rock which is thrown or which flows out of a volcano: Two villages were destroyed by the river of boiling *lava*.

lavatory (lav-a-to-ry) *lavatories* 1. a room in which one may wash one's hands and face. 2. a water-closet.

law 1. a rule by which the behaviour or way of life of the people of a country or town are controlled: A new *law* has just come into force to control prices. 2. all the *laws* of a country: It is against the *law* to steal other people's property. 3. what is sure to happen under certain conditions: Sir Isaac Newton discovered the *law* of gravity.—The winds and waves obey the *laws* of nature. **lawful** allowed by *law*: I am my father's *lawful* heir. **lawless** not obeying the *law*: The wild west was full of *lawless* men. **lawyer** a person who has studied law and deals with matters having to do with it; a solicitor: The contract for the sale of this house has been drawn up by a *lawyer*.

lay *laid, laying* 1. put in a certain position: How many bricks can this bricklayer *lay* in an hour?—*Lay* down your burden. 2. produce (of animals): The hen has *laid* four eggs in five days. 3. put or keep down: Shall we *lay* the carpet this morning?—A sprinkling of water will *lay* the dust. 4. arrange: The fire has been *laid*, so now we can *lay* the table for tea. 5. put on a tax: More duties have been *laid* on motor oil. 6. put down money: Heavy bets are being *laid* on the result of the race. **lay-by** a place at the side of a main road where cars and lorries may park for a limited time.

layer (lay-er) 1. a thickness of material laid over another: How many *layers* of cement will be needed on this path? 2. a shoot of a plant fastened down to take root. 3. fasten down a shoot of a plant in soil so that it will take root: The gardener has *layered* the carnations.

lazy 1. not willing to work: 'You are *lazy* knaves, and here ye lie' (Shakespeare, *Henry VIII*). 2. a time when one is not working: I'm having a *lazy* day in the garden tomorrow. **laziness** being *lazy*.

lead (rhymes with *said*) 1. a soft, heavy metal used for making roofs and pipes, and for mixing with other metals. 2. a name commonly given to graphite, the material used in '*lead*' pencils. **leaden** made of *lead* or looking like *lead*: 'The sun was lost in a *leaden* sky' (Henry Newbolt, *Songs of the Fleet*).

lead (rhymes with *need*) led, leading 1. guide, show the way: Our guide *led* us along a narrow path. 2. take by the hand, or by a strap, rope etc.: 'You can *lead* a horse to the water but you can't make him drink' (proverb). 3. direct: Who is *leading* the singing in church this morning? 4. go first: The favourite *led* all the way to the winning-post. 5. be a way to: A narrow path *led* to the cottage. 6. live: I intend to *lead* a busy life. 7. action of guiding: You can't go wrong if you follow my *lead*. 8. first place: The favourite took the *lead* at the start. 9. a strap for *leading*: 'All dogs must be kept on the *lead*' (notice in a public park). 10. an electric flex taking current to the place where it is needed: 11. the principal part in a play: The *lead* is a brilliant actor. **leader** a person who *leads*: The first violinist is usually the *leader* of an orchestra.

league 1. a group of nations, societies or persons working for a common cause: Great Britain was a member of the *League of Nations*. — Would you like to join the *league* against cruel sports? 2. a group of clubs playing the same sport: Which team is top of the *league* this season?

leak 1. a crack or a hole through which gas or liquid may escape or enter: The water came in through a *leak* in the roof. 2. pass in or out through a *leak*: Water has *leaked* through the ceiling and spoilt the carpet. 3. the passing of secret information: News has *leaked* to the press of a coming change in the government. **leakage** a *leak*: There has been a *leakage* of military secrets to a foreign power.

lean leaned or leant, leaning 1. containing no fat, not fat: Jack Sprat, who could eat no fat, was *lean*; his wife, who could eat no *lean*, was fat. 2. poor, producing little: Owing to the lack of rain the corn harvest has been *lean* this year. 3. be in or put into a sloping position: First I *lean* backwards, then I *lean* forwards. — Have you seen the *Leaning* Tower of Pisa? 4. be or put in a sloping position against something: *Lean* against me. — He *leaned* the ladder against the wall. 5. depend on: I will try my best but I shall *lean* on you for support.

leap leapt or leaped, leaping 1. jump: He escaped by *leaping* over a wall. 2. a jump: With a great *leap*, he was over the wall and away. **leap-frog** a game in which players *leap* over others who are stooping. **leap year** one year in four in which February has 29 days.

learn learnt or learned, learning 1. come to know through effort: It takes many years to *learn* a language well. 2. come to know through being told, reading etc.: We have just *learned* of your brother's success.

leash a leather strap for holding a dog; a lead: This terrier is dangerous and should always be kept on a *leash*.

leather (leath-er) material for clothes, shoes and other articles of use made from the skins of animals: I only wear shoes with *leather* soles.–This book has been bound in *leather*.

ledge 1. a narrow shelf: The cliff narrowed down to a dangerous *ledge*.–The cat was sleeping peacefully on the window-*ledge*. 2. a reef or line of rocks under the sea or under other bodies of water.

ledger (led-ger) a book in which the accounts of a business are kept.

leg 1. one of the limbs on which a human being or an animal walks: He has had a lame *leg* since the accident.–The cook was carving a *leg* of lamb. 2. that part of a garment which covers the *leg*: Have you noticed the tear in the *leg* of your trousers? 3. one of the supports of a piece of furniture: Don't sit on the chair; it has a broken *leg*. 4. that part of the cricket field to the left rear of a batsman: He hit the ball to *leg* for four (runs). 5. a stage or any given distance in a relay race or a journey: The first *leg* of the journey was completed within two days. **-legged** having *legs*: A grasshopper is a long-*legged* insect. **legless** having no *legs*. **leggings** coverings for the *legs*.

legacy (leg-a-cy) a gift of property given to a person through the will of another person who has died: The *legacy* he inherited included a house and a considerable sum of money.

legal (le-gal) 1. connected with the law: My solicitor looks after all my *legal* affairs. 2. allowed by law: It is not *legal* to park a car on a double yellow line.

legend (leg-end) a story made up in the past which is believed by some to be true: Tennyson wrote about the *legends* of King Arthur in verse. **legendary** told about in *legend*: The days of our week are named after the *legendary* gods of the Anglo-Saxons.

legible (leg-i-ble) capable of being read easily: Her handwriting is perfectly *legible*. **legibly** in a *legible* manner: Please write your name and address *legibly*.

legislate (leg-is-late) make laws: Parliament has recently *legislated* against imposing the death penalty. **legislation** laws, making laws: We must study the recent *legislation* on landlord and tenant. **legislature** the body of people making the laws (in Great Britain, Parliament). **legislative** having to do with laws: *Legislative* action will soon be taken on the question of pollution.

leisure (lei-sure) spare time; time when one is not working: I do not have enough *leisure* for playing golf.

lemon (lem-on) a pale yellow fruit with very sour juice, used for flavouring. **lemonade** a drink made from *lemon* juice, sugar and water.

lend *lent*, *lending* give something for a certain length of time on condition that it is returned: Please *lend* me your pencil.

length 1. how long anything is: What is the *length* of the River Thames? 2. how long something lasts: We had not expected him to speak at such great *length*. **lengthen** make longer: Your dress is too short and needs *lengthening*.

lenient (le-nient) merciful, not inclined to punish: Some magistrates are more *lenient* than others.

lens a piece of glass specially made with one or both sides curved, for use in spectacles, microscopes, telescopes, cameras etc.: As his sight gets worse, he needs stronger *lenses*.

Lent the period of forty days before Easter set aside for fasting and worship: Many Christians observe *Lent*.

lentil (len-til) a plant with a seed like a small bean, used for food.

leopard (leop-ard) a large, fierce, animal of the cat family, living in Africa and southern Asia: The *leopard's* skin is covered with black spots.

leper (lep-er) a person suffering from *leprosy*, a skin disease which eats into the body and slowly destroys parts of it.

less not so much: If you wish to lose weight, eat *less* bread and put *less* sugar in your coffee.

lesson (les-son) 1. something to be learnt or taught: My sister is having piano *lessons*. 2. a period of time given to learning one subject: Our third *lesson* this morning is English. 3. a passage from the Bible read as part of a church service: We shall take for our first *lesson* the Twenty-Third Psalm.

lest for fear that; in order not to: Keep away from the fire *lest* you burn yourself.

let 1. allow to: *Let* me take you for a walk.– Don't *let* the rope slip. 2. hire, rent: If this house is to *let* will you please *let* it to me? **let in** allow to come in: Open the window and *let* some air in. **let off** excuse, fire off: May I please be *let off* school today?–We are *letting off* fireworks this evening.

lethal (leth-al) causing death: *Lethal* gases are escaping from the stove.

letter (let-ter) 1. a sign representing a sound: There are 26 *letters* in the English alphabet. 2. a written message: I had a *letter* from my brother yesterday. **lettering** printed or written words: We could not read the *lettering* on the signpost.

lettuce (let-tuce) a garden plant with large tender green leaves eaten in salads.

level (lev-el) 1. a horizontal line or surface: We are now well above sea *level*. 2. having a horizontal surface: The football field is quite *level*. 3. flatten: The earthquake *levelled* the whole town. 4. raise (a gun etc.): He *levelled* his rifle and took aim. **spirit level** an instrument containing an air bubble which shows when a surface is exactly *level*.

lever (le-ver) 1. a bar or other instrument used for lifting weights, forcing open doors etc. 2. move or open something with a *lever*: It took two men to *lever* the heavy crate on to the truck.

levy (lev-y) *levies, levied, levying* 1. impose (a tax, fine etc.): A tax is *levied* every year on all dog owners. 2. a tax or fine.

liable (li-a-ble) 1. responsible by law: I am not *liable* for your debts. 2. likely: If you wear those shoes you are *liable* to have sore feet.

liberal (lib-er-al) 1. generous, giving freely: He has been a *liberal* contributor to the hospital funds. 2. plentiful: We have a *liberal* supply of food. 3. a member of the *Liberal* Party, a British political party. **liberality** generosity, giving freely: We thank you for your *liberality*.

library (li-bra-ry) *libraries* a place where books are kept: The British Museum has one of the largest *libraries* in the world.– People may borrow books from a public lending *library*. **librarian** a person who looks after a *library*.

licence (li-cence) a statement giving permission to a person or persons to do something or own something: Do you possess a driving *licence*?

license (li-cense) give a licence to: '*Licensed* to sell tobacco' (notice outside a shop).

lie 1. make a statement which one knows is not true: He is *lying* to you. 2. stretch out on a flat surface: He is *lying* on the grass. 3. be in a certain position: Don't leave things *lying* about. 4. be situated: England *lies* between France and Scotland. **liar** a person who does not tell the truth.

lieutenant (lieu-ten-ant) (pronounced *leftenant*) a junior officer in the army next below a captain; in the navy next below a *lieutenant*-commander.

life *lives* 1. that which *lives*, grows and produces young: Is there *life* on any of the planets? 2. a human being: Many *lives* were lost in the fire. 3. a way of living: *Life* in the country is quiet and peaceful. 4. the time between birth and death: I have lived all my *life* in England. 5. the biography of a person: I am reading the *life* of Charles Dickens. 6. energy, interest, activity: The child is full of *life*. **lifetime** the length of time one *lives*: This leather coat will last me a *lifetime*.

light 1. that which makes it possible to see things; the opposite of dark: He was reading by the *light* of a lamp.– It was already getting *light* when we awoke. 2. anything that gives *light*: Have you seen the *lights* of New York?– I can't find my way without a *light*. 3. make burn: *Light* the fire, it's cold. 4. make bright: How many candles shall I *light*? 5. of a pale colour: Her dress was *light* green in colour. 6. not heavy: This van can only carry *light* weights. 7. gentle: I felt a *light* touch on my arm. 8. (of sleep) not deep: I awoke out of a *light* sleep. 9. (of travel) without much luggage: We're travelling *light* on this journey. **light-headed** dizzy. **light-hearted** cheerful.

lighten (light-en) 1. make or grow lighter: If you can carry this parcel it will *lighten* my load. 2. make brighter: The sky *lightened* towards dawn. **lightning** flashes of light in the sky produced by atmospheric electricity. **lightning conductor** a rod of metal which, by taking *lightning* to the ground, prevents it doing damage to buildings.

like 1. be fond of, enjoy: Do you *like* oranges? 2. desire to have or do something: Would you *like* an orange?– I would *like* to go for a walk. 3. similar to, resembling: Isn't he *like* his brother! 4. in such a way: He behaved *like* a perfect gentleman. **likeable** pleasant, friendly: She is a very *likeable* person. **likely** probable, probably: What time are you *likely* to arrive? **liking** fondness: I have a great *liking* for oysters. **likeness** resemblance, portrait: There is not a great *likeness* between the twins.

lily (li-ly) *lilies* a plant, of which there are many kinds, growing from a bulb: On the surface of the pond floated water *lilies* of many colours. **lily-of-the-valley** a small white flower with a sweet scent.

limb 1. the leg or arm of a human being or animal: I ache in every *limb*. 2. the branch of a tree: The budgerigar was perched on the highest *limb* of the oak tree.

lime 1. a white powder made by burning *lime*stone, used for making cement and whitewash. 2. a tree with sweet-smelling yellow blossom and fruit resembling a lemon. **quick-lime** burnt *lime* before water is added. **slaked lime** *lime* after the addition of water. **lime-kiln** an oven specially made for burning *lime*stone. **limelight** a powerful white light used for lighting the stage of a theatre. **in the limelight** to be the object of public interest.

limit (lim-it) 1. a boundary line: The police chased the car beyond the city *limits*. 2. a point beyond which one must not go: There is a *limit* to the amount of money I can spend. 3. put a *limit* on: You must *limit* the number of cigarettes you smoke each day. **limitless** without *limit*: The desert seemed *limitless*. **limited company** (shortened to *Ltd.*) a company whose members are liable only to the amount of money they hold in shares.

limp 1. not stiff, drooping: The flowers are *limp* from lack of water. 2. walk lamely, resting the weight on one foot more than another: After his injury the player *limped* off the field. 3. a jerky movement: You are walking with a bad *limp* this morning.

line 1. a length of thread, wire, rope or string: Two pairs of socks are hanging on the *line*. 2. a long mark made by a pen, pencil, brush etc.: I drew a *line* along the edge of the paper. 3. a row of persons or things: Along the side of the road grew a *line* of trees. 4. a railway track or route: Be careful how you cross the *line*.—This is the main *line* between London and Bristol. 5. method: You are working out the problem along the wrong *lines*. 6. kings, members of families etc., following one another: I am the last of my *line*. 7. military posts joined together for defence: Spies are active behind the enemy *lines*. 8. kind of work or activity: What is his *line* of business? 9. a row of

words on a page: He read the letter slowly, *line* by *line*. 10. any goods to be bought and sold: We have an excellent *line* in overcoats this month. 11. mark with *lines*: His face was *lined* with old age. 12. be placed in a *line* or *lines*: We found ourselves on a road *lined* with trees. 13. cover the inside of: We will *line* the box with thick layers of paper. **linesman** a person who watches the boundary *line* of a football pitch or tennis court and judges when the ball is out of play. **liner** a ship or aircraft travelling on a certain route or *line*: The *Queen Elizabeth 2* is a famous *liner*. **lining** a layer on the inner side of something (a coat, a box etc.).

linen (lin-en) 1. cloth made from flax: The table was laid with a clean white *linen* cloth. 2. articles made from *linen*: You will find all the *linen* in this drawer.

linger (lin-ger) be slow, stay near a place: He *lingered* by the fountain. **lingering** lasting a long time: He suffers from a *lingering* illness.

link 1. one ring of a chain: A chain is only as strong as its weakest *link*. 2. something which connects other things: This is the last *link* in the chain of evidence. 3. join or be joined with: The discovery of the fingerprints *linked* him with the crime. 4. a torch once used to light people along the streets, often carried by a *link*-boy. **links** a golf course.

lion (li-on) a large animal of the cat family found in Africa and southern Asia: The *lion* is called the King of Beasts. **lioness** a female *lion*.

lip 1. the fleshy fold above and below the mouth: Not a word shall pass my *lips* (I will say nothing). 2. part of the edge of a vessel which sticks out so that liquids may be poured from it: Who broke the *lip* of the milk-jug? **lip-reading** a method used by the deaf of watching the *lips* to find out what others are saying. **lipstick** a stick of coloured substance used for colouring the *lips*.

liquid (liq-uid) 1. a substance such as water or oil, that flows freely and can be poured out. 2. in the form of a *liquid*: Since his operation he has been able to take only *liquid* food. **liquidate** bring to an end; kill. **liquor** a drink containing alcohol: He was taken to the police station under the influence of *liquor*. **liquorice** a black substance taken from the root of a plant of the same name and used in drinks, medicines and sweets.

list 1. a number of names or figures in a row or column: Is my name on the voting *list*?–Take the shopping *list* with you. 2. make a *list*: He has *listed* everything he needs to build the wall. 3. lean over, or a leaning over to one side: The ship *lists* badly.–It has a bad *list*.

listen (lis-ten) 1. try to hear: If you *listen* you will hear the cuckoo. 2. pay attention: I've said it all before but you weren't *listening*. **listen in** *listen* to a radio broadcast or eavesdrop. **listener** one who *listens*; one who *listens* to the radio.

literature (lit-er-a-ture) 1. stories, poems, essays, biographies etc. published in books etc.: He knows a great deal about French *literature*. 2. written material sent to people as advertisements: Have you any *literature* about the latest electric heaters? **literary** having to do with the writing of books etc.: He is a *literary* man, and his *literary* earnings are high. **literate** able to read and write: Most people in Great Britain are *literate*. **literacy** the ability to read and write.

litter (lit-ter) 1. all kinds of waste paper, bottles, cartons etc. scattered about: *Litter* spoils the countryside. 2. straw used as bedding for animals. 3. the young of an animal immediately after birth: Our sow has had a *litter* of twelve pigs. 4. leave odds and ends about: We have been asked not to *litter* the study with waste paper. 5. a couch or a stretcher used to carry people: 'There is a *litter* ready: lay him in it' (Shakespeare, *King Lear*).

little (lit-tle) 1. small: What a pretty *little* butterfly! 2. short: I will spend a *little* time with you.–It's only a *little* way. 3. not much, a small quantity or amount: Will you have a *little* cheese? 4. slightly: I feel a *little* better today.

live (rhymes with *give*) 1. be alive: This plant will not *live* through the winter. 2. dwell: He has *lived* all his life in the village. 3. feed, keep alive by means of: Cattle *live* on grass.–He cannot *live* on his wages. 4. pass one's life: 'They *lived* happily ever after.' **living** a means of keeping alive, a way of life: I am earning a good *living*. **living room** the room which a family uses during the day for recreation and entertaining.

live (rhymes with *hive*) 1. being alive, having life: Under the stone I could see a *live* lizard. 2. burning hot: The old man lit his pipe with a *live* coal. 3. unexploded: The wagon was full of *live* ammunition. 4. carrying electricity: He received a shock from touching a *live* wire. 5. not recorded: The concert is being broadcast *live*. **lively** bright, gay, exciting: The evening passed in *lively* conversation.

liver (liv-er) 1. an organ of the body which helps in the digestion of food. 2. the *liver* of an animal used as food: *Liver* and bacon are on today's menu.

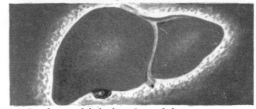

load 1. that which is placed in or on anything to be carried: The last wagon-*load* of hay was brought in. 2. the amount which can be carried: That horse is bearing too heavy a *load*. 3. put *loads* on to a person, an animal or a vehicle: They *loaded* the truck with bags of cement. 4. put a bullet into a gun or a film into a camera: He *loaded* his camera with a new roll of film. **load-shedding** cutting off or cutting down the supply of electric current from a power station.

loaf *loaves* 1. a large piece of bread baked in a special shape: The shop-window was full of newly-baked *loaves*. 2. meat, sugar etc., prepared and shaped like a *loaf*. 3. waste time or spend time idly: He does nothing but *loaf* at street corners.

loathe 1. be disgusted by: We *loathe* the smell of this polluted stream. 2. dislike: I *loathe* working inside on sunny days. **loathsome** disgusting: During the Great Plague (1666), the population of London was attacked by a *loathsome* disease.

lobby (lob-by) *lobbies, lobbied, lobbying* 1. an entrance hall: The guests were assembled in the *lobby* of the hotel. 2. a large room in the House of Commons where visitors may interview members. 3. try to persuade members of the House to aid or prevent the passing of a Bill: The officers of our association will be *lobbying* their members tomorrow.

lobe the lower part of the ear: Some women have their *lobes* pierced so that they can wear earrings.

local (lo-cal) 1. having to do with a certain district: Our *local* councillor is a brilliant speaker. 2. concerning a part and not the whole: The injury was *local* and was cured in a week. **locality** a certain place: There are few restaurants in this *locality*. **locate** find the position of; place something: The source of the trouble was *located* in the right arm.—A new clinic is to be *located* in this area. **location** the place where a thing happens; a place other than the film studio, where a film is photographed.

lock 1. a means of shutting a door, cupboard, drawer etc., so that it cannot be opened without a key: A new *lock* has been fixed on the front gate. 2. an enclosed part of a canal where boats can be raised or lowered by means of changing the level of water. 3. the small portion of hair forming a curl: She cut a *lock* of hair from her head and gave it to me. 4. fasten with a *lock*: Every night we *lock* all the doors. 5. fasten in or out with a *lock*: He was *locked* out and had to climb in through a window. 6. become fixed or jammed, not able to be moved: The car could not be used because the brakes were *locked*. **locker** a small cupboard where things can be *locked*: His books are stored in a *locker* at school. **locket** a small case for a portrait or a *lock* of hair, usually worn on a chain round the neck. **locksmith** a man who makes and mends *locks*. **lock-keeper** a person who looks after the machinery of a *lock* in a canal.

locomotion (lo-co-mo-tion) the power to move from place to place. **locomotive** a railway engine: There are very few steam *locomotives* still operating.

locust (lo-cust) a winged insect, a kind of grasshopper living in parts of Africa and Asia, which flies in great swarms and devours crops and vegetables.

lodge 1. a small house at the entrance to the grounds of a country estate, occupied by a gatekeeper or servant. 2. a house used during the hunting or shooting season: You will see a shooting-*lodge* on the high moors. 3. the room used by the porter at the entrance to a college, factory or a block of flats: 'For the key, please apply at the porter's *lodge*'. 4. the place where members of a society meet: How long has he been a member of this *lodge*? 5. receive as a guest: The evacuees were *lodged* in the homes of the townspeople. 6. pay for bed and board in another person's house: I am *lodged* at the home of a friend. 7. become fixed in a place: The splinter was *lodged* in the lion's paw. 8. place a statement with the authorities: We have *lodged* a complaint about the state of our drains. **lodger** a person who *lodges* in another person's house. **lodging** a room, or rooms, in another person's house in which one lives: Come to my *lodging* for tea. **lodging-house** a house which takes *lodgers* which is not a hotel.

loft 1. a room in the highest part of a house, stable or barn, used for storing things: We were surprised to find all kinds of antiques when we cleaned out the *loft*.— He brought down another bale from the hay*loft*. 2. part of a church: The children love to play in the organ *loft*.

logic (log-ic) 1. the study of methods of reasoning: He is studying *logic* at university as part of a philosophy course. 2. the ability to convince people by clear reasoning: I was impressed by the *logic* of his arguments. **logical** arrived at through reasoning: He put forward a *logical* argument for selling the property.

loiter (loi-ter) go slowly towards a place, stand about, loaf: Don't *loiter* on your way to school.

lonely 1. alone, with no company: I feel *lonely* without my dog. 2. not often visited: We were lost for hours on the *lonely* moor. **loneliness** being *lonely*: Many old people suffer through *loneliness*.

long 1. having great distance from end to end: This is a *long* road. 2. having much time from one point to another: Will you be here *long*? 3. desire very much: We *long* to see him again. **longing** a great desire: His *longing* for adventure persuaded him to join the army. **long-sighted** able to see things far away but not near to the eyes. **long-winded** inclined to talk for a very *long* time.

longitude (lon-gi-tude) distance east or west, in degrees, from Greenwich: Liverpool is on the 3rd line of *longitude* west.

loom 1. a machine for weaving cloth. 2. appear indistinctly: Out of the morning mist *loomed* the ghostly shape of a tank.

loop 1. a rope, thread, wire, line etc. which curves and crosses itself: To tie a knot, make a *loop* with string, draw one end through the *loop* and tighten it. 2. make a *loop*: She *looped* back the curtains to let in the sun. **loop the loop** fly an aeroplane in a *loop*: The airman *looped the loop* several times before he landed.

loose 1. free from restraint, not kept on a lead, or in a purse, box, or prison: A dangerous snake has broken *loose*. 2. not tight: The light has gone out; there's a *loose* connection somewhere.—I like my clothes to be *loose*-fitting. **loosen** make free; make less tight: At last we reached the prisoner and *loosened* his bonds.

loot 1. something stolen or taken away by force: The soldiers returned from the war laden with *loot*. 2. take by force or steal: The disorder in the streets was accompanied by much *looting*.

lose *lost, losing* 1. cease having something and be unable to find it: I have *lost* my watch. 2. fail to do or get something: He *lost* his train and was late home. 3. be defeated: Our team played well but *lost* the match. 4. (of a clock or watch) go slow: My watch *loses* a minute in every hour. 5. waste (time, chances, effort etc.): Quick, you must not *lose* a moment! **be lost** be unable to find one's way; disappear: They were *lost* in the dense forest.—Ten men were *lost* in the mining disaster.

loss 1. *losing*, being *lost*: I reported the *loss* of my watch at the police station. 2. not winning: The *loss* of one game deprived our team of the championship. 3. waste: The escape of steam is causing a *loss* of power in the engine. 4. something *lost* or destroyed: There was a great *loss* of life when the ship sank.

lotion (lo-tion) a liquid used for healing and cleansing the skin: I bought a bottle of hand *lotion* at the chemist's.

lottery (lot-ter-y) *lotteries* a scheme for raising money by the sale of tickets, some of which, picked out by chance after the sale, give the owners the right to claim prizes.

loud 1. noisy; not soft: He answered me in a *loud* voice. 2. (of colours) bright, vivid: The colours of the curtains were too *loud* for the rest of the room.

lounge stand, sit or lie about lazily: He does nothing but *lounge* about the house all day.

love 1. feeling of great fondness and affection for people, things or activities: 'Let brotherly *love* continue' (Epistle to the Hebrews).–We became friends through our *love* of sailing. 2. have a feeling of affection for: 'Do you *love* me, master?' (Shakespeare, *The Tempest*). 3. enjoy: I *love* playing the guitar. **lovely** beautiful, enjoyable: There was a *lovely* sunset last night.–We spent a *lovely* evening together. **lóver** a person who *loves*: He is a *lover* of good food.–'It was a *lover* and his lass' (Shakespeare, *As You Like It*). **lovingly** in a *loving* manner.

low 1. not high, of little height: He jumped over the *low* wall. 2. not as high as is normal: We can walk far out from the shore at *low* tide. 3. weak: I feel rather *low* this morning. 4. small: Prices of apples are at their *lowest* this week. 5. neither loud nor high in tone: He played the *low* notes on a trombone.–They were speaking in *low* voices. 6. almost gone: Supplies of meat are running *low*. 7. in a *low* position: The messenger bowed *low* before the prince. **lower** bring or come down: It is time they *lowered* the cost of public transport.

loyal (loy-al) true to: He is a *loyal* friend of yours.–We are all *loyal* subjects of the Queen.

lubricate (lu-bri-cate) put oil or grease into parts of a machine to make it work smoothly. **lubrication** *lubricating* or being *lubricated*: How much would the *lubrication* of my car cost?

luck chance, good or bad fortune: What *luck* did he have in the lottery?–We wish you good *luck*. **lucky** having or bringing good *luck*: You were *lucky* to escape with your life.–He won by a *lucky* chance.

luggage (lug-gage) bags, trunks etc. used when one goes on a journey: Please attach labels to all your *luggage*.

lull 1. make quiet, become quiet: Mother was *lulling* the baby to sleep. 2. an interval of quiet: They were able to make some repairs during a *lull* in the storm. **lullaby** a song sung by a mother to *lull* a child to sleep.

lumber (lum-ber) 1. move heavily and noisily: An elephant came *lumbering* down the road. 2. timber sawn and split into planks: Tons of *lumber* floated down the stream to the sawmills. 3. useless and old articles stored away: We must clear all the *lumber* out of this attic. 4. fill or load with useless articles: I don't want to be *lumbered* with all your old books.

luminous (lu-mi-nous) giving out light, reflecting light: Traffic is guided at night by *luminous* reflectors on the road surface.

lump 1. a piece of solid matter without regular shape: Large *lumps* of clay were scattered about the field. 2. a swelling: What caused the *lump* on your neck? 3. put together in one heap: Coats, hats, shoes and other garments had been *lumped* together without order.

lunatic (lu-na-tic) 1. a mad person: 'He hath been a *lunatic*' (Shakespeare, *The Taming of the Shrew*). 2. mad, very foolish: Running in front of a moving car was a *lunatic* thing to do. **lunacy** madness, mad or foolish actions: It is sheer *lunacy* to think of climbing that rock.

lunch 1. a meal taken at midday or shortly after: He has been invited to a *lunch* at the Mansion House. 2. have *lunch*: We are *lunching* today with my grandparents.

lung one of the two organs with which human beings and animals breathe: He filled his *lungs* with the fresh air of the mountainside.

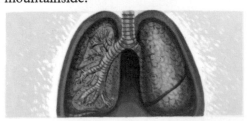

lunge 1. a thrust as in fencing. 2. a forward movement of the body. 3. make a *lunge*: He *lunged* and struck his opponent on the thigh.

lurch 1. suddenly lean or roll to one side: The wounded man *lurched* across the room and then fell. 2. a sudden roll: The ship gave a *lurch*.

lurk remain in hiding, waiting to attack: Hostile Indians were *lurking* in the woods.

luscious (lus-cious) very pleasing to taste: He took a big bite of the *luscious* pear.

lustre (lus-tre) 1. brightness: The pearls shone with a brilliant *lustre*. 2. glory: 'The two kings, equal in *lustre*, were now best, now worst' (Shakespeare, *Henry VIII*).

luxury (lux-u-ry) 1. having and enjoying costly food, clothing and everything that is pleasant; much more than one needs: He has lived a life of *luxury*. 2. something not really needed but which gives very great pleasure: For the first time in my life I enjoyed the *luxury* of a sauna bath. **luxurious** enjoying *luxury*; supplying *luxury*: He lives in *luxurious* surroundings.

lynch kill someone without authority: A crowd of angry men attacked the gaol and *lynched* the prisoner. **lynch-law** the practice of *lynching* victims without trial.

M

macadam (ma-cad-am) broken stone, crushed and rolled, used to surface a road. **macadamize** construct a road of *macadam*: The main road through our village is being *macadamized*.

macaroni (mac-a-ro-ni) wheat flour mixed with water and made into long hollow tubes: In Italy *macaroni* is an important part of many meals.

macaroon (mac-a-roon) a sweet cake or biscuit made of the whites of eggs, sugar, a little flour, and almond paste or coconut.

mace 1. a heavy club covered with spikes and used as a weapon by soldiers in the Middle Ages. 2. an ornamental staff carried before the mayor of a town or an important official as a symbol of his office: The mayor, preceded by his *mace-bearer*, walked in procession to the cathedral. 3. a spice made from nutmegs.

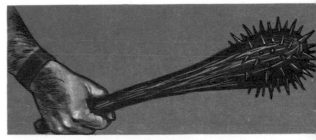

machine (ma-chine) a device made up of many parts, all working together to do a task more quickly than a person could do it by hand: Most *machines* work by electric power but some, such as sewing *machines* and lawn-mowers may be worked by hand or foot. **machinery** *machines* or mechanical devices: New *machinery* has been installed in this factory. **machinist** a person who works a *machine*: My brother is a *machinist* in a shoe factory.

mackerel (mack-er-el) a fish found in the North Atlantic which is caught for food: A *mackerel* has dark cross markings on its back.

mackintosh (mack-in-tosh) a rainproof coat. The earliest *machintoshes* were made of cloth treated with rubber but many are now made of other materials.

mad 1. diseased in mind, insane: 'Masters, help; my master is *mad*' (Shakespeare, *The Taming of the Shrew*). 2. (of animals) furious and violent: There is a *mad* bull in that field. 3. foolish: He has the *mad* idea of leaving the country for ever. **madness** being *mad*; a *mad* or foolish action: It would be *madness* to go into the burning house. **madden** make *mad* or angry.

magazine (mag-a-zine) 1. a book with a paper cover coming out at regular periods (weekly, monthly etc.) which contains articles and stories: He was a regular reader of the Strand *Magazine*. 2. a place where ammunition and explosives are stored: The defenders could no longer hold out after the *magazine* had been destroyed. 3. that part of a gun which holds the cartridges. 4. that part of a camera which holds the film.

magic (mag-ic) 1. the supposed power of making things happen by the help of spirits or mysterious beings: Many people still believe in *magic*. 2. tricks done by a conjurer to entertain an audience. 3. able to produce *magic*: The conjurer produced three doves out of his *magic* box. **magician** a person who is believed to have *magic* power or who does conjuring tricks: 'The King ordered the *magicians* to be brought, to tell what his dreams meant' (The Book of Daniel).

magistrate (mag-is-trate) a person, called a Justice of the Peace, who acts as a judge in a police court: The young man was taken before a *magistrate* and charged with theft.

magnet (mag-net) a piece of iron which has the property of attracting other pieces of iron or steel: We used a *magnet* to pick up the pins from the carpet. **magnetic** having to do with a *magnet*; having power to attract. **magnetic field** the area round a *magnet* in which objects are affected by it. **magnetic needle** a *magnetized* steel rod which, if left to swing freely, points north and south. **magnetic tape** tape specially made for use in a tape-recorder. **magnetism** the force exerted by a *magnet*. **magnetize** transfer *magnetic* force to a piece of iron or steel, usually by stroking it with a *magnet*: One of the blades of my pocket knife is *magnetized* and will pick up pins.

magnificent (mag-nif-i-cent) 1. splendid: The duke lives in a *magnificent* country house. 2. superb: We listened to the *magnificent* playing of the violinist.

magnify increase the apparent size of: This lens *magnifies* everything a hundred times. **magnifying glass** a glass (or lens) which makes things look larger.

mahogany (ma-hog-a-ny) a tropical American tree with a dark reddish-brown wood much used in the making of fine furniture.

maid, maiden 1. a young unmarried woman: 'I heard a *maid* sing in the valley below' (old song). 2. a girl who works as a servant for a family: House*maids* and nurse*maids* are rare these days. **maiden aunt** unmarried aunt. **maiden name** the surname of a woman before she marries. **maiden over** (in cricket) an over of six balls from which no runs are scored. **maiden speech** (in Parliament) the first speech given by a new member.

mail 1. the government organization for collecting and delivering parcels and letters between one place and another: The postman is late this morning; there must be something wrong with the *mail*. 2. the letters and parcels carried: I received a large amount of *mail* this morning. 3. armour of metal links worn by soldiers in the Middle Ages: The knight was clothed in *mail* from head to foot.

maim injure so badly that some part of the body cannot be used: Our neighbour was badly *maimed* in the train crash.

maintain (main-tain) 1. keep, preserve: Friendly contact with other nations is being *maintained*. 2. support, provide with food, clothing etc.: I have a large family to *maintain*. 3. hold on to an argument, insist: In spite of all evidence to the contrary the prisoner *maintained* his innocence. 4. keep in repair: The house and grounds cost a great deal to *maintain*.

majesty (maj-es-ty) a condition, appearance or sound of great splendour: At last the ruler appeared in all his *majesty*. **majestic** splendid in every way: The chorus sang a *majestic* hymn of praise. **'Your (His, Her) Majesty'** a title used in addressing, or speaking of, a king, queen, emperor or empress.

major (ma-jor) 1. an army officer ranking between a captain and a lieutenant-colonel. 2. greater: The *major* part of his life has been spent in the navy. **major-general** an army officer ranking between a brigadier and a lieutenant-general. **major scale** the scale beginning and ending with 'doh' (doh, ray, me, fah, soh, la, te, doh). **majority** the greater number: The *majority* of our friends live in this road.–The motion to close the road was carried by a small *majority*.

make *made* 1. construct: I am *making* a new shelf for my books. 2. earn: You can *make* more money by working overtime. 3. bring about, cause: She always *makes* a fuss when the kettle boils over. 4. cause to be: Too much cream will *make* you ill. 5. cause to do: I couldn't *make* the radio work.–Don't *make* me laugh! 6. be or become: Do I *make* myself clear?–You'll *make* a good lawyer if you study hard. 7. amount to: Two and two *make* four. 8. raise to a certain position: He was *made* captain of our cricket team. 9. kind of manufacture: This radio is a different *make* from the one I had before. **make off** go away, run away: The thieves *made off* with all her jewels. **make for** go in the direction of: The car was *making for* Bristol. **make up** put together: Ask the chemist to *make up* the prescription. **make-up** cream, lipstick etc. to *make* a woman's face more beautiful: Your face is too pale, you need more *make-up*. **maker** the person *making* a thing; God: We sent the watch back to the *maker*.–'Kneel before the Lord our *Maker*' (Psalm 95).

malady (mal-a-dy) *maladies* a disease or illness: John suffers from a rare *malady*.

malaria (ma-lar-i-a) a fever introduced into the body by the sting of the mosquito. **malarial** giving or causing *malaria*: The expedition was lost in a *malarial* swamp.

male a man, a boy, or the 'he' of any animal.

malice (mal-ice) the wish to cause injury or suffering to other persons: 'What *malice* was between you?' (Shakespeare, *Othello*). **malicious** showing *malice*: Take no notice of *malicious* gossip.

malignant (ma-lig-nant) 1. showing a desire to cause injury: Goblins were believed to be *malignant* fairies. 2. (of diseases) causing danger to life.

mallet (mal-let) a tool like a hammer, usually of wood: Small *mallets* are used by sculptors to shape their statues and long-handled *mallets* by polo players to strike the ball.

malnutrition (mal-nu-tri-tion) weakness caused through not eating enough food: The people of many parts of the world suffer from *malnutrition*.

mammal (mam-mal) one of the class of animals of which the female feeds its young with milk from the breast, and which is warm-blooded: Man is a *mammal* and so are the elephant, whale and bat.

mammoth (mam-moth) 1. a huge elephant with a hairy coat and long tusks, that once lived on earth. 2. very great, very large: A *mammoth* stadium is being built.–Its construction will be a *mammoth* task for the architects and builders.

manage 1. handle, control: He can *manage* all kinds of boats. 2. be able to do, to live etc.: If I am ill you will have to *manage* without me.–Have you enough money to *manage*? **management** the handling of an institution, business etc.; the people who handle affairs: The firm failed because of bad *management*.–If you want a job here you must apply to the *management*. **manager** a person who controls or *manages* a business: Where is the *manager* of the hotel?

mane the long hair that grows on the neck of a horse, and round the head of a lion: He seized the horse by the *mane* and leapt on its back.

manger (man-ger) a long trough or box open at the top, from which horses eat: Jesus was born in a stable and his first bed was a *manger*.

mangle (man-gle) 1. crush, damage, tear, injure badly. 2. a machine with rollers through which clothes are passed after washing to smooth or dry them. 3. put garments etc. through a *mangle*.

mania (ma-nia) 1. great excitement or enthusiasm: He has developed a *mania* for billiards. 2. madness accompanied by violence and exaggerated excitement. **maniac** a madman: The king was stabbed in his carriage by a *maniac*.

manicure (man-i-cure) 1. professional care of the hands and fingernails: I have made an appointment for a *manicure* on Thursday morning. 2. care for the hands and fingernails: My nails are *manicured* once a week. **manicurist** a person whose occupation is *manicure*.

manifest (man-i-fest) 1. appear: No sooner had we started the journey than trouble *manifested* itself. 2. show: He does not *manifest* much liking for music. **manifesto** a public declaration by a ruler, political party, or revolutionary group: On taking over the government, the army issued a *manifesto* declaring its aims.

manipulate (ma-nip-u-late) 1. handle skilfully: The pilot *manipulated* the controls to land the aeroplane safely. 2. arrange things, sometimes unfairly, to gain certain ends: The situation was *manipulated* to his own advantage.

manner (man-ner) 1. the way a thing is done: Slowly, in a calm *manner*, the officer proceeded to remove the fuse. 2. ways of behaving among people: Your table *manners* are excellent.–It is bad *manners* to push in front of others. 3. kind: 'What *manner* of man is he?' (Shakespeare, *Twelfth Night*)

manoeuvre (ma-noeu-vre) 1. a planned movement of troops or war vessels: By a skilful *manoeuvre* Nelson drew up his ships opposite the enemy line. 2. planned movements in the training of military forces: Traffic was stopped while the army was out on *manoeuvres*. 3. change the position of: Slowly the driver *manoeuvred* his lorry along the winding street.

mantle (man-tle) 1. a loose cloak without sleeves: She wore a silk *mantle* over her evening dress. 2. something that covers: A *mantle* of snow covered the hills. 3. a hood or cover fixed over a flame, which becomes hot and glows, giving light.

manual (man-u-al) 1. done with hands: Every person in the camp was forced to do *manual* labour. 2. a small book of instructions; a handbook: Did you borrow my engineering *manual*? 3. the keyboard of an organ: The organ in this church has three *manuals*.

manufacture (man-u-fac-ture) 1. make by machinery: This firm *manufactures* all kinds of woollen goods. 2. the making of goods by machinery: Sheffield is noted for the *manufacture* of cutlery. 3. the thing or material that is made: Here is a list of our *manufactures*. **manufacturer** a person or a firm *manufacturing* anything.

manure (man-ure) 1. animal waste or other manufactured substances spread on the ground to make it more fertile: The cart was carrying a load of *manure*. 2. to spread *manure* on the soil.

manuscript (man-u-script) a book, a piece of music or an article for a journal written out by hand or with a typewriter: I have sent the *manuscript* of my latest play to the B.B.C.

map 1. a diagram or drawing of the earth, a part of the earth, the moon, a planet or the heavens: He set off with a *map* of London in his pocket.–Have you seen the latest *map* of the moon? 2. make a *map* of: The astronomer has *mapped* this part of the heavens.

marauder (ma-raud-er) a person who robs and plunders: A band of *marauders* ransacked the house.

marble (mar-ble) 1. limestone, often white, sometimes with coloured markings, used for building, and making statues: On the mantelshelf stood a small *marble* statue. 2. a small ball made of glass or baked clay used by children in the game of *marbles*.

march 1. walk in time, taking steps of the same length: We *marched* to the music of the band. 2. make a person (or persons) *march*: The captives were *marched* off to the gaol. 3. the act of *marching*: On the third day we began our long *march* home. 4. a piece of music to which one can *march*: 'Colonel Bogey' is a famous military *march*.

mare a female horse.

margin (mar-gin) 1. the blank space between the writing or printing and the edge of a page: The teacher wrote remarks in red ink in the *margin*. 2. the difference between the buying and selling price. 3. an amount over and above what is necessary.

marine (ma-rine) 1. having to do with the sea: My brother is a *marine* painter, my father a *marine* engineer and my sister studies *marine* life. 2. having to do with ships: Lloyds deals with *marine* insurance. 3. a soldier who may serve on board ship: The Royal *Marines* is a distinguished regiment. **mercantile (or merchant) marine** all the merchant ships of a country. **mariner** a sailor: 'Ye *mariners* of England that guard our native seas–' (Thomas Campbell).

mark 1. a line, dent, scratch, stain, etc.: My little dog has a brown *mark* on his back. 2. a sign: Please accept the book as a *mark* of my affection. 3. a printed sign indicating a brand name: All goods manufactured by this firm bear our trade*mark*. 4. grade: Did you get a good *mark* for your English? 5. something aimed at: The arrow was wide of the *mark*. 6. the place where a race starts: On your *mark*! Get set! 7. the number in a series of manufactured articles: My car is a Jaguar *Mark* II. 8. put a *mark* or *marks* on: All school clothing should be *marked* with your initials. 9. have *marks* on: The leopard is *marked* with spots and the zebra with stripes. 10. notice, pay attention: 'Fairy king, attend and *mark*; I can hear the morning lark' (Shakespeare, *A Midsummer Night's Dream*). 11. a unit of German money: How many *marks* does beer cost in Germany?

market (mar-ket) 1. a place to which people may go to buy and sell: 'This little pig went to *market*' (nursery rhyme). 2. trade in a certain kind of produce: Trading was brisk on the wool *market* today. 3. a place or a country where one may sell goods: Our firm is always seeking new *markets* for its products. 4. take to a *market* to sell: We have *marketed* twenty pigs today. **market garden** a garden where vegetables, fruit, salad plants etc. are grown to be sold at *market*. **marketplace** an open space, usually in the centre of a town, where *markets* are held on certain days.

marriage 1. the ceremony at which a man and a woman become husband and wife: A *marriage* has been arranged between these two young people. 2. the state of being *married*: Their *marriage* was a great success. **marry** take in *marriage*: My sister has *married* an Italian musician.–They were *married* in the cathedral.

marsh an area or expanse of low, wet land; a swamp: The *marsh* is rich in all forms of wildlife.

marshal (mar-shal) 1. a military officer of the highest rank, known as a field-*marshal* in the army, an air-*marshal* in the Royal Air Force. 2. an officer responsible for arranging important state functions: The Earl *Marshal* of England is in charge of arrangements for all state processions, coronations, royal marriages and funerals. 3. arrange in order: The army was *marshalled* in battle order.

marsupial (mar-su-pi-al) a mammal whose young are born when they are only partly developed, and are then transferred to a pouch on the mother's stomach: A kangaroo is a *marsupial*.

martial (mar-tial) having to do with war: The band played *martial* music.—The commander placed the town under *martial* law.

martyr (mar-tyr) 1. one who suffers death rather than give up his religion: Stephen was the first Christian *martyr*. 2. put a person to death: Many people were *martyred* for their beliefs during the Wars of Religion. **be a martyr to** suffer from: He was a *martyr to* rheumatism. **martyrdom** death or suffering: I have just read about the *martyrdom* of Thomas More.

marvel (mar-vel) 1. something to be wondered at: Television is one of the *marvels* of the modern age. 2. wonder at, be surprised at: I *marvel* at what they do to help their neighbours. **marvellous** wonderful: We had a *marvellous* journey through the Alpine passes.

mascot (mas-cot) a person, animal or thing that is supposed to bring good luck: The *mascot* of our school football team is a panda dressed in a red coat.

masculine (mas-cu-line) 1. of or like a man: She prefers *masculine* clothes to dresses. 2. a class of words in grammar: The word 'man' is *masculine* gender.

mask 1. a covering for the face worn as a disguise or to hide the features: At our Guy Fawkes party we danced round the bonfire wearing *masks*. 2. a breathing apparatus to protect the wearer against smoke and poisonous gases: The rescuers put on their *masks* before entering the mine. 3. put on or wear a *mask*: The men *masked* themselves before attacking the coach.

mason (ma-son) a person who builds or works in stone: A large number of *masons* are building the new cathedral.

masquerade (mas-quer-ade) 1. a party or ball at which all the guests wear masks. 2. pretend by disguise or other methods to be another person: The king used to *masquerade* as a ploughman.

mass 1. a large quantity: There is a *mass* of letters in answer to the advertisement. 2. a large lump or number without shape: The roses made a *mass* of colour in front of the house. 3. join or come together: The crowds were already *massing* in front of the gates. **mass meeting** a large number of people meeting to give their views about something. **mass production** the making of large numbers of articles, all alike, with machines. **Mass** the celebration of holy communion in a Roman Catholic church.

massacre (mass-a-cre) 1. the merciless killing of large numbers of innocent people: King Herod ordered the *massacre* of all the male children in the city. 2. carry out a *massacre*: Thousands were *massacred* when the fortress was captured.

massage (mas-sage) 1. treatment of the body by rubbing and pressing to make the muscles and joints less painful: What you need is a course of *massage*. 2. rub, knead and press the muscles and joints: The footballer had cramp and had to be *massaged* for several minutes.

mast a tall upright pole which supports the sail of a boat or ship.

master (mas-ter) 1. a person who rules and controls: May I speak to the *master* of the house? 2. a person whose skill at a certain kind of work is recognized: My father is a *master* plumber. 3. the captain of a merchant ship: I was glad to hear that you had at last got your *master's* ticket (to qualify you to command a ship). 4. the way of addressing a boy or young man: This letter is addressed to *Master* Thomas Green. 5. a male teacher: Have you met your new chemistry *master* yet? 6. the holder of a university degree above that of bachelor: My brother is a *Master* of Science. 7. learn a subject thoroughly: It is not difficult to *master* the elements of shorthand. 8. control: I found it difficult to *master* my temper. **masterpiece** a picture, poem, novel, piece of music etc. recognized by all as being extremely good: One of Reynolds' *masterpieces* was recently auctioned. **masterful** liking to control or order others. **mastery** complete control of some activity: We were all amazed at his *mastery* of the piano.

mastiff (mas-tiff) a large, powerful dog, used mainly as a watchdog.

mat 1. a piece of material usually woven, for covering floors, putting under ornaments, on the dining table etc.: He closed the door and wiped his feet on the *mat*. 2. tangle or be tangled together: The dog's hair was *matted* with mud.

mate 1. a ship's officer below the rank of captain: Some ships have first, second and third *mates*. 2. one of a pair of animals or birds: The blackbird is singing to his *mate*. 3. (of animals) become one of a pair or a couple.

material (ma-te-ri-al) 1. the substances out of which a thing is made or with which things are done: I have enough *material* for two dresses.—Where are the writing *materials*? 2. having to do with the body and its needs: The nurse attends to all my *material* comforts. 3. (of the law) very important: The case had to be tried again because more *material* evidence had appeared. **materialize** become real: We planned to build a factory and hoped one day our plans would *materialize*.

maternal (ma-ter-nal) having to do with a mother: The child is in need of *maternal* care.—My *maternal* grandmother is my mother's mother.

mathematics (math-e-mat-ics) the study of numbers and measurements (length, breadth, area, time, amount): Arithmetic, algebra and geometry are all parts of *mathematics*. **mathematical** having to do with *mathematics*: Our son is a *mathematical* genius.

matinee (mat-i-nee) the afternoon performance at a theatre or cinema: Seats in this theatre are less expensive at *matinees*.

matter (mat-ter) 1. all material things of which the universe is composed: Everything we see around us is some kind of *matter*. 2. something to think or talk about: Here are a few *matters* for your consideration.—This is no laughing *matter* (nothing to joke about). 3. things printed or written: Printed *matter* advertising our goods is sent out regularly. 4. importance, something wrong: You haven't smiled all morning; what's the *matter*? 5. be important: Does it *matter*?—Yes, it *matters* a great deal.

mattress (mat-tress) a large thick pad, which may be of wool and contain springs, or of feathers, foam rubber etc., made specially to sleep on: My bed needs a new spring *mattress*.

mature (ma-ture) 1. ripen, become ready for use, become fully developed: This cheese is delicious when it has *matured*. 2. fully grown up, adult: He is only a boy but he has the mind of a *mature* person. 3. well thought out: After *mature* consideration the government has decided to build a new airport.

maul injure by rough treatment: The hunter was *mauled* by a lioness.

maximum (max-i-mum) the greatest number, quantity, amount: Nobody ever scores the *maximum* marks in this subject.—We are seeking the *maximum* value for our money.

may *might* 1. possibly, have been, will, etc.: I *may* be in to lunch today. 2. be allowed: *May* I have the next dance please? 3. hope that: God bless the Queen; long *may* she reign. 4. (with a capital) the fifth month of the year: Jane's birthday is on the 15th of *May*.

mayor (rhymes with *fair*) the chief officer and head of the corporation of a town or city. **mayoress** the wife of a *mayor*, the woman a *mayor* or a lady *mayor* chooses as companion in office for the year: Both the *mayor* and *mayoress* wore their gold chains.

maze 1. a confusing network of paths: Theseus boldly entered the *maze* to slay the minotaur (an old Greek legend). 2. anxiety or confusion of mind.

meadow (mead-ow) a field where grass is grown, usually for making hay: 'Let us dance in the green *meadow*' (folk tune).

mean 1. plan, think of doing: I didn't *mean* to hurt you. 2. intend to say: Please tell me what these words *mean* in English. 3. be of value: What you say *means* little to me. 4. looking poor or weak: This part of the city has many *mean* little streets. 5. of low rank: The prince would speak to the *meanest* of his subjects. 6. selfish: Don't be *mean*; give your little brother a sweet. **means** money, the way in which things are done: Don't live beyond your *means*.—What are our best *means* of letting everybody know?

measure (meas-ure) 1. the size, weight, amount etc.: Buy your sweets here and we will give you good *measure*. 2. something with which size, amount, weight etc. is found: She took a tape-*measure* to find out how long the table was. 3. laws or actions to bring about a result: New *measures* have been taken to prevent smuggling. 4. find the size, weight or amount: Please *measure* the length and breadth of this carpet. 5. be a certain size etc.: The table *measures* three metres. **measurement** the figures found by *measuring*: I have written down the *measurements* of your new carpet.

meat 1. the flesh of animals (not including that of fish and birds): What kind of *meat* are we having today? 2. food in general. **meatless** not eating *meat*: We have at least two *meatless* days a week.

mechanic (me-chan-ic) a skilled workman who makes and repairs machinery: This car should be taken to a motor *mechanic*. **mechanical** having to do with machinery; done without thought: This road carries all kinds of *mechanical* transport.—My job at the factory is purely *mechanical* (i.e. I do not have to think). **mechanism** the working parts of a machine: If your clock has stopped, you had better have the *mechanism* checked.

medal (med-al) a badge, usually a flat piece of metal with a design on it, given to a person for long service, bravery or for some other reason: He was proud to receive his *medal* from the Queen herself.

meddle (med-dle) busy oneself in other people's affairs without being asked: Who has been *meddling* with my tools?

medicine (med-i-cine) 1. the study of the means of preventing or curing disease: My son is going to university to read *medicine*. 2. the substances taken to help cure illnesses: I take a teaspoonful of this *medicine* three times a day. **medical** having to do with *medicine*: This university has a very good *medical* school.

medieval (med-i-e-val) having to do with the Middle Ages (about A.D. 800 to 1500): We are studying *medieval* history.–Who was the most powerful *medieval* monarch?

mediocre (me-di-o-cre) not very good, not very bad, of about average ability: Our team won the match, but it was a *mediocre* game.

meditate (med-i-tate) think about: He sat in a corner, *meditating* on some mischief. **meditation** silent, deep thought; reflection: He sat there, deep in *meditation*.–Have you read the *Meditations* of the Roman emperor, Marcus Aurelius?

medium (me-dium) *media* 1. the means by which something is done: Among the best *media* for advertising is the local paper. 2. not too much, not too little: He is a man of *medium* height.–Eat neither too much nor too little; keep to a happy *medium*. 3. a person who acts as a link, especially in spiritualism: This is a book by a famous *medium* about spiritual healing.

meet *met* 1. come upon, come face to face with: I first *met* him at an art exhibition. 2. get to know, be introduced to: I should like you to *meet* my wife. 3. come together by arrangement: Shall we *meet* at dinner? 4. satisfy, pay: I can't *meet* your bill until next week. 5. join: Our ways *met* at a lonely place on the moor. **make both ends meet** have enough to live on. **meeting** coming together by chance or arrangement: The next *meeting* will be on Tuesday.

megaphone (meg-a-phone) a large horn into which one speaks and which magnifies the voice so that it can be heard a long distance away: The steward announced the next event through the *megaphone*.

melancholy (mel-an-cho-ly) 1. sad: Why am I so *melancholy*?–We were sad to hear the *melancholy* news. 2. sadness: Loneliness is one of the most frequent causes of *melancholy*.

melody (mel-o-dy) *melodies* 1. a tune: I shall now sing you an old English *melody*. 2. tunefulness: All day long we hear the *melody* of bird song. 3. the chief part when two or more sing or play: The *melody* is first played by the violin to the accompaniment of the other instruments. **melodious** sweet sounding: This composer has written many *melodious* tunes.

member (mem-ber) a person who belongs to a society or group: My father is a *member* of the bowling club. **membership** being a *member*, the number of *members*: His *membership* was renewed last week.–The club has a *membership* of several hundred.

memory (mem-o-ry) *memories* 1. the power to bring back to mind things that have happened in the past: Have you a good *memory* for faces?–No, I have a far better *memory* for dates. 2. a period of time which a person can remember: This is the hottest summer in living *memory*. **memorial** something chosen or made to remind people: I will meet you at the war *memorial*.–Take this ring as a *memorial* of our friendship. **memorize** learn by heart; commit to *memory*: You must all *memorize* your parts before the next rehearsal.

menace (men-ace) 1. danger, threat: The building of factories in the forest would be a *menace* to wild life. 2. threaten: The lack of rain is *menacing* crops in most parts of the country.

menagerie (me-nag-er-ie) a place where wild animals are brought together in cages, especially in a travelling circus: The *menagerie* has been visited by several thousand people.

mend 1. repair: Would you please *mend* the hole in my sleeve. 2. become better in health: The boy will soon *mend* if he rests in the sunshine. **invisible mending** the repair of clothes so that no trace of the hole or tear may be seen.

mental (men-tal) having to do with the mind: He is good at *mental* arithmetic.

mention (men-tion) 1. speak or write about something: I will *mention* the matter to your uncle. 2. referred to, being noticed or spoken well of: There was no *mention* of his bravery in the newspapers but he was *mentioned* in several dispatches.

menu (men-u) a list of the courses being served in a meal: I will give the order as soon as I've seen the *menu*.

mercenary (mer-ce-na-ry) a professional soldier who is paid to fight in a foreign army: The troops were reinforced by a thousand *mercenaries*.

merchant (mer-chant) 1. a trader who buys and sells goods: Antonio was a *merchant* living in Venice. 2. a person who deals in a certain kind of goods: The coal *merchant* delivers coal once a week. 3. having to do with *merchants* and trading: Which country has the largest *merchant* navy? **merchandise** goods in which *merchants* deal: England imports all kinds of *merchandise* from abroad.

mercury (mer-cu-ry) a heavy liquid that shines like silver: *Mercury* is most commonly used in thermometers and barometers.

mercy (mer-cy) *mercies* a decision not to punish a person for his offence, pity: The king showed *mercy* to his captives and spared their lives. **merciful** showing *mercy*: 'Be *merciful*, great duke' (Shakespeare, *Henry V*). **merciless** showing no mercy: 'The foe is *merciless*, and will not pity' (Shakespeare, *Henry VI*).

mere being nothing more than: He gave a *mere* wave.–Don't punish him; he's a *mere* child. **merely** only, simply: I *merely* wanted to give you a little advice.

merge join together: Our two firms are now *merged* into one large trading concern.–The sea *merged* with the sky on the horizon. **merger** the joining of two or more businesses etc.: Have you read about the latest *merger* between the three companies?

merit (mer-it) 1. some quality that deserves praise; worth: The great *merit* of this machine is that it needs no attention. 2. deserve: Your plan *merits* serious thought.

mermaid (mer-maid) a maiden described in fairy tales, who has a fish's tail instead of legs, and lives in the sea.

merry (mer-ry) gay, bright, happy, joyful: Here comes Robin Hood with his *merry* men!–'A *merry* Christmas, my good fellow' (Dickens, *A Christmas Carol*). **merriment** being *merry*.

mess 1. dirt, filth, disorder: After we had pulled down the shed we had to clear away the *mess*. 2. trouble: How am I to get out of this *mess*? 3. the place used in the army and navy to eat and for entertainment: Could you please take me to the Officer's *Mess*?

message (mes-sage) 1. news, information: A radio *message* informed us that we could enter port.–Take this *message* to the managing director. 2. an errand: I have been carrying *messages* all day. 3. an important statement: The Prime Minister's *message* to the country appeared in all the newspapers. **messenger** a person carrying a *message*: The telegram has been delivered by special *messenger*.

metal (met-al) any hard substance such as tin, copper, lead, iron or gold, which comes from ore dug from the ground: What kind of *metal* is the statue made of?

meteor (me-te-or) a shooting star; a solid body rushing from outer space into the earth's atmosphere and causing a bright streak in the sky as it burns up. **meteorite** a piece of stone or metal that has fallen to earth from outer space: A great *meteorite* has fallen in the Sahara Desert.

meter (me-ter) 1. an apparatus for recording measurements on a dial: The man has called to read the gas *meter*. 2. measure with a *meter*: All water used by householders is soon to be *metered*. **parking meter** an apparatus measuring the amount of time a car has been parked in one place.

method (meth-od) 1. a way of doing things: There are various *methods* of paying money, in cash, by cheque, or by postal order. 2. order in doing something: We shall not finish this in time unless we use some other *method*. **methodical** doing things in an orderly way: We need *methodical* workers in our head office.

metre (me-tre) 1. a unit of length equal to 39·37 inches: What does this carpet measure in *metres*? **metric** of the *metre*. **metric system** the system of measurement based on the *metre*, now widely used. 2. a poetic measure: Blank verse is one of the many kinds of *metre* used by poets.

metropolis (me-trop-o-lis) the most important city in any country: London is England's *metropolis*. **metropolitan** having to do with a *metropolis*: The *Metropolitan* Police Force was set up by Sir Robert Peel.

mew the sound made by a cat: I heard a

mew at the door.—It was the cat, *mewing* to be let in.

micro- (mi-cro) a word meaning small, from which we form other English words. **microbe** a tiny living creature too small to be seen: *Microbes* exist everywhere; some cause diseases and others are necessary to human life. **microphone** an instrument which changes sound into electricity so that it can be sent great distances. **microscope** an instrument to enlarge things too small to be seen by the naked eye.

midget 1. a very small person: The *midgets'* act at the circus was very amusing. 2. very small: *Midget* submarines did important work during the war.

might great strength, great power: 'Old Tubal Cain was a man of *might*' (a very strong man—from a poem by C. Mackay). **mighty** great, powerful: The little boat was alone on the *mighty* ocean.

migrate (mi-grate) 1. go from one place to another to live: Many English people have *migrated* to Australia. 2. (of birds) travel to another part of the world to live during certain seasons of the year: In the winter swallows *migrate* to warmer countries. **migration** the movement of people or birds to other places.

mild 1. gentle in manner and speech toward others: He is the *mildest* of people and would never hurt anybody. 2. not strong or sharp in flavour: He prefers *mild* cigarettes. 3. (of the weather) not too cold: The morning was *mild*. 4. not severe: Since it was his first offence he was given a *mild* sentence.

mile a measure of distance, just over 1,609 metres. **milestone** a stone set up by the roadside giving distances to the most important places.

military (mil-i-ta-ry) having to do with soldiers, armies, or land battles: In some countries all men have to undergo *military* training. **militarism** a belief in the importance of *military* strength. **militarist** believing in *militarism*. **militant** ready and willing to fight for a cause: A group of *militant* workers were among the first to strike.

million (mil-lion) one thousand thousand (1,000,000). **millionaire** a very rich man who is worth a *million* or *millions*, as of pounds, dollars, francs, marks etc.

mimic (mim-ic) *mimicked*, *mimicking* 1. a person who is clever at imitating other persons or animals. 2. imitate, especially for a joke: He makes everybody laugh when he *mimics* his friend. **mime** a play in which few words are spoken, and in which imitation is the most important part.

mince cut or chop into small pieces: I *minced* the onions after the meat. **mincemeat** currants, raisins, sugar, apples, suet and spices mixed together: Have we enough *mincemeat* to make three *mince* pies?

mind 1. brain; that part of the person which remembers, thinks and directs the actions of the body: He may be old and weak but his *mind* is still quite clear. 2. intention: What have you in *mind* for tomorrow?—I thought I would work but I have changed my *mind*. 3. be careful about: '*Mind* the doors! *Mind* your heads!' 4. be troubled by, object: Do you *mind* if I smoke?

mine 1. possessive form of I: That box is *mine*. 2. a hole or tunnel in the earth for digging out coal, iron or minerals: The *mine* produced a thousand tons of coal a day. 3. a metal case filled with explosive which blows up when disturbed: *Mines* have been placed at the entrance to the harbour. 4. dig for coal or other minerals: This company is *mining* for gold. 5. lay explosive mines: The entrance to the harbour has been *mined*. 6. sink with *mines*: The battleship was *mined* and it sank in twenty minutes. **minefield** an area of land on which explosive *mines* have been placed. **miner** a person who works in a *mine*. **mineral** a substance such as iron, gold, lead or copper dug from the earth by *mining*.

mingle (min-gle) mix: Several policemen in plain clothes *mingled* with the crowd.

miniature (min-i-a-ture) 1. a very small portrait of a person or a scene: On the shelf was a *miniature* of grandfather in a splendid uniform. 2. on a very small scale, tiny: My favourite hobby is the growing of *miniature* trees.—Have you ever been on the *miniature* railway?

minimum (min-i-mum) the very smallest amount or number: Only the *minimum* of effort is necessary to complete the work.—'We give the maximum value at the *minimum* price' (notice in a shop).

mink a small animal living near the water whose fur is very valuable: She has never wanted to own a *mink* coat.

minor (mi-nor) 1. less important: He was dragged out of the burning car with only *minor* injuries.—I have read the works of most of the *minor* poets. 2. the younger of two brothers: The headmaster sent for Jones *minor*. **minor scale** the scale beginning and ending with 'lah' (lah, te, doh, ray, me, fah, soh, lah). **minority** the smaller number; a small number of foreign people living in a country: Only a small *minority* voted to repair the road; the majority voted to close it.—In England there are several *minorities* belonging to various nations, such as Italians, Chinese and Poles.

minstrel (min-strel) 1. a person who sings and tells funny stories: One of the most famous television entertainments is the Black and White *Minstrels*. 2. one of a class of medieval musicians who sang or recited accompanied by an instrument.

mint 1. a plant which has a pleasant smell and which is used in the making of sauces and flavourings: There are many varieties of *mint*, such as green *mint*, orange *mint* and pepper*mint*. 2. a place where coins are made: The Royal *Mint* manufactures coins for many countries. 3. make coins: New coins were *minted* when decimal coinage was introduced.

minus 1. less: What is 24 *minus* 12? 2. without: When I reached home I found that I was *minus* my wrist-watch.

minute (min-ute) the sixtieth part of an hour: My interview with the manager lasted twenty *minutes*. **minutes** the record of what has been said and decided on in a meeting: The chairman asked the secretary to read the *minutes* of the last meeting. **minute** (pronounced *my-newt*) very small: The floor of the car was covered with *minute* fragments of glass.

miracle (mir-a-cle) 1. something that cannot be explained by the laws of nature: Christ's first *miracle* was the turning of water into wine. 2. a most fortunate happening, hard to explain: It is a *miracle* that the driver was not killed. **miraculous** like a *miracle*: 'Your husband has made a *miraculous* recovery,' said the doctor.

mirror (mir-ror) 1. a surface which reflects objects, once made of polished metal, but now usually of glass; a looking glass: He saw his own face reflected in the *mirror*. 2. reflect: The calm surface of the pond *mirrored* my face in the water.

mischief (mis-chief) 1. things done without thought, which cause annoyance to others: I don't mind what games you play as long as you keep out of *mischief*. 2. damage: Much *mischief* has been done at the public baths by vandals. 3. a person who is fond of *mischief*, not usually intending harm: Wait till I catch you, you little *mischief*! **mischievous** causing *mischief*; full of *mischief*: This was done by *mischievous* boys.—Beware of *mischievous* gossip.

miserable (mis-er-a-ble) 1. very unhappy: The loss of my bracelet has made me *miserable*. 2. bad, poor: What *miserable* weather!—It was a *miserable* performance. **misery** being *miserable*, suffering: The bad harvest has caused much *misery* among farmers.

misfortune (mis-for-tune) bad luck: While skiing I had the *misfortune* to break my arm.

mislead (mis-lead) *misled* lead or guide wrongly; cause others to do the wrong things: It is easy to *mislead* a person when giving street directions.

missile (mis-sile) something which is thrown or shot: The infantry advanced into a hail of *missiles*. **guided missile** a *missile* which can be shot into the air and guided to its destination.

mission (mis-sion) 1. a number of persons sent out to do a special piece of work: The *mission* has been sent to investigate the causes of the disaster. 2. a body of religious teachers sent to convert people to a religion: There are still many Christian *missions* in India. 3. the work one feels one has to do in life: My *mission* is to find homes for the poor. **missionary** a member of a religious *mission*: A band of *missionaries* has begun work in the jungles of Brazil.

mist 1. water vapour in the air through which it is difficult to see: Drive carefully, there are patches of *mist* on the motorway.–As we neared the town the *mist* thickened into a dense fog. 2. be covered with *mist* or vapour: As soon as she entered the warm room her spectacles became *misted* over. **misty** having *mist*: It's very *misty* this morning.

mistake (mis-take) *mistook, mistaken* 1. a wrong idea or deed: Your book is full of spelling *mistakes*. 2. make an error: He *mistook* the road and found himself in Bristol. **mistaken** in error: He has the *mistaken* idea that this house is his.

mistress (mis-tress) a woman who is in charge of a house, a family or school: The *mistress* of the house should sign the receipt.–The new French *mistress* at school is very nice.

mix 1. put together and stir so that one substance cannot be distinguished from another: '*Mix* the flour and sugar thoroughly before adding water' (from a recipe for making a cake). 2. carry on more than one activity at the same time: I am *mixing* business with pleasure. **mixed up** confused in mind: Don't interrupt me when I am adding, or I'll get *mixed up*. **mixture** various things put together: 'Take the *mixture* three times a day' (instructions on a medicine bottle).–We are trying to invent a new smoking *mixture*.

moan 1. a low sound of pain: All night long we could hear the *moans* of the wounded. 2. a low sound: Can't you hear the *moan* of the wind in the trees? 3. make such a sound. 4. speak with groans, complain: 'What a miserable place this is!' he *moaned*.

moat a deep, wide ditch round a castle, a fort or a large house, dug out and filled with water, to defend it against enemies.

mob 1. a disorderly crowd of people: An angry *mob* gathered round the prison gate. 2. crowd round to attack or to cheer: The crowd rushed on to the ground and *mobbed* the referee.–He left the theatre by a rear entrance to avoid being *mobbed* by his admirers.

mobile (mo-bile) 1. able to move or be easily moved: He broke his leg some weeks ago but is now *mobile* again. 2. moving, changing: *Mobile* troops on motor vehicles were on all the main roads. 3. a structure with many hanging parts which is moved continually by currents of air.

mock 1. make fun of by copying: He speaks with a lisp and the other boys *mock* him. 2. not real: *Mock* turtle soup is made from a calf's head. **mockery** *mocking*, an offensive imitation: His trial without a jury was a *mockery* of justice.

model (mod-el) 1. a small copy: I would very much like to see your new *model* railway. 2. a pattern to be copied: Take this as your *model*.–She is a *model* of patience. 3. something of which many copies are to be made: Have you seen the new *model* in our range of small cars? 4. a person who poses for artists or sculptors; a person employed to wear clothes for buyers to see: Before she became an actress she worked as a *model*. 5. shape from clay or some other soft substance: I like *modelling* in plasticine. 6. work as a *model*: She is *modelling* the latest fashions in hats. 7. copy the ways of another person: He is *modelling* himself on his professor. **modelling** the art of making *models*: The artist is an expert in *modelling* animals and birds.

moderate (mód-er-ate) neither too small nor too great, too little or too much: I bought this house for a *moderate* sum, as I have only a *moderate* income. **moderate** (mod-er-áte) 1. keep oneself, one's wishes, needs etc. from becoming extreme: If you *moderate* your demands a little I may be able to pay you. 2. become less: At last the wind is *moderating*. **in moderation** not too much, not too little: You will come to no harm if you eat *in moderation*.

modern (mod-ern) 1. of present and recent times: Space travel is a *modern* development.—I am studying *modern* history. 2. the very latest: 'We specialize in making the most *modern* kitchen equipment' (an advertisement). **modernize** bring up to date: The latest edition of the dictionary has been completely *modernized*.

modest (mod-est) 1. not thinking too highly of oneself or one's abilities: 'She is young, and of a noble, *modest* nature' (Shakespeare, *Henry VIII*). 2. not large in size or amount: My father left me a *modest* sum of money. **modesty** being *modest*.

modify (mod-i-fy) 1. change, make different: We have *modified* the design of the car to suit the needs of disabled drivers. 2. reduce, make more suitable: When he knew we could not pay the price he *modified* his demands. **modification** *modifying* or being *modified*: The *modification* of the design has pleased most of our customers.

moist damp; slightly wet: He rubbed the window with a *moist* cloth.–Don't sit down; the grass is still *moist*. **moisten** make *moist*: The shirts should be *moistened* before they are ironed. **moisture** damp; vapour.

mole 1. a small dark spot on the human skin. 2. a small dark-grey animal covered with fur which burrows under the ground. **molehill** a pile of soft earth which the *mole* throws up while burrowing.

molecule (mol-e-cule) the smallest particle of matter that can exist unchanged: *Molecules* are made up of still smaller particles called atoms.

molest (mo-lest) interfere with or annoy: If you *molest* the cat she may scratch you.

moment (mo-ment) 1. a very short period of time: The earthquake only lasted a few *moments*. 2. a point in time: I knew you the *moment* I saw you. **momentary** lasting for a very short time: The pain will only be *momentary*.

momentum (mo-men-tum) speed increased by movement: An object gains *momentum* as it falls.

monarch (mon-arch) a ruler: A *monarch* may be a king, a queen, an emperor, an empress, a duke or a duchess. **monarchist** a person who believes that the head of a country should be a *monarch* (and not, for instance, a president or dictator).

monastery (mon-as-ter-y) a building in which monks live: There are many *monasteries* to be seen in England.

Monday (Mon-day) the second day of the week: The beaches were crowded on Easter *Monday*.

money (mon-ey) 1. metal coins or printed pieces of paper used by people when buying and selling: I felt in my pocket and found I had no *money*.–How much *money* have you? 2. amounts of *money* in banks: Most of my *money* is in the National Bank. **monetary** of *money*: The pound is the *monetary* unit in Great Britain, the franc in France and the lira in Italy.

mongrel (mon-grel) a dog whose parents are of different breeds: *Mongrels* are often very intelligent.

monitor (mon-i-tor) 1. a child who helps a teacher with special tasks, such as keeping order or supervising work. 2. a person who is employed to listen to foreign broadcasts to collect news.

monk a man living as a member of a religious group apart from the world in a building called a monastery: A *monk* wears a special gown, known as a habit.

monkey (mon-key) 1. an animal that is one of a group of higher primates, the most closely related of the mammals to man, found in Africa, Asia and South America: The troop of *monkeys* swung through the trees, chattering noisily. 2. play, behave mischievously: Who's been *monkeying* with my tools?

monsoon (mon-soon) a seasonal wind which blows over India and southern Asia: The south-west *monsoon* brings rain; if it fails serious famines occur.

month 1. one of the twelve parts into which the year is divided: In which *month* were you born? 2. a period of about 28 days or 4 weeks: I haven't seen you for a whole *month*. **monthly** happening once a *month*: Will you be coming to our *monthly* meeting?

monument (mon-u-ment) a statue, pillar, etc., usually set up as a memorial to a great person or event: I will meet you at the Nelson *monument* in Trafalgar Square. **monumental** having to do with a *monument*; something of outstanding value: Beethoven's Fifth Symphony is one of the most *monumental* pieces of music ever composed.

mood state of mind or feeling: I will speak to father when he's in a better *mood*. **moody** having *moods* that change quickly: *Moody* people are not easy to please.

moon 1. the satellite nearest the earth and which moves round it, whose light is reflected to the earth at night: Whoever thought that men would one day walk on the *moon*! 2. a heavenly body moving round one of the planets: Jupiter has twelve *moons*. 3. move about lazily with nothing special to do: We found him *mooning* about in the garden. **moonbeam** a ray of light from the *moon*.

moor 1. an area of uncultivated land, often covered by heather and rough grass: Every autumn we shoot grouse on the Scottish *moors*. 2. make a boat or ship fast to the quay or landing-stage. **moorings** the place at which a boat is *moored*; the ropes or chains fastening it: In the storm ten boats broke loose from their *moorings*.

moral (mo-ral) 1. a lesson taught by a story: What is the *moral* of the Parable of the Sower? 2. having to do with right and wrong, good and evil: 'Treat others as you would like them to treat you' is a *moral* teaching. **morals** standards of behaviour accepted by society. **morality** the kind of *morals* one believes in and practises: The people of this country are strict Christians and have high standards of *morality*. **morale** the state of discipline and the spirit of an army, a school, a team etc.: If we can keep our *morale* we are certain to win the trophy.

morbid (mor-bid) unpleasant, unhealthy (of ideas and thoughts): His fear of ghosts arises from a *morbid* imagination.

more 1. greater in number, amount, size.: There's no *more* money in my purse.— May I have a little *more* jelly please? 2. greater in extent or degree: You must practise *more* if your piano playing is to improve.—'It is *more* blessed to give than to receive' (The Acts of the Apostles). 3. again: I would like to see you once *more* before you go to France.

morning (mor-ning) 1. the early part of the day before noon: Our milk is delivered at 8.00 every *morning*. 2. having to do with the *morning*: Have they brought the *morning* paper yet?—I always read it before my *morning* walk.

morose (mo-rose) bad-tempered, sulky: Why is Henry so *morose* today?

morphia (mor-phia) a drug made from opium which is given to relieve pain: The doctor gave him a *morphia* injection to lessen the pain.

mortal (mor-tal) 1. certain to die: All men are *mortal*. 2. something causing death: He received a *mortal* wound in the attack. 3. a human being: 'I pray thee, gentle *mortal*, sing again' (Shakespeare, *A Midsummer Night's Dream*). **mortality** number of deaths caused, death rate: The *mortality* caused by the earthquake was great. **mortuary** a building in which corpses are kept until the time of burial.

mortar (mor-tar) 1. a mixture of cement, lime, sand and water used to hold bricks and stone together in a building. 2. a bowl of hard material in which drugs etc. are powdered with a pestle. 3. a very short cannon which throws shells at high angles into the air, to drop at the place intended: This morning the enemy launched a *mortar* attack.

mortgage (mort-gage) 1. a written agreement to take a loan on property promising to give up the property if the debt is not paid in the time stated: I have taken out a *mortgage* on my house. 2. make such an agreement: I have *mortgaged* my house to buy the field which adjoins it.

mosquito (mos-qui-to) *mosquitos* a small flying insect the female of which feeds on the blood of living beings: Some *mosquitos* carry the malaria germ.

most 1. the greatest in number, quantity, quality, etc.: Who has *most* marks?—This is the *most* beautiful picture in the exhibition. 2. the greater number, the greater part of:—*Most* people get colds at some time. I had a cold *most* of the winter. 3. very: I heard a *most* interesting story yesterday. **mostly** chiefly, nearly all: The goods we make are *mostly* for use in the house.—This fruit drink is *mostly* water.

moth a winged insect resembling a butterfly: The grubs of some *moths* eat and make holes in woollen cloth. **moth-eaten** eaten by *moths* and full of holes; of no use. **mothproof** proof against *moths*: The curtains are entirely *mothproof*.

mother (moth-er) 1. the female parent: I have to help *mother* before I can come out and play. 2. care for, as a *mother* does: She needs *mothering*! **mother-in-law** the *mother* of one's husband or wife. **mother tongue** the language one has spoken from birth: My *mother tongue* is English. **mother country** one's native land.

motion (mo-tion) 1. movement: 'Do not open the door while the train is in *motion*.' 2. a certain way of moving; a gesture: She went through the *motions* of sweeping the floor. 3. an item for discussion in a meeting: We will now take your *motion* about increasing our membership. 4. make a movement: He *motioned* to me to go and sit next to him. **motionless** with no movement: The sick dog lay on the floor, *motionless*.

motive (mo-tive) 1. causing motion: Electricity provides the *motive* power in this factory. 2. something causing action: He has done all this through *motives* of kindness.—Don't be influenced by selfish *motives*.

motor (mo-tor) 1. an engine, a machine that supplies power to make other machines work: He took the electric *motor* out of the washing-machine to repair it. 2. travel by car: We *motored* all the way to Land's End. **motorist** a person who drives a car: This road is not to be used by *motorists*. **motorway** a road for the use of *motor* vehicles only.

mould 1. soft, fine earth used for making plants grow quickly: This flower-bed needs more leaf-*mould*. 2. a container into which molten material (lead, jelly etc.) is poured so that it will take its shape when solid: This is a plastic *mould* for making chessmen. 3. give a shape: The sculptor *moulded* the clay into the figure of a dancer. 4. a growth like fine hair which forms on certain substances: There's green *mould* on that piece of cheese. **mouldy** covered with *mould*: Don't eat that cheese, it's *mouldy*.

mound a small pile of earth, a small hill: If you stand on the *mound* you can see the next village.

mount 1. go up, get on: He was unable to *mount* the stairs.–He *mounted* his horse and galloped off. 2. grow in size or amount: His debts are *mounting* up. 3. put something in position: I am having your photograph *mounted* (put in a frame or *mount*). 4. the article or animal on which a person or thing is *mounted*: The general rode up on his grey *mount*. 5. used in the name of a mountain: There is snow on the slopes of *Mount* Everest.

mountain (moun-tain) a very high hill: Ben Nevis is the highest *mountain* in Scotland. **mountaineer** a person who climbs *mountains*. **mountainous** with many *mountains*: Switzerland is a *mountainous* country.

mourn feel great sorrow for: We *mourn* the loss of our grandmother. **mourner** a person who *mourns* another who has died. **mournful** sad: He answered me in a *mournful* tone. **mourning** sadness; black clothes worn when a person has died: The whole family were in *mourning* at the funeral.

moustache (mous-tache) hair growing on the upper lip of a man.

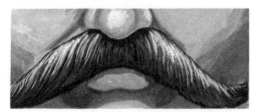

mouth 1. the opening in the face through which human beings and animals take in food, and by which sounds and speech are made: 'My *mouth* shall speak of wisdom' (Psalm 49). 2. the entrance or outlet of many other objects: He stood at the *mouth* of the cave.–A number of boats were anchored near the *mouth* of the river. **mouthful** as much as the *mouth* will hold: He took a *mouthful* of soup. **mouthorgan** a harmonica. **mouthpiece** the part of a pipe or a musical instrument which is placed in or against the *mouth*: This pipe needs a new *mouthpiece*.

move 1. put a thing in a different place: We *moved* the chair in front of the fire. 2. change position: The policeman *moved* cautiously towards the half-open window. 3. go to live or work in another place: My firm is *moving* to Birmingham. 4. cause strong feelings of pity, sorrow etc.: I was *moved* to tears by her sad story. 5. put forward a subject to be decided or discussed: Mr Chairman, I *move* that we erect a new sports pavilion. 6. a change of position in a game: The next *move* is mine.

movement (move-ment) 1. a changing from one position to another: Any *movement* you make will frighten the bird. 2. a part of a machine which moves: There's something wrong with the *movement* of my watch. 3. the effort of a group of people to change conditions: I am writing a history of the Trade Union *movement*. 4. a section of a musical composition: The orchestra played the final *movement* of Beethoven's Fifth Symphony.

mow *mowed, mown* 1. cut down; cut the grass: I shall *mow* the lawn this morning. 2. destroy: The attacking force was *mown* down by machine-gun fire. **mower** a machine that *mows*.

Mr (shortened form of *mister*) the title placed before a man's name. **Mrs** (shortened form of *missis*) the title placed before the name of a married woman. **Messrs** the shortened form of the French word *Messieurs*, used in English as the title placed before the names of more than one man: Would *Messrs* Jones, Brown and Robinson please come with me.

mud wet, soft, sticky earth: He fell in the *mud*, ruining his new suit. **muddy** covered with *mud*: His suit is *muddy* from falling in the *muddy* road.

muddle (mud-dle) 1. bring to disorder and confusion: I'm completely *muddled* by all your stories.–You've *muddled* everything up. 2. confusion of things and ideas: Everything in the office was in a *muddle*.

mule 1. an animal which is the young of a mare and a male donkey: 'The messenger is now unloading of his *mules*' (Shakespeare, *Antony and Cleopatra*). 2. a flat slipper which leaves the heel exposed. 3. a machine for spinning cotton and wool: The spinning-*mule* was invented two hundred years ago.

multiply (mul-ti-ply) 1. add a number to itself a certain number of times: If you *multiply* 9 by 5 the result is 45. 2. increase in number: Rabbits become a pest if they are allowed to *multiply*. **multiplication** *multiplying*, being *multiplied*: We obtained the answer by *multiplication*. **multiple** having many parts: He was brought into hospital suffering from a *multiple* fracture.

multitude (mul-ti-tude) 1. a great number: The audience asked a *multitude* of questions. 2. a great number of people: Christ preached to the *multitude*.

mumble (mum-ble) speak indistinctly so that people can hardly hear: A good actor never *mumbles* his words.

mummy (mum-my) *mummies* the dead body of a human being preserved by the use of spices and chemicals: Several Egyptian *mummies* may be seen in the British Museum. **mummify** embalm and dry a dead body so as to preserve it.

mumps a disease in which the glands of the neck swell painfully.

munch chew: He walked along *munching* an apple.

municipal (mu-ni-ci-pal) having to do with a town or city: We pay our rates at the *municipal* offices. **municipality** a town or city which governs itself: This *municipality* has its own water supply and bus services.

munitions (mu-ni-tions) guns, shells, bombs, rockets etc. for use in war: Victory depends on a plentiful supply of *munitions*.—*Munitions* factories have been set up in all parts of the country.

murder (mur-der) 1. the unlawful killing of a person: The man was brought into court charged with *murder*. 2. kill a person unlawfully: We read in the newspaper that the grocer's wife had been *murdered*. **murderer** a person who *murders*: The hunt for the *murderer* is still going on.

murky (mur-ky) dark, dismal, gloomy: Why are you going out on such a *murky* night?

murmur (mur-mur) 1. a low, soft, continuous sound: We heard the *murmur* of voices in the distance. 2. make such a sound: 'I *murmur* under moon and stars' (Tennyson, *The Brook*).

muscle (mus-cle) the strong tissues in the body of an animal which control the movements: He walks to work every day to develop his leg *muscles*. **muscular** having to do with *muscles*: *Muscular* fatigue may result from too much exercise.—The wrestler was short, with *muscular* arms and legs.

museum (mu-se-um) a building in which interesting objects are displayed, especially those dealing with nature, ancient history, arts and science: A large collection of objects dealing with the two World Wars can be seen in the Imperial War *Museum*.

mushroom (mush-room) 1. a fungus that can be cultivated and eaten: Can you distinguish a *mushroom* from a toadstool? 2. gather *mushrooms*: Shall we go *mushrooming* in the morning?

music (mu-sic) 1. sounds made by the human voice or by instruments which create melody and harmony, usually giving pleasure to those who listen: We danced to the *music* of the piano and violin.–The procession passed through the street to the sound of solemn *music*. 2. written signs which consist of instructions as to what to sing or play: He composes *music* but he can't write *music*. **musical** enjoying or making *music*: I am *musical* and play several *musical* instruments. **musician** a person skilled in composing or performing *music*.

musket (mus-ket) an old type of gun which could be fired from the shoulder: Soldiers used the *musket* before the rifle was invented. **musketeer** a soldier whose chief weapon was the *musket*.

muslin (mus-lin) a fine cotton cloth from which light dresses, curtains, sheets and pillowcases are often made.

mussel (mus-sel) a small creature protected by a black shell, living in the sea. *Mussels* are delicious to eat.

must 1. have to: You *must* obey the orders you have received. 2. need to: We *must* find out the times of the trains. 3. may be supposed to: You *must* be tired after your journey.

mustard (mus-tard) 1. a plant with yellow flowers and hard seeds in pods: Do you see that field of *mustard*? 2. the seeds of the *mustard* plant, ground and made into a hot-tasting sauce: Will you have *mustard* on your beef?

muster (mus-ter) 1. an assembly or parade of soldiers. 2. call troops together for inspection or for action: We *mustered* all the men and marched them off. 3. summon, call forth: He had to *muster* all his courage to climb the steep cliff.

mute 1. silent, not speaking: We gazed at the scene in *mute* astonishment. 2. not sounded: The 'n' in 'column' is *mute*. 3. made to sound more softly: In the hospital ward the nurses spoke with *muted* voices. 4. a piece of bone or metal put over the strings of a stringed instrument or a pad put into the bell of a wind instrument to muffle the sound. 5. a person who is unable to speak: The emperor was attended by a number of *mutes*.

mutilate (mu-til-ate) injure or damage a person or animal by breaking, tearing or cutting: The corpse was badly *mutilated* in the train crash. **mutilation** *mutilating*, being *mutilated*.

mutiny (mu-ti-ny) *mutinies* 1. a rebellion of soldiers, sailors, prisoners etc. against those who are in charge: Thousands of lives were lost in the Indian *Mutiny*. 2. rebel against authority: The sailors *mutinied* when provisions ran short. **mutineer** a person who has *mutinied*: The *mutineers* were condemned to long prison sentences.

mutter (mut-ter) mumble, say something in a low voice so it cannot be heard: 'Did I hear someone *muttering*?' asked the teacher.

mutton (mut-ton) the meat of the sheep, used as food: Tonight we are having leg of *mutton* for dinner.

mutual (mu-tu-al) shared, held in common: We have a *mutual* respect for each other.–Our society exists for *mutual* aid (members helping each other).

muzzle (muz-zle) 1. the mouth of a gun or pistol; the end from which the shot comes: I found myself facing the *muzzle* of a revolver. 2. the jaw, mouth and nose of an animal: I felt the dog's warm *muzzle* in the palm of my hand. 3. a device of straps and wires placed over an animal's mouth to prevent it from biting. 4. put such a device in place: All dogs allowed in the streets must be *muzzled*. 5. stop newspapers or people from saying what they think: News is scarce from some countries because the press is *muzzled*.

mystery (mys-tery) *mysteries* something impossible to understand: How he discovered my secret is still a *mystery*. **mysterious** full of *mystery*: We shall never discover the truth about his *mysterious* disappearance.

myth a story handed down from olden times, usually about superhuman beings such as gods, fairies, and legendary heroes: I have studied the *myths* of Greece and Rome. **mythical** existing only in *myths*: Thor was the ancient *mythical* god of thunder. **mythology** the study of *myths*; the collected *myths* of people.

N

nag 1. continually ask, scold or find fault with: You won't get what you want by *nagging*. 2. an old, tired-looking horse: Here comes the old-clothes man with his *nag*.

nail 1. a hard plate growing on the tops of and at the ends of fingers and toes: It's a bad habit to bite your *nails*. 2. a thin pointed piece of metal used for hammering into wood etc.: You need only a hammer and *nails* to fix the bookshelves. 3. fasten with a *nail* or *nails*: I had to *nail* two new boards on the fence.

naked (na-ked) 1. without clothes. 2. without covering: 'Do not place near a *naked* light' (instruction on a packet). 3. not disguised in any way: Do you want me to tell you the *naked* truth?

napkin (nap-kin) 1. a piece of cloth used during a meal to protect the clothing and to wipe one's hands and lips: The table was laid with a linen cloth and *napkins*. 2. a towel, usually of cloth, folded and fastened between a baby's legs; a **nappy**.

narrow (nar-row) 1. neither wide nor broad, measuring little in width compared with length: We found ourselves at the edge of a long, *narrow* lake. 2. near, close: You have had a *narrow* escape. **narrow-minded** not tolerant of the opinions or behaviour of other people.

nasty (nas-ty) 1. dirty, unpleasant: This medicine has a *nasty* taste. 2. bad-tempered: If you tease the dog much longer he may turn *nasty*. 3. dangerous: Be careful, there's a *nasty* bend in the road. 4. having done harm: He has had a *nasty* accident with his car.

nation (na-tion) a body of people who have the same government, usually speak the same language and have similar customs and ways of life: The Prime Minister spoke to the *nation* on radio last night. **national** having to do with a *nation*: Most *nations* have their own *national* anthems and *national* flags. **nationality** being a member of a *nation*: People of all *nationalities* meet at the United *Nations* building in New York. **nationalism** a love of one's own *nation*, sometimes a desire to fight for its independence. **nationalize** put under the control of a *national* government: In Great Britain the railways and the coalmines have been *nationalized*.

natural (nat-u-ral) 1. having to do with or produced by nature: Much of England is now supplied with *natural* gas from the North Sea. In this forest the animals live in their *natural* state. 2. being such by nature; born such: My son is a *natural* musician.—It is *natural* for a cat to catch mice. **naturalist** a person who studies animals and plants. **naturalize** give a person the right to become a citizen of a country other than the one in which he was born: He was born in England but is now a *naturalized* American. **naturalization papers** the papers which prove that a person has taken another nationality. **naturally** by nature, in a *natural* way: Her hair curls *naturally*.— She is *naturally* good at games.

nature (na-ture) 1. the universe: The earth, sea, sky and all that are in them are part of *nature*. 2. simple life not using many of the things man has made: There are still races in remote parts of the world living in a state of *nature*. 3. qualities that belong to certain persons, animals or things: 'Let bears and lions growl and fight, for 'tis their *nature* to'. (Isaac Watts, *Divine Songs*).—I like people with generous *natures*.

navigate (nav-i-gate) 1. manage and steer a boat or aircraft: He successfully *navigated* the canoe through the rapids. 2. sail over: Captain Cook *navigated* the Pacific as far as Australia. **navigation** the act and science of *navigating*: I have begun my studies in *navigation*.–He is employed in coastal *navigation*. **navigator** a person who *navigates*: Sir Francis Drake, a distinguished *navigator*, sailed round the world.

navy (na-vy) a country's warships and those who man them: It is now a year since I joined the *navy*. **naval** of the *navy*: Nelson won several *naval* victories.

neat 1. tidy: This is *neat* work. 2. liking tidiness: He is a *neat* worker. 3. clever: He found a *neat* way of solving the problem. 4. with nothing added: The old man drinks his whisky *neat*.

nebula (neb-u-la) *nebulae* a cluster of stars resembling a cloud of light: The Milky Way is a long line of star-clusters or *nebulae*. **nebulous** like clouds; vague not thoroughly worked out: There are thousands of *nebulous* patches in the night sky.–My plans for the coming year are still *nebulous*.

necessary (nec-es-sa-ry) 1. having to be done: It is *necessary* for me to go to the meeting. 2. that which is important and cannot be ignored: Sleep is *necessary* to all human beings. **necessitate** make *necessary*: Your plan *necessitates* careful thought. **necessity** something *necessary*: I depend on my parents for all the *necessities* of life.

neck 1. that part of the body which connects the head to the trunk: He had a red scarf round his *neck*. 2. the *neck* of an animal used for food: We had *neck* of mutton for lunch. 3. something like a *neck*: He seized the bottle by the *neck* and threw it. 4. part of a piece of clothing that covers the *neck*: A new shirt, sir? What size *neck* do you take?

nectar (nec-tar) 1. the drink of the gods in Greek mythology. 2. the sweet liquid collected from flowers by bees. 3. any sweet drink.

need 1. a want, a lack of something: There is a great *need* for manual workers in this industry. 2. poverty; misfortune: The recent floods have left many families in great *need*. 3. want, require: I *need* a new pen. **needy** poor, in *need*: 'The *needy* shall not always be forgotten' (Psalm 9).

negative (neg-a-tive) 1. expressing a refusal, usually with 'no' or 'not': When I asked him whether he would like an ice-cream his answer was in the *negative*. 2. a photographic plate or film on which the light parts of the subject are dark and the dark parts are light.

neglect (neg-lect) 1. fail to give time and care to: He *neglected* his training and was not picked for the team. 2. omit to do something: Don't *neglect* to write every week. 3. the state of being *neglected*: The whole room was in a state of *neglect*. **neglectful** *neglecting* things: He is *neglectful* of his studies. **negligent** in the habit of *neglecting*. **negligence** the habit of *neglecting*: He was dismissed for general *negligence*.

negotiate (ne-go-ti-ate) 1. talk about something in order to come to a decision: A treaty is being *negotiated* between the two countries. 2. conclude, arrange (a sale, treaty, rent or loan): A mortgage on this property should not be too difficult to *negotiate*. **negotiation** the act of *negotiating*: *Negotiations* are proceeding for the sale of the house.

Negro (ne-gro) a member of one of the black-skinned races which came originally from central and southern Africa.

neigh (pronounced *nay*) 1. whinny, make the cry of a horse: The mare galloped off, *neighing*. 2. the cry of a horse: Did you hear a *neigh* in the field?

neighbour (neigh-bour) 1. a person who lives near another: My *neighbour* lent me his ladder while mine was being mended. 2. a person near to another: Don't copy the answers from your *neighbour*. 3. a country near another: Our nearest *neighbour* is France. **neighbourhood** a district, a district near to: There have been several burglaries in this *neighbourhood*.

neither (nei-ther) 1. not one or the other: I tried both pairs of shoes but *neither* one fitted. 2. nor: He doesn't drink coffee and *neither* do I.

nephew (neph-ew) the son of one's brother or sister: The old man left all his money to his *nephew*.

nerve 1. one of the small fibres carrying messages between the brain and all parts of the body: Paralysis may result from damage to the *nerves*. 2. boldness, courage: I haven't the *nerve* to ask for more money.–You need plenty of *nerve* to make a parachute jump. **nervous** of the *nerves*, easily frightened, restless: He is suffering from a *nervous* breakdown.–Don't be *nervous*; the dog won't bite you.

nest 1. the place in which birds, animals or insects choose to lay and hatch eggs: We found a crow's *nest* in the trees.–Don't sit near the wasps' *nest*. 2. a number of things that fit together: A *nest* of tables stood in the corner. 3. a hiding-place: The artillery was ordered to shell the machine-gun *nest*. 4. make a *nest*: Don't disturb the swallows while they are *nesting*. **nestle** lie close and in a comfortable position: The cat *nestled* in front of the fire.–*Nestle* close to your mother.

net 1. material made by knotting string, wire, hair etc., for various purposes: *Nets* are designed to hold hair, to divide the two parts of a tennis court, to catch animals and fish, or to fence off an area. 2. catch with a *net*: He has *netted* ten large fish today. **netball** a game played mainly by girls in which a ball has to be thrown into a *net* hung from a pole. **network** lines, rivers, railways, roads, canals crossing each other: England is crossed by a *network* of railways.

neuralgia (neu-ral-gia) pains in the face and head along the path of a nerve. **neuritis** inflammation of the nerves in any part of the body, causing great pain.

neutral (neu-tral) 1. on neither side in a war or quarrel: Throughout recent wars Switzerland has remained *neutral*. 2. a *neutral* country: In recent wars the trade of *neutrals* has been badly affected. 3. in a motor, the gear position in which power is not transferred from the engine to the working parts: When you stop the car you apply the brake and put the gear in *neutral*. **neutrality** being *neutral*: I want to keep strict *neutrality* in this quarrel. **neuter** (in grammar) the gender which is neither masculine nor feminine: The word 'boy' is masculine, 'girl' is feminine and 'hat' is *neuter*.

new 1. never known, possessed, seen or heard before: How do you like my *new* suit? 2. coming or beginning again: Happy *New* Year!–I shall dig up the *new* potatoes this afternoon. 3. existing but not known or knowing before: That's a *new* story to me.–I'm *new* to this country. **newborn** just born: The shepherd brought in a *newborn* lamb. **newcomer** a *new* arrival: *Newcomers* to this city are welcome. **new-laid** just laid: *New-laid* eggs for sale. **newly** recently: The *newly* married couple will be living in Brighton.

newt a small reptile like a lizard, living mainly in water but also on land, which feeds on larvae and tiny water creatures.

nibble (nib-ble) 1. bite off small bits: He sat at the table *nibbling* at a hot cross bun 2. bite gently: The fish are *nibbling* all the time but I haven't caught one yet.

nice 1. pleasant, agreeable: '*Nice* day today!' called the milkman. 2. friendly: He's an extremely *nice* person. 3. clever, requiring skill and accuracy: He played the piano with a *nice* sense of timing. **nicely** very well: '*Nicely* played!' the umpire called.

niche 1. a place shaped out of a wall in which ornaments may be put: A small statue of the Virgin stood in the *niche*. 2. a place in life or in one's work where one is happy and doing well: At last I've found my *niche* as a dress designer.

nick a small cut made by a knife or axe in wood, or cut out of stone: With his axe he cut a *nick* in the tree-trunk to act as a guide.

nickname (nick-name) 1. a name which is not a person's real name but is used by friends: My name is Robert but my *nickname* is Bobby. 2. give such a name: He practises weight-lifting, so we *nick-named* him Muscles.

nicotine (nic-o-tine) a substance in tobacco which if taken in large quantities is poisonous: *Nicotine* is so called because the man who first brought tobacco to France in 1560 was called Nicot.

niece the daughter of one's brother or sister.

night the dark period of time between sunset and sunrise on the following day: It rained all *night*. **nightdress, night-gown** a loose garment worn in bed. **night-light** a small light, either candle or electric bulb, used to light a bedroom during the dark hours. **nightingale** a small bird of the thrush family that sings sweetly both day and *night*.

nimble (nim-ble) 1. moving quickly: I tried to catch him but he was too *nimble* for me. 2. having a quick mind: 'You have a *nimble* wit, I think' (Shakespeare, *As You Like It*). **nimbly** in a *nimble* manner: I tried to hit him but he sprang *nimbly* to one side.

nine the number 9 coming after 8 and before 10: Divide these *nine* boys into groups of three. **nineteen** the number 19, *nine* plus 10. **ninety** the number 90, *nine* multiplied by 10 or 10 groups of *nine*: He lived to the age of *ninety*.

nip 1. press hard between finger and thumb, pinch or bite: Your dog *nipped* my leg.—If you want large flowers, you should *nip* off the side shoots. 2. stop something growing: The frost has *nipped* all the young plants in the bud. 3. a biting quality, as in cold air: The air has a distinct *nip* this morning.

nitrogen (ni-tro-gen) a gas which forms four-fifths of the air we breathe: *Nitrogen* is used in fertilizers, explosives and dyes.

no 1. not one, not any: 'We have *no* bananas today,' said the greengrocer.—'I have *no* money,' I replied. 2. the opposite of 'yes': Are you coming? *No*, I'm not.—I refuse to take *no* for an answer.

noble (no-ble) 1. good, righteous, of excellent character: 'Oh, *noble* judge!' (Shylock in Shakespeare's *Merchant of Venice*). 2. one of high rank or birth: Here comes the king with his *nobles*. 3. splendid, admirable: It was a *noble* scheme. **nobly** in a *noble* way: He entertained his guests *nobly*.

nobody (no-bod-y) no person: I knocked, but *nobody* answered.

nod 1. make a sign of agreement or greet a person by bowing the head slightly: The porter *nodded* as I passed him on the platform. 2. let the head fall forward as if going to sleep: The old man was *nodding* in his armchair. 3. move backwards and forwards as with the wind: The poet saw the daffodils *nodding* in the breeze. 4. a *nodding* of the head: Give me a *nod* when you want the window opened.

noise 1. a sound of any kind: Did you hear a *noise* next door? 2. a loud, harsh, unpleasant sound: Don't make a *noise* or you'll wake the baby. **noiseless** with no *noise*: He entered with *noiseless* steps. **noisy** with much *noise*, making much *noise*: This aircraft is too *noisy*.–The room was full of *noisy* children.

nomad (no-mad) a person, usually one of a tribe which wanders from place to place, having no fixed home: The only *nomads* left in England are a few gipsies.

nominate (nom-i-nate) 1. to appoint a person to a duty or office: I *nominate* Mr Brown as my deputy. 2. put a person forward to be elected: How many people have been *nominated* for the committee? **nomination** *nominating*: I wish you would accept *nomination* for the office of treasurer. **nominee** a person *nominated*: We were glad to see our *nominee* elected.

non- a prefix which indicates a negative– not being or doing something: **non**alcoholic, not containing alcohol; **non**destructible, which cannot be destroyed; **non**descript, not easy to describe, of no special kind: His boat is neither a canoe nor a rowing boat; it is quite *non*descript. **non-**edible, that cannot be eaten; **non**intoxicating, not making a person intoxicated; **non-**inflammable, not catching fire: *Non*-inflammable nightdresses should be worn by all children; **non**sense, foolish talk or behaviour: How could you believe such *non*sense!

none not any, not one: 'When she got there the cupboard was bare, and so the poor dog had *none*' (not one bone).–I had some sugar yesterday but there's *none* left this morning.

noon the middle of the day, 12 o'clock: Morning school ends at *noon*.

noose a loop in a rope or a piece of string with a slip knot tied in it: He pulled at the rope and the *noose* tightened round the cow's neck.

normal (nor-mal) regular, usual: What is the *normal* rate at which a child grows?– For a boy of seven he is below *normal* size.

north 1. the direction in which the left arm points when one faces the sunrise: He pointed with his staff towards the *north*.– I returned yesterday from the *north* of Scotland. 2. to, from, at the *north*: I am travelling *north* this morning.–The magnetic needle points towards the *North* Pole.–The *North* Star can be seen in winter. **north-east** half-way between *north* and east: We travelled *north-east* and eventually reached the cabin. **north-easter** the wind blowing from the *north-east*. **north-west** halfway between *north* and west. **northerly** in or from the *north*: They followed a *northerly* course for two days. **northern** having to do with the *north*: A meteor flashed across the *northern* sky.

nose 1. the part of the face just above the mouth through which one breathes and is able to smell. 2. a good sense of smell: This dog has a good *nose* for rabbits. 3. go with great care: Slowly we *nosed* our way through the dark cave. **nosegay** a small bunch of flowers: The little girl presented a *nosegay* to the Queen. **nostril** one of the openings of the *nose*.

not a word used to make another word or words have an opposite, negative meaning: He is *not* going to school today.–Do *not* lean out of the windows.–I told you *not* to climb that ladder.

notable (no-ta-ble) 1. worth noticing: What were the most *notable* events of last month? 2. famous, outstanding: We are showing the work of this country's most *notable* painters.

notch 1. a nick, a small V-shaped cut: Cricketers once counted the runs that had been scored by cutting *notches* on a stick. 2. make *notches*: He *notched* the bough in two places and fastened the swing to it.

nothing not a thing: I can find *nothing* wrong, but the car still won't go.–What are you carrying in that bag? *Nothing*.

notice (no-tice) 1. information about something: The preacher read the *notices* of the week's events.–The *notice* informed the public of the danger of fire. 2. warning of a coming event within a fixed time: I have given in my *notice* to leave my present employment. 3. attention: I told him to be careful but he took no *notice*. 4. see, hear, observe: You passed me in the street and didn't *notice* me. **notice-board** a board on which announcements or *notices* are fixed.

notify (no-ti-fy) give notice about: We must *notify* the authorities of the outbreak of smallpox.–Have we been *notified* of your change of address?

notion (no-tion) idea, opinion, feeling: I have a *notion* that I am being followed.

nought 1. nothing: All our plans came to *nought*. 2. the figure 0 indicating nothing: Add a *nought* to the end of the number.–Shall we play *noughts* and crosses?

noun the name of a person, place, thing or quality: There are three *nouns* in the sentence, 'John is measuring the length of this fence.' (John, length, fence)

nourish (nour-ish) feed, keep alive and make grow: We need more rain to *nourish* the growing corn. **nourishment** food, anything which *nourishes*: The patient is now able to take liquid *nourishment*.

novel (nov-el) 1. a long, fictional story: I love Kenneth Grahame's *novels*. 2. new, not thought of before: His mind is full of *novel* ideas. **novelty** 1. newness: The *novelty* of wearing uniform soon stopped. 2. something new: Our shop stocks *novelties* in chidren's toys.

November (No-vem-ber) the eleventh month of the year.

now 1. the present time: You must decide *now* when you are going to France. 2. the present moment: Don't wait, do it *now*. **nowadays** in our own times: People once travelled by coach and horse, but *nowadays* we go by air. **now and then** from time to time: I enjoy going to the theatre *now and then*.

nowhere (no-where) in no place, not anywhere: I searched the room but could find my camera *nowhere*.–It was *nowhere* to be found.

nozzle (noz-zle) the metal pipe at the end of a hose or a pair of bellows etc. through which the water or air comes: The fireman turned the *nozzle* of the hose on the burning house and a stream of water put out the fire.

nuclear (nu-cle-ar) concerned with a nucleus: *Nuclear* energy is used to supply power to ships and machinery.–A *nuclear* device has been exploded underground. **nuclear reactor** an apparatus which produces *nuclear* energy.

nucleus (nu-cleus) *nuclei* the central part of anything around which other parts are grouped: We have six good players who will provide the *nucleus* of our football team.–The central core of an atom is called the *nucleus*.

nude naked, undressed: There was a *nude* figure in the painting.

nudge 1. a light touch or push: Give him a *nudge* to wake him up. 2. give a slight push: He's not listening; *nudge* him.

nugget (nug-get) a lump, usually of metal, especially gold: The miner saw on the ground a shining yellow *nugget*.

nuisance (nui-sance) something or somebody causing trouble or offence to others:

This refuse-tip smells so badly that it is a public *nuisance*.

numb 1. not able to feel: The wind was so cold that the ends of his fingers went *numb*. 2. make *numb*: The dentist *numbed* the gum before filling the tooth.

number (num-ber) 1. a quantity, a few, many: A *number* of spectators were injured when the car ran off the track. 2. one issue of a magazine or journal: 'This exciting story will be continued in our next *number*.' 3. a single part of a stage performance: After his *number* the comedian was loudly applauded. 4. give a *number* to: The exhibits had been *numbered* incorrectly. 5. consider: I *numbered* him among my best friends.

numeral (nu-mer-al) a word or figure standing for a number: 1, 2 and 3 are Arabic *numerals*. I, II and III are Roman *numerals*. **numerous** very many, great in number: You have made *numerous* mistakes in this exercise.

nun a woman living apart from society as a member of a religious group, in a building called a nunnery or convent.

nurse 1. a trained person who works in a hospital, taking care of the sick and injured: The *nurse* visited all the wards to make sure the patients were comfortable. 2. take charge of people who are sick: If you are to recover your mother will have to *nurse* you. 3. hold a child or an animal close and fondle it: You should not *nurse* the kitten so much. 4. care for specially: The tiny plants are *nursed* under glass. **nursery** 1. a room in which small children are looked after by a *nurse*maid. 2. an establishment where young plants are grown: I bought a dozen geraniums at the local *nursery*.

nut 1. the hard fruit of certain trees, enclosed in a shell: What kind of *nuts* would you like, pea*nuts*, wal*nuts* or hazel*nuts*? 2. a hollow piece of metal into which a bolt can be screwed: The handle had been fixed to the door with a *nut* and bolt. **nutmeg** the hard seed of the fruit of an East Indian tree.

nymph a goddess of Greek and Roman mythology who lived in the sea, hills, trees etc.: 'Sea *nymphs* hourly ring his knell' (Shakespeare, *The Tempest*).

oak 1. a large tree with very hard wood used for making furniture, ships and floors: The wooden ships in the British navy were usually made of *oak*. 2. the wood of the *oak*: The village has many timber houses built with *oak* beams.

oar a long pole with a blade at one end used for rowing a boat: The *oars* were too light to propel the boat very fast.

oasis (o-a-sis) *oases* a place in the desert where water is to be found and where trees grow: The travellers hoped to fill their water bags at the next *oasis*.

oat a grass-like plant used for food for men and animals: *Oats* and hay are fed to horses. **oatmeal** meal made from *oats*: Every morning in winter we have *oatmeal* porridge for breakfast.

oath 1. a promise to do something, with the help of God. 2. a declaration made with God as a witness that what one is about to say is true. 3. a swear word: Uttering *oaths* and curses, the thief struggled to free himself. **on oath** having sworn on the Bible to tell the truth: The witness gave his evidence *on oath*.

obey (o-bey) do what one is told to do: Children should *obey* their parents. **obedience** *obeying*: I will act in *obedience* to your orders. **obedient** *obeying*: Man Friday was Robinson Crusoe's *obedient* servant.

object (ób-ject) 1. something that can be seen or touched: I want you to make a list of all the *objects* in the house. 2. an aim: My *object* is to recover the lost jewels. 3. something which appears strange, uncommon or pitiful: The starving child was an *object* of pity. **object** (ob-ject) not to be in favour of something: The residents are *objecting* to the new motorway going through the village. **objection** statement or act of *objecting*: They have stated their *objections* to their Member of Parliament. **objectionable** not liked, unpleasant: This cheese has a most *objectionable* smell.

oblige (o-blige) 1. force: I was *obliged* to give up my work because of illness. **obliged** grateful: I am *obliged* to you for your prompt reply to my letter. **obliging** always ready to help: We found the local people very *obliging*. **obligation** something that ought to be done: I am under an *obligation* to pay back the money. **obligatory** that has to be done: Swimming lessons are *obligatory* in this school.

oblique (ob-lique) slanting: Take a horizontal line and from a point on it draw an *oblique* line (any line that does not make a right angle).

oblivion (ob-liv-i-on) being forgotten: All his early mistakes have passed into *oblivion*. **oblivious** forgetting, not knowing about: He continued running, *oblivious* of the panic around him.

obscene (ob-scene) indecent, disgusting: The player was sent off the field for using *obscene* language.

obscure (ob-scure) 1. dark, not easy to see, hidden: By midday we had reached an *obscure* part of the forest. 2. not easy to understand: I find the meaning of this poem *obscure*. 3. hide: We stole out of our hiding place when the clouds *obscured* the moon. **obscurity** being *obscure*, unknown: The artist spent his whole life in *obscurity*.

observe (ob-serve) 1. see and notice: I *observed* a car going dangerously fast. 2. mention: She *observed* that our provisions were running out. 3. keep, celebrate: The king's birthday was *observed* with processions and fireworks. **observation** *observing*, being *observed*, the act of noticing or remarking: The house was kept under constant *observation*. **observer** one who *observes*: He is a keen *observer* of the habits of birds.

obstacle (ob-sta-cle) something that makes difficult: The greatest *obstacle* to climbing the mountain was lack of oxygen.

obstinate (ob-sti-nate) not willing to give way or yield to others: He is *obstinate* and refuses to take his medicine.– The enemy put up an *obstinate* resistance. **obstinacy** being *obstinate*: A mule is well-known for its *obstinacy*.

obtain (ob-tain) acquire, get: Where can I *obtain* a copy of today's newspaper?

obvious (ob-vi-ous) clear, easy to understand: It is *obvious* that he can't go with us while he is ill.

occasion (oc-ca-sion) 1. a time when something happens: I have been wounded on two *occasions*. 2. a reason: 'I will go and sit and weep till I can find *occasion* of revenge' (Shakespeare, *The Taming of the Shrew*). **occasional** happening from time to time: He smokes an *occasional* cigar.

occupy (oc-cu-py) 1. live in: Do you know who *occupies* Number 11? 2. take possession of: Our troops *occupied* the town without resistance. 3. fill space: All the seats are *occupied*. 4. fill time: How shall I *occupy* my days? 5. fill the mind: I am fully *occupied* in writing a book. 6. fill a position: For three years he has *occupied* the post of Inspector of Taxes. **occupation** 1. taking possession: The *occupation* of the enemy post cost 2 killed and 6 wounded. 2. what one does for a living or to fill one's time: Gardening is a pleasant *occupation*.

occur 1. happen: The accident *occurred* on the south-bound carriageway. 2. come to mind: It *occurred* to me that you may need help. 3. be found: Mistakes *occur* frequently if you are not very careful. **occurrence** something that happens: Dreams are a nightly *occurrence* with most people.

ocean 1. a large body of water, larger than a sea: There are five *oceans* in the world. 2. having to do with an *ocean*: Have you ever been on a long *ocean* voyage?

octave (oc-tave) in music, the space between one doh and the next higher doh (C to C, D to D, etc.): How many *octaves* are there on your piano?

October (Oc-to-ber) the tenth month of the year.

octopus (oc-to-pus) *octopuses* a sea animal with an oval body and eight arms, each ending in a sucker.

oculist (oc-u-list) a specialist who examines and treats diseases of the eye: When his sight began to fail the doctor sent him to an *oculist*.

odd 1. not even, will not divide by 2: 3, 5 and 7 are all *odd* numbers. 2. one of a pair when the other is not there: I felt in my pocket and found I had two *odd* gloves. 3. one of a set apart from all the others: There are only three aces here; who has the *odd* one? 4. not regular: We need a man to do *odd* jobs in the greenhouse. 5. strange, not normal: How *odd* that you should find me here.—He's an *odd* sort of person. **oddity** being *odd*, something which is unusual or *odd*: A four-leaf clover is an *oddity*.

offence (of-fence) crime, sin, wrongdoing: Yesterday I was fined for a parking *offence*. **offend** irritate in mind or feelings: I'm sorry I *offended* you by my rudeness. **offender** a person who *offends*, usually against the law: The magistrate is usually lenient with young *offenders*. **offensive** irritating, causing *offence*: Her nasty behaviour was highly *offensive*.

offer (of-fer) 1. say that one is willing to give or pay for something: I *offered* him a good sum for the horse. 2. the act of *offering*, saying that one is willing to do something: His *offer* to buy the horse has not been accepted.—Are there any other *offers*?

office (of-fice) 1. a place of business: He works in an *office* from nine until five. 2. a government department: Have you seen the latest circular from the Home *Office*? 3. a position of power and authority: How long has the Prime Minister been in *office*? **officer** a person commanding others in the forces or who is in a position of authority: Have you seen the *officer* in charge of equipment?—The customs *officer* searched my luggage.

official (of-fi-cial) 1. a person holding a position of responsibility in a society or in government: We were visited by an *official* of the Gas Board. 2. having to do with a position of authority; a formal ceremony: This is an *official* report of the disaster.—The ambassador was given an *official* reception at the Mansion House. **officiate** carry out an *official* duty: Would you please *officiate* as our Chairman this evening?

oil 1. grease and fat obtained from animals and plants, or liquid from the ground that does not mix with water and which usually burns: *Oil* is used for lubricating and driving machinery.—Certain kinds of *oil* are taken as medicine. 2. apply *oil*, put *oil* on or in: If you *oil* the hinges the door will stop squeaking. **oilcake** food for cattle made from seeds after the *oil* has been pressed out. **oilfield** an area where *oil* is found, usually by drilling into the earth. **oilskin** a coat made of cloth treated with *oil* to keep out water. **oily** 1. like *oil*, having *oil* on: Go and wash your *oily* hands. 2. unpleasantly smooth in manner.

ointment (oint-ment) a paste made from medicines with oil or grease, and used for putting on the skin to heal sores and bruises.

omen (o-men) something which is regarded as a sign of future good or bad fortune: The Indians regarded the bird as an evil *omen*. **ominous** threatening: He greeted my remark with an *ominous* silence.

omit (o-mit) 1. miss out, not include: A whole chapter has been *omitted* from this book. 2. not do something: Why did you *omit* doing this exercise? **omission** missing out, something not done: The *omission* of an important sentence altered the meaning of the letter.

once 1. at some time in the past: *Once* I used to be good at tennis. 2. at one time: *Once* a year I visit my old school. **at once** immediately: He telephoned for an ambulance *at once*.

one 1. the sign of figure 1: Two *ones* are two, three *ones* are three etc. 2. a single: I used to have two pens, but now I have only *one*. 3. the same: We all live under *one* roof.– We all go *one* way. 4. a special person: 'Sleep, my little *one*; sleep, my pretty *one*.' 5. any person: *One* never knows what will happen in the future. **one another** each other: Why do they quarrel with *one another*? 6. some time in the future: I'll see you *one* day.

only (on-ly) 1. single, one group: He is my *only* friend.–We three were the *only* people to be admitted. 2. no more than: *Only* five visitors are allowed in at one time.–This room is for members *only*. 3. merely, simply: I *only* did it for a joke. 4. but: I would buy it, *only* it costs too much.

opaque (o-paque) that cannot be seen through: The room was divided in two by an *opaque* screen.

open (o-pen) 1. letting things or persons in or through: The gate was *open* and we went in. 2. without cover or roof: I love the *open* air. 3. spread out: He sat with an *open* book on his knee. 4. public, admitting all people: This is an *open* competition. 5. able to be changed: I have an *open* mind on this matter. 6. make *open*: *Open* the door and let me in! 7. extend: He *opened* the book and started to read. 8. let people know that a place is *open*: The Mayor *opened* the bazaar with a speech. 9. become *open*: The sun is shining and the flowers are *opening*. 10. begin: The symphony *opens* with a roll of drums.

opening 1. a gap: He escaped through an *opening* in the wall. 2. foundation, beginning: I was at the *opening* of the new swimming baths. 3. a vacant position: We have an *opening* for a wages clerk. **openly** publicly: 'Dare you . . . maintain such a quarrel *openly*?' (Shakespeare, *Titus Andronicus*)

opera (op-e-ra) a play in which the actors sing all the words and are accompanied by an orchestra: Beethoven's only *opera* is called *Fidelio*.

operate (op-er-ate) 1. work or make work: Do you know how to *operate* the washing machine? 2. cut into the body to treat a disease or the result of an accident: The surgeon *operated* on the injured man. **operator** a person who manages a mechanical device: My sister is a telephone *operator*.

opinion (o-pin-ion) the way a person thinks: Please give me your honest *opinion* of my plan.

opportunity (op-por-tu-ni-ty) chance, time when a chance arises: Have you had an *opportunity* to read my essay yet?

oppose (op-pose) be against: I am strongly *opposed* to your going on this journey. **opposition** being *opposed*; resistance: She married in *opposition* to her parents' wishes.

opposite (op-po-site) 1. facing: Who lives in the house *opposite*? 2. complete difference: 'Long' is the *opposite* of 'short'.– Black and white are *opposites*.

oppress (op-press) 1. rule with cruelty: The king *oppressed* his subjects with harsh laws. 2. feel uncomfortable in mind or body: We are *oppressed* by sorrow. **oppression** *oppressing*, being *oppressed*: This nation will one day rise against *oppression*. **oppressive** unjust, hard to bear: We have to obey *oppressive* laws.– How *oppressive* this hot weather is!

optical (op-ti-cal) having to do with sight: The telescope and the microscope are both *optical* instruments. **optician** a person who makes and sells *optical* instruments: I had to go to the *optician* to have my eyes tested.

optimist (op-ti-mist) a person who is always hopeful and inclined to look on the bright side of things: An *optimist* believes that everything happens for the best.

oracle (or-a-cle) 1. a statement given by a priestess at a shrine in ancient Greece as the answer of a god to an enquiry about the future. 2. a person who can be trusted to give good advice.

orator (or-a-tor) a public speaker of great skill: He was a brilliant *orator*, able to persuade vast audiences to agree with his opinions.

orbit (or-bit) 1. the path followed by a satellite or planet around a body such as the earth or sun: The earth follows an *orbit* round the sun. 2. the path followed by an earth satellite round the earth: The astronauts boarded the space-craft while it was in *orbit*.

orchestra (or-ches-tra) a group of performers on various musical instruments including strings, woodwind, brass and percussion playing compositions together: I have heard some of the world's most famous *orchestras* in London.

ordinary (or-di-na-ry) 1. usual, average: Part of my *ordinary* duty is to see that all doors are locked. 2. not bad, not good: I thought the exhibition was extremely *ordinary*. **ordinarily** in the *ordinary* way: *Ordinarily*, I leave home at eight every morning.

ore rock or earth from which metals can be extracted: Rich deposits of iron *ore* have been found in Spain.

organ 1. a single part of the body which does its own special work: The eye is the *organ* of sight and the ear of hearing. 2. a musical instrument with a keyboard and pedals often placed in churches and large assembly halls: Most *organs* produce sound by means of forcing air through pipes, but there are also many electric *organs*. **organism** any form of animal or plant life: A drop of water is full of tiny *organisms*. **organist** a person who plays an *organ*.

organize (or-gan-ize) form and put into working order: We are *organizing* a campaign to prevent cruelty to animals. **organization** *organizing*, an *organized* body: Can you help with the *organization* of this campaign?–Will you become a member of our *organization*? **organizer** one who *organizes*.

Orient (o-ri-ent) the East; the countries east of the Mediterranean Sea; Asia, especially China and Japan: Most of the goods we sell are imported from the *Orient*. **Oriental** of the *Orient*: We went to an exhibition of *Oriental* rugs.

origin (or-i-gin) the beginning: The *origin* of our friendship was a common interest in chess.–The *origins* of this custom go back to the Middle Ages. **original** 1. first: My *original* intention was to write a book. 2. new: My evening dress is an *original* design. **originally** at first: This building was *originally* a water mill. **originate** begin: Printing *originated* in ancient China.

ornament (or-na-ment) 1. something that adds beauty: Candlesticks, vases, and many other small *ornaments* were arranged on the table. 2. make more beautiful by adding *ornaments*: His uniform was *ornamented* with gold lace on the collar and sleeves. **ornamental** having *ornament*: There is an *ornamental* fountain in the public gardens.

ought should: You *ought* to apologize for insulting him.—He *ought* to have been an architect.—If he continues to train he *ought* to win a gold medal.

ounce a unit of weight used in Great Britain, one-sixteenth of a pound.

out 1. not at home: I rang but you were *out*. 2. not in: Unfortunately the tide was *out*. 3. at another place: He is *out* of the country for a week. 4. not a secret any longer: The results of the election are *out* at last. 5. into the open, showing: The sun came *out* at three o'clock. 6. not burning: Who let the fire go *out*? 7. ended: I must finish this job before the day is *out*. 8. loudly: Call *out* if you need me. 9. in error: You are ten *out* in your reckoning.—Your watch is ten minutes *out*. 10. (in cricket) dismissed, bowled, caught etc.: The captain was *out* for a duck and the whole team were *out* for 55. 11. without: We're *out* of currants.—I was *out* of breath from running. 12. apart, away from the rest: I've taken *out* all the green apples. 13. (with other words) **outbreak** the start of some trouble, a war etc. **outburst** a bursting forth (of temper, rage etc.). **outcast** a person cast *out*, turned away from family, society etc. **outdoor** the open air: Most people are fond of *outdoor* games. **outcome** the result: I shall go alone, whatever the *outcome*. **outdistance** go faster than others: The favourite horse was *outdistanced* in the final lap of the race. **outgrow** grow too big for: He has *outgrown* all his clothes. **outhouse** a small building near or joined to a main building. **outlaw** a person who is not protected by law; a criminal. **outlive** live longer than: The old man has *outlived* all his friends. **outnumber** be more in number than: Our little force was greatly *outnumbered* by the enemy. **outpatient** a patient of a hospital who travels from home for treatment. **output** the things produced: We are trying in every way to increase our *output* of fine cloth. **outset** beginning: It was clear from the *outset* that the champion driver would win. **outward** to the *outside*, on the *outside*: Our ship left port and is now *outward* bound. **outwit** get the better of others by cunning or by a trick: They *outwitted* their guards with their clever disguise.

outcry (out-cry) a general protest: There was an *outcry* when it was learnt that the school was to be closed.

outing (out-ing) a trip for pleasure: We were taken on an *outing* to Brighton.

outlay (out-lay) expenditure, money put down to start a business: In two years we should get back all our *outlay*.

outlet (out-let) 1. a way out for liquids, water etc.: This water tank has only one *outlet*. 2. a way of releasing: Football is a wonderful *outlet* for a boy's energy.

outline (out-line) 1. a line showing the shape of an object: The *outline* of a ship appeared on the horizon. 2. a short summary: Will you give us an *outline* of your plans?

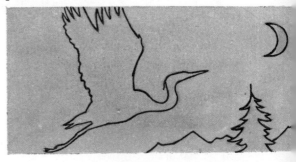

outlook (out-look) the view, the prospect: What a beautiful *outlook* there is from the top of this hill.—With trade in this state the *outlook* for our firm is bad.

outrage (out-rage) a cruel or violent act, a shocking act: Two bomb *outrages* are reported in this morning's news.

outside (out-side) 1. the outer side: The *outside* of the house was painted green. 2. out of doors: Would you like to come *outside* for a moment?

outstanding (out-stand-ing) 1. easily noticed: This tower is an *outstanding* part of the landscape. 2. not yet accounted for: Most debts have been collected but there is still much money *outstanding*.

oval (o-val) having the general form of an egg: The race took place on an *oval* track.

oven (o-ven) an enclosed heated space used for cooking: I am baking twelve loaves in the *oven*.

over (o-ver) 1. from standing erect, to fall on one side or the other: He fell *over* on the ice. 2. to or from: My uncle has just come *over* from Canada.—The traitor went *over* to the other side. 3. left: When we had paid all the bills there was very little money *over*. 4. more, more than: He is well *over* average height.—Only adults *over* 18 years of age are admitted. 5. ended: Run away, children, the fun is all *over*. 6. covering: He had a mask *over* his eyes. 7. above: Let me put my umbrella *over* you. 8. governing: Who is *over* you in this department? 9. again: I went through the sum three times *over*. 10. out and down from: Don't let the milk boil *over*. 11. across: The dog jumped *over* the stile. 12. (with other words) **overcoat** a coat put on *over* all one's other clothes. **overcrowd** put too many into a small space: The little room was *overcrowded* with children. **overdo** do too much: He is working hard but he should not *overdo* it. **overdue** late, should have arrived already: The 10.30 train is 15 minutes *overdue*. **overflow** flow over the edges. The reservoir is *overflowing*. **overhang** hang over: We took shelter under an *overhanging* cliff. **overhead** above: A squadron of aeroplanes flew *overhead*. **overhear** hear things one is not intended to hear: I *overheard* them making their plans. **overnight** through the night: We stayed *overnight* at the hotel on the beach. **overrule** decide against: My decision to buy more machinery was *overruled* by the general manager. **overrun** conquer and occupy a country: Within three days the country was *overrun* by the enemy.

overseas beyond the sea: My brother has been *overseas* for the last year. **oversight** something not seen, neglected: Through an *oversight* your gas bill for the last quarter was not sent. **overtake** catch up and pass: He was *overtaken* in the last lap of the race. **overthrow** defeat and put an end to: The government has been *overthrown*. **overtime** time worked longer than the normal hours: We get paid more than the usual rate for *overtime*. **overweight** weighing more than usual: As you are *overweight* I would advise you to go on a diet. **overwhelm** cover *over*, crush completely: I felt *overwhelmed* with unhappiness.—The enemy forces *overwhelmed* our tiny army. **overwork** work too hard or too long: He has been *overworking* recently and is very tired.

overboard (o-ver-board) over the side of a ship: One of the passengers fell *overboard*.

overcome (o-ver-come) be too strong for: In the end we shall *overcome* all obstacles.—Three firemen were *overcome* by fumes.

overdraft (o-ver-draft) money lent by the bank to someone whose account is overdrawn: The manager allowed me to have an *overdraft* for two months.

overgrown (o-ver-grown) covered with something that has grown over it: The whole garden was *overgrown* with weeds.

overhaul (o-ver-haul) examine and put right: I am having my car *overhauled* today.

overlook (o-ver-look) 1. see from above: My room *overlooks* the railway. 2. not notice: I *overlooked* the mistakes in your calculations. 3. not count: You made a bad mistake, but this time I'll *overlook* it.

overturn (o-ver-turn) upset, turn over: A barrel of apples was *overturned* in the street.

owe 1. need to pay: How much do I *owe* you for this tennis racket? 2. feel a debt to: I *owe* all my success to my parents.

own 1. possess: Who *owns* this red bicycle? 2. confess: He *owned* to having taken the bicycle. 3. the property of a person: This watch is yours; my *own* is in my pocket.

oxygen (ox-y-gen) a gas with no taste, smell or colour: *Oxygen* forms about one-fifth of the air, and without it, living beings could not exist.

oyster (oy-ster) a small flat shellfish that is cultivated to eat or for the pearls some varieties produce.

P

pace 1. the distance covered in one step: Two *paces* forward—march! 2. the speed at which one walks: We will slacken our *pace*.—Try to keep *pace* with me. 3. walk slowly and regularly: He *paced* up and down the room. 4. measure by stepping: He *paced* out the length of the tennis court.

pacify (pac-i-fy) make quiet and calm: My apology was enough to *pacify* him.

pack 1. a bundle: Off he went, with his *pack* on his back. 2. a number of dogs kept for hunting: A *pack* of hounds ran across the field. 3. a number of wolves travelling together. 4. the set of 52 playing cards: He took the *pack* and shuffled the cards. 5. put things together into a container: Is my lunch *packed* yet?—Have you finished *packing* for the holiday yet? 6. crowd: The stands were *packed* with excited spectators. 7. put paper or other material round fragile things to keep them safe: Please *pack* this crockery with care. **package** a parcel or bundle: The postman delivered a heavy *package* today. **packet** a small parcel: Where did you buy that *packet* of sweets?

pad 1. soft material made into a small cushion to give comfort or protection: He was kneeling on a *pad*, scrubbing the floor. 2. a guard for the leg when playing certain games: The batsman struck at the ball but it bounced off his *pad* and hit the wicket. 3. sheets of writing paper fastened together at one edge: He scribbled the message on a *pad* and gave it to the boy. 4. the soft part under the feet of certain animals: The lion had a large thorn in its *pad*. 5. a small cushion of absorbent material soaked with ink, for inking rubber stamps. 6. put a *pad* or *pads* on or into something: The doctor *padded* the wound with gauze before he bandaged it.

paddle (pad-dle) 1. a short oar held in both hands and used to move a canoe through the water. 2. send a canoe or other craft through the water with a *paddle*: We *paddled* hard, and our raft finally reached the shore. 3. walk in the water with bare feet: The children took off their shoes and stockings and *paddled* in the sea.

paddock (pad-dock) a small field where horses are exercised or where they are brought together before a race.

page 1. one side of a leaf of paper in a book, journal or newspaper: The story is continued on *page* 36. 2. a boy who served at court in the Middle Ages: Along came the knight, followed by his *page*. 3. a boy who serves in a hotel or club. 4. call a person's name aloud in a hotel or club.

pageant (pag-eant) 1. an outdoor entertainment in which scenes from history are usually shown: He is playing the part of Oliver Cromwell in our town *pageant*. 2. a great celebration in which there is a procession of people wearing costumes of past ages etc. **pageantry** great display with scenery, costume and entertainment: The coronation was celebrated with splendid *pageantry*.

pail 1. a bucket of metal, wood or plastic with a handle for carrying it. 2. a *pail* filled with something: I need a *pail* of water to wash the windows.

pain 1. suffering through illness or injury: He lay in great *pain*.–'Where do you feel the *pain?*' asked the doctor. 2. threat: Ten captives are in prison under *pain* of death. 3. hurt, give *pain*: 'Your conduct has *pained* me greatly', said the headmaster. **pains** effort, care: I am taking great *pains* with this model. **painful** giving *pain*: He has a *painful* sore on his knee. **pain-killer** something to take *pain* away. **painless** with no *pain*: The extraction of my tooth was quite *painless*.

paint 1. colouring matter that can be put on a surface with a brush, spray or by other means: In front of the fence was a sign which read 'Wet *paint*'. 2. spread *paint* on: He is *painting* the door a bright red. 3. make a picture by *painting*: When are you going to *paint* my portrait? **painter** a person who *paints*; an artist who *paints* pictures: Rembrandt was one of the greatest *painters* of all time. **painting** a picture or design: Have you seen the *paintings* in the National Gallery?

pair 1. two things of a kind, matched for use together: I have bought a new *pair* of shoes. 2. two parts of an article joined together: Have you a *pair* of scissors? 3. two married persons: The happy *pair* set off on their honeymoon. **Pair off** group in twos, go two by two: The children were *paired off* for the game of musical chairs.

pale 1. of a whitish appearance, without much colour: Why do you look so *pale*? 2. light in colour: I particularly like your *pale* blue dress. 3. a long pointed stick put in the ground and used as part of a fence. **paling** a fence of *pales*: The ground was fenced off by a high wooden *paling*.

palm 1. that part of the inner surface of the hand between the wrist and the fingers. 2. a tree that grows in warm climates: A *palm* has a long trunk with large wide leaves at the top.–Dates and coconuts grow on *palms*. **palmist** a person who claims to be able to tell fortunes and read the character by looking at the *palm* of the hand.

pamphlet (pamph-let) a thin paper-covered book, usually on a subject of general interest: Our party has issued a new political *pamphlet*. **pamphleteer** a person who writes *pamphlets*.

pan 1. a metal dish, usually shallow and sometimes with a handle, used for cooking: She put the *pan* on the fire to heat the milk. 2. what a *pan* holds: He spilt a *pan* of boiling water on his foot. **pancake** a thin flat cake of eggs, flour and milk, fried in a *pan*: We eat *pancakes* on Shrove Tuesday.

panda (pan-da) a mammal from the Himalayas and central China, with a black and white body and large black patches around its eyes.

pane 1. a single sheet of glass in a window: Do you hear the rain rattling on the window*pane*? 2. a thin sheet of wood, part of a door or of panelling.

panel (pan-el) 1. a separate part of the surface of a door, wall or ceiling, framed like a picture. 2. a piece of material put into a dress, of a different colour or pattern from the rest. 3. a body of speakers answering questions or taking part in a game, usually with an audience: 'Listeners are invited to telephone their questions to the members of our *panel*' (radio announcement). **panelled** with *panels*: The room was beautifully *panelled* in dark oak. **panelling** *panels* on a wall: We all admired the oak *panelling*.

panic (pan-ic) 1. fear and terror spreading to everybody: When the cry of 'fire' was raised, *panic* seized the audience. 2. be struck with terror; rush about in confusion: 'Don't *panic*,' shouted the manager, 'the danger is over.'

panorama (pan-o-ra-ma) 1. a view over a wide area: When we reached the top of the hill, a vast *panorama* spread out below us. 2. a scene which is constantly changing: In the pageant the whole *panorama* of modern Britain is placed before us.

pant 1. breathe hard and quickly as one does after exertion: He rose to the surface of the water *panting* for breath. 2. a short, quick breath; a gasp.

pantomime (pan-to-mime) a kind of play with music usually based on a fairy tale: Every Christmas our parents take us to the *pantomime*.

pantry (pan-try) a small room in a house where the food is kept: He opened the *pantry* door and greedily snatched a cake.

paper (pa-per) 1. material made from wood, rags etc., and pressed into thin sheets to be used for writing, printing, drawing and wrapping: He took a sheet of *paper* and began to write. 2. a newspaper: Have you seen today's *paper*? 3. a set of examination questions: Today's *paper* was very difficult. 4. an essay, usually read out to an audience: The professor read a *paper* on the composition of rocks. 5. a document: Every ten years we receive census *papers* to complete. – This house is mine, and I have the *papers* to prove it. 6. paste *paper* on a wall or a ceiling: Our dining room has just been *papered*. **paperhanger** a person who pastes *paper* on the walls of rooms.

parable (par-a-ble) a story told for the purpose of teaching a lesson: Christ used *parables* in his teaching.

parachute (par-a-chute) a device which when dropped from the air opens like an umbrella and is used for landing troops, provisions etc.: For three weeks the shipwrecked sailors were supplied by *parachute*.

parade (pa-rade) 1. gather together for inspection, drilling, marching etc.: The company will *parade* at dawn. 2. a gathering together: The *parade* will take place on the *parade* ground. 3. a display: Many attractive people attended the fashion *parade*. 4. a promenade (by the sea, in public gardens etc.): We met him walking along the *parade*.

paradise (par-a-dise) 1. heaven. 2. a place of extreme beauty and happiness: You have made this garden a *paradise*. 3. a state of perfect happiness.

paraffin (par-af-fin) 1. oil obtained from coal and petroleum, used for burning: He poured more *paraffin* in the stove and soon the room was warm. 2. using *paraffin*: The room was lit by a single *paraffin* lamp. **paraffin wax** a kind of wax used for making candles, polishes etc.

paragraph (par-a-graph) 1. a group of sentences dealing with one subject: When you change the subject you should start a new *paragraph*. 2. a short item in a newspaper: We have inserted a *paragraph* in the newspaper announcing the birth of our son.

parallel (par-al-lel) 1. (of lines) being the same distance apart throughout their length: The opposite sides of a square are *parallel*. 2. a line of latitude: Birmingham is on the 52nd *parallel*. **parallelogram** a figure whose opposite sides are *parallel*.

paralyse (par-a-lyse) make unable to move or feel with part or all of the body: After a fall from his horse his legs were *paralysed*. **paralysis** being *paralysed*: The accident caused *paralysis* of the lower limbs. **paralytic** accompanied by *paralysis*: He was rendered helpless by a *paralytic* stroke.

paratroops (par-a-troops) soldiers specially trained to be landed by parachute. **paratrooper** a soldier belonging to the *paratroops*.

parcel (par-cel) something wrapped and tied up for storing, carrying, sending etc.: He left the *parcel* in the luggage office. **parcel post** a department of the Post Office dealing with the posting of *parcels*.

parch make dry, dry up with heat, especially of the sun: Nothing would grow in the *parched* soil.

parchment (parch-ment) the skin of sheep, goats etc. dried and prepared for use as a writing material: The poem was written in Latin on a small sheet of *parchment*.

pardon (par-don) 1. forgiveness: 'I beg your *pardon*,' said the young man. 2. forgive: 'I pray you, *pardon* me' (Shakespeare, *The Merry Wives of Windsor*). 3. excuse from punishment: On the king's coronation many prisoners were *pardoned*.

pare take away the outer part: He was *paring* his fingernails.—Shall I *pare* the apple for you? **parings** pieces or parts *pared* off: She threw the *parings* in the dustbin.

parent (par-ent) a father or mother: My *parents* are both in England this month. **parentage** fatherhood, motherhood, ancestry: He is of royal *parentage*. **parental** of a *parent*: The child is in need of *parental* care.

parish (par-ish) 1. part of a county which has its own church and priest: Our *parish* consists mostly of farms. 2. having to do with a *parish*: Our *parish* church was built 800 years ago. **parishioner** an inhabitant of a *parish*: The vicar visits his *parishioners* regularly.

park 1. a public recreation ground with gardens etc.: The band is playing by the pond in the *park* this afternoon. 2. the private grounds round a large house. 3. a place of great beauty specially preserved for visitors: The Lake District is one of our national *parks*. 4. a place where cars may be left for a period: Could you please direct me to the car *park*? 5. leave a car for a time: May I *park* my car here while I visit the shops?

parliament (par-lia-ment) a body of people elected by voters, whose members meet to make laws: The *Parliament* of Great Britain meets at Westminster. **parliamentary** having to do with *parliament*: The activities of *Parliament* are reported in a number of volumes known as Hansard's *Parliamentary* Debates.

parole (par-ole) 1. the freeing of a prisoner before his sentence is completed, after his promise of good behaviour. 2. the promise of a prisoner that, if allowed more freedom, he will not try to escape: Because of his former good conduct the prisoner was released on *parole*.

parrot (par-rot) a bird with a hooked bill and brightly coloured feathers: Our *parrot* can repeat most things that are said to it.

part 1. a portion or division: The shopkeeper lost *part* of his stock in the fire. 2. a share in what is being done: My *part* in the work was not important.—Have you learnt your *part* in the play yet? 3. a side in a quarrel: Thank you for taking my *part*. 4. a section of a book; an instalment of a story: Have you read *Part* Seven yet? 5. a necessary piece of machinery: He had to go to the dealer to buy a spare *part*. 6. one of the pieces sung or played which makes up a whole musical composition: I sing the tenor *part*.—Have you brought the second violin *part*? 7. separate: We shook hands and *parted*.—The referee *parted* the two fighters. **part with** give up, give away: I will give it to you but I hate *parting* with it. **parting** 1. leaving: '*Parting* is such sweet sorrow' (Shakespeare, *Romeo and Juliet*). 2. the line where the hair is *parted*: She has a *parting* on the left side of her head.

particle (par-ti-cle) a tiny piece: A *particle* of grit was blown into my eye.—He doesn't show a *particle* of sense.

particular (par-tic-u-lar) 1. special: I have my own *particular* reason for keeping quiet. 2. not easy to please: He is very *particular* about what he eats. 3. detail: Give *particulars* of any illnesses you have had.

partition (par-ti-tion) 1. division into parts: Before its *partition* India was governed by the British. 2. a wall between rooms: The sitting room has been divided in two by a *partition*. 3. divide into parts: As the family increased some of the rooms had to be *partitioned*.

partner (part-ner) 1. a person who joins with others in some activity or business: I cannot give you an answer until I have consulted my *partners*. 2. a person who plays, dances etc., with another: The first prize was won by Mr Green and his *partner*. 3. be a *partner* to: Will you *partner* me in this game? **partnership** being a *partner*, a business run by *partners*: He is in *partnership* with his brother.

party (par-ty) 1. a number of persons working for the same cause: Are you a member of the Conservative *Party*? 2. a group of people travelling or working together: A rescue *party* was sent out early this morning. 3. a group meeting by invitation, for pleasure or entertainment: Our Christmas *party* was held in the chairman's office. 4. a person who is concerned in some activity: I was never *party* to the fraud.

pass 1. move to and beyond: I *passed* by your window. 2. go by (of time): The year is *passing* too quickly. 3. give: Would you please *pass* the salt. 4. succeed in an examination: I *passed* my driving test the first time I tried. 5. give a judgment: The judge *passed* sentence. 6. send a ball to a player of the same side: He *passed* to the centre forward, who scored. 7. success in a test: I got a *pass* in history. 8. a piece of paper giving permission to go somewhere: 'Show your *passes* please,' said the doorkeeper. 9. the act of *passing* to another player: It was a clever *pass* to the centre forward. 10. a narrow path between high hills: We shan't be able to ride through the *pass* before sunset. **passbook** the book issued by a bank to a customer with particulars of the money he puts in and takes out. **passport** a document carried by a travel-ler in foreign countries. **password** a secret word known only to a few, which enables a person to be recognized as belonging to a particular group of people.

passage (pas-sage) 1. voyage from one place to another: We had a rough *passage* across the Atlantic. 2. going past: All will be forgiven with the *passage* of time. 3. a tunnel or corridor: The old castle had many underground *passages*. 4. an extract: The Bishop read a *passage* from St Mark's gospel. 5. the passing of a bill in Parliament. **passenger** a person who is taken on a journey by bus, boat, train, taxi etc.: All *passengers* were ordered off the bus.

passion (pas-sion) 1. strong feeling of love, anger, hatred etc: When he read the letter he flew into a *passion*. 2. the suffering and death of Jesus. **Passion Week** the week before Palm Sunday. **passion-flower, passion-fruit** a climbing plant with a brilliant flower, some kinds of which bear fruit which can be eaten. **Passion play** a play which deals with events in the life of Jesus.

past 1. gone by: 'The winter is *past*, the rain is over and gone' (*The Song of Solomon*). 2. time gone by: All this happened in the long distant *past*. 3. the earlier days of a person's life: I never talk about my *past*. 4. after: I will meet you at half *past* six. 5. by: a squadron of aeroplanes flew *past*. 6. beyond: I could once run 2 kilometres but I'm *past* it now.

pasteurize (pas-teur-ize) heat liquids, especially milk, to a high temperature to kill any germs that they may contain.

pastime (pas-time) anything which serves to make time pass pleasantly: My favourite *pastime* is golf.

pasture (pas-ture) 1. a field of grass for the feeding of cattle: There are twenty cows in the *pasture*. 2. land of this kind: The rain has greatly improved the *pasture* this month. 3. put cattle or sheep on a *pasture*: On these moors we *pasture* hundreds of sheep.

pat 1. strike lightly with the open hand or with a flat object: The dog likes being *patted*. 2. a tap with the open hand: He gave me a *pat* on the back. 3. a small piece of butter. 4. just right, without stopping: He recited the poem off *pat*.

patch 1. a piece of material used to mend a hole or strengthen a weak place: His coat had leather *patches* on the elbows. 2. a piece of silk or plaster used to cover up an injured eye. 3. a small differently coloured part of a surface: My fox terrier is white with a round black *patch* on its right side. 4. a small piece of ground, especially for growing plants: We have food all the year from our vegetable *patch*. 5. put a *patch* on: My trousers have been *patched* at the knees. **patchwork** material made up of *patches*: The bed was covered with a large *patchwork* quilt. **patch up** repair: He came to the rally in an old *patched up* car.

patent (pat-ent) 1. a government grant giving a person the sole right to manufacture something he has invented: I have taken out a *patent* for my new fly-catcher. 2. the invention protected by a *patent*: The fly-catcher is my own *patent*. 3. obtain a *patent*: I have had my fly-catcher *patented*. 4. protected by *patent*: This shop sells *patent* medicines.

path 1. a narrow track made by animals or people walking: Follow the *path* across the field. 2. the way a thing moves: From age to age the earth follows its *path* round the sun. **pathless** with no *paths*.

pathetic (pa-thet-ic) sad: The woman's *pathetic* case upset us.

patience (pa-tience) 1. the ability to suffer pain, sadness, hardship etc. without complaining: She bore her illness with *patience*. 2. a card game which can be played by one person. **patient** 1. having *patience*: I see I must be *patient* a little longer. 2. a person who is being treated by a doctor: 'How is your *patient*, doctor?' asked the nurse.

patriot (pa-tri-ot) a person who loves his country and is ready to defend it: He lived and died a true *patriot*. **patriotic** loving one's country, praising one's country: They marched along, singing *patriotic* songs. **patriotism** love of one's country.

patrol (pa-trol) 1. go back and forth to keep watch: All night long they *patrolled* the city walls. 2. the act of *patrolling*: We have a hundred men on *patrol*. 3. the group or person on *patrol*: Our little force was attacked by an enemy *patrol*.

patron (pa-tron) a person who gives support to some person or cause: Our Society has many distinguished *patrons*. **patron saint** a saint who is believed to protect a certain church or group: St Crispin is the *patron* saint of shoemakers. **patronage** encouragement by a *patron*; custom given to a shop: 'We thank you for your valued *patronage*' (notice in a shop window). **patronize** 1. help, give custom to: He has always *patronized* the same tailor. 2. behave as if one is consciously descending from a superior position: Her elder brother irritated her with his *patronizing* manner.

pattern (pat-tern) 1. a model or drawing to guide a person making something: She spread the dress *pattern* out on the carpet. 2. a model on which to base one's life: Take the life of Captain Scott as your *pattern*. 3. a small sample: The traveller always carried his book of *patterns*. 4. a design: I like the *pattern* of your wallpaper.

pauper (pau-per) a person who has no means of existence and has to rely on others for support: Having spent his fortune, he ended his life a *pauper*. **pauperism** complete poverty: His family was reduced to *pauperism*.

pause 1. a short stop: People emerged from the shelters during a *pause* in the bombing. 2. a sign in music ⌢ to show that a note or rest is to be lengthened. 3. make a short stop: He *paused* in the middle of a sentence and looked round his audience.

pave 1. put stones on a road or path to make walking easier: The ground was muddy so the path was *paved* with stones. 2. make things easier: Hard work helped to *pave* his way to success. **pavement** a *paved* path running along the side of a street: He tripped on the kerb and fell flat on the *pavement*.

paw 1. the foot of an animal that has claws: He always carries a rabbit's *paw* for luck. 2. beat the ground with the forefoot: The horse *pawed* the ground impatiently.

pawn 1. place valuables in another person's care as a pledge for money borrowed: He had to *pawn* his watch to buy food. 2. being pawned: He put his watch in *pawn*. 3. a piece in the game of chess. **pawnshop** a shop whose owner takes goods as pledge for money lent. **pawnbroker** the person keeping a *pawnshop*.

pay *paid*, *paying* 1. give money for goods: I *paid* very little for this camera. 2. give back money: ' "When will you *pay* me?" said the bells of Old Bailey' (nursery rhyme). 3. give (visits, compliments, attention etc.): *Pay* heed to what I say. 4. be to one's benefit: It *pays* to advertise. 5. money received for work: We receive our *pay* every Friday. **payment** *paying*: The *payment* to this grocer was due last week.

pea the small seed of the *pea* plant: *Peas* are taken from the pods in which they grow and are eaten as vegetables.

peace 1. freedom from war or fighting: *Peace* was declared between the two countries two months after the war began. 2. quiet: I love getting away from the busy city to the *peace* of the moors. **peaceful** quiet: It was a *peaceful* day with hardly a breath of wind.

peach 1. a tree which bears round, juicy fruit with a stone-like seed. 2. the fruit of the *peach* tree.

peacock (pea-cock) a large male bird with a splendid tail of coloured feathers which it spreads out like a fan. **peahen** the female of the *peacock*.

pear 1. a tree with sweet juicy fruit usually coloured green or yellow. 2. the fruit of the *pear* tree.

pearl 1. a hard, round silvery formation found in some oyster-shells: We watched the Japanese girls diving for *pearls*. 2. made of *pearls*: She wore a *pearl* necklace at the ball. **pearl barley** grains of barley looking like small *pearls*.

peasant (peas-ant) a person who works on the land and who is usually poor: There are still many *peasants* in Europe.

peat partly-decayed plants found on moors and bogs, used for fuel and for putting on the land: They were warming their hands before a *peat* fire.

pebble (peb-ble) a small stone which has been made round by the action of the sea, or a stream: It was difficult to paddle from the beach because of the large *pebbles*. **pebbly** full of *pebbles*: We crossed the *pebbly* bed of a stream.

peck 1. hit with the beak intending to injure: The brown hen has been badly *pecked* by the others. 2. pick up food by *pecking*: The hens *pecked* the corn till it was all finished. 3. a blow or a scar made with a beak: The mark was made by a *peck* on the leg.

peculiar (pe-cul-iar) 1. belonging to, done by only one group or person: This style of violin playing is *peculiar* to him. 2. strange: What a *peculiar* animal the kangaroo is!

pedal (ped-al) 1. part of a machine worked by the feet: He pressed hard on the *pedals* and the bicycle climbed the hill. 2. having *pedals*: In our church there is a fine *pedal* organ. 3. use a *pedal* or *pedals*: When the knife-grinder *pedalled* the stone began to turn.

pedlar (ped-lar) a person who goes from house to house selling small articles.

peel 1. the skin of fruit and of some vegetables: Don't leave banana *peel* on the pavement. 2. take off the *peel*: He *peeled* the orange with a pocket-knife. 3. come off easily: The paint is *peeling* with the heat of the sun. **peeler** an instrument for *peeling*. **peelings** *peel* that has been taken off: He ate the orange and threw the *peelings* away.

peer 1. look closely at: He *peered* into the darkness but could see nothing. 2. an equal: The law says that a man must be judged by his *peers*. 3. a member of the higher nobility: Most British *peers* sit in the House of Lords. **peeress** a woman *peer*; the wife of a *peer*. **peerless** having no equal: 'You, so perfect and so *peerless*, are created of every creature's best' (Shakespeare, *The Tempest*).

peevish (peev-ish) easily irritated, cross: It is a pity he is such a *peevish* child.

peg 1. a pin of wood or other material driven into something to fasten parts together, to hang things on, to make fast, to stop a hole and for many other purposes: On the wall was a row of *pegs* for hanging clothes. 2. fix with a *peg*: In a few minutes we had *pegged* down the tent firmly. 3. mark out with *pegs*: In the rush for gold, several claims had already been *pegged* out.

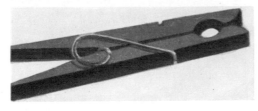

pellet (pel-let) 1. a little ball the size of a pill, of food or medicine. 2. a small bullet, a piece of small shot such as that used in airguns.

pelt 1. throw things: We were *pelted* with snowballs. 2. fall heavily: By the time we reached home the rain was *pelting* down. 3. the skin of an animal with or without hairs: The trapper was carrying a load of *pelts* to the store.

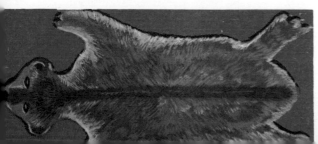

pen 1. an instrument for writing: The first *pens* were made of feathers, then of steel, but today most people use ball-point *pens*. 2. a small enclosure for domestic animals: He let the sheep out of the *pen*. **penfriend** a person, especially in another country, with whom one keeps up a friendship through letters. **penholder** a holder in which the steel nib of a *pen* is placed for writing. **penknife** a small pocket-knife made originally for making and mending *pens* of feathers.

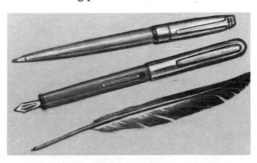

penal (pe-nal) having to do with punishment: Theft and assault are among the most common *penal* offences.—Devil's Island was once a famous French *penal* settlement. **penalize** subject a person or a player in a game to a *penalty*: The centre forward was *penalized* for foul play. **penalty** punishment for doing wrong or for breaking rules: In many countries the death *penalty* has been abolished.—You must pay the *penalty* for your foolishness.

pencil (pen-cil) 1. a tube of wood containing a hard substance in the middle with which one can write: Lead *pencils* contain material called graphite, which will make marks on paper. 2. mark with a *pencil*: He handed to the manager a *pencilled* note.

pendulum (pen-du-lum) a piece of brass, stone or other material swinging freely by a rod, string, chain or rope from a fixed point: The *pendulum* is used for controlling the movements of clocks.

penetrate (pen-e-trate) 1. pierce into: The bullet had *penetrated* his right shoulder.—Our lamps were too dim to *penetrate* the fog. 2. spread: The smell of cooking *penetrated* the whole building. **penetrating** piercing: She has a high, *penetrating* voice. **penetration** the power of *penetrating*; influencing the affairs of another country.

penguin (pen-guin) a seabird of the Antarctic whose wings are used for swimming and not for flying.

peninsula (pen-in-su-la) a piece of land almost surrounded by water: A *peninsula* is connected to the mainland by an isthmus or narrow neck of land. **peninsular** having to do with a *peninsula*: An army commanded by the Duke of Wellington fought in the *Peninsular* War.

penitence (pen-i-tence) sorrow for something done wrong, for sin. **penitent** sorry for things done wrong: The Prodigal Son returned, *penitent*, to his father. **penitentiary** a prison in which the chief aim is to reform prisoners.

penny (pen-ny) A British bronze coin once worth one-twelfth of a shilling, but now worth one-hundredth of a pound.

pension (pen-sion) a regular payment made by the state or by a former employer to a person who is disabled, old, a widow etc.: My grandfather's *pension* is paid to him monthly by cheque. **pensionable** entitling one to draw a pension: I have put in thirty years of *pensionable* service. **pensioner** a person receiving a *pension*.

pentathlon (pen-tath-lon) a competition in the Olympic Games in which a competitor takes part in five events.

people (peo-ple) 1. men, women and children: Thousands of *people* crowded into the stadium. 2. those belonging to nation, state or country: 'Tell old Pharaoh to let my *people* go' (Negro spiritual). 3. fill with *people*: 'The world must be *peopled*' (Shakespeare, *Much Ado about Nothing*).

pepper (pep-per) 1. a hot-tasting powder made from various plants and used for flavouring food. 2. a plant which produces red or green seed-pods used for food: The red *peppers* burnt my tongue. 3. pelt, shower: The crowd *peppered* him with small stones.

per cent for each hundred: 10 *per cent* is one tenth or ten out of every hundred. **percentage** 1. number in each hundred: What *percentage* of these apples is (or are) bad? 2. a number out of the whole: Quite a large *percentage* is (or are) bad.

perch 1. the place where a bird rests, usually a stick or rod: The budgie flew on to his *perch*. 2. a high seat: From my *perch* on the roof I saw the whole match. 3. sit, rest: Hundreds of sparrows *perched* on the rooftops. – The giant's castle was *perched* on a high cliff.

perennial (per-en-nial) 1. a plant that lasts for a long time: My garden is well stocked with *perennials*. 2. living through the winter: This is a *perennial* wallflower. 3. lasting a long time, rising again and again: Now we come to this *perennial* question of cheaper railway fares.

perfect (pér-fect) 1. without a single fault: This is a *perfect* example. 2. accurate: The artist took a piece of chalk and drew a *perfect* circle. 3. complete, absolute: He's a *perfect* stranger to me. **perfect** (per-féct) make *perfect*: I am busy *perfecting* my latest invention. **perfection** being or making *perfect*: The *perfection* of my invention took a year.

perforate (per-for-ate) 1. make small holes in: *Perforate* the can so that it pours more easily. 2. make a line of holes in paper so that it can be torn easily: I bought a *perforated* pad of notepaper.

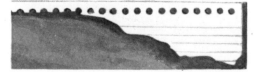

perform (per-form) 1. do: Have you *performed* all the tasks I gave you? 2. act, sing, do tricks etc., for an audience: This evening we are *performing* a play by Shakespeare. **performance** action; *performing* of a play: The English team gave a miserable *performance*. – We do two *performances* nightly. **performer** a person who *performs* or acts.

perfume (per-fume) 1. scent; a prepared liquid which gives off an agreeable smell: He bought her a small bottle of expensive *perfume*: 2. smell: These flowers have a lovely *perfume*. 3. give a *perfume* to: 'The air shall be *perfumed*' (Shakespeare, *Henry VI, part 2*).

perhaps (per-haps) it may be, possibly: *Perhaps* the postman will bring a letter.

peril (per-il) danger: As long as we stay here we are in *peril*. **perilous** dangerous: This was the end of our *perilous* journey.

period (pe-ri-od) 1. a length of time: I am going to America for a *period* of six weeks.—We are studying the Tudor *period* at school. 2. a full stop at the end of a sentence. 3. having to do with a certain *period* or *periods*: The play takes place in the reign of Queen Victoria, and all the players wear *period* dress. **periodic** coming at regular intervals: I am subject to *periodic* attacks of influenza. **periodical** a newspaper or magazine coming out at regular intervals: What *periodicals* do you wish us to deliver?

periscope (per-i-scope) an instrument which contains mirrors so that one may look from behind a wall, in a trench or under the sea at an object: We could not get into the ground but we saw the match through a *periscope*.

perish (per-ish) 1. die: Thousands have *perished* in the recent floods. 2. lose its quality: The elastic band broke because the rubber had *perished*. **perishable** *perishing* or going bad quickly: *Perishable* food must be taken to market and sold as soon as possible.

permanent (per-ma-nent) intended to last for ever: He had a *permanent* pain in his leg after falling from the horse. **permanent wave** a way of treating the hair so that waves or curls are put in which last until they have grown out.

permit (per-mit) allow: May I be *permitted* to smoke?–'Dogs not *permitted* unless on a lead' (notice on a park gate). **permit** (per-mit) a paper giving written permission to do something or go somewhere: You cannot enter the factory without a *permit* from the management. **permission** consent: May I have your *permission* to leave?

perpetual (per-pet-u-al) 1. continuing or lasting for ever: The planets run their *perpetual* course round the sun. 2. often repeated: I am tired of your *perpetual* requests for money. **perpetuate** keep from being forgotten: His memory is *perpetuated* by a large monument in the public park. **in perpetuity** for ever: This land has been granted to our village *in perpetuity*.

perplex (per-plex) worry, confuse: I was *perplexed* by his story. **perplexity** being *perplexed*: I was in such *perplexity* that I did not know what to do next.

persecute (per-se-cute) annoy, oppress, treat cruelly: Christians were *persecuted* under the Roman Emperors. **persecution** *persecuting*, being *persecuted*: Thousands fled from the country because of *persecution*.

persevere (per-se-vere) keep on: You are sure to succeed if you *persevere* with your studies. **perseverance** constant trying: It was entirely due to his *perseverance* that the new art gallery was built.

persist (per-sist) 1. refuse to change: If you *persist* in talking you will have to leave the room. 2. last, endure: The ships cannot leave port as long as the bad weather *persists*. **persistence** continuation: The *persistence* of dry weather is causing a scarcity of fruit. **persistent** continuing: We asked, but were met by *persistent* refusals.

person (per-son) a human being: She was the only *person* I knew in the room. **personnel** staff, *persons* employed in a firm, a government department or in the forces. **personnel officer** a *person* in a firm whose work is to deal with the affairs, grievances etc. of employees.

personal (per-son-al) 1. private: What I do in my spare time is a *personal* matter. 2. in person, not through anybody else: I shall make a *personal* appearance at court. 3. of a person: His *personal* appearance was attractive.—I shall leave all my *personal* property (not including land etc.) to my youngest son. **personate** see *impersonate*.

personality (per-son-al-i-ty) 1. all that makes up a person's character: She has an attractive *personality* and is liked by all. 2. a well-known person: I am a friend of several *personalities* in the theatre.

perspire (per-spire) give off a salty fluid through the pores of the skin, sweat: This hard work makes me *perspire*. **perspiration** sweat: Beads of *perspiration* stood on his forehead.

persuade (per-suade) make a person do something by reasoning with him: Can't I *persuade* you to come with me to the conference? **persuasion** the act of *persuading*: It was his *persuasion* that brought me here. **persuasive** good at *persuading*: He has a *persuasive* way of talking.

pest something that causes trouble and destruction: Foxes are a *pest* to the poultry-farmer. **pesticide** a substance which destroys *pests* in the home, the farm and the garden. **pestilence** a plague: The Black Death was the worst *pestilence* Europe has ever known.

pestle an instrument used in a mortar for crushing substances.

pet 1. an animal, bird etc. cared for and kept as a companion: Mary's *pet* lamb followed her to school. 2. fondle: My dog does not like being *petted*.

petal (pet-al) part of the flower which stands out from the centre like a coloured leaf: The garden path was strewn with rose-petals.

petition (pe-ti-tion) 1. a request, usually written and signed by a number of persons: A *petition* has been presented to the government to build a new road. 2. draw up and present a *petition*: We are *petitioning* the teacher to be excused from games today.

petroleum (pe-trol-eum) oil found underground and refined to make petrol, paraffin and many other products. **petrol** refined *petroleum*, used to drive cars and other machines.

petticoat (pet-ti-coat) an underskirt worn by women and children.

petty (pet-ty) 1. small, not important: I am tired of listening to your *petty* grievances. 2. trivial: Don't listen to *petty* gossip. **petty cash** a fund set aside to make small payments. **petty officer** an officer in the navy who does not hold a commission.

pew a long wooden seat with a back, usually fixed to the floor of a church.

phantom (phan-tom, pronounced *fantom*) a ghost; an image in a dream: 'Slowly the *phantom* raised its head' (from a ghost story).—In his dream, the old sailor saw a *phantom* ship approaching.

pharmacist (phar-ma-cist, pronounced *farmacist*) a person licensed to mix drugs and prepare medicines. **pharmacy** a shop where medical preparations are sold.

pheasant (pheas-ant, pronounced *fesant*) a long-tailed bird which is shot for sport and whose flesh is used for food.

phenomenon (phe-nom-e-non, pronounced *fenomenon*) *phenomena* 1. anything which is observed: The rainbow is a *phenomenon* of nature. 2. something or somebody remarkable or unusual: A double rainbow is a very rare *phenomenon*. **phenomenal** remarkable, unusual: Even as a child, Mozart was a *phenomenal* performer on the piano.

philosophy (phi-los-o-phy, pronounced *filosofy*) 1. a system of thought dealing with the nature and meaning of life, the world and the mind: We are studying the *philosophy* of medieval times. 2. an attitude towards life which helps a person to face misfortune, illness, danger and death. **philosopher** 1. a student of *philosophy*. 2. a person whose life is guided by his personal *philosophy*: Socrates was an ancient Greek *philosopher* who taught and practised his own *philosophy*.

phlegm (pronounced *flem*) 1. a thick fluid that gathers in the nose and throat and is expelled by coughing. 2. slowness to act. **phlegmatic** not easily roused or put into a temper: It is often said that English people are *phlegmatic*.

phone (pronounced *fone*) see **telephone**.

phosphorus (phos-phor-us, pronounced *fosforus*) a yellowish substance that easily catches fire and shines faintly in the dark. **phosphorescent** giving out light without burning: We gazed through the night at the *phosphorescent* crests of the waves.

photograph (pho-to-graph, pronounced *fotograf*) or **photo** 1. a picture produced by light passing into a camera through its lens on to light-sensitive film. 2. take a *photograph*: He was *photographed* feeding the ducks in the park. **photographer** a person who takes *photographs*. **photographic** having to do with *photographs*: Here is an unused reel of *photographic* film. **photofinish** the finish of a race that is so close that the winner can only be decided by consulting a *photograph*.

phrase (pronounced *frase*) 1. a group of words which form part of a sentence: 'How sweet the moonlight sleeps upon this bank' is a sentence; 'upon this bank' is a *phrase*. 2. put into words: His speech could not have been better *phrased*.

physical (phys-i-cal, pronounced *fisical*) 1. having to do with material things: Man, with his telescopes, is exploring the *physical* universe. 2. having to do with the body: Every morning he does *physical* exercises. **physician** a doctor of medicine who treats bodily ailments. **physic** medicine.

physics (phys-ics, pronounced *fisics*) sciences that deal with matter and energy: The study of light, heat and sound is a branch of *physics*.

piano (pia-no) a musical instrument played by striking keys on a keyboard: The keys of a *piano* operate hammers which produce notes by striking metal strings. **pianist** a person who plays a *piano*.

pick 1. pluck, gather, pull: The children were *picking* flowers in the field. 2. separate, tear apart: An old lady sat in a corner, *picking* rags. 3. choose: He *picked* the biggest apple.—They are *picking* the team for the championship. 4. use an instrument to do something: I can *pick* this lock with a compass. 5. choice: Take your *pick* of all these prizes. 6. a heavy tool with a handle and an iron head which has two pointed ends: He dug up the road with a *pick* and shovel. **pick up** 1. lift: Don't *pick up* the baby unless he begins to cry. 2. gain: He slowly *picked up* speed as he went down the hill. **pick-up** the arm of a record player that goes over the record and produces the tune. **pick on** find fault with: We were all there; why *pick on* me?

picket (pick-et) 1. a small group of men, or one man, on guard duty: We walked in the shadow to avoid being seen by the *picket*. 2. a group of strikers standing outside the gates of a place of work to persuade other workers not to enter: The strikers had posted a strong *picket* at the gate. 3. place soldiers on guard, or men at a factory gate: The works were *picketed* day and night.

pickle (pick-le) 1. a mixture of vinegar, salt water etc. that is used to preserve and flavour meat, fish and vegetables: We will put these onions in *pickle*. 2. food that is *pickled*: At the grocers I bought a jar of *pickles*. 3. put things in *pickle*: The cucumber we cannot eat today we will *pickle*.

picnic (pic-nic) *picnicked*, *picnicking* 1. a pleasure trip on which food is taken to be eaten out of doors: We went for a *picnic* in the woods. 2. go on such a trip: We *picnicked* under a large oak.

picture (pic-ture) 1. a drawing or painting: His walls were covered with *pictures*. 2. a beautiful object: What a charming *picture* she made on the swing. 3. what one sees on a screen: I wish we could get a better *picture*. **picturesque** being like a *picture*: We had a view of a *picturesque* valley. **pictorial** shown in *pictures*: This is a *pictorial* history of England.—We have an excellent *pictorial* record of our wedding.

pie a baked dish consisting of meat or fruit covered with pastry: 'Four and twenty blackbirds baked in a *pie*' (nursery rhyme).

piece 1. a part of something: Would you like a *piece* of cake? 2. an example or instance of something: I shall give you a *piece* of advice. 3. one article of a set or collection: I have bought a dinner service of a hundred *pieces*. 4. a particular length, weight, quantity in which goods are prepared for sale: We sell our cloth by the *piece*. 5. a coin: We found hundreds of gold *pieces* buried in the field. 6. a single composition, a single task: Would you please play this *piece*?—You have done a fine *piece* of work. 7. put together from the *pieces*: He has *pieced* together all the parts and built an engine. **piecemeal** bit by bit: This floor will have to be laid *piecemeal*.

pier 1. a structure built out into the sea to serve as a landing place for ships, or for pleasure: We sat in the sun on the end of the *pier*. 2. a pillar which helps to support a bridge: The bridge had three *piers* and four arches.

pierce 1. make a hole with a sharp instrument: The arrow had *pierced* his shield. 2. sound sharply through: The cry of an owl *pierced* the air. 3. show through: A faint light *pierced* the darkness.

pig an animal bred on farms whose flesh is eaten as pork and bacon.

pigeon (pi-geon) a bird of the dove family: Some *pigeons* are trained to carry messages.

pigment (pig-ment) colouring matter: The paint was made darker by adding a brown *pigment*.

pike 1. a large, slender, fierce fish which lives in fresh water. 2. a weapon with a long shaft and a small metal head once used by infantrymen.

pile 1. a number of things lying upon each other: He chose a large book from the *pile*. 2. a heavy timber pole, sometimes pointed at the lower end and driven into the ground: These houses stand on a marsh and are built on *piles*. 3. the raised hair-like surface on cloth or on a carpet: Velvet has a thick *pile*. 4. put into a pile: The bricks had been *piled* up by the garden gate. **atomic pile** an apparatus for producing atomic energy.

pilfer (pil-fer) steal, especially in small quantities: There have been many complaints about *pilfering* from stores. **pilferer** a person who *pilfers*: 'Pilferers will be prosecuted' (notice in a large store).

pilgrim (pil-grim) one who journeys, especially a long distance, to some sacred place: The *pilgrims* were on their way to the shrine of St Thomas of Canterbury. **pilgrimage** a journey made by *pilgrims*: As a boy, King Alfred went on a *pilgrimage* to Rome.

pill a small round ball of some medical substance, to be swallowed: Take one *pill* three times a day. **pillbox** 1. a small box for holding *pills*. 2. a small fort with thick concrete walls.

pillar (pil-lar) 1. an upright column of stone, wood, metal etc. used as a support or as a monument: The roof of the temple is supported by sixteen *pillars*. 2. a person who supports a cause: He is a *pillar* of the community. 3. something shaped like a *pillar*: In their wanderings in the desert the Israelites were guided by a *pillar* of smoke by day and a *pillar* of fire by night. **pillar-box** an iron box in the shape of a *pillar* in which letters are posted for collection and distribution.

pillow (pil-low) 1. a bag filled with soft material on which one may rest the head, especially when sleeping: I fell asleep as soon as my head touched the *pillow*. 2. anything serving as a *pillow*: Jacob took the stone he had used as a *pillow* and set it up as a pillar. 3. rest one's head: We *pillowed* the injured man's head on a pile of sacks. **pillowcase, pillowslip** the cotton, linen or nylon cover drawn over a *pillow* before use.

pilot (pi-lot) 1. a person who takes a ship in and out of harbours or through channels which are not well known: Once in the river mouth we took the *pilot* on board. 2. a person who controls an aeroplane. 3. steer: He *piloted* us safely through the dangerous waters. 4. experimental: This is only a *pilot* scheme.

pimple (pim-ple) a small inflamed swelling or spot on the skin: The boy's face is full of *pimples*; it is *pimply*.

pin 1. a small, slender, pointed piece of metal or wood used to fasten things together: A card with my name on it was fastened to my lapel with a *pin*. 2. any kind of device for fastening in which the main part is a *pin*: The box was full of safety-*pins*, drawing-*pins*, hair*pins* and hat*pins*.—The *pin* has come out of my brooch. 3. a wooden peg used for various purposes: Rolling-*pins* and nine-*pins* are not really *pins*. 4. fasten with a *pin*: The professor *pinned* the notice on the board. **pincushion** a small cushion or pad in which *pins* are stuck ready to be used. **pinafore** a loose dress worn to protect the clothing when doing work, so called because it was *pinned* 'afore' or in front.

pincers (pin-cers) a tool for gripping things and taking nails out of wood.

pinch 1. take firmly between the thumb and forefinger: Somebody *pinched* me to stop me falling asleep. 2. hurt through being too tight: My new shoes are *pinching* me. 3. the act of *pinching*: I felt a *pinch* on my arm and awoke. 4. anxiety, usually caused by being without something: After a fortnight with no wages he began to feel the *pinch*. 5. that which can be taken up between the thumb and forefinger: The old man took a *pinch* of snuff.

pine 1. an evergreen tree which has small needle-shaped leaves and cones which carry its seeds. 2. become thin through sorrow or anxiety: The poor child is *pining* for its parents. 3. desire very much: I *pine* for a sight of my old home.

pineapple (pine-ap-ple) a large juicy fruit grown in the tropics, so called because the fruit bears some resemblance to the pine cone.

pink 1. a light red colour: Tea was laid on a *pink* tablecloth. 2. a sweet-smelling garden flower: In June the garden is full of *pinks*. 3. punch cloth or leather with small holes for ornament. 4. (of a petrol engine) make high-pitched sounds: The engine is *pinking* and needs attention. **pinking shears** scissors with notched edges specially made to cut cloth so that it will not fray.

pint one eighth of a gallon in liquid measure: Ask the milkman to leave a *pint* this morning. (1·75 *pints* = 1 litre).

pipe 1. a hollow tube through which water, gas, steam, etc., can flow: The ground floor was flooded because of a burst *pipe*. 2. a tube of wood, clay, etc., with a bowl at one end and mouthpiece at the other, used for smoking: There he sat, puffing away at his *pipe*. 3. a musical instrument: We watched the little man playing a *pipe* and dancing. 4. take water, gas etc. through *pipes*: Does your house have *piped* water? 5. sing or talk in a thin, high voice: 'I didn't do it!' *piped* the little mouse (nursery story). 6. trim: The dress was *piped* with purple braid.— Mother is *piping* the birthday cake. **piper** a person who plays the *pipe*.

piracy (pi-racy) 1. capturing another vessel at sea. 2. operating an illegal service etc.

pirate (pi-rate) a person who commits robbery on the sea.

pistol (pis-tol) a small gun held in one hand: The revolver and the automatic are two kinds of *pistol*.

piston (pis-ton) a movable cylinder made to fit inside a hollow tube or cylinder, which can be pushed up and down by steam or gas pressure to supply power to an engine.

pit 1. a deep hole in the ground: We dug a *pit* and threw in all the rubbish. 2. a small scar left on the body as a result of some disease. 3. the seats behind the stalls on the ground floor of a theatre: We were able to book seats in the front row of the *pit*. 4. the place at which racing car drivers stop to refuel and get necessary repairs: The champion lost three minutes' valuable time by having to stop at the *pit*. 5. make small holes in the skin: His face was *pitted* with the scars of smallpox. 6. match: David *pitted* his skill against the strength of the giant Goliath.

pitch 1. set up: We *pitched* our tent by the side of the stream. 2. throw: He *pitched* the ball in my direction.—Three men *pitched* the hay on to the cart. 3. put music into a certain key: I can't sing this tune because it is *pitched* too high. 4. fall: The drunken man *pitched* forwards on to his face. 5. move up and down: The ship was *pitching* heavily in the gale. 6. (in cricket) put the stumps into the ground ready for play: Wickets were *pitched* after lunch. 7. a prepared ground on which a game is played: The spectators stood round the netball *pitch*. 8. a place where a street trader puts his wares: I pay a low rent to the Council for this *pitch*. 9. the slope of a roof: A high-*pitched* roof enables the snow to slide off. 10. a black substance like tar used to mend leaks in boats and fill cracks in pavements. **pitchfork** a large fork for *pitching* hay. **pitched battle** a battle fought in prepared positions.

pitcher (pitch-er) 1. a large vessel with a handle and lip, used for holding liquids: 'You shall meet a man bearing a *pitcher* of water: follow him' (The Gospel according to St Mark). 2. the player in a baseball game who throws the ball to the batter.

pity (pi-ty) 1. a feeling of sorrow for the sufferings of others: Have *pity* on the blind man. 2. reason for being sorry: It's a great *pity* that you won't be able to join us. 3. feel sorrow for other people's sufferings: 'Do you *pity* him? No, he deserves no *pity*' (Shakespeare, *As You Like It*). **pitiful** causing pity: There he lay, a *pitiful* creature.

place 1. a position, where a thing should be or is: 'A *place* for everything and everything in its *place*' (proverb). 2. a city, town, building etc.: I like this *place*.—I never visit crowded *places*. 3. a position on a surface, in a book etc.: How did you get that sore *place* on your arm.—I dropped the book and I've lost my *place*. 4. rank, position among people, employment: Every man should be kept in his *place*.—I've found you a *place* in our export department. 5. position in a competition or race: I would like him to get first *place*. 6. another name for a street: I live in St Ann's *Place*. 7. duty: It is your *place* to distribute the circulars. 8. put: *Place* your tickets in this box. 9. identify: I've seen him many times but I can't *place* him.

plague 1. an epidemic, the spread of disease: The war was followed by a widespread *plague*. 2. a disaster caused by something other than disease: The whole country has been visited by a *plague* of locusts. 3. annoy: Don't *plague* me with so many questions.

plaid (rhymes with *had*) 1. a long piece of cloth worn over the shoulders as part of the Scottish national dress. 2. a piece of cloth with a design of coloured checks and squares: I like your *plaid* skirt.

plain 1. easy to see, hear, understand: Please tell us the story in *plain* language. 2. simple: Only *plain* food is served here. 3. out of uniform: The house was surrounded by police in *plain* clothes. 4. honest: I know you like *plain* dealing. 5. not good-looking: 'You are called *plain* Kate' (Shakespeare, *The Taming of the Shrew*). 6. an area of flat country: Military manoeuvres are now being held on Salisbury *Plain*.

plait 1. twist lengths of hair, wool, straw, to make a kind of rope: He *plaited* the horse's tail. 2. hair, rope etc. that has been *plaited*: She wore her hair in two *plaits*.

plan 1. a drawing showing the details and positions of the parts of a piece of land, a building or a machine: The architect has submitted his *plans* of the new Town Hall to the Council. 2. a scheme for doing things in the future: What are your *plans* for this summer? 3. Work out the details for a garden, house etc.: The positions of trees in the park are now being *planned*. 4. make arrangements for the future: We are *planning* a long holiday in Spain.

plane 1. a tree with broad leaves and thin bark which falls off in large flakes. 2. an aeroplane: He went to Paris by *plane*. 3. a surface: A ball gathers speed as it rolls down a sloping *plane*. 4. a tool which has a sharp blade fitted into it, designed to smooth wood and metal. 5. smooth with a *plane*: The edge needs *planing* off this door to make it close. 6. a flat surface.

planet (plan-et) one of the heavenly bodies that moves round the sun: From the *planet* Earth, spacecraft have already been sent to other *planets*.

plank a long flat piece of timber used mostly for walking on and making floors: We crossed the stream by walking along a narrow *plank*.

plant 1. a living thing that is not an animal and is smaller than a tree: Spring is the time for putting *plants* in the garden. 2. machinery etc.: Our factory is being equipped with new *plant*. 3. put *plants*, trees etc. into a garden or other cultivated ground: Have you *planted* your tomato *plants* yet? 4. found, set up, establish: The British people *planted* colonies in all parts of the world. **plantation** an area of land on which trees are *planted*; an estate on which cotton, sugar, tobacco etc. are grown: Sugar is produced on *plantations* in the West Indies. **planter** a person who grows crops on a *plantation*.

plaster (plas-ter) 1. a soft mixture of lime, sand and water used for covering walls. 2. a cloth on which medicine has been spread, to lay on an injury or painful place: Let me put a *plaster* on that sore finger. 3. cover a wall with *plaster*. 4. cover thickly: The players came off the field *plastered* from head to foot with mud. **plasterer** a workman who puts *plaster* on walls and ceilings.

plastic (plas-tic) 1. easy to mould and make into shapes: Modellers make use of clay and other *plastic* materials. 2. made of *plastic* materials: She washed the tea cups in a *plastic* bowl.

plate 1. a shallow dish with edges slightly turned up, used for meals and other purposes: A hungry man leaves nothing on his *plate*.–How much did you put on the collection *plate*? 2. articles of gold and silver for use at meals and in churches: The wealthy man owned a valuable collection of *plate*. 3. a thin flat sheet: On the door was a metal *plate* bearing the doctor's name. 4. cover with gold, silver etc.: Bring out the silver-*plated* teapot. **plate glass** thick glass suitable for putting into shop windows etc.

plateau (pla-teau) *plateaux, plateaus* an area of flat land high above sea level.

platform (plat-form) 1. a raised floor in a hall for use by public speakers: The Mayor and aldermen sat on the *platform*. 2. the raised area along the side of the tracks in a railway station: We waited on the *platform* for the express to arrive.

platinum (plat-i-num) a hard, greyish white and very valuable metal used for making scientific apparatus and jewellery: This *platinum* brooch belonged to my grandmother.

platoon (pla-toon) a body of soldiers of two or more sections, being part of a company and commanded by a lieutenant.

play 1. take part in a game for pleasure: 'Boys and girls come out to *play*' (nursery rhyme). 2. pretend: Shall we *play* soldiers? 3. do, perform (jokes, tricks etc.): He's always *playing* pranks on people. 4. take part in a game: They are *playing* football. 5. perform on a musical instrument: I am learning to *play* the violin. 6. perform in a drama or *play*: He is *playing* the part of Mark Antony in *Julius Caesar*. 7. games taken part in for pleasure: The children are at *play*. 8. a drama for the stage: This is one of the *plays* of Bernard Shaw. 9. things done in a game: The referee is on the field to see fair *play*. **player** a person who *plays* a game or is in a drama: 'All the world's a stage and all the men and women merely *players*' (Shakespeare, *As You Like It*). **playful** full of fun, always wanting to *play*: He brought home a *playful* kitten. **playmate** a person with whom one *plays*.

plead 1. put forward the case of a person in a court of justice: My solicitor *pleaded* my case. 2. make an earnest appeal: The man *pleaded* for mercy. 3. make an excuse: It's no good *pleading* ignorance of the law. 4. use arguments for or against something: I am *pleading* the cause of the old and infirm. **plea** statement, request, excuse: The lawyer entered a *plea* of guilty.

please 1. find something agreeable: Are you *pleased* with your birthday presents? 2. like, wish, choose: I will do what I *please*. 3. a polite form of asking: *Please* sign here.—*Please* pass the salt. **pleasant** *pleasing*, agreeable, giving enjoyment: We spent a *pleasant* evening in their *pleasant* house. **pleasure** feeling of being happy; enjoyment: 'Sweet is *pleasure* after pain' (Dryden, *Alexander's Feast*).

pledge 1. something given as a security that the giver will pay a debt or do what is required of him: 'What *pledge* have we of thy firm loyalty?' (Shakespeare, *Henry VI, part 3*). 2. a promise: I give you my *pledge* that I will not trespass again. 3. put in pawn, give as security. 4. promise: I am *pledged* to keep the matter secret. 5. drink the health of: I *pledge* the bride and bridegroom.

plenty (plen-ty) a large number or quantity; as much or more than is needed: Don't hurry; we've *plenty* of time.—Eat it up, there's *plenty* more. **plentiful** in *plenty*: Apples are *plentiful* this year.

pliers (pli-ers) small pincers with long jaws for bending wire, holding small objects etc.

plight 1. a sad or awkward situation: With no money and no home they were in a terrible *plight*. 2. promise: I never go back on my *plighted* word.

plimsoll (plim-soll) a rubber-soled canvas shoe, laced to fit the foot: I forgot to bring my *plimsolls* to school.

plod walk or work, slowly but without pause: 'The ploughman homeward *plods* his weary way' (Gray's *Elegy*). **plodder** a person who works slowly but steadily and usually succeeds.

plot 1. a secret plan: They made a *plot* to steal the jewels. 2. the plan or story of a novel or play: You cannot write a story unless you have a *plot*. 3. a small piece of ground: In the centre of the garden was a grass *plot*.—I have bought a *plot* of land on which to build my house. 4. plan secretly: Guy Fawkes was one of those who *plotted* to blow up the Houses of Parliament. 5. make a plan or diagram: We are *plotting* a graph to show the month's rainfall.

plough 1. an agricultural implement for cutting and turning up the soil: Some *ploughs* are drawn by horses, others by tractors. 2. a group of seven stars in the constellation of the Great Bear: The *Plough* is only visible in the sky during the winter months. 3. turn up the soil with a *plough*: This competition is to decide who can *plough* the straightest furrow. 4. work at something slowly and with perseverance: It took me three months to *plough* through this French grammar.

pluck 1. pull out from the place of growth, as feathers, flowers etc.: She was *plucking* a goose for dinner. —2. take hold and pull: He was idly *plucking* the strings of his guitar. 3. courage in face of difficulties: He had the *pluck* to own up. **plucky** having *pluck*, needing *pluck*: It was a *plucky* rescue.

plug 1. a piece of wood or other material used to stop up a hole: He pulled out the *plug* and the water ran out of the bath. 2. a device for making a connection with an electric supply: He took the *plug* to pieces and put in a new fuse. 3. a place where the water supply can be connected to a hose: On the pavement in front of the the house you will see a notice saying 'fire *plug*'. 4. stop, fill up by putting in a *plug*: Can you *plug* the leak in this tank? 5. connect: I have *plugged* in your electric sewing machine.

plum 1. a tree bearing soft sweet fruit with a smooth skin and a stone-like seed. 2. the fruit of the *plum*: I love stewed *plums*. **plum pudding** boiled pudding containing dried fruits and spices, usually eaten at Christmas time.

plumber (plumb-er) a workman who puts in and repairs pipes etc. in connection with water supply and drainage, both inside and outside. **plumbing** the water-pipes, tanks and cisterns in a building: As there's no hot water today, there must be something wrong with the *plumbing*.

plump 1. well filled out, rather fat: She was a *plump* little girl. 2. fall heavily: He was tired, and *plumped* into the armchair.

plunder (plun-der) 1. rob people by force: The invading armies *plundered* the town. 2. what is taken illegally: They went away carrying their *plunder*.

plunge 1. thrust something in: He *plunged* his hand into the hot water. 2. dive: He *plunged* into the canal to rescue the drowning boy. 3. the act of *plunging*: Let's take a *plunge* in the sea. **take the plunge** do something difficult, disagreeable or risky: I'm not sorry I *took the plunge* and bought the house.

plural (plu-ral) meaning more than one thing or person: The *plural* of 'man' is 'men'.

plus added to: Two *plus* two is four.

pneumonia (pneu-mo-nia) inflammation of the lung: *Pneumonia* is a very serious illness. **double pneumonia** inflammation of both lungs.

poach 1. trespass and take game from another person's land: Two men were brought to court for *poaching*. 2. take something that belongs to another person. 3. cook an egg by dropping it without the shell into boiling water: We often have *poached* eggs for breakfast.

pocket (pock-et) 1. a small bag inserted into a garment for carrying things: He had a penknife in his trouser *pocket*. 2. money: I shall be out of *pocket* if I change jobs. 3. a string bag at the corner of a billiard table: He shot the red ball straight into the *pocket*. 4. suitable for the *pocket*: I need a clean *pocket*-handkerchief. **pocket-money** a small allowance of money which one can spend as one pleases.

pod a long seed vessel carried by plants like the pea and the bean: We sell dried peas, frozen peas, canned peas and peas in the *pod*.

poem (po-em) a piece of writing in verse: In our school magazine are several *poems*.

poet (po-et) a person who writes poems: A famous *poet* came to school and read some of his poems to us. **poetess** a woman *poet*. **poetic** having to do with poetry: The story is *poetic* in form. **poetry** poems, the writing of poems: We are studying the *poetry* of Dylan Thomas.

point 1. the sharp end, as of a dagger, a pen, pencil, needle etc.: The *point* of my pencil is broken. 2. a tip: He stood on the *point* and looked out to sea.—The champion received a blow on the *point* of the chin. 3. a dot: Where do I put the decimal *point*? 4. a position in time or space: We had reached the *point* of no return (there was no turning back). 5. a mark to indicate temperature, pressure or water levels: The thermometer was now well below freezing *point*. 6. a mark showing a score in competitions etc.: He lost *points* through knocking down too many hurdles. 7. use: What's the *point* of being here an hour before time? 8. idea: What's the *point* of all this extra work? 9. a place on a railway line where a train shifts from one track to another: The wheels rattled over the *points*. 10. show, be directed towards: The hand of the clock *pointed* to twelve.—Don't *point* that gun at me! 11. fill in the spaces between bricks with new mortar: Your chimney badly needs *pointing*. **pointer** 1. anything that *points*: The *pointer* showed that we were flying too low. 2. a dog trained to stand with its nose in the direction where game is to be found.

poison (poison) 1. a substance which if absorbed may destroy life: The rodent officer used *poison* to destroy the rats. 2. destroy or injure with *poison*: Discharge from the chemical works has *poisoned* the fish in this river. **poisoner** a person who kills by means of *poison*. **poisonous** containing *poison*: Do you know which of the wild plants are *poisonous*?

poke 1. thrust against or through something with the finger, a stick etc.: Somebody *poked* me in the ribs.—Who *poked* a hole in this cushion? 2. the act of *poking*: It's time you gave the fire a *poke*. **poker** an iron bar for *poking* the fire.

pole 1. a long, rounded, slender piece of wood or metal: The street was lined with telegraph *poles*. 2. one of the two ends of the imaginary line drawn through the earth from north to south, on which the earth turns: The Norwegian explorer Roald Amundsen discovered the South *Pole*. 3. one of the two ends of a magnet. **polar** having to do with the *poles* of the earth: They made their way slowly through the *polar* ice. **pole-vault** a leap over a high horizontal bar with the help of a long *pole*.

police (po-lice) 1. an organized force whose work is to maintain order, deal with crime and see that laws are kept: Police were on duty all day in Trafalgar Square. 2. keep order in a place: The armed forces are now *policing* the boundary between the two countries. **policeman, policewoman** a member of the *police* force.

policy (pol-i-cy) 1. a plan of action: Our *policy* is to try to keep everybody off the streets. 2. an agreement between an insurance company and a person or persons: I have two *policies* for life insurance and one for fire insurance.

polio (pol-i-o) a shortened form of the word **poliomyelitis**, an infectious disease of the spinal cord which may cause paralysis.

polish (pol-ish) 1. make shiny by rubbing: I have washed and *polished* the car today. 2. the surface obtained by *polishing*: The table looks better with a high *polish*.

polite (po-lite) showing good manners towards others in behaviour and speech: When you meet your uncle try to be *polite*. **politeness** being *polite*: What *politeness* to offer me your seat!

politics (pol-i-tics) 1. the science or art of government: We are studying *politics* at the university. 2. the conduct of a country's affairs: He plays a prominent part in *politics*. **political** having to do with *politics*: *Political* power is in the hands of the party which controls parliament. **politician** a person taking part in *politics*: My book should be interesting to *politicians* of all parties.

poll 1. voting at an election: There was a heavy *poll* (a large number of people voted). – Our candidate came out at the head of the *poll*. 2. receive a certain number of votes: Our candidate *polled* 12,500 votes. **polling day** the day of the election.

pollen (pol-lĕn) the fine powdery yellowish grains formed on flowers, which fertilize other flowers and produce seed: *Pollen* is carried from flower to flower by bees and by the wind.

pollute (pol-lute) make dirty: The rivers are being *polluted* by chemical waste from factories. **pollution** the act of being *polluted*, the state of being *polluted*: Humanity may suffer from the *pollution* of the seas.

polo (po-lo) a ball game resembling hockey, played on horseback with long mallets and a wooden ball. **water-polo** a water game played by swimmers using a large inflated ball.

pond a body of water smaller than a lake, often artificially formed, used as a drinking-place for cattle or for pleasure in a park: We went skating on the frozen *pond*.

pony (po-ny) a small horse: The children ride on *ponies* on the beach. **ponytail** a style of hairdressing in which the hair is tied at the back of the head and hangs loose.

pool 1. a pond, a small body of standing water: There is a paddling-*pool* for children in the park. 2. a place to swim in.

3. a still, deep place in a stream or river: The *Pool* of London lies in the Thames below London Bridge. 4. an amount of money staked by a number of people on the results of races, football etc.: He won the first prize in a football *pool*. 5. put money together for the use of all: If we *pooled* our money we could buy a car.

poor 1. having little property or money: Let us do what we can to help *poor* people. 2. not good: This cloth is of very *poor* quality. 3. deserving pity or help: The *poor* child has no shoes. **poorly** 1. not well done: The room was very *poorly* decorated. 2. in *poor* health, ill.

pop 1. a sharp, short noise: The cork flew out of the bottle with a *pop*. 2. go or come quickly: I just *popped* in to show you what I have bought. 3. make a short sharp noise: Don't you hear the corks *popping*? 4. a shortened form of the word *popular* applied to certain pieces of art, music and singers: I'm very fond of *pop* music. **popgun** a small toy gun that shoots corks.

pope the Bishop of Rome, head of the Roman Catholic Church.

popular (pop-u-lar) 1. of the people: A *popular* government is one elected by the people. 2. liked by people: This teacher is very *popular* with his pupils.

porcelain (porce-lain) delicate china pottery with a shiny surface.

porch a covered entrance leading to the door of a house or other building: Some of the finest *porches* in the country are to be seen in our churches.

pore 1. a tiny opening in the skin of a person or animal: I was sweating at every *pore*. 2. read or study with steady attention: He *pored* over his book until his eyes became tired. **porous** having *pores*, allowing liquid to pass through: The soil in our garden is dry and *porous*.

pork the flesh of pigs used as food.

porridge (por-ridge) a breakfast dish made by boiling oatmeal in water and adding milk.

port 1. a harbour: The ship sailed into *port*. 2. a town with a harbour: London is one of the largest *ports* in the world. 3. the left side of a ship or aircraft, facing forward. 4. a sweet dark red wine which originally came from Portugal. **porthole** a small hole or opening in the side of a ship which lets in light and air: I could see the cliffs of Dover through the *porthole*.

porter (por-ter) 1. a person who carries luggage: The hotel *porter* took my luggage to the taxi. 2. a doorkeeper: 'Shall I be a *porter* at the gate?' (Shakespeare, *The Comedy of Errors*). **portable** that can be carried: I always take my *portable* typewriter with me.

portion (por-tion) a part, a share: 'Tear off this *portion* and hand it to the attendant' (instruction on a ticket).—Please give me a very small *portion* of potatoes.

portray (por-tray) 1. make a picture, drawing, or carving of something. 2. describe in words; act as if on the stage: He *portrayed* the character of the ancient King with great skill. **portrayal** description, playing of a part: It was a wonderful *portrayal* of Scrooge. **portrait** a drawing, painting or photograph of a person or animal: I am glad you are having your *portrait* painted.

pose 1. take or hold a position for an artist to draw or paint: Every morning I *pose* for the students at the School of Art. 2. pretend to be what one is not: He loves to *pose* as an expert on antiques. 3. a position taken up for a portrait: Here is her portrait in a most attractive *pose*. 4. a pretence: His use of long words is only a *pose*.

position (po-si-tion) 1. a place: We must find another *position* for this bookcase. 2. a way of holding the body: I couldn't stand in this *position* for long. 3. a rank: I wish you could reach a higher *position* in class.—He has obtained a *position* as chief engineer. 4. a state: We are not in a *position* to take any more orders.

positive (pos-i-tive) 1. certain, very sure: I am *positive* that he is the man I saw last night. 2. helpful: He gave me several *positive* ideas. 3. showing light and shade as seen in the original, the opposite of a negative (in photography).

possess (pos-sess) 1. have, own: Do you *possess* a film projector? 2. keep control: You must *possess* yourself a little longer. 3. take control of a person: I don't know what *possessed* him to write that letter. **possession** ownership, something *possessed*: We entered into *possession* of the house today.—We lost all our *possessions* in the recent floods. **possessive** wanting to own or acquire: He is too *possessive*; he wants everything he sees.

possible (pos-si-ble) that can be done, that can happen: I would like your answer as soon as *possible*.—Patches of fog are *possible* on all roads this morning. **possibility** being *possible*: There is a *possibility* of thunderstorms during the afternoon.

post 1. a place where a person should be on duty: Every man will remain at his *post* until morning. 2. a place where soldiers are put: Along the frontier there is a line of fortified *posts*. 3. a position: I have applied for a *post* as a teacher. 4. the delivery of letters: How many *posts* a day do you receive? 5. an upright piece of wood used as a support, for displaying notices etc.: The gate was supported by two strong *posts*. 6. put at a *post*: Men have been *posted* all along the route to guide the cyclists. 7. put letters into a pillar-box or take to a *post* office: I *posted* three parcels this morning. 8. put up a notice for all to see: News of the election results was *posted* in front of the school.—'Bill-*posting* strictly prohibited' (notice painted on a wall). **postage** payment for sending letters etc.: The cost of *postage* will be increased from June 1st. **postal** having to do with the *Post* Office: *Postal* services are very good in this town.

poster a notice displayed publicly: We read the election results on a *poster* in town. **postal order** a money order bought and cashed at a *post* office.

post- a prefix which means after or later than, from which many words have been formed:
postmortem a medical examination made of a person after death. **postpone** put off until another time: The match was *postponed* because of bad weather. **postponement** act of *postponing*: The match was played after several *postponements*. **postscript** a short message added to a letter after it has been signed (usually denoted by the letters *PS*): *PS* don't forget to let me know when you will arrive.

pot 1. a vessel of earthenware or metal, usually round and deep, used mostly in and about the house: Here are plant*pots*, tea*pots*, coffee*pots* and flower*pots*. 2. put in a *pot*: Have you *potted* the young plants yet? 3. shoot at, hit with a shot: I *potted* a fine duck on the marsh today. **potherb** any herb whose leaves, roots etc. are used for cooking. **pothole** 1. a hole in the road made by the wheels of vehicles or through subsidence 2. a deep hole or cave among rocks. **potholer** a person who explores *potholes* as a hobby. **pot roast** roast meat cooked slowly in a *pot* in the oven. **potter** a person who makes *pots*. **pottery** 1. all kinds of *pots*. 2. the making of *pots*: I am attending a *pottery* class at evening school.

potato (po-ta-to) *potatoes* a plant whose fleshy tuber is eaten as a vegetable: *Potatoes* may be boiled and mashed, roasted, baked or cooked in many other ways.

pouch 1. a small bag: Look in my pocket for my tobacco *pouch*. 2. a kind of bag in which a marsupial, such as the kangaroo, carries its young.

poultry (poul-try) 1. birds, mainly chickens, ducks, geese and turkeys, reared on farms for food. 2. the meat of *poultry*: We are having *poultry* for Christmas dinner. **poulterer** a person who sells *poultry* for food.

pounce jump or swoop down suddenly: He knelt with his rifle cocked, waiting for the lion to *pounce*.

pound 1. 16 ounces in weight: 14 *pounds* (2·2 *pounds* = 1 kilo) make one stone. 2. a hundred pence, expressed as £1: I gave him a £1 note and he gave me 50 pence change. 3. a place where stray animals are kept: If you have lost your dog, he may have been taken to the *pound*. 4. strike heavily: He *pounded* on the door until somebody came and opened it. 5. crush: The iron ore is *pounded* and then put into a furnace.

pour 1. send a liquid flowing in a stream out of a vessel: Would you please *pour* me a cup of tea? 2. come flowing out or in: Water was *pouring* from the roof. – Crowds *poured* into the stadium to see the match. 3. (of rain) come dropping down: Come under my umbrella, it's *pouring*.

poverty (pov-er-ty) being poor: The family lived in terrible *poverty*.

powder (pow-der) 1. material that has been ground to dust and is used for many purposes: We had to surrender to the enemy because we had no more (gun)*powder*. – I am using a new kind of (face)*powder*. 2. use face *powder*. **powder magazine** a place where gun*powder* is stored.

power (pow-er) 1. ability to do things, strength: He used all his *power* to open the door. 2. force that can be used to do work: This is a nine horse*power* engine. 3. control: At last I have you in my *power*! 4. a person or persons having authority: 'Some blessed *power* deliver us.' (Shakespeare, *A Comedy of Errors*). 5. a state which has great authority in the world: The great *powers* have agreed on methods of stopping piracy. 6. the right: I have been given the *power* to award the prizes. **powerful** having much *power*: A *powerful* crane was lifting the stones. – There are many *powerful* reasons why you should go. **powerless** without *power*: I was *powerless* to stop him.

practical (prac-ti-cal) 1. real, not just in the mind: I could do with some *practical* help. 2. clever at doing things: He does all our household repairs; he's a very *practical* person. **practically** almost, very nearly: It is *practically* impossible to buy fresh vegetables at this time of year.

practice (prac-tice) 1. constant repetition of something in order to improve: Have you done your piano *practice* today? 2. something done regularly: It is our *practice* to close the shop every Wednesday afternoon. 3. some kinds of business: He has set up in *practice* as a solicitor (doctor etc.). 4. a business of this kind: He has sold his *practice* and retired. 5. the doing of a thing which has been planned: We have at last put our plans into *practice*.

practise (prac-tise) 1. do something repeatedly in order to become skilful: I *practise* the violin for an hour every day. 2. work in certain professions: He *practises* as a doctor.

prairie (prai-rie) a wide area of treeless land on which grass grows: There are large *prairies* in North America.

praise 1. say good things about: He was *praised* by all for his skill in winning the championship. 2. the act of *praising*; being *praised*: His skill deserves *praise*. 3. worship: *Praise* the Lord; all *praises* be to God. **praiseworthy** worthy of being *praised*: He was given a medal for his *praiseworthy* act.

pram (short for **perambulator**) a small carriage in which a baby is wheeled.

prance 1. move by springing on the hind legs, as a horse does. 2. dance and leap about: We saw the lambs *prancing* in the meadow.

prank mischievous trick: He is always playing *pranks* on people.

pray 1. make requests or give thanks to God: 'Fools, who came to scoff, remained to *pray*' (Goldsmith, *The Traveller*). 2. ask a person: 'Mistress, your father *prays* you leave your books' (Shakespeare, *The Taming of the Shrew*). **prayer** the act of *praying*: Repeat the Lord's *Prayer* after me. **prayerbook** a book containing *prayers*. **The Prayer Book** the book of *prayers* used in the Church of England.

preach 1. put forward a religious teaching: St Augustine *preached* Christianity to the Saxons. 2. advise, recommend, urge: He went from one country to another *preaching* revolution. **preacher** a person who *preaches*, especially in church.

precede (pre-cede) go before: The entry of the king was *preceded* by a flourish of trumpets. **preceding** coming before: In the *preceding* week we travelled all over France.

precious (pre-cious) 1. very valuable: The crown is ornamented with *precious* stones. 2. dear, much loved: My little dog is very *precious* to me.

precipice (prec-i-pice) a cliff whose face overhangs the land below: They fought on the edge of the *precipice*. **precipitous** high and overhanging like a *precipice*: They determined to climb the most *precipitous* face of the mountain.

precise (pre-cise) 1. exact: Please give me *precise* details of your requirements. 2. careful not to make mistakes: You can rely on what he does, for he is very *precise*. **precision** being accurate: We owe a great deal to his *precision*. **precision tools** tools which measure very accurately small distances, quantities etc.: *Precision tools* are very necessary in modern industry.

predict (pre-dict) say what is going to happen in the future: The weatherman *predicts* a week of rain. **prediction** what is *predicted*: Their *prediction* came true and the rivers flooded.

prefabricate (pre-fab-ri-cate) make the parts of a building, ship or other construction separately, to be put together on the site: *Prefabrication* is a modern process. **prefab** (short for *prefabricated*) a *prefabricated* house: The *prefab* we bought was not expensive.

prefer (pre-fer) like one thing or person rather than another: Which of these footballs do you *prefer*? **preference** what is *preferred*: My *preference* is for the white one.

prefix (pre-fix) a word or syllable placed in front of another word to alter its meaning: The *prefix* non- usually gives a word an opposite meaning.

prehistoric (pre-his-tor-ic) belonging to the days before recorded history: The tools of *prehistoric* man have been dug up in many parts of Britain.

premier (pre-mier) the prime minister or first in rank: The *premier* of New Zealand is visiting this country. **premiership** the office of *premier*: As his party had the most members in the Commons, he was offered the *premiership*.

prepare (pre-pare) get ready, make ready: We must *prepare* for a long struggle.–A meal has already been *prepared*. **preparation** *preparing*, something *prepared*: The fire has been lit in *preparation* for the meeting. **preparatory** in *preparation*; *preparing*: *Preparatory* steps have been taken to repair the footpath.

prescribe (pre-scribe) order the use of: Several medicines have been *prescribed* by the doctor. **prescription** what is *prescribed*, usually written on a small sheet to be presented to the chemist: This *prescription* should help to cure you.

present (pre-sent) 1. at the place agreed; not absent: All the members were *present* at the meeting. 2. a gift: She received a *present* of a box of chocolates. 3. now: Up to the *present* we have had no news. **presently** soon: I will see you *presently*.

present (pre-sént) 1. give: He was *presented* with a gold watch. 2. put forward: We are *presenting* a petition to the government. 3. introduce: May I *present* my cousin. 4. perform (a play): The Dramatic Society are *presenting* a play by Sheridan this week. **presentation** being *presented*: We are all going to the *presentation* of prizes at school.

preserve (pre-serve) 1. save, keep from harm: 'Now good angels, *preserve* the king' (Shakespeare, *The Tempest*). 2. keep from going bad: What is the best method of *preserving* apples? 3. keep in good repair: This is a well-*preserved* timber cottage. 4. jam: This is the best quality raspberry *preserve*. 5. a place where animals, birds, insects, trees etc. are kept free from interference: My cousin is the warden of a large nature *preserve*. **preservation** *preserving*, being *preserved*: Lectures are being given on the *preservation* of food.

preside (pre-side) take charge of a meeting, a business, the work of an organization etc.: The Chairman *presided* over the meeting. **president** the person who *presides* over a government, a government department, a company etc.: The first *President* of the United States was George Washington. **presidency** the period a *president* is in office: Much good work was done during his *presidency*. **presidential** having to do with a *president*: He never neglected his *presidential* duties.

press 1. push: *Press* the button and the bell will ring. 2. push with force, crowd: Ten people were injured by the crowd *pressing* against the turnstiles. 3. urge, demand: We are *pressing* for an enquiry into the matter. 4. a machine for squeezing or *pressing*: Two men were working the wine*press*. 5. a printing machine: This is a mechanical printing *press*. 6. the printing and newspaper business; reporters: The *press* will not be admitted to the trial.

pressure (pres-sure) 1. a pressing of one thing on another: A barometer measures the *pressure* of the atmosphere. – With a little more *pressure* we should be able to close the lid. 2. force, compel people to do something. 3. something which oppresses: We are all alarmed by the *pressure* of rising prices. **pressurized** made so that atmospheric *pressure* and temperature can be controlled: This aeroplane has a *pressurized* cabin.

pretend (pre-tend) 1. make believe: Let's *pretend* to be cowboys and Indians. 2. try to make others believe things that are not true: It's no good *pretending* you didn't know. 3. claim: I don't *pretend* to know everything about dogs. **pretence** *pretending*, excuse, claim: He stopped me on the *pretence* of wanting to know the time. – I make no *pretence* to great knowledge.

pretty (pret-ty) 1. attractive, pleasing but not beautiful: She is a *pretty* girl. 2. fairly: I've a *pretty* good idea of what you want.

prevent (pre-vent) stop something from happening: His quick action *prevented* a fire. – You won't get the money if I can *prevent* it. **prevention** *preventing*: The *prevention* of illness is better than its cure. **preventive** something which *prevents*: Do you know a good *preventive* of rust?

preview (pre-view) view of a film, a play, an exhibition, goods on sale etc. before they are shown to the public: Today is the *preview* of the Motor Show.

previous (pre-vious) coming before: All this happened on a *previous* visit. **previously** before: The detective had *previously* questioned the suspect.

prey 1. a living being killed and eaten by another: The tiger roams the jungle searching for its *prey*. 2. hunt another animal for food: The big fishes *prey* on the little ones. 3. cause anxiety to: The crime he committed *preyed* on his conscience.

price 1. what something costs: I asked the *price* of the table. 2. ask or fix the *price* of something: Have you *priced* the table? – The shopkeeper was *pricing* the goods in his window. **priceless** having a value beyond all *price*: In the glass case was a collection of *priceless* jewels.

prick 1. puncture, make a hole in: He *pricked* the toy balloon. 2. cause pain by *pricking*: Have you *pricked* your finger? 3. a small hole made by something sharp: Look at all the *pricks* in this paper. 4. pain caused by being *pricked*: The *prick* of the thorn still hurts my leg. **prickle** 1. a small point sticking out: Don't touch the *prickles* on that hedgehog. 2. give a feeling of being *pricked*: My ear *prickled* after it was stung by a gnat. **prickly** having *prickles*: Don't touch that nettle; it's *prickly*!

pride 1. a feeling of satisfaction at having done something well or having people's respect: Every one of these men has *pride* in his work. 2. a thing or person to be proud of: He is my *pride* and joy. 3. too high an opinion of one's own importance: *Pride* goes before a fall (proverb). 4. be proud of: He *prides* himself on his knowledge of astronomy.

priest 1. a clergyman, usually in the Roman Catholic Church or the Church of England: The *priest* visits all the invalids in his parish. 2. a minister of any religion: The Buddhist *priests* in Thailand wear yellow robes.

primary (pri-ma-ry) 1. first in rank of importance: My *primary* concern is for your safety. 2. first in time or order: My son's first school will be the local *primary* school. **primary colours** (paints) red, yellow and blue, from which all other colours can be made.

prime 1. chief: The *Prime* Minister is the head of the government. 2. very good indeed: We have some *prime* ribs of beef today. 3. give a person all the facts: He has been well *primed* and is ready to answer any question. **primer** 1. a first textbook on any subject: Take out your French *primers*. 2. the first coat of paint put on an unpainted surface.

primitive (prim-i-tive) 1. having to do with the earliest times: *Primitive* man did not know how to make fire. 2. simple: Some races today use *primitive* tools.

prince 1. in Great Britain the son or grandson of a king or queen: Edward II of England was the first *Prince* of Wales. 2. a ruler: *Princes* and lords may flourish (Goldsmith, *The Traveller*). **princess** in Great Britain the daughter or granddaughter of a king or queen, or the wife of a *prince*.

principal (prin-ci-pal) 1. most important: The *principal* rivers of England are the Thames and the Severn. 2. the head of a college. 3. a sum of money which a person owns and which he can invest: I have invested the *principal* in government stock.

principle (prin-ci-ple) 1. a rule which guides a person's behaviour: It is a sound *principle* to look before you leap. 2. the law on which the working of a machine is based: A motor car engine and a steam engine work on the same *principle* – the movement of a piston in a cylinder. 3. the elements of a subject: You should study the *principles* of geometry.

print 1. make a mark on paper, cloth etc. by pressing with inked type or coloured designs: My book of poems has been *printed*. 2. make a photograph on paper from a negative. 3. letters, designs etc. in *printed* form: I can't read this small *print*. 4. marks left by the finger, the foot, the hand, an animal's paw etc.: The footprints led out of the garden and along the road. **printer** a person who *prints* for a living: I have taken the programme of the concert to the *printer*.

prior (pri-or) 1. at or of an earlier time: I am sorry but I have a *prior* engagement. 2. first: Your son has a *prior* claim to the money. **priority** the right to be considered before all others: 'Good quality is our first *priority*' (notice in a shop).

prison (pris-on) a building in which criminals and others condemned by the courts are locked up: Escape from this *prison* is almost impossible. **prisoner** a person kept in *prison* or some other form of captivity: The *prisoners* of war were put into a barbed wire enclosure.

private (pri-vate) 1. having to do with one person or a group: He came to a door marked '*PRIVATE. MEMBERS ONLY.*' 2. secret: For your *private* information, I am leaving tomorrow. 3. personal: Most of his time is spent on his duties as Mayor; he has hardly any *private* life. 4. a soldier who is not an officer: *Private* Perkins was awarded the Military Medal. **privacy** being alone, the right to be alone: I value my *privacy*.

prize 1. the reward of victory in a contest: The first *prize* was a book token. 2. having won a *prize*: The farmer brought his *prize* bull to market. **prize-fight** a boxing match for money. **prize money** money got by the sale of something captured in battle, or money won in a competition: The *prize money* was divided among the crew.

probable (prob-able) likely to happen or prove true: It is *probable* that we shall visit London this week. **probably** most likely: We shall *probably* visit London. **probability** being *probable*: The *probability* is that it will rain and we shall stay at home.

probation (pro-ba-tion) 1. a period in which a person is tested for suitability before being given a post: My *probation* is now nearly over. 2. a period in which offenders are allowed to go free providing they commit no further offences: The young man was put on *probation* for a year.

problem (prob-lem) 1. a difficult question to be answered: The class was set four mathematical *problems* to do at home. 2. something in life which presents difficulties: I am faced with the *problem* of finding a new post. 3. offering *problems*: He is a real *problem* child.

proceed (pro-ceed) 1. move forward or onward: We *proceeded* to discuss the terms of the will.–The caravan *proceeded* towards the next oasis. 2. come forth: 'A law shall *proceed* from me' (Isaiah, chapter 51). **proceeding** action: We followed the *proceedings* of the meeting with interest. **proceeds** (pró-ceeds) profits: The *proceeds* of the bazaar will help to pay for our new organ.

process (pro-cess) 1. actions which go on: We watered the seed and watched the slow *process* of growth. 2. things which are done in order: We stopped at the next town and began the *process* of unloading.

procession (pro-ces-sion) a line or body of persons moving along in an orderly manner: The band was followed by a cheerful and noisy *procession*.

proclaim (pro-claim) make known to all: When his father died the prince was *proclaimed* king. **proclamation** *proclaiming*; that which is *proclaimed*: We heard the *proclamation* of the outbreak of war.

procure (pro-cure) obtain, get: Where can I *procure* a pump to blow up my tyre?

prodigal (prod-i-gal) wasteful: Don't be too *prodigal* of your food.–The *prodigal* son wasted his money.

produce (pro-duce) 1. make, grow, create: We *produce* the very best crops of wheat. –The factories of Lancashire *produce* cotton goods. 2. show: All tickets must be *produced* at the door. 3. cause: His article in the newspaper *produced* many letters of protest. 4. make a line longer: *Produce* the line AB to a point C. 5. bring something before the public: When is the next play to be *produced*? **produce** (pró-duce) something *produced*: Much of our dairy *produce* comes from our own farms.

product (pro-duct) 1. something produced: All our *products* are of the highest quality. 2. the result when two numbers are multiplied: 8 is the *product* of 2 and 4. **production** producing, the quantity produced: We specialize in the *production* of mirrors and our *production* is increasing month by month. **productive** producing, able to produce: The new methods are highly *productive*.

profession (pro-fes-sion) the kind of work which needs special education and training: The medical *profession* interests me particularly as a career. **professional** having to do with a *profession*: I started my *professional* training last month.–He is a *professional* (golfer, boxer, footballer, musician etc.). **professor** a university teacher who directs one branch of learning: I have had an interview with the *professor* of oriental languages.

proficient (pro-fi-cient) skilled at a particular thing: He is a highly *proficient* swimmer. **proficiency** being *proficient*: I have a certificate for *proficiency* in woodwork.

profile (pro-file) 1. the outline of the side view of a face: Let me draw you in *profile*. 2. a short outline of a person's life.

profit (pro-fit) 1. advantage from some activity: I have made a good *profit* on the sale. 2. bring or obtain some gain: He has *profited* by the advice he received. **profitable** bringing *profit*: Selling these goods is hard work but very *profitable*.

programme (pro-gramme) 1. list of what is to happen in a concert, a sports meeting, the names of the cast of a play etc.: I found it impossible to follow the events without a *programme*. 2. a plan of what is to be done: I have been given my *programme* of studies for this year. **program** 1. the facts that are put into a computer. 2. put facts into a computer. **programmer** a person who supplies facts to a computer.

progress (prog-ress) 1. forward movement, advancement: 'He is making good *progress*' (school report). 2. make *progress*: The patient is *progressing* favourably.

prohibit (pro-hib-it) forbid: Smoking is *prohibited* in this theatre. **prohibition** an order forbidding something: There is a *prohibition* against striking matches in the woods. **prohibitive** likely to prevent the use of: The price of butter is *prohibitive*.

project (pro-ject) 1. plan: A new airport is being *projected* near the coast. 2. throw an outline or a picture on a screen. 3. throw a missile into space. 4. stand out: A shelf of rock *projected* from the vertical face of the cliff. **project** (pró-ject) a plan: There are several *projects* for building houses on this land. **projectile** a missile thrown or shot: Several *projectiles* landed in the residential areas of the town. **projector** a machine that *projects* a picture: I have *projectors* for both slides and films.

prolong (pro-long) 1. make longer in space: *Prolong* this line to a point on the side of the triangle. 2. make longer in time: The interview was *prolonged* and difficult. **prolongation** being *prolonged*: The *prolongation* of the interview caused me to miss my train.

promenade (prom-e-nade) 1. a place where one can walk, especially in public and for pleasure: Let's walk along the *promenade*. 2. go up and down a *promenade*: Some people were *promenading*, others were listening to the band.

prominent (prom-i-nent) 1. standing out, easily seen: You will recognize him by his *prominent* chin. 2. well-known, important: He holds a *prominent* position in the Civil Service. **prominence** being *prominent*; that which is *prominent*: He rose to *prominence* through his novels.

promontory (prom-on-to-ry) a cliff or high point of land standing out from the coastline: A lighthouse stood on the *promontory*.

promote (pro-mote) 1. raise in rank or position: He was *promoted* to chief clerk. 2. organize: We are *promoting* a new company and shares will soon be on the market. **promotion** a raising in rank: The reasons for his *promotion* are well known.—He won *promotion* through his gallantry in the field.

prompt 1. without delay, on time: He is always *prompt* in doing what is asked. 2. be the reason for doing something: I was *prompted* to come by the letter you sent. 3. remind an actor of his words when he forgets them: He had to be *prompted* several times in the first act. **prompter** a person who *prompts* actors in a play. **promptitude** being *prompt*: His *promptitude* in sounding the alarm prevented the fire from spreading.

pronoun (pro-noun) a word used instead of a noun: Did Harry give the key to John? Yes, he (*pronoun*) gave it (*pronoun*) to him (*pronoun*).

pronounce (pro-nounce) 1. make the sounds of words: You do not *pronounce* the p in psalm. 2. declare: 'I do *pronounce* you man and wife' (from the marriage service). 3. give as an opinion: The gala was *pronounced* a great success. **pronunciation** the way words are *pronounced*: If you want a good part in the play you must improve your *pronunciation*.

proof 1. facts which show that a thing is true: The postmark on my letter is a *proof* that I was in London. 2. a first copy of something printed to make sure that it is satisfactory: Here are the *proofs* of the wedding photographs. 3. giving safety or protection against: The marshal rode through the streets in a bullet-*proof* car.

prop 1. a stick or pole used to prevent things from falling: The clothes line is held up by a clothes *prop*. 2. any other kind of support. 3. support: The lintel of this door needs *propping* or it will collapse.

propagate (prop-a-gate) 1. increase the numbers: Some plants are *propagated* by seeds, others by taking cuttings. 2. spread: We must try to stop the *propagation* of false rumours. **propaganda** 1. teachings, news etc. spread far and wide: The government has started a *propaganda* campaign to increase road safety. 2. false, misleading information.

propel (pro-pel) drive forward: Our canoe is *propelled* by a paddle.–A jet-*propelled* air liner came in to land. **propeller** a shaft with curved blades that whirl round to drive a boat or an aeroplane forward. **propulsion** a way of *propelling*: Most planes now have jet *propulsion* but rocket *propulsion* is employed to lift spacecraft.

proper (prop-er) 1. as it should be, as they should be: You cannot go down a mine without the *proper* clothing and tools. 2. correct: What is the *proper* thing to do when you receive a prize? **proper noun** the name of a person or place: In the sentence 'John lives in Bristol' there are two *proper nouns*, 'John' and 'Bristol'.

property (pro-per-ty) 1. everything which is owned: My real *property* consists of land and buildings; my clothing, money and jewellery are my personal *property*. 2. what a thing does; how it may be recognized: One of the *properties* of a liquid is to take the shape of the vessel into which it is placed.–This ointment has great healing *properties*. 3. a piece of furniture or decoration on a stage; anything handled by an actor: All the *properties* are now ready for the first scene.

prophecy (proph-e-cy) a statement as to what is going to happen: My *prophecy* of fine weather came true. **prophesy** to say what is going to happen: I *prophesied* fine weather and I was right. **prophet** a person who *prophesies* or teaches: 'Beware of false *prophets*'–people who bring the wrong teachings.

proportion (pro-por-tion) 1. relation of one thing to another: The field is long in *proportion* to its breadth.–The work was too hard in *proportion* to the money received; it was out of all *proportion*.–Flour and sugar should be mixed in the *proportions* stated. 2. part: There is a very small *proportion* of gold in this rock.

propose (pro-pose) 1. put forward plans or ideas: I *propose* that we camp here for the night. 2. ask a person to marry one: He *proposed* to Sarah yesterday evening. 3. suggest a person for an office: I *propose* Mr Jones as our Chairman for the coming year. **proposal** something *proposed*: Your *proposal* that we should camp here is a good one.–She accepted his *proposal* of marriage. **proposition** a plan or scheme to be considered or adopted: The *proposition* was to camp in the mountains for the night.

proprietor (pro-pri-e-tor) a person who owns a business, hotel etc.: Who is the *proprietor* of this cafe? **proprietress** a woman *proprietor*.

prosecute (pros-e-cute) 1. carry on, continue to do something: The detectives are *prosecuting* an enquiry into the recent thefts. 2. bring to trial in court: 'Trespassers will be *prosecuted*' (notice outside a private estate). **prosecution** *prosecuting*, being *prosecuted*: If you enter these grounds you will be liable to *prosecution*.

prospect (pros-pect) 1. a view: From the top of the hill there is a delightful *prospect* of fields and woods. 2. something expected: You will have good *prospects* as a salesman in this firm.–He has every *prospect* of a quick recovery. 3. search: In 1849 thousands of men went *prospecting* for gold in California. **prospective** possible, or likely: We have already many *prospective* buyers for these houses. **prospectus** a printed account giving details of a business, a school, a book, etc.: We are sending you our latest *prospectus*.

prosper (pros-per) be successful, do well: May you *prosper* in your work. **prosperous** *prospering*: He owns a *prosperous* farm in Wales. **prosperity** being successful: We wish you *prosperity* in all you do.

protect (pro-tect) keep from harm or danger: This thick coat will *protect* you from the cold. **protection** 1. *protecting*, being *protected*: The president was under the *protection* of a bodyguard.–You need *protection* against the cold. 2. the state of being *protected*: I place myself under your *protection*. **protective** that *protects*: *Protective* clothing is being issued to the rescue party. **protector** a person or thing that *protects*.

protest (pro-test) speak against: The prisoners *protested* about the poor food. **protest** (pró-test) a statement *protesting* against something: They handed their written *protest* to the governor of the prison. **Protestant** a member of a Christian church which is not Roman Catholic.

prototype (pro-to-type) the original or the model, the first of a series from which others are copies: The *prototype* of the new aeroplane has been flown for the first time today.

proud 1. showing a reasonable pride: I am *proud* to be a member of this school. 2. showing too much pride, having too high an opinion of oneself: 'Take her hand, *proud* scornful boy' (Shakespeare, *All's Well That Ends Well*). 3. splendid: A *proud* ship sailed into the harbour.

prove 1. show proof or show that a thing is true: The police suspect him of the theft but they cannot yet *prove* it. 2. turn out: We trusted him but he *proved* to be dishonest.

provide (pro-vide) 1. furnish, supply: Can anybody *provide* me with an umbrella? 2. prepare beforehand: *Provide* against accidents by inflating your tyres to the correct pressure. 3. state as being necessary: This agreement *provides* that instalments shall be paid monthly.

providence (prov-i-dence) the way God's care over his creatures is shown: Again *providence* stepped in and saved our lives. **provident** careful to provide for future needs. **providential** as though done by *providence*: Our escape was *providential*.

province (prov-ince) 1. a large division of a country: The governors of every *province* were summoned to the capital. **the provinces** all parts of the country outside the capital: The French President is making a tour through the *provinces*. 2. a branch of learning, a department of business: I am afraid that questions of finance are outside my *province*.

provincial (pro-vin-cial) 1. having to do with a *province*: The *provincial* government has the right to levy certain taxes. 2. typical of the *provinces* as contrasted with the capital: He speaks with a broad *provincial* accent.

provision 1. preparation for the future: We have made *provision* for any emergency. 2. a part of a legal document, an agreement etc. which says what must happen under certain circumstances: A *provision* in the will states that the money shall go to the younger son if the elder one dies first. 3. supply with food, stores etc.: When we had been fully *provisioned* we set off on our long journey. **provisions** food, stores etc.: Every Friday we buy *provisions* for the following week.

provoke (pro-voke) 1. stir up, arouse, call forth: The news of the leader's imprisonment *provoked* a riot. 2. cause to do something: The insult *provoked* her to slam the door in his face. 3. make angry: Don't *provoke* me any further. **provocation** *provoking*, being *provoked*: She cried at the slightest *provocation*.

prowl 1. go about in search of prey, plunder or whatever may be found: A cat was *prowling* among the bushes. 2. the action of *prowling*: Keep your doors locked; thieves are on the *prowl*. **prowler** an animal or person who *prowls*. Beware of *prowlers*.

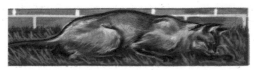

pry *pried*, *prying* 1. peer, peep curiously: We *pried* into the dark hole but could see nothing. 2. enquire curiously: She's always *prying* into other people's business. 3. find out by enquiring: At last we *pried* the secret out of him.

public (pub-lic) 1. the people who make up the state, the nation, community: This park is open to the *public* from 8 am to dusk. 2. having to do with the people: This is a *public* recreation ground. **public house** or **pub** a house where alcoholic drinks are sold and consumed on the premises. **publican** a keeper of a *public* house. **publication** publishing, making or made known to the *public*: I was pleased to hear of the *publication* of your book.—Have you seen our latest *publication*? **publicity** being known and recognized by all: He is a famous actor but he hates *publicity*. **publish** make known to the *public*; print a book or periodical: The magazine is *published* every Thursday.—**publisher** a person or firm which *publishes* books, magazines etc.

puddle (pud-dle) a small pool of water, especially dirty water, as in a road after rain: 'He stepped in a *puddle* up to his middle and never went there again.' (nursery rhyme, *Doctor Foster*)

puff 1. a short, quick blast of wind or breath: A *puff* of wind blew off his hat.— He took several *puffs* at his pipe. 2. a soft pad for putting powder on the face: On the dressing-table was a powder *puff*. 3. pastry filled with jam, cream etc.: Do you like jam *puffs*? 4. make *puffs*: The goods train came *puffing* round the curve. 5. swell, make to swell: The little frog *puffed* up his chest. **puffy** swollen: His face was red and *puffy* from crying.

pull 1. use force to draw or haul in a certain direction: The tractor was *pulling* the plough.—Stop *pulling* my hair. 2. the action of *pulling*: 'Give a long *pull*, a strong *pull* and *pull* all together, boys!' (from an old folk-play)

pulley (pul-ley) a wheel with the rim hollowed out so that ropes or chains can run over it: *Pulleys* are used for lifting heavy weights.

pulp 1. the soft, fleshy part of fruit: He skinned the plum, threw away the stone and ate the *pulp*. 2. material such as rags or wood, torn up, beaten, crushed and mixed with liquid as in the making of paper: This is a machine for making wood *pulp*. 3. make into *pulp*, become like *pulp*: These old books and magazines will be sent for *pulping*.

pulpit (pul-pit) raised platform in a church enclosed by a wooden frame from where a clergyman delivers his sermon.

pulse 1. the regular throbbing of the arteries caused by the pumping of blood by the heart: The doctor placed his fingers on my wrist and felt my *pulse*. 2. any regular throb: Below decks we felt the *pulse* of the ship's engines. 3. throb: A swift chase after the bus sent the blood *pulsing* through my veins.

pump 1. a machine for forcing liquids or gases through pipes: The only water in the village was from a *pump* on the green. 2. a light shoe used for dancing. 3. force liquids etc. through pipes: You have *pumped* enough air into those tyres.

punch 1. a tool for piercing or stamping materials or for making holes: He knocked the nail deep into the wood with a metal *punch*. 2. a blow: A *punch* on the chin sent him reeling backwards. 3. a drink made by mixing wine and spirits with hot water and fruit juice. 4. make a hole, stamp a design etc. with a *punch*: A row of holes had been *punched* in the leather to take the laces. 5. strike hard with the fist: The boxer had been badly *punched* about the face and body.

punctual (punc-tu-al) arriving or doing a thing at the time fixed, not late: The train is always *punctual*.

punctuate (punc-tu-ate) 1. put into a piece of writing all the stops, commas, question marks etc. 2. interrupt: His speech was *punctuated* with cries of anger from the hall. **punctuation** putting in full stops, commas and other *punctuation* marks.

puncture (punc-ture) 1. a small hole made by pricking with a stone or a pointed instrument: We stopped by the roadside to mend a *puncture*. 2. make a *puncture*: To get out the splinter it was necessary to *puncture* the skin.

punish (pun-ish) 1. subject to a penalty, pain, loss, imprisonment etc. for some offence: 'I shall have to *punish* you for breaking the window', said the headmaster. 2.

treat roughly: It was a *punishing* cross-country race. **punishment** *punishing*, being *punished*: My *punishment* was to do more homework.

puny (pu-ny) very small, very weak: 'What a *puny* little creature!' said the lion.

pupil (pu-pil) 1. a person who is learning under the instruction of a teacher: My sister teaches the piano to several *pupils*. 2. the dark opening in the centre of the eye.

puppet (pup-pet) a doll which moves either on strings or is worked by the hand thrust inside it: Some *puppets* are string *puppets*, others are glove *puppets*. **puppeteer** a person who gives *puppet*-shows.

purchase (pur-chase) 1. buy: I should like to *purchase* this pair of skates. 2. something bought: At the price, it was a very good *purchase*. 3. a firm grip for holding or raising something: Don't try to lift until I get a good *purchase* on this end.

pure 1. not mixed with anything else: The *pure* air of the country is good for you. 2. clean, without evil: 3. simply, nothing but: He talks *pure* nonsense. **purify** make *pure*: We need a fan to *purify* the air. **purity** being *pure*: We guarantee the *purity* of our products.

purpose (pur-pose) an aim, what one means to do: What is your *purpose* in coming to see me? **purposely**, on purpose; by intention and not by chance: I came here *purposely* to warn you.

purr 1. make a low continuous murmuring sound as a cat does: The cat lay on the rug, *purring* contentedly. 2. the sound of *purring*: When I stroked it, the cat gave a contented *purr*.

purse 1. a small bag, pouch or case for carrying money: My *purse* was empty by the end of the week. 2. money: The winner of the fight will receive a large *purse*. 3. draw the lips together into tiny wrinkles: She *pursed* her mouth and refused to answer.

pursue (pur-sue) 1. follow, intending to overtake, capture, kill etc.: The fugitive was *pursued* by three policemen. 2. work at, spend one's time: I am still *pursuing* my hobby of coin-collecting. **pursuit** 1. the act of *pursuing*: The whole village followed in *pursuit*. 2. the way one spends one's time: His whole life is spent in the *pursuit* of pleasure.

push 1. use force to move something away: The old man was *pushing* a cart up the hill. 2. press: He *pushed* the button and the bell rang. 3. press oneself forward: I *pushed* through the crowd to see what was happening. 4. the act of *pushing*: If you give a good *push* the door will open.

put move something into a place or position: 'Put down that gun,' said the detective.—He *put* the money into his pocket.—He *put* a cross opposite his name.—Another satellite has been *put* into orbit round the earth.

putty (put-ty) 1. a paste made of whiting and linseed oil and used for fixing panes of glass, stopping up holes in woodwork etc. 2. any person who is easily influenced.

puzzle (puz-zle) 1. something difficult to understand: Where he can have gone is a complete *puzzle*. 2. a problem to be worked out: I do the crossword *puzzle* on the train every morning. 3. be perplexed about something: I am *puzzled* what to do about my lost watch. 4. think hard about something: He kept trying until he had *puzzled* it out.

pyjamas (py-jam-as) a jacket and trousers worn for sleeping in at night.

pyramid (pyr-a-mid) 1. an object with a base of three or more sides and sloping surfaces which meet at a point. 2. one of the great stone structures built by the ancient Egyptians as royal tombs.

Q

quack 1. the cry of a duck: '*Quack, Quack*!' said the little duck. 2. make the cry of a duck: The ducks *quacked* until they were fed. 3. a person who pretends to possess knowledge or qualifications which he does not possess: A *quack* doctor addressed the crowd in the market place. 4. something given by a *quack*: Surely you don't expect that *quack* medicine to cure you?

quadruple (quad-ru-ple) 1. four times or by four times: In the last two years my income has *quadrupled*. 2. a number four times that of another: 32 is the *quadruple* of 8. **quadruplet** one of four children born to one mother at the same time: All the *quadruplets* are alive and healthy.

quaint strange or odd, but in an interesting and pleasing way: I've bought an old-fashioned house in a *quaint* old village.

quake 1. tremble, shake: Suddenly the earth *quaked* under our feet.–When she saw the horrible creature she began to *quake* with fear. 2. an earthquake: A severe *quake* has shaken the two towns.

qualify (qual-i-fy) 1. be well suited for something: I am well *qualified* by experience to give you advice. 2. obtain certificates etc. giving a person the authority to take up a certain profession: He has *qualified* as a doctor. **qualification** the certificate or the training that allows a person to take up a profession: What are your professional *qualifications*?

quality (qual-i-ty) 1. a certain degree of goodness: The food was of high *quality*. 2. a feature which distinguishes a person or thing from others: This leather has special *qualities* of toughness and strength.

quantity (quan-ti-ty) size, weight, amount, number: You need only add a small *quantity* of water.–A boat came in bringing large *quantities* of oranges.

quarantine (quar-an-tine) 1. a period, originally of forty days, when a person or animal is kept away from all others to prevent the spread of disease: All dogs entering Great Britain must be kept in *quarantine* for six months. 2. put and keep in *quarantine*: The new arrivals have been *quarantined* to prevent the spread of fever.

quarrel (quar-rel) 1. a disagreement: I can hardly remember the cause of our *quarrel*. 2. take part in a *quarrel*: I don't want to *quarrel* with you.–They *quarelled* as to who was to have the largest share.

quarry (quar-ry) 1. an open place in the ground from which stone is dug: Some of the finest stone in England is dug from this *quarry*. 2. take stone from a *quarry*: Large quantities of slate are *quarried* in Wales. 3. an animal, a bird or a person who is pursued or hunted: We followed our *quarry* for several hours.

quart a measurement of liquids; two pints, a quarter of a gallon: I need two *quarts* of milk.

quarter (quar-ter) 1. one of four equal parts: Would you like a *quarter* of this cake?–It's a *quarter* (of an hour) past three. 2. a direction, a district: We take passengers to all *quarters* of the town. 3. a place to live in: We were soon moved to better *quarters*. 4. mercy granted to an enemy: We will fight on; we want no *quarter*. 5. divide into *quarters*: I *quartered* the cake and gave one *quarter* to each boy. **quarterly** happening once every three months: The debt will be paid in ten *quarterly* instalments. **quartet** a group, or a piece of music for a group of four singers or players: We need a bass to sing in our *quartet*.

quay a man-made landing place where ships can be unloaded and loaded.

queen 1. a female ruler (e.g. Elizabeth I, Victoria, Elizabeth II). 2. the wife of a king. 3. a girl chosen to represent a group or society: She has been chosen Railway (Hospital, Caravan etc.) *Queen* for the coming year. 4. a bee, wasp or ant which produces eggs: The worker bees crowded round the *queen*. 5. a piece in the game of chess; a card in the pack next in importance to the king.

queer 1. strange, odd, peculiar: At midnight we heard a *queer* noise in the library. 2. suspicious: Don't trust all the *queer* characters you meet. 3. sick, not well: I'd better go home, as I feel rather *queer*.

quench 1. put out: The flames were *quenched* with jets of water. 2. put an end to: I would like something to *quench* my thirst.

query (que-ry) 1. a question: I have a *query* about the delay in paying these accounts. 2. doubt, question: I would like to *query* these figures.

quest a search: The *quest* for oil in the North Sea is making good progress.

question (ques-tion) 1. a word or sentence that requires an answer: I would like to ask a *question*. 2. something to be discussed, to be decided: The *question* is, who is to go?—Let us decide that *question* first. 3. doubt: I will accept your word without *question*. 4. ask a *question* or *questions*: We should like to *question* you.

queue 1. a line of people or vehicles waiting their turn: Take your place in the *queue*, please.—The accident caused a *queue* two miles long to form. 2. form a *queue*: They were *queueing* all morning to get into the stadium.

quick 1. fast moving: *Quick* as lightning, he sprang out of the way. 2. hasty: You have too *quick* a temper. 3. intelligent: she had a very quick mind. **quickly** in a *quick* manner: He ran *quickly* to my side. **quicken** make or become *quicker*: As our pursuers came nearer, we *quickened* our pace.

quiet (qui-et) 1. silent, still: It was a *quiet* evening. 2. restful: Let's have a *quiet* day. 3. free from trouble: He likes a *quiet* life. 4. freedom from disturbance: I'd like a few minutes *quiet* from everyone. **quieten** make or become *quiet*: I will try to *quieten* the baby.

quilt 1. a thick cover for a bed made by stitching two thicknesses of material with soft warm padding between them. 2. make a *quilt*.

quintuplet (quin-tu-plet) one of five children born to one mother at the same time.

quit leave, go away: Here is your notice to *quit*; you must leave the house within a week.

quite 1. entirely: Are you *quite* cured? 2. more or less: He is *quite* a good goalkeeper. 3. truly: His success was *quite* a surprise to us.

quiver (quiv-er) 1. tremble or make tremble: The leaves *quivered* in the breeze. 2. the case in which an archer carries his arrows.

quiz a test usually given out loud to a number of people: Today we had a poetry *quiz*. **quizmaster** one who asks questions in a *quiz*, usually on television or radio programmes.

quoit 1. a metal ring used in the game of *quoits*, thrown from a distance at a peg in the ground. 2. a rubber ring used in the game of deck tennis.

quote 1. repeat in speech or in writing the words of another: I *quoted* from the speech of Sir Winston Churchill. 2. name a price which a person will charge: I can *quote* you a reasonable price for a thousand bricks. 3. a punctuation mark placed before and after something *quoted*. **quotation** 1. something *quoted*: Do you know any *quotations* from Shakespeare? 2. a price *quoted*: I will accept your *quotation* for building a new greenhouse.

R

rabbi (rab-bi) 1. a teacher of the Jewish law. 2. the principal officer of a Jewish synagogue corresponding to the minister of a Christian church.

rabbit (rab-bit) 1. a small, long-eared animal which burrows in the ground. 2. the flesh of the *rabbit* used as food: We had *rabbit* for dinner.

rabble (rab-ble) 1. a disorderly crowd, a mob: Fighting broke out among the *rabble* in the square. 2. a scornful way of referring to a crowd or to the lowest class of people: 'The *rabble* call him lord' (Shakespeare, *Hamlet*).

rabies (ra-bies) an infectious disease of the brain which affects animals, especially dogs, and which can be passed on to people through being bitten.

race 1. a contest of speed: We went to see the boat *race* last Saturday. 2. a group of persons, a tribe or a nation believed to have the same ancestors: England was colonized by people of three *races*, the Angles, the Saxons and the Jutes. 3. one of the main natural divisions of living beings: Men and women belong to the human *race*. 4. the strong stream of water that turns a millwheel, a mill*race*. 5. compete in speed with another person: I'll *race* you to the next bus-stop. 6. make something go fast: He *raced* the engine until it became hot. 7. train animals or birds to compete in *races*: My uncle *races* his pigeons every week. **racing** having to do with *races* and speed tests: The earl keeps a *racing* stable and his son runs a *racing* yacht. **racer** any person, animal or thing that *races*.

rack 1. a framework or a stand specially made to hold things: Hang your hat on the *rack*.–The plates were draining on the plate *rack*. 2. A medieval instrument of torture designed to stretch the limbs of those who were placed on it.

racket (rack-et) 1. a loud confused noise, din, uproar: They made such a *racket* we could not hear ourselves speak. 2. A dishonest way of getting money: The offer of thousands of prizes was all part of the *racket*. 3. (sometimes spelt *racquet*) a light bat having a network of cord stretched on an oval frame, used in playing tennis, badminton and some other games.

radar (ra-dar) a device by which the position of an object can be found by measuring the time in which the echo of a radio wave returns to its source and the direction from which it comes (short for

Ra[dio] d[etecting] a[nd] r[anging]): The position of the enemy submarine was found by *radar*.

radiant (ra-diant) 1. shining, sending out light: 'Hide me from the *radiant* sun' (Shakespeare, *Cymbeline*). 2. looking joyful, delighted: When she saw the dress she was to wear, she was *radiant*.

radiate (ra-di-ate) 1. send out rays or lines like rays from a centre: Our new electric fire *radiates* heat to all parts of the room. 2. spread out in rays or as if in rays: Light *radiates* from an electric lamp above the entrance.–A number of avenues *radiate* from the city centre. **radiation** *radiating*, something *radiated*: All those living near the atomic reactor were evacuated owing to the dangers of *radiation*. **radiator** an apparatus for *radiating* heat: The room is heated by two electric *radiators*.

radio (ra-di-o) 1. communication by wireless telegraphy: We have at last had a *radio* message from the island. 2. broadcasting: We heard the good news on the *radio* last night. 3. a wireless, a device for receiving *radio* broadcasts. **radiogram** a gramophone and *radio* receiver combined.

radish (rad-ish) a plant grown in gardens for its red root which is eaten with salad: She bought a bunch of *radishes* at the greengrocer's.

radium (ra-dium) a metal which sends out rays capable of penetrating solid matter: *Radium* is used in the treatment of diseases.

radius (ra-dius) 1. the distance from the centre to the circumference of a circle. 2. an area within a fixed distance of a certain point: All drivers of cars within a *radius* of 15 kilometres were questioned by the police.

raffia (raf-fia) fibre from the leaf-stalks of a palm-tree growing in Madagascar: *Raffia* is used for making matting, baskets, hats and other articles, and for tying plants and cut flowers.

raffle (raf-fle) 1. a method of raising money by selling tickets and choosing the prize-winning numbers by lot. 2. dispose of by *raffle*: A large doll is being *raffled* to raise money for the club.

raft a floating platform made of various materials, such as tree-trunks, rubber, planks, empty barrels etc. tied together and used as a substitute for a boat: In 1947 the Kon-Tiki expedition crossed the Pacific Ocean on a *raft*.

rafter (raft-er) one of the sloping beams or timbers which hold up the outer covering of a roof.

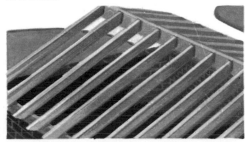

rag 1. a piece of cloth torn from a larger piece: He polished the window with a clean *rag*. 2. old, torn clothing: He wore no hat and his clothes were in *rags*. **ragged** in *rags*: After he was rescued he changed his *ragged* clothes for a new suit.

rage 1. fury, violent anger: When he heard the news he fell into a *rage*. 2. something about which people are enthusiastic or which is in fashion: Embroidered waistcoats were the *rage* in grandfather's day. 3. act or speak with great anger, furiously: He *raged* about the room like a madman. 4. move with violence: The storm *raged* all day long.

raid 1. a sudden attack: Two men were injured in the *raid* on the bank. 2. a sudden attack by an enemy force: Many London buildings were destroyed in the air *raids*.—He won the Victoria Cross for leading a *raid* on an enemy strongpoint. 3. make or take part in a *raid*: Last night the police *raided* a number of clubs.

rail 1. a bar of wood or metal making part of a fence: He climbed the wooden *rails* and jumped down into the field. 2. a steel bar fastened to the ground to help provide a track on which vehicles may run: The train was travelling too fast and ran off the *rails*. 3. the railway: The parcel was too heavy to go by post so we sent it by *rail*. 4. a bar of wood or metal put into a certain place and having a certain use: There was a towel-*rail* in the bathroom.—Keep your hand on the *rail* as you come down the stairs. **railing** a barrier made of *rails* with posts to support them: The

sports ground was enclosed by high steel *railings*. **railway** a track on which trains run, all the engines etc. that run on it, the buildings, stations etc. and the people who manage it: My brother works on the *railway*.

rain 1. water in drops falling from the clouds to the earth: He went out in the *rain*. 2. a fall of *rain*: There was heavy *rain* last night. 3. anything falling like *rain*: The French horsemen rode into a *rain* of arrows. 4. fall in drops from the clouds: 'The *rain* it *raineth* every day' (Shakespeare, songs from *King Lear* and *Twelfth Night*). 5. fall, send down: He *rained* blow after blow on his unfortunate victim. **rainbow** a large coloured arch in the sky seen opposite the sun during a *rain*storm. **rainfall** the amount of *rain* falling on one area during a fixed period: The south-east of England has the lowest *rainfall*. **rainproof** able to keep out rain: He put on his *rainproof* coat. **rainy** having much rain: We don't walk far on *rainy* days.

raise 1. lift up; move to a higher position: After much effort the submarine was *raised* from the sea bed.—We *raised* our glasses in a toast to the Queen. 2. set up, erect: A monument was *raised* in memory of those killed in the war. 3. make appear: My jokes always *raise* a smile. 4. make louder: If I *raise* my voice you will be able to hear me. 5. bring up (a question): I would like to *raise* an objection. 6. make grow, produce: He is in Australia *raising* cattle. 7. get: We are *raising* money for the new organ.

raisin (rai-sin) a dried grape used in cookery.

rake 1. a tool with a long handle and teeth for gathering hay, grass, or leaves together and for breaking the surface of the ground. 2. gather together with a *rake*: The harvesters were *raking* up the hay. 3. search thoroughly: They *raked* among the rubbish but could not find the bracelet.

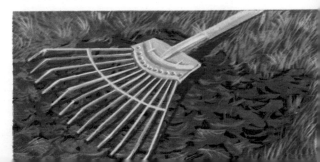

rally (ral-ly) 1. bring or come together ready for action: We must *rally* round our leader: 2. begin to recover, gain strength: The patient is *rallying* and will improve. 3. (in tennis) the return of the ball several times by both sides before a point is scored. 4. a large gathering to bring about new efforts: Our party held a successful *rally* at the Albert Hall. 5. a competition between car drivers in which strict rules are followed to test performance.

ram 1. a male sheep. 2. drive or force by heavy blows: The loose earth had to be *rammed* down the hole. 3. pack tight: He hastily *rammed* his clothes into the suitcase. 4. run into or strike: The gunboat *rammed* and sank an enemy submarine.

ramble (ram-ble) 1. walk about in a leisurely manner; take a long walk for pleasure: For two hours we *rambled* through the fields. 2. grow in many directions with long shoots: The honeysuckle had *rambled* over the fence into the next garden. 3. talk of various things without keeping to one subject: He wanted to talk so I just let him *ramble* on. 4. a leisurely walk: The day is ideal for a *ramble* in the country.

ramp 1. a sloping walk or passageway: To reach the departure platform we have to ascend a steep *ramp*. 2. a sloping way from one level to another: The car's wheels slipped on the icy *ramp*.

rampart (ram-part) a long wide bank of earth, usually having a wall on top, erected to defend a fort or strong point: The attacking force scaled the *rampart* and took the fort by storm.

ramrod (ram-rod) an iron rod for ramming powder and shot into a cannon or muzzle-loading gun, or for cleaning the barrel of a rifle.

ramshackle (ram-shack-le) held together loosely, in danger of collapsing or falling to pieces: We were forced to stay the night in an old *ramshackle* hut.

ranch a large farm, especially in North America or Australia, for raising cattle, sheep or horses. **rancher** a person who owns or works on a *ranch*.

rancid (ran-cid) having an unpleasant stale smell or taste: The butter was so *rancid* that we could not eat it.

random (ran-dom) done, made, happening etc. without any aim or purpose: We took a *random* sample to test the quality.– The enemy aircraft dropped bombs at *random*.

range 1. set in order in a row or rows: Spectators of the boat race were *ranged* along the river banks. 2. go through or over: I have *ranged* the countryside to find specimens of this plant.–Our talk *ranged* over a variety of matters. 3. extend in two directions: The boundary *ranges* east and west along this line. 4. vary within certain limits: The price of these chairs *ranges* from the cheap to the very expensive. 5. a row or line: Before reaching the lake we had to cross a *range* of mountains. 6. a piece of ground with targets for shooting: We spent two hours on the rifle *range*. 7. the distance to which a bullet or shell may be fired. 8. the extent between two limits: Her voice has a *range* of 3 octaves. 9. a stretch of land for grazing: There are thousands of cattle on the *range*. 10. a large stove for cooking, having an oven and points for heating various articles at the same time: Dinner was being cooked on the kitchen *range*.

rank 1. a row: There is a taxi *rank* at the station. 2. a number of soldiers, police etc. standing or marching side by side. 3. position in a scale, grade, standing: A major is an officer of a higher *rank* than a captain.–He is a musician of the highest *rank*. 4. arrange in order: I *rank* you among my best friends. 5. growing too fast: He took a scythe and cut down the *rank* growth of weeds. 6. smelling or tasting bad: At the door we were met by the *rank* odour of stale food. 7. thorough: He stands no chance of winning; he is a *rank* outsider.

ransack (ran-sack) 1. search thoroughly: I *ransacked* the drawer but could not find the papers I wanted. 2. plunder: The castle was *ransacked* and everything of value stolen.

ransom (ran-som) 1. a sum of money paid to free a prisoner or to recover goods which have been taken: The kidnappers demanded a large *ransom* in return for the boy's freedom. 2. pay the price demanded: The king was *ransomed* by his nobles.

rap 1. strike with a quick blow: He *rapped* on the door but nobody answered. 2. a quick, smart blow: Give another *rap* on the door.

rapid (rap-id) quick, speedy: These bushes are well known for their *rapid* growth.— He is a *rapid* worker. **rapids** that part of a river which flows swiftly, over a steep slope in the bed. **rapidly** quickly: The police car approached *rapidly*.

rapture (rap-ture) great joy, delight: His return was greeted with cries of *rapture*. **rapturous** with *rapture*: He was given a *rapturous* welcome.

rare 1. unusual, uncommon, not often found: She wore a necklace of *rare* jewels. 2. (of the air) thin: The Olympic athletes found training difficult in the *rare* atmosphere of the highlands. **rarity** something uncommon: A four-leaf clover is a *rarity*.

rascal (ras-cal) 1. a dishonest person: This *rascal* is not to be trusted. 2. a mischievous child: The little *rascal* has eaten all my sweets.

rash 1. with too much haste; without enough thought: You were *rash* to send that letter. 2. a breaking out of tiny red spots on the skin: We realized that the child had measles when we saw the *rash*.

rasher (rash-er) a thin slice of bacon: I had two *rashers* for breakfast this morning.

raspberry (rasp-berry) a small red berry with many seeds that grows on a bush: *Raspberries* are made into jam, as well as being made into pies.

rat a long-tailed rodent resembling but much larger than a mouse.

rate 1. a measured speed, height, weight, quantity, temperature or price: The car descended the hill at a dangerous *rate*.— Could you please tell me the new postage *rates*? 2. a tax on land and buildings: Our *rates* have been increased because of the cost of a new Council Office. 3. class, grade: This is a first-*rate* tape recorder.— The performance at the Opera House was only third-*rate*. 4. set a value on: I do not *rate* highly my chances of winning. 5. set a value on property on which to fix a *rate*: Our house is *rated* far too high.

rather (rath-er) 1. more gladly, more willingly: I'd *rather* stay at home than go for a walk. 2. to a certain extent: He's a *rather* good tennis player.

ration (ra-tion) 1. a fixed allowance given for a period: Every man received his *ration* of food. 2. the allowance of food given to a member of the armed forces: He went to draw his *rations* for the journey. 3. limit the issue of food etc.: Petrol will be *rationed* as long as the strike lasts.

rattle (rat-tle) 1. give out a number of short sharp sounds: The door *rattled* with the force of the wind. 2. make something *rattle*: He *rattled* the knocker several times. 3. talk quickly: She *rattles* on but nobody listens. 4. a series of short, sharp sounds: We heard the *rattle* of machine-gun fire. 5. a baby's toy that produces a *rattling* sound.

ravage (rav-age) 1. destroy or damage greatly: London was *ravaged* by the great plague of 1665. 2. rob, plunder and destroy: The countryside was *ravaged* by the invading armies. 3. destruction: It took years to repair the *ravages* of war.

rave 1. talk wildly or angrily: At the height of his fever the patient began to *rave*. 2. talk or write with foolish enthusiasm: She *raved* about the latest fashions. **raving** talking wildly: He behaved like a *raving* madman.

ravel (rav-el) separate (a rope, a piece of cloth etc.) into threads: She trimmed the edge with pinking shears so that the cloth would not *ravel*.

raven (ra-ven) 1. a large black bird resembling a crow. 2. black and glossy: In the box lay a lock of *raven* hair.

ravine (ra-vine) a long, deep, narrow valley: Flowing through the *ravine* was a stream of clear water.

raw 1. uncooked: I prefer vegetables *raw*. 2. not prepared or manufactured: *Raw* cotton is imported into Lancashire.—In fixing the prices we must consider the cost of the *raw* materials we have bought. 3. damp, cold: There's a *raw* wind blowing this morning. 4. not trained: The sergeant was drilling a squad of *raw* recruits. 5. sore, not healed: The doctor cut the sleeve and exposed the *raw* wound on the arm.

ray 1. a beam of light, heat or energy: Do not expose yourself to the direct *rays* of the sun. 2. one of the many lines coming from a central point. 3. a large fish with a flat body.

raze tear down, destroy: A whole street of houses was *razed* to the ground by fire.

razor (ra-zor) a sharp-edged tool used for shaving the hair from the face and body.

re- a prefix meaning again. **re** is added to many words and their altered meaning may easily be guessed, as in **reappear**: The sun *reappears* every morning at dawn. **rearrange**: I have *rearranged* the flowers in the vase. **rearm**: This country is surrounded by enemies and has been forced to *rearm*. **rebound**: The ball *rebounded* from the wall and he caught it in both hands. **recall**: Our ambassador has been *recalled* for talks with the Prime Minister.—I can *recall* the days when there were hardly any motor cars on the roads. **reclaim**: These marshes have been *reclaimed* and now corn is grown there. **recondition**: The engine of my car was very old but has now been *reconditioned*. **reconstruct**: The building which was destroyed by fire has been *reconstructed*.—The detectives are trying to *reconstruct* the circumstances of the crime. **recount**: There may have been a mistake, so we shall have to *recount* the votes. **re-enter**: We were able to *re-enter* the room after the smoke had cleared away. **refill**: He *refilled* his water bottle at the tap. **refit**: I am having the brakes *refitted* to my bicycle. **refloat**: The sunken submarine was *refloated* at the third attempt. **refuel**: The champion lost the first place in the race when he stopped at the pit to *refuel*. **regain**: He *regained* the lead after three laps. **rehouse**: Our tenants have been *rehoused* in the new flats. **reissue**: The book has been *reissued* in a new edition. **rejoin**: I was able to *rejoin* the party by taking a short route. **remount**: He fell from his horse but was able to *remount* without trouble. **reopen**: The exhibition closes on Friday and *reopens* on Monday morning. **repay**: If you lend me the money I will *repay* you within three days. **replace**: Kindly *replace* the books on the shelves after use. **reprint**: So many readers have asked for the recipe that we are *reprinting* it. **reset**: His broken arm was badly set and had to be *reset*. **rewrite**: This exercise is badly done and you must *rewrite* it.

reach 1. stretch out the hand for and take: He *reached* up and grabbed the clock from the mantelpiece. 2. go to: I hope to *reach* Bristol this evening. 3. extend as far as: The sound did not *reach* to the back of the hall. 4. the distance to which the hand will stretch: The champion boxer has the advantage of a long *reach*.–The book is well within my *reach*. 5. a distance: Is there a good hotel within easy *reach*? 6. part of a river or a canal between two bends: There is good fishing along this *reach*. **reach out** *reach* for, stretch out the hand for: He *reached out* for the bottle.

read 1. look at and understand the meaning of something written or printed: I am afraid I cannot *read* your writing.–He is learning to *read* music. 2. understand the meaning of: The gipsy will *read* your palm.–I can almost *read* your thoughts. 3. study: I am *reading* history at the university. 4. indicate, show: The barometer *reads* 20°C. **reader** 1. a person who *reads*: My son is a keen *reader* of detective stories. 2. a lecturer in a university. 3. a book from which one may practise *reading*: We have a new French *reader* this term.

reading (read-ing) 1. the action of one who reads: Do you prefer *reading* to listening to the radio? 2. a way of understanding something: According to my *reading* of this agreement you should pay the money. 3. the figure on a dial: Every two hours we take the thermometer *reading*. 4. an entertainment which consists of *reading*: He gave a *reading* from the poems of John Masefield. 5. one of the stages in putting a bill through Parliament: The bill was thrown out in its second *reading* in the Commons.

ready (read-y) 1. completely prepared, in a fit condition: We are all packed and *ready* to go.–Dinner is *ready*. 2. quick in seeing, speaking, writing etc.: He always had a *ready* answer. 3. within reach, in a fit condition for use: 'All money *ready* please,' said the conductor. 4. likely to do something at any time: I had run so hard I was *ready* to drop. 5. prepared beforehand: 'We specialize in *ready-cooked* food' (notice in a shop window). **readily** promptly, quickly: I will *readily* help you. **readiness** in a prepared state: We had everything in *readiness* for the journey.

real (re-al) 1. true, not imagined: This story comes from *real* life. 2. genuine, not imitation: The necklace is of *real* pearls. **reality** the state of being *real*. **in reality** actually, in fact: You think I deceived you but *in reality* I am your best friend.

realize (re-al-ize) 1. understand clearly: We fully *realize* that you cannot do the work alone. 2. make something come true: At last my dreams were *realized*. 3. obtain a profit through selling or work: My land *realized* a high price at the auction.

realm 1. a kingdom: The marriage of the princess was proclaimed throughout the *realm*. 2. region: Goblins and gnomes only exist in the *realms* of fantasy.

ream a standard quantity among those who sell paper. A *ream* was formerly 480 sheets. Paper is now usually sold in *reams* of 500 sheets.

reap 1. cut and take in a harvest of grain: The harvesters have *reaped* three fields. 2. get as a result or a reward: He has *reaped* the fruits of his labour.

rear 1. the back part of anything: We took our seats in the *rear* of the train. 2. at the back: Would you please close the *rear* window. 3. raise and care for a young person or animal: On this farm we are *rearing* pigs. 4. raise to an upright position: The angry lion *reared* its head. 5. rise on the hind legs: At the sound of firing the horse *reared*.

reason (rea-son) 1. the cause of a belief or an event: What was the *reason* for your absence? 2. the power to understand: The tragedy made him lose his *reason*. 3. good sense, a knowledge of what is right: He was obstinate and refused to listen to *reason*. 4. use one's *reason*: Man's power to *reason* has helped him to make use of the forces of nature. 5. argue: After I had *reasoned* with him he promised to apologize. **reasonable** fair, acting according to *reason*: The price I am asking is *reasonable*.—He is a *reasonable* person.

reassure (re-as-sure) give a person confidence, remove doubts: I can *reassure* you that your secrets are safe with me.

rebel (re-bel) 1. one who rises in arms against a ruler: The countryside was swarming with *rebels*. 2. having to do with a *rebel* or *rebels*: Our army marched into *rebel* territory. **rebel** (re-bél) rise in arms, resist: 'Both young and old *rebel*' (Shakespeare, Richard II). **rebellion** *rebelling*: The chief nobles rose in *rebellion*.

recapitulate (re-ca-pit-u-late—sometimes shortened to *recap*) go over or repeat the main points of a plan, discussion or report: 'To get all this quite clear in our minds,' said the chairman, 'let me *recapitulate*.' **recapitulation** the repeating of the main points of an argument.

recede (re-cede) 1. go back: The tide *receded*, leaving the boats high and dry. 2. appear to go back: As we crossed the plain the mountains *receded* into the distance.

receive (re-ceive) 1. get, accept: I *received* many presents for my birthday.—We were glad to *receive* news of our son.—Please *receive* our apologies. 2. admit: I have been *received* into the church. 3. entertain, welcome: Members of the trade unions were *received* by the Prime Minister. **receiver** 1. a person who *receives*: He is a *receiver* of stolen goods.—The property of the bankrupt is now in the hands of the Official *Receiver*. 2. an apparatus for *receiving* broadcast programmes; a radio or television *receiver*.

recent (re-cent) having happened, being done or made not long ago: I have now recovered from my *recent* illness. **recently** a short time ago: I heard *recently* that he was in Brazil.

reception (re-cep-tion) 1. receiving, being received: A hotel has been booked for the *reception* of the Italian football team. 2. a way of receiving or being received: The speech met with a tumultuous *reception*. 3. the receiving of guests: All the guests were invited to the wedding *reception*. 4. the quality of radio or television signals received: We listened to the Queen's broadcast and the *reception* was excellent. **receptive** able to receive ideas quickly: He has a very *receptive* mind. **receptionist** a person employed to receive guests in a hotel, patients in a surgery or callers.

recess (re-cess) 1. a short time when work or business is stopped: Parliament is in *recess* until October. 2. a space in the wall of a room that is set back: There was room in the *recess* for a small table and two chairs. 3. an inner part, kept secret or not easily reached: The hunters penetrated the dark *recesses* of the forest.

recipe (rec-i-pe) (pronounced *ressipy*) a set of directions telling how something, especially a cooked dish, is prepared: I should like to have the *recipe* for this cake.

recite (re-cite) 1. repeat the words from memory: He *recited* the poem from beginning to end. 2. give a list or an account: The strikers *recited* their complaints to the manager. **recital** 1. an account, *reciting*: I went to the *recital* of Dickens' works last night. 2. a musical performance: The pianoforte *recital* was well attended. **recitation** the act of *reciting*, what is *recited*: The *recitation* of their complaints took a full hour.—I have bought a book of humorous *recitations*.

reckless (reck-less) not caring what happens: The motorist was fined for *reckless* driving.

reckon (reck-on) 1. calculate the number or amount: I have *reckoned* up my debts and find I can pay them. 2. consider: He is *reckoned* to be the best player on the field.

recognize (rec-og-nize) 1. be able to know again: I *recognize* that tune.—He has grown so much that I hardly *recognized* him. 2. admit: I *recognize* that I made a bad mistake. 3. agree: Everybody *recognizes* him to be the greatest living chess player.

recoil (re-coil) 1. draw back: She *recoiled* in horror from the spectacle. 2. rebound, come back: The results of your bullying will one day *recoil* on your own head. 3. (of a gun) rebound of the weapon on firing: The *recoil* was so powerful that it bruised his shoulder.

recollect (rec-ol-lect) remember: I *recollect* hearing Caruso sing. **recollection** remembering: My *recollection* of past days is very clear.

recommend (rec-om-mend) 1. speak well of; put forward as worthy: I can *recommend* this toothpaste. 2. advise: I have been *recommended* to stay indoors on very cold days. **recommendation** *recommending*, a statement in favour of a person or thing: I am trying this toothpaste on your *recommendation*.—We have read your letters of *recommendation* and wish to offer you the job.

recompense (rec-om-pense) 1. repay, reward: I will *recompense* you for your trouble in copying these letters. 2. a reward or payment: He was made a knight as a *recompense* for his public services.

reconcile (rec-on-cile) 1. become friends after a quarrel: After we had both apologized, we became *reconciled*. 2. be satisfied with: He was not thought good enough for the first team and had to *reconcile* himself to a place in the second.

reconnoitre (rec-on-noi-tre) inspect or survey the position of an enemy to estimate his strength: Before the attack the whole area had to be *reconnoitred*. **reconnaissance** the act of *reconnoitring*: Our aircraft made a thorough *reconnaissance* of the enemy positions.

record (re-cord) 1. an account in writing, or taken in any other way, to be preserved: Here is a *record* of the number of times you have been late. 2. things known about the past history of a person or thing: He has a criminal *record*. 3. a disc, a magnetic tape, a film etc., on which sound or pictures have been made: I have bought the latest *record* of Beethoven's Fifth Symphony.—The film provides a detailed *record* of the Queen's visit. 4. the best, highest, largest etc. so far *recorded*: He has broken the *record* for the high jump.—The temperature last Sunday was the highest on *record*. **record** (re-córd) 1. keep for reference: I have *recorded* all the events in my diary. 2. make a gramophone *record* or tape *recording*: His voice has been *recorded* on tape. 3. mark on a scale: A high rainfall was *recorded* in many places yesterday. **recorder** 1. an apparatus that *records* sounds: Would you like to hear a few songs on my tape *recorder*? 2. a musical instrument similar to a flute. **recording** a piece of music, a speech etc. *recorded* on magnetic tape or on a disc, to be played back when required: We may be able to find the song in one of the B.B.C. *recordings*.

recover (re-cov-er) 1. get again or regain something lost: The diamond necklace was *recovered* by the police. 2. become well again: She is *recovering* from a cold. 3. regain a state or a position once held: The farmers are slowly *recovering* from the effects of the bad harvest. **recovery** *recovering*, being *recovered*: His *recovery* from influenza is complete.—She thanked the police for the *recovery* of her necklace.

recreation (rec-re-a-tion) refreshment of body or mind by some agreeable pastime: My favourite *recreation* is a game of tennis. **recreation ground** an open piece of land on which games can be played.

recruit (re-cruit) 1. a new member of a society, a recently enlisted member of the forces: The police force needs *recruits* urgently. 2. obtain new members: Our object is to *recruit* 1,000 policemen a month. 3. get back: I am slowly *recruiting* my health and strength.

rectangle (rec-tan-gle) a four-sided figure with four right angles.

rectify (rec-ti-fy) put right: It took me hours to *rectify* all the mistakes.

rector (rec-tor) 1. a Church of England clergyman in charge of a parish. 2. a person in charge of certain universities and other institutions.

recuperate (re-cu-per-ate) recover: The patient has been sent to the south coast to *recuperate*.—He never *recuperated* his losses from the fire. **recuperation** recovery of health or fortunes: After his *recuperation* he went back to work.

recur (re-cur) 1. happen again: I am faced with *recurring* demands for money. 2. come again to the mind: This nightmare *recurs* continually.

red the colour of blood. **redden** make *red*: The flames from the burning building *reddened* the sky.

redeem (re-deem) 1. get back by payment: He pawned his watch on Monday and *redeemed* it on Friday. 2. set free by paying a ransom: King Richard I was *redeemed* from captivity and returned home. 3. fulfil: Now that your promises have been *redeemed* you are free to go. 4. compensate, make up for: His bad temper is *redeemed* by his great generosity.

reduce (re-duce) 1. make smaller in size, amount, extent or number: What are you doing to *reduce* your weight? 2. change to a different form or condition: Within a few hours the house was *reduced* to ashes. **reduction** *reducing*, being *reduced*: 'Great price *reductions* this week' (a newspaper advertisement).

redundant (re-dun-dant) no longer needed: Now that we have changed our methods, all this old machinery is *redundant*. **redundancy** being *redundant*: Owing to the new methods of production many men were faced with *redundancy*.

reed 1. the straight stalk, usually hollow, of various tall grasses growing in marshy places: The baby Moses was found in a basket, hidden among the *reeds* by the bank of the Nile. 2. a piece of cane or metal put into the mouthpiece of musical instruments such as the oboe, clarinet and bassoon and which helps to produce the sound.

reef 1. a narrow ridge of rock or sand lying near the surface of the water: Our little ship struck a *reef* and capsized. 2. part of a sail that can be rolled up and tied to reduce the area exposed to the wind.

reek 1. a strong unpleasant smell: We were met at the door by the *reek* of stale fish. 2. smell strongly and unpleasantly: His breath *reeked* of alcohol.

reel 1. a roller or cylinder on which to wind something: I have bought a *reel* of film for my camera.—Would you pass the *reel* of cotton? 2. a gay Scottish dance. 3. rock or sway under a blow or a shock: A blow on the chin made him *reel*. 4. walk unsteadily: The drunken man came *reeling* along the pavement. 5. seem to rock or sway: The scene *reeled* before his eyes and he fell in a dead faint.

refer (re-fer) 1. send, pass to, hand to: The dispute about wages was *referred* to a committee of masters and men. 2. direct the attention to: For further information we *refer* you to page 44. 3. turn to for information: He often had to *refer* to the book on the desk. 4. speak about: When I talk about people arriving late, I am not *referring* to anybody here. **referee** a person to whom questions are *referred*; a person who controls certain games and matches such as football, boxing, hockey etc.

reference (ref-er-ence) 1. the act of referring: *Reference* to a good textbook will give you all the facts you need. 2. a person to whom one refers for details about another person's character: Would you please act as a *reference* for me? 3. a written statement concerning a person's character: He brought with him a long *reference* from his headmaster. 4. a note telling where certain facts may be found: At the end of the book there was a long list of *references* to standard works on the subject.

refine (re-fine) purify: Sugar from sugar-beet and sugar-cane is *refined* for use in the home. **refined** purified; well-mannered, cultured: He was a gentleman of the most *refined* manners. **refinement** good manners, speech and taste: The play was vulgar and showed a complete lack of *refinement*. **refinery** a building where raw products are *refined*: A large oil *refinery* is to be built at the mouth of the river.

reflect (re-flect) 1. cast back (light, heat, sound etc.): He saw his face *reflected* in the shop window. 2. bring praise or blame: Your success in the final examination *reflects* great credit on all who taught you. 3. think carefully: Before you make a decision, pause and *reflect*. **reflection** 1. anything *reflected*: We saw the *reflection* of the moon in the still water. 2. thought: On further *reflection* I have decided not to call in the police: 3. blame: There are some mistakes in your calculations, but this is no *reflection* on your ability.

reform (re-form) 1. improvement, putting right what is wrong: We are pressing the government to bring in *reforms* in taxation. 2. improve, make or become better: He has given up drink and is now a *reformed* character.

refrain (re-frain) 1. keep oneself fro... doing something: We are asked to *refrain* from smoking during the performance. 2. the chorus, repeated at the end of each verse, of a song: We all joined in the *refrain*.

refresh (re-fresh) give new strength by taking food, drink or rest: We rose from sleep greatly *refreshed*. **refreshment** that which *refreshes*: We stopped for *refreshment* at an inn.—*Refreshments* were provided after the play.

refrigerate (re-frig-er-ate) preserve by freezing. **refrigeration** the preservation of food by freezing. **refrigerator** a box, cabinet or a small room in which food is kept cold to preserve it: He took a bottle of fresh milk out of the *refrigerator*.

refuge (ref-uge) 1. shelter or protection from danger etc.: We took *refuge* from the storm in a hut. 2. a place or means of *refuge*: Our only *refuge* was in flight. 3. a low platform in the middle of a street on which people may take *refuge* from traffic while crossing. **refugee** a person who has taken *refuge* in another place, especially a foreign country: The roads were crowded with *refugees*, seeking safety.

refund (re-fund) 1. give back or repay money: All your expenses on the journey will be *refunded* later. 2. money given back: I had been charged too much for electricity and applied for a *refund*.

refuse (re-fúse) be unwilling to do something: The messenger *refused* to accept the bribe. **refusal** the act of *refusing*: I was very disappointed by your *refusal* to help. **refuse** (ré-fuse) that which is thrown away as worthless: *Refuse* is collected from this street on Mondays. **refuse dump** a place where household *refuse* is thrown after being collected.

regard (re-gard) 1. look on a person or thing with a particular feeling; consider: I *regard* him as one of my best friends. 2. pay attention to: Why don't you *regard* my advice? 3. a look, gaze: His *regard* was fixed on a stain on the victim's clothing. 4. thought, attention: He does what he likes without *regard* to other people's feelings. 5. respect: We have a high *regard* for his honesty. 6. kind thoughts: Please send your brother my *regards*.

regatta (re-gat-ta) a meeting at which races of yachts, rowing boats and other vessels are held: There were crowds at Henley *Regatta* this week.

regent (re-gent) a person who rules a country at a time when the monarch is too young, too old or too ill: For ten years George IV was Prince *Regent* of England. **regency** the period when a *regent* is ruling.

regiment (reg-i-ment) 1. an army unit consisting of two or more battalions, and commanded by a colonel: 'He led his *regiment* from behind' (W. S. Gilbert, *The Gondoliers*). 2. a large number: Vast *regiments* of beggars roamed the countryside. 3. organize, put under strict discipline: Children at this school have little freedom; they are too *regimented*. **regimental** having to do with a *regiment*: He plays the big drum in the *regimental* band.

region (re-gion) 1. a part of the earth's surface: Icebergs are drifting south from the polar *regions*. 2. part of the body: I feel a pain in the *region* of the left kidney. **regional** having to do with a *region* or *regions*: The *regional* wines of Italy have their own distinct flavours.

register (reg-is-ter) 1. a list of names: The teacher began to mark the *register*.—Lloyd's *Register* is a list of all known seagoing ships. 2. range of a voice or of a musical instrument: The opera singer has a *register* of three octaves. 3. a device for recording numbers or measurements: The cashier rang up the amounts of my purchases on the cash *register*. 4. cause to be recorded: We have *registered* the baby's birth this morning.—As an alien he has to *register* with the police. 5. show on the dial of an instrument: What temperature does the thermometer *register* this morning? 6. show on the face: His face *registered* astonishment. 7. pay a fee to send a letter by special post: The contents of the envelope were valuable and it had to be *registered*. **registrar** 1. an official who keeps records of births, marriages and deaths. 2. a doctor in a hospital training to be a specialist. **registration** recording; sending by *registered* post. **registry** a place where *registers* are kept. **register office** (usually called *registry* office) a place where births, deaths, and marriages are recorded and where marriages can take place.

regret (re-gret) 1. feel sorry: I *regret* being late for the appointment. 2. feeling of sorrow: We learnt with *regret* of your recent illness. **regrets** feelings of sorrow about what has been lost or done: Though my attempt failed, I have no *regrets*.

regular (reg-u-lar) 1. even, well arranged: The girl had dark hair, blue eyes and *regular* features.—Posts were set up at *regular* intervals along the road. 2. happening at fixed times: The patient's pulse was *regular*. 3. a professional soldier, the professional *(regular)* army: My brother first joined the territorials but is now a *regular*. **regularity** being *regular*: The aeroplanes flew over every few minutes with unfailing *regularity*.

regulate (reg-u-late) 1. control, direct according to a rule or method: Measures have been taken to *regulate* the traffic in the centre of the city. 2. control by mechanical means: The temperature of the water is *regulated* by a thermostat. 3. adjust, put in order: The clock is slow and needs *regulating*. **regulation** 1. a rule or order: The safety *regulations* forbid standing in the aisles. 2. according to rule or order: *Regulation* dress must be worn at the parade.

rehearse (re-hearse) practise: This is the last time we shall *rehearse* the play. **rehearsal** *rehearsing*: Everybody must be present at the dress *rehearsal* (the last before the performance, when all the players are in costume).

reign 1. period in which a ruler is in office: The *reign* of Queen Victoria lasted nearly sixty-four years. 2. be in office as a monarch: 'Edward still lives and *reigns*' (Shakespeare, *Richard III*).

rein 1. a long narrow strap fastened to the bridle, by which the movements of a horse or other animal are controlled: He pulled at the *reins* and the animal came to a halt. 2. control: During the king's illness his eldest son took up the *reins* of government.

reindeer (rein-deer) a kind of deer with branched antlers found in arctic regions, kept for transport and for its milk, meat and hide.

reinforce (re-in-force) 1. strengthen with some added piece of material: The wall was in danger of collapsing and had to be *reinforced* with steel rods. 2. make stronger with more men, materials, ships etc.: The defending army had to be *reinforced* to withstand the enemy attacks. **reinforcements** men, ships, materials etc. to increase the strength of an army, fleet or air force.

reinstate (re-in-state) put back into a former position or state: After a long debate the chairman was *reinstated* and took charge of the meeting.

reject (re-ject) 1. throw away as being useless: Many of the apples were *rejected* because they had gone bad. 2. refuse to accept: Why did he *reject* my advice 3. refuse to grant (a demand): My appeal for mercy was *rejected*. **reject** (ré-ject) something *rejected*: We are selling off *rejects* at a very cheap price. **rejection** being *rejected*, *rejecting*: All his appeals for mercy met with a firm *rejection*.

rejoice (re-joice) be glad: 'I hear thee and *rejoice*' (Wordsworth, *To the Cuckoo*).– 'I should *rejoice* now at this happy news' (Shakespeare, *Henry IV*, *part 2*). **rejoicing** great joy, merrymaking: The duke returned to his people amid great *rejoicing*.

relate (re-late) 1. tell: I have an interesting story to *relate*. 2. think of at the same time: I find it hard to *relate* the good character of this man with the accounts of his bad conduct. 3. have connection with: Bring me all the facts *relating* to the bank robbery.

relation (re-la-tion) 1. connection: There is a *relation* between the moon and the tides. 2. the telling: We listened to his *relation* of the events during his journey. 3. a person in the same family: She is a *relation* of mine by marriage.

relative (rel-a-tive) 1. a person connected with another by blood or marriage. 2. two or more things considered in relation to each other: We discussed the *relative* merits of the two cars.

relax (re-lax) 1. become or make less firm or tight: He *relaxed* his grip on the animal's throat. 2. make less strict: Discipline was *relaxed* on board while there was no threat of attack. 3. use less effort and energy: He spent the afternoon *relaxing* in a deck chair. **relaxation** *relaxing* or being *relaxed*; recreation: Periods of *relaxation* are necessary for all who work hard.–My favourite *relaxations* are chess and riding.

relay (re-lay) 1. a set of men, animals etc. taking turns: For the next stage of the journey we needed a new *relay* of horses. – They finished in time by working through the night in *relays*. 2. a team race in which one member takes up the race from another: We have a first-class team for the swimming *relay*. 3. pass on a message or a broadcast programme by *relays*: 'This programme is *relayed* by satellite direct from Washington' (television announcement).

release (re-lease) 1. set free: All the prisoners were *released*. 2. let go: He *released* his hold on the rope. 3. allow news to be published: News of the disaster has just been *released*. 4. *releasing*, being *released*: He arrived home two hours after his *release*.

relic (rel-ic) 1. something that has survived from the past and is valued: In the museum are many Stone Age *relics*. 2. the remains of a saint or martyr kept after death: Pilgrims returned from the Holy Land bringing *relics* of the saints.

relief (re-lief) 1. the lessening or removal of pain or distress: The injection gave the patient immediate *relief*. – To our great *relief* the ship arrived safely. 2. something bringing *relief*: *Relief* arrived in the shape of a small boy with a note. 3. reinforcements of troops sent to help those besieged in a town or fort: When we saw the distant campfires we knew *relief* was near. 4. release from a post of duty by the arrival of others to occupy it: The party worked all day without *relief*. 5. a design or figure that stands up from the surface from which it has been cut: The memorial consists of the figure of an angel in high *relief*. **relieve** give or bring *relief*: He was given drugs to *relieve* the pain. – The town was *relieved* and the enemy fled to the hills.

religion (re-li-gion) 1. the belief in a god who controls the affairs of men. 2. one of the many systems of worshipping such a god: Christianity, Islam and Buddhism are the three great *religions* of the world. **religious** 1. believing in and worshipping God: My tutor was a *religious* man. 2. having to do with *religion*: I have made progress with my *religious* studies.

relish (re-lish) 1. something used to give flavour to a dish: She had a cupboard full of sauces and *relishes*. 2. pleasure in something: He sat down and ate his dinner with great *relish*. 3. find pleasure in: I still *relish* a game of chess.

rely depend: I am *relying* on you to keep my secret. **reliable** that may be *relied* on: He is a *reliable* worker. – I learn from a *reliable* source that he is in America.

remain (re-main) stay, be left after others have gone or been taken: We *remained* at our post until the danger had passed. – After everybody had taken his share there *remained* only three oranges. **remains** what is left; ruins: The *remains* of the meal were thrown to the dogs. – Yesterday we visited the *remains* of Corfe Castle. **remainder** persons or things left over: Three hundred of the people filled the hall and the *remainder* heard the music outside through a loud speaker. Take 16 from 20 and what is the *remainder*?

remark (re-mark) 1. say: 'I saw you in the street yesterday,' she *remarked*. 2. notice: I *remarked* a change in her behaviour. 3. something said: He made a few *remarks* about the work to be done. **remarkable** unusual, extraordinary: There is a *remarkable* change in the weather today.

remedy (rem-e-dy) 1. a cure: Do you know a good *remedy* for colds? 2. cure; put right: There is nothing in your complaint that cannot be *remedied*. **remedial** intended to *remedy*: Every morning she has to do *remedial* excercises to strengthen her wrist.

remember (re-mem-ber) 1. call to mind things which are past: I *remember* the house where I was born. 2. send or give greetings to: *Remember* me to your sister. **remembrance** *remembering,* being *remembered*: Wreaths are laid at the monument on *Remembrance* Day.

remind (re-mind) cause a person to remember something: *Remind* me to lock the door. **reminder** something intended to *remind*: A *reminder* to pay our gas bill arrived this morning.

remit (re-mit) 1. excuse punishment or payment of a debt: One year of his prison sentence has been *remitted*. 2. send money in payment: Please *remit* by cheque or postal order. **remission** pardon of sins; freeing from debt or punishment: John the Baptist preached repentance and *remission* of sins. **remittance** money sent.

remnant (rem-nant) 1. a part or a number remaining: The *remnants* of the feast were fed to the birds. 2. an odd piece of cloth or material not sold: We are selling off *remnants* at a great reduction in price.

remote (re-mote) 1. far away: Our missionaries work in *remote* parts of the earth. 2. long ago: This pot was made in the *remote* past. 3. faint: You haven't the *remotest* idea what I am talking about.— There's just a *remote* possibility that you will meet him.

remove (re-move) 1. take off, take away: *Remove* your hat when you enter the house. 2. put an end to; get rid of: Can you *remove* this stain from my coat? 3. dismiss: The treasurer was *removed* from office. 4. move from one place, especially a house or place of business, to another. **removal** act of *removing*: Our *removal* took place yesterday. **remover** 1. a person who moves furniture etc. when people *remove*. 2. something that *removes*: I have bought a bottle of stain *remover*.

renew (re-new) 1. do a thing again: I have *renewed* my library subscription for another year. 2. make new or as good as new: The decorations of this room need *renewing*. 3. replenish, replace with the same kind of thing: We chopped wood to *renew* our supplies before the winter. **renewal** being *renewed*: The *renewal* of our friendship gave us great pleasure.

renovate (ren-o-vate) restore to good condition: Our church hall has recently been *renovated*.

renown (re-nown) fame: 'John Gilpin was a citizen of credit and *renown*'. (William Cowper) **renowned** famous: The *renowned* pianist Jan Paderewski was once president of Poland.

rent 1. payment made regularly for the use of a building or other property: The *rent* for your farm is due next week. 2. pay or charge *rent*: Do you *rent* this farm? Yes, it is *rented* to us by the owner. 3. a tear or open place in cloth or other material: The barbed wire made a long *rent* in his sleeve.—We caught a glimpse of the moon through a *rent* in the clouds.

repair (re-pair) 1. put into working order again: Has my radio been *repaired*? 2. put right a wrong or wrongs: All these mistakes can be *repaired*. 3. *repairing*, being *repaired*: The *repair* of his watch will not take long. 4. state, condition: The bicycle is in very good *repair*. **repairer** one who *repairs*.

repeat (re-peat) 1. do or say again: The man was almost deaf and I had to *repeat* my question. 2. say what has been learnt or what has been said by others: I can *repeat* the whole poem.—Don't *repeat* malicious gossip. 3. other, similar: There will be a *repeat* performance on Tuesday.—We are looking for *repeat* orders. **repeated** said or done again and again: I had to face *repeated* threats to my life.

repel (re-pel) 1. drive or thrust back: The enemy attack was *repelled*. 2. make one feel dislike or disgust: We were *repelled* by the filthy state of our new quarters.

repent (re-pent) be sorry for something done or said: 'Marry in haste, *repent* at leisure' (proverb).—I *repent* ever having lent him the money. **repentance** regret: I hope your *repentance* is sincere.

replenish (re-plen-ish) fill up again: Our stock of coal needs *replenishing* for the winter.

reply (re-ply) 1. answer: Have you *replied* to your brother's letter? 2. an answer: I knocked three times but there was no *reply*.

report (re-port) 1. give an account, news or information: The man on watch *reported* seeing a sail in the distance. 2. present oneself: You will all *report* for duty at eight o'clock. 3. make a complaint: Two boys were *reported* for trespassing. 4. a statement, an account of some event: I have read your *report* on the state of our roads.—Your school *report* this term was not a good one. 5. a noise as from an explosion: We heard a loud *report* from the direction of the gasworks. **reporter** a person employed by a newspaper to *report* events of interest.

repose (re-pose) 1. rest, sleep, lie quietly: You may *repose* on this couch for a while. 2. rest, sleep: 'Goodnight, and good *repose*' (Shakespeare, *Julius Caesar*). **repository** a place where things may be stored: This cupboard is a *repository* for all kinds of junk.

represent (rep-re-sent) 1. stand for, be a symbol of: The wavy lines *represent* trees in the distance.—These symbols *represent* sounds in music. 2. pretend to be: The man at the door *represented* himself as a police officer. 3. speak or act for others: He *represents* us in Parliament.—All the women's organizations were *represented*. **representative** a person who *represents* a group of people, or a firm to sell its products: Who is your *representative* in Parliament?—You will shortly receive a visit from our *representative* in your area.

reprieve (re-prieve) 1. put off or delay the punishment of a person: The prisoner was *reprieved* for a month until further enquiries had been made. 2. the postponement of a punishment: We were glad to have news of his *reprieve*.

reprimand (rep-ri-mand) 1. reprove a person for a fault: He was brought before the captain and *reprimanded* for disobeying orders. 2. a reproof, especially by an official: He received a severe *reprimand*.

reproach (re-proach) 1. blame or find fault with a person: He *reproached* her for being too generous with her money. 2. blame: Your conduct in this matter has been beyond *reproach* (blameless). 3. a matter for blame: 'The untidiness of this classroom is a *reproach* to you all,' said the teacher.

reproduce (re-pro-duce) 1. make a copy of something seen or heard: He *reproduced* the scene in a fine oil painting.—I have heard my voice *reproduced* on a gramophone record. 2. increase through breeding, seeds or in any other way: Rabbits *reproduce* quickly and often become pests. **reproduction** *reproducing*, something *reproduced*: This portrait is a poor *reproduction* of the original.

reptile (rep-tile) a cold-blooded animal such as a lizard, a crocodile or snake, that creeps or crawls.

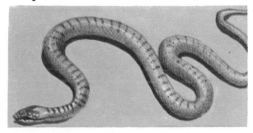

republic (re-pub-lic) a country whose governors are elected by the people and which has a president instead of a monarch.

repulse (re-pulse) 1. beat off, drive back, repel: The attacking force was *repulsed* with heavy losses. 2. reject, refuse to accept: All my offers of help were *repulsed*. 3. *repulsing*, being *repulsed*: The *repulse* of my offers of help ended our friendship. **repulsive** causing a feeling of disgust: She fainted at the *repulsive* sight.

reputation (rep-u-ta-tion) the opinion of people about a person, a group of persons or things: Our mayor is a man of blameless *reputation*.—These raincoats have a wonderful *reputation* for good wear.

request (re-quest) 1. the act of asking for something: This is my last *request*. 2. the thing asked for: Your *request* is willingly granted. 3. ask, make a *request*: Silence is *requested* during the performance.

require (re-quire) 1. need: We *require* two more typists in our office.—These plants *require* watering every morning. 2. desire, order, demand: I *require* you to be at your post when the whistle blows. **requirement** something demanded: We can meet all your *requirements*. **requisite** a necessary thing: This shop stocks all kinds of fishing *requisites*.

rescue (res-cue) 1. deliver from imprisonment, violence, danger etc.: Twelve people were *rescued* from the burning building. 2. *rescuing*, being *rescued*: The fire brigade went to the *rescue*.—My *rescue* from the sea was a miracle. **rescuer** a person who *rescues*, has *rescued*: The child's *rescuer* vanished into the crowd.

resemble (re-sem-ble) be like: You *resemble* your mother. **resemblance** likeness: There is a family *resemblance* between all the brothers and sisters.

resent (re-sent) feel angry at: I *resent* having to wear a uniform. **resentful** feeling or showing anger: Don't feel *resentful*. **resentment** feeling angry, injured etc.: He showed his *resentment* by slamming the door behind him.

reserve (re-serve) 1. keep back or save for future use: I have *reserved* tomorrow for a visit to the zoo. 2. keep for a special purpose: These seats are *reserved* for my guests. 3. book, or pay beforehand for something: I have *reserved* two rooms at the hotel. 4. something that has been *reserved*: We had sufficient *reserves* of food to last seven days. 5. a place kept apart for special use: Near to us is a nature *reserve* where many rare butterflies are to be found. 6. a lack of warmth or friendliness: At first I was treated with great *reserve*, and few people spoke to me. **reserves** military forces held back for use when needed: He served five years in the army and is now in the *reserves*; he is a *reservist*. **reservation** the act of *reserving*; what is *reserved*: I have a *reservation* at the hotel.—Three tribes live on this Indian *reservation*. **reservoir** a place, either natural or made by man, where water is stored for use in the home and industry.

reside (re-side) live, have one's home: I *reside* in Birmingham. **residence** the place where one *resides*. **resident** a person living in a certain place: The *residents* on this estate have formed a club. **residential** consisting mainly of houses, flats etc.: This is a *residential* district.

resign (re-sign) 1. give up an office or a claim: He *resigned* his post as general manager owing to illness. 2. accept willingly: He has at last *resigned* himself to living alone. **resignation** *resigning*, being *resigned*: He handed in his *resignation* yesterday.

resin (res-in) a sticky sap that flows from certain trees when cut: *Resin* is used in making varnish, lacquer and many other substances in general use.

resist (re-sist) 1. strive against, oppose: 'If he do *resist*, subdue him' (Shakespeare, *Othello*).—The prisoner was charged with *resisting* arrest. 2. be proof against, undamaged by: I want to buy a dish which *resists* the heat of the oven. 3. withstand, not give in to: Although these cakes are so good I must *resist* them. **resistance** *resisting*, the force that *resists*: My plans for the new building met with great *resistance*.—The car did not reach maximum speed because of the *resistance* of the wind. **resistant** capable of *resisting*: Is this material rain-*resistant*?

resolve (re-solve) 1. choose to do, settle on, decide: I have *resolved* to tell the truth. 2. decide on by the vote of a group of people: It was *resolved* to re-elect the chairman. **resolution** determination, the act of *resolving*: I made a New Year *resolution* to give up smoking.—The *resolution* to re-elect the chairman was rejected.

resort (re-sort) 1. turn to for help or use: When he could not earn enough money, he *resorted* to theft. 2. go often to a place: During the hot weather we *resort* to the swimming baths. 3. resource: When he failed to earn enough money, stealing became his last *resort*. 4. something or some place *resorted* to: Every summer we visit a different holiday *resort*.

resource (re-source) 1. wealth, supplies of anything at hand when needed: I would use all my *resources* to have you freed. This country has great *resources* of precious metals. 2. pastimes resorted to to keep the mind occupied. 3. qualities needed to meet difficulties: He needed all his *resources* to tackle the problem. 4. an action resorted to when all else has failed: My last *resource* was to sell everything I possessed.

respect (re-spect) 1. high regard and admiration: I have the greatest *respect* for his abilities. 2. a detail, particular: I agree with you in some *respects*, but on the whole I think you are wrong. 3. think highly of: We *respect* him greatly for his long and distinguished service. **respects** greetings: Please give my *respects* to your father. **respectable** worthy of *respect*, of some importance. **respectful** showing *respect*: The servant greeted the visitor with a *respectful* bow.

respirator (res-pi-ra-tor) an apparatus through which a person can breathe when the air is rare as in high altitudes, or polluted by smoke or poisonous gases: Firemen, wearing *respirators*, brought out the three children.

respond (re-spond) 1. answer: The mayor *responded* to the toast with a witty speech.—When I read the letter she *responded* with a sigh of relief. 2. do something in answer: The patient is *responding* well to treatment.—The car *responds* immediately to a touch on the footbrake. **response** answer: Her *response* to my request was immediate.—The choir and congregation joined in the *responses*.

responsible (re-spon-si-ble) 1. expected as a duty to do a thing or a service: I will make you *responsible* for seeing that all the doors are locked. 2. reliable, trustworthy, capable: Our security officer is a thoroughly *responsible* person. 3. a post needing a *responsible* person: The post of a security guard is a very *responsible* one. **responsibility** being *responsible*, something for which one is *responsible*: You will take *responsibility* for locking all the doors. – Your post is one of great *responsibility*.

rest 1. freedom from work or movement: We stopped half way up the hill for a short *rest*. – He brought the machine to *rest*. 2. sleep: Did you have a good night's *rest*? 3. a device which supports: This chair has an arm*rest* and is also fitted with a foot*rest*. 4. a sign in music marking an interval of silence. 5. what is left: She shared out half the cake and put the *rest* in the cupboard. 6. be still, not moving: We *rested* under a tree. 7. give *rest* to: I will sit here and *rest* my weary limbs. 8. support or be supported by: His arm *rested* on the table. 9. be directed to: My gaze *rested* on a strange object by the door. **restful** quiet, peaceful: What a *restful* place this is. **restless** never quiet, unable to *rest*: We were alone on the *restless* ocean. – He suddenly awoke out of a *restless* sleep.

restaurant (res-tau-rant) a place where meals are served to customers: We had lunch at the *restaurant* round the corner.

restore (re-store) 1. give back: We *restored* all the stolen property to its owners. 2. repair, make as it was before: This painting has been cleverly *restored*. 3. bring back to one's former state: I was *restored* to my post as cashier. **restoration** *restoring*, being *restored*: This office looks after the *restoration* of lost property. **restorative** capable of *restoring*, something which may *restore*: Do you know of a good hair *restorative*?

restrain (re-strain) hold back from action; keep under control: It was difficult to *restrain* my laughter. **restraint** *restraining*, being *restrained*: He kept the big dog under *restraint*.

restrict (re-strict) keep within limits, not going to extremes: You should *restrict* your smoking to three cigarettes a day. **restriction** a limitation, that which keeps something within limits: Speed *restrictions* are in force on this road.

result (re-sult) 1. happen because of something that has happened before: His illness *resulted* from long exposure to the cold. 2. bring about, cause: The hot weather *resulted* in the sale of all the ice-cream. 3. that which *results*; which is produced by a cause: Have you seen this afternoon's football *results*? – This certificate is the *result* of a year's hard work. 4. something found by calculation or study: If you add 2 and 4 the *result* is 6.

resurrect (res-ur-rect) 1. raise from the dead: Lazarus was *resurrected* by Jesus. 2. bring back: Old English songs and dances are being *resurrected* in many places. **resurrection** bringing back. **Resurrection** the rising again of Jesus Christ after his burial.

retail (re-tail) the sale of goods from a shop to the public in small quantities: Most shops buy goods wholesale in large quantities and sell by *retail*, making a profit. **retailer** a person who sells by *retail*.

retain (re-tain) 1. keep possession of, hold: I am *retaining* this pocket-knife until I know who owns it. – This piece of cloth will *retain* its colour for ever. 2. keep in mind: I *retain* memories of my schooldays, but I can't *retain* the prices of the goods I bought only yesterday. 3. hire by paying a fee: We have *retained* a solicitor to plead my son's case in the juvenile court. **retainer** a servant of a person of high rank: An old family *retainer* opened the door and admitted us. **retention** *retaining*, being *retained*: I am angry at the *retention* of my passport by the police. **retentive** having the power to *retain*: If you can remember this poem you must have a very *retentive* memory.

retire (re-tire) 1. withdraw, go to a place apart: Shall we *retire* while the tables are being cleared? 2. go to bed: We *retired* early last night. 3. (of an army) go back: The force of the enemy attack compelled our troops to *retire*. 4. give up work: He *retired* at the age of sixty. **retired** having *retired*: He is a *retired* schoolmaster. **retiring** shy, reserved: She has a *retiring* disposition. **retirement** the state of having *retired*: Most of my *retirement* is spent gardening and walking.

retreat (re-treat) 1. move back in face of an enemy: The general commanded his troops to *retreat*. 2. the signal for *retreating*: The bugler sounded the *retreat*. 3. a place where one can be alone: I spend hours in my *retreat* in the woods.

retrieve (re-trieve) 1. get into one's possession again: Within two years I had *retrieved* all my losses. 2. rescue: Through the kindness of a friend he was *retrieved* from ruin. 3. (of a dog) find and fetch killed or wounded game. **retriever** a dog used for *retrieving* killed and wounded game.

return (re-turn) 1. go or come back to a place: We *returned* to London by the next train. 2. take, give, pay, carry, put or send back: Please *return* the keys to the caretaker.—I have *returned* the book to its place on the shelf. 3. elect a person to a seat in Parliament: The Conservative candidate was *returned* by a good majority. 4. going or coming back: He awaited my *return* with impatience. 5. a report or statement: I have just filled in my income tax *return*. **returns** money obtained from business deals or sales 'Small profits, quick *returns*' (If you take little in profit you sell your goods more quickly).

reveal (re-veal) 1. make known: At last the truth was *revealed*. 2. show, display: A flash of lightning *revealed* a form huddled in the doorway. **revelation** revealing, making known, something made known: The *revelation* of my secret surprised them all.

revenge (re-venge) 1. do harm or injury to another in return for injury done to you or your friend: He never forgets to *revenge* an insult. 2. the harm or injury done: His only thought was to get his *revenge*.

revenue (rev-e-nue) money coming in; all the money the government receives in taxes and by other means. **Inland Revenue** money received through taxation. **revenue officer** a customs officer who checks goods brought into a country, in order to collect the due tax.

revere (re-vere) regard with great respect; treat as being sacred. **reverence** a feeling of deep respect: The pilgrims bowed their heads in *reverence* before the altar. **Reverend** the title of a clergyman.

reverse (re-verse) 1. opposite to: We will take these names in the *reverse* order (the last first).—He walked a short way in the *reverse* direction (towards the place from which he had started). 2. turn the other way: Please *reverse* the charge (so that the person receiving the phone message pays the bill). 3. make to go the opposite way: He *reversed* the car into the side road. 4. do the opposite: I have *reversed* the order in which I will pay these bills. 5. the opposite: You may think I am rich but in fact I am just the *reverse*. 6. a defeat, misfortune: My failure in the examination was a great *reverse*.

review (re-view) 1. go over again: You had better *review* your expenses and see if you can economize. 2. inspect troops etc.: The Queen *reviewed* the regiment this morning. 3. think over what has passed: This week our reporter will be *reviewing* the events of the football season. 4. report on a book or a play. 5. a military or naval inspection: We went to London to see the great *review*. 6. a report on a book or a play: I am disappointed with the *review* of my novel. 7. a periodical which contains articles on literature, the arts and events of the day.

revise (re-vise) read again carefully, think about again: Have you *revised* your work for tomorrow's examination? – I have *revised* my opinion about this man. **revision** *revising*, being *revised*: The *revision* of my work did not take long.

revive (re-vive) 1. make or become conscious or active again: The plants have *revived* after the rain. 2. put into use or come into use again: We have *revived* our Whitsuntide Carnival. **revival** being *revived*, *reviving*: The discovery of a spring of fresh water brought a *revival* of our hopes.

revoke (re-voke) take back or withdraw: Your permit to use this land as a playground has been *revoked*. **revocation** withdrawing, *revoking*: After the *revocation* of the permit to use the land we had to play in the street.

revolt (re-volt) 1. rise in rebellion: The peasants *revolted* against their overlords. 2. turn away in disgust: We were *revolted* by the terrible sight. 3. the act of rebelling: The Peasants' *Revolt* was quickly crushed. **revolting** disgusting: We were shocked by his *revolting* behaviour.

revolution (rev-o-lu-tion) 1. the complete overthrow of a government: France became a republic after the *Revolution* of 1789. 2. a complete change in ways of doing things: If we are to sell our products we must have a complete *revolution* in our selling methods. 3. the act of going round: In 24 hours the earth makes one complete *revolution* round the sun.

revolve (re-volve) 1. go round in a circle: The moon *revolves* round the earth. 2. think over: Before I acted I *revolved* the problem in my mind. **revolver** a pistol which has a *revolving* cylinder carrying the cartridges, enabling it to be fired a number of times without reloading.

reward (re-ward) 1. that which is given for some service or work of special value: A *reward* is offered for the recovery of the money. 2. give a *reward*: The girl who saved the boy was *rewarded* by his parents.

rheumatism (rheu-ma-tism) a disease which affects the joints and the muscles: *Rheumatism* is very painful, causing inflammation and stiffening of the joints. **rheumatic** having to do with *rheumatism*: For the last two years he has had *rheumatic* pains.

rhinoceros (rhi-noc-er-os) a large, heavily-built animal with a grey skin and one or two horns on its snout: The *rhinoceros* is found in Africa and Asia.

rhododendron (rho-do-den-dron) a large evergreen shrub bearing pink, purple or white flowers.

rhubarb (rhu-barb) a garden plant with large green leaves, and thick, juicy stalks that may be stewed or made into pies.

rhyme 1. the agreement in the ends of lines of verse, or words: *fill* and *kill*, *dart* and *cart*, *beam* and *team* are *rhymes*. 2. a poem with *rhymes* in it: How many nursery *rhymes* do you know? 3. be in *rhyme*; end with the same sound: *Hill rhymes* with *fill* and *tie* with *lie*. 4. make verses with *rhymes*: Most poets are good at *rhyming*.

rhythm (rhy-thm) 1. a regular beat in music, speech, dancing or movement: The audience began to clap in *rhythm* with the music. 2. the way in which certain events follow each other: Summer and winter, day and night occur in endless *rhythm*. **rhythmical** in *rhythm*: We joined in the *rhythmical* steps of the dance.

rib 1. one of the curved bones that run from the backbone to the front of the body, over the chest, protecting the heart and lungs: He fell and broke a *rib*. 2. the *rib* of an animal with the meat on it: We had *rib* of beef for dinner: 3. something like a *rib* in shape: One of the *ribs* of my umbrella is broken. 4. a raised line in cloth.

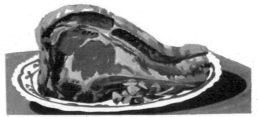

ribbon (rib-bon) 1. a band of silk or other cloth used for decoration: She wore a green *ribbon* in her hair. 2. a piece of *ribbon* used for some special purpose: He wore the dark red *ribbon* of the Victoria Cross. 3. a long thin piece of material: As I came through the forest my clothes were torn to *ribbons*.

rice the seeds or grain of a grass that grows in warm climates: *Rice* is an important food in many Eastern countries.

rich 1. wealthy, having much money or property: A legacy from his uncle made him a *rich* man. 2. valuable, costly, expensive: '*Rich* and rare were the gems she wore' (Thomas Moore). 3. fertile, having many natural resources: This land is *rich* enough to bear two crops a year. — The rocks they found proved to be *rich* in minerals. 4. containing much butter, fat, sugar, eggs etc.: I am afraid I cannot digest *rich* foods. **riches** wealth: 'Give me neither poverty nor *riches*' (*The Book of Proverbs*). **richly** 1. expensively. 2. thoroughly: You *richly* deserved your punishment.

rid 1. clear, make free of: 'I can *rid* your town of rats,' said the piper. 2. **get rid of** free oneself of: I am going to *get rid of* this old car. **riddance** being delivered or *rid* of: 'Good *riddance*,' he sighed as his unwelcome visitor departed.

riddle (rid-dle) 1. a question designed to puzzle others: I asked him a *riddle* which he could not answer. 2. something which is difficult to answer: Where the coins had disappeared was a complete *riddle*. 3. a sieve for stones or cinders: He passed the earth through a *riddle* and threw the stones on the path. 4. shake a *riddle* to pass things through. 5. fill with holes: The aeroplane crashed to the ground *riddled* with bullets.

ride *rode ridden* 1. be carried by: He *rode* off on his horse. — Can you *ride* a bicycle?

2. the time when one *rides*; a journey: We went for an hour's *ride* this morning. — It's a long *ride* between here and Edinburgh. **rider** a person who *rides*: Both horse and *rider* fell into the river.

ridge 1. a long, narrow chain of hills, or raised area: Our path lay along a *ridge* with valleys on both sides of us. 2. a raised strip: The furrows between the *ridges* were flooded with water.

ridicule (rid-i-cule) 1. words or actions intended to make fun of something or someone: If you go out dressed like that you will be an object of *ridicule*. 2. make fun of: I don't like being *ridiculed* because of my long hair. **ridiculous** absurd, laughable: He looks *ridiculous* in that little hat.

rifle (ri-fle) 1. search in order to rob: The whole room had been *rifled*. 2. a gun with a long barrel, fired from the shoulder: He went out into the woods armed with a *rifle*. **rifle range** a place where people may practise shooting with a *rifle*.

rig 1. fit out a ship with masts, sails etc.: The vessel had been *rigged* for a long voyage. 2. put together: When the snow started to fall we *rigged* up a shelter for the night. **rigging** the ropes which support the masts and sails of a ship: Boys were climbing the *rigging* like monkeys.

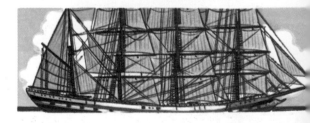

right 1. good, according to law: You did *right* to tell me about it. 2. accurate: Is your watch *right*? — Make sure every detail of your account is *right*. 3. best: We need the *right* person to do this work. 4. well: My leg doesn't feel *right*. 5. (of an angle) neither acute nor obtuse: This road runs at *right* angles to the main road.

6. the *right* side—the side which is on the east when one faces north: Hold up your *right* hand. 7. straight: 'Keep *right* on to the end of the road' (a song). 8. correct: Did you get the two sums *right*? 9. as things should be: I've tried, but nothing seems to go *right*.—It serves him *right*! 10. that which is good: 'I laboured all I could to do him *right*' (Shakespeare, *Richard II*). 11. a just claim: Everybody has the *right* to use a public highway. 12. order: It is time we put things to *rights*. **righteous** doing what is *right*: He answered his accusers with *righteous* fury. **rightful** just, according to law: He is the *rightful* owner of this land.

rigour (rig-our) strictness, harshness, sternness: He was punished with the utmost *rigour* of the law. **rigorous** stern; severe: He was given a *rigorous* training for the dangerous mission.

rim an outer edge, border or margin: We had to force the tyre off the *rim* before we could mend the puncture.—He wore spectacles with thick tortoiseshell *rims*.

rind the thick firm skin or covering of fruits etc.: He ate the cheese and threw away the *rind*.

ring *rang, rung* 1. give out a clear musical sound: Can't you hear the bell *ringing*? 2. a loud clear sound: We hear the *ring* of happy laughter. 3. the sound of a bell: There was a *ring* at the door. 4. make something *ring*: *Ring* the bell! 5. be filled, echo: The room *rang* with children's voices.—The whole town *rang* with praise of the hero. 6. a circular band of metal, usually gold, to wear on the finger: She wore a wedding *ring*. 7. any circular band: This engine needs a set of new piston *rings*. 8. a circle: 'Last night the moon had a golden *ring*' (Coleridge, *The Ancient Mariner*). 9. a group of people: He was a member of a *ring* of forgers. 10. an enclosure for a circus or for some sport: The two boxers entered the

ring at the same time. 11. surround, make a *ring* round: I have *ringed* some of these figures in pencil. 12. put a *ring* on: These birds have been *ringed* so that we can trace their movements.

rink a sheet of ice prepared for skating, or a smooth floor prepared for roller-skating.

rinse 1. dip in water to get rid of dirt, soap etc.: *Rinse* out the milk-bottles before you return them. 2. a cleaning through *rinsing*: She gave the cloth a *rinse* before hanging it out to dry. 3. something in which hair is *rinsed* in order to alter its colour: Did you notice Mrs Jones's blue *rinse*.

riot (ri-ot) 1. disturbance of the peace by a group of people: The police arrived in force to quell the *riot*. 2. make a *riot*: When the people heard the news they *rioted* in the streets.

rip 1. tear, pull, cut apart: His sleeve had been *ripped* from shoulder to wrist. 2. a torn place: The balloon came down because of a *rip* in the material which allowed gas to escape. **ripsaw** a saw used to saw wood along the grain.

ripe 1. ready for reaping or gathering: She brought in a basketful of *ripe* apples. 2. fully developed in body and mind: He had reached the *ripe* age of thirty. 3. ready to have things done: This plot of land is now *ripe* for development (to be built on). **ripen** become *ripe*: The fields were full of *ripening* corn.

rise *rose*, *risen* 1. get up, stand up: I usually *rise* at seven.—He *rose* from his chair to welcome me. 2. appear above the horizon: The sun *rises* late in winter. 3. come to life: Lazarus *rose* from the dead. 4. increase; come to a higher position: When will prices stop *rising*?—Her voice *rose* to a scream. 5. slope upwards: At this point the ground *rose* sharply. 6. rebel: The whole countryside *rose* in arms. 7. start: The river *rises* in a lake among the hills. 8. a slope: The memorial could be seen on top of the *rise*. 9. increase: The sudden *rise* in temperature has pleased the farmers.

risk 1. chance of danger, injury or loss: There is a *risk* of fire if you strike matches here. 2. take the *risk* of injury, danger or loss: He *risked* his life to save the drowning child. **risky** full of *risk*: It would be *risky* to walk along the edge of the cliff.

rite a ceremony: 'Let us use him with all respect and *rites* of burial' (Shakespeare, *Julius Caesar*).

rival (ri-val) 1. one who wants the same thing as another, or to do something better than another: We have always been *rivals* on the sports field. 2. be as good as: What game could *rival* the old English game of cricket? **rivalry** being *rivals*, competition: There has been a long *rivalry* between the two universities.

river (riv-er) 1. a large stream of water: Shall we take a boat on the *river* today? 2. a large stream: A *river* of lava flowed from the volcano.

rivet (riv-et) 1. a metal pin or bolt used for fastening metal plates or pieces together: The small end of a *rivet* is flattened with a hammer so that it will not come loose. 2. drive in *rivets*: The blades of scissors are usually *riveted* together.

road 1. an open way, specially prepared to carry traffic: Cars and lorries thundered along the *road* all day long. 2. a way to a place or a state: We took the *road* to Leicester.—'The *road* to hell is paved with good intentions' (proverb). 3. the name of a *road* or street: 'Go straight along Whitechapel *Road* and turn right into New *Road*.'

roam wander about with no fixed purpose or direction: We found him *roaming* about in the wood.

roar 1. a loud, deep noise, as of a lion or thunder: With a *roar* the tiger sprang towards him. 2. make such a sound: We heard the sea *roaring* below us.—When he heard the story he *roared* with laughter.

roast 1. bake in an oven; cook over or in front of a fire: From the kitchen came the delicious smell of *roasting* meat.—Every Christmas we *roast* chestnuts on the fire. 2. a piece of meat for *roasting* or one already *roasted*: He put an enormous *roast* on the table.

rob steal from others, or take things from them by force: He was *robbed* of his watch by a pickpocket.—The room had been *robbed* of everything of value. **robber** a person who *robs*: *Robbers* broke into the bank during the night. **robbery** *robbing*, having *robbed*: He was convicted of *robbery* with violence.

robe 1. a long loose garment worn by men or women: She wore a long flowing *robe*. —Here comes the mayor in his *robes* of office. 2. put a *robe* or *robes* on; wear *robes*: In a corner of the picture was an angel *robed* in white.

robin (rob-in) a small bird having a red or reddish breast: 'A *robin* redbreast in a cage puts all heaven in a rage' (William Blake).

robot (rob-ot) 1. a machine made to act and do certain things as if it were a person. 2. a person who acts like a machine: Under the influence of the drug he was a mere *robot*.

rock 1. a large stone standing on land or jutting from the sea: Our ship capsized and landed us on a deserted, barren *rock*. 2. a hard sweet made with various flavours: He offered me a piece of pineapple *rock*. 3. stone: The parachute landed on a shelf of solid *rock*. 4. move to and fro, from side to side: 'When the wind blows the cradle will *rock*' (nursery rhyme).

rocket (rock-et) a tube-shaped device filled with material that burns very fast so that the gases push it into the air: *Rockets* are used as signals of distress, for saving lives and for putting spacecraft into orbit.

rod a thin stick, wand or staff: 'Aaron cast down his *rod* before Pharaoh and it became a serpent' (*The Book of Exodus*).— *Rods* are used for hanging curtains, for fishing and for many other purposes.

rodent (ro-dent) the order of mammals known specially for their long sharp teeth, used for gnawing, nibbling and biting: Mice, rats, squirrels, beavers and rabbits are *rodents*.

rogue 1. a scoundrel, rascal, a dishonest person: Can you recognize the man who robbed you among these pictures of *rogues*? 2. a person who is fond of playing tricks: 'Keep out of mischief, you little *rogue*,' said his uncle.

roll 1. move by turning over and over: The ball *rolled* to my feet and I kicked it. 2. move between two surfaces; turn over and over: He took down the map from the wall and *rolled* it up. 3. move or advance in a stream or with a *rolling* motion: Wait till the clouds *roll* by.—The tide came *rolling* in. 4. flatten by *rolling* something on it: He was *rolling* the cricket pitch. 5. make a long low sound: All day long the noise of battle *rolled* across the hills. 6. move from side to side: The ship was *rolling* heavily in the storm. 7. something that is *rolled*: He put a new *roll* of film into his camera.—The draper cut a piece of cloth from the *roll*. 8. a *rolling* movement: He walks with a *roll*, like a sailor. 9. a long low sound: The skies became dark and we heard a *roll* of thunder. 10. a list of names: 'I will call the *roll* now', said the teacher. **roller** a cylinder used to *roll* things or a machine containing such *rollers*: He was pushing the *roller* across the lawn.

romance (ro-mance) 1. a story of adventure or love, quite unlike what really happens: My sister reads nothing but *romances*. 2. something unreal, attractive, picturesque: The old castle seemed a place of mystery and *romance*. **romantic** having to do with *romance*: Where does she get her *romantic* ideas about the East?— We stayed the night at a *romantic* old inn.

romp 1. play or frolic in a noisy manner: A number of children were *romping* on the grass: 2. come first easily, as in a race: The horse *romped* home in record time. 3. a frolic: They had a *romp* on the grass before going home.

roof 1. the top covering of a building, a tent, or a vehicle: They had only just left the house when the *roof* fell in. 2. put a *roof* on: We had to *roof* the hut before we could use it. **roofing** material used to make *roofs*.

rook 1. a large black bird like a crow: The *rooks* are building their nests in the trees. 2. (in chess) a castle. 3. make money by cheating: He *rooked* all the other players of everything they had. **rookery** a place, usually a number of high trees, where *rooks* live and breed.

room 1. a portion of space within a building separated from others by walls or partitions: We were shown into a large *room* and told to wait. 2. space: Is there *room* for me on this bench? 3. opportunity: 'There is *room* for improvement in this subject' (school report). **roommate** a person who lives in the same *room* as another, sharing costs. **roomy** having plenty of space or *room*: It was a *roomy* house, with four bed*rooms*.

roost 1. a pole or branch on which birds may sleep or rest. 2. (of birds) rest, sleep: The rooks are *roosting* in the elm trees.

root 1. that part of a plant or tree that is under the ground and provides its nourishment: We cannot take out this tree unless we dig down to the *roots*. 2. that part of a hair, tooth or nail which resembles a *root* in its position or use: This comb pulls my hair out by the *roots*. 3. the source or essence of a matter: The doctor is trying to get to the *root* of your illness. 4. make *roots* when put into the ground: These roses are *rooting* nicely. 5. stand still with fear, terror etc.: At the awful sight he was *rooted* to the spot. 6. turn up; search: The pigs were *rooting* in the ground for nuts.

rope 1. a strong thick cord, usually of twisted strands of material: The prisoners were tied together with strong *ropes*. 2. tie or bind with a *rope* or *ropes*: The bull was *roped* to the tree.—He was *roped* to the mast. 3. lasso: During the day the cowboys *roped* more than a hundred cattle.

rosary (ro-sa-ry) 1. a series of prayers used in the Roman Catholic Church. 2. a string of beads used to count these prayers when reciting them.

rose 1. a bush which has prickles on its stems and bears a sweet-smelling flower. 2. the flower of the *rose* tree: On the table was a bowl of red *roses*. **rosy** having the colour of red *roses*: The little girl has *rosy* cheeks. **rosette** a small bunch of ribbons resembling a *rose*, used as an ornament or badge: The supporters of the football club wore large blue *rosettes*.

rot 1. decay, become soft or weak due to decay: Much of the wood of the floor has *rotted*. 2. make a thing decay: The damp has *rotted* the window-frames. 3. decay, *rotting*: The whole floor had to be renewed because of dry *rot*. **rotten** decayed, not in good condition: The branches of the apple-trees were *rotten* and had to be sawn off.—Most of the eggs in the box were *rotten*.

rotate (ro-tate) 1. move or make move round a central point: He *rotated* the bicycle wheel to examine its spokes. 2. follow in a regular way: The farmer *rotates* his crops to make the best use of the soil. **rotation** going round, following in a set order: Day and night are caused by the *rotation* of the earth.

rouge a red cosmetic used for colouring the cheeks.

rough 1. uneven, not smooth: He found it difficult to walk on the *rough* ground without shoes. 2. neither calm nor quiet: The ship rolled and tossed on the *rough* sea. 3. disorderly, violent: He loves playing *rough* games.—He went to live in one of the *roughest* quarters of the city. 4. not easy, with harsh treatment: I had a *rough* childhood. 5. badly finished; incomplete: This is a *rough* model of a boat.—I have done a *rough* sketch of the garden. 6. a person who is rowdy, impolite and violent: He was assaulted in the street by a gang of *roughs*. 7. make *rough*: You should *rough* up the leather with a file before you stick on the new rubber sole. **roughly** 1. in a *rough* manner: This child has been *roughly* treated. 2. about: It will be *roughly* two weeks before you hear from me.

round 1. like a ball or a circle in shape: Everybody knows the earth is *round*. 2. returning to the point at which it started: The *round* trip took two days. 3. something which is complete: I bought a *round* dozen. 4. a regular series of visits: Every morning the postman does his *round*. 5. a single part of a match: He was knocked out in the third *round*. 6. a song for two or more groups singing the same melody but beginning at different times: One of the best-known *rounds* is 'Three blind mice'. 7. in a circle: The earth moves *round* the sun. 8. changing direction: He went *round* the corner to the post office. 9. on all sides: We sat *round* the fire eating chestnuts.—He looked *round* at his audience and smiled. 10. make or become *round*: When singing your lips should be well *rounded*. 11. go *round*: As we *rounded* the Cape the weather began to clear. **rounders** a game for two teams played with a bat and ball, in which players run *round* a prepared course and back to the starting-point.

roundabout (round-a-bout) 1. using a longer way round: We approached the house by a *roundabout* route. 2. a circular platform with wooden horses on which children ride, and which goes round and round; a merry-go-round. 3. a place where roads join, where traffic, instead of going across, moves round a circular or oval space: When entering a *roundabout*, always give way to the traffic approaching from the right. (One of the rules of the *Highway Code*.)

rouse 1. bring out of sleep, wake up: I was *roused* by the sound of voices. 2. become or make more active, angry or enthusiastic: His insults *roused* me to a fury.—The meeting began with a *rousing* speech by the chairman.

rout 1. complete defeat and flight: 'Shame and confusion! All is on the *rout*.' (Shakespeare, *Henry VI, part 2*). 2. put an enemy to flight: The French were completely *routed*.

route a way or road taken or planned: We shall take the shortest *route* from here to Manchester. **routine** a regular way of doing things: When visitors call unexpectedly it upsets my daily *routine*.

rove wander about; roam: I spent all day *roving* through the woods. **rover** a person who wanders: 'I've been a *rover* for many a year' (old song).

row (rhymes with *so*) 1. a number of people or things in a line: A *row* of bottles stood on the shelf. 2. make a boat move by pulling on oars: We had to *row* to the nearest island for fresh water.

row (rhymes with *now*) 1. a noisy dispute or quarrel: There was a *row* between two bricklayers. 2. a commotion, uproar: The police were called to stop a *row* outside a public house.

royal (roy-al) having to do with a king or queen: The *Royal* Family appeared on the balcony of Buckingham Palace.—The name '*royal*' is given to many societies, regiments etc. by special *royal* grant. **royalist** a supporter of a king or queen; a supporter of King Charles I in the Civil War (1642–49). **royalty** 1. *royal* position or persons: The garden fete was attended by *royalty*. 2. payment of money to those who own land, those who have written books or music: This singer has earned huge sums in *royalties* on his records.

rub 1. move one thing backwards and forwards on another, pressing so as to make it dry, to clean it, smooth it, polish it, or for pleasure: He was *rubbing* his face with his hands.—*Rub* out those pencil marks in your book.—If you *rub* harder your shoes will shine. 2. move backwards and forwards: Your chair is *rubbing* against the wall. 3. the act of *rubbing*: Give your shoes a *rub* before you go out.

rubber (rub-ber) 1. an elastic material made from the juice that comes from certain trees when the bark is cut: *Rubber* is one of the most valuable products of modern times. 2. a piece of *rubber* specially made for erasing pencil marks. 3. three games between the same persons in whist or bridge; a contest decided by winning two games out of three.

rubbish (rub-bish) 1. waste material, litter, thrown away as being of no use: You should either put your *rubbish* in the dustbin or burn it. 2. nonsense: I have seldom read such *rubbish* as this essay.

rucksack (ruck-sack) a kind of knapsack carried on the back by hikers.

rudder (rud-der) 1. the plate of wood or metal fixed to the stern of a boat for the purpose of steering. 2. a similar device fixed to an aeroplane to enable it to move right or left.

ruddy (rud-dy) 1. having a red face, a sign of good health: The farmer's boy had a *ruddy* complexion. 2. reddish in colour: After the sun sank a *ruddy* glow remained in the western sky.

rude 1. impolite, rough in manner: It is *rude* to speak with your mouth full. 2. rough, not well finished: We made a *rude* boat to carry us across the river. **rudeness** being *rude*: I shall not excuse such *rudeness* another time.

rue 1. repent: If you sell this house you'll *rue* it one day. 2. a small evergreen herb with a strong scent and bitter-tasting leaves.

ruffian (ruf-fian) a violent, lawless man, a rough brute: He was attacked by a gang of *ruffians*.

ruffle (ruf-fle) 1. destroy the smoothness of something: A light wind *ruffled* the surface of the water.–Don't *ruffle* my hair; I've just brushed it. 2. gather cloth together to make tiny folds. 3. a strip of cloth, lace etc., drawn together at one edge and used as a trimming on dress: In her portrait, Queen Elizabeth I wears a large *ruffle* round her neck. **ruffled** annoyed: He is easily *ruffled*, so be careful what you say.

rug 1. a small, usually thick carpet used as a floor covering: Two kittens were playing on the *rug*. 2. a large thick piece of woollen cloth or blanket used as a covering: The old lady's knees were covered with a green *rug*.

rugged (rug-ged) 1. roughly broken, rocky, uneven: We slowly climbed the *rugged* side of the mountain. 2. wrinkled, furrowed: The old man had a *rugged* face. 3. severe, hard: Out in the wilds the peasants live a *rugged* life. 4. sturdy, strong and honest but with rough manners: A *rugged* old labourer told us the story of his life.

ruin (ru-in) 1. destruction, complete downfall: Carelessness and over-spending brought him to *ruin*. 2. being decayed, destroyed: The old house has fallen into *ruin*. 3. cause the destruction of: A severe earthquake *ruined* the whole town. **ruins** remains: We visited the *ruins* of an old monastery. **ruinous** in *ruins*, causing *ruin*: The price of meat is *ruinous*.

rule 1. a law or custom generally followed, which tells people how to behave: He was disqualified for not obeying the *rules* of the club. 2. a piece of wood or metal with a straight edge used for measuring and drawing straight lines: He marked off the distance with a steel *rule*. 3. govern: Oliver Cromwell *ruled* England for many years. 4. decide: The chairman has *ruled* that the subject shall not be discussed in this meeting. 5. make a line or lines with a *rule*: She *ruled* a margin down the left-hand side of the page. **ruler** 1. a person who *rules*: The new king was a kind and merciful *ruler*. 2. a *rule* for making lines etc. **ruling** a decision: The chairman's *ruling* must be obeyed.

rumble (rum-ble) 1. make a deep, heavy continuous sound: The thunder *rumbled* all day. 2. a *rumbling* sound: We heard the *rumble* of wheels long before we saw the coach arrive.

rummage (rum-mage) 1. search through a place by turning things over and moving them about: You may find what you want if you *rummage* in the drawer. 2. various odds and ends: We arc holding a *rummage* sale in the church hall on Saturday for the scouts.

rumour (ru-mour) 1. gossip, things talked about which may not be true: There is a *rumour* that a new airport is to be built here. 2. report by *rumour*: I have heard it *rumoured* that the plans have already been drawn up.

run *ran*, *run* 1. move more quickly than walking, so that both feet are off the ground at the same time: If you *run* you may catch the bus. 2. stand as a candidate for election: He is *running* for Parliament. 3. go, move: Our ship *ran* on the rocks.—The trains are *running* late this morning. 4. flow: The river *runs* through a deep valley.—Who left the tap *running*? 5. work, be in good or bad order: The engine is not *running* very well. 6. transport by car, ship etc.: I'll *run* you home in my car. 7. cause to *run*, flow or move: I'll *run* the car into the garage.—He *ran* a jugful of water. 8. come back again and again: I've got a tune *running* through my head. 9. move, or cause to move into another state: The well has *run* dry.—Take care not to *run* into debt. 10. manage, organize: Who is *running* this business? 11. extend or make in a certain direction: A bookcase *ran* along the wall. 12. the act of *running* or moving: He set off at a *run*. 13. a trip or journey: It is a four-day *run* to New York. 14. an enclosed space: You'll find him in the chicken-*run*. 15. a single score made by batsmen running from one wicket to the one opposite: The Australians declared at 550 *runs*. 16. a number of notes sung or played in order: All this morning he has been practising *runs* on the violin. 17. a number of happenings: We have had a *run* of bad luck this season. **runaway** a person, animal etc. *running* away: He received a medal for stopping a *runaway* horse. **runway** a prepared surface along which an aeroplane can take off and land.

runner (run-ner) 1. a person or animal that runs: How many *runners* are in the next race? 2. a smuggler or smuggling vessel: The gun-*runners* landed their cargo on a deserted part of the beach. 3. a long piece of cloth placed on a sideboard. 4. a long stem which grows from a plant and takes root: The strawberry plant has put out four *runners*.

rung one of the crosspieces forming the steps of a ladder: Don't use the ladder until the fourth *rung* has been replaced.

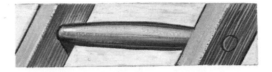

rural (ru-ral) having to do with the country and not the town: We are spending our holidays in *rural* surroundings.

rush 1. go fast or cause to go fast: At the call of 'Fire!' the crowd *rushed* out of the building.—Medicines and supplies were *rushed* to the spot. 2. come or pass rapidly: Tears *rushed* to her eyes. 3. attack and capture quickly: The crowd *rushed* the gaol and let out the prisoners. 4. hurry: I'm already late; I must *rush*. 5. the act of *rushing*: There was a sudden *rush* for the doors. 6. great activity: The shops are preparing for the Christmas *rush*. 7. sudden demand: When the hot weather came there was a sudden *rush* on cool drinks. 8. the stem of a plant which grows on marshy ground. **rush hours** the times when most people fill the trains and buses on their way to and from work.

rust 1. a red or orange-coloured coating which forms on iron when exposed to the air and the damp: The machine had not been used and was covered with *rust*. 2. a disease of plants in which the leaves and stems become spotted and turn a reddish colour. 3. become covered with *rust*; decay because of *rust*: The wire fence had *rusted* away. **rusty** 1. covered with *rust*: I found a tin of *rusty* nails. 2. suffering through lack of use or neglect: My Spanish was *rusty*, but I tried my best to talk to him. **rustless** that does not *rust*: These kitchen utensils are made of *rustless* steel.

rustic (rus-tic) 1. having to do with the countryside, simple, homely: The cottage was approached through a charming *rustic* garden.–He has lived many years in town but has not lost his *rustic* speech. 2. made of roughly worked branches: All kinds of *rustic* garden furniture are sold here. 3. a countryman with country accent and manners.

rustle (rus-tle) 1. make a number of soft, light sounds as of leaves, silk or papers rubbing together: The leaves were *rustling* in the breeze. 2. the sound made when something *rustles*: There was a *rustle* of silk when Jane walked by. 3. steal cattle or horses: A gang of outlaws *rustled* my herd last night.

rut 1. a furrow or track in the ground made by the wheels of vehicles: Since the building operations began, our road has become full of *ruts*. 2. a way of life that has not changed for a long time: I have worked so long as a clerk that I am now in a *rut*. 3. make *ruts* in the ground: The road had been badly *rutted* with the passing of heavy lorries.

ruthless (ruth-less) without any pity or mercy: We were faced by a *ruthless* enemy.–'Ruin seize thee, *ruthless* king!' (Gray, *The Bard*).

rye a plant or grass whose grain is used for making flour, and as food for cattle.

S

Sabbath (Sab-bath) the day of rest and worship: Saturday, the seventh day of the week, is the *Sabbath* day for Jews and Sunday, the first day of the week, for Christians.

sabotage (sab-o-tage) 1. the deliberate damaging of machinery by discontented workers. 2. interference with a country's production by resistance workers or enemy agents during war time. 3. commit acts of *sabotage*: During the war the enemy transport system was *sabotaged* by the blowing up of railway lines and goods depots.

sabre (sa-bre) a heavy one-edged sword with a curved blade, used by cavalry.

saccharin (sac-cha-rin) a substance made from coal-tar which is about 400 times as sweet as sugar and is used as a sugar substitute.

sack 1. a large oblong bag made of coarse cloth or paper, used for carrying goods such as coal, cement, flour, potatoes etc. 2. discharge from employment: Owing to lack of work more than half the staff had to be *sacked*. 3. plunder or loot during time of war: The city was *sacked* and burnt.

sacred (sac-red) 1. having to do with God or religion: On Sunday there is to be a concert of *sacred* music. 2. solemn: The prince made a *sacred* vow to go on a pilgrimage. **sacrament** a solemn religious ceremony: Baptism, the marriage service and holy communion are some of the *sacraments* of the Christian Church.

sacrifice (sac-ri-fice) 1. offer a life or something of value to a god: The tribe *sacrificed* a goat to their local god.–He *sacrificed* his life for the good of his country. 2. something *sacrificed*: They hoped that the *sacrifice* of a goat would bring rain.–The money gained was not worth the *sacrifice* of his spare time. 3. the selling of something at a loss: He sold the house at a great *sacrifice* (far below its value).

sad sorrowful, mournful; causing sorrow: She was *sad* to lose her kitten. **sadden** make *sad*: We were all *saddened* by the bad news. **sadness** being *sad*: What is the cause of your *sadness*?

saddle (sad-dle) 1. a seat for a rider on a horse or other animal, or on a bicycle: He leapt into the *saddle* and was away at a gallop. 2. put a *saddle* on: Our horses are *saddled* and we are ready to go. 3. have hard work, great responsibility etc.: When my father died I was *saddled* with all his debts. **saddler** one who makes *saddles* and harness.

safari (sa-fa-ri) an expedition lasting several days for hunting or taking photographs of wild life.

safe 1. free from danger, unhurt: How I wish I were *safe* at home! 2. secure, not causing harm: Is this bridge *safe*?—The bathing is *safe* on this beach. 3. a steel or iron box in which valuables may be kept: The burglars had broken open the *safe*. **safety** being *safe*; a *safe* place: We do everything possible for the *safety* of our passengers.

saga 1. an old story about the deeds of gods and heroes, especially of the Danes and Northmen. 2. the story of a family told in a series of books: I have read all the volumes of 'The Forsyte *Saga*'.

sail 1. a canvas sheet spread out to catch the wind and make a boat move through the water: Our *sails* are spread to catch the wind. 2. a device with four arms fixed on the side of a windmill to catch the wind. 3. a voyage or excursion in a boat: We went for a *sail* on the river. 4. move forward over water: 'They *sailed* away for a year and a day' (Edward Lear). 5. set off on a sea voyage: We *sail* for Canada tomorrow. 6. control a boat or ship: He *sailed* his boat from Dover to Calais. **sailor** a member of a ship's crew: 'Home is the *sailor*, home from the sea' (Robert Louis Stevenson).

saint a person declared by the Church to be worthy of worship through the holiness of his life: Pilgrims visited the shrine of *Saint* Thomas à Becket at Canterbury. **saintly** very holy; very good: She is a person of *saintly* character.

sake reason, good: I'll help you for your father's *sake* (because he was my friend).—Keep out of mischief for your own *sake* (so that you will not be punished).

salad (sal-ad) a dish of uncooked green plants or other vegetables served cold with meat, eggs, cheese etc.: We had chicken *salad* for lunch. **salad dressing** a mixture of oil, vinegar, cream etc. to be eaten with *salad*. **fruit salad** a mixture of fruits, cut up and eaten cold.

salary (sal-a-ry) a fixed payment, usually monthly, for work done: He receives a good *salary* as a cashier in a bank.

sale 1. the exchange of money for goods: We made a profit on the *sale* of our car. 2. the offering of goods at prices that are lower than usual: Good bargains can be found at the January *sales*. 3. the selling of goods by auction: He buys furniture at all the local *sales*. **salesman, saleswoman** people who are employed to sell goods either in or out of a shop.

salient (sa-lient) 1. prominent; most important: He repeated the *salient* points of his argument. 2. a place in a battle front where a wedge has been driven into the enemy line.

saliva (sa-li-va) the liquid which is always present in the mouth, keeping it moist and helping to digest food.

sallow (sal-low) (of the human skin) pale yellow, unhealthy-looking: He developed a *sallow* complexion from living so long in Africa.

saloon (sa-loon) 1. a room in a hotel or a ship in which people may meet together, to dine. 2. a room set apart for a special purpose: I met him in the billiard *saloon*.– Every good public house has its *saloon* bar. **saloon car** a motor car with a solid roof seating four or more persons.

salt 1. a white substance obtained by mining or from sea water, and used to flavour and preserve foods: These potatoes need *salt*. 2. a chemical which contains an acid and a mineral: Epsom *salts* and Glaubers *salts* are well-known medicines. 3. an old sailor: The old *salt* had a store of wonderful tales. 4. put *salt* on: Have you *salted* the potatoes? 5. containing *salt*: We took with us a supply of *salt* beef.–He was ordered by the doctor to bathe regularly in *salt* water. **salty** containing *salt*; having the taste of *salt*.

saltpetre (salt-pe-tre) a white powder used in making gunpowder, in preserving food, as medicine and as a fertilizer.

salute (sa-lute) 1. a greeting between officers and men of the forces which consists in raising the right hand to the forehead and bringing it down to the side again. 2. a firing of guns to show respect and honour to a country or a person: The president's visit was honoured by the firing of a *salute* of twenty guns. 3. greet: He *saluted* her by raising his hat.

salvage (sal-vage) 1. save property from loss in a fire or some other disaster: Very little was *salvaged* from the floods. 2. the property saved: We were able to buy our equipment cheaply at a *salvage* sale. 3. waste material saved for use again: Every week old rags and newspapers are collected for *salvage*. 4. payment given to those who have saved property: The members of the crew each received a share of the *salvage* for bringing in the damaged vessel.

salvation (sal-va-tion) 1. saving, having been saved, especially from sin or its results: 'Salvation is far from the wicked' (Psalm 119). 2. that which saves somebody: The help given by his friends has been his *salvation*.

same 1. not another: I met you and your cousin on the *same* day.–When they were questioned they all made the *same* answer. 2. no different: It's all the *same* to me whether we go today or tomorrow. 3. in a similar way: Do you feel the *same* about it as I do?

sample (sam-ple) 1. one of a number of things intended to show what the rest are like: Our traveller goes out every day with his case of *samples*. 2. try, take a *sample* of: Would you like to *sample* my home-brewed beer?

sanction (sanc-tion) 1. permission to do something: I have the *sanction* of the author to produce the play. 2. the action of one or more states towards another, usually through stopping trade, to force it to fulfil some duty.

sanctuary (sanc-tu-a-ry) 1. a holy place, especially in a church, where people were formerly able to take refuge from arrest: This is the altar at which he claimed *sanctuary* from his pursuers. 2. a country to which people of other countries go for refuge: Great Britain has given *sanctuary* to refugees from all parts of the world.

sand 1. a large number of tiny fragments of rock as seen on the seashore: He took a handful of *sand* and let it drop between his fingers. 2. rub with *sand* to smooth or polish. **sands** large areas of *sand* on the seashore: We took the children to play on the *sands*. **sandpaper** tough paper with *sand* glued to it, used for smoothing rough surfaces.

sandal (san-dal) a kind of shoe consisting of a sole with thongs or straps to fasten it to the foot.

sandwich (sand-wich) 1. two or more slices of bread with meat, eggs, lettuce, tomato etc. between them: Do you like ham *sandwiches*? 2. crush between two persons: I was *sandwiched* between my two cousins and couldn't move.

sane healthy in mind; not mad. **sanity** being *sane*: We were all certain of his *sanity*.

sanguine (san-guine) hopeful, cheerful: My sister is rather *sanguine* in temperament.

sanitary (san-i-ta-ry) 1. having to do with health or conditions such as cleanliness which make for health: The *sanitary* inspector has ordered the disinfection of this building. 2. favourable to health: We would all like to work under *sanitary* conditions. **sanitation** measures, especially drainage, taken to protect health: We could not live in the house because of its poor *sanitation*.

sap 1. the liquid in a plant which takes food to all its parts: Rubber is made from the *sap* of a tree.—In spring the *sap* rises and plants begin to grow. 2. a tunnel made by soldiers to take them nearer to the enemy. 3. drain away the strength: His health has been *sapped* by overwork and late hours. **sapling** a young tree.

sarcasm (sar-casm) harsh and hurtful remarks, taunts: Nobody likes him because of his *sarcasm*. **sarcastic** using *sarcasm*: His *sarcastic* remarks were the cause of our quarrel.

sardine (sar-dine) a small fish which is caught and preserved in olive oil or tomato sauce: Would you like *sardines* for supper?

sari (sa-ri) a long piece of cotton or silk forming the outer garment of Hindu women, one end of which is worn over the head or shoulder.

sash 1. a long band of cloth or silk worn over the shoulder as part of a uniform, or round the waist for decoration. 2. a framework in which panes of glass are set and which can be made to move up and down as part of a window. **sashcord** the cord which moves on a pulley and raises or lowers the *sash*.

satchel (satch-el) a leather or canvas bag with a shoulder-strap used for carrying schoolbooks: 'The whining schoolboy with his *satchel* and shining morning face creeping like snail unwillingly to school' (Shakespeare, *As You Like It*).

satellite (sat-el-lite) 1. a small body or a moon which moves round a planet: The earth has one *satellite*, Mars two, Saturn nine and Jupiter twelve. 2. a country which is dominated and politically controlled by another more powerful one. 3. a man-made device, usually containing scientific instruments, put into orbit round the earth: The news is being relayed from the United States by *satellite*.

satin (sat-in) a material of silk or rayon, smooth and shiny on one side, used mainly for ribbons and dresses: Cinderella wore a dress of pink *satin* to the ball.

satire (sat-ire) a kind of writing or speaking which shows up the evil or foolishness in people by mocking or casting ridicule on them: '*Satire* should, like a polished razor, wound with a touch' (Lady Mary Wortley Montagu). **satirical** mocking: His answers are nearly always *satirical*. **satirist** a writer who uses *satire* as his method of attack.

satisfaction (sat-is-fac-tion) being contented; something that makes one contented: The news of your safety gave us all great *satisfaction*. **satisfactory** giving *satisfaction* or pleasure: Your last French exercise was highly *satisfactory*. **satisfy** give contentment or *satisfaction*: I am *satisfied* that you have told me the truth.– To *satisfy* his curiosity he looked into the cupboard.

saturate (sat-u-rate) 1. make or become wet: I had been out in the rain so long that I was completely *saturated*. 2. make one substance take in the greatest possible amount of another: This water is *saturated* with salt, and can dissolve no more.

Saturday (Sat-ur-day) the seventh and last day of the week; the Jewish Sabbath.

sauce a preparation, usually liquid, which can be eaten with food to give it an added flavour: Mint *sauce* is eaten with lamb and apple *sauce* with pork. **sauceboat** a vessel in which *sauce* is served at table. **saucer** a small, round shallow dish to hold a cup. **saucepan** a small pan for boiling or stewing. **saucy** impertinent, impudent: 'You will show yourself too *saucy* by asking for *sauce* or any dainty thing.' (Hannah Woolley, The Gentlewoman's Companion, 1675)

sauna (sau-na) a kind of steam bath, originally used by the people of Finland.

saunter (saun-ter) stroll, walk in a leisurely way: I saw him *sauntering* along the promenade.

sausage (sau-sage) chopped up meat mixed with seasoning, and sometimes with bread, packed into a special skin: Have you any pork *sausages* today? **sausage meat** chopped up meat used for making *sausages*. **sausage roll** cooked *sausage* with a covering of pastry.

savage 1. wild, rugged: To reach our goal we had to cross a *savage* wilderness. 2. uncivilized: David Livingstone journeyed among the *savage* tribes of central Africa. 3. fierce, wild: The *savage* beasts of the jungle came looking for their prey. 4. a primitive, uncivilized person: The *savages* in this part of the world live by hunting and fishing. 5. be attacked, bitten, trampled on etc.: The farmer was *savaged* by an angry alsatian. **savagery** being *savage*, *savage* behaviour: The attack on unarmed civilians was an act of the utmost *savagery*.

save 1. rescue from loss, danger, injury or death: I was *saved* from drowning by a life guard. 2. put aside for use at a later time: We are *saving* our money for a holiday in France. 3. avoid wasting: I *save* time by cycling to work. 4. except: 'None shall be mistress, *save* I alone' (Shakespeare, *Twelfth Night*). **saviour** a person who rescues another. **The Saviour** Jesus Christ.

savour (sa-vour) 1. taste, flavour: Do you like the *savour* of herbs in the sauce? 2. taste and enjoy: He *savoured* the wine and pronounced it excellent. 3. seem to have present in it: Your remark *savours* of impudence. **savoury** tasting or smelling good, with a salty, not a sweet taste.

saw *sawed*, *sawn* 1. a tool for cutting, with a thin metal blade containing a row of sharp teeth: He cut branches off the tree with a *saw*. 2. use a *saw*: He *sawed* two branches off the tree. 3. move backwards and forwards: He was *sawing* away at his fiddle. 4. an old or wise saying: Our preacher has an old *saw* for almost every occasion. **sawdust** tiny bits of wood which fall off when *sawing*. **sawmill** a mill where wood is cut by mechanically operated *saws*. **sawyer** a person employed to *saw* wood.

saxophone (sax-o-phone) a musical wind instrument made of brass, with keys on which the fingers are pressed to select the notes.

say *said* 1. utter words: What did you *say*?— I *said* I was ready to go. 2. give an opinion: What would you *say* this bicycle cost? 3. advise, command: Do as I *say* and don't argue. 4. repeat: We shall now *say* the Lord's Prayer. 5. opinion: Let every man have his *say*. **saying** a well-known remark or proverb: 'Live and let live' is a *saying* worth remembering.

scab the crust which forms over a sore when it is healing: When the wound has healed the *scab* drops off.

scabbard (scab-bard) the case into which the blade of a sword or dagger is put for safety: He drew his sword from its *scabbard*.

scaffold (scaf-fold) 1. a kind of frame carrying a platform, put up against walls for builders and painters to work on. 2. a platform on which executions took place. **scaffolding** the framework of a *scaffold*: Three men were injured when the *scaffolding* gave way.

scald 1. hurt through burning with hot liquid or steam: She *scalded* her leg with boiling water from the kettle. 2. clean by the use of boiling water or steam: You ought to *scald* this bottle before using it. 3. a burn caused by hot liquid or steam: He received a nasty *scald* through a leaking steampipe.

scale 1. one of the thin, flat, hard plates that covers the skin of certain fishes and reptiles: Scrape the *scales* off the fish before you cook it. 2. small flakes of skin that come loose and fall off. 3. marks at regular distances for measuring: If we consult the *scale* on a thermometer we can find the temperature of the room. 4. the proportion between the small measurements on a map or diagram and the real distances: On the map before us we can see the whole district on a small *scale*. 5. the size or extent: At present we are growing vegetables on a very small *scale*. 6. in music, notes going up or down in order: My lesson this week is to practise the *scale* of G. 7. one of the pans of a balance or weighing machine: He used a pair of *scales* to weigh the sugar. 8. scrape *scales* from: We *scale* the fish before we cook it. 9. drop off in *scales*: Do you see the plaster *scaling* off the wall? 10. climb a wall, a hill, cliff etc.

scallop (scal-lop) 1. a kind of shellfish which has grooves on its shell: *Scallops* are good to eat. 2. a curved edging put on cloth for ornament: Her dress had a sleeve with *scallops* at the wrist.

scalp 1. the skin and hair of the head: The Indians of North America used to take the *scalps* of their enemies as trophies of victory. 2. take an enemy's *scalp*.

scalpel (scal-pel) a small light knife used by surgeons when performing operations.

scamp 1. a worthless rascal. 2. a mischievous person. 3. do work carelessly: The painting of this door has been badly *scamped*.

scamper (scam-per) run quickly, hastily: The kittens *scampered* off among the bushes.

scan 1. look very carefully at something: The captain *scanned* the horizon for signs of an enemy vessel. 2. look quickly over something: I just have time to *scan* the morning paper before hurrying off to work.

scandal (scan-dal) 1. disgraceful behaviour; the offence caused by it: The man's treatment of his children was a *scandal*. 2. careless or harmful gossip: Never listen to *scandal*. **scandalous** shocking: His *scandalous* behaviour was reported in the newspapers.

scant very little: He paid *scant* attention to the warnings I gave him. **scanty** very small in size, amount, quantity etc.: The news we have so far received is *scanty*.

scapegoat (scape-goat) one who is made to bear the blame for the misdeeds of others.

scar 1. a mark remaining after a wound or damage: The fall left a long *scar* on his forehead. 2. make a *scar* or *scars* on: The polished table was badly *scarred* with burns.

scarce 1. not enough for the need or the demand: Petrol is *scarce* in time of war. 2. rarely seen or met with: In this collection there are many *scarce* books. **scarcity** smallness of supply: The bad harvest has caused a *scarcity* of apples this year. **scarcely** not quite, hardly: I am so lame I can *scarcely* walk.

scare 1. make afraid, frighten: She was *scared* by the sound of footsteps on the stairs. 2. drive away: Small boys were *scaring* away the birds. 3. a sudden fright; a time when many people become afraid: You gave me a *scare*. **scarecrow** an object dressed in old clothes, set up to imitate the figure of a man, to *scare* away birds.

scarf *scarves* a long strip of material worn round the neck or over the head for warmth or decoration.

scatter (scat-ter) 1. send or throw in many directions: She *scattered* fragments of bread on the lawn. 2. go in many directions: The crowd *scattered* as soon as they heard the alarm. **scattered** set apart from each other: Small villages were *scattered* about the valley.

scavenger (scav-en-ger) a creature that feeds on the remains of animals, birds or insects: Vultures are the *scavengers* of the desert.

scene 1. the place where something happened: London is the *scene* of many of Dickens' novels. 2. something which happens: There were *scenes* of great rejoicing when our football team won the cup. 3. an outbreak of anger in front of others: I know you are disappointed, but there's no need to make a *scene*. 4. a view spread out before the eye: We were charmed by the *scene* of fields and trees in autumn. 5. part of a play; a division of one of its acts: We will now rehearse Act 5, *scene* 1 of *The Tempest*. **scenery** 1. the appearance of a place or a landscape: Some of the finest *scenery* in England is to be found in the Lake District. 2. the hangings, painted woodwork etc., on a stage: The members of the cast have made and painted all the *scenery*.

scent 1. smell: I love the *scent* of roses. 2. a perfume: She was given a bottle of *scent* for her birthday. 3. the smell left behind by animals, which can be followed by certain dogs: The hounds followed the *scent* of the hare. 4. the way to a discovery: The detectives are now hot on the *scent* of the thief. 5. give a *scent* to: The air was *scented* with honeysuckle.

sceptre (scep-tre) a rod or wand held in the hand as a symbol of power by a king or ruler.

schedule (sched-ule) 1. a list or statement giving the time allowed for each part of a process, a journey etc.: This *schedule* allows us four weeks to finish the work. 2. make plans for certain dates and times: The train is *scheduled* to arrive at 10.30.

scheme 1. a plan, either secret or not secret: We have a *scheme* to get him out of prison.—This is a *scheme* for constructing the new road. 2. make a plan: The two men were *scheming* to break into the food store.

schnorkel (schnor-kel–also **snorkel**) 1. a device on a submarine which takes in and expels air so that the submarine can remain under water for long periods. 2. a tube which enables a person swimming under water to breathe and thus remain below the surface for long periods.

scholar 1. a learned person: He is a famous Greek *scholar*. 2. a student or pupil: How many *scholars* are there in your class? 3. a student who because of merit is granted money to enable him to go on with his studies. **scholarship** 1. learning or knowledge. 2. a regular sum of money granted to enable a person to continue his studies: He has won a *scholarship* to Cambridge University.

school 1. a place in which children are given education: My brother goes to a comprehensive *school*. 2. a period in which teaching is given: I will see you after *school*.—There will be no *school* today. 3. all the students or pupils attending a *school*: The headmaster spoke to the whole *school* about punctuality. 4. a department of a college or university: He is head of the medical *school*. 5. a large number of fish, whales etc. swimming and feeding together. 6. teach or train: My dog has been *schooled* to follow at my heels. **schooling** education, teaching: He has had very little *schooling* but he reads well. **schoolfellow, schoolmate** a pupil who goes to the same *school* at the same time as another.

science (sci-ence) knowledge obtained by examining and seeing how things work: Chemistry, physics and astronomy are *sciences*. **science fiction** stories dealing with real or imagined discoveries in *science*, especially in space travel. **scientific** having to do with *science*: The professor's laboratory was full of *scientific* instruments. **scientist** an expert in any of the branches of *science*.

scissors (scis-sors) a cutting instrument consisting of two blades joined at a point so that they can be brought together for cutting.

scoff 1. mock: They *scoffed* at my efforts to ride a bicycle. 2. ridicule: 'I have too long borne your bitter *scoffs*' (Shakespeare, *Richard III*).

scold find fault with, blame angrily: He was *scolded* for coming late to school. **scolding** a severe reprimand: My father gave me a *scolding* for staying out late at night.

scoop 1. a small deep shovel with a short handle for ladling flour, sugar etc. 2. the large bucket at the end of a mechanical shovel used to pick up earth etc.: A huge *scoop* was used to dig the foundations of the building. 3. use a *scoop*, make a hole: The shovel *scooped* out a huge hole in the ground.

scooter (scoo-ter) 1. a child's toy steered by a handlebar, with two small wheels and a board between them on which one foot is placed while the other pushes on the ground to move it. 2. (or **motor-scooter**) a motor bicycle with small wheels and a low seat.

scope 1. the opportunity to act or work freely: His position as manager offers full *scope* for his abilities. 2. power, province: Dealing with complaints from customers is outside my *scope*.

scorch 1. mark by burning: The iron was too hot and *scorched* the cloth. 2. become marked by heat, the sun etc.: We sat down on the *scorched* grass to rest.

score 1. a record of points made by competitors in a game: The final *score* was 2 goals to 1. 2. a copy of the music showing all the vocal and instrumental parts: When I go to a concert I always take the *score* with me. 3. twenty: 'The days of our years are three*score* years and ten' (Psalm 90). 4. win points in a game: The centre forward *scored* two goals. 5. keep a record of points gained (especially in cricket): We must have somebody to *score*. 6. mark with cuts, lines or scratches. 7. make a *score* for an orchestra or group: We are *scoring* this waltz for a string orchestra. **scorer** a person who keeps the *score* in a game, a person who *scores* points or goals: He is the best goal *scorer* in our team.

scorn 1. contempt, a feeling that something is not worthy of respect: We treated his explanation with the *scorn* it deserved. 2. look down on or feel that somebody or something is unworthy: He *scorned* my advice. **scornful** showing *scorn*: Her *scornful* glance hurt his feelings.

scoundrel (scoun-drel) a villain, a wicked person: This *scoundrel* stole my watch.

scour 1. clean dirt, grease or rust off by rubbing: The pan was so dirty it had to be *scoured*. 2. look everywhere: The police *scoured* the whole countryside to find the missing girl.

scout 1. a soldier, a warship or an aeroplane sent out to reconnoitre or discover the enemy's position and movements. 2. a member of a road patrol belonging to an organization whose work is to help motorists: We telephoned the Automobile Association and a *scout* came to our assistance. 3. act as a *scout*: I was *scouting* around for people with a knowledge of machinery. **boy scout** a member of the organization for boys founded by Baden Powell in 1908. **scoutmaster** an officer who leads a troop of boy *scouts*.

scowl 1. frown, look angry and bad-tempered: Why are you *scowling* at me? 2. a frown: 'I didn't do it,' he said with an angry *scowl*.

scramble (scram-ble) 1. make one's way in a hurry by using hands and feet, over rough ground: We had to *scramble* over large rocks. 2. struggle with others to get things: The children *scrambled* in the street for sweets. 3. cook eggs in a pan by mixing them with butter, milk etc.: I'll have *scrambled* eggs on toast, please. 4. a struggle: There was a *scramble* to get the best seats.

scrap 1. bits of paper, things no longer wanted: He copied down the address on a *scrap* of paper. 2. food left over after meals: The *scraps* were given to the dog. 3. throw away as useless, set aside to be broken up: I've *scrapped* my old typewriter and bought a new one. **scrapbook** a book in which photographs, newspaper cuttings etc. are pasted.

scrape 1. make clean by drawing a sharp instrument over a surface: Before we could decorate the room we had to *scrape* off the old paint. 2. hurt or damage by *scraping*: He fell and *scraped* the skin off his elbow. 3. rub across something: The branches *scraping* across the window prevented me from sleeping. 4. put together by effort or with difficulty: We have managed to *scrape* together enough money to buy a radio. 5. a *scraping* sound: We heard the *scrape* of the shovel as he cleared away the snow. 6. something that is *scraped*: Let me see that *scrape* on your leg. 7. a difficult situation: I won't help you if you get into any more *scrapes*.

scratch 1. mark by rubbing, making lines with something sharp or rough: Who *scratched* the paint off this door? 2. hurt oneself through being *scratched*: His legs were badly *scratched* by thorns. 3. scrape with claws, fingernails or anything else: The cow was *scratching* itself against a post. 4. use nails or claws for digging: The hens were *scratching* in the farmyard. 5. remove a name from a list: The horse was *scratched* from the race. 6. a mark or sound produced by *scratching*: We heard a *scratch* at the door.

scrawl 1. write carelessly or poorly: He *scrawled* his name on the blackboard. 2. careless or poor writing: 'I refuse to give a mark for such a *scrawl*,' said the teacher.

scream 1. utter a loud, sharp cry: 'Leave me alone,' she *screamed*. 2. a loud, sharp cry: I heard a sudden *scream* of pain.

screech 1. make a harsh, shrill cry or noise: Parrots were *screeching* in the dense forest. 2. a harsh shrill cry or noise: With a *screech* of the brakes the car came to a stop.

screen 1. anything that can be used to protect or hide: There was a folding *screen* in front of the door to keep out the draughts. 2. white or silver material stretched on a frame on which slides or films can be projected. 3. the cinema: My uncle writes plays for the *screen*. 4. a sieve through which stones, grain or sand can be sieved. 5. hide, shelter: The house is *screened* from view by an avenue of trees. 6. show on a *screen*; make a film of: I hear they are *screening* the life of Captain Scott.

screw 1. a metal peg or nail with a groove in the head and a spiral ridge called a thread which can be driven into wood with a *screwdriver*. 2. the propeller of a ship or an aeroplane: A twin-*screw* ship has two *screws* or propellers revolving in opposite directions. 3. fasten with *screws*: He *screwed* down the lid of the box. 4. twist, alter the shape; force: She *screwed* up the paper and threw it in the fire.–He *screwed* up his courage and plunged into the icy water. **screwdriver** a tool fitting into the head of a *screw* to drive it in or take it out by turning.

scribble (scrib-ble) scrawl, write badly and carelessly: He *scribbled* his name on the back of the box.

script 1. handwriting, printing in imitation of handwriting: I received a circular letter printed in *script*. 2. the text of a play given to the cast for rehearsal: The prompter always has his *script* ready. **script-writer** a person who writes *scripts* for radio, television, etc. **scriptures** the sacred books of various religions. **The Holy Scriptures** the Bible.

scroll a roll of paper or parchment especially one on which there is writing: In ancient times all books were written on *scrolls*.

scrub 1. rub hard with a brush, using soap and water: This paint needs *scrubbing* to clean off the dirt. 2. land covered with low trees and shrubs: We travelled for days through miles of waterless *scrub*.

scruff the back of the neck: He took the offender by the *scruff* of the neck and threw him out.

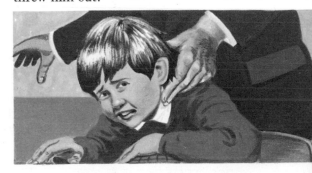

scrutiny (scru-ti-ny) 1. very close and detailed examination: The taxi-driver was subjected to a long *scrutiny*. 2. a re-count of votes after an election: 'I demand a *scrutiny*' said the defeated candidate. **scrutineer** a person who sees that election papers are properly counted. **scrutinize** examine in great detail.

scuffle (scuf-fle) 1. a confused struggle or fight: There were several *scuffles* between the supporters of the two teams. 2. take part in a *scuffle*: They *scuffled* until the police dispersed them.

scullery (scul-le-ry) a small room where the dirty work of the kitchen (such as washing up the dishes) is done.

sculpture (sculp-ture) 1. the art of forming figures in wood, stone, marble, granite, clay, plastics etc.: I am taking a course in *sculpture* at the art school. 2. a single piece of such work: The room was filled with fine *sculptures*. 3. make *sculptures*, decorate in *sculpture*: The columns of the temple are *sculptured* in marble.

scum 1. a layer of froth or unwanted matter which settles on the top of liquids: The pond was covered with green *scum*. 2. worthless, or seemingly worthless people: 'Ours (our army) is composed of the *scum* of the earth' (The Duke of Wellington, 4th November, 1831).

scurry (scur-ry) 1. go or move quickly and in haste: The mouse *scurried* behind the cupboard. 2. a *scurrying* rush: We heard the *scurry* of little feet on the stairs.

scurvy (scur-vy) 1. a disease brought about by a shortage of vitamin C causing the gums to swell and bleed, spots to appear on the skin and a feeling of weakness. 2. mean, dishonest: That was a *scurvy* trick to play on a little child.

scuttle (scut-tle) 1. scurry away. 2. make holes in the bottom or sides of a ship to sink it: Rather than be captured, the captain *scuttled* his ship. 3. a box or any container for holding coal.

scythe 1. a tool with a long curved blade fastened to a handle, for mowing grass etc.: The farm labourer sharpened his *scythe* with a stone. 2. cut down with a *scythe*.

sea 1. the salt waters that cover nearly three-quarters of the earth's surface, each part having its own name: Oil has been found under the North *Sea*.–The Caspian *Sea* is the largest salt-water lake in the world. 2. the state of the *sea*: There's a stormy *sea* running this morning. 3. a large quantity or number: He looked out on a *sea* of faces. **seasick** sick from the motion of the *sea*.

seal 1. a furry marine mammal with flippers, mainly found in cold waters in both the northern and southern hemispheres: *Seals* return to land to give birth to their young. 2. a piece of metal on which there is a design which can be stamped on wax. 3. the piece of wax or other material with the design stamped on it as proof that a document is genuine: King John set his *seal* to the Magna Carta in 1215. 4. put a *seal* on; close tightly: The police *sealed* the room so that its contents could be examined later. **sealed orders** instructions given to an officer which must not be opened until a given time or place. **sealing-wax** wax used for *sealing* letters or documents.

seam 1. a line where two pieces of material are sewn together: These *seams* are coming undone. 2. a layer of coal or another mineral between layers of different rock: A thick *seam* of coal has been found in Yorkshire. **seamstress** (or **sempstress**) a woman who earns her living by sewing.

search 1. look carefully in order to find: We *searched* the room for the missing money. 2. the act of *searching*: All day long the *search* went on. **searchlight** a powerful light which can throw a beam in any direction.

season (sea-son) 1. one of the four divisions of the year–spring, summer, autumn and winter. 2. the time of the year when something is at its best or is done: We are now at the beginning of the football *season*. 3. flavour food by adding spices or sauces: He does not like highly-*seasoned* dishes. **in season** ripe, ready for use: Cherries are *in season* in spring. **seasoning** substances added to food to give it an appetizing flavour.

seat 1. something used for sitting on: Let me find you a *seat*. 2. the part of the chair etc. on which one sits. 3. the part of the body or of a garment on which one sits: How did you tear the *seat* of your trousers? 4. a large house, particularly one in the country; a place where something is carried on: Westminster is the *seat* of the British government. 5. have *seats* for: This hall *seats* a thousand people. 6. sit down: Please be *seated*.

secede (se-cede) withdraw from an alliance or an association: *Two states which disagreed with the rest seceded from the alliance.* **secession** act of *seceding*: *Their secession was deeply regretted.*

second (sec-ond) 1. one of the sixty parts of a minute: *The clap of thunder lasted ten seconds.* 2. next after the first in order, place, time, rank etc.: *February is the second month of the year.* 3. another: *May I have a second helping please?* 4. like one which has gone before: *He thinks he's a second Napoleon.* 5. one who helps a boxer or wrestler between rounds: *He would not listen to the advice of his second.* 6. one who supports a person fighting a duel. 7. speak in a meeting in support of a motion: *Mr Jones proposed the vote of thanks and Mr Smith seconded it.* **secondary** coming after the first in time, order, importance etc.: *Children go first to a primary and then to a secondary school.* **second-hand** used, not new: *We bought an excellent second-hand car.*

secret (se-cret) 1. something not to be told to any other person: *Can you keep a secret?* 2. a reason not generally known: *What is the secret of his success?* 3. kept from others: *This letter contains secret information.* 4. quiet, not well known: *He took us to a secret place in the woods.* **secrecy** being *secret*, able to keep *secrets*: *This is an affair of the utmost secrecy.* **secrete** put in a *secret* place: *The dog secretes his bones in a corner of the garden.* **secretive** in the habit of keeping *secrets*, not revealing one's thoughts: *Why are you so secretive about your actions?*

secretary (sec-re-tary) 1. a person who deals with correspondence, keeps records etc. for a business, a person or an organization: *Please telephone my secretary if you wish to see me.* 2. a high official of an organization or a government: *The Secretary of the Trades Union Congress is meeting the Secretary of State for Home Affairs this morning.* **secretarial** having to do with *secretaries*: *The college teaches all aspects of secretarial work.*

section (sec-tion) 1. a part cut off, one of the parts into which something may be divided: *How many sections are there in this catalogue?* 2. one of the parts which, put together, make a whole: *We are building the garden hut by bolting together the sections.* 3. a division or part of a body of people (soldiers, police etc.). **sectional** supplied in *sections*: *We have bought a sectional greenhouse and are erecting it ourselves.*

sector (sec-tor) part of a circle cut off by two lines drawn from the centre to the circumference.

secure (se-cure) 1. free from fear, safe: *Once all the doors had been locked we felt secure.* 2. fastened: *Not likely to fall, be moved etc.: All the windows are secure.* 3. sure, certain: *Our victory is secure.* 4. make *secure* or fast: *A great river barrier is to be erected to secure London against floods.* 5. get something: *I have secured a ticket for the Cup Final at Wembley.*

security (se-cur-i-ty) 1. freedom from fear or danger: *For people to be happy they must live in security.* 2. something of value handed over as a guarantee that a debt will be paid or some other obligation carried out: *If you lend me this money you may have my jewellery as security.*

sedative (sed-a-tive) a medicine which calms or soothes: *The patient was given a sedative after the accident.* **sedation** being under the influence of a *sedative*: *The patient remained under sedation for four hours.*

sedition (se-di-tion) words, writings or actions intended to cause discontent or rebellion against a government: *After his fiery speech he was imprisoned for sedition.* **seditious** of the nature of *sedition*: *Their leader was arrested for circulating seditious pamphlets.*

285

see, *saw, seen* 1. have or use the power of sight: You can *see* a long way from the attic window. 2. notice, observe: I *saw* him walking down the street. 3. understand: I don't *see* what you're laughing about. 4. have experience or knowledge: I *saw* a good deal during my days in the army. 5. visit, be visited: I went to *see* the doctor but he was too busy to *see* me. 6. accompany: Let me *see* you to the bus. 7. allow: I can't *see* an animal suffer and do nothing. 8. find out: Go and *see* who is knocking. 9. make sure, attend to: Please *see* that all your things are put away.

seed 1. that part of a plant from which another plant will grow. 2. sow with *seed*: There are bare patches in the lawn which need *seeding*. 3. remove *seed* from: I have bought a bag of *seeded* raisins. 4. produce *seed*: Most flowers bloom in spring and *seed* in summer and autumn. **seedling** a young plant grown from *seed*.

seek *sought* 1. look for. 2. ask for: You ought to *seek* your teacher's advice.

seem appear to: There *seems* to be a mistake here.

seep leak slowly: Water was *seeping* through the roof of the hut.

see-saw a children's game played on a plank balanced at the middle so that the ends rise and fall.

segment (seg-ment) 1. a part cut off from a circle by a straight line. 2. a part into which something divides naturally: Would you like a *segment* of this orange?

segregate (seg-re-gate) set apart from the main body: The doctor said we must *segregate* those children who had measles.

seize 1. take hold of suddenly: The alarm was sounded and we all *seized* our weapons. 2. grasp with the mind: The author *seized* upon the idea for a book suggested by his son. 3. take possession of: The smuggled goods were *seized* by the customs officers. **seizure** 1. *seizing*: Our officers have reported the *seizure* of a thousand gold watches. 2. a sudden attack of illness: He suffered a brain *seizure* and is unable to move.

seldom (sel-dom) not often: I *seldom* go to the cinema.

select (se-lect) choose in preference to another: He *selected* two ripe apples out of the basket. **selection** choosing; things chosen: Were you present at the *selection* of the team?—This is a fine *selection* of brooches. **selector** a person who chooses: The *selectors* of the cricket team met this morning.

selfish thinking more of one*self* than of others: It would be *selfish* not to pay your share of the expenses.

sell *sold* 1. exchange for money: I have *sold* my camera. 2. keep things to *sell*: We *sell* all kinds of leather goods. 3. be *sold*: Cold drinks *sell* well in this hot weather.

semaphore (sem-a-phore) a means of signalling by holding flags in both hands, different letters of the alphabet being shown by the positions in which flags are held at arm's length.

semi- (sem-i-) a prefix meaning half, as *semi*circle, *semi*conscious, *semi*skilled. **semicolon** (;) a punctuation mark indicating a rather greater separation between the parts of a sentence than that shown by a comma.

senate (sen-ate) 1. the most important law-making body in ancient Rome. 2. one of the legislative bodies, usually the smaller one, known as the Upper House, which makes laws in some countries, as in the United States, France, and Italy. 3. the ruling body in some universities. **senator** a member of the *senate* of a country.

send *sent* cause or order to go or be carried: The king *sent* a messenger to ask for peace.

senior (se-nior) 1. older in years: He is my *senior* by five years. 2. of higher rank: You must consult your *senior* officer. 3. (after a person's name) the elder of two persons in a family bearing the same name, usually abbreviated to *snr.*: John Thompson *snr.* sends you his good wishes.

sensation (sen-sa-tion) 1. feeling: I felt a *sensation* of warmth as I opened the door. 2. a state of excitement felt by a large number of people: The news of the burglary caused a great *sensation*. **sensational** causing a *sensation*, giving news in a way which causes a *sensation*: 'Sensational drop in house prices' (newspaper headline).

sense 1. one of the five powers of sight, hearing, touch, taste or smell by which we are conscious of ourselves and all around us: Dogs have a keen *sense* of smell. 2. having and using one's *senses*; being sane: It's time he came to his *senses* and stopped behaving foolishly. 3. feeling, being conscious of: Have you no *sense* of shame? 4. meaning: I can read the poem but I can't understand the *sense*. **sensible** showing good *sense*, conscious of: Every *sensible* person agrees with you. **senseless** foolish; unconscious: It was *senseless* to go without an umbrella.—He fell *senseless* to the ground.

sensitive (sen-si-tive) 1. quick to feel or be conscious of things: My eyes are very *sensitive* to light. 2. easily hurt or offended: You are far too *sensitive* about your appearance.

sentence (sen-tence) 1. a group of words which make a statement or ask a question:

The *sentences* in the last paragraph are far too long. 2. a decision by a judge or magistrate on the punishment to be given to an offender: Everybody thought the *sentence* of two years was light. 3. give punishment: The thief was *sentenced* to a year's imprisonment.

sentiment (sen-ti-ment) a feeling; all one feels about a person, or a subject: Because of family *sentiment* I try and spend Christmas with my parents. **sentimental** affecting the feelings; easily moved, showing *sentiment* or tender feeling: She spends her spare time reading *sentimental* novels.

sentry (sen-try) a soldier stationed at a place to keep guard: 'Who goes there?' called the *sentry*. **sentry-go** the duty performed by a *sentry* walking his beat.

separate (sép-a-rate) not joined together: This story is told in ten *separate* instalments. **separate** (sep-a-ráte) make or become *separate*: This machine *separates* the cream from the milk. **separation** separating, being *separate*: We met again after a *separation* of three years. **separator** a machine used for *separating* cream from milk.

September (Sep-tem-ber) the ninth month of the year.

septic (sep-tic) caused by infection from disease germs: The wound was not cleaned and turned *septic*.

sequel (se-quel) 1. an event which follows another: The *sequel* of my visit was an invitation to dinner the following night. 2. a novel which continues the story of a previous novel: Have you read the *sequel* to *The Prisoner of Zenda*? **sequence** following on: A *sequence* of bad harvests caused a terrible famine.

serenade (ser-e-nade) 1. the performance of a piece of music especially a love song, in the open air at night. 2. a composition: He sang a *serenade* under her window. 3. perform a *serenade*: Every night he *serenades* her under her balcony.

serene (se-rene) 1. calm, clear: We have had a week's *serene* weather. 2. peaceful, happy: He lived to a *serene* old age. **serenity** being *serene*: I love the *serenity* of this remote valley.

sergeant (ser-geant) 1. non-commissioned officer in the army ranking above a corporal. 2. a police officer ranking between a constable and an inspector. **sergeant-major** an officer ranking above a *sergeant*; a non-commissioned officer of the highest rank.

series (ser-ies) 1. a number of events happening after each other and all having to do with each other: This month we have had a *series* of rainy days. 2. a set of articles issued at the same time: We are issuing a new *series* of books on great writers. **serial** anything published or broadcast in instalments at regular intervals: Read the first instalment of the new *serial*.

serious (se-ri-ous) 1. of solemn character or appearance: Don't look so *serious*. 2. important: Now we come to the *serious* question of your career. 3. bringing possible danger: Pneumonia is a *serious* illness. 4. earnest: 'A *serious* worker' (school report).

sermon (ser-mon) 1. an address or speech given from a pulpit in church on a religious subject. 2. a serious talk: The headmaster gave us a *sermon* on being punctual.

serpent (ser-pent) 1. a snake. 2. a sly, crafty person: 'He is a very *serpent* in my way' (Shakespeare, *King John*).

serum (se-rum) 1. the thin liquid part of the blood. 2. liquid taken from that part of the blood of an animal which has had a certain disease and which, when injected into a human being, may prevent him from getting it.

serve 1. do work for wages: I *served* as a head waiter. 2. do duty: He *served* under Montgomery in the desert. 3. wait on: Is anybody *serving* at this counter? 4. fulfil a need: This screwdriver will *serve* my purpose. 5. spend time: I *served* five years in the Life Guards. 6. (tennis) start play by striking a ball over the net: It's my turn to *serve*. **servant** one who *serves* in any way: He is a civil *servant* (a paid *servant* in a government department).– Domestic *servants* (*servants* in households) are difficult to find.

service (serv-ice) 1. being a servant: He has been in our *service* since leaving school. 2. a department of government: The postal *service* is very good in this town. 3. help: How can I be of *service* to you? 4. plates, dishes etc. for use at table: How much is this dinner *service*? 5. a religious ceremony: We go to Communion *service* every Sunday morning. 6. the act of *serving* in tennis: He does not play well but he has a very good *service*. 7. the keeping of an apparatus in working order: My car needs a *service* this week. **serviceable** giving good *service*: This is a good, *serviceable* lawn mower.

session (ses-sion) 1. a meeting of a court, of Parliament or a conference: The Archbishop of Canterbury spoke during the afternoon *session*. 2. a university term: During the spring *session* we shall be doing most of our experiments.

set 1. go down (of the sun, moon and stars): At what time does the sun *set* today? 2. put something into a certain state or condition: *Set* your watch before we go. 3. cause somebody to do a thing: I will *set* you to work peeling potatoes. 4. put something in a place where it will grow, work, do what is wanted: I have seen a mouse; we must *set* a trap. 5. fit music to words: This poem was *set* to music by Vaughan Williams. 6. become firm or solid: Don't step on the concrete until it has *set*. 7. a number of things grouped together: In the glass case we saw a beautiful *set* of chessmen. 8. an apparatus for receiving radio or television programmes: There is no sound at all; there must be something wrong with the *set*.

settle (set-tle) 1. go and live in another place: Many Frenchmen *settled* in Canada. 2. come to rest on: The butterfly *settled* on a cabbage leaf. 3. become or make calm: Don't go out until the wind has *settled*. 4. sink or cause to sink: The house had been left empty and dust had *settled* everywhere. 5. decide on, make an agreement: We have *settled* our differences and are friends again. 6. pay: I have a number of accounts to *settle* before the end of the month. 7. put in order: I want to *settle* all my affairs before I leave England. **settler** a person who has *settled* in a new land to develop it: My ancestors were among the first *settlers* in New Zealand.

settlement (set-tle-ment) 1. the settling of a debt, quarrel etc.: After the *settlement* of the strike the men went back to work. 2. a group of people settled in a new colony: At first the small *settlement* had difficulty finding water supplies.

seven (sev-en) the number between 6 and 8: There are *seven* days in a week. **seventeen** 7 added to 10 = 17. **seventy** 7 multiplied by 10 = 70: My grandfather is *seventy* years old.

several (sev-er-al) being more than two or three but not many: I called on him *several* times but he was not at home.

severe (se-vere) 1. violent: I have a *severe* headache. 2. strict, stern: He will work better if you are not too *severe* with him. 3. plain, without decoration: Your dress is far too *severe* to wear at a Christmas party. **severity** being *severe*: His father punished him with his usual *severity*.

sew (rhymes with *so*) *sewed*, *sewn* fasten cloth, leather etc. by making stitches with needle and thread: Will you please *sew* a button on my trousers? – We found the notes *sewn* up in a canvas bag.

sewer (sew-er) an underground drain made of wide pipes which carries waste away from houses and factories: A *sewer* is being dug to serve the new housing estate. **sewage** waste material from houses etc. which flows through the *sewers*. **sewage farm** a place where *sewage* is treated with chemicals and made into fertilizer.

sex being male or female: We shall be able to tell the *sex* of the chick after a few days.

sexton (sex-ton) a man who is charged with taking care of the church, its contents, and the graveyard, ringing the bell, grave-digging etc.

shabby (shab-by) 1. very much worn: He wore a *shabby* pair of trousers. 2. dressed in *shabby* clothes. 3. unfair, mean: He played a *shabby* trick in leaving me to pay the bill.

shack a small roughly built house: The old man lived in a *shack* in the woods.

shackle (shack-le) 1. a ring of iron for fastening the wrist or the ankle, usually connected by a chain to the floor or wall: The prisoner was unable to walk because of the heavy *shackles* he wore. 2. put *shackles* on: He was *shackled* and flung into a dark dungeon.

shade 1. partial darkness caused by cutting off the direct rays of light: It's cooler in the *shade*. 2. a different degree of colour: The fields were in all *shades* of green. 3. something to shield or partly cover: Long John Silver wore a black eye-*shade*. 4. cut off the direct rays of light from: This tree will *shade* us from the hot sun. 5. darken: He *shaded* the drawing with a pencil. **shading** shadow put on a drawing to give light and *shade*. **shady** giving *shade* from the sun: It is cooler on the *shady* side of the street.

shadow (shad-ow) 1. an area of shade: We did not see him standing in the *shadow* of the wall. 2. the shape thrown on the ground, a wall etc. by the cutting off of rays of light: 'I have a little *shadow* that goes in and out with me' (Robert Louis Stevenson). 3. the slightest trace: There is not a *shadow* of doubt about it. 4. darken by *shadows*: Clouds *shadowed* the whole scene. 5. follow a person to watch his movements: He was *shadowed* all day by detectives.

shaft 1. a long pole or rod forming the main part of a spear, lance or arrow. 2. a ray or beam: A *shaft* of sunlight fell on the trees. 3. the handle of an axe, hammer or other tool of the same kind: He seized the hammer by the *shaft*. 4. one of the bars of wood between which the horse is harnessed to pull a cart: We backed the mare into the *shafts*. 5. a long narrow space, usually vertical, to contain a lift in a building, or the cage in which miners descend into a mine: The lift was stuck in the *shaft* for more than an hour.

shaggy (shag-gy) rough and coarse: He stroked the dog's *shaggy* coat.

shake *shook*, *shaken* 1. move quickly up and down or from side to side: He *shook* the sand out of his shoes. 2. become or make weaker: The earthquake has *shaken* the foundations of the houses. 3. *shaking*, being *shaken*: If he doesn't wake up, give him a *shake*. 4. a glass of milk with flavour added and *shaken*: I'll have a milk *shake*. **shaky** weak, unreliable, unsafe: The legs of this chair are very *shaky*.

shallow (shal-low) not deep: We cannot sail this boat in *shallow* water.

sham 1. pretend to be: You're not hurt, you're only *shamming*. 2. a pretence: All his promises are a *sham*. 3. pretended, not real: The General directed a *sham* battle on Wimbledon Common.

shambles (sham-bles) 1. a place of slaughter: The battlefield was a *shambles*. 2. a place of confusion: Clear away all those toys; this playroom is a *shambles*.

shame 1. the feeling one has after doing something foolish or dishonourable: I am filled with *shame* at not having thanked you for your present. 2. something to be sorry about: What a *shame* that you won't be able to come. 3. cause others to feel *shame*: You have *shamed* your family. 4. make a person do something through *shame*: Finally he was *shamed* into paying his share of the bill. **shameful** bringing *shame*: His behaviour towards his mother was *shameful*.

shampoo (sham-poo) 1. wash the hair or clean upholstery and carpets with a special preparation. 2. the act of *shampooing*: I'll have a *shampoo* and set. 3. the preparation used: I bought a bottle of special *shampoo* at the chemist's shop.

shanty (shan-ty) 1. a small, roughly-made hut or cabin: He lives in a *shanty* on the edge of the wood. 2. a song sung by sailors in rhythm with their work: 'Haul away Joe' is a well-known sea *shanty*.

shape 1. form, as seen by the eye: I don't like the *shape* of this lampshade. 2. arrangement; fitness: My affairs are in a very bad *shape*. 3. give a shape to: He is *shaping* clay into a ball. **shapely** of a pleasing *shape*.

share 1. a part: If you do a *share* of the work you'll have a *share* of the profits. 2. divide: They *shared* out the last parcel of food. 3. join with others in using: We have our own bedroom and sittingroom but we *share* the kitchen and bathroom.

shark a fish that lives in oceans and which ranges in size from 30 cm to 13·5 m: *Sharks* have a reputation for being the most dangerous of all marine animals.

sharp 1. with a keen edge for cutting or piercing: Don't let the little boy play with that *sharp* knife. 2. having a point or angle: We came to a *sharp* turn in the road. 3. shrill, piercing: We heard a *sharp* cry of pain. 4. quickly seeing, hearing, understanding etc.: What *sharp* eyesight you must have! 5. severe, harsh: King Alfred was given a *sharp* scolding for burning the cakes. 6. quick: You should go for a *sharp* walk before dinner. 7. promptly: I'll meet you at eight *sharp*. 8. suddenly: Turn *sharp* left at the crossroads. **sharpen** make *sharp*: He *sharpened* his knife on a stone.

shatter (shat-ter) 1. suddenly break in pieces: The glass fell to the floor and *shattered*. 2. weaken, destroy: His health was *shattered* by overwork.

shave 1. cut hair off the face, head etc. with a razor: Every morning my father *shaves* before breakfast. 2. come very near to touching: The lorry *shaved* our car by a fraction. 3. a narrow miss: That was a narrow *shave*. **shaving** a very thin slice of wood *shaved* off a larger piece with a plane or chisel.

shawl a piece of material worn chiefly by women as a covering for the shoulders or head: Wrap the baby in a *shawl* before you go out.

she 1. a female person: '*She* wheels her wheelbarrow through streets broad and narrow' (*Cockles and Mussels*, a song). 2. a female animal; the way of referring to a ship (even though it may have the name of a male): 'Our flagship was *The Lion* and a mighty roar had *she*' (a song).

sheaf 1. a bundle of corn, bound up after reaping: The *sheaves* were thrown on to a cart and taken to the barn. 2. a large bunch of flowers: The bride carried a *sheaf* of lilies. 3. a bundle of papers laid on top of one another and tied together.

shear *shorn* remove by cutting with a sharp instrument: In early spring the farmers *shear* the sheep. **shears** a tool for *shearing* consisting of two blades riveted together: Take the *shears* and cut the hedge.

sheath a case or covering for a sword, dagger etc.: He rattled his sword in its *sheath*. **sheathe** put into a *sheath*: 'Draw your swords and *sheathe* them not' (Shakespeare, *Titus Andronicus*).

shed 1. let fall: In autumn the trees *shed* their leaves. 2. take off: In hot weather we *shed* our thick clothing. 3. spread: The sun *shed* its light into every corner of the garden. 4. a building used for storing things, keeping animals etc.: 'Once in royal David's city stood a lowly cattle-*shed*' (Christmas carol).

sheep a short, stocky domestic animal which eats grass and is reared for wool and meat.

sheer 1. very thin, almost transparent: On the counter were several pairs of *sheer* stockings. 2. complete: It would be *sheer* lunacy to attempt to climb that rock. 3. very steep: Over the edge of the cliff was a *sheer* drop.

sheet 1. a large rectangular piece of cloth used for covering a bed. 2. a covering: The ground was covered by a *sheet* of ice. 3. a thin piece of material: We need three *sheets* of glass in the greenhouse.—He drew a circle on a large *sheet* of paper.

shelf 1. a thin slab of wood, stone or other material standing out from a wall and used for holding things: On the *shelf* stood a clock and two candlesticks. 2. a ledge standing out from a vertical face of rock: The rescuers were lowered on to the *shelf* by means of a rope. **shelve** put on a *shelf*; put aside for a time: We cannot decide this matter today; we'll *shelve* it until we have more time.

shell 1. the hard outer covering of eggs, nuts, some seeds and certain animals: We ate the nuts and threw away the *shells*. 2. the outer framework of a building, ship etc.: Only the *shell* of the factory remained after the explosion. 3. a metal case filled with explosive, fired from a gun: As we charged, *shells* exploded all around us. 4. take something out of a *shell*: The girls were *shelling* peas for dinner. 5. fire *shells*: Last night the enemy positions were heavily *shelled*. **shellfish** an animal living in water and having a *shell*, such as the mussel, oyster, lobster, crab and shrimp.

shelter (shel-ter) 1. something which gives refuge from rain, danger etc.: On our first night we built a rough *shelter* from the branches of trees. 2. protection: We took *shelter* in a barn until the storm cleared. 3. be a *shelter* for, give *shelter* to: The high wall *sheltered* us from the snow. 4. take *shelter*: Let us *shelter* under these trees.

shepherd (shep-herd) 1. a person who looks after sheep: The *shepherd* rescued the sheep from the snowdrift. 2. look after and guide people: Slowly the teacher *shepherded* his children across the busy road.

sheriff (sher-iff) in the United States, the chief officer for carrying out the law in a county. **High Sheriff** (in England) an officer of the Crown who carries out certain duties in some counties and cities.

sherry (sher-ry) a fortified wine first produced in southern Spain but now a name given to wines made elsewhere in imitation of Spanish *sherry*.

shield 1. a piece of defensive armour carried on the arm and used to protect a soldier in battle: The champion came out of his tent armed with sword and *shield*. 2. a picture of a *shield* on a coat of arms. 3. a kind of screen to give protection from gunfire, wind, dust etc. 4. protect: I cannot tell lies to *shield* you from punishment.

shift 1. move from one place or position to another: The boy *shifted* restlessly in his seat. 2. a group of workmen who work the same hours: One week I work the day *shift* and the next week the night *shift*. **shiftless** lazy, not willing to work. **shifty** deceitful, not to be trusted.

shilling (shil-ling) a British coin today equal to five pence.

shimmer (shim-mer) shine with a soft, continually moving light: The reflection of the moon *shimmered* on the surface of the lake.

shin 1. the front part of the leg below the knee as far as the ankle: He will not be able to play in the next match because he has been kicked on the *shin*. 2. climb quickly: The little boy *shinned* up the tree like a monkey.

shine *shone* (*shined*) 1. give out or reflect light: We saw a light *shining* in the distance.–The sun *shone* all day. 2. do a thing well: I'm afraid I don't *shine* at spelling. 3. make *shine*: Have you *shined* your shoes yet? 4. brightness, polish: All the *shine* has gone from these old coins. **shiny** having a *shine*: He showed me his *shiny* new watch.

shingle (shin-gle) 1. a thin oblong piece of wood used like a tile for covering roofs and sometimes walls: The church spire needs new *shingles*. 2. small pebbles on the seashore made round in shape by the action of water: We could not walk on the *shingle* in our bare feet. 3. put *shingles* on a roof or wall: The church spire has been newly *shingled*. **shingles** a disease in which inflamed spots appear on the skin, most often round the waist.

ship 1. a vessel, larger than a boat, that sails the seas: 'I saw three *ships* come sailing by' (carol). 2. send in a *ship*: We *shipped* most of our furniture to Australia. 3. take members, or become a member of a *ship's* crew: I *shipped* as a cook on a sailing vessel. **ship-shape** in good order: We inspected the rooms and found everything *ship-shape*. **shipwreck** destruction of a ship by storm, collision, striking rocks etc. **shipwright** a person who builds *ships*. **shipment** goods sent by *ship*: Your *shipment* of woollen blankets will arrive on the 16th. **shipyard** a place where *ships* are built or repaired.

shirk avoid doing work or duty: You will make no progress if you *shirk* your homework.

shirt a loose-fitting garment with buttons down the front, a collar and long or short sleeves: He wore his new *shirt* at the picnic.

shiver (shiv-er) 1. shake or tremble with cold, fear, excitement etc.: The very thought of a cold bath makes me *shiver*. 2. a trembling movement: I felt a *shiver* go down my spine.

shoal 1. a sandbank, a place where water is shallow: Our boat was stuck for two hours on a *shoal*. 2. a large number of fish swimming together: We put out to sea when we heard that a *shoal* of herrings was approaching.

shock 1. a sudden and violent blow or collision: The *shock* of the collision badly dented one of the cars. 2. the effect of an electric current passing through the body: He touched a live wire and received an electric *shock*. 3. the effect of some injury or bad news: The news of his death was a great *shock* to us. 4. a number of sheaves of corn put together in a field to dry, supporting each other so that rain will run off them. 5. cause *shock*, suffer *shock*: We were *shocked* to hear the bad news.

shoe *shod* 1. put a *shoe* or *shoes* on: You need to be well *shod* in this bad weather. 2. a curved band of iron nailed to the hoof of a horse: I had to call at the blacksmith's because my horse had lost a *shoe*. 3. an outer covering for the foot: My *shoes* need mending. **shoehorn** a shaped piece of horn or metal used to make a *shoe* slip on to the foot more easily. **shoetree** a device of metal or wood put into *shoes* when they are not being worn to help keep them in shape.

shoot *shot* 1. aim and fire from a gun, a bow etc.: 'I *shot* an arrow into the air' (Longfellow). 2. hit, wound or kill by *shooting*: The prisoner was sentenced to be *shot* at dawn. 3. send out quickly; come or go quickly: Flames *shot* up from the burning ship. 4. grow quickly: Your son has *shot* up in the last month! 5. cause sharp darting pains in a part of the body: Pains *shot* through his arm. 6. pass through or over quickly: We *shot* the rapids and were soon in calmer waters. 7. take photographs or make films: *Shooting* starts in the studio at dawn tomorrow. 8. a new or young growth on a plant: We cut off the old branches and tied up the new *shoots*.

shop 1. a building where goods are sold: The main street has two rows of *shops*. 2. a place where machines and other goods are made and repaired: Ten men were working in the engineering *shop*. 3. go to *shops* to buy things: I *shopped* all morning without finding what I wanted. **shopkeeper** a person who carries on business in a *shop*. **shoplifter** a person who steals goods from *shops*. **shop-soiled** damaged through being handled or left too long in a *shop*-window: These *shop-soiled* garments are being sold half-price. **shop-steward** an official of a trade union who represents workers in a factory.

shore the land along the side of the sea, a lake or a river: The two boys walked along the *shore* picking up pebbles.

short 1. not long in time or space: He made a *short* speech. 2. not enough of: We have run *short* of bread. 3. not saying much; speaking quickly and abruptly: Please be *short* and to the point. 4. suddenly: He was pulled up *short* in the middle of his speech. 5. easily falling to crumbs and breaking, as does pastry containing fat. **shortage** not having enough: There is a *shortage* of eggs in the shops. **shorten** make *shorter*: Your dress needs *shortening* a little. **shorthand** a way of writing rapidly using simple strokes instead of letters. **short-sighted** unable to see distant objects clearly.

shot 1. the noise made when a gun is fired: We heard several *shots* in the distance. 2. an attempt to hit by shooting: After several *shots* he hit the target. 3. a number of small pellets of lead contained in the cartridge of a sporting gun. 4. a person who shoots: He is a very good *shot*. 5. a heavy metal ball used in a throwing competition: He is a champion at putting the *shot*.

shoulder (shoul-der) 1. that part of the body where the arm (in man) or foreleg (e.g. in a sheep) is joined. He carried the ladder on his *shoulder*. 2. take on the *shoulder*: 'Shoulder arms!' shouted the sergeant. 3. take responsibility or do work: I am prepared to *shoulder* the responsibility for finishing the job. 4. push: I *shouldered* my way through the crowd.

shout 1. call or cry out loudly: I heard him *shouting* for help. 2. a loud cry: The king was received with *shouts* of joy.

shove 1. push: The engine failed and we had to *shove* the car to the side of the road. 2. push rudely and roughly: 'Stop *shoving*' cried the little boy. 3. a good strong push: Give it a *shove* and it will roll down the hill.

shovel 1. a tool resembling a spade with a blade like a scoop, used for moving earth, snow, coal etc. 2. use a *shovel*: We had to *shovel* away the snow before we could leave the house.

show 1. display, allow to be seen: He *showed* me his collection of foreign stamps. 2. guide, conduct, point out: Could you *show* me the way to the bus stop? 3. make others understand; prove: His face *showed* how delighted he was. 4. be visible: The pattern of the wallpaper still *showed* under the coat of paint. 5. the act of *showing*: The vote was decided by a *show* of hands. 6. display, a collection of things displayed: Are you going to the cattle *show*? **showcase** a case with a glass top or front in which things of interest are displayed. **showman** a man who organizes public *shows* such as circuses.

shower (show-er) 1. a short fall of rain, hail or snow: 'April *showers* bring May flowers.' 2. a large number, coming at the same time: The troops advanced through a *shower* of bullets.–He had to answer a *shower* of questions. 3. a *shower*-bath: We have installed a *shower* in our bathroom. 4. send or give in large numbers: The B.B.C. was *showered* with letters about the programme.

shrapnel (shrap-nel) a hollow shell or bomb containing an explosive charge and bullets which can be made to scatter in all directions at a given time after firing.

shred 1. a piece, especially a narrow strip cut or torn off: His coat was torn to *shreds* by the brambles. 2. the smallest bit: There's not a *shred* of truth in his story.

shriek 1. scream: 'Come away from that fence,' *shrieked* his mother. 2. a scream: His jokes brought *shrieks* of laughter from the audience.

shrill high-pitched and piercing: 'Hear the *shrill* whistle' (Shakespeare, *Henry IV, part 1*).

shrimp a small, long-tailed shellfish used for food.

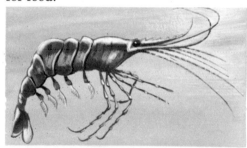

shrine a building devoted to something or somebody highly respected, or to a saint: The Canterbury Pilgrims journeyed to the *shrine* of St Thomas.

shrink *shrank, shrunk* 1. become or make less through heat, cold or moisture: I can't wear this shirt because it has *shrunk* in the wash. 2. move back; be unwilling or afraid to do something: I would not *shrink* from telling the truth.

shrivel (shriv-el) become wrinkled and dried up through heat, cold, dryness or old age: All our best flowers are *shrivelled* with the heat.

shrub a bush or small tree with many stems growing up from the ground: All we could see was an expanse of dry grass and a few small *shrubs*. **shrubbery** a garden or part of a garden where *shrubs* are cultivated.

shrug 1. raise and lower the shoulders to show that one doubts, does not care etc. 2. such a movement: He answered with a *shrug* of the shoulders.

shudder (shud-der) 1. tremble, as from horror, fear or cold: The very memory of that day makes me *shudder*. 2. a trembling of the body: A *shudder* passed through me when I looked into the room.

shuffle (shuf-fle) 1. walk, dragging the feet: The man *shuffled* along the floor. 2. do things in a clumsy way: He *shuffled* into his clothes. 3. mix playing cards in a pack to alter their positions. 4. avoid doing what one should: He always *shuffles* out of his duties. 5. a *shuffling* movement: He gave the cards a *shuffle*.

shun keep away from a place or a person; avoid: She is shy and *shuns* company.

shunt move a train from one railway track to another: Our carriage was *shunted* on to a siding until the Edinburgh express had passed.

shut 1. close: *Shut* the door. 2. become closed, remain closed: The cupboard door won't *shut*. 3. cease business: This shop *shuts* at 6 p.m. 4. hurt or pinch by *shutting*: Don't *shut* your fingers in the door. 5. keep in; keep out: I found myself *shut* in a yard with high walls.–The big tree *shuts* out the light from this room. **shutter** a movable cover for a window: 'Now stir the fire and close the *shutters* fast' (William Cowper).

shuttle (shut-tle) a boat-shaped piece of wood by means of which thread is carried from side to side of a loom, weaving between the threads. **shuttlecock** a piece of cork with feathers in it, struck with a racket to and fro in badminton and battledore.

shy 1. timid, uncomfortable when others are present: She felt too *shy* to say a word. 2. easily frightened away: Deer are *shy* animals. 3. start or turn away as in sudden fear: The sudden approach of a car made my horse *shy* and throw me.

sick 1. not well in body or mind: He has been *sick* in hospital for a month. 2. *sick* in the stomach: Too many sweets will make you *sick*. 3. those who are ill: There were not enough nurses to care for the *sick*. **sick bay** part of a ship reserved for those who are ill. **sicken** 1. be in the early stage of an illness: I am afraid she is *sickening* for influenza. 2. make one feel *sick*: They were *sickened* at the sight of so much suffering. **sickly** 1. weak: He's a *sickly* little boy. 2. likely to make one feel *sick*: There was a *sickly* smell in the kitchen.

side 1. one of the surfaces of an object: A cube has six *sides*. 2. one of the surfaces not including top or bottom, front or back: Go to the *side* entrance. 3. either of the two surfaces of paper, cloth, leather, plastic etc.: 'Write on both *sides* of the paper' (instructions at an examination). 4. either the right or left parts of a human body, or that of an animal: I have a pain in my right *side*. 5. part of an area or a thing: Let us walk along the sunny *side* of the street. 6. one of two groups opposed to each other: Where is the captain of our *side*? 7. descent through a parent: He is French on his mother's *side*. 8. take the part of in a quarrel: Only a few people *sided* with him. **sideways** towards the *side*; with one *side* turned towards the viewer: He jumped *sideways* and the stone missed him. **siding** a short railway track lying at the *side* of a main line.

siege the process of surrounding and capturing a fortified place by cutting off supplies, bombarding, attacking etc.: The *siege* of Troy lasted ten years.

sieve 1. a utensil, the bottom of which is perforated or made of wire net, used to separate fine particles of matter from coarse ones, or liquids from solids: The soup must be passed through a *sieve* before it is served. 2. pass through a *sieve*: These seeds will grow better if the soil is *sieved* before they are sown.

sift pass through a sieve: We always *sift* the flour when baking. **sifter** a small kitchen utensil like a sieve: We need another sugar-*sifter*.

sigh 1. let out one's breath audibly as from sorrow or relief. 2. long for: It's no good *sighing* for the days that are gone. 3. the act or sound of *sighing*: 'I shall never find it,' she said with a *sigh*.

sight 1. the power to see: He lost his *sight* at an early age. 2. something well worth seeing: The woods in autumn are a beautiful *sight*. 3. seeing, being seen: If you catch *sight* of him, let me know. 4. the distance one can see: At last we came in *sight* of land. 5. something that looks odd or ugly: You look a *sight* in that hat. 6. a device on a gun, a compass etc. which guides the eye: I shall fire when I have him in my *sights*. 7. get *sight* of: We *sighted* an aeroplane coming towards us.

sign 1. a mark or figure used instead of the word or words it represents: The *signs* for two plus four are 2 + 4. 2. words or pictures painted on a board to give information to people: Do you know what these traffic *signs* mean? 3. something that shows the existence of another thing: His face bore all the *signs* of a life of hard work. 4. a movement made instead of speaking: The policeman made a *sign* to me to cross the road. 5. write one's name: *Sign* on the dotted line, please. 6. show by a *sign*: The policeman *signed* to us to cross the road. **signature** a person's name, written by himself.

signal (sig-nal) 1. a movement or a device used to give an order or some information: The bell is a *signal* for changing lessons. 2. something which causes action: The sound of the referee's whistle was the *signal* for a general invasion of the pitch. 3. make a *signal*, tell by means of a *signal*: The leader *signalled* to us to follow him.

signify (sig-ni-fy) 1. make known by speech, signs or action: He *signified* his agreement with a nod of the head. 2. be a sign of; mean: The gathering clouds *signify* the approach of a storm. **significance** meaning, importance: The discovery of North Sea gas has already been of great *significance* to Britain. **significant** important, having a special meaning: In his speech he made some *significant* remarks on road safety.

silence (si-lence) 1. absence of noise, sound or speech: We listened to his words in complete *silence*. 2. make *silent*: We brought the dog into the house to *silence* his howling. **silencer** a device fitted to the exhaust pipe of a petrol engine or on to a gun to reduce the noise. **silent** saying nothing, making no noise: Charlie Chaplin acted in many *silent* films.—The letter 'k' is *silent* in the word 'know'.

silhouette (sil-hou-ette) 1. a picture in black, or an object seen in outline with the light behind it: Turn sideways and I will draw you in *silhouette*. 2. be shown or seen in *silhouette*: We saw the horse *silhouetted* against the evening sky.

silk material manufactured from the fine shiny thread made by *silk*worms: She wore a dress of blue *silk*. **silkworm** a kind of caterpillar which spins the fine thread of *silk* to make its cocoon. **silky** smooth, soft: The baby has *silky* hair.

silly (sil-ly) foolish, stupid: It would be *silly* of you not to apologize.

silver (sil-ver) 1. a shiny white metal used for making ornaments, coins, mirrors and utensils for the dining table: 'Bobby Shafto's gone to sea, *silver* buckles at his knee' (Songs for the Nursery, 1805). 2. coins once made of *silver* but now of metal resembling *silver*: I have no notes; I shall have to pay you in *silver*. 3. resembling *silver*: 'This precious stone (England) set in a *silver* sea' (Shakespeare, *Richard II*). **silversmith** a person who makes articles of *silver*. **silverware** articles, especially for use on the table, made of *silver*. **silver wedding** the 25th wedding anniversary. **silvery** like *silver*.

similar (sim-i-lar) having a likeness or resemblance: The twins always wear *similar* clothes. **similarity** likeness: There is a great *similarity* between them.

simmer (sim-mer) keep a liquid very hot, just at boiling point: Let the soup *simmer* for fifteen minutes.

simple (sim-ple) 1. easy to understand, do or use: Mending your clock is a *simple* job and needs only *simple* tools. 2. unlearned, ignorant: '*Simple* Simon met a pieman' (nursery rhyme, 1764). 3. plain, with no decoration or luxury: The house is built in a very *simple* style. 4. with nothing added or altered: I'm telling you the *simple* truth. **simply** in a *simple* manner, only, completely: I'm *simply* a labourer. **simpleton** a foolish person. **simplicity** being *simple*. **simplify** make easier or more understandable: The problem of crossing the river was *simplified* when the rain ceased.

sin 1. wrong-doing, any serious offence: 'I will be sorry for my *sin*' (Psalm 38). 2. a mistake, something that is not sensible: It's a *sin* to spend so much money when we need it for other things. 3. do wrong, commit a *sin*. **sinful** wrong, wicked.

since 1. between a particular past time and the present: *The house was burnt down but has since been rebuilt.–He left home two years ago and we have not seen him since.* 2. ago, before now: *All this happened in times long since past.*

sincere (sin-cere) honest, not deceitful: *I am sincere in wanting to help you.* **sincerely** in a *sincere* way: *He is sincerely sorry for what he did.* **sincerity** being *sincere*.

sinew (sin-ew) a cord or tendon which fastens the muscles to the bones: *Prehistoric man made thread from the sinews of animals.* **sinewy** strong: *'The smith, a mighty man is he with large and sinewy hands'* (Longfellow, *The Village Blacksmith*).

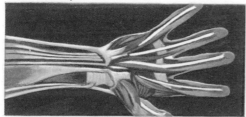

sing 1. make music with the voice, with or without words: *The birds are singing in the park.* 2. make a humming sound: *The kettle is singing; put the tea in the pot.* **singer** a person who *sings*, especially in public. **singsong** a meeting of friends who *sing* together informally.

singe 1. burn the ends of hair: *The cat singed its fur by sitting too close to the fire.* 2. make brown or black by burning: *I singed my shirt with a hot iron.* 3. a slight burn.

single (sin-gle) 1. one only: *You haven't eaten a single cake.* 2. not married: *Do you intend to stay single all your life?* 3. only to be used by one person. 4. having only one set of petals: *In the garden was a bed of single dahlias.* 5. a single run in cricket; a game between two people: *We went to see the singles final at Wimbledon.* 6. a one-way ticket for a train, bus etc.: *He took a single to Leeds.*

singlet (sin-glet) a vest, a garment worn under a shirt.

singular (sin-gu-lar) 1. one person or thing: *'Man' is the singular of 'men' and 'woman' of 'women'.* 2. strange: *It is very singular that he never speaks to his old friends.* 3. outstanding: *He was given the George Medal for an act of singular courage.*

sink *sank, sunk* 1. go down: *The ship sank in the storm.* 2. go down, cause to go down in sound, in strength, in value etc.: *Her voice sank to a whisper.* 3. a basin of stone, porcelain etc. with a pipe to drain away the water: *The old woman was at the kitchen sink washing crockery.* **sinker** a small lead weight fastened to a fishing line to keep it under water: *The fish swallowed the bait, hook, line and sinker.*

sip 1. drink a little at a time: *'The sweetest girl I ever saw was sipping cider through a straw'* (an old song). 2. a very small quantity drunk at a time: *Would you like a sip of apple juice?*

sir 1. a respectful form of address used to a man: *Follow me, sir.* 2. the title of a knight or baronet: *Sir Francis Drake was a great English seaman.*

sister (sis-ter) 1. the daughter of the same parents as another person: *My sister works in Italy.* 2. a senior nurse in a hospital. 3. a nun in the Catholic Church. **sister-in-law** the wife of one's brother or the *sister* of one's husband or wife.

sit *sat, seated* 1. rest on the lower part of the body: *Sit down and make yourself comfortable.* 2. perch, remain on eggs until they hatch: *The hen has been sitting for a week.* 3. hold a meeting of parliament, a committee etc.: *The finance committee sits tomorrow evening.* 4. make *sit*: *We sat the little boy on a wall where he could see the fireworks.*

site 1. a place on which anything has been or is situated: This is the *site* of an old Roman temple. 2. a place where a building is to be erected: The *site* for the new Town Hall has been cleared of buildings. 3. erect a building somewhere: We have decided to *site* the new Law Courts in the town centre.

situation (sit-u-a-tion) 1. condition: I was in an awkward *situation*, owing more money than I could pay. 2. place where a town, building etc. is: This house is in a pleasant *situation*, with a view across the valley. 3. employment: I looked through the '*situations* vacant' column of the newspaper. **situated** in a certain place or condition: Our house is *situated* at the crossroads.

six the number between five and seven: I had *six* hours' sleep last night. **sixteen** 6 added to 10 = 16. **sixty** 6 multiplied by 10 = 60. **six-shooter** a revolver with which *six* shots can be fired without reloading.

size 1. the largeness or smallness of a thing: Look at the huge *size* of this egg. 2. one of a number of measures of clothing, shoes etc.: Do you take *size* 8 shoes? 3. a sticky substance mainly used with a brush to close up the pores or holes in paper, plaster etc. to make painting easier. 4. apply *size*: You will need to *size* this wall before you paint it.

skate 1. a metal blade which can be fixed to the sole of a shoe or boot to make it possible to glide on icy surfaces: He fell on the ice when one of his *skates* came loose. 2. a large sea fish used as food. 3. go on *skates*: It was freezing and people were *skating* on the ponds. **roller-skate** a *skate* which has four small wheels instead of a blade and which is used on smooth surfaces.

skeleton (skel-e-ton) 1. the bones of a human or other animal fitted together as they would be in life: There are two human *skeletons* in the museum. 2. the framework of any kind of construction: There is a *skeleton* of a large block of flats in the middle of town. 3. the main parts of a plan, a map, scheme etc. which remains to be finished: Here is a *skeleton* project for our next annual sports day. **skeleton key** a key which will open many different locks.

sketch 1. a rough drawing: He took a pencil and drew a rapid *sketch* of the ship. 2. a short description, the outline of a plan: Before I begin to write the story I shall make a *sketch* of its chief characters and events. 3. make a *sketch* or *sketches*: I *sketched* the old lady drawing water from the well.

ski 1. one of a pair of long, slender pieces of hard wood, metal or plastic which can be fitted to a shoe and used for gliding over snow. 2. travel on or use *skis*: Is the snow firm enough for us to *ski*?

skid 1. the slipping movement of the wheels of a car or other vehicle especially when driven too fast over a slippery surface: The car suddenly went into a *skid*. 2. make such a slipping movement: We had barely turned the corner when we *skidded* into a lamp-post.

skiff a small boat, light enough to be sailed or rowed by one person.

skill the ability to do something well: Because of his great *skill* with the bat he was selected for his county cricket team. **skilful** having *skill*: I have never met a more *skilful* chess player. **skilled** trained, having *skill* and experience: There is a great shortage of *skilled* workmen in the building industry.

skim 1. remove scum, cream, grease etc. from the surface of a liquid: She *skimmed* the fat off the soup before it was served. 2. move quickly and lightly over: Hovercraft and speedboats *skimmed* the waters of the bay. 3. read a thing very quickly: After *skimming* through the book I decided to buy it.

skin 1. the outer covering of the body of a human being, animal, vegetable or fruit: The sun had tanned his *skin* a dark brown. 2. the solid layer which forms on milk when it cools: Do you like the *skin* of the rice pudding? 3. take off the *skin*: The poacher *skinned* the rabbit and cooked it.

skip 1. spring, jump or leap lightly: The lambs were *skipping* in the field. 2. jump, using a *skipping*-rope. 3. pass over without reading: I have read most of the book but I *skipped* the longest chapters.

skipper (skip-per) the captain of a small ship or boat; the captain of a football or cricket team.

skirmish (skir-mish) 1. a short, sharp fight between small bodies of men or two fleets: Two men were lost in a *skirmish* with the enemy. 2. take part in a *skirmish*.

skirt 1. a garment, the lower part of a dress or coat that hangs from the waist: Her *skirt* was torn and covered with mud. 2. pass along the edge or side of: We took the road which *skirted* the lake.

skittle (skit-tle) 1. a game in which a ball is rolled along an alley to knock down a number of bottle-shaped pieces of wood. 2. one of the pieces of wood used in the game of *skittles*. 3. get members of a cricket team out one after the other: The whole team was *skittled* for 25 runs.

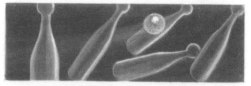

skull the bony framework of the head which encloses the brain: The cyclist fell off his machine and fractured his *skull*.

skunk a small, striped, North American mammal with a bushy tail which when attacked sends out an evil-smelling fluid.

sky the space we see above us, containing sun, moon stars and clouds: The sun shone in a cloudless blue *sky*. **skyline** the outline of hills, buildings etc. seen against the *sky*.

slack 1. loose, not tight: He let the reins go *slack* and the horse trotted slowly along. 2. careless, not attending to work: Your marks are low this term because you have been *slack*. 3. not active or having much work to do: Business is *slack* this month. 4. be careless or lazy: If you want to win a prize you can't afford to *slack*. 5. that part of a rope which hangs loosely: He took up the *slack* in the rope and fastened it firmly round the post. 6. coal dust: He put *slack* on the fire and it burnt all night. **slacken** become or make *slack*: At a signal from the shore the ship *slackened* speed. **slacker** a person who is lazy, who *slacks*: You must do your share of the duller jobs; we don't like *slackers*.

slake satisfy one's thirst: He *slaked* his thirst with a jug of cold water.

slam 1. shut or be shut noisily: Don't *slam* the door. 2. dash or knock with force: He *slammed* the book on the table. 3. the noise made when something is *slammed*: We heard the *slam* of the front door and footsteps running down the path.

slander (slan-der) 1. an untrue statement that injures another person's good name or reputation: The man was condemned to pay damages for *slander*. 2. utter *slander* about another person.

slang 1. certain words and phrases used in conversation but not used in good speech or writing: Soldiers, sailors, school-children and tramps all have their own kind of *slang*. 2. use vulgar language to another person.

slant 1. slope: The roof *slanted* steeply. 2. present news so that it supports only one side or point of view: You would think from the way this story has been *slanted* that the injured man had only himself to blame. 3. a slope: The post has been put in on the *slant* instead of straight up.

slap 1. strike with the open hand or something flat: 'Hello,' he said, *slapping* me on the back. 2. put something down with a loud quick noise: He *slapped* the book on the table. 3. put paint on carelessly: He *slapped* on the paint, letting it run down the door. 4. a quick blow with the hand or something flat: You didn't deserve that *slap*.

slash 1. make long slits or cuts: The cushion had been *slashed* with a razor. 2. strike with sharp strokes: We made a path by *slashing* our way through the long grass. 3. slit a garment for decoration: The sleeves of the coat had been *slashed* to show the yellow silk lining. 4. a long cut or wound: The spike had made a long *slash* in his leg.

slate 1. a fine-grained blue-grey rock that can be split into large flakes and is used for covering roofs: The building was in ruins and the *slates* had fallen off the roof. 2. sheet of *slate* in a wooden frame used for writing: Schoolchildren used to do their sums on *slates*. 3. cover a roof with *slate*: The roof of the old house has just been *slated*.

slaughter (slaugh-ter) 1. kill animals or people: Owing to foot and mouth disease thousands of cattle have had to be *slaughtered*. 2. killing: We must do all we can to avoid further *slaughter* on Britain's roads.

slave 1. a person who is owned by another person and made to work for no wages: The ancient kings of Egypt had thousands of *slaves*. 2. in the power of: He was a *slave* to drink as long as he lived. 3. work very hard: To feed her children she *slaved* for years at the sewing-machine. **slavery** being a *slave*, having *slaves*: The prisoners were sold into *slavery*.

slay *slew*, *slain* kill, usually in battle: The giant was *slain* by David.

sledge 1. a low platform on runners of steel made to slide on snow or ice: Large *sledges*, called sleighs, are usually drawn by horses. 2. a large hammer used by a blacksmith. 3. ride on a *sledge*: There had been a heavy fall of snow, so we were able to go *sledging*.

sleep *slept* 1. rest both body and mind, closing the eyes and becoming uncon-scious: Have you *slept* well? 2. provide room for *sleeping*: We can *sleep* twenty people in this hotel. 3. the state of being *asleep*: He walks in his *sleep*. **sleepless** without *sleep*: We passed a *sleepless* night in the cave. **sleepy** needing *sleep*: Lie down if you feel *sleepy*.

sleeper (sleep-er) 1. a person who *sleeps*: Some people are heavy *sleepers*, others are light *sleepers*. 2. a heavy beam of wood or sometimes of concrete on which rail-way lines are laid. 3. a train on which there are bunks for *sleeping*: We took the *sleeper* to Vienna.

sleet 1. snow or hail and rain falling to-gether: He went out into the driving *sleet* to rescue the child. 2. fall as *sleet*: It was *sleeting* hard when we arrived home.

sleeve 1. that part of a dress or coat that covers the arm: The jacket fits well except that the *sleeves* are too short. 2. an envelope for a gramophone record: On the *sleeve* there was a portrait of Beethoven.

slender (slen-der) 1. long and narrow: He cut a *slender* branch from the tree to make a bow. 2. slim: She would like to keep her *slender* figure. 3. poor, slight: My father had to bring up a large family on a *slender* income.

slice 1. a thin, broad, flat piece cut from something: I had two *slices* of toast for breakfast. 2. a utensil with a broad, flat blade: The cook used a fish *slice* to turn the food in the pan. 3 cut into *slices*: He *sliced* the bacon with a sharp knife.

slick 1. smooth, skilful: With a *slick* movement the conjurer produced a pack of playing cards. 2. a patch of oil discharged on water by a ship: A large oil *slick* is being blown towards the beach.

slide 1. move smoothly on a slippery surface: A number of children were *sliding* on the frozen pond. 2. move quietly: He *slid* out of the room without saying good-bye. 3. the act of *sliding*: We are going for a *slide* on the ice. 4. the slope down which one may *slide*: The children made a *slide* in the school playground. 5. a colour photograph which can be projected on a screen: He brought several *slides* showing scenes of London. 6. a small piece of glass on which things are placed to be examined through a microscope.

slight 1. small in amount: There is a *slight* smell of burning. 2. slim, slender: We saw a *slight* figure disappear in the distance. 3. treat rudely, neglect: I felt *slighted* when nobody spoke to me. 4. rude or neglectful treatment: I shall never forget the *slight*. **slightly** a little: I feel *slightly* better this morning.

slim 1. slender. 2. small, not very good: You have a very *slim* hope of getting what you want. 3. do things to make one *slim*: Some people *slim* by avoiding heavy meals, others take exercise.

slime 1. thin, soft, sticky mud: He fell in the pond and was covered with green *slime*. 2. the sticky substance left behind by snails: The pathway was covered with thin trails of grey *slime*. **slimy** like *slime*, covered with *slime*.

sling *slung* 1. a band of material put round an object to lift it: His arm was in a *sling*. 2. a piece of leather joined to cords and used to throw stones: The boy put a stone in the *sling* and aimed it at the tin. 3. the act of throwing with a *sling*: David *slung* the stone and killed the giant Goliath. 4. suspend so that a thing hangs or is lifted: We *slung* our hammock between two trees.

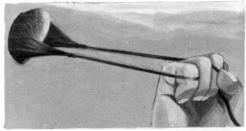

slink *slunk* go away quietly as if in fear, cowardice or shame: He *slunk* out of the room in disgrace.

slip 1. slide suddenly and lose one's balance: I *slipped* and fell on the ice. 2. move quietly and quickly: I *slipped* past without her seeing me. 3. escape: He *slipped* out of my grasp. 4. put on or off quickly: *Slip* on your coat and take this to the post. 5. the act of *slipping*, making mistakes: I made a *slip* in adding your bill. 6. a loose cover or garment: The *slip* covers on the couch need washing. 7. a small piece of paper: He wrote his address on a *slip* of paper. 8. a small twig cut from a plant to be put in the soil to take root: Would you like a couple of *slips* from this rose tree? 9. a fielder in

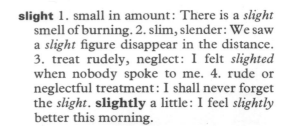

cricket: The last batsman was caught by the second *slip*. **slipknot** a knot tied so that it *slips* along the string round which it is tied. **slipstream** the stream of air forced back by the propeller or jet engine of an aeroplane. **slipper** a light shoe which can be easily *slipped* on for wear in the house. **slippery** smooth, easy to slide on: The recent frost had made the ground *slippery*.

slit 1. a straight narrow cut or opening: We looked through a *slit* in the wall and saw them coming. 2. make a *slit* or narrow opening: He *slit* the envelope and took out the letter. 3. be *slit* or cut along its length: The arm of my coat was *slit* on the barbed wire.

slog 1. hit hard as in boxing, cricket etc.: He *slogged* the ball to the boundary. 2. keep on, walk or work hard: I've been *slogging* away at these sums for hours. **slogger** a person who hits hard; a person who works with determination: He isn't brilliant, but he's a *slogger*.

slogan (slo-gan) an easily remembered cry or phrase used by a party or a group or to advertise something: 'We dye to live' (the *slogan* of a firm of dyers).

sloop a sailing vessel with one mast.

slop splash: Whitewash had been *slopped* all over the floor. **slops** waste water and liquid used in the home. **sloppy** 1. wet, full of puddles. 2. carelessly done: 'Bad spelling, untidy writing; a *sloppy* piece of work' (a teacher's remark on an exercise book).

slope 1. a slanting position: We measured the *slope* of the roof. 2. land which rises and falls: We went skiing on the mountain *slopes*. 3. be in a slanting position: The roof *slopes* at an angle of 45 degrees.

slot a narrow opening designed to receive narrow objects, especially coins: He put the money into the *slot* of the parking meter. **slot-machine** a machine with a *slot* into which one puts coins in order to obtain goods, play games of chance etc.

sloth 1. laziness, idleness. 2. a South American mammal which lives in trees, eats leaves and fruits and moves very slowly.

slouch sit, stand or walk in a lazy way, with drooping head or bent shoulders: He spends his time *slouching* about the streets.

slough 1. a marsh: 'On his way to the Eternal City Pilgrim passed through a *slough* whose name was Despond.' (John Bunyan, *The Pilgrim's Progress*) 2. cast off: Every year the snake *sloughs* its skin.

sloven (slov-en) a person who is untidy, dirty and careless about his dress, appearance, work and habits. **slovenly** of or like a *sloven*: This work is *slovenly* and must be done again.

slow 1. taking a long time; not quick: The *slow* train stopped at every station. 2. not acting or learning quickly: I am good at English but *slow* at arithmetic. 3. (of watches and clocks) showing a time earlier than the correct time: The reason that I'm late is because my watch is *slow*. 4. go *slower*: Slow down before reaching the traffic lights.

sludge thick mud; sewage: At the sewage works *sludge* from houses and factories is made into fertilizer.

slug 1. a slow-moving creature that looks like a snail but has no shell: During the night the *slugs* ate a number of seedlings in the garden. 2. a small pellet for firing from a gun.

sluggish (slug-gish) slow-moving, not active: When the river reaches the plain it becomes *sluggish* and overgrown with weeds. **sluggard** a lazy person.

sluice a channel for conducting water to places where it is needed: The level of the water in the *sluice* can be controlled by the opening or closing of a *sluice*gate.

slum a dirty street, dwelling or part of a city inhabited by the poorest people: In most towns today the *slums* are being cleared and new dwellings built.

slumber (slum-ber) 1. sleep quietly and peacefully: 'You have waked me too soon; I must *slumber* again' (Isaac Watts, *The Sluggard*). 2. sleep: After tossing about on my bed I fell into a troubled *slumber*.

slump 1. fall heavily: Tired with running, I *slumped* on the grass. 2. a sudden fall in trade, prices etc.: Thousands were put out of work because of a *slump* in the cotton trade.

slur 1. pronounce words indistinctly: He is hard to understand because he *slurs* his speech. 2. join two notes in music, passing without break from one to the next. 3. a remark intended to damage another person's reputation or character: I do not want to cast a *slur* on your good name.

slush soft snow, partly melted: My feet are wet from walking through the *slush*.

sly cunning; doing things secretly: The *sly* fox waited until the farmer had left the field.

smack 1. a slap with the open hand: I gave the horse a *smack* and he galloped away. 2. a blow: With a mighty *smack* he sent the ball soaring over the spectators' heads. 3. a small boat: When evening comes the fishing *smacks* put out to sea. 4. give a blow with the open hand: 'If you do that again I'll *smack* you,' said the child's mother. **smacking** blows with the palm of the hand: The little boy did it again and was given a *smacking*.

small little, not large: I have only a *small* garden. **small change** coins of silver and copper of *small* value. **smallholding** a piece of land on which vegetables etc. are grown for the market. **smallpox** a disease which spreads from one person to another, often leaving lasting scars on the body.

smart 1. bright, clean, well-dressed: You look very *smart* in that new suit. 2. clever: He is a *smart* boy and top of his class. 3. vigorous: Let's go for a *smart* walk. 4. severe: He received a *smart* scolding for staying out late. 5. feel or cause a sharp pain: Peeling onions makes my eyes *smart*. **smarten** make or become *smart*: We must *smarten* up the room for the party tonight.

smash 1. break or be broken: Don't *smash* all the crockery in the house. 2. collide, break through: At the bottom of the hill the lorry *smashed* into a house. 3. a violent breaking or collision: The dishes fell to the floor with a loud *smash*.

smear 1. spread dirt, ink, oil etc. over something: He drew his hand over the inky page and *smeared* the writing. 2. spread over: She *smeared* her face and neck with suntan lotion. 3. a dirty or greasy mark made by *smearing*: Who made that black *smear* on the wall?

smell 1. be aware of by means of the nose: Can you *smell* something burning? 2. give out a *smell*: This cheese *smells* of onions. 3. something one is aware of by *smelling*: There's a *smell* of turpentine in this room. 4. the act of *smelling*: Take a *smell* of this milk and tell me if you think it is sour.

smelt separate metal from its ore by melting it: The first metal to be *smelted* by man was copper.

smile 1. a look of pleasure, happiness or amusement on the face: She greeted us with a *smile*. 2. give a *smile* to express happiness or any other feeling: He *smiled* a sickly *smile* and left without an explanation.

smirk 1. smile in a silly, disagreeable way. 2. such a smile: 'Take that irritating *smirk* off your face,' shouted the sergeant.

smith a person who works in iron or other metals: 'The *smith*, a mighty man is he' (Longfellow, *The Village Blacksmith*).

smock a loose garment worn over other clothes for protection. **smocking** Embroidery stitches used to gather cloth into a pattern, usually of diamond shapes.

smoke 1. the cloud, often brown, grey or black, given off when something burns: A column of *smoke* rose from the burning ship. 2. give off *smoke*: The ruins were still *smoking* on the following day. 3. draw the *smoke* from burning tobacco or other substances into the mouth and let it out again: Do you *smoke* a pipe or cigarettes? 4. dry and preserve meat, fish etc. by the use of *smoke* from wood fires: *Smoked* salmon is very expensive. **smoker** 1. a person who *smokes* tobacco. 2. the compartment of a train for the use of those who *smoke*. **smokestack** a tall chimney which lets out *smoke* from a furnace or a factory. **smoky** giving out *smoke*, full of *smoke*: This room is *smoky* because the chimney needs sweeping.

smooth 1. not rough to the touch: The ice on the pond was as *smooth* as glass. 2. free from lumps: 'Beat the mixture until it is quite *smooth*' (from a recipe). 3. with no bumping or shaking: We reached Dover safely after a *smooth* Channel crossing. 4. make *smooth*: He *smoothed* the surface of the board with sandpaper. 5. get rid of difficulties: A visit to the headmaster helped to *smooth* over my son's problems.

smother (smoth-er) 1. kill by depriving of air necessary to life. 2. put out a fire by keeping air from it: A few buckets of sand were thrown on the fire to *smother* it. 3. cover: I came home from the match *smothered* in mud.–She *smothered* the child's face with kisses. 4. hold back: News of the disaster was *smothered* before it reached the newspapers.

smoulder (smoul-der) burn or smoke without flame: The fire was still *smouldering* when we got up next morning.

smudge 1. a dirty mark or smear: There were several black *smudges* on the wall. 2. make a dirty mark or smear: Try not to *smudge* the pages of your exercise book. 3. become smeared: I can't help it, this ink *smudges* very easily.

smug very satisfied with what one is or does: You may have won the game but you shouldn't be so *smug* about it.

smuggle (smug-gle) 1. carry goods illegally in or out of a country without paying customs duties: He was fined heavily for *smuggling* cameras into England. 2. take things or people to places against the rules: By some means or other a skeleton key was *smuggled* into the prison cell.– Everything is being done to stop the *smuggling* of arms into the country. **smuggler** a person who *smuggles* goods.

snack a light meal eaten quickly: We stopped the car by the roadside for a *snack*.

snag 1. something (a branch, a rock etc.) sticking up out of the ground or the bed of a river: He caught his foot on a *snag* and fell into the bushes. 2. a difficulty that has not been expected: The best plans seldom work without *snags* appearing.

snail a small animal with a soft body and shell that lives in water and on land: The *snail* moves slowly, carrying its shell on its back.

snake a serpent; a long crawling reptile without legs: Many *snakes* are poisonous and can kill people with their bite.

snap 1. seize or try to seize with the teeth: Don't stroke the dog, he may *snap* at your hand. 2. break, open or close with a sudden sharp sound: The branches *snapped* as he forced his way through the bushes. 3. take a quick photograph: I *snapped* him as he was coming round the corner. 4. the sound of something being broken or closed: The lion's jaws closed with a *snap*. 5. a sudden short period of cold weather: This cold *snap* will damage the fruit trees. 6. a fastener on clothing etc.: The dress was made to fasten at the waist by means of a *snap*.

snare 1. a trap with a noose used for catching animals and birds: The poacher caught only one rabbit in his *snares*. 2. anything intended to catch or trap a person unawares: He did not realize there was a *snare* in the question. 3. catch in a *snare*: They went out into the fields by night to *snare* rabbits.

snarl 1. show the teeth and growl: The dog *snarled* and would not let me pass. 2. speak roughly and harshly: 'What business is it of yours?' he *snarled*. 3. the action or sound of *snarling*.

snatch 1. make a sudden effort to seize something with the hand: He *snatched* up his clothes and ran out of the burning room. 2. get something quickly: While the van was being loaded he *snatched* a hasty breakfast. 3. the act of *snatching*: The thief made a *snatch* at my handbag. 4. a bit, a fragment of something: In the distance I heard *snatches* of a well-known song.

sneak 1. go quietly in a sly manner; slink: While the others were not looking he *sneaked* past the doorway. 2. a sly, deceitful person: I didn't tell anyone; I wouldn't be such a *sneak*.

sneer 1. smile or curl the lip in a manner which shows scorn; say scornful words. 2. the act of *sneering*: 'I won't waste my time with sneaks,' he said with a *sneer*.

sneeze 1. send out air suddenly through the nose and mouth: 'Speak roughly to your little boy, and beat him when he *sneezes*' (Lewis Carroll, *Alice's Adventures in Wonderland*). 2. the act of *sneezing*: 'Coughs and *sneezes* spread diseases.'

sniff 1. draw air through the nose in short breaths: The dog raised his head and *sniffed* the air. 2. the act of *sniffing*: One *sniff* is enough to make you ill.

snip 1. cut with scissors or shears in small quick strokes: He *snipped* off a curl from the baby's head. 2. a cut or slit made by *snipping*: One *snip* of the scissors and the lock of hair fell to the ground. 3. a small piece *snipped* off: Take a *snip* of this silk to the shop and see if you can match it.

snipe 1. fire shots from a hiding place: The soldiers were *sniping* from roofs and windows. 2. a bird with a long bill that lives in the marshes. **sniper** a person who fires shots from a hiding-place.

snob one who imitates and seeks the friendship of those of wealth or high rank in society and despises those whom he thinks are less important than he is: 'It is impossible, in our condition of society, not to be sometimes a *snob*' (Thackeray, *The Book of Snobs*). **snobbish** of a *snob* or like a *snob*: He is too *snobbish* to speak to his own brother. **snobbery** *snobbishness*, being *snobbish*.

snoop prowl around enquiring in a mean, sly manner into other people's business: Every few hours the manager comes *snooping* around. **snooper** a person who *snoops*.

snore breathe noisily with harsh sounds while asleep: I was kept awake all night by your *snoring*.

snort 1. force the breath violently through the nose in excitement or anger: The horse *snorted* and galloped away. 2. express or say in this way: 'Not I!' he *snorted* angrily. 3. the act of *snorting*: With a violent *snort* of anger the huge animal charged.

snout the long nose and sometimes the jaws of an animal that stand out from the face: The pig thrust his *snout* into the trough and gobbled up the food.

snow 1. small white flakes of frozen water which fall slowly to the ground in winter: 'The *snow* lay round about, deep and crisp and even' (*Good King Wenceslas*). 2. drop as *snow*: Last Sunday it *snowed* all day. **snowball** a ball of *snow* made by rolling *snow* till it grows large, or rolling it in the hands for throwing. **snowdrift** *snow* blown by the wind into a large heap: The road was blocked by *snowdrifts*. **snowflake** one of the tiny flakes made up of small crystals of *snow*. **snowplough** a machine driven by a motor for pushing *snow* away from roads and railways. **snowy** bringing *snow*; covered with *snow*; the colour of *snow*: The old man's hair was *snowy* white.

snub 1. treat with scorn, slight: I tried to explain my actions but he *snubbed* me into silence. 2. *snubbing* behaviour: I cannot forgive the *snub* I received from him. 3. short and turned up at the tip: He has red cheeks and a little *snub* nose.

snuff 1. sniff: The horse *snuffed* the air and reared its head. 2. put out a candle by removing the burnt end of the wick: He *snuffed* out the candle with his fingers. 3. powdered tobacco taken into the nose by sniffing: He opened his *snuff* box and took a pinch of *snuff*.

snuffle 1. breathe with sniffing sounds as if one has a cold in the head: I've been *snuffling* all morning. 2. the act of *snuffling*.

snug 1. warm, comfortable: 'Here Skugg lies, *snug* as a bug in a rug' (Benjamin Franklin in a letter, 1772). 2. fitting closely and comfortably: I have bought you a *snug* little coat for winter. **snuggle** get close so as to be warm and comfortable: The puppy *snuggled* close to its mother.

soak 1. become or make wet through: *Soak* the raisins in water for four hours. 2. take in liquid: The blotting paper *soaked* up the ink. 3. make very wet: The rain *soaked* us all to the skin. 4. go through: The rain has *soaked* through the roof in several places.

soap 1. a substance made from fat or oil and used for washing: I went to the shop for a cake of *soap*, a packet of *soap* flakes and some *soap* powder. 2. put *soap* on; rub with *soap*: She *soaped* the clothes well before rinsing them. **soapsuds** the foam or froth made through rubbing *soap* with water. **soapy** with *soap*, like *soap*: I upset a bucket of *soapy* water all over the floor.

soar 1. fly high: A lark *soared* into the sky. 2. fly high without visible movement of the wings: There were several eagles *soaring* round the summit of the mountain. 3. go high: The price of vegetables has *soared* because of scarcity.

sob 1. weep, drawing in a breath sharply: 'All the birds of the air went a-sighing and a-*sobbing*' (*Cock Robin*). 2. the action or sound of *sobbing*: The child's *sobs* could be heard from the next room.

sober (so-ber) 1. quiet, thoughtful, solemn in manner and speech: I was forced to take notice of his *sober* judgment. 2. not drunk: He has been *sober* for the last six months. **sobriety** being *sober*: If you are to work for us, we insist on complete *sobriety*. **sober down** become quiet: After all the excitement the children finally *sobered down*.

soccer (soc-cer) association football: I love going to *soccer* matches.

social (so-cial) 1. having to do with friendship and companionship: We are members of a *social* club. 2. having to do with the life of people as a whole, living in communities: We are studying the *social* customs of this part of England. 3. of human society, its ranks, its classes: The Lord Mayor's banquet is an important *social* function. 4. having to do with the problems of the poor, those who are ill, the old, children etc.: My daughter is hoping to do *social* work as a career. **socialism** the belief that all the main industries and wealth of a country should be under the control of its people.

society (so-ci-e-ty) 1. a body of individuals living as members of a community: The police force exists to protect *society* against those who wish to damage it. 2. companionship, company: I enjoy the *society* of people who are interested in music. 3. having to do with people of high rank, of fashion: She reads all the *society* gossip and goes to all the *society* weddings. 4. an organization of persons formed for a special purpose: He is a Fellow of the Royal Geographical *Society*.

sock a short stocking which does not reach to the knee: You need a clean pair of *socks* today.

socket (sock-et) a hollow specially made so that another thing may fit into it: We need a new *socket* for this electric light bulb.

sod a piece of grass taken from the earth with its roots: When the new Town Hall was to be built, the Lady Mayoress turned the first *sod*.

soda (so-da) a substance used in the making of soap, glass and other materials, and for washing and cleaning: *Soda* (sodium bicarbonate) is used in baking and as a medicine. **soda-water** water into which a gas (carbon dioxide) has been added to make it bubble.

sodden (sod-den) 1. wet through, soaked through: Our clothes were *sodden* with rain and we had to change them. 2. heavy through not being cooked long enough: She was disappointed to find that the bread was *sodden*.

sofa (so-fa) a long upholstered seat with back and arms: He stretched out on the *sofa* to read.

soft 1. easily altering in shape when pressed: Rest your head on this *soft* cushion. 2. not loud: The orchestra played *soft* music. 3. gentle. 4. not cold or fierce: A *soft* breeze blew in from the sea. 5. (of water) free from impurities and good for washing: Rain water is the *softest* of all water. 6. not containing alcohol: I should like lemonade or some other *soft* drink. 7. a certain kind of sound: The first *c* in *circle* and the *g* in *gentle* are both *soft*; in the words *club* and *glow* both these letters are hard. **soften** make or become *soft*: He squeezed the putty to *soften* it.

soggy 1. soaked; heavy with water: It took a long time to walk through the *soggy* field. 2. heavy: The bread was too *soggy* to eat.

soil 1. earth, dirt, ground, especially that in which plants and trees are grown: The *soil* in the garden is very fertile. 2. make dirty: She took the *soiled* clothing to the laundry.

solace (sol-ace) 1. something that gives comfort in trouble: I turned for *solace* to my best friend. 2. comfort, console or cheer a person: I *solaced* myself with the thought that things might have been worse.

solar (so-lar) having to do with the sun: The earth is part of the *solar* system; it receives *solar* heat and revolves completely round the sun in one *solar* year.

solder (sol-der) 1. metal which can be easily melted and applied with a hot iron to join the surfaces of harder metals together. 2. use *solder*: The radio set would not work because one of the points needed *soldering*.

soldier (sol-dier) 1. a member of an army: 'Ben Battle was a *soldier* bold, and used to war's alarms' (Tom Hood). 2. an army commander: Field-Marshal Montgomery was one of the greatest British *soldiers*. 3. serve in an army: He spent ten years *soldiering* in India. 4. keep working in spite of difficulties: The government is *soldiering* on until the next election.

sole 1. a flat fish with a hook-like snout that swims in the sea. 2. the under part of the foot: The *soles* of his feet were hard from walking barefoot. 3. the bottom part of a boot or shoe: Your boots need new *soles*. 4. the only, the single: I am my father's *sole* heir and shall inherit all his possessions.

solemn (sol-emn) 1. grave, sober, serious in speech, voice, tone, face etc.: He greeted me with a *solemn* handshake. 2. serious in intention: I have sworn a *solemn* oath to pay all my debts. 3. carried out with serious ceremony: Everyone stood in *solemn* silence during the playing of the Last Post. **solemnity** seriousness, ceremony: The Emperor was crowned with *solemnity*. **solemnize** perform with ceremony: The marriage was *solemnized* at three o'clock.

solicitor (so-lic-i-tor) a person who advises people on questions of law and prepares documents dealing with legal matters: If you wish to make a will, you should consult your *solicitor*.

solid (sol-id) 1. not hollow; having the interior completely filled up: This is a *solid* silver bracelet. 2. not liquid or gas: When water freezes it becomes *solid* ice. 3. strong, firm: This castle is built on foundations of *solid* rock. 4. firm, that can be relied on: I am doing this with the *solid* support of all my partners. 5. having length, breadth and thickness: The cube and the sphere are *solid* objects. 6. not liquid or a gas: Iron, wood, stone, copper and tin are all *solids*. **solidify** become *solid*: When water freezes it *solidifies*.

soliloquy (so-lil-o-quy) the act of talking to oneself: 'To be or not to be' is the beginning of Hamlet's famous *soliloquy*.

solitary (sol-i-tar-y) 1. with no friends or companions: He lives a *solitary* life in the country. 2. single: I failed to be present on one *solitary* occasion. **solitude** being alone: I like spending part of every day in *solitude*.

solo (so-lo) a piece of music or other performance by a single person: Will you sing a *solo* in Church next Sunday?–She made a *solo* flight from England to Australia. **soloist** a person who performs a *solo*.

solution (so-lu-tion) 1. the answer, or the way of finding an answer, to a problem or mystery: It took a week to find a *solution* to the crime. 2. dissolving or the result of dissolving something in liquid. **solve** reach a *solution*, find the answer to a problem: We never *solved* the mystery of the missing diamond.

some 1. a number of: *Some* people prefer the radio, others prefer television.–I went to buy *some* sweets. 2. a quantity of: I spent *some* time in America last year. 3. about: I arrived at the airport *some* two hours ago. **somebody** a person: Is *somebody* calling? **somehow** by *some* method, in *some* way: No trains are running today but I'll get home *somehow*. **something** *some* article; event, happening, etc.: I'm longing for *something* to happen. **sometime** at *some* time: I'd like to have a talk with you *sometime*. **sometimes** now and then, at times: *Sometimes* I buy ice cream and *sometimes* chocolates. **somewhat** rather: I was *somewhat* surprised to see you here. **somewhere** in or at *some* place: I'm sure you'll find your camera *somewhere* in the house.

son the male child of a parent: My *son* is a doctor. **son-in-law** the husband of one's daughter.

song 1. singing: Did you hear the *song* of the birds at dawn? 2. a piece of music with words: I will now sing a *song* about a grandfather clock.

sonnet (son-net) a poem of 14 lines which rhyme according to a definite scheme: Shakespeare wrote many *sonnets*.

soon 1. within a short time after the present: We shall *soon* know the result of the examination. 2. early: How *soon* do you want me to return your book? **as soon as** when: I came *as soon as* you called. **sooner** earlier; rather: I would *sooner* lose my fortune than my reputation.

soot black powder formed when something burns: Clouds of *soot* rose from the chimney.

soothe 1. make quiet, calm: She rocked the baby to *soothe* it. 2. make a pain less: This lotion will *soothe* the bites on your leg.

sop 1. a piece of bread soaked in milk or soup. 2. soak, take up liquid: *Sop* up the spilt water with this cloth. **sopping** wet through: He came into the house *sopping* wet.

soprano (so-pra-no) 1. the highest part sung by a person: My wife sings *soprano* and I sing tenor. 2. a woman or a boy who sings *soprano*: Have you ever heard Maria Callas, the famous *soprano*?

sorcerer (sor-cer-er) a man who is supposed to practise magic through contact with evil spirits: 'I am subject to a tyrant, a *sorcerer*' (Shakespeare, *The Tempest*). **sorcery** evil acts by a *sorcerer*: 'By *sorcery* he got this isle' (Shakespeare, *The Tempest*).

sordid (sor-did) 1. dirty, wretched, filthy: Few people in this city live in *sordid* conditions. 2. mean, dishonest: I will not make money by such *sordid* methods.

sore 1. tender, painful: His eyes are *sore* from reading too much. 2. a *sore* place: Two of the *sores* refuse to heal. **sorely** severely: I was *sorely* tempted to leave my job.

sorrow (sor-row) sadness, grief: We were forced to part, to our great *sorrow*. **sorry** feeling *sorrow* or regret: I am very *sorry* if I offended you.

sort 1. a group of things which are in some way alike: Scientists have discovered a new *sort* of mineral.—What *sort* of music do you like best? 2. separate into groups of things resembling each other: I have *sorted* my books into fiction and non-fiction.

soul 1. the spiritual part of man distinct from the physical. 2. a person: There wasn't a *soul* in the place. 3. a spirit: They prayed for the *souls* of their heroes. 4. energy, life: He puts his heart and *soul* into his singing.

sound 1. something that can be heard: 'The *sound* of his horn brought me from my bed' (John W. Graves, *D'ye Ken John Peel*?). 2. healthy: Your heart and lungs are *sound*. 3. good: He awoke from a *sound* sleep. 4. make something *sound*: The enemy attacked and the alarm was *sounded*.

soup a liquid food made by boiling meat, fish or vegetables in water, and adding seasoning and sometimes milk: We started lunch with a bowl of chicken *soup*.

sour 1. having a sharp taste, the opposite of sweet: I don't know how you can suck those *sour* lemons. 2. having fermented: The milk has turned *sour*. 3. bad-tempered: He greeted me with a *sour* look. 4. turn something *sour*: The hot weather has *soured* the milk.

source 1. the place where a stream or river rises: The explorer John Speke discovered the *source* of the Nile. 2. the origin from which anything rises: Malaya is the *source* of much of the world's rubber.

souse 1. plunge into water or throw water on. 2. be soaked or drenched: At the end of the day's sailing we were *soused* to the skin. 3. preserve in salted water or vinegar: *Soused* herrings are my favourite fish.

south 1. the direction in which the right arm points when one faces the sunrise: We are spending our holiday in the *south* of France. 2. to, at, from etc., the *south*: We were travelling *south* towards Naples. **south-east** halfway between *south* and east. **south-west** halfway between *south* and west. **southerly** in or from the *south*: There is a *southerly* wind blowing this morning. **southern** having to do with the *south*: The constellation of the *Southern* Cross can be seen in Australia and New Zealand.—We are playing a cricket team from the *southern* counties.

souvenir (sou-ve-nir) something given or kept for remembrance: He brought home a beer mug as a *souvenir* of his holiday in Germany.

sovereign (sov-er-eign) 1. the ruler of a country; a king, queen or emperor: I have made a list of all the *sovereigns* of England from the time of the Norman Conquest. 2. a British gold coin no longer in circulation: The gentleman pressed a gold *sovereign* into the little boy's hand. 3. having supreme power, self-governing: Many countries which were once ruled by Britain are now *sovereign* states.

soviet (so-vi-et) in Russia, a council of workers, a higher council, part of the Russian machinery of government. **Soviet Union** the Union of *Soviet* Socialist Republics ruled by a council called the Supreme *Soviet*.

sow *sowed*, *sown* (rhymes with *grow*) put seed into the ground: Have you *sown* your lettuces yet?

sow (rhymes with *now*) a fully grown female pig: 'There was an old farmer who had an old *sow*' (folksong).

soya soya bean a plant and its seed, the seed used as a valuable food for human beings and animals: The oil from the *soya bean* is used as food, as well as in the manufacture of soap and candles.

space 1. that in which all things exist and move: The stars and the planets all exist in *space*. 2. the distance between things: Please sign your name in the *space* provided. 3. a place in which there are no people or things: There was plenty of *space* to turn round. 4. a period of time: 'In short *space*, it rained' (Shakespeare, *Henry IV, part 1*).

spade 1. a tool for digging with a broad iron blade and a long handle. 2. one of the four suits in a pack of cards.

spaghetti (spa-ghet-ti) a food eaten mainly in Italy, made from wheat and sold in the form of long string-like pieces.

span 1. the distance between the tip of the thumb and the tip of the little finger when the hand is extended. 2. the distance between the supports of a bridge: The bridge crosses the river in a single *span*. 3. go over and across: At this point the river is *spanned* by a stone bridge.

spangle (span-gle) 1. a small piece of glittering material: She wore a dress covered with *spangles* to the fancy-dress ball. 2. sprinkle or glitter with *spangles*: 'Oh say, does that Star-*spangled* Banner yet wave?' (*The Star-Spangled Banner*).

spank 1. hit with the open hand, usually as a punishment for a child. 2. a blow with the open hand: He deserves a good *spank* (or *spanking*).

spanner (span-ner) a tool for gripping or turning the head of a bolt, a screw or a nut.

spar 1. a strong pole used for the mast of a ship, or to support its sails. 2. part of the framework supporting the wing of an aeroplane. 3. practise boxing, making the motions of attack and defence: The champion was *sparring* with his *sparring* partner in the gym.

spare 1. not punish, harm or destroy: The king showed mercy and *spared* my life. 2. find money, time, thought etc.: We should *spare* a thought for the homeless. 3. more than one needs at the time: Every car should carry a *spare* tyre. 4. thin, lean: Abraham Lincoln was tall and *spare*.

spark 1. a tiny glowing particle thrown off by burning wood or by one hard body striking another: The wheels of the train threw off *sparks*. 2. the least little bit: He doesn't show a *spark* of interest in this subject. **sparkle** shine, give out flashes of light: His eye *sparkled* at the sight of the new car.

sparking plug a device in the cylinder of a petrol engine which creates the electric *spark* to set it in motion.

sparrow (spar-row) a small, brownish-grey bird: The *sparrows* have built a nest in the barn.

spasm 1. the sudden abnormal contraction of a muscle. 2. a sudden short attack: In the middle of the speech he had a *spasm* of coughing. 3. any sudden burst of activity: His interest in model railways comes and goes in *spasms*. **spasmodic** taking place irregularly: I have made *spasmodic* efforts to stop smoking.

spastic (spas-tic) 1. disabled because of faulty links between the brain and parts of the body, bringing about spasmodic movements. 2. a person suffering in this way.

spatter (spat-ter) scatter or dash in small drops or particles: The passing car *spattered* mud all over me.

speak *spoke*, *spoken* 1. use language; talk in conversation: You *speak* too quickly. 2. talk to an audience: Who is *speaking* at the conference this year? **speaker** 1. a device which is part of a radio or television set, or which can be attached, to magnify the sound. 2. a person who makes speeches. **The Speaker** the officer who acts as chairman in the British House of Commons, of The House of Representatives in the United States, or some other similar assembly.

spear 1. a weapon for thrusting or throwing consisting of a long wooden handle on to which is fixed a sharp head of iron or steel: The natives of the island were armed with long *spears*. 2. pierce with a *spear*: They stood waist-deep in the river *spearing* fish.

special particular, not common: The safe has to be opened with a *special* kind of key. **specially** particularly: We came *specially* to hear you sing. **speciality** something one does or makes unusually well: Chinese food is our *speciality*. **specialize** be an expert: I *specialize* in old silver. **specialist** one who *specializes*, an expert: The doctor sent him to a blood *specialist*.

species (spe-cies) a group of individuals having features which distinguish them from other groups: The power to reason distinguishes the human *species* from all others.

specific (spe-cif-ic) exact, precise: I gave you *specific* orders about spending this money. **specify** mention, giving all details: The contract *specifies* concrete foundations of an exact depth and thickness. **specification** an account in detail of the materials and work to be done: I have asked for *specifications* for building a porch in front of the house.

specimen (spec-i-men) one thing taken to represent others like it: We have collected *specimens* of shells from the coasts of Britain.

speck a small spot of a different colour from its background: By this time the ship was a mere *speck* on the horizon. **speckle** 1. one of many small marks or spots on a background. 2. make or show such marks: This egg was laid by the *speckled* hen.

spectacle 1. a great show or display in public or in a theatre, circus etc.: Trooping the Colour is one of several *spectacles* to be seen in London. 2. a sight worth remembering: The view of the valley from the mountain-top was a remarkable *spectacle*. 3. something seen as unworthy, sad, ridiculous: Wearing a pink feather in her hair, she made an absurd *spectacle*. **spectacles** two glass lenses fixed in a frame resting on the nose, designed to assist a person to see better: He wore a pair of gold-rimmed *spectacles*. **spectacular** making a *spectacle*: Last night we were present at a *spectacular* firework display. **spectator** a person who looks on: At the end of the cricket match a large number of *spectators* rushed on to the field.

spectre a ghost: The *spectre* appeared at midnight.

spectrum (spec-trum) a band of colours formed when a beam of light passes through a piece of glass of certain shape: The colours of the *spectrum* are red, orange, yellow, green, blue and violet.

speculate (spec-u-late) 1. think or meditate: I *speculated* what I should do if I won the pools. 2. buy and sell goods, shares in business companies etc. hoping for profits but risking losses. **speculation** the act of *speculating*: It was a good *speculation* to buy the houses; they are worth much more now. **speculator** a person who *speculates*.

speech 1. the manner of speaking: If you want to be an actor you must improve your *speech*. 2. a talk given to an audience: The President's *speech* on television was watched by a vast audience. 3. the power to speak: Of all the animals only man has the power of *speech*. **speechless** unable for some reason to speak: When he threw the book at me I was *speechless* with anger.

speed *sped* 1. swiftness in moving, travelling or doing things: 'In skating over thin ice, our safety is in *speed*' (Ralph Waldo Emerson). 2. rate of *speed*: Aeroplanes can now fly at twice the speed of sound. 3. move along: The car *sped* down the road. 4. drive a car faster than is allowed: He was fined for *speeding*. **speedy** quick: We wish you a *speedy* recovery.

spell *spelt* 1. name or write the letters of a word in their proper order: How do you *spell* your name? 2. a form of words supposed to have magic power: The witch cast a *spell* on the poor woodcutter. 3. a period of time: The cold *spell* came as a surprise. **speller** a person who *spells*: I was never a good *speller*. **spelling** the way a word or words are *spelt*: The *spelling* of some words differs in the United States from their *spelling* in England.

spend *spent* 1. pay money for goods: I *spent* all my money on sweets. 2. pass time: We *spent* an hour or two in the fairground. 3. use up: He *spent* all his energy making a model aeroplane.

sphere 1. a solid body which appears to be round from whatever point it is seen: The earth is a *sphere*. 2. the surroundings in which a person moves and works, the company he keeps: I am quite out of my *sphere* among people who are interested in music.

sphinx 1. a stone statue in Egypt with a lion's body and a man's head. 2. a

monster in Greek mythology who asked passers-by a riddle and killed all who could not answer it.

spice a substance, usually part of a plant or tree (ginger, nutmeg, cinnamon etc.) used to flavour food: I do not like cakes with too much *spice* in them.

spider (spi-der) a small creature with eight legs which lives on insects: Many *spiders* spin webs in which they catch flies and other insects.

spike 1. a sharp, pointed piece of metal: His coat hung from one of the *spikes* of the railings. 2. an ear of grain, such as barley; a number of small flowers growing on one stem: He plucked a few *spikes* of lavender. **spiked** having *spikes*: All those competing in the race must wear *spiked* running shoes.

spill *spilt* 1. allow liquid to run or fall from a container: He *spilt* his tea on the tablecloth. 2. upset: The carriage wheel came off and the passengers were *spilt* into the ditch. 3. a fall from a horse, bicycle, carriage etc.: Turning the corner on his bicycle he had a bad *spill*. 4. a small piece of wood or paper used for lighting candles, pipes of tobacco etc.: On the shelf was a small vase containing *spills*.

spin *spun* 1. make cotton, wool or other material into threads so that it can be woven: The old lady sat at the door of her cottage *spinning*. 2. (of a spider) make a web. 3. tell a story: He *spun* us a long yarn about having missed the bus. 4. make a thing go round and round: The little boy was *spinning* a top. 5. move quickly: We were *spinning* along at a good speed. 6. go round quickly: A blow on the chin sent him *spinning*. 7. a *spinning* movement: The bowler put a *spin* on the ball and it hit the wicket. 8. a short ride: Get your bicycle and we'll go for a *spin*. **spinning wheel** an old-fashioned, simple machine with a wheel and pedal for *spinning* cotton or wool into threads. **spin bowler** a bowler who *spins* the ball as he delivers it. **spindrier** an electrical machine that dries clothes after washing by *spinning* them in an enclosed space. **spindle** a long rod on which thread is wound as it is *spun*.

spinach (spin-ach) a garden plant with green leaves which is eaten as a vegetable.

spine 1. the backbone: The *spine* or *spinal* column consists of a number of small bones through which runs the *spinal* cord containing the most important nerves of the body. 2. a thorn or sharp point: The hedgehog is covered with small *spines* which protect it from enemies.

spinster (spin-ster) an unmarried woman.

spiral (spi-ral) 1. something which starts at a central point and moves from it in a long curve, winding around itself. 2. going upwards, onwards or in any other direction in circles: The aeroplane ascended leaving behind it a *spiral* trail of vapour.

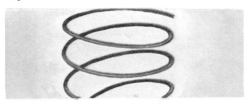

spire a tall structure on top of a church or other building which rises gradually to a point: The *spire* of Salisbury Cathedral is one of the highest in the world.

spirit (spir-it) 1. that part of a human being thought of as separate from the body, the soul: I am too ill to join you but I shall be with you in *spirit*. 2. a ghost, fairy, goblin or elf: 'Spirit, fine *spirit*, I'll free thee within two days for this' (Shakespeare, *The Tempest*). 3. state of mind, way of thinking or feeling: He is in good *spirits* this morning. 4. take away in secret: The child has been *spirited* away and nobody knows where he is. **spirits** drinks which contain alcohol: 'This house is licensed to sell wine and *spirits*.' **spirit level** an instrument with a glass tube containing *spirit*, used to test whether a surface is level or not. **spirited** full of *spirit*, lively: He was riding a *spirited* horse.

spiritual (spir-it-u-al) 1. having to do with the soul or spirit: We had a long discussion on *spiritual* matters. 2. having to do with the Church: Bishops and archbishops are *spiritual* lords. 3. a religious song originally sung by Negroes in the United States. **spiritualism** the belief that one may receive messages from and communicate with the *spirits* of people who have died.

spit *spat* 1. a rod or bar on which meat is cooked over a fire: Three chickens were roasting on the *spit*. 2. the liquid which forms in the mouth and which helps to digest food. 3. send out from the mouth: He ate the plum and *spat* out the stone. 4. send out with a *spitting* noise: The engine puffed out smoke and *spat* out red sparks. 5. fall in a few small drops, as rain: You'd better bring your umbrella; it's *spitting*.

spite 1. a desire to harm others or cause damage: You broke my model railway out of *spite*. 2. hurt another person because of *spite*: He put a high wall round his garden to *spite* his neighbours. **spiteful** showing *spite*: Nobody likes *spiteful* people. **in spite of** in defiance of: I shall go to work *in spite of* the doctor's orders.

splash 1. spatter, wet or soil by dashing drops of a liquid: Don't *splash* the water all over the kitchen. 2. the sight or sound of *splashing*: The stone fell into the river with a *splash*. 3. a mark left by a *splash*, a patch of colour: There are *splashes* of ink on the page.

splendid (splen-did) magnificent, gorgeous, excellent: We had a *splendid* time at the carnival. **splendour** magnificent appearance, colour: There were scenes of great *splendour* when the king was crowned.

splice 1. join two ends of rope, string etc. together. 2. join two pieces of wood so that they overlap. 3. the join made in rope, string, wood etc. by *splicing*: The work was so cleverly done that the *splice* could hardly be seen. 4. the part of the handle of a cricket bat that fits into the blade.

splint a thin strip of wood or other material used to keep a broken bone in position until it heals: His leg was in *splints* for some weeks after the accident.

splinter (splin-ter) 1. a small piece of wood, metal etc., with sharp edges, broken off a larger piece: The sergeant was severely wounded by a shell *splinter*. 2. break off or split off as *splinters*: The wooden bowl crashed to the floor and *splintered*.

split 1. break or cause to break into two or more parts, pull or knock apart: The prisoners were set to work *splitting* logs. 2. divide: The teacher *split* the class into two sections. 3. a crack or break: Let me mend that *split* in the back of your coat. **the splits** the feat of sinking to the floor, extending the legs at right angles to the body: Only trained acrobats and dancers are able to do *the splits*.

splutter (splut-ter) 1. make a sound as if spitting: Two lamb chops *spluttered* in the frying pan. 2. talk quickly in an excited way, so that the words are not clearly heard: When he was caught loitering in the playground he *spluttered* out an excuse.

spoil *spoilt*, *spoiled* 1. damage, make of less value: The bad weather has *spoilt* the fruit on the trees.—'Tweedledum said Tweedledee had *spoiled* his nice new rattle' (Lewis Carroll, *Through the Looking-glass*). 2. injure a person's character by unwise treatment: These children have been *spoiled* through always having their own way. 3. become bad: Ripe peaches should be eaten quickly or they will *spoil*. 4. things that have been stolen or taken by force: The army returned from the war carrying their *spoils*.

spoke one of the bars of wood or metal connecting the hub of a wheel with its rim.

spokesman (spokes-man) a person who is chosen to speak for a group: A *spokesman* of the party tells us that a special meeting is to be held today.

sponge 1. an animal that lives in the sea. 2. the framework or skeleton of this animal, made up of elastic material full of holes and used for washing and cleaning. 3. a piece of rubber or plastic material made for this purpose: We washed the car with a *sponge* and clean water. 4. get goods from a person or live at his expense: 'You've *sponged* on me for long enough,' said her uncle.

sponsor (spon-sor) 1. a person who makes himself responsible for another: As your godfather I am your *sponsor* until your eighteenth birthday. 2. an advertiser who pays for a radio or television programme in return for the advertisement of his goods.

spontaneous (spon-ta-neous) done without thinking beforehand or being urged by other persons: After the disaster we received several *spontaneous* offers of help.

spook a ghost: Don't go into that cellar, there are *spooks* about. **spooky** making a person feel uncomfortable and afraid: There's something *spooky* about the old house on the hill.

spool a reel on which thread, wire, photographic film, typewriter ribbon, magnetic tape etc. is wound.

spoon 1. a utensil consisting of a shallow bowl and a handle used in the kitchen and for eating: She stirred the jam with a wooden *spoon*. 2. use a spoon: The hungry man hastily *spooned* up the porridge. **spoonful** as much as a *spoon* will hold: Add a small *spoonful* of salt to the potatoes.

sport 1. an activity carried on for exercise, usually including much movement of the body: Hunting, fishing, shooting, racing and many other kinds of games are all *sports*. 2. fun: Don't take me seriously; I only said it for *sport*. 3. a meeting for athletic contests: We hold our school *sports* on Tuesday. 4. show proudly: He came to the dance *sporting* a bow tie.

spot 1. a small mark or stain on cloth etc. or on the skin: A leopard cannot change its *spots*. 2. a place: What a lovely *spot* to pitch our tents. 3. become marked with *spots*: The window was *spotted* with raindrops. 4. recognize: Can you *spot* him in the crowd? **spotty** with many *spots*. **spotless** very clean, with no *spots*: The shirt came *spotless* out of the wash. **spotlight** a projector which throws a circle of light on to a particular place or person.

spout 1. a pipe or tube through which a liquid is poured: This teapot has lost its *spout*. 2. come out, send out with great force: Water *spouted* from the hole in the road.

sprain 1. injure or twist a joint: I fell and *sprained* my ankle. 2. the injury caused by *spraining*: It was a bad *sprain*.

sprawl sit or lie with arms and legs stretched out in a careless way: He lay *sprawled* on the grass.

spray 1. water or other liquid broken up into very small drops falling or blown through the air: We walked along the promenade and were drenched with *spray*. 2. liquid prepared for certain purposes to be applied as a *spray*: I went into the shop for a bottle of hair *spray*. 3. the apparatus used for *spraying*: We used a garden *spray* to kill the pests. 4. scatter liquid in small drops: We *spray* the fruit-trees early in spring.

spread 1. stretch out, unfold: He *spread* out the plan on the table. 2. lay on; cover a larger space: They are *spreading* tar on the road. 3. extend or become extended over a wide area: The Great Plague *spread* from London to other parts of England. 4. take time: You can *spread* the payments over three years. 5. *spreading*: We are interested in the *spread* of knowledge.

sprig a small twig, shoot or branch of a tree: The old lady plucked a *sprig* of mint.

spring *sprang*, *sprung* 1. jump: He heard a sound and *sprang* out of bed. 2. come into being, grow: The fine weather is making the plants *spring* up. 3. the act of *springing*: With a sudden *spring* the lion threw itself on the hunter. 4. a piece of metal which, when pulled, returns quickly to its original shape: My watch needs a new *spring*. 5. the ability to *spring*: This elastic band has lost its *spring*. 6. the season of the year when the weather becomes warmer and everything begins to grow: In Britain *spring* begins in March; in Australia it begins in September.

sprinkle (sprin-kle) scatter in small drops or particles: The men *sprinkled* salt on the frozen path. **sprinkling** a very small amount *sprinkled* on: She put a *sprinkling* of salt in the soup. **sprinkler** a device for *sprinkling*: When water is scarce we are not allowed to use *sprinklers* to water the lawn.

sprint 1. make a short quick run: He *sprinted* along the road to catch the bus. 2. a short quick run: Everybody cheered when he won the *sprint*.

sprout 1. begin to grow: The corn is *sprouting* in the fields. 2. a small shoot which has just appeared. **Brussels sprouts** green buds which grow on the stem of a cabbage plant and are eaten as vegetables.

spry active, nimble: Grandfather is a *spry* seventy-year-old.

spur 1. a pointed device attached to the heel of a horseman's boot to urge the horse on: He dug in the *spurs* and the horse broke into a gallop. 2. anything that makes a person work harder or be more active: The *spur* of hunger forced him to seek work. 3. the hard spike on the leg of a cock. 4. urge on: He *spurred* his horse to a gallop.

spurt 1. squirt or gush out: Water *spurted* out of the burst pipe. 2. a sudden burst: A few *spurts* from the hose put out the fire.—He made one last *spurt* towards the winning post.

sputnik (sput-nik) an artificial satellite put into space, especially the first Russian satellite.

sputter (sput-ter) make a spitting sound: The candle *sputtered* and went out.

spy 1. a person who keeps secret watch on the actions of others: I knew I was being shadowed by a police *spy*. 2. one employed by a government to get secret information about military affairs of other countries: He was sentenced to be shot as a *spy*. 3. watch in secret: Those men have been employed to *spy* on me. 4. see: 'I *spy* with my little eye, something beginning with B' (a children's game).

squabble (squab-ble) 1. quarrel noisily: The thieves were *squabbling* about the division of the loot. 2. a noisy quarrel: I don't like *squabbles* about things that don't matter.

squad a small number of people working together: We need a *squad* of workers to pick up the litter. **squadron** a unit of cavalry, warships or aircraft fighting together: He led his *squadron* into the attack.

squalid (squal-id) dirty, filthy, wretched: Outside the large towns many people live in *squalid* conditions.

squall 1. a sudden strong wind which quickly dies away: The little boat was overturned in a *squall*. 2. a sudden cry, especially of a baby: All day we listened to the *squalls* of children. 3. cry out in pain, anger, fear etc.: 'Don't *squall*; I shan't hurt you,' said the doctor.

squander (squan-der) spend (money, time etc.) wastefully: The Prodigal Son *squandered* his money and returned home penniless.

square 1. a flat shape with four equal sides and four right angles. 2. an open space in a town with streets and buildings all round it: 'A nightingale sang in Berkeley *Square*' (a song). 3. the result when a number is multiplied by itself: The *square* of 4 is 16. 4. an instrument for drawing and measuring right angles. 5. shaped like a *square*: The table had a *square* top. 6. fair, honest: We give every customer a *square* deal. 7. complete, satisfying: I haven't had a *square* meal for days. 8. having to do with a number multipled by itself: 3 *squared* is 9 and the *square* root of 16 is 4. 9. make *square*, give a *square* shape to: I am *squaring* the corners of this piece of wood (making them right angles).

squash 1. crush: Don't *squash* those strawberries. 2. put down: The rebellion was *squashed* within a week. 3. a fruit drink: I have bought a bottle of orange *squash*. 4. a game played with rackets, sometimes called *squash*-rackets.

squat 1. sit on one's heels: A group of natives *squatted* in front of the hut. 2. settle on land or in a house without permission: The house had only been empty a week when a family started *squatting* in it. 3. short and thick: We saw the *squat* figure of a man walking down the road. **squatter** a person who enters and settles in property without permission.

squeak 1. a short, sharp, high-pitched cry: We heard a faint *squeak* from behind the door. 2. make or utter *squeaks*: 'Let me go,' *squeaked* the little mouse.

squeal 1. a shrill high-pitched cry, louder than a squeak: The little pig gave a loud *squeal* as I picked it up. 2. give a *squeal*: The children *squealed* with delight when the clown entered the circus ring.

squeamish (squeam-ish) 1. easily made sick: All this rich food has made me feel *squeamish*. 2. easily shocked, disgusted: We needn't go to the cinema if you feel *squeamish* about horror films.

squeeze 1. press something: He *squeezed* my hand. 2. press oneself against others: The little boy *squeezed* to the front of the crowd. 3. the act of *squeezing*: Her mother gave the baby a *squeeze*. 4. escape: 'That was a narrow *squeeze*,' he said as the car brushed past him. **squeezer** a device for *squeezing*: Bring me the lemon *squeezer*.

squelch 1. make a splashing or sucking sound: My boots *squelched* in the thick mud. 2. a *squelching* sound: He withdrew his foot from the mud with a loud *squelch*.

squib a small firework that can be thrown by hand.

squint 1. have eyes which look in different directions: You will recognize the man because he *squints*. 2. look with eyes half closed: He *squinted* into the sun, trying to see who was calling. 3. a crossing of the eyes: He needs a pair of spectacles to help cure his *squint*.

squire 1. a man who owns most of the land in a certain district: 'My little ones came running out to tell me that the *squire* was come, with a crowd of company' (Oliver Goldsmith, *The Vicar of Wakefield*). 2. in the Middle Ages, a young man who attended a knight and who would himself one day be a knight.

squirm 1. twist the body, wriggle: He showed me a caterpillar *squirming* on a leaf. 2. feel uncomfortable: She *squirmed* with embarrassment when he was cross with her for being late.

squirrel (squir-rel) a small rodent, with grey or red fur and a bushy tail, which lives among trees and eats nuts.

squirt 1. force out liquid in a jet from a narrow opening: The firemen *squirted* water on to the burning building. 2. a small quantity of liquid *squirted*: May I have a *squirt* of soda water in this lemonade, please?

stab 1. pierce or wound with a sharp knife or other instrument: He had been *stabbed* in the back. 2. a wound made by *stabbing*: There were more than ten *stab* wounds on the body. 3. (of a pain) feeling like a *stab*: He complained of *stabbing* pains in the neck.

stable (sta-ble) 1. a building in which horses are sheltered and fed: Jesus was born in a *stable* because there was no room at the inn. 2. put horses into a building to rest and feed: You can *stable* your horses in this shed for the night. **stabling** *stables* etc. for horses: There is good *stabling* in the village.

stack 1. a large heap or pile: The haymakers were piling hay on the *stack*. 2. a large amount: There is a *stack* of applications for this post. 3. pile up: When you have washed the dishes you should *stack* them carefully.

stadium (sta-dium) a large open space with seats all round it: A huge *stadium* is being built for the next Olympic Games.

staff 1. a stick, pole or rod used for walking, climbing, or as a weapon: The old man leant on his *staff*. 2. a pole used to support a flag. 3. a number of assistants working together under a headmaster, a manager etc.: I have recently joined the *staff* of this school. 4. (or *stave*) the five parallel lines on which notes of music are written.

stag an adult male deer: The *stag* was caught by its horns in the thick undergrowth.

stage 1. the platform in a theatre on which the actors perform: A conjuror performed marvellous tricks on the *stage*. 2. everything having to do with the theatre: I hope to go on the *stage* when I have finished my training. 3. a platform: The speaker stood on a *stage* in the open air. 4. a part of a journey, a single step in a process or growth: The next *stage* of our cruise took us to New Zealand.–Our team was knocked out of the contest at a very early *stage*. 5. put something (a play etc.) on the *stage*: Our dramatic society is *staging* a play by Shakespeare for seven days. **stagecoach** a coach drawn by horses which regularly carried passengers from place to place before the days of railways. **stagestruck** eager to go on the *stage*, to become an actor or actress.

stagger (stag-ger) 1. walk unsteadily: The drunken man *staggered* along the pavement. 2. shock, amaze: We were *staggered* to hear that he had disappeared. 3. arrange things, especially working hours, so that they do not come together: By *staggering* working hours we are hoping to ease the pressure on buses and trains in the rush hour.

stagnant (stag-nant) (of water) not flowing or moving: *Stagnant* water is unfit to be drunk by human beings.

stain 1. make dirty marks or marks of a different colour: Your fingers are *stained* with red ink. 2. make wood etc. a different colour with specially prepared liquid: I shall *stain* this cupboard the colour of dark oak. 3. the liquid used for *staining*: You need a can of dark oak *stain*. 4. a patch of colour or a dirty mark: There were *stains* of blood on the dead man's collar. **stainless** (of knives, forks, garden tools etc.) that will not *stain* or become rusty: This carving knife is made of *stainless* steel.

stair one of a number of steps leading up or down: You will find a café at the top of the *stairs*. **staircase,** *stair*way, a flight of *stairs*, a number of *stairs* leading from one level to another.

stake 1. a post driven into the ground to support or hold something: The bull was tied to a *stake*. 2. a post to which a person was bound who was to be burnt to death: Joan of Arc was burnt at the *stake* in 1431. 3. support with a *stake*: Have you *staked* your tomato plants yet? 4. risk: I would *stake* everything on the success of this mission.

stale 1. no longer fresh: We throw our *stale* bread to the poultry. 2. heard or seen before: That joke is *stale*. 3. having lost freshness or vigour through too much practice.

stalk 1. that part of a plant which supports a leaf, flower or fruit: I plucked a rose with a long *stalk*. 2. walk with slow, stiff strides: He *stalked* angrily out of the room. 3. move quietly in pursuit of something: Our party was *stalking* game in the woods all morning.

stall 1. a place in a stable for one horse or cow: The horse was feeding in its *stall*. 2. a small shop with an open front, a table on which goods are placed for sale: I bought a newspaper at the *stall* in the station. 3. (of an engine) stop suddenly and unexpectedly: My engine *stalled* and I had to push the car to the side of the road. **the stalls** the seats in a theatre nearest the stage.

stallion (stal-lion) a full-grown male horse from which foals are bred: The king rode into battle on his white *stallion*.

stalwart (stal-wart) 1. tall and strong: His bodyguard was made up of *stalwart* men-at-arms. 2. firm, reliable, enthusiastic: His *stalwart* supporters cheered his speech.

stamen (sta-men) that part of a flower, often in the centre, which bears the pollen.

stammer (stam-mer) 1. speak with sudden stops and pauses, or repeating parts of words: 'P-p-put that c-c-candle on the t-t-table,' he *stammered*. 2. the act of *stammering*: I wish I could cure my *stammer*.

stamp 1. put the foot down with force: He planted the tree and *stamped* down the soil all round it. 2. put a mark on something: You will find my name *stamped* on all my linen. 3. the act of *stamping*: The bull gave a *stamp* of rage and ran towards us. 4. put a postage *stamp* on a letter. 5. a device with a design or words cut into it which is used for printing: I put my name and address on the back of my letters with this rubber *stamp*. 6. a piece of printed paper, made to be stuck on letters as a sign that the postage on them has been paid: I had to buy more *stamps* at the post office.

stand *stood* 1. keep an upright position on the feet: There were no empty seats on the bus so we had to *stand* all the way. 2. rise to one's feet: The audience *stood* when 'God Save the Queen' was played. 3. remain: My offer to lend you the money still *stands*. 4. be in a certain position: The barometer still *stands* at 'fine'. 5. put in a certain place: He *stood* the ladder against the wall. 6. be in a certain place: This lamp *stands* on the table. 7. bear: I can't *stand* all this noise. 8. a position: We took our *stand* on top of a small hill. 9. a piece of furniture made to hold things: You will find an umbrella-*stand* in the hall. 10. a stall; a place where things are exhibited: He sells papers at a news-*stand*. 11. a structure from which people may watch sports, races and matches: The Queen and her party took their places on the royal *stand*.

standard (stand-ard) 1. a flag, banner or other object raised on a pole to rally an army, to indicate loyalty to a ruler etc.: King Charles I raised his *standard* at Nottingham. 2. a pole on which something may be placed: At the corner of the road is a lamp-*standard*. 3. a measure or level by which weights, lengths, sizes or values may be compared: As wages increase, it is hoped that the *standard* of living will rise. 4. most widely used: I have bought a *standard* edition of the works of Charles Dickens.

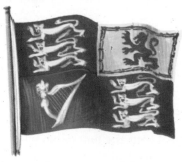

stanza (stan-za) a group of lines forming part of a poem: I will recite to you the first *stanza* of Gray's *Elegy*.

staple (sta-ple) 1. a piece of metal shaped like the letter U with two points: A *staple* can be hammered into a wall to hold electric wires. 2. a small strip of metal which, when pressed over papers with a special *stapling* machine, fastens them together. 3. the chief product of any country or region: Rubber is the *staple* product of Malaya.

star 1. one of the bodies (not a planet) that may be seen in the sky at night: Do you know how to recognize the North *Star*? 2. a figure with 5 or 6 points: Every *star* on the flag of the United States represents one state. 3. a leading actor or performer: There were many *stars* at the Royal Command Performance. 4. take the chief part in a performance or a film. **starfish** a marine animal having the shape of a five-pointed *star*. **starry** lit by *stars*, shining: The sky was *starry*, and there was no moon.

starch 1. a solid white substance with no taste obtained from wheat, potatoes etc.: *Starch* in some form is an important part of our diet. 2. *starch* prepared for stiffening linen and for use in industry. 3. use *starch* to stiffen garments: Collars which have been slightly *starched* will keep their shape better.

stare 1. look for a time with the eyes wide open: We *stared* with surprise at the strange insect. 2. the act of *staring*: He looked at me with an impertinent *stare*.

start 1. begin: Everyone suddenly *started* laughing.—What time in the morning do you *start* work? 2. set out: If we want to arrive before midnight we must *start* early. 3. move suddenly: I *started* in surprise when he entered. 4. set in motion: I could not *start* the engine. 5. a sudden movement: When the alarm rang I woke with a *start*. 6. beginning: Let's make a *start*. 7. the amount of time or the distance by which one *starts* in front of the rest: He had a good *start* but I soon caught up with him.

startle (star-tle) give a shock, a surprise, make a person start suddenly: We were all *startled* when he flung open the door.

starve be hungry; suffer through not having: They were lost in the desert and *starved* to death.—This child is *starved* of affection. **starvation** the condition of being *starved*: During the famine thousands died of *starvation*.

state 1. the condition in which a person or a thing is: The house is in a bad *state* of repair. 2. all the people under one government; the government under which they live: The railways of this country are run by the *state*. 3. having to do with the *state*: We travelled on the Italian *State* Railways. 4. having to do with ceremony: The ambassador was received in *state*. 5. express in words: Please *state* your needs at the counter. **stately** majestic, magnificent: A *stately* procession moved along the main street. **statement** something *stated*: The Minister of Transport will issue a *statement* this afternoon. **statesman** a person who takes an important part in managing the affairs of *state*: William Ewart Gladstone was one of Britain's greatest *statesmen*.

static (stat-ic) not changing; at rest: For ten years the population has remained *static*. **static electricity** electricity in the atmosphere which interferes with the sending or receiving of wireless signals.

station (sta-tion) 1. a position in which one remains: All men will remain at their *stations* for the next hour. 2. a building used for a particular purpose: Notice of the blaze was telephoned to the fire *station*. 3. a place where railway trains stop. 4. put at a certain place: Police were *stationed* all round the building. **stationary** remaining in the same place: The car ran into the back of a *stationary* lorry.

stationer (sta-tion-er) a person who sells writing paper, pens and other writing materials. **stationery** all kinds of writing materials: Our address is printed on all our *stationery*. **The Stationery Office** the government department which publishes and distributes government books, papers and pamphlets.

statistics (sta-tis-tics) the science dealing with the collection and use of numerical facts: Last month's trade *statistics* show an increase of imports.

statue (stat-ue) the figure of a person or animal represented in stone, wood, bronze, plastic or any other material: The *statue* of Eros, the Greek god of love, stands in the middle of Piccadilly Circus in London. **statuary** *statues*: In the museum there is a room full of Greek *statuary*. **statuette** a small *statue*.

statute (stat-ute) a law made by a person or a body such as parliament having the power to make laws: In England *statutes* were once made by the king; today every *statute* is an act of Parliament.

staunch 1. loyal, trustworthy: He has been my *staunch* friend for many years. 2. stop the flow of: A tourniquet was wound round his arm to *staunch* the flow of blood.

stave 1. break, smash: The side of the house was *staved* in by a runaway bus. 2. avoid: By borrowing money he managed to *stave* off the danger of being made bankrupt. 3. the five lines (or *staff*) on which the notes of music are written.

stay 1. remain: '*Stay* where you are!' shouted the policeman. 2. stop: I bought a sandwich to *stay* my hunger. 3. the length of time one remains: We are only here for a short *stay*.

steady (stead-y) 1. firm, fixed, not likely to fall: Is this ladder *steady*? 2. not changing speed or direction: We rowed all morning against a *steady* current. 3. regular, not changing: 'A *steady* worker' (from a school report). 4. make *steady*: I had to hold the ladder to *steady* it. **steadily** in a *steady* manner: Supplies of vegetables are *steadily* increasing.

steak a thick slice of meat or fish: He ate two beef *steaks* for dinner.

steal *stole*, *stolen* 1. take something belonging to another: 'Who *steals* my purse *steals* trash' (Shakespeare, *Othello*). 2. move, come or go very quietly and secretly: 'Around the walls to *steal* he *stole*' (part of an old rhyme).

steam 1. the vapour into which water turns when it boils: The kitchen was filled with clouds of *steam*. 2. surplus energy: We sent the children out to play in the garden to let off *steam*. 3. give off vapour: I sat down to a *steaming* bowl of soup. 4. move by *steam* power: Our boat *steamed* slowly through the fog. 5. cook by means of *steam*: I love *steamed* fish. **steam power** the power by which machines are run through producing *steam* in a boiler.

steel iron which has been hardened by heat and mixed with small quantities of other substances: This knife is made of the best Sheffield *steel*.

steep 1. having a sharp slope: '*Steep* hill: descend in low gear' (notice to motorists). 2. soak in water or another liquid: I like herrings *steeped* in brine.

steeple (steep-le) the tower of a church which has a spire rising above its roof: 'Turn again Whittington,' rang the bells from a hundred *steeples*. **steeplechase** a race across country on foot or on horseback in which many obstacles (hedges, fences etc.) are met.

steer 1. guide a car, boat, ship etc. in the required direction: We *steered* west in the hope of reaching land. 2. an almost fully grown male calf raised for beef.

stem 1. the main part of a tree or plant above ground. 2. the stalk which supports a leaf, flower or fruit: This vase will only hold flowers with short *stems*. 3. the long slender part of a tobacco-pipe or a wineglass: The glass fell to the floor and broke at the *stem*. 4. stop, dam up (a stream): We tried to *stem* the flood by putting down sandbags. 5. the upright timber at the forward end of a ship or boat to which the side timbers or metal plates are joined.

stench a very disagreeable smell: The *stench* of rotting eggs was overpowering.

step 1. move by lifting up the foot and putting it down again in a new position: I *stepped* backwards into a puddle. 2. the movement of one foot made by *stepping*: Don't come a *step* nearer! 3. the sound made by somebody walking: We heard *steps* (or foot*steps*) on the stairs. 4. a movement of the feet in time with others in marching or dancing: 'Keep in *step*!' said the teacher. 5. a very short distance: My friend lives only a couple of *steps* from here. 6. a move towards some purpose: We are taking *steps* to save the building from ruin. 7. a level place for the foot when going up or down: Don't fall over the *step* as you come in. **step-ladder** a folding ladder with *steps* fitted into its frame. **stepping stone** a stone on which one may *step* in crossing a stream.

step- a prefix indicating a relative through the remarriage of a widowed parent. **stepfather** the husband of one's widowed mother. **stepmother** the wife of one's widowed father. **stepbrother, stepsister** the child of an earlier marriage of one's *stepfather* or *stepmother*. **stepdaughter, stepson** the child of an earlier marriage of one's husband or wife.

stereo (ster-e-o) or **stereophonic** having to do with sound reproduced through two speakers from a radio or gramophone: The whole of Beethoven's Fifth Symphony is being broadcast in *stereo*.

stern 1. strict, severe: Discipline is *stern* on this ship. 2. the back part of a ship: The liner struck an iceberg and shook from stem to *stern*.

stethoscope (steth-o-scope) an instrument used by doctors to listen to a patient's breathing and beating of the heart.

stew 1. cook by boiling slowly in a closed vessel: Do you like *stewed* pears? 2. *stewed* meat: We are having a *stew* for dinner.

steward (stew-ard) 1. one who manages the property and money matters of another person. 2. a man who arranges for the comfort of passengers on a ship or aircraft: We went to see the *steward* about our lost baggage. 3. a man who organizes a dance, a race meeting or any public function: A few rowdy visitors had to be thrown out by the *stewards*. **steward-ess** a woman *steward*.

stick *stuck* 1. a piece of wood broken off a tree or shrub: We met an old woman gathering *sticks*. 2. a piece of wood cut and trimmed for walking or any other purpose: The little boy was knocking apples off the tree with a *stick*. 3. something shaped like a *stick*: The teacher picked up a *stick* of chalk. 4. pierce or puncture with a pointed instrument: He burst the balloon by *sticking* a pin into it. 5. join with, be joined with: The pages of this book are *stuck* together. 6. put something into a certain position: Don't *stick* your hands in your pockets. 7. become fixed, come to a stop: I was *stuck* in the mud. **sticky** that *sticks*: He put his *sticky* hands on my new dress.

stiff 1. not easily bent: I went out into the cold and now I have a *stiff* neck.—Have you a piece of *stiff* cardboard? 2. not easy to do: We were faced with a *stiff* climb to the top of the mountain. 3. blowing strongly: The ship sailed on in a *stiff* breeze. **stiffen** make or become *stiff*: The lapels of this coat need *stiffening*.

stifle (sti-fle) 1. make unable, be unable to breathe properly: The heat in the room was *stifling*. 2. keep back, put down: He *stifled* a yawn.

stile a series of steps to enable people to get over a gate or a fence: We had to help the old lady over the *stile*.

still 1. quiet, not moving: We stood perfectly *still* until he had gone. 2. at or up to this time: Are you *still* working? 3. even, yet: I need *still* more time to finish the work. 4. and yet, but: You've made all these promises but I *still* don't trust you.

stilt one of two poles, each of which has a support for the foot some distance above the ground: When I was quite small I learnt to walk on *stilts*.

stimulate (stim-u-late) excite, rouse to action or effort: A rise in the rate of bank interest is *stimulating* people to save. **stimulant** a drink that makes people more active: Tea, coffee, brandy and whisky are all *stimulants*. **stimulus** something that *stimulates*: A little encouragement would be a great *stimulus* to harder work.

sting *stung* 1. the sharp pointed organ of an insect or animal which injects poison into the body: The wasp carries its *sting* in its tail. 2. the pain or injury caused by a *sting*. 3. prick or wound with a *sting*: While plucking flowers I was *stung* by a bee. 4. give or feel a sharp pain: The cut on my hand *stung* painfully for hours.

stink *stank*, *stunk* 1. have a bad smell: The food *stank* through being allowed to go bad. 2. a bad smell: There was a *stink* of rotten eggs.

stir 1. move or make move: A gentle wind *stirred* the leaves. 2. move round and round as with a stick or a spoon: He poured milk into his tea and *stirred* it. 3. excite: The sight of the blind child *stirred* pity in all who saw her. 4. excitement: News of the royal marriage caused quite a *stir*.

stirrup (stir-rup) a footrest which hangs down from the saddle of a horse: He put his foot in the *stirrup*, mounted and galloped off.

stitch 1. one complete movement of a needle, pulling a thread between two holes made in cloth: I had to put a few *stitches* into the coat before I could wear it. 2. make *stitches* with needle and thread: The doctor had to *stitch* the wound on her forehead. 3. various movements of the needle in knitting, crochet and other kinds of work with thread, cotton, silk etc. 4. a sharp pain in the side often caused by running.

stock 1. goods for sale: We have a good *stock* of children's books. 2. goods stored: We need a large *stock* of firewood for the winter. 3. liquid in which meat and vegetables have been stewed, used to make soup etc. 4. keep for sale: We *stock* many kinds of radio and television sets.

stocking (stock-ing) a covering of wool, cotton, nylon or silk for the foot and leg: She wore a pair of elegant black *stockings*.

stoke put fuel on a fire, especially for an engine or a furnace. **stoker** a man who attends to the fires of an engine or furnace. **stokehold** the place where a ship's furnaces are *stoked*.

stole 1. (of the church) a narrow strip of silk or other material worn by a priest over the shoulders and which hangs down in front. 2. a collar of fur or other material worn over the shoulders by women.

stomach (stom-ach) the pouch in the body in which food is held and digested: He has a weak *stomach* and cannot digest solid food.

stone 1. the substance of which rocks are made: On the hill stood the figure of a man carved out of *stone*. 2. a piece of *stone*: We picked the *stones* from the soil and built them into piles. 3. the rather large and hard seed inside plums, peaches, cherries and some other fruit. 4. throw *stones* at: 'Three times I was beaten with sticks and once I was *stoned*' (St Paul writing to the Corinthians). **stony** 1. having many *stones*: We made our way along a *stony* path. 2. without feeling or expression: They listened to his story in *stony* silence.

stool 1. a seat with no back: The milkmaid sat on the three-legged *stool*. 2. a short low support for the feet: In front of the old man's chair was a wooden *stool*.

stoop 1. bend the body forwards and downwards: He *stooped* to pick up the pin. 2. behave badly, unwisely, selfishly etc.: He will *stoop* to any mean action to get what he wants. 3. a position in which the head and shoulders are held forward: The old man walks with a slight *stoop*.

stop 1. make an end of movement; cease from, leave off: He *stopped* the bus in front of the theatre. 2. fill up a hole or opening: He soldered the kettle to *stop* the leak. 3. prevent: He clutched at a branch to *stop* himself from falling off the cliff. 4. a halt: The car came to a sudden *stop*. 5. a place at which public vehicles (buses, trains etc.) *stop*: I'll meet you at the bus *stop*. 6. a punctuation mark: Every sentence should end with a full *stop*. 7. something that *stops* anything from moving: We had to keep the door open with a doorstop. **stoppage** something being *stopped*: There is a *stoppage* in the pipe and the water won't come through. **stopper** an object which closes a hole: When you put away the bottle, see that the *stopper* is in. **stopwatch** a watch used to time races etc. that can be started and *stopped* when needed to measure the time taken.

store 1. supply or stock of something kept until needed: We have a good *store* of hay for the animals. 2. a place where things are kept for use later: Our furniture is in *store*. 3. a place where things are kept to sell: We went to the furniture *store* to buy a wardrobe. 4. keep for future use: The dog *stores* his bones in a hole in the ground. 5. put things into a warehouse: While we were out of the country our furniture had to be *stored*.

stork a wading bird with long neck, legs and bill: The *stork* built its nest on the top of the Town Hall.

storm 1. a disturbance of the air, with strong wind, rain, or hail, snow, thunder, lightning, or dust: The snowstorm raged all night. 2. a violent and sudden attack: The town was taken by *storm*. 3. a violent outburst: The speaker's words were received with a *storm* of cheering. 4. shout in anger: He *stormed* about the room in a violent temper. 5. capture by *storm*: The fort was *stormed* at midnight. **stormy** 1. accompanied by *storms*: We cannot go out in this *stormy* weather. 2. accompanied by outbursts of temper etc.: I had a *stormy* interview with the manager.

story (sto-ry) an account, either fiction or true, about an event: Shall I tell you the *story* of my life?

stout 1. not fat, but of solid build: I am getting *stout* as I grow older. 2. strong, stalwart: Robin Hood arrived with a body of *stout* companions. 3. strong in construction, not likely to wear out quickly: You need a pair of *stout* shoes for walking. 4. a strong, dark beer, heavier than ale.

stove a kind of box made of metal or brick in which a fire can be lit and from which heat can be obtained for heating or cooking: In the living room we have a gas *stove* but the other rooms are warmed by electric *stoves*.

stow pack into something (a ship, a trunk, a cupboard etc.): Before leaving he *stowed* his belongings into a large packing case. **stowaway** a person who has hidden himself on a ship or aircraft in order to make a journey without paying.

straddle (strad-dle) stand or sit across something with the legs wide apart: The mare stood still and allowed him to *straddle* her.

straggle (strag-gle) 1. go, come or spread in a scattered, irregular way: A number of small houses *straggled* along the side of the road. 2. fall behind or stray from the march. **straggler** one who *straggles*: The enemy lay in wait to cut off *stragglers*.

straight 1. going one way without turns or bends: We walked along a *straight* road to the church. 2. level: Put your hat on *straight*. 3. honest: I will give you a *straight* answer. 4. free from wrong doing: He has kept *straight* for the last year. 5. directly: Don't forget to come *straight* home. 6. in good order: I want to put the office *straight* before I go on holiday. 7. the *straight* part, especially of a racecourse: The horse caught up with the others along the *straight*. **straighten** make *straight* or tidy: *Straighten* your clothes before you go out. **straightforward** 1. honest: He told me the story in a *straightforward* way. 2. easy to understand or do: Once you've done it, it becomes perfectly *straightforward*.

strain 1. stretch tightly: The rope was *strained* to breaking-point. 2. exert to the limit: We had to *strain* our ears to hear

what she said. 3. weaken or injure by *straining*: He *strained* a muscle competing in the long jump. 4. pass liquid through a sieve or cloth: The cook *strained* the soup before it was served. 5. being *strained*: The rope snapped under the *strain*. 6. something that *strains*: Paying the heavy fine was a great *strain* on my resources. 7. music: We heard the *strains* of the national anthem over the radio. 8. breed: We hope to breed a *strain* of cattle that will resist foot and mouth disease.

strait a narrow passage of water connecting two large bodies of water. **straits** a desperate condition: If you go on wasting money you will soon be in financial *straits*. **strait-jacket** a stiff garment designed to prevent a lunatic from struggling or harming himself.

strand 1. drive ashore: We found a shark *stranded* on the beach. 2. each of the strings or yarns which are twisted together to make a rope or cord. 3. a string (of beads, pearls etc.). **stranded** left in a helpless position with no money, friends or transport: We were *stranded* in France because of a railway strike.

strange 1. unusual: What a *strange* thing to say! 2. not used to; out of one's usual surroundings: The new office was *strange* to her at first. 3. not known, met or seen before: This handwriting is *strange* to me. **stranger** a person whom one does not know: 'I have been a *stranger* in a *strange* land (*The Book of Exodus*).

strangle (stran-gle) kill by squeezing the throat and preventing breathing: The victim was found *strangled* in the wood. **strangulation** being *strangled*: The doctor said that death was from *strangulation*.

strap 1. a narrow strip of leather or other material for holding, lifting, pulling etc.: As the bus rocked, the standing passengers held tightly on to the *straps*. 2. attach by a *strap*: We *strapped* the luggage on to the roof of the car. 3. beat with a *strap*.

strategy (strat-e-gy) the art of planning a military campaign or managing any important business affair: The faulty *strategy* of the generals caused them to lose the battle. **strategic** having to do with *strategy*: It was thought wise to make a *strategic* retreat (a retreat which could provide stronger positions).

stratosphere (strat-o-sphere) the layer of thinner air which surrounds the earth, lying above the atmosphere.

straw 1. the stalks of wheat, barley, and other kinds of cereal after the grain has been taken off: *Straw* is used for making hats, mats, as bedding for cattle and for thatching roofs. 2. a single stalk of *straw*; a narrow hollow paper tube: She asked for a *straw* to drink her lemonade. **strawberry** a plant that grows close to the ground and produces red fruit which is delicious to eat.

stray 1. turn away from the right path, get lost: Two sheep have *strayed* on the moor. 2. any wandering, homeless or friendless creature: This is a home for *stray* cats and dogs.

streak 1. a long narrow mark, smear or band of colour: The evening sky was marked with *streaks* of red. 2. mark with a *streak* or *streaks*: The green leaf was *streaked* with yellow. 3. move quickly: Ten racing cars were *streaking* round the track. **streaky** having *streaks*: Have you any *streaky* bacon?

stream 1. a body of flowing water, a river or brook: 'Still glides the *stream* and shall for ever glide' (Wordsworth). 2. a flow of water, liquid, gas, people, words: *Streams* of molten lava flowed down the mountainside. 3. run, flow: Blood *streamed* from her forehead. 4. wave or blow: As she ran her long hair *streamed* in the breeze. 5. move: Crowds *streamed* out of the stadium after the match. **streamer** a long narrow flag, strip of paper; anything that will wave in the wind: *Streamers* waved from windows as the king passed by. **streamlined** having a shape that offers least resistance to the air, so that a *streamlined* aeroplane or car can travel at greater speed.

street 1. a public way through a town or village with houses or shops on one side or both sides: 'She wheeled her wheelbarrow through *streets* broad and narrow' (*Cockles and Mussels*). 2. the people in a *street*: After he had won the medal the whole *street* came out to shake hands with him.

strength 1. being strong: 'It is excellent to have a giant's *strength*' (Shakespeare, *Measure for Measure*). 2. something that makes strong: Samson's *strength* lay in the hair of his head. 3. power as measured by numbers: The enemy faced us in *strength*. **strengthen** make stronger: This post needs *strengthening* or the roof will fall in.

strenuous (stren-u-ous) full of force and energy: Our batsmen faced a *strenuous* attack from the Yorkshire spin bowlers.

stress 1. strain, pressure: He cannot bear the *stress* of extra work. 2. emphasis: In this school we lay special *stress* on good manners. 3. emphasis on a word or part of a word when speaking: In the word 'recreation' the *stress* is on the third syllable. 4. lay emphasis on: Again I must *stress* the need for extra care.

stretch 1. draw out, reach out: *Stretch* your arm to its full length. 2. make longer, wider etc. by pulling: These shoes pinch; they'll have to be *stretched*. 3. extend: The forest *stretches* to the other side of the hill. 4. the act of *stretching*: Another *stretch* on the rope and the boy was pulled out of the pond. 5. an extent or a period of time: I have driven this lorry for ten hours at a *stretch*. **stretcher** a framework, usually of two poles with canvas between them, for carrying sick or injured persons.

strew *strewed*, *strewn* scatter far and wide: They *strewed* rose petals all over the pavement.

strict 1. stern, requiring obedience: John was set to work under a *strict* master. 2. complete: I'm telling you this in *strict* confidence. 3. exact: I am giving you a *strict* account of all that happened.

stride *strode*, *stridden* 1. walk with long steps: He *strode* out of the room. 2. pass over or across in one step: Can you *stride* that ditch? 3. the distance covered in one step: He took three long *strides*, then jumped. 4. an amount of progress: He is making rapid *strides* with his French.

strife quarrelling, fighting: The *strife* between the parties reached its highest point just before the election.

strike *struck* 1. hit, deliver a blow or thrust: He *struck* the table with his fist. 2. produce (fire, sparks etc.) by hitting or rubbing: He *struck* a match. 3. occur, come into the mind: It *struck* me that you may be short of money. 4. move in a certain direction: We *struck* across the fields. 5. take down, lower: We *struck* camp and continued our journey. 6. come upon or find: We have *struck* oil in the North Sea. 7. take root, put into soil to take root: I am *striking* a few geranium cuttings. 8. refuse to work in order to get better pay, shorter hours etc.: The workers are *striking* for an extra week's holiday. 9. the act of *striking*: The coal *strike* has lasted ten weeks. **striker** a person who *strikes*: The *strikers* walked in procession to the House of Commons. **striking** 1. that *strikes*: Could you please repair this *striking* clock? 2. causing great interest: The professor made a *striking* discovery.

string *strung* 1. a piece of cord thinner than a rope for tying parcels etc.: I cut the *string* on the parcel with a pair of scissors. 2. a piece of cord stretched tightly for some purpose: I need new *strings* for my violin. 3. a number of objects (beads, pearls etc.) threaded on a *string*. 4. a line of people or objects: A *string* of cars waited until the road was clear. 5. put a *string* or *strings* on: My tennis racket needs *stringing*. 6. put objects on a *string*: A number of girls sat at the table *stringing* beads. **stringy** like *string*, having tough fibres: The bacon this morning was too *stringy* to eat. **string band** a band made up of *stringed* instruments. **string beans** a kind of bean, the pods having *stringy* parts down the side.

strip 1. take off clothes, covers etc.: The boys *stripped* off their clothes and dived into the pool. – The decks of the ship were *stripped* for action. 2. rob, plunder, take away: The house was *stripped* of everything of value. 3. a narrow piece: This *strip* of land belongs to me. **strip cartoon** a number of pictures following each other and telling a story. **strip lighting** lighting by long *strips* of glass tube instead of bulbs.

stripe 1. a broad or narrow line or band of a different colour from the background: The flag of the United States is the Stars and *Stripes*. 2. a badge shaped like a V on the jacket sleeve of a British soldier or police officer: A lance-corporal or bombardier in the army has one *stripe*, a corporal two and a sergeant three. **striped** marked with *stripes*.

strive *strove*, *striven* 1. struggle: 'I *strove* with none, for none was worth my strife' (Walter Savage Landor). 2. try hard: We *strive* to please all our customers (notice in a shop).

stroke 1. the act of striking; a blow: The brave little tailor killed seven flies at one *stroke*. 2. a mark made by one movement of the pen or brush: He gave away all his money at one *stroke* of his pen (his signature). 3. one of a number of regular movements, or sounds: 'At the third *stroke* it will be 5-45 precisely' (time check on the telephone). 4. a sudden attack of illness of the brain: The old man died of a *stroke*. 5. pass the hand gently across something: Don't *stroke* the dog; he may bite.

stroll 1. a quiet, slow walk: Let's go for a *stroll* in the park. 2. take a *stroll*.

strong 1. having great strength of body, or part of the body: The Olympic weight-lifters are all *strong* men. – You need *strong* nerves to climb great heights. 2. having the power in mind and will: He set to work with a *strong* determination to succeed. 3. great in numbers: A *strong* force of police was sent to deal with the riot. 4. not easily yielding or giving way: The prison is surrounded by a *strong* wall. 5. forceful: There is a *strong* wind blowing. 6. having much flavouring in it: I don't like *strong* tea. 7. affecting the taste, smell, sight etc.: There's a *strong* smell of gas.

strop a leather strap for sharpening a razor.

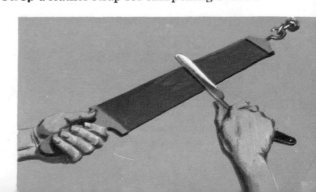

structure (struc-ture) 1. anything that is built: Westminster Abbey is a majestic *structure*. 2. the way in which a thing is formed, put together, built etc.: A doctor understands the *structure* of the human body.

struggle (strug-gle) 1. fight; work hard, make efforts: He *struggled* to free himself from the policeman's grasp. 2. hard work, *struggling*: When the alarm was raised there was a *struggle* to reach the exit.

stub 1. the remains of a pencil, a cigarette, a cigar etc.: He put the *stub* in the ashtray. 2. strike, put out: I *stubbed* my toe on a rock. **stubble** the stumps of grain after harvesting: Farmers turn their cattle on to the *stubble*. **stubby** short and thick: The pianist has *stubby* fingers.

stubborn (stub-born) obstinate; not yielding: Our army met with *stubborn* resistance.

stud 1. a small button or fastener that can be passed through two holes to bring together pieces of material: Has anybody seen my collar-*stud*? 2. a large-headed nail driven into a door, shield etc., as an ornament. 3. put *studs* into something: The soles of my shoes are *studded* to prevent slipping. 4. scatter on a surface: The king's cloak was *studded* with diamonds.

studio (stu-di-o) 1. the workroom of an artist, painter or sculptor. 2. a room specially equipped for broadcasting radio or television programmes, or where films are made for the cinema.

study (stud-y) 1. spend time and energy in learning things, especially from books: How long have you been *studying* Ger-

man? 2. examine carefully: We are *studying* your letter and will give you an answer later. 3. the act of *studying*: Our *studies* of your report reveal several errors. 4. a room used for *study*: You will find the professor in his *study*. 5. a composition or exercise done as a practice or to give practice to others: This portrait is only a *study*.– I have begun to practise Chopin's piano *studies*. **student** one who *studies* in a school or university or who strives to learn: *Students* in the Modern Language Department sat for their examinations today.

stuff 1. the material out of which something is made: How much *stuff* did you have to buy to make that dress? 2. any sort of material: What sort of *stuff* did you put in the cushions? 3. pack tightly into something: I *stuffed* the cushion with feathers. 4. pack flavouring (herbs, breadcrumbs, sausage meat etc.) into a bird before cooking. 5. fill the inside of a dead bird, animal, reptile etc. to preserve its natural form for exhibition: A *stuffed* owl stared down at us from the wall. **stuffing** material used to *stuff* things, either for cooking or other purposes: Who likes bread *stuffing*? **stuffy** 1. (of a building) badly ventilated. 2. (of a person) old fashioned, easily shocked.

stumble (stum-ble) 1. strike the foot against something: He *stumbled* and fell over the kerb. 2. walk unsteadily. 3. discover a thing by accident: At last I *stumbled* on the explanation.

stump 1. the lower end of a plant or tree left when the main part has been cut off: He sat on a tree *stump* to rest. 2. the part of anything left when the rest has been broken or cut off: He took a *stump* of pencil and wrote down the address. 3. each of the three upright sticks in cricket which make up the wickets: The ball hit the middle *stump*. 4. put a batsman out when he is not standing in the crease, by touching the *stumps* with the ball. **stumpy** short and thick: The tailor was a *stumpy* little man.

stunt 1. check the growth of: The trees on the slopes had been *stunted* by the fierce winds. 2. a performance showing skill or strength: Various acrobatic *stunts* took place at the air display. 3. something done to attract attention: Men dressed as clowns walked the streets as part of the advertising *stunt*.

stupid (stu-pid) foolish, dull in mind: He's *stupid* enough to believe anything. **stupidity** being *stupid*: It would be sheer *stupidity* to go out in this weather.

stupor (stu-por) being nearly unconscious through drink, drugs or any other cause: Most of the time he is in a drunken *stupor*. **stupefy** make almost unconscious; shock: He was *stupefied* by drink.–Everybody was *stupefied* by the shocking news. **stupefaction** being *stupefied*.

sturdy (stur-dy) 1. strongly formed or built: Your son is a *sturdy* child. 2. firm, loyal: The castle had a thousand *sturdy* defenders.

stutter (stut-tcr) stammer: 'Y-Yes, sir,' he *stuttered*. **stutterer** a person who stammers.

sty 1. a small building for pigs. 2. (or *stye*) a small pimple or inflamed spot on the edge of the eyelid.

style 1. a way of speaking, writing or doing a thing: Do you like the *style* of most modern buildings? 2. a fashion: This overcoat is in the latest *style*. 3. design: Our latest model cars are *styled* by the best designers. **stylish** fashionable: He always dresses in *stylish* clothes.

subdivide (sub-di-vide) divide a part of something into smaller parts: The novel is divided into books and *subdivided* into chapters.

subdue (sub-due) 1. defeat, overcome: After a long struggle the rebels were *subdued*. 2. make quiet: The child's sobbing became gradually *subdued*.

subject (súb-ject) 1. something talked about, thought about, studied, written etc.: The *subject* of my sermon this morning is the parable of the Sower. 2. one who is under the rule of the sovereign: We are loyal *subjects* of the Queen. 3. under the government of another ruler: The Roman emperor ruled many *subject* races. 4. being likely to have: The little boy is *subject* to headaches. 5. depending on: Everything I have done is *subject* to your consent. **subject** (sub-ject) subdue, bring under control: Rome *subjected* all the surrounding lands to her rule.

subjugate (sub-ju-gate) subdue, conquer: The native tribes were soon *subjugated*. **subjugation** conquering, conquest: The *subjugation* of England by William the Conqueror took some years.

sublet (sub-let) let part of a building or house of which one is already a tenant: I rent the house from my landlord and *sublet* two rooms.

sublime (sub-lime) grand, perfect: What *sublime* scenery there is in the Lake District!

submarine (sub-ma-rine) 1. under the sea: The ship is laying a *submarine* cable. 2. a ship which is equipped to be navigated under water.

submerge (sub-merge) 1. sink out of sight: Before we could fire at the submarine it had *submerged*. 2. be under water: The tanker hit a *submerged* rock and its cargo of oil began to leak.

submit (sub-mit) 1. surrender, put oneself under the control of: The motorist had to *submit* to a blood test. 2. put forward, offer, suggest: I beg to *submit* my report on the state of our playing fields.–Have you *submitted* the plans of your house to the Council yet? **submission** the act of *submitting*: The town was starved into *submission* by our army.

subnormal (sub-nor-mal) below normal: We have had many days of *subnormal* temperature.

subscribe (sub-scribe) 1. give money with many other people towards some object: Everybody in the street has *subscribed* to the hospital fund. 2. agree to take and pay for regularly: Would you like to *subscribe* to our school magazine? **subscriber** a person who *subscribes*. **subscription** subscribing, money *subscribed*: I have renewed my *subscription* to the hospital fund.

subside (sub-side) 1. sink to a lower level: At last the floods have *subsided*. 2. quieten down: The storm *subsided* and the sun came out.

subsidy (sub-si-dy) money granted by a government or public body towards some object: Farmers are asking the government for a *subsidy* to bring down food prices. **subsidize** give money to help: 'I can no longer *subsidize* your extravagances,' said his father.

subsist (sub-sist) be kept alive: This family cannot possibly *subsist* on what the father earns. **subsistence** means of being kept alive: He hardly earns a *subsistence* wage (enough to live on).

substance (sub-stance) 1. matter, a kind of matter: Lead is a *substance* which melts at a low temperature. 2. the main thing talked about, studied etc.: Now I am coming to the *substance* of my speech. 3. property; wealth: The Prodigal Son wasted his *substance* in a distant country.

substantial (sub-stan-tial) 1. strong, large: Before you go you must have a *substantial* breakfast. 2. on the whole: We differ on small points but we are in *substantial* agreement on the main features of the plan.

substitute (sub-sti-tute) 1. a person or thing acting in the place of another: He smokes herbs as a *substitute* for tobacco. 2. act as a *substitute*: Do you mind if I *substitute* tinned cream for fresh cream?

subterranean (sub-ter-ra-nean) underground: Before the earthquake we heard loud *subterranean* rumblings.

subtitle (sub-ti-tle) 1. a second title for a book or play, usually of an explanatory nature. 2. words in English projected on to a foreign-language film to help viewers to understand what is being said.

subtract (sub-tract) take away: *Subtract* 5 from 12 and the answer is 7. **subtraction** the act of *subtracting*: He has not learnt simple *subtraction* yet.

suburb (sub-urb) a district, usually mainly of houses, lying immediately outside a city or town: They live in a garden *suburb* outside London. **suburban** having to do with a *suburb*: Every morning I go to the office on the *suburban* (railway) line.

subversive (sub-ver-sive) intending to cause the downfall of a government or other powerful body by spreading rumours, making people distrust it etc.: The three men were taken to court for distributing pamphlets, and were found guilty of *subversive* conduct. **subversion** *subversive* conduct. **subvert** try to destroy in this way.

subway (sub-way) an underground passage taking people from one place to another, especially under streets: The road was too busy for children to cross safely and a *subway* had to be built.

succeed (suc-ceed) 1. have the desired result: All my plans have *succeeded*. 2. do what one intended to do: I *succeeded* in raising enough money to buy the boat. 3. take the place of another because of descent, election or in any other way: Queen Elizabeth II *succeeded* her father King George VI. **success** *succeeding*. The expedition was a great *success*. **successful** achieving *success*: My son has become a *successful* lawyer.

succession (suc-ces-sion) 1. the way one thing comes after another: There has been a *succession* of crimes in this district. 2. the right of *succeeding* to a title: The two princes both claimed *succession* to the throne.

succumb (suc-cumb) 1. yield: He *succumbed* to temptation and took the money. 2. die: The pilot of the plane *succumbed* to his injuries.

such 1. of the same kind, extent etc.: We have never had *such* bad weather before. 2. so big, good, bad, much etc.: I get *such* pleasure from seeing you; you are *such* a good friend. 3. this, that, these, those: *Such* are my thoughts about the election.

suck 1. draw into the mouth by the action of the lips and tongue: She was *sucking* lemonade through a straw. 2. draw in other ways: The plants *suck* up moisture from the earth. 3. put into the mouth and roll with the tongue: Don't *suck* your thumb. 4. draw in by *suction*: The little boat was *sucked* into the whirlpool. **sucker** 1. an organ in some animals by which they can attach themselves to a surface. 2. a new growth coming up from the underground root of a plant: It is necessary to take off all the *suckers* from rose-trees. **suction** 1. removal of air or a liquid so that things are *sucked* into the vacuum: A vacuum cleaner collects dust by *suction*. 2. attaching by *sucking*: The foot of a fly sticks to a wall by *suction*.

sudden (sud-den) quick, coming without warning: We were caught in a *sudden* snowstorm. **suddenly** in a *sudden* way: The platform *suddenly* collapsed.

sue 1. make a claim against another person in a court of law: If your car runs into mine I shall *sue* you for damages. 2. ask: After the army had been defeated the king *sued* for peace.

suede (pronounced *swade*) soft leather finished on the flesh side with a napped surface: I like your black *suede* shoes.

suet (su-et) hard fat taken from round the kidneys of sheep and cattle and used for the making of pastry etc.: I bought beef *suet* at the butcher's shop.

suffer (suf-fer) 1. feel pain, injury or loss: Do you *suffer* badly from colds? 2. endure, undergo: His parents *suffered* hardships in order to give him a good education. **suffering** pain, hardship: The recent earthquake has brought *suffering* to thousands.

suffice be enough; satisfy: Will this amount of money *suffice*? **sufficient** enough: The dinner was *sufficient* for all the guests.

suffocate (suf-fo-cate) 1. cause difficulty in breathing: This room is so stuffy that I'm almost *suffocated*. 2. kill through being deprived of air: Ten people were *suffocated* in the fire at the hotel.

suffrage (suf-frage) the right to vote in elections: In Great Britain there is universal *suffrage* (all adults have the right to vote). **suffragette** a woman who, in the early years of the twentieth century, worked for women's *suffrage*.

sugar (sug-ar) 1. a sweet substance extracted from the *sugar* cane and *sugar* beet, and used to sweeten drinks and foods. 2. sweeten, coat with *sugar*: Do you like *sugared* almonds?

suggest (sug-gest) 1. bring a plan or idea before a person's mind to be thought about or acted on: I *suggest* that we examine all the letters. 2. bring an idea into the mind: The idea of tunnelling under the wall *suggested* itself to us.

suggestion (sug-ges-tion) 1. suggesting: I came here at your own *suggestion*. 2. something suggested: On his *suggestion* we knocked at every door in the street. 3. something that suggests: There was a *suggestion* of boredom in his manner.

suicide (su-i-cide) 1. the intentional killing of oneself: The jury brought in a verdict of *suicide* while of unsound mind. 2. a person who kills himself intentionally: There were ten *suicides* in this city last year. 3. something which is likely to damage a person or a cause: If we give money away like this we are committing financial *suicide*. **suicidal** very harmful to oneself: During his nervous break-down he became *suicidal* for a short period.

suit 1. a set of garments, or armour, intended to be worn together: Did you notice the man in the grey *suit*? 2. a case in a law court: A *suit* for slander was brought against me. 3. one of the four sets of cards—hearts, diamonds, spades or clubs. 4. be satisfactory: Would Friday *suit* you? 5. look well with: This make-up *suits* your pale complexion. **suitable** such as to *suit*; right for the purpose: Are these shoes *suitable* for hard walking?

suite 1. a company of followers attending on another person: The ambassador has arrived with his *suite*. 2. a set of rooms in a hotel: They have been given a *suite* at the Savoy. 3. a number of articles of furniture which go together in one room: We bought a bedroom *suite* and a dining room *suite* at the sale.

sulk show by one's face and manner that one is in a bad temper: He sat all morning in a corner, *sulking*. **sulky** bad-tempered: If he doesn't always win he becomes *sulky*.

sullen (sul-len) 1. bad-tempered, sulky: All through the meeting he sat in *sullen* silence. 2. dismal, gloomy: It won't be possible to picnic in this *sullen* weather.

sulphur (sul-phur) a light yellow substance that burns with a blue flame and has a strong smell: *Sulphur* is used in the making of matches and gunpowder, medicine and rubber.

sultry (sul-try) hot and damp: The weather is far too *sultry* for me to work.

sum 1. the total obtained by adding numbers or amounts together: 25 is the *sum* of 12, 8 and 5. 2. a problem in arithmetic: This morning I got all four *sums* correct. 3. an amount of money: The total *sum* missing from the bank was enormous. **sum up** say briefly; make a judgment on: The judge *summed up* the evidence before the jury retired.

summary (sum-ma-ry) a short account giving the main points only: I will give you a *summary* of what happened.

summer (sum-mer) the second and warmest season of the year: In Britain *summer* begins in June; in Australia it begins in December.

summit (sum-mit) 1. the highest point; the top: After four hours' climb we reached the *summit* of the mountain. 2. the highest point of one's hopes, fortunes etc.: With the conquest of England, Duke William reached the *summit* of his power. 3. a meeting between heads of state: If peace is to be achieved there must be *summit* talks.

summon (sum-mon) 1. call for the presence of: He was *summoned* to appear before the magistrate. 2. rouse, gather up, call into action: 'Imitate the action of the tiger; stiffen the sinews, *summon* up the blood' (Shakespeare, *Henry V*). **summons** an order to appear, a command to do something: I received a *summons* to appear in court.

sun 1. the star from which the earth and all the other planets receive light and heat: In summer the *sun* rises early in the morning. 2. the *sun's* light and heat: 'The birds are faint with the hot *sun*' (John Keats). 3. any star which has satellites: There are millions of *suns* in the heavens. **sunbeam** a ray of *sun*light. **sunburn** a place where the skin is made brown or is burnt by the *sun's* rays. **sundial** a device for telling the time from observing a shadow thrown by the *sun*. **sunlight** the light given off by the *sun*. **sunrise** the rising of the *sun* in the morning. **sunset** the setting or going down of the *sun* in the evening. **sunny** 1. having much *sun*light: We set off on a *sunny* morning. 2. cheerful: She is popular everywhere thanks to her *sunny* disposition.

sundae (sun-dae) a portion of ice-cream with fruit or syrup poured over it, often with cream, chopped nuts etc. on top.

sundry (sun-dry) various, several: I have met him on *sundry* occasions.

superb (su-perb) wonderful, magnificent: He gave a *superb* performance as Hamlet.

superficial (sup-er-fi-cial) 1. being near the surface, not deep: His wounds were only *superficial*. 2. faint, slight: He bears a *superficial* resemblance to his cousin. 3. not thorough or detailed: I have only a *superficial* knowledge of astronomy.

superfluous (su-per-flu-ous) more than is wanted: What shall we do with the *superfluous* wrapping-paper?

superhuman (su-per-hu-man) above or beyond what is human, having more than human power: It would need a *superhuman* effort to finish the job in such a short time.

superimpose (su-per-im-pose) put one thing on top of another: To show the relative sizes of the two countries, here is a map of Britain *superimposed* on one of India.

superintend (su-per-in-tend) oversee, direct, supervise: Who is *superintending* the building of these houses? **superintendent** a person who *superintends*, a manager: My father is a Sunday school *superintendent*.

superior (su-per-i-or) 1. higher in rank: He is my *superior* officer. 2. better: This cloth is of *superior* quality. 3. greater in numbers: Our army was defeated by *superior* forces. 4. better than other people: He thinks himself too *superior* to join our group. **superiority** being better: The *superiority* of these goods has been proved by the way they sell.

superman (su-per-man) *supermen* a man having more than human powers: *Supermen* have never existed but have been imagined and written about by many authors.

supermarket (su-per-mar-ket) a large store selling all kinds of goods where people can serve themselves.

supersede (su-per-sede) replace by some other thing or person thought to be more suitable: Washing machines have *superseded* the washtub.

superstition (su-per-sti-tion) the belief in magic, witchcraft; the fear of what is unknown or mysterious: It is a common *superstition* that one should not walk under a ladder. **superstitious** having to do with *superstition*: She is full of *superstitious* fears about the future.–Are you a *superstitious* person?

supervise (su-per-vise) watch and direct work that is being done: My duty is to *supervise* the laying of a new drainage system. **supervision** *supervising*: The work is being done under the *supervision* of the chief clerk. **supervisor** one who *supervises*: I asked the advice of the *supervisor* of studies.

supper (sup-per) the last meal of the day: 'Little Tommy Tucker sings for his *supper*' (nursery rhyme).

supple (sup-ple) 1. bending easily without breaking: The rods used by the chimney-sweep are of *supple* cane. 2. moving easily: When we grow older our limbs become less *supple*.

supplement (sup-ple-ment) 1. something added later to a book; an extra addition to a newspaper or journal: The latest *supplement* to the encyclopedia has just appeared. 2. add to something: For years I needed to *supplement* my income by working at night. **supplementary** additional: He needs a small *supplementary* grant to finish his course at college.

supply 1. provide with what is needed: We are *supplied* with milk by the local dairy. 2. what is *supplied*: I have a good *supply* of coal for the winter.

support (sup-port) 1. bear or hold up: This bridge will *support* heavy lorries. 2. maintain, provide for: He has a large family to *support*. 3. help, strengthen: Our cause is being *supported* by members of all political parties.—This hospital is *supported* by gifts from the public. 4. that which *supports*: Additional *supports* are needed if the building is not to collapse.

suppress (sup-press) 1. put an end to: Efforts are being made to *suppress* the traffic in drugs. 2. keep back something from being known or seen: News of the disaster has so far been *suppressed*. **suppression** *suppressing*, keeping back: *Suppression* of the truth will do you no good. **suppressor** a device fitted to a motor or electrical appliance to stop interference with radio or television reception.

supreme (su-preme) highest in quality or importance, greatest: His was an act of *supreme* courage.—The *supreme* moment of his life occurred when he was presented with the medal. **supremacy** *supreme* authority or power: Rome achieved *supremacy* over all surrounding lands.

sure 1. certain, without doubt: I am not *sure* where I left my umbrella. 2. reliable, to be depended on: This is a *sure* remedy for your sore throat. **surely** certainly: *Surely* you are mistaken.

surf the white foam seen when the waves break on the shore or on the rocks. **surfboard** a board used for the sport of riding the *surf*.

surface (sur-face) 1. the outer face or outside of an object: A cube has six *surfaces*.— He smoothed the rough *surface* of the wood with a plane. 2. the top of a liquid: The sun shone bright on the *surface* of the lake. 3. the outward appearance: We shall only know the truth if we look below the *surface* of this matter. 4. give a *surface* to: This road is *surfaced* with concrete. 5. come to the *surface*: For want of air the submarine was forced to *surface*.

surge 1. a forward movement: We watched the *surge* of the waves. 2. move forward, rise: The crowd *surged* towards the scene of the riot.

surgeon (sur-geon) a doctor who is qualified to perform operations: The surgeon performed the difficult operation with skill. **surgery** 1. the practice of treating disease and injuries by operations: *Surgery* is needed to cure your illness. 2. the room in which people wait before they consult the doctor. **surgical** having to do with *surgery*: The exhibition contains *surgical* instruments in use a hundred years ago.

surname (sur-name) a name which a person has in common with the other members of his family: My Christian name is George; my *surname* is Smith.

surpass (sur-pass) do better than: His performance in the race *surpassed* all previous records.

surplice (sur-plice) a loose-fitting white gown with wide sleeves worn over a cassock by clergymen and members of church choirs.

surplus (sur-plus) the amount remaining after all needs have been met: As a result of the good harvests there is a large world *surplus* of wheat.

surprise (sur-prise) 1. come upon, discover suddenly: The watchman *surprised* the burglar breaking into the safe. 2. astonish: I am *surprised* to see you here. 3. the act of *surprising*: The enemy force was taken completely by *surprise*. 4. the feeling of being *surprised*: I can understand your *surprise* at seeing me here. 5. sudden, unexpected: The landlord paid us a *surprise* visit. **surprising** causing *surprise*: The train travelled at a *surprising* speed.

surrender (sur-rend-er) 1. give up: The town was *surrendered* to the enemy. 2. yield, give up hope: He *surrendered* himself to despair. 3. the act of *surrendering*: The leaders carried a banner with the words 'No *surrender*!'

surround (sur-round) 1. be all round: The house is *surrounded* by thick woods. 2. shut in all round: The enemy forces *surrounded* us. 3. the part of the floor left uncovered between the walls and the carpet: The room has a plain brown carpet and a linoleum *surround*. **surroundings** everything that is or was around: At Whipsnade you may see animals in their natural *surroundings*.

survey (sur-vey) 1. take a general view of: 'I am monarch of all I *survey*' (William Cowper, *The Solitude of Alexander Selkirk*). 2. measure and find the extent of land: We are having our estate *surveyed*. 3. examine the condition of a house or a building: Before you buy a house you should have it *surveyed*. 4. a statement giving the results of *surveying* land, a house etc.: Our *survey* proves that considerable repairs are needed. **surveyor** a person whose work is to *survey* land or buildings.

survive (sur-vive) live longer than: This old woman has *survived* all her relatives. **survivor** a person who has *survived*: The *survivors* of the recent fire are being treated in hospital.

suspect (sus-péct) 1. guess, imagine: I have always *suspected* that he was not telling the truth. 2. have a feeling that a person is guilty: We *suspect* him of theft (but we cannot yet prove it). **suspect** (sús-pect) a person who is *suspected* of something: The police have now interviewed all the *suspects*. **suspicion** *suspecting*: He was arrested on *suspicion* of housebreaking. **suspicious** showing or causing *suspicion*: I'm very *suspicious* about the truth of what he says.–He acted in a *suspicious* manner.

suspend (sus-pend) 1. hang, remain in the air or in a liquid: A large side of bacon was *suspended* from the ceiling. 2. stop: The banks have *suspended* payment until the crisis is over. 3. bar or prevent a person carrying on his usual activities for a limited time: After the match two players were *suspended*. **suspender** an elastic band or strap for keeping up socks or stockings. **suspension** *suspending*, being *suspended*. **suspension bridge** a bridge the roadway of which is *suspended* from cables hanging between great towers of steel or other building materials.

suspense (sus-pense) uncertainty about something; not being sure: We were in a state of *suspense* until the doctor told us the patient was out of danger.

sustain (sus-tain) 1. hold up, keep from falling: These brackets are not strong enough to *sustain* the weight of the heavy trunk. 2. suffer, undergo: The pilot of the aeroplane *sustained* serious injuries.

swab 1. a large mop used on board ship for cleaning decks. 2. a piece of sponge, cotton-wool etc. for cleaning the mouth of a patient or taking a specimen from the throat etc. 3. the material collected by a *swab*: Examination of the *swab* showed that he was not suffering from any disease.

swagger (swag-ger) 1. walk or talk in an insolent, proud and overbearing manner: He *swaggers* about as if he owns the place. 2. the act of *swaggering*: He entered the room with his usual insolent *swagger*.

swallow (swal-low) 1. let something go down the throat to the stomach: He *swallowed* a hasty breakfast, put on his coat and left. 2. make disappear: The great wave came and *swallowed* up the boat. 3. a small bird that migrates to warm countries in winter and comes back to Britain every summer: 'Gathering *swallows* twitter in the skies' (John Keats).

swamp 1. an area of soft, wet, marshy ground: If you stray from the road you may get lost in the *swamp*. 2. flood or drench with water: The boat was *swamped* by a huge wave. 3. be plunged into or overwhelmed with: I can't see any more visitors; I'm *swamped* with work.

swan a large graceful swimming bird with a long slender neck, usually white in colour.

swarm 1. a great number of birds or insects moving together: The sky was blackened by a *swarm* of locusts. 2. (of bees) move round the queen when migrating to form a new hive or colony. 3. appear or move in large numbers: Crowds *swarmed* into the football stadium.

swarthy (swarth-y) having a dark-coloured skin and complexion: We were stopped in the street by a *swarthy* beggar who asked us for money.

swathe wrap tightly round and round: He lay in bed, his head *swathed* in bandages.

sway 1. move unsteadily from side to side: The trees were *swaying* in the wind. 2. control, direct: He makes mistakes by being *swayed* too easily by other people.

swear 1. declare solemnly before God that what one says is true: 'I *swear* by almighty God that what I am about to say is the truth, the whole truth and nothing but the truth' (oath taken by a witness in court). 2. make a promise: I have *sworn* to give up smoking. 3. use bad language: Don't *swear* at me.

sweat 1. give up moisture through the skin: This hot weather makes me *sweat*. 2. moisture given out through the skin when *sweating*: 'His brow is wet with honest *sweat*' (Longfellow, *The Village Blacksmith*). **sweater** a knitted jersey, usually of thick wool, worn by athletes during exercise, or by other people for warmth or casual wear.

sweep *swept* 1. move dust or dirt away with a brush or broom: Have you *swept* the carpet? 2. push away, clear away as if with a brush: The wind has *swept* the snow into deep drifts. 3. pass over: A hurricane *swept* over the country. 4. move over or along lightly: Her long skirts *swept* the ground as she walked. 5. extend: Follow the road which *sweeps* round the base of the mountain. 6. the act of *sweeping* or clearing away: He gave the stable a good *sweep*. 7. a person whose work is to *sweep* chimneys: Little Tom was made to go up the chimneys by his master, the cruel *sweep*.

sweet 1. tasting like sugar: Is your coffee *sweet* enough? 2. pleasing: Revenge is *sweet*.—She is a *sweet*-tempered person. 3. sugar, boiled and with other things added: Would you like a *sweet* or a biscuit? 4. a *sweet* dish, a pudding. **sweeten** make sweet: 'All the perfumes of Arabia will not *sweeten* this little hand' (Shakespeare, *Macbeth*). **sweetheart** a person who is loved by another, of the opposite sex: 'Take your *sweetheart's* hat' (Shakespeare, *The Winter's Tale*).

swell *swelled*, *swollen* 1. increase in size, amount etc.: My leg is *swollen* from a snake-bite. 2. the rise in the level of water: Many boats were carried away by the *swell*. 3. the rise and fall of the waves: It will be dangerous to take the boat out in this *swell*. **swelling** a *swollen* place, especially on the body.

swelter (swel-ter) suffer from great heat; perspire: With no shelter from the sun we lay on the sand *sweltering*.

swerve suddenly change direction: The car *swerved* off the road and hit a tree.

swift quick, speedy: 'They were *swifter* than eagles; they were stronger than lions' (*The Second Book of Samuel*).

swill 1. kitchen refuse given to pigs. 2. wash by flooding with water: He *swilled* out the stables. 3. drink heavily: Don't sit there *swilling* tea. 4. a cleaning with water: Give the tub a good *swill* before it is used again.

swim *swam*, *swum* 1. move along in water by movements of the arms and legs or (of fishes) with the fins and tail: Goldfish were *swimming* in the pool.– I am learning to *swim*. 2. cross by *swimming*: This is my third attempt to *swim* the English Channel. 3. move on a surface: Bubbles *swam* on the soapy water. 4. seem to be moving: The room *swam* before my eyes. 5. the act of *swimming*, a time when one *swims*: Every morning I go for a short *swim* in the lake. **swimmer** a person who *swims*.

swindle (swin-dle) 1. cheat a person of his money: The old man was *swindled* out of his savings. 2. a process, a piece of *swindling*: The appeal for subscriptions is a *swindle*. **swindler** a person who *swindles*.

swine 1. a pig. 2. a coarse, disgusting person.

swing *swung* 1. make something move to and fro: He *swings* his arms as he walks. 2. turn or make something turn: As I *swung* round I saw him disappear round a corner. 3. move with a circular movement: The athlete *swung* the heavy hammer before he threw it. 4. a *swinging* movement: One second passes at every *swing* of the pendulum. 5. a seat hanging from above by ropes or chains so that one may sit in it and *swing*. 6. a strong rhythm in music or poetry: What a marvellous *swing* that tune has!

swirl move with a whirling motion: The wind sent dust and sand *swirling* about the streets.

swish 1. move or set moving swiftly through the air with a hissing sound: He *swished* his cane and struck the flower from its stalk. 2. a *swishing* sound: With a *swish* of its tail the horse galloped off.

switch 1. a device on railway lines to direct trains on to another track. 2. a device to put an electric light, cooker, etc. off and on. 3. a supple, easily-bending branch of a tree used as a stick: With his *switch* he urged the horse into a trot. 4. turn electric current on or off: It's getting dark; *switch* on the lights. 5. move a train from one line to another: The slow train was *switched* on to a siding to let the express pass. 6. change: I had to *switch* the conversation to another less painful subject. **switchback** 1. a mountain road having many sharp bends. 2. (railways) a zig-zag arrangement for climbing steep slopes.

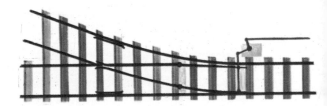

swoon 1. a fainting fit: She fell down in a *swoon*. 2. have a fainting fit: 'What! Did Caesar *swoon*?' (Shakespeare, *Julius Caesar*).

swoop 1. come down with a swift rush: The eagle *swooped* on its prey. 2. a swift movement: In a single *swoop* on their headquarters the whole gang was captured.

sword a weapon that consists of a long steel blade fixed to a hilt or handle: *Swords* are no longer used in battle but are still part of the ceremonial uniform of officers.

syllable (syl-la-ble) a part of a word which may be split from other parts: Sat-ur-day is a word of 3 *syllables* and Sun-day is a word of 2 *syllables*.

syllabus (syl-la-bus) the plan or outline of a course of studies: I have just received next year's chemistry *syllabus* from the evening school.

symbol (sym-bol) a sign, mark or object which represents something else: The cross is the *symbol* of Christianity and the white flag a *symbol* of surrender.–Many *symbols* such as + and −, × and ÷ as well as several letters of the alphabet, are used in mathematics.

sympathy (sym-pa-thy) a feeling of friendliness and agreement existing between people: We are in complete *sympathy* with your suggestions. **sympathize** feel *sympathy* for: We *sympathize* with you on the loss of your father. **sympathetic** showing *sympathy*: The children sang to a *sympathetic* audience.

symphony (sym-pho-ny) a long, elaborate musical composition consisting of 3 or more movements, played by a large orchestra: Among the finest *symphonies* are those written by Beethoven.

symptom (symp-tom) a sign or indication of something: These red spots on the skin may be a *symptom* of measles.

synagogue (syn-a-gogue) a building used by Jews as a place of worship.

syncopate (syn-co-pate) change the rhythm of music, placing the accent on beats which are not normally accented. **syncopation** the act of *syncopating*; a tune which has been *syncopated*.

syndicate (syn-di-cate) a number of firms in commerce which combine to do business or supply goods: Most of what is sold in this shop is supplied by a large *syndicate*.

synopsis (syn-op-sis) the brief outline of a book, a play etc.: Before I submitted my latest novel to the publisher I sent a *synopsis*.

syringe (syr-inge) a device which draws in liquid and forces it out again in a stream: *Syringes* are used for spraying and for injecting fluids into the body.

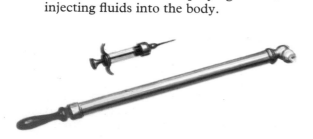

syrup (sy-rup) a thick, sweet, sticky liquid made by boiling sugar in water: *Syrup* can be given various flavours or used as a medicine.

system (sys-tem) 1. a number of parts making a whole or working together: Great improvements need to be made to the British railway *system*.–We are now studying the solar *system* (the sun and the planets). 2. a set of ideas or principles: The British *system* of government is based on election by the people. 3. a plan or method: It is impossible to work well unless I have some *system*. **systematic** based on a *system*: The town council has started a *systematic* destruction and rebuilding of slum areas.

T

tab 1. a small loop fastened on a garment for hanging. 2. a label: Every plant carries a *tab* bearing its name.

table (ta-ble) 1. a piece of furniture consisting of a flat top, usually on four legs: She put a vase of flowers on the *table*. 2. a *table* for some special use: Would you be so kind as to lay the *table* in the dining room. 3. a list in which facts are arranged in an orderly manner: Before I buy a book I always look at the *table* of contents.

tableau (tab-leau, pronounced *tablo*) a grouping of persons to represent a scene or a picture, with no words or actions.

tablet (tab-let) 1. a writing pad containing many sheets of paper fastened together along the top. 2. a flat piece of wood, stone or metal on which words have been written: On the wall was a *tablet* bearing the names of those who died in the war. 3. a cake of soap. 4. a small flat pellet of medicine: If you have a headache take one of these *tablets*.

tack 1. a small nail with a large head for fastening down carpets etc. 2. a long stitch for fastening pieces of cloth together until they can be properly sewn. 3. fasten with *tacks*: We *tacked* the carpet down to keep it from slipping. 4. sew with *tacking* stitches: If I *tack* the dress you will be able to try it on. 5. sail in a zigzag direction to make the best use of the wind: To reach harbour we had to *tack*.

tackle (tack-le) 1. ropes and pulleys needed for lifting heavy weights, for raising or lowering the sails of ships etc. 2. equipment needed for a special purpose: You can buy fishing *tackle* at this shop. 3. the act of stopping an opponent in football or rugby: That was a fine *tackle*! 4. deal with a problem, set to work on a task: Nobody else would fix the door so I *tackled* the job myself.

tact great skill and understanding in dealing with people; ability to handle difficult situations without giving offence: He showed great *tact* in persuading the men to go back to work. **tactful** having or showing *tact*. **tactless** lacking or not showing *tact*: It was very *tactless* of you to tell them to go home.

tadpole (tad-pole) the young of a frog or toad: When a *tadpole* develops into a frog its legs grow and it loses its tail.

taffeta (taf-fe-ta) a shiny, stiff silk or rayon cloth: *Taffeta* is often used for lining dresses.

tag 1. a piece of card, paper or other tough material to mark or label something: Every article in the shop bore a *tag* giving its price. 2. the binding of metal, plastic or other hard material at the end of a shoelace, string, cord etc.: *Tags* are put on the ends of ropes and laces to prevent them from fraying. 3. a game in which one child chases and tries to touch another. 4. fasten on: Before the sale, price labels were *tagged* on to all the shoes.

tail 1. the movable part which grows at the back or end of the body of an animal: A dog wags its *tail* when it is pleased and a cat when it is angry. 2. something resembling a *tail*: He fastened a *tail* to his kite. 3. the side of a coin opposite to that which usually carries the portrait of a monarch, a president etc.: 'Heads or *tails*!' he called, tossing the coin. 4. to move or follow in a line. **tail-light** the light at the rear end of a car or other vehicle. **tail-spin** a spiral dive of an aeroplane in which the *tail* spins in wider circles than the front.

tailor (tail-or) one whose business it is to make or mend outer garments: 'She went to the *tailor's* to buy him a coat' (*Old Mother Hubbard*).

take *took*, *taken* 1. hold with arms, teeth, hands or an instrument: He *took* the thief by the collar and threw him out. 2. capture, possess: Twenty prisoners were *taken* in the raid. 3. steal, borrow: Who's *taken* my pencil? 4. use up: It *took* an hour to walk to the station. 5. accept: 'What will you *take* for this cricket bat?' I asked the shopkeeper. 6. buy regularly: Every morning we *take* 'The Times'. 7. find out: The doctor *took* my temperature. 8. receive into the body: He has *taken* no food all day. 9. carry, accompany: I'm *taking* the children for a week's holiday. 10. occupy: Please *take* a seat. 11. undergo, enjoy: He *took* a bath after the game. 12. write down: The secretary *took* notes during the meeting. 13. consider: I *take* you to be an honest man. 14. perform: Shall we *take* a walk? 15. require: It *takes* courage to sail round the world alone.

talc a soft, smooth mineral that can be split into thin plates or ground into very fine powder. **talcum powder** a very fine white powder made from *talc* which is perfumed and used on the body.

tale 1. a story: I will tell you a *tale* about a giant. 2. a report: They all brought different *tales* about the accident.

talent (tal-ent) a special natural ability to do a thing well: He was born with a *talent* for drawing. **talented** having a *talent*: He is a *talented* violinist.

talk 1. speak, say things: We *talked* about our travels. 2. be able to speak: The baby can't *talk* yet. 3. give information: They tried to make him *talk*. 4. discuss, *talk* about: All evening they *talked* about nothing but chess. 5. make somebody do a thing or be in a certain state by *talking*: I've *talked* myself hoarse with no result. 6. a conversation: Now let's have a *talk* about the future. 7. a lecture, an address: We listened to a *talk* on astronomy. 8. a rumour: Have you heard the *talk* about the factory closing?

tall 1. (of persons) of more than average height: He is *tall* for his age. 2. (of objects) high: The *tall* chimney fell with a crash.

tallow (tal-low) hard fat or suet, usually from animals, used for the making of candles, soap etc.

tally (tal-ly) 1. a ticket or label. 2. match or agree: We both added the figures up but your answer does not *tally* with mine.

talon (tal-on) a claw, especially that of a bird of prey, an eagle, a hawk etc.

tambourine (tam-bou-rine) a small drum consisting of a circular wooden frame with skin stretched over it, and in the frame small metal plates which give a jingling sound when it is shaken: The *tambourine* is played by being shaken and tapped with the fingers.

tame 1. (of animals) accustomed to living with human beings: *Tame* animals, such as cattle, horses, cats and dogs are of great use to men. 2. dull, not interesting: The sermon was so *tame* that the old man fell asleep. 3. make *tame*: I have not yet found it possible to *tame* a fox. **tamer** a person who *tames* animals: The lion-*tamer* walked boldly into the cage.

tamper (tam-per) interfere, meddle: The door would not open because the lock had been *tampered* with.

tan 1. yellowish brown: She bought a pair of *tan* shoes. 2. make an animal's skin or hide into leather. 3. become brown through being burnt by the sun: Some people *tan* easily. 4. the brown colour one becomes through being in the sun: She came home from her holiday with a deep *tan*. **tanner** a person who *tans* hides.

tandem (tan-dem) 1. a bicycle made for two persons to ride on, one behind the other. 2. one behind the other: Most of the party had their own bicycles, but my wife and I were riding *tandem*.

tang a sharp flavour, or distinctive smell or taste: We sniffed the *tang* of the sea a few miles from the coast.

tangent (tan-gent) 1. a straight line touching but not cutting a curve or a circle. 2. a sudden change from one subject or one action to another: He flew off at a *tangent* and began to talk about fishing.

tangerine (tan-ger-ine) a small, loose-skinned variety of orange.

tangle (tan-gle) 1. an amount of string or hair twisted together and difficult to undo: The puppy had made a *tangle* of the ball of string. 2. a confusion: I tried to make my way out of the *tangle* of traffic in the square. 3. make a *tangle*: Who has *tangled* my ball of wool?

tango (tan-go) 1. a South American dance with a strong rhythm. 2. the music for a *tango*: When we entered the restaurant the orchestra was playing a *tango*.

tank 1. a large container for carrying liquid or gas: The water *tank* supplies all the houses in the street. 2. an armoured fighting vehicle first used in the war of 1914–18: It was impossible to stop the advance of the enemy *tanks*. **tanker** 1. a ship which carries petroleum 2. a heavy lorry carrying petroleum: In the collision the *tanker* spilt much of its cargo on the road.

tankard (tank-ard) a large drinking mug, usually for beer, with a handle and sometimes a hinged lid.

tantalize (tan-ta-lize) torment by making a person hope for things he can never get: Don't *tantalize* him with your stories of hidden treasure.

tap 1. a device for controlling the flow of liquid from a pipe: Who turned the *tap* on? – Who left the *tap* running? 2. a quick, light blow: I felt a *tap* on my shoulder. 3. make a hole to let liquid come out: Rubber trees are *tapped* in order to get the valuable sap from which rubber is obtained. 4. get information by secret means: We did not realize that our telephone had been *tapped*. 5. give a *tap* to: He *tapped* at the window before opening the door.

tape 1. material in narrow strips for tying up parcels, for use in making garments, and other purposes: I shall need insulating *tape* to fix this electric light. 2. magnetic *tape* specially prepared to record sound: We recorded his speech on *tape*. 3. fasten, bind with *tape*: A plaster was put over the wound and it was securely *taped*. 4. record on magnetic *tape*: Would you allow me to *tape* your speech? **tape measure** a length of *tape* with marks on indicating measurements. **tape recorder** a machine into which *tapes* can be inserted for recording sounds.

taper (tap-er) 1. become or make smaller at one end: The conductor's baton *tapers* off to a point. 2. a long, very thin candle: 'The *taper* burneth in your closet, sir' (Shakespeare, *Julius Caesar*).

tapestry (tap-es-try) cloth in which threads are woven by hand to make a design or picture: The Bayeux *Tapestry* shows scenes of the Norman conquest of England.

tar 1. a black substance made from coal, thick and very sticky when hot, and hard when cold: *Tar* is used for preserving timber and making roads. 2. put *tar* on: 'Newly *tarred* road. Proceed with caution.' (notice to motorists). **tarmac** a mixture of *tar* and small stones, used to surface roads, and runways for aeroplanes. **tarpaulin** thick canvas treated with *tar* to make it waterproof: The furniture was packed on a lorry and covered with a large *tarpaulin*.

tarantula (ta-ran-tu-la) the name given to large poisonous spiders found in southern Europe and America.

tardy (tar-dy) 1. moving slowly. 2. late or behind time: It was extremely *tardy* of me not to have written sooner.

target (tar-get) 1. any object to be aimed at: The archers were practising aiming at the *target*. 2. anything aimed at other than by throwing or firing: Our *target* is to finish painting the house by tomorrow.

tariff (tar-iff) 1. list of goods and services supplied by an hotel: A printed *tariff* was displayed in the window. 2. list of taxes levied on imported goods: Many countries try to protect their own industries by putting *tariffs* on goods from abroad.

tarnish (tar-nish) 1. (of metals) lose colour or brightness: In the drawer we found a candlestick of *tarnished* copper. 2. cause to *tarnish*: Exposure to the air will *tarnish* most metals.

tarry (tar-ry) stay for a time: If you *tarry* too long in this place they will catch up with you.

tart 1. a small piece of pastry shaped like a saucer, its centre filled with fruit, jam etc.: A fruit *tart* has a crust of pastry covering the fruit. 2. sour in taste: This apple is very *tart*.

tartan (tar-tan) 1. woollen cloth with stripes of different colours crossing at right angles: Every Scottish clan has its own *tartan*. 2. cloth with a *tartan* pattern: She wore a *tartan* skirt.

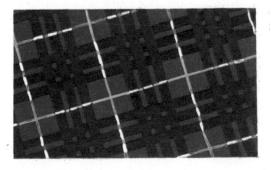

tartar (tar-tar) a hard, chalky substance deposited on the teeth: When the dentist cleans our teeth he first scrapes off the *tartar*.

task 1. a piece of work, a duty to be done: One of my *tasks* is to sweep out the stables every morning. 2. strain, overwork: Do not *task* your strength by carrying loads which are too heavy.

tassel (tas-sel) an ornament consisting of a bunch of thin cords or threads tied at one end to make a knob or ball: From each side of the banner hung a *tassel* of gold cord.

taste 1. the sense by which the flavour of something is known when taken into the mouth: Lemon juice is sour to the *taste*. 2. the kind or degree of flavour that substances give when taken into the mouth: I like the sweet *taste* of honey. 3. a small quantity of: Do have a *taste* of this cake! 4. a liking for: I have a *taste* for rich foods. 5. the sense or knowledge of what is good in certain things or actions: I admire his *taste* in classical music. 6. be conscious of the *taste* of something: I can *taste* almonds in this cake. 7. try something by its *taste*: The waiter poured wine into the glass for me to *taste*. 8. know, experience: Have you ever *tasted* the fun of foreign travel? **tasteless** showing little *taste*; having no *taste*: The arrangement of the exhibition was dull and *tasteless*.

tatter (tat-ter) a rag, a piece torn off: His clothes were in *tatters* after walking for a week. **tattered** ragged: We sent him upstairs to take off his *tattered* clothes.

tattoo (tat-too) 1. a signal on a drum to call soldiers or sailors to retire to their quarters. 2. a continuous tapping: He continued to beat a *tattoo* on the table with his finger tips. 3. an outdoor military entertainment: Did you see the Royal *Tattoo* on television? 4. prick the skin and make coloured designs in it: Once the skin has been *tattooed* the designs cannot be easily removed.

taunt 1. an insulting remark intended to hurt a person's feelings: We went on with our work and took no notice of his *taunts*. 2. to insult in a scornful way: 'That's right, run off and tell your mother,' he *taunted*.

taut tightly stretched: As long as the wind remained strong, all the ropes were kept *taut*.

tavern (tav-ern) an inn, a place where food and drink can be bought and consumed.

tax 1. money paid by the people of a country towards the cost of its government, defence, health services, education etc.: *Taxes* are levied on income, on property, on profits and many other items. 2. a strain: Serving on the committee has been a great *tax* on her strength. 3. lay *taxes* on: The peasants were heavily *taxed*. 4. be a strain on: His health was *taxed* through overwork. **taxation** raising money by *taxes*: The government is trying in vain to reduce *taxation*.

taxi (ta-xi) 1. a car which one may hire to be driven from place to place: We must take a *taxi* to the station. 2. (of an aeroplane) move along the ground: The plane *taxied* along the tarmac.

tea 1. the dried leaves of an evergreen plant grown in Asia. 2. the drink made by pouring boiling water on the leaves: Would you prefer *tea* or coffee? 3. a regular time when *tea* is drunk: It's four o'clock; would you like to stay to *tea*? **teatime** the time when *tea* is regularly served.

teach *taught* give instruction: I *teach* mathematics. **teacher** a person who *teaches*. **teaching** the work of a *teacher*, that which is *taught*: I earn my living by *teaching*.

team 1. a number of persons playing on the same side in a match: There are eleven players in a cricket *team*. 2. a number of persons doing something together: I have brought my *team* of dancers to perform in this town. 3. two or more horses or oxen drawing a cart, a plough etc.: The farmer was ploughing with his *team*. **teamwork** the combined effort of a *team* working well together.

tear (rhymes with *fair*) *tore*, *torn* 1. pull apart or in pieces by force: We *tore* up a whole newspaper to light the fire. 2. become *torn*: This cloth *tears* easily. 3. rush at great speed: I watched him as he *tore* along the street on his motorcycle.

tear (rhymes with *ear*) a drop of salty water that comes from the eyes: I laughed so hard that the *tears* ran down my face.

tease 1. make fun of another person, sometimes causing annoyance: He *teased* the little girl till she begãn to cry. 2. a person who likes to *tease* others.

technical (tech-ni-cal) having to do with great skill in some industry (engineering, weaving, printing etc.) or in the arts (painting, music etc.): Carpentry needs a great deal of *technical* knowledge and skill. **technician** a person expert in the methods of a particular art or industry. **technique** skill, or method of doing things expertly: He is learning all the *techniques* of colour printing.

tedious (te-di-ous) boring, making one weary or tired: Many of the jobs in this factory are very *tedious*.

teem 1. contain in large numbers: This lake *teems* with fish. 2. be present in large numbers: The sky was alive with a *teeming* multitude of locusts.

teens numbers (in age) between 12 and 20: This shop specializes in clothes for young people in their *teens* (sometimes called *teen*agers).

teetotal (tee-to-tal) not drinking or approving of drinking alcoholic drinks: I didn't know you were *teetotal*. **teetotaller** a person who is *teetotal*.

tele- part of a word meaning distant, which refers especially to sight and sound. **telegram** a communication sent by *tele*graph. **telegraph** a system of communication by the use of electric current along wires, or by wireless. **telephone** communication with persons a long way off through an apparatus that transmits speech. **teleprinter** an instrument that prints messages as they come in over long distances. **telescope** an instrument with lenses that makes distant objects appear much nearer. **television** still or moving pictures transmitted over great distances.

tell *told* 1. give information about something: Did you *tell* him what I said? 2. relate (a story or an experience): Shall I *tell* you the tale about the hare and the tortoise? 3. order: *Tell* him to stop playing the piano. 4. distinguish: Can you *tell* the difference between margarine and butter? 5. reveal (secrets): I asked you not to *tell*. **telltale** a person who *tells* another's secrets.

temper (tem-per) 1. the state of one's mind: You can stroke the dog; he has a very good *temper*. 2. an angry state of mind: Don't go near him, he's in a *temper*. **temperament** the way a person thinks, feels and acts: The two brothers are completely different in *temperament*.

temperance (tem-per-ance) 1. self-control, being moderate in all things such as eating, drinking, smoking etc. 2. avoiding all intoxicating drinks. **temperance hotel** a hotel in which no alcoholic drinks are served. **temperate** 1. behaving with moderation or *temperance*: Though he had been insulted he answered in *temperate* language. 2. not too hot, nor too cold: I should prefer to live in a country with a *temperate* climate.

temperature (tem-per-a-ture) heat and cold as measured in degrees on a thermometer: What is the *temperature* at which water boils?

tempest (tem-pest) a violent storm: 'From the shore the *tempest* beat us back' (Shakespeare, *Henry VI, part 2*). **tempestuous** violent, stormy: The weather is too *tempestuous* to sail today.

temple (tem-ple) 1. a building used for the worship of a god: We are excavating the remains of an ancient Greek *temple*. 2. the flat part of the head between the ear and the forehead.

temporary (tem-po-ra-ry) lasting or intended to last only a short time: I have obtained a *temporary* post in a bank.

tempt 1. attempt to persuade a person to do evil: Eve was *tempted* by the serpent. 2. appeal, seem very good: Your offer *tempts* me to buy the chair. 3. attract a person to do something: The fine weather *tempted* us to go for a stroll in the park. **temptation** being *tempted*; something that *tempts*: It was hard to resist the *temptation* to finish the cake.

ten the number (10) coming after 9 and before 11: *Ten* men went to mow a meadow.

tenant (ten-ant) a person who pays rent for the use of a building or of land: Every week the landlord collects the rent from his *tenants*. **tenement** a house or a portion of a house rented by a *tenant* as a separate dwelling: Two large houses have been divided into *tenements*.

tender (ten-der) 1. not hard; easy to chew: The steak we had for dinner was very *tender*. 2. easily broken, soft, delicate: My skin is still *tender* after being sunburnt. 3. very young: This food is not suitable for children of a *tender* age. 4. kind, soft-hearted, easily hurt: Be kind and *tender* hearted. 5. an estimate of work to be done: The council are asking for *tenders* for the building of a hall. 6. offer, put in a *tender*: I have *tendered* my resignation as your secretary.

tendon (ten-don) the thick cord that joins a muscle to a bone: The player had to leave the field after pulling a *tendon*.

tendril (ten-dril) a thread-like part of a plant that reaches out and twists round anything that can give the plant support: The vine had wound its *tendrils* around the trellis.

tennis (ten-nis) a game played on a *tennis* court by two or four players in which they hit a ball backwards and forwards over a net with a racket.

tenor (ten-or) 1. the third part, next to the lowest (or bass) in four-part harmony; music written for this part; a person who sings this part: Enrico Caruso was one of the greatest *tenors* who ever lived. 2. the general meaning of a speech, the general course of one's life: The accident upset the peaceful *tenor* of his life.

tense 1. tightly drawn or stretched: In the game of tug-of-war both sides hold the rope *tense* until the referee says 'Pull!' 2. (of the nerves) strained: The whole audience was *tense* with excitement. 3. that part of a verb which shows the time: 'Will be' is in the future *tense*, 'am' is in the present *tense* and 'was' is in the past *tense*. **tension** being *tense* or strained: Relations between the two countries were in a state of *tension*.

tent a movable shelter of skins, coarse cloth or specially treated canvas supported by poles and held in place by ropes fastened with pegs.

tentacle (ten-ta-cle) a slender flexible boneless growth on some animals which acts as a feeler, a limb and a means of catching prey: An octopus has eight *tentacles* armed with suckers.

tepid (tep-id) moderately warm: Rinse your hair with *tepid* water.

term 1. a fixed period of time: The President of the United States is elected for a *term* of four years. 2. the parts in which the year of a school, college etc. is divided: He was absent for the whole of the summer *term*. 3. something agreed to: Before you book at the hotel you should enquire about *terms* (i.e. the prices charged). 4. relations between people: We have not been on speaking *terms* for the last two years. 5. words expressing clear meanings in science etc.: Myopia is the *term* used by an optician for short-sightedness.

terminal (ter-mi-nal) 1. taking place at the end of each *term*: We have just had our *terminal* examinations. 2. the end of a railway, or an air line: We leave from Heathrow *terminal* tomorrow. 3. a place where electric points are joined: Your electric battery has positive and negative *terminals*. **terminate** end: My work with this firm *terminates* today. **terminus** the station at the end of a railway line, bus line etc.: All passengers must leave the bus at the *terminus*.

terrace (ter-race) 1. a flat piece of ground rising like a step, or with a steep slope above the lower part: On the hillside were a number of *terraces* planted with vines. 2. a row of houses all joined together: We live in a house at the end of a long *terrace*. 3. form land into *terraces*: In front of the house is a *terraced* lawn.

terrible (ter-ri-ble) 1. causing terror: There has been a *terrible* crash on the motorway. 2. causing discomfort: I can't bear this *terrible* cold. **terrific** *terrible*, making one afraid: The tanker drove down the road at a *terrific* speed. **terrify** fill with fear or horror: I am *terrified* of walking home in the dark. **terror** great fear: I have a particular *terror* of floods.

terrier (ter-ri-er) a small active dog, once used to hunt burrowing animals such as rabbits or foxes: There are fox *terriers*, Scottish *terriers*, Irish *terriers*, bull *terriers* and many other kinds.

territory (ter-ri-to-ry) 1. any area of land: This *territory* gets very little rain. 2. an area of land occupied by a particular race or ruled by one ruler: We discovered that we were in Indian *territory*.

terse brief in speech; going straight to the most important point: Explain your business, and please be *terse*.

test 1. a trial for quality, speed etc.: Has your car had its annual *test* yet?–He came out top in the intelligence *test*. 2. apply or carry out a *test*: My car was *tested* yesterday.–His heart was *tested* and has been proved sound. **test match** one of a series of matches played at agreed times between the best teams of the cricket-playing nations.

testament (tes-ta-ment) 1. a written statement saying what a person wishes to be done with his property after his death: 'This is the last will and *testament* of me . . .' (from a printed will form). 2. one of the two main divisions of the Bible: You will find the Book of Isaiah in the Old *Testament*.

testify (tes-ti-fy) 1. give evidence in favour of or against a person: My brother *testified* against the thief. 2. declare: He *testified* that he had not been in the town when the crime was committed. **testimony** a statement declaring that something is true: The witness gave his *testimony* under oath.

testimonial (tes-ti-mo-ni-al) 1. a statement in writing made by one person to testify to the abilities or good qualities of another person: 'Applicants for this post are required to enclose three *testimonials* in support of their applications.' 2. a present given to a person when he leaves a post, usually by the firm's management or his fellow-workers.

tether (teth-er) 1. a rope, chain etc. by which an animal is fastened to prevent it moving too far. 2. fasten by a *tether*: The goat was *tethered* to a stake in the meadow.

text 1. the printed part of a book, not including illustrations: This book has 100 pages of *text* and 20 of photographs. 2. the original words of an author: The book was translated from the German *text*. 3. a short sentence or phrase, usually out of the Bible, on which a preacher bases his sermon. **textbook** a book which gives instructions in a subject: I have learnt all the lessons in the *textbook*.

textile (tex-tile) having to do with the making of cloth: The latest *textile* machinery has been installed in our factory. **textiles** all kinds of cloth.

than a word used in comparisons: I am older *than* you but your work is better *than* mine.– I can type more quickly *than* I can write.

thank say that one is grateful: Have you *thanked* your uncle for the present he gave you? **thank you** a polite expression: Will you have a biscuit? Yes, *thank you*. **thankful** grateful, expressing *thanks*: I am *thankful* for the help you gave me. **thankless** showing no *thanks* or gratitude; bringing no reward: He is very *thankless* considering all that has been done for him.

that 1. a word which points out: Do you know *that* boy?– This is a bigger towel than *that* one. 2. a word which refers to a word used before: It's the radio next door *that* is making all the noise. 3. a word which joins two phrases: I knew very well *that* you would be here.

thatch 1. a covering of straw, heather or other material over the roof of a house: The birds had made holes in the *thatch*. 2. cover a roof with such materials: The cottage has been newly *thatched*.

thaw (of the temperature) 1. rise above freezing point: It's *thawing* and the snow is melting. 2. a time when the snow melts: The rivers were soon swollen because of the quick *thaw*.

theatre (thea-tre) 1. a place either in a specially designed building or in the open air where plays are performed and entertainments given. 2. a room where lectures are given; a room in which operations are performed: The patient was taken to the operating *theatre*. 3. a place where important things happen or have happened: The major fought in all the principal *theatres* of war. **theatrical** having to do with the *theatre*: Ten *theatrical* performances are being given here this winter.

theft the act of stealing: He was convicted of *theft*.

their the possessive form of 'they'; belonging to them: Have you seen *their* house? **theirs** something belonging to them: I didn't know this house was *theirs*.

them a word referring to things, animals or people already known: Your toys are all over the floor; put *them* away. **themselves** *them*: They were washing *themselves* in the stream.

theory (the-o-ry) 1. the general principles of any subject: You can learn the *theory* of flight while on the ground but for practice you must fly in an aeroplane. 2. a belief put forward: Many novels have been based on the *theory* that Mars is inhabited.

therapy (ther-a-py) a kind of medical treatment: Occupational *therapy* is a means of exercising certain parts of the body through occupations approved by doctors. **therapeutic** having to do with healing: In various parts of Britain there are *therapeutic* springs where patients may take (drink or bathe in) the waters.

there 1. in, to or at a certain place: Don't sit *there*, sit here. 2. used with is, was, can be, seems to be etc.: *There's* a hole in this bucket.– *There* seems to be a broken tile on the roof. 3. used as an exclamation: *There*! What did I tell you! **therefore** for that reason: I have no ticket, *therefore* I can't go with you.

thermo- (ther-mo-) part of a word concerning temperature or heat. **thermometer** an instrument that measures temperature. **thermos flask** a flask which will keep cold things cold and hot things hot for several hours. **thermostat** a device which will keep the temperature of a room, water-tank, or oven even and unchanging.

these plural of *this*; persons or things that are nearer to the speaker than others are: *These* children are hungry.

they plural of *she*, *he* and *it*; a word referring to more than one person, animal or thing: After a week *they* let me out of prison.

thick 1. some distance from side to side, from front to back, from top to bottom: Is the ice *thick* enough for skating? 2. with parts close together: He stroked the cat's *thick* fur. 3. partly solid: I asked for a plate of *thick* soup. 4. husky, hoarse, not clear: The cold had given him a *thick* voice. 5. the most crowded or active part: He dashed into the *thick* of the fight. **thicken** make *thick* or *thicker*: The ice on the pond will *thicken* if the cold weather lasts. **thickness** being *thick*: There's a good *thickness* of ice on the pond now. **thicket** a place where bushes are *thick*: Robbers were hiding in the *thicket*.

thief *thieves* a person who steals: Nobody saw the *thief* leave the house. **thieve** steal: 'Somebody has been *thieving*,' said the headmaster.

thigh the upper part of the leg between the knee and the hip.

thimble (thim-ble) a small cap, usually of metal, worn on the tip of the finger when sewing to push in the needle.

thin 1. the opposite of thick, having edges or surfaces close together: May I have a *thin* slice of bread? 2. not fat, not carrying much flesh: He has become very *thin* since his illness. 3. not thickly packed: The lawn was covered with *thin* grass. 4. not *thick* (of liquids): He ordered a plate of *thin* soup. 5. not strong in sound: He answered in a *thin* voice. 6. make or become *thin*: The fog is beginning to *thin*.

thing 1. an object which exists: Do these *things* all belong to you? 2. the state a person, a business etc. is in: *Things* aren't going very well just now. 3. an action: Of all the *things* I do I like swimming best. 4. clothing, equipment, especially when going out: Put on your *things* and we'll go. 5. a subject: There's another *thing* I want to talk about.

think *thought* 1. form an idea in the mind: Be quiet a moment and let me *think*. 2. have an opinion about something; believe: We all *think* you should see a doctor. 3. turn over in the mind, meditate: I was *thinking* what I would do if I had lots of money. 4. have an idea: I've just *thought* of a plan.

third 1. next after the second in time, place, order, importance etc.: I am *third* in the class this term.–March is the *third* month of the year. 2. one of three equal parts: We will divide the apple into three parts and take one *third* each. **thirteen** (13) the number coming between 12 and 14; 10 plus 3. **thirty** (30) the number coming between 29 and 31; 10 multiplied by 3.

thirst 1. the feeling caused when one needs to drink: The horse drank from the stream to quench its *thirst*. 2. a great desire: Ever since their fight he has had a *thirst* for revenge. **thirsty** having a *thirst*: 'If your enemy is *thirsty*, give him water' (*The Book of Proverbs*).

this a word which points out, meaning the one nearer to us, or the one just mentioned: Would you rather have *this* apple or that one?

thistle (this-tle) a wild plant with prickly leaves and purple flowers: The *thistle* is the emblem of Scotland.

thong a narrow strip of hide or leather used to fasten things, or as the lash of a whip: The stick hung from its hook on a leather *thong*.

thorn a spine or prickle on a plant: Rose-trees and blackberry bushes bear *thorns*. **thorny** 1. having *thorns*: These plants are too *thorny* to handle without gloves. 2. difficult; causing trouble: How are we going to solve this *thorny* problem?

thorough (thor-ough) complete: We carried out a *thorough* search of the room.
thoroughbred an animal of pure breed whose parents were of the same strain, not mixed with any others: 'Up came the troopers mounted on their *thoroughbreds*' (*Waltzing Matilda*).

those plural of *that*; persons or things that are farther away from the speaker than others: Do *those* shoes belong to you?

though 1. in spite of the fact that: *Though* he is only four years old he is quite tall. 2. even if: Strange *though* it may seem, I have never been to London. **as though** as if: He talks *as though* he knows all about repairing engines.

thought 1. the act of thinking, meditation: I spent some minutes in deep *thought*. 2. care: He gives no *thought* to his appearance. 3. idea: A *thought* has just struck me. 4. an opinion: I'd like your *thoughts* on this matter. 5. expectation: I had no *thought* of meeting you here. **thoughtful** showing *thought* or care: That was very *thoughtful* of him. **thoughtless** showing no *thought* or care; selfish: How could you be so *thoughtless* as to forget her birthday?

thousand (thou-sand) a number (1,000), 10 times as large as 100, 100 times as large as 10.

thrash 1. beat, whip: Why are you *thrashing* your dog? 2. beat, win a match or contest: Our team *thrashed* the visitors, winning by three goals to one. 3. move with violence: Before we could land it the fish *thrashed* about in the water for a long time.

thread 1. a very thin length of cotton, wool, silk, linen etc.: I need a reel of white cotton *thread* to sew on this button. 2. a line of thought: If you interrupt you will make me lose the *thread* of my story. 3. the spiral ridge that runs round a screw: This screw will not hold fast because the *thread* is worn away. 4. put *thread* through

the eye of a needle, through beads etc. 5. make a way through a number of people: She *threaded* her way to the front of the crowd. **threadbare** worn thin so that the *threads* of the cloth are plainly visible: He wore a dark green *threadbare* coat.

threat 1. a spoken intention to do harm to another: I shall take no notice of your *threats*. 2. a sign of future trouble: When underground rumblings occurred everybody knew there was a *threat* of an earthquake. **threaten** utter *threats*, warn of future trouble: The landlord is *threatening* to turn us out.

three the number (3) coming after 2 and before 4. '*Three* blind mice; see how they run' (nursery rhyme).

thresh separate the grain from the stalk by beating it either by hand or with a machine: The corn is ready for *threshing*. **thresher** a *threshing* machine.

threshold (thresh-old) 1. the piece of horizontal wood lying across the bottom of a doorway: He tripped and fell over the *threshold*. 2. the opening, the beginning: We are on the *threshold* of great discoveries.

thrift care in the use of money and goods; avoiding waste: If your funds are to last you will need to exercise great *thrift*. **thrifty** economical management: 'Here's to the housewife that's *thrifty*' (Sheridan, *The Rivals*).

thrill 1. a sudden feeling of keen excitement: It was a great *thrill* to go to the Royal Garden party. 2. cause a *thrill*: His victory in the Olympic games *thrilled* the whole nation. 3. feel a *thrill*: We were all *thrilled* by the news of your engagement. **thriller** a novel, play or film in which mystery and excitement are the main features.

thrive 1. grow strong and healthy: The baby is *thriving* on this new food. 2. prosper: As the demand for our goods grows, our business continues to *thrive*.

throat 1. the front part of the neck: I took him by the *throat* and shook him. 2. the passage by which food and air passes from the mouth to the stomach and lungs: I had a fishbone stuck in my *throat*.

throb 1. beat rapidly and with force: My heart was *throbbing* with excitement. 2. a strong vibration: In the distance we heard the loud *throb* of the engine.

throne the chair on which a king, queen or other ruler sits during ceremonies: 'Here is my *throne*; bid kings come bow to it' (Shakespeare, *King John*). **the Throne** the royal authority of the King or Queen: We are all loyal to *the Throne*.

throttle (throt-tle) 1. hold tightly by the throat and stop a person breathing: This tight collar is *throttling* me. 2. control the flow of steam, petrol etc. to an engine by opening or closing a valve. 3. the valve which controls the flow of fuel to an engine: He opened the *throttle* and the car shot forward.

through 1. in at one end, one side, one surface and out at the other: The train went *through* the tunnel. 2. by means of; because of: You failed *through* your own laziness. 3. from beginning to end of a period of time: I lay awake the whole night *through*. 4. non-stop: You will do the journey faster if you catch a *through* train. 5. connected (on the telephone): Will you put me *through* to the manager, please? **throughout** completely; everywhere in: This coat is lined with fur *throughout*.

throw *threw, thrown* 1. hurl, make a thing go through the air either by a quick movement of the arm or by machine: He *threw* the ball back to the bowler. 2. put on quickly: *Throw* on your coat and we'll go for a walk. 3. make a rider fall to the ground: His leg was broken when his horse *threw* him. 4. the act of *throwing*: 'Good *throw*!' shouted the crowd when the ball hit the stumps.

thrush 1. a bird, common in Britain, which sings sweetly: 'That's the wise *thrush*; he sings each song twice over' (Browning, *Home Thoughts from the Sea*). 2. a disease, mainly affecting children, in which small whitish spots appear in the mouth.

thrust 1. push hard, drive with force: He *thrust* a pistol into my hand. 2. the act of *thrusting*, a push, a drive: The allies were driven back by the enemy *thrust*.

thud 1. a sudden, dull sound: He fell to the floor with a *thud*. 2. make a *thud*: We heard the sound of his fists *thudding* against the door.

thumb 1. the short thick inner finger of the human hand, next to the first, or index, finger. 2. the place for the *thumb* in a glove. 3. turn over with the *thumb*: He was idly *thumbing* the pages of a book.

thump 1. strike or beat with the fist or something heavy: Don't *thump* on the door! 2. a heavy blow, the sound of a heavy blow: We heard the *thump* of heavy boots on the wooden floor.

thunder (thun-der) 1. the loud noise that comes with a flash of lightning due to a discharge of electricity in the air: The lightning flashed, the *thunder* roared. 2. a noise that sounds like *thunder*: The *thunder* of the guns could be heard in all the neighbouring villages. 3. make *thunder*: Do you hear it *thundering*? 4. make a noise like *thunder*: The engine came *thundering* along the rails. 5. shout, attack in words: 'Halt!' *thundered* the sergeant. **thunderstorm** a storm in which there is *thunder* and lightning.

Thursday (Thurs-day) the fifth day of the week.

thus in this way: '*Thus* let me live, unseen, unknown' (Pope, *Ode to Solitude*).

tick 1. a light sharp clicking sound like that made by a clock: You can only hear the *tick* of the clock. 2. a tiny mark put at the end of exercises and against figures and names when they are checked: Against every figure on the list there was a *tick*. 3. a small bloodsucking insect that buries itself in the skin of certain animals. 4. the outside cover of a mattress or pillow. 5. make a *tick* (sound): This clock *ticks* too loudly. 6. make a *tick* (writing): I have *ticked* all the numbers on this sheet.

ticket (tick-et) 1. a small piece of paper or card showing that one has paid the fare on a bus, train etc., or been given admission to a theatre, cinema or other public building: 'Tickets please,' called the inspector. 2. a label attached to goods to show their price: After I had bought the case of spoons the assistant took off the price *ticket*. 3. mark with a *ticket*: All the articles in the window have now been *ticketed*.

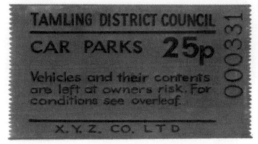

tickle 1. touch or stroke with the fingers to create a tingling feeling on the skin: 'If you *tickle* us do we not laugh?' (Shakespeare, *The Merchant of Venice*). 2. please, delight: The story *tickled* my sense of humour. 3. a *tickling* feeling: I've got a *tickle* behind my right ear. **ticklish** 1. easily made to laugh and squirm when *tickled*. 2. puzzling, difficult, needing careful thought: What a *ticklish* situation we're in!

tide 1. the regular rise and fall of the sea on the coasts: The *tide* comes up at 10.00 this evening. 2. the rise and fall of one's luck, fortunes, people's opinions etc.: 'There is a *tide* in the affairs of men which taken at the flood leads on to fortune' (Shakespeare, *Julius Caesar*). **tidal** having to do with the *tides*: The Thames is *tidal* as far as Teddington, Surrey. **tidal wave** a large, destructive wave produced by an earthquake or the like.

tidings (ti-dings) news: Have you any *tidings* of your brother?

tidy (ti-dy) 1. in order: Make sure that everything in the office is *tidy*. 2. having *tidy* habits: She is a very *tidy* person. 3. make *tidy*: We *tidied* up the room after the party.

tie 1. fasten by means of rope etc.: The Indians had *tied* him to a post. 2. make the same score as another. Two horses *tied* for first place. 3. something that *ties*: We are bound together by family *ties*. 4. a band worn round the neck, under a collar, and *tied* in front. 5. something that prevents one from doing all one wants: My business *ties* prevent me from taking a long holiday. 6. a result in which two competitors or teams finish equal: The cricket match ended in a *tie*. 7. a curved line joining two notes of music that are to be played or sung without a break.

tier (rhymes with *fear*) one of a number of rows of seats rising one above the other so that all spectators can see well: The seats in the new sports pavilion rise steeply in *tiers*.

tiff 1. a slight quarrel: We had a *tiff* yesterday but are friends again today. 2. a fit of bad humour: I told him what I thought and he went off in a *tiff*.

tiger (ti-ger) a large fierce animal of the cat family living in Asia: *Tigers* have yellowish fur striped with black. **tigress** a female *tiger*.

tight 1. fastened, close-fitting: Put the cakes into an air*tight* tin (close-fitting so that air cannot get in). 2. stretched: Every day she walks on the *tight*rope. 3. firm, difficult to undo: The knot is so *tight* I shall have to cut the string. **tighten** make or become *tighter*: The ropes need *tightening* to keep the tent from falling down. **tights** a close-fitting garment covering the body from the waist downwards, and the legs.

tile 1. a thin slab or plate of baked clay used for covering roofs, lining walls, paving etc.: The bathroom *tiles* are blue. 2. put *tiles* in place: The workmen were *tiling* the swimming pool.

till 1. up to the time of: He sings from morning *till* night. 2. a drawer in a shop in which money is kept: While the shopkeeper was out somebody robbed the *till*. 3. cultivate land: We live by *tilling* the soil. **tiller** 1. a person who *tills* the soil. 2. a lever fitted to the top side of a rudder for steering a boat: The yacht sailed better with the captain at the *tiller*.

timber (tim-ber) 1. wood ready for use in building: Stacks of *timber* caught fire last night in the *timber* yard. 2. trees which are growing to provide *timber*: A huge forest of *timber* has been destroyed by fire. 3. the large pieces of *timber* already built into houses, ships etc.: The tempest made the *timbers* of the old ship creak.

time 1. the passing of seconds, minutes, hours, days, months, years etc.: *Time* seemed to stand still. 2. a measured period of *time*: I have spent a long *time* making this table. 3. a point or moment in *time*: 'I will sit down now, but the *time* will come when you will hear me' (Benjamin Disraeli, in the House of Commons, 7 December 1837). 4. an occasion, a repeated happening: Don't say it again, I heard you the first *time*. 5. a word which indicates multiplication: What is five *times* nine? 6. a way in which one feels or has felt: We had a marvellous *time* at the beach yesterday. 7. a way of measuring *time*: When do we start summer*time* this year? 8. a measurement of *time* in music: This song is in 4 *time*, with 4 beats in a bar. 9. measure the *time* taken by; fix a *time* for: Will you *time* me in the flat race? **time bomb** a bomb set to explode at a certain *time*. **timetable** a list showing on what day and at what *time* certain things are to happen.

timid (tim-id) easily alarmed, quick to take fright: Deer, mice and rabbits are *timid* animals.

tin a shiny white metal which looks like silver, used in plating other metals, especially in the making of cans for preserving food. **tin foil** very thin sheets of *tin* used in wrapping tobacco, sweets or for use in cookery.

tinder (tin-der) soft material that easily catches fire from a spark: *Tinder* was used for making fires before matches were invented. **tinderbox** a box containing flint, steel and *tinder*.

tinge 1. give a slight touch of colour to: The morning sky was *tinged* with yellow. 2. add a slight amount of: Her admiration of his courage was *tinged* with envy. 3. a slight degree: There was a *tinge* of regret in her voice.

tingle (tin-gle) 1. have a feeling of slight stings or prickly pains from cold, a sting or a blow: A cold bath will make you *tingle* all over. 2. a *tingling* feeling.

tinker (tin-ker) 1. a person who journeys from place to place mending kettles, pots and pans. 2. try to mend; play with something that is not working: He's in the shed *tinkering* with his motorcycle.

tinkle make a number of short ringing sounds: I can hear the school bell *tinkling*.

tinsel (tin-sel) cheap material made of metal cut out in thin strips to give a sparkling effect: The Christmas tree was decorated with *tinsel*.

tint 1. a pale colour: *Tints* are obtained by adding white to colours and shades, by adding black.—There were *tints* of green and gold in the evening sky. 2. colour lightly, give a *tint* to.

tiny (ti-ny) very small: The *tiny* girl unexpectedly won the race.

tip 1. the thin pointed end of: He touched the dog with the *tip* of his cane. 2. a small piece added to the end of something: He chalked the *tip* of his billiard cue. 3. a small present of money given in return for service: Will you give the waiter a *tip* or shall I? 4. a useful piece of information: If you take my *tip* you'll keep out of his way. 5. make something slant, set it on one end, turn it upside down: With a mighty heave he *tipped* the large table over. 6. empty out: She *tipped* the dirty water down the drain. 7. strike with a sharp, light blow: The batsman *tipped* the ball into the wicket-keeper's hands. 8. give a *tip* or *tips* to: I had to *tip* the taxi-driver. **tip-off** a piece of secret information, a warning: The gang was captured as a result of a *tip-off*. **tiptoe** walk on the *tips* of one's toes.

tire make weary: This hot weather *tires* me out. **tired** weary in body and mind; bored: You must be *tired* of this place. **tireless** never *tired*: He is a *tireless* worker. **tiresome** troublesome, boring, tedious: I listened for an hour to her *tiresome* complaints.

tissue (tis-sue) 1. part of the material of which an animal or plant is made: The body is held together by muscular *tissue*. 2. a very light woven fabric. 3. a number, a mass: He answered with a *tissue* of lies. **tissue paper** very thin paper used for wrapping delicate articles.

title (ti-tle) 1. the name of a book, play, story, song, picture etc. 2. a special name to show a person's occupation, rank: His surname is Grant; his *title* is Professor. 3. the right to own or succeed to: The king's eldest son has given up his *title* to the throne.– I have a legal *title* to this land.

toad an animal that looks like a frog and which lives mainly on land. **toadstool** an umbrella-shaped fungus: Many *toadstools* are poisonous.

toast 1. make bread brown and crisp by heating it in front of a fire or under a grill: Every morning I *toast* bread for the family's breakfast. 2. make a speech and drink the health of a person: Before anybody is allowed to smoke we shall *toast* the Queen. 3. *toasted* bread: I'll have *toast* and coffee this morning.

tobacco (to-bac-co) a plant with large leaves which are dried and used for smoking: *Tobacco*, cigars, cigarettes and snuff are all sold by the tobacconist.

toboggan (to-bog-gan) 1. a long narrow light sledge curved upwards and backward, at the fronts used originally for transport over snow but now mainly for sport. 2. take part in sport with a *toboggan*: We spent all day *tobogganing* on the icy slopes.

today (to-day) this day; on this day: We hope to see you later *today*.

toe 1. one of five divisions in the front part of the foot: 'She has bells on her fingers and rings on her *toes*' (*Ride a Cock-horse*, 1784). 2. that part of the sock, stocking or boot that covers the *toe*: I have kicked out the *toe* of my shoe playing football.

toffee (tof-fee) a sweet made with sugar or treacle boiled with butter, and sometimes nuts.

together (to-geth-er) 1. in each other's company: We've been *together* now for forty years. 2. with each other (of things): He gathered *together* his belongings and left. 3. at the same time: All *together*, hip, hip, hip, hurrah!

toil 1. long, hard work: 'I have nothing to offer but blood, *toil*, tears and sweat' Winston Churchill, 13 May 1940). 2. work hard: We *toiled* all day to get the boat refloated.

toilet (toil-et) 1. the act or process of dressing, including bathing, arranging the hair etc.: Every morning my sister spends an hour at her *toilet*. 2. lavatory.

token (to-ken) 1. a sign, symbol: They waved a white flag as a *token* of surrender. 2. something used instead of money: In some countries people have to buy *tokens* in order to use a public telephone. 3. something done not seriously but as a gesture: The enemy made only a *token* resistance.

tolerate (tol-er-ate) endure silently: I have *tolerated* his bad manners long enough. **tolerable** fairly good; just good enough to be *tolerated*: The service in the hotel was *tolerable*.

toll 1. the payment required to pass over a road, bridge etc.: In Italy they pay a *toll* to use the motorways. 2. payment taken, sacrifice: Every year the motorcar takes a heavy *toll* in human lives. 3. cause a large bell to ring slowly and regularly for summoning people to church or for announcing a death.

tomahawk (tom-a-hawk) a light axe used by the North American Indians as a weapon and tool.

tomato (to-ma-to) a soft red or yellow fruit with a juicy centre and many seeds, eaten with meat and in salads.

tomb a place dug out of the earth or cut out of a rock into which a dead body is put: The *tomb* of the Egyptian king, Tutankhamen, was discovered in 1922. **tombstone** a stone raised as a memorial over a grave or *tomb*.

tomboy (tom-boy) a girl who likes to play rough, noisy games.

tomorrow (to-mor-row) the day after this day: 'Think today and speak *tomorrow*' (a proverb).

ton, tonne a measure of weight: In Great Britain a *ton* equals 2,240 pounds (about 1016 kilos).

tone 1. a sound: He spoke in an angry *tone*. 2. the spirit, character of a group of people: The *tone* of the meeting was good-humoured. 3. amount of light or shade in a colour: The picture is painted in different *tones* of red. 4. the interval between certain notes of music: Between the notes C and D there is a full *tone*, between E and F a semi*tone*. 5. give a certain sound or colour to a thing: You should *tone* down some of the lighter parts of the portrait. 6. give health and vigour to a person: You need some of this medicine to *tone* you up. **tonic** 1. a medicine that gives strength: The doctor gave him a nerve *tonic*. 2. the keynote of a musical scale.

tongs a tool consisting of two arms for picking things up: I can't find the sugar *tongs*.

tongue 1. in man and many other animals, an organ in the mouth which can move, and which is the chief means of taste and in man, of speech: He put the tablet on his *tongue* and swallowed it. 2. a language: My mother *tongue* is English. 3. an animal's *tongue* used as food: Would anybody like a *tongue* sandwich? 4. something like a *tongue*: *Tongues* of flame leapt up from the burning building.

tonight (to-night) the night after this day: Are you going to the concert *tonight*?

tonsil (ton-sil) one of two oval masses of tissue situated at the back of the throat: If you open your mouth wide in front of a mirror you will be able to see your *tonsils*.

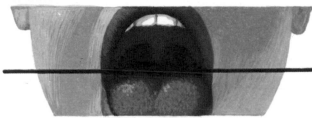

too 1. in addition, also, as well: If you're going to the park may I come *too*? 2. more, lower, higher, dearer, cheaper etc. than is required or allowed: These pears are *too* expensive.—The handle of the kettle is *too* hot to hold.

tool 1. an instrument held in the hand in order to do certain work: Spades, chisels, screwdrivers, planes and saws are all *tools*. 2. a person who is used by another person for his own benefit: The swindler used the bank clerk as his *tool*.

toot 1. a short sharp sound as from a whistle or horn: He gave a *toot* on the horn and the boy jumped out of the way. 2. give such a sound: He came to the door when I *tooted* the horn.

tooth *teeth* 1. one of the hard white structures attached to the upper and lower jaws, used for biting and chewing food: 'You have a fine set of *teeth*,' said the dentist. 2. a hard spike sticking out in a rake, a comb or a saw: This comb has lost two of its *teeth*.

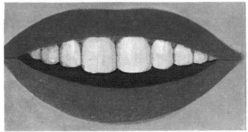

top 1. the highest point: 'He marched them up to the *top* of a hill and he marched them down again' (*The Grand Old Duke of York*). 2. the upper edge: Turn to the *top* of the next page. 3. the upper surface: There are scratches on the *top* of this table. 4. the first place: I am *top* of the class again this term. 5. the leaves of certain vegetables standing above the ground: We gave the turnip *tops* to the cattle. 6. a toy with a pointed tip on which it can be made to spin: He plays for hours with his spinning-*top*. 7. reach the *top*: Our team has *topped* the league again this season. 8. take the *top* off: We must *top* and tail the gooseberries before they are cooked.

topic (top-ic) something talked about, a subject for discussion: The strike and the resignation of the Prime Minister were the chief *topics* of the day. **topical** having to do with *topics* of the day.

topple (top-ple) turn upside down or fall over: The pile of bricks came *toppling* down.

topsy-turvy (top-sy tur-vy) in complete confusion, upside down: Since I was ill all my affairs have been *topsy-turvy*.

torch 1. a light made with wood soaked in oil or tallow to make it burn brightly: They gave me a *torch* to light my way along the street. 2. an electric light that can be carried by hand: Make sure you have an electric *torch* at your bedside. **torchlight** the light of *torches*: We stood at the window watching the *torchlight* procession.

torment (tor-ment) 1. give great bodily or mental pain to: I am *tormented* by violent headaches. 2. worry, pester: Don't *torment* me with any more questions. 3. suffering, pain: Can anybody put an end to this *torment*?

tornado (tor-na-do) a violent whirlwind in which winds rush round a centre carrying homes and everything else before them: A signal was received that a *tornado* was approaching.

torpedo (tor-pe-do) 1. a large metal shell shaped like a cigar which after being fired will propel itself towards a target: A *torpedo* explodes on contact. 2. fire or to be hit by a *torpedo*: The ship sank within minutes of being *torpedoed*.

torpid (tor-pid) inactive, dull, slow: He suffers from a *torpid* liver. **torpor** being inactive and slow: There was no buying or selling; the market was in a state of *torpor*.

torrent (tor-rent) a river or stream rushing violently downhill: 'The roaring *torrent* is deep and wide' (Longfellow, *Excelsior*). **torrential** in *torrents*, caused by *torrents*: We have had a week of *torrential* rain.

torrid (tor-rid) (of weather) very hot: The *torrid* zone is that part of the earth lying between the tropics.

tortoise (tor-toise) a four-legged reptile with a hard shell on its back: Some *tortoises* live on land and some swim in fresh water.

torture (tor-ture) 1. cause severe physical or mental suffering: The prisoners were *tortured* to make them tell what they knew. 2. the suffering caused by *torturing* or being *tortured*: The captives were put to the *torture*.

toss 1. throw up into the air: The umpire *tossed* the coin and it came down heads. 2. move up and down or from side to side: 'Ten thousand saw I at a glance, *tossing* their heads in sprightly dance' (Wordsworth, *The Daffodils*). 3. a *tossing* movement: 'Not I,' she replied with a *toss* of the head.

tot 1. a very small child. 2. add up: When we *totted* up the bills we found we had spent a great deal of money. 3. a small portion of drink.

total (to-tal) 1. complete: The expedition was a *total* failure. 2. the amount: He added up all the items and arrived at the *total*. 3. find the *total*: He *totalled* up the bills. 4. amount to: The money taken at the door *totalled* more than we expected. **totalizator** (or **tote**) a machine which registers bets on a racecourse so as to divide the *total* amount won, less taxes, expenses etc. between the winners.

totem (to-tem) an object in nature, often an animal, considered as an emblem of a family or a related group of people: An image of the *totem* was carved and painted by the American Indians and set up on a *totem* pole.

totter (to-ter) 1. walk with unsteady steps, swaying and rocking: The baby *tottered* along the corridor. 2. sway and rock as if about to fall: The great tower *tottered* and fell.

touch 1. bring a part of the body into contact with another object so as to be able to feel it: Somebody *touched* me on the elbow. 2. (of objects) be in contact: Put the apples on the tray but don't let them *touch* each other. 3. strike or press lightly: He *touched* the ball and it went over the fence. 4. cause feelings of sorrow, sadness, pity, gratitude etc.: We were greatly *touched* by your kind letter. 5. one of the five senses: Fur is soft and smooth to the *touch*. 6. the act of *touching*: I felt a *touch* on my arm. 7. a stroke etc.: I'm just adding the finishing *touches* to the painting. 8. a small amount: There was a *touch* of sarcasm in his voice. 9. a slight attack: I have a *touch* of rheumatism this morning. **touchy** quickly or easily offended. **in touch** in communication: Even if you leave, we'll keep *in touch* by writing.

tough 1. not easily cut or broken: The beef was very *tough*. 2. strong, hard-wearing: You need *tough* shoes for climbing. 3. able to endure hardship: You have to be *tough* to be a paratrooper. 4. difficult, unpleasant: We were faced with a *tough* problem. 5. severe, violent: The struggle was long and *tough*. 6. lawless, disorderly: That night we went into the *toughest* parts of the city. **toughen** make *tough*, become *tough*.

tour 1. a journey beginning and ending at home, visiting many places in succession: The company is going on *tour* to perform a series of plays. 2. (chiefly military) a period of duty at one place: I finished my *tour* of duty yesterday. 3. travel from place to place: They are *touring* Spain this summer. **tourist** a person making a *tour*, especially for pleasure. **tourist agency** a business company which arranges *tours*. **tourism** organized *touring*: Britain receives large sums of money each year from *tourism*.

tournament (tour-na-ment) 1. a trial of skill in a game in which competitors play a series of contests: There were more spectators than ever at this year's tennis *tournament*. 2. in the Middle Ages, a contest between armed knights on horseback.

tourniquet (tour-ni-quet) a device for checking bleeding by stopping the flow of blood from an artery: A simple *tourniquet* can be made with a bandage, tightened by twisting.

tout 1. a person who harasses and worries people to buy things, sells information about racehorses etc.: There were several *touts* at the gates of the ground selling tickets at ten times the official price. 2. act as a *tout*: Men stood outside the shop *touting* for customers.

tow 1. drag or pull by means of a rope or chain: The ship had to be *towed* into port. 2. the act of *towing*: The car had to be given a *tow* before the engine would start. 3. broken fibres of material used for making rope, for cleaning oily machinery etc. **towrope** the rope used for *towing*.

towards (to-wards) 1. in the direction of: We continued walking *towards* the mountain range. 2. concerning, about: What are your feelings *towards* your old enemy? 3. as a help to: We are contributing *towards* a present for our secretary who is retiring.

towel (tow-el) a cloth for wiping or drying something wet: In the bathroom you will find a hand-*towel* and a bath-*towel*. **towelling** material out of which *towels* are made. **towel-rail** a rail over which a *towel* is placed.

tower (tow-er) 1. a very high building either standing alone or as part of a collection of buildings: The *Tower* of London is composed of many small buildings, also called *towers*. 2. a person supporting another person: 'The King's name is a *tower* of strength' (Shakespeare, *Richard III*). 3. be higher than: The new London office blocks *tower* over the other buildings. 4. be greater than, to have more ability than: As a playwright Shakespeare *towers* over all others.

town 1. an inhabited area, larger than a village, smaller or less important than a city: I would rather live in a village than a *town*. 2. The nearest large *town*; in England, usually London: The newspaper shows what's happening in *town* this weekend. 3. the people living in a *town*: The whole *town's* talking about the royal visit.

toxic (tox-ic) poisonous: *Toxic* fumes are being given off during this experiment.

toy 1. a child's plaything: It's bedtime; put all your *toys* away. 2. made as a *toy*: He plays with *toy* soldiers. 3. play with; amuse oneself with: All the time he talked he was *toying* with his watchchain.

trace 1. make a plan, diagram or map: He *traced* out the plan of the building. 2. copy by drawing over transparent paper: Your homework is to *trace* the map of Africa. 3. print in a curved, broken manner as if with difficulty: *Traced* faintly on the paper were the words 'not here, not there'. 4. follow (footprints, marks etc.): We *traced* him to his uncle's house. 5. a mark or sign showing somebody or something has been at a place or that something has happened there: We saw *traces* of a struggle. 6. a very small amount: *Traces* of blood were found on his sleeve. **tracer** (bullet or shell) a missile which when fired leaves a line of flame or smoke behind it. **tracing** a drawing made by the process of *tracing*, with *tracing* paper.

track 1. a mark or marks left by a vehicle, a human being, or an animal: We followed the *tracks* of the wounded lion. 2. a rough roadway made by the passing of many feet or wheels: We followed a narrow *track* across the moors. 3. the rails, sleepers etc. on which a railway runs. 4. a line of travel: The astronomers are following the *track* of the newly-discovered comet. 5. a course laid out for running or racing: A new running *track* is being made on the sports field. 6. follow *tracks*: The woodcutter was an expert in *tracking* animals. 7. having to do with a *track*: Most of the *track* events (running) were won by the Russians. **tracker** a person who follows the *tracks* of wild animals.

tract 1. a stretch of land: The party had to make their way across a frozen *tract* to reach their cabins. 2. a group of organs in the body: We are studying the digestive *tract* (having to do with the digestion of food). 3. a pamphlet, usually on religion, printed and distributed in large numbers: She stood at the street corner handing out *tracts* to the passers-by.

traction (trac-tion) the act of drawing or pulling; the power to pull loads: Steam *traction* has now been superseded by petrol and electric *traction*. **tractor** a powerful motor vehicle used for doing work mainly on farms. **traction engine** a heavy steam engine on wheels, once used for rolling the surfaces of roads and pulling heavy loads.

trade 1. buying, selling and exchanging goods between individual people or countries: Here is a list of firms in the book *trade*. 2. a way of making a living: Employees in the building *trade* are on strike. 3. people in certain businesses: This wholesale house sells only to the *trade*. 4. carry on *trade*: We *trade* in secondhand cars. 5. exchange: I *traded* my camera for a projector. **tradesman** a person who keeps a shop or delivers goods: Please use the *tradesman's* entrance. **trade in** give up an article plus a certain amount of money in exchange for another one of the same kind: I have *traded in* my old car for a newer model. **trademark** a symbol shown on goods to distinguish one maker's goods from those of another.

tradition 1. the handing down of customs, beliefs, legends etc. from one generation to another: Here is a story that has come down to us by *tradition*. 2. beliefs etc. handed down by *tradition*: There is a *tradition* that Queen Elizabeth I slept in this bed.

traffic (traf-fic) 1. the coming and going of persons, vehicles, ships etc. along an agreed way of travel: *Traffic* on the motorways is increasing every year. 2. the business done by a railway, an airline etc.: Twice as much *traffic* has been handled this year as ten years ago. 3. trading: Efforts are being made to control the drug *traffic*. 4. trade: The Hudson Bay Company *trafficked* in furs with the North American Indians.

tragedy (trag-e-dy) 1. a play with an unhappy ending: *Hamlet* is one of the greatest *tragedies* ever written. 2. an unhappy event: Twelve people were killed in the recent mining *tragedy*. **tragic** having to do with *tragedy*: He met a *tragic* death while flying over Alaska.

trail 1. a stream of dust, smoke, people etc. behind something moving: The aeroplane left a long *trail* of white vapour behind it. 2. a line, mark or scent left by an animal or person: We followed the *trail* of blood through the forest. 3. a path or track worn across a wild region: The *trail* led us across a barren desert. 4. drag or be dragged along: The little boy *trailed* a toy engine behind him. 5. set something floating after itself: Off went the car, *trailing* clouds of dust. 6. (of plants) grow along the ground and over walls etc. **trailer** 1. a vehicle *trailed* along behind another. 2. a few short extracts from a film shown in order to advertise it in advance.

train 1. a set of carriages or wagons connected to a locomotive: We took the *train* to Leeds. 2. a number of persons, vehicles etc. travelling together: A *train* of mules carried our baggage through the pass. 3. a series: I will tell you the *train* of events that led to our meeting. 4. part of a long dress that trails on the ground: The bride wore a dress with a long *train*. 5. teach, bring up (a child or an animal): The dog is being *trained* to guard the house. 6. make grow in the required direction: I *trained* the apple tree along the wall. 7. aim: Our guns were *trained* on the enemy's supply lines. **trainer** 1. a person who *trains* (people or animals). 2. an aeroplane used for *training* pilots. **training** physical fitness: I was not in good *training* so I lost the race.

traitor (trai-tor) a person who betrays his friend, a group of people or his country: He was condemned to death as a *traitor*.

tram an electric car running along a street: *Trams* in London have been replaced by buses. **tramlines** the lines on which *trams* run.

tramp 1. tread or walk heavily: We heard the sound of *tramping* feet. 2. go on foot: He *tramped* the streets all day looking for his dog. 3. the act of *tramping*: I have spent the last six weeks on the *tramp*. 4. the sound of a heavy tread: We heard the *tramp* of the policeman's feet. 5. a person who goes from place to place doing odd jobs but no regular work: We spent the night in a hostel for *tramps*. **trample** 1. tread heavily: The cows have *trampled* on the flower beds. 2. treat harshly; show no consideration for: He *tramples* on everybody's feelings.

tranquil (tran-quil) quiet, calm: We spent a week in a *tranquil* country house. **tranquility** calm, peace.

trans- a prefix meaning across or from one to another, which is used with many words. **transaction** business taking place between people. **transcribe** copy writing. **transcription** copying, sometimes from shorthand notes. **transfer** (trans-fér) change jobs or property: He has been *transferred* to our new branch at Luton. **transfer** (tráns-fer) an example of *transferring*: I am writing for my *transfer* to another branch. **transfix** pierce through: The lion was *transfixed* by the hunter's spear. **transform** change into another shape or kind: The witch *transformed* the frog into a prince. **transfusion** taking blood from one person and injecting it into another. **transgress** break a law or a commandment: I have promised not to *transgress* again. **transgression** the act of *transgressing*: 'Blessed is he whose *transgression* is forgiven' (Psalm 32). **transistor** a device which replaces the valve in radio sets, hearing aids and other equipment of the same kind. **transit** taking or being taken from one place to another: Our furniture was delayed in *transit*. **transition** a change from one condition to another: In some countries the *transition* from hot to cold weather occurs quickly. **translate**

put into another language: I *translated* the letter from English into French. **transmit** send, allow to pass through: The message was *transmitted* by radio. **transparent** that can be seen through: Glass is *transparent*. **transplant** plant in another place: I have *transplanted* the chrysanthemum to another part of the garden. **transport** (trans-pórt) carry to another place. **transport** (tráns-port) the means of carrying.

trap 1. a device for catching animals: We set a *trap* to catch the mouse. 2. a trick or plan to deceive people: When the Inspector questioned him, the prisoner fell into the *trap* and confessed everything. 3. a U-shaped section of a drainpipe or ventilation pipe which, being filled with liquid, prevents impure air and bad smells from getting into places where people live. **trapdoor** a door in the floor, a ceiling or a roof, which can be lifted up.

trapeze (tra-peze) a swing consisting of a short horizontal bar attached to the ends of two suspended ropes: A *trapeze* is used for gymnastic exercises and in circuses.

trash anything worthless; nonsense: 'I have never read such *trash*,' my brother said, laughing.

travel (trav-el) 1. go from place to place, make a journey: 'I never *travel* without my diary' (Oscar Wilde, *The Importance of Being Earnest*). 2. go from place to place on business: My father *travels* to Switzerland on business once a week. 3. pass over: My eyes *travelled* over all the things in the shop. 4. *travelling*: I have spent nearly all my life in *travel*. 5. journeys: Shall I tell you about my *travels* to the Far East?

traverse (trav-erse) go across, pass over: He *traversed* the Sahara by camel.

tray a flat, shallow piece of wood, plastic or metal with raised edges used for carrying things: The waitress brought tea on a *tray*.

treacherous (treach-er-ous) 1. disloyal to a friend; deceitful: It was a *treacherous* act to reveal our hiding-place. 2. not firm, not secure: Walk on the track or you may fall into the *treacherous* bog. **treachery** betrayal of trust; disloyalty: I didn't think he could be guilty of such *treachery*.

treacle (trea-cle) a dark sticky liquid obtained in the refining of sugar.

tread *trod, trodden* 1. step, walk: *Tread* carefully among the flowers. 2. trample, crush: When you plant the tree, *tread* down the soil around the roots. 3. sound of walking: We heard the heavy *tread* of marching feet. 4. the part of a stair on which the foot is placed: These stairs need new rubber *treads*. 5. the part of a tyre which is in contact with the ground: The *tread* of these tyres is wearing thin. **treadle** a lever worked by foot to make a machine move: If you work the *treadle* you will be able to stitch the leather.

treason (trea-son) the betrayal of one's country: *Treason* is one of the most serious crimes that can be committed.

treasure (treas-ure) 1. valuables (gold, silver, jewels etc.): The divers are looking for *treasure* in the sunken ship. 2. something which is greatly valued: Priceless art *treasures* are on exhibition in this gallery. 3. value highly: Look after these photographs; I *treasure* them. **treasurer** the person who looks after the money matters of a company or a society. **The Treasury** the department of government which looks after the finances of the country. **treasury** a book containing valuable information or literary extracts: This guide is a *treasury* of interesting facts.

treat 1. behave towards: I shall always *treat* you as a friend. 2. consider: Do you wish me to *treat* your proposal seriously? 3. give medical aid to: The doctor is *treating* my grandmother for rheumatism. 4. pay for food, drink etc. for a person: I'm *treating* you to a good lunch. 5. anything that gives pleasure: For a *treat* she took us to the cinema. **treatment** the way of *treating* or being *treated*: I am undergoing *treatment* for rheumatism. **treaty** an agreement made between nations: This country has signed a commercial *treaty* with its neighbour.

treble (tre-ble) 1. soprano; the highest part in a piece of music: I will sing the *treble* part. 2. the person singing this part: Are all the *trebles* here? 3. three times as much: Nuts have gone up to *treble* the price they were last Christmas. 4. make or become three times more: My wages have *trebled* in the last year.

tree 1. a large perennial plant with a thick stem, or trunk, and branches from which grow twigs and leaves: Timber is obtained from the trunks and branches of *trees*. 2. a piece of wood for a special purpose: Boots and shoes are stretched on a shoe*tree*; the body of a cart or waggon rests on an axle*tree*. **treeless** with no *trees*: We marched for days across a *treeless* plain.

trek 1. (in South Africa) a long journey made by ox-wagon. 2. any long journey: We started our *trek* into the interior.

trellis (trel-lis) a frame made of light pieces of wood crossing each other: A *trellis* was fixed to the wall, covered with a climbing vine.

tremble (trem-ble) 1. shake from a feeling of fright, cold etc.: The dog was brought into the house, wet and *trembling*. 2. vibrate: The ground *trembled* beneath us. 3. be very worried: I *tremble* to think what can have happened to him. 4. the action of *trembling*. **tremor** a shaking: We have had several earth *tremors* lately.

tremendous (tre-men-dous) very great, dreadful, awful: He knew he was facing a *tremendous* task.—With a *tremendous* roar the building came crashing down.

trench 1. a ditch: *Trenches* were dug across the field to drain off the water. 2. a deep ditch dug as a protection for soldiers: Our heavy guns bombarded the enemy *trenches*.

trend a general course or direction: The *trend* of the road is towards the south-west.

trespass (tres-pass) 1. go on other people's land without permission: He was caught *trespassing* on government property. 2. an offence, sin or wrong: 'Forgive us our *trespasses* as we forgive them that *trespass* against us' (*The Lord's Prayer*).

trestle (tres-tle) a frame consisting of a horizontal bar on two pairs of spreading legs: The table top rested on two *trestles*. **trestle bridge** a bridge resting on a framework made in *trestle* fashion.

trial 1. a testing: I don't know whether the rope will be strong enough but we'll give it a *trial*. 2. an examination in a law court. At his *trial* he pleaded not guilty. 3. a thing, a person or an experience that annoys or tests: His lameness is a constant *trial* to him. 4. done to test something: Let's take a *trial* run in the new car.

triangle (tri-an-gle) 1. a flat figure with three sides and with three angles. 2. a musical instrument made from a triangular steel rod which produces a light, ringing sound. **triangular** in the shape of a *triangle*.

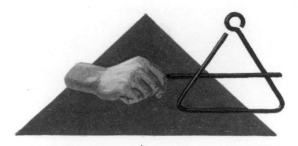

tribe a group of people of the same race, with the same language and customs: The ancient Israelites consisted of twelve *tribes*. **tribal** having to do with *tribes*: *Tribal* organization and customs still survive in some parts of the world.

tribunal (tri-bun-al) a group of people acting as judges in order to hear appeals against such things as high rents, unjust prison sentences etc.: The House of Lords is the highest *tribunal* in Great Britain.

tribute (trib-ute) 1. a payment demanded regularly by a ruler or conqueror from those he rules or has conquered: The Romans demanded *tribute* from all their subject states. 2. something done or said to show respect or to honour a person: We present this gold watch as a *tribute* to you on your retirement. **tributary** 1. a state paying *tribute* to a more powerful one. 2. a small stream flowing into a larger one.

trick 1. something done to deceive: The invitation was a *trick* to capture him. 2. a mischievous act: He's up to his *tricks* again. 3. a clever act, a feat of skill: I know a large number of *tricks* with cards. 4. one round of a card game: We won all the *tricks*. 5. deceive: You *tricked* me with your fine promises. **tricky** 1. likely to deceive: He brought the player down with a *tricky* tackle. 2. needing skill: Getting the canoe over the rapids was a *tricky* business.

trickle (trick-le) 1. flow in drops: The rain *trickled* down the windowpane. 2. a thin stream: A *trickle* of blood flowed from her cut knee.

tricycle (tri-cy-cle) a cycle with three wheels, one in front and the other two behind, one on each side.

trifle (tri-fle) 1. something of little importance or value: We need not quarrel over *trifles*. 2. a small sum of money: I only paid a *trifle* for it. 3. a little: I'm a *trifle* disappointed that I was not invited. 4. a dish consisting of sponge cake soaked in wine, covered with cream, custard, jam etc.: We had strawberry *trifle* for tea. 5. not treat seriously: I'm not in the mood to be *trifled* with. 6. amuse oneself, play with: He sat *trifling* with a cigarette holder. 7. waste time.

trigger (trig-ger) 1. a lever on a rifle, gun or pistol by which it is fired: He pressed the *trigger* and the gun went off. 2. start: An unfortunate remark by a foreman *triggered* off the strike.

trigonometry (trig-o-nom-e-try) that branch of mathematics which deals with the relations between the sides and angles of triangles.

trill 1. a sound made by the voice or an instrument which shakes between two notes: The song ends in a *trill* on the highest note. 2. make such a sound: We heard the birds *trilling* before dawn.

trim 1. tidy, neat: The old lady lived in a *trim* little cottage. 2. make neat: This hedge needs *trimming*.—I have just had my hair *trimmed*. 3. decorate: Who *trimmed* your hat? 4. state, condition: You'll win the race if you can keep in good *trim*. **trimming** things used for decoration: Did you save our Christmas *trimmings* from last year?

trinity (tri-ni-ty) 1. a group of three. 2. *Trinity* (in Christianity) Three Persons in one God, Father, Son and Holy Ghost.

trinket (trin-ket) a small jewel or ornament: The shop window was full of worthless *trinkets*.

trio 1. a group of three: Those comedians are a comical *trio*. 2. something to be sung or played by a group of three: We are rehearsing a string *trio*.

trip 1. step lightly or nimbly: She came *tripping* along the street in her new sandals. 2. stumble: He *tripped* and fell over a stone. 3. make somebody stumble: I didn't fall, I was *tripped*. 4. cause a person to make a mistake or say something he had not intended to say: 'Ah, I *tripped* you up there, didn't I?' 5. a journey for pleasure or business: He has just returned from a business *trip* abroad.

tripe part of the stomach of the cow, washed, cooked and used as food: A favourite dish in this district is *tripe* and onions.

triple (tri-ple) 1. made up of three parts: The *Triple* Alliance was made between Germany, Austria-Hungary and Italy in 1882.—This piece of music is in *triple* time (three beats in a bar). 2. make three times as big: I have *tripled* my income this year. **triplet** one of three children born to the same mother at the same time. **triplicate** of which three are alike: This statement must be typed in *triplicate* (making 3 copies). **tripod** a stool with three legs; a three-legged support for a camera.

triumph (tri-umph) 1. victory; the rejoicing at the winning of a victory: The soldiers returned to scenes of *triumph* in the streets. 2. win a victory: He has *triumphed* over his blindness. **triumphant** rejoicing at having *triumphed*: 'Now to London with *triumphant* march' (Shakespeare, *Henry VI, part III*).

trivial (triv-i-al) not important: He was summoned for a *trivial* motoring offence.

trolley (trol-ley) 1. a small cart with two or four wheels which is pushed by hand: Scouts are collecting wastepaper on their *trolley*. 2. a small table for use in the home, which runs on tiny wheels, one on the end of each leg: Tea was served from a *trolley*. 3. the wheel on a tramcar or bus which connects it to an overhead electric cable. **trolleybus** a bus, not running on rails, which takes power from an overhead cable.

trombone (trom-bone) a large wind instrument consisting of a curved brass tube widening into a bell, which produces notes by sliding one part of the tube in and out of the other.

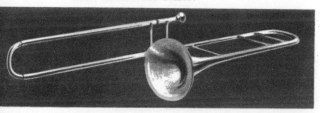

troop 1. a company of cavalry: The *troop* galloped into battle. 2. a company of boy scouts. 3. soldiers: The general rode into battle at the head of his *troops*. 4. a group of children, people, animals etc. on the move: A *troop* of children came along the road. 5. come or go together: They came *trooping* through the school gates. **trooper** a soldier in a cavalry regiment. **trooping the colour** the ceremony of carrying the flag or colours before *troops*.

trophy (tro-phy) 1. something kept in memory of a victory or success: All the colonel's hunting *trophies* were on exhibition in his hall. 2. a prize: He has carried off the swimming *trophy* for the third year running.

tropic (tro-pic) a line of latitude just over $23\frac{1}{2}$ degrees north (*tropic* of Cancer) and another just over $23\frac{1}{2}$ degrees south (*tropic* of Capricorn) of the equator. **the tropics** that part of the world between these two lines. **tropical** having to do with the *tropics*: He is taking on the journey a supply of *tropical* clothing.

trot 1. a pace faster than a walk but slower than a run: The horse kept up a steady *trot*. 2. go at this pace: He was *trotting* along happily when the shaft broke.

trouble (trou-ble) 1. bring about worry, anxiety, discomfort: His lame leg *troubles* him now and then. 2. take special care to do something: Please, do *trouble* to answer this letter. 3. worry, anxiety: These weeds are a constant source of *trouble*. 4. something causing work, discomfort: It's too much *trouble* to make such a long journey. 5. disturbance, unrest: The government has had to face great labour *troubles*. 6. illness: For years he has had heart *trouble*. **troublesome** causing *trouble*: He has a *troublesome* cough.

trough (pronounced *troff*) 1. a long open box out of which animals feed: The farmer's wife poured the pigs' food into the *trough*. 2. a hollow between waves. 3. an area of low pressure in the atmosphere: 'A *trough* of low pressure is approaching the north-western coast.'

trousers (trou-sers) 1. an outer garment covering the lower part of the body and each leg separately: I went to buy a new pair of *trousers*. 2. having to do with *trousers*: I have torn a *trouser* leg.

trousseau (trou-sseau, pronounced *trooso*) a set of clothes, linen etc. which a bride brings with her at marriage.

trowel (trow-el) 1. a tool with a flat blade for applying cement, plaster etc. 2. a tool with a curved blade used in the garden: He put the blade of the *trowel* into the ground and gently lifted out the plant.

truant (tru-ant) a girl or boy who stays away from school without the consent or knowledge of his teacher and parents: 'You've been playing *truant* again,' said the headmaster severely.

truce a short pause in fighting by agreement on both sides: During the *truce* the wounded were carried off the battlefield.

truck 1. a small barrow on two wheels used by a railway porter: The porter piled our luggage on to his *truck*. 2. an open railway carriage used for carrying heavy goods: A train went past drawing several cattle *trucks*.

trudge walk wearily: He *trudged* the streets all day looking for work.

true 1. not lying or fiction: Is it *true* that you are leaving school? 2. loyal, faithful: You have been a *true* friend to me. 3. exact, accurate: I agree that this is a *true* copy of my father's will. 4. rightful: He is the *true* heir to the throne. 5. the right position: This post is out of *true*. **truly** truthfully, sincerely, really: That was a *truly* noble action.

trumpet (trum-pet) 1. any of a family of musical wind instruments of brass consisting of a tube curved round upon itself: My brother plays the *trumpet* in a military band. 2. make known everywhere: The hero's praise was *trumpeted* throughout the kingdom.

trunk 1. the main stem of a tree: He carved his initials on the *trunk* of the oak tree. 2. the body of a person or an animal without the head or limbs. 3. a large box for holding clothes and other articles: All my most valuable things are kept in a *trunk* in my bedroom. 4. an elephant's nose or snout: The elephant moved the log out of the way with his *trunk*. **trunks** short garments stretching from hip to thigh and worn for running, swimming etc. **trunk call** a telephone call to a distant place. **trunk road** a main road used chiefly by long-distance traffic.

truss 1. a bundle: There were several *trusses* of hay in the barn. 2. tie up: When we found him he was *trussed* up like a chicken.

trust 1. faith, belief in the goodness, justice etc. of somebody: I am sure you can put your *trust* in her to keep a secret. 2. responsibility: He occupies a position of great *trust*. 3. have faith, belief in: I can *trust* him to tell the truth. 4. hope: I *trust* you are quite well again. **trustworthy** worthy of being *trusted*: He called together a few *trustworthy* companions. **trusty** an old-fashioned way of saying *trustworthy*: He swung his *trusty* sword.

try 1. attempt to do something: I am *trying* to learn Latin. 2. test: *Try* this medicine for your cold. 3. bring a case into a court of law: He is being *tried* for theft today. 4. an attempt: Come on, it's worth a *try*. 5. (in Rugby football) a score of three points earned by putting the ball down behind the opposite touchline. **trying** annoying, irritating: It was a very *trying* time while he was unemployed.

tub 1. a broad, round, wooden open vessel used for holding rainwater, or for washing clothes etc. 2. a vessel for bathing in, a bath*tub*. 3. as much as a *tub* holds: In a corner of the garden there was a *tub* of water.

tube 1. a hollow cylinder of metal, glass, rubber etc. for holding or taking liquids from one place to another: The water runs along a *tube* into the boiler. 2. a small metal container with a screw top for holding things that can be squeezed out, such as paint, toothpaste, mustard, etc. 3. an underground railway: Every morning I go to work by *tube*. **tubing** material of rubber or plastic which can be cut into *tubes* for various purposes.

tuber (tu-ber) a thick underground stem or shoot from which new plants will grow: The potato is a *tuber*.

tuberculosis (tu-ber-cu-lo-sis) an infectious disease which may affect any part of the body, but which mostly affects the lungs.

tuck 1. a fold in material, stitched down either to make the material shorter or for ornament: Your sleeve is too long; I shall have to put a *tuck* in it. 2. fold in, push into the required space: He *tucked* his napkin under his chin.

Tuesday (Tues-day) the third day of the week.

tuft a bunch of feathers, hairs, grass, flowers, leaves etc. held at the base: All that we could see was sand and a few *tufts* of coarse grass.

tug 1. pull with force: They *tugged* at the oars. 2. a hard pull: He gave a *tug* and the rope broke. 3. a small boat used to *tug* other boats: *Tugs* were used to pull the wreck off the rocks. **tug-of-war** a contest in which two teams pull against each other on a rope.

tulip (tu-lip) a bell-shaped plant which grows on a tall stem from a bulb: *Tulips* of all colours grew in the flowerbeds.

tumble (tum-ble) 1. fall: He *tumbled* down the stairs. 2. roll about, turning one way and the other: All night I *tumbled* sleeplessly in bed. 3. put in disorder through *tumbling* or tossing about: The bedclothes were *tumbled* in confusion. 4. make fall; send falling: The horse bolted, *tumbling* the rider off the saddle. **tumbler** 1. a flat-bottomed drinking glass with no stem. 2. an acrobat.

tumour (tu-mour) a diseased growth or swelling in some part of the body.

tumult (tu-mult) 1. the uproar or disturbance made by a crowd: He tried to make his voice heard above the *tumult*. 2. a confused state of mind: When I heard of the accident my mind was in a *tumult*. **tumultuous** noisy, in a *tumult*: He tried his best to quieten the *tumultuous* crowd.

tuna (tu-na) a large fish from the ocean whose flesh is used for food.

tune 1. a series of notes following each other and forming a melody: He walked along the street whistling a *tune*. 2. agreement in pitch or harmony: He always sings in *tune*. 3. put the strings of a musical instrument in *tune*: We are having our piano *tuned*. 4. adjust the various parts of a machine or engine: I'm *tuning* in to the B.B.C. programme. **tuner** a person who *tunes* musical instruments.

tunic (tu-nic) 1. a coat or jacket worn as a part of a military uniform. 2. a loose, sleeveless dress worn by a girl or woman, and gathered at the waist by a belt: You will need to bring your gym *tunics* to school tomorrow.

tunnel (tun-nel) 1. an underground passage: The train entered the *tunnel*. 2. make an underground passage: The prisoners escaped by *tunnelling* under the wall.

turban (tur-ban) 1. a man's headdress made by winding a length of cloth round the head. 2. a similar headdress worn as a hat by women.

turbulent (tur-bu-lent) violent, tumultuous: Nothing could control the *turbulent* mob.–'Will no one free me of this *turbulent* priest?' (King Henry II speaking of Thomas à Becket). **turbulence** being *turbulent*: *Turbulence* in the atmosphere may bring thunderstorms to all districts.

tureen (tu-reen) a large deep dish with a cover for holding soup, vegetables etc. at table.

turf 1. the covering of grass with its matted roots on a field, a lawn etc.: The bowling green was covered with fine *turf*. 2. lay *turf* on land: We are having our front garden *turfed*. **the turf** a racecourse, the pastime, occupation or profession of racing horses. **turf accountant** a person who has an establishment for taking bets on horseracing.

turkey (tur-key) 1. a large domesticated bird. 2. the flesh of the *turkey*: We had *turkey* for dinner at Christmas.

turmoil (tur-moil) disturbance, trouble, confusion: The classroom was in a *turmoil* on the teacher's return.

turn 1. face a different way; go round: The earth *turns* round the sun. 2. change in condition: The caterpillar *turns* into a butterfly. 3. pass: It's just *turned* four o'clock. 4. move round: I caught sight of him as he *turned* the corner. 5. make go, send: We *turn* the cat out every night. 6. the action of *turning*: A few more *turns* and the screw was firmly in the wood. 7. a change of direction: Drive carefully; there are sudden *turns* in the road here. 8. a change in condition: He has taken a *turn* for the better. 9. a chance to do something: It's my *turn* to bat. 10. a good or bad action: One good *turn* deserves another. 11. a short performance on the stage: His *turn* was loudly applauded. 12. a performer: His is one of the best *turns* I have ever seen. **turnstile** a gate with bars at the top which *turn* and let a person through, once admission had been paid: A *turnstile* often has a device which records the number of people going through.

turnip (tur-nip) a plant with a thick fleshy root which is eaten as a vegetable and given as food to cattle.

turpentine (tur-pen-tine) an oily substance which comes from cone-bearing trees and which is used for mixing paints, removing stains etc.

turquoise (tur-quoise) 1. a greenish-blue precious stone. 2. the colour of the *turquoise*: She wore a *turquoise* dress to the ball.

turtle (tur-tle) a large marine reptile whose soft body is protected by a shell, like that of a tortoise.

tusk a long pointed tooth, grown as one of a pair on elephants, walruses, wild boar etc.: Ivory is obtained from the *tusks* of elephants.

tussle (tus-sle) 1. a wrestle: After a brief *tussle* the thief was taken to the police station. 2. struggle: I *tussled* with the problem for an hour before I solved it.

tutor (tu-tor) 1. a person who instructs another in some branch of learning: He was unable to go to school, so he had to have a private *tutor*. 2. teach privately: I had to be specially *tutored* to pass the examination.

tweed 1. a coarse woollen cloth often woven with threads of different colours, either hand-woven in Scotland or reproduced by machine elsewhere. 2. articles made from this cloth: Last time I saw him he was wearing a *tweed* jacket. **tweeds** a suit of clothes made of *tweed*.

tweezers (tweez-ers) very small pincers or tongs for picking up small objects, pulling out hairs etc.: *Tweezers* are used to pluck hairs from the eyebrows.

twelve the number coming after 11 and before 13; a dozen.

twenty (twen-ty) the number coming after 19 and before 21: 'There's not one wise man among *twenty*' (Shakespeare, *Much Ado About Nothing*).

twice two times: 'Hear *twice* before you speak once' (proverb).

twig a small shoot from the branch or stem of a tree: The bird sat on the *twig* singing.

twilight (twi-light) the light in the sky just before the sun rises and just after it sets: We went for a walk in the *twilight*.

twin 1. one of two children or animals born to the same mother at the same time: My sister and I are *twins*. 2. one of a set of two: In one of our bedrooms there are *twin* beds.

twine 1. string or cord: The parcel was tied with *twine*. 2. wind: The ivy had *twined* itself round and round the chimney.

twinge 1. a sudden sharp pain: Every now and then I get *twinges* of rheumatism. 2. a sudden unexpected feeling: I never think of him without a *twinge* of regret that we quarrelled.

twinkle (twin-kle) 1. shine with quick, flickering gleams of light, as a star does: '*Twinkle, twinkle, little star*' (Jane Taylor). 2. (of a person) be bright with amusement or pleasure: Her eyes *twinkled* with mischief. 3. a *twinkling* light: The *twinkle* of light from the window told us that somebody was in the cottage. 4. a sparkle in the eyes: 'Don't you believe it,' she said with a *twinkle* in her eye.

twirl turn or make turn round and round: He sat by the fire *twirling* his thumbs.

twist 1. turn or wind a number of strands, threads etc. one around the other: We made a rope by *twisting* together pieces of long grass. 2. turn one end or part of some thing: He *twisted* the cap off the tube of paint. 3. move, making a spiral shape: Smoke *twisted* upwards from the chimney. 4. turn, curve: The road *twisted* and turned through the valley. 5. change position; move restlessly: He *twisted* about in pain. 6. a sudden jerk; a *twisting* movement: I screamed as he gave my arm a *twist*. 7. something made by *twisting*: She took a *twist* of cotton and started to sew. 8. the direction given to a ball: The bowler gave the ball a *twist* and it hit the middle stump.

twitch 1. give a sudden sharp jerk or movement: Every now and then his face *twitched*. 2. a sudden quick jerk or pull: I felt a *twitch* at my sleeve. **twitch-grass** a kind of coarse grass that grows as a weed in gardens: I wish we could get rid of the *twitch-grass* in this flowerbed.

twitter (twit-ter) 1. chirp: The birds *twitter* in the trees. 2. the sound of birds chirping; the sound of excited voices: The *twitter* of children's voices could be heard in the next room.

two the number coming after 1 and before 3: 'There were *two* horses in a stall—one called Peter and one called Paul' (children's rhyme).

two-way in two directions. **two-way street** a street in which traffic goes both ways. **two-way stretch** elastic material which stretches both ways. **two-way switch** an arrangement by which electric current can be switched on or off at two points.

tycoon (ty-coon) a businessman of great wealth and power.

type 1. a kind or sort: We are selling furniture of an entirely new *type*. 2. blocks of metal with letters on them used for printing: We are having the pamphlet set in *type* today and it will be printed tomorrow. 3. a kind or size of printing: The warning to the public was printed in a large bold *type*. 4. use a *type*writer: I am learning to *type*. **typewriter** a machine on which, by pressing keys, one can print letters on paper. **typist** a person who is employed to *type*.

typhoid (ty-phoid) an infectious fever which causes inflammation of the intestines: *Typhoid* is often caused by eating and drinking impure food or drink.

typhoon (ty-phoon) a violent storm, or hurricane, with fierce winds.

tyrant (ty-rant) a king or ruler who uses his power unjustly: *Tyrants* have often obtained their power by force. **tyrannical** of or like a *tyrant*. **tyranny** the cruel or unjust use of power: 'Let us rise up in arms and put an end to this *tyranny*,' shouted the rebel leader.

tyre a band of metal or rubber fitted on to the rim of a wheel to make a good running surface: Before going on a long journey, make sure that your *tyres* are inflated to the correct pressure.

U

ugly (ug-ly) 1. not pleasing in looks: The room was full of *ugly* furniture. 2. disagreeable, threatening danger or difficulty: The weather turned *ugly* when we were half way across the channel.

ukulele (u-ku-le-le) a small musical instrument with four strings resembling a guitar, popular in Hawaii.

ulcer (ul-cer) an open sore either on the outside or inside of the body which discharges poisonous matter: He has had an operation for a stomach *ulcer*. **ulcerated** having formed an *ulcer* or *ulcers*: She has an *ulcerated* leg.

ultimate (ul-ti-mate) 1. the last, the final: My *ultimate* aim is to become a doctor. 2. the one beyond which it is impossible to go: The hydrogen bomb has been called the *ultimate* deterrent. **ultimatum** 1. a list of demands sent by one party to another with notice that if they are not met within a fixed time measures will follow. 2. a statement of conditions.

ultraviolet (ul-tra-vi-o-let) belonging to that part of the spectrum which the human eye cannot see: *Ultraviolet* rays are used in the treatment of skin diseases.

umbrella (um-brel-la) a covering of nylon, cotton or plastic over a folding frame, fixed on a handle: An *umbrella* is carried as a shelter from rain.

umpire (um-pire) 1. a person who acts as judge in a game (especially cricket or tennis) or a dispute: The *umpire* declared that the batsman had been run out. 2. act as judge in a game or dispute: We have asked the headmaster to *umpire* our match.

un- a prefix meaning either 1. the opposite of (*un*happy, *un*kind) or 2. a reverse of the action (*un*button, *un*lock, *un*roll). The meaning of most of these words can be guessed. A few of the more difficult ones or those already used in this dictionary are given:
unable: I am *unable* to go to school because I am ill. **unaware**: I was quite *unaware* that I had taken your seat. **unbeaten**: The boxing champion remains *unbeaten*. **unbroken**: I have had eight hours of *unbroken* sleep. **uncertain**: I am *uncertain* whether or not I can meet you tomorrow. **uncomfortable**: This chair is very *uncomfortable*. **unconscious**: He had been knocked *unconscious* by a blow on the head. **uncover**: The police have *uncovered* a plot to steal the jewels. **undo**: I cannot *undo* this knot. **uneasy**: I became very *uneasy* when he did not come back. **uneven**: Write down all the *uneven* numbers between 1 and 10. **unexpected**: It was an *unexpected* pleasure meeting you. **unexploded**: An *unexploded* bomb has been discovered under the bridge. **unfit**: This meat is *unfit* to eat. **unfortunate**: It was *unfortunate* that I should lose my new watch. **unhappy**: We are very *unhappy* that you are leaving us. **unjust**: You were *unjust* to punish him. **unlike**: The twins are *unlike* each other. **unload**: The ship's cargo has been *unloaded*. **unlucky**: He was very *unlucky* to miss the train. **unpack**: We could not change our clothes until we had *unpacked*. **unpleasant**: We had a most *unpleasant* holiday; it rained the whole time. **unreal**: The ending of this story is quite *unreal*; it would never have happened like this in real life. **unsettled**: We can't go out for the day in such *unsettled* weather. **unsightly**: This street is spoilt by the *unsightly* advertisements. **unsteady**: Let me help you; you are very *unsteady* on

your feet. **untie**: I can't *untie* my shoe-lace. **untrue**: What he said about me was *untrue*. **unusual**: This stormy weather is *unusual* for summer. **unwanted**: Please take all *unwanted* refuse to the dump. **unwilling**: I am most *unwilling* to sell my piano.

unanimous (u-nan-i-mous) of one mind; in complete agreement: We arc *unanimous* about the need for a new public library.

uncanny (un-can-ny) mysterious: Every night we hear *uncanny* noises upstairs.

uncle (un-cle) the brother of one's mother or father; the husband of one's aunt: 'An old religious *uncle* of mine taught me to speak' (Shakespeare, *As You Like It*).

uncouth (un-couth) rough in manners and behaviour: An *uncouth* young man insulted me as I passed.

under 1. beneath: We buried the treasure *under* a heap of stones. 2. lower in rank, age, height, depth etc. than: Persons *under* the age of 18 are not allowed in. 3. being acted on: This road is *under* repair.

under- (un-der) a prefix meaning either 1. placed *under* in position (*under*ground) or rank (*under*secretary), or 2. not as much, large etc. as is needed (*under*paid, *under*production). The meanings of these are easy to guess: **underclothes**: In winter we wear woollen *underclothes*. **underdone**: This meat has not been cooked long enough; it is *underdone*. **underexpose**: The last film I took was *under-exposed* and the prints were very dark. **underground**: The miners spend much of their working day *underground*. **undergrowth**: We could not find our ball in the *undergrowth*. **underline**: Write your name at the top of the page and *underline* it.

undercarriage (un-der-car-riage) the landing gear of an aircraft: The aeroplane crashed because the *undercarriage* would not come down.

undercover (un-der-cov-er) done out of sight; secret: During the war he lived in enemy country as an *undercover* agent.

undergo (un-der-go) *underwent* experience or pass through: In our journey through the forest we had to *undergo* much hardship.

underhand (un-der-hand) deceitful, secretive: I don't approve of your *underhand* methods.

undermine (un-der-mine) gradually make weaker: His health was *undermined* by drink.

underneath (un-der-neath) below, at a lower place: You will find your football boots *underneath* the bed.

underrate (un-der-rate) place too low a value or estimate on (especially on a person): We lost the match because we *underrated* our opponents.

undersell (un-der-sell) *undersold* sell goods at a lower price than one's competitors.

understand (un-der-stand) *understood* 1. know the meaning of: I do not *understand* the orders you have given me. 2. get to know, learn or hear: I *understand* you have joined the navy. 3. view or accept with sympathy: If you don't invite me to the wedding I shall quite *understand*. **understanding** 1. agreement: We have come to an *understanding* about working overtime. 2. power to grasp with the mind: He has a good *understanding* of physics. 3. sympathy with others; seeing things from another's point of view: The headmaster showed great *understanding* in excusing me from school.

understudy (un-der-study) 1. an actor who takes the place of another who is unable to appear. 2. study another person's part in a play in case he may not be able to appear: I am *understudying* the part of Shylock.

undertake (un-der-take) *undertook, undertaken* 1. agree to do something: I have *undertaken* to build a garden shed. 2. promise: I can't *undertake* to be there in time. **undertaking** 1. a piece of work, a task: The expedition to the North Pole was a dangerous *undertaking*. 2. something one has *undertaken* to do. **undertaker** a person whose business is to prepare the dead for burial and to take charge of funerals.

uniform (u-ni-form) 1. the same: He picked out a number of boys of *uniform* size.– This refrigerator keeps food at a *uniform* temperature. 2. a dress worn by all members of an organization (police, traffic wardens, the army, navy, air force etc.): It is the first time I have seen you in *uniform*.

union (u-nion) 1. joining; things, states or societies joined: The United States of America is a *union* of states. 2. being joined in marriage or in some other way: We look forward to this business partnership being a happy *union*.

unit (u-nit) 1. a single person, thing or group: We have decided to visit ten family *units*, each with three children. 2. a body of soldiers: After a week's leave he returned to his *unit*. 3. a quantity, length, amount etc. used as a standard of measurement: The metre is a *unit* of length and the gram is a *unit* of weight. **unite** become one, join together: England and Scotland were *united* in 1706. **unity** being *united*, agreeing: Let us live together in *unity*.

universe (u-ni-verse) the earth, the planets, the stars, space; all of matter and energy: Astronomers are exploring the *universe* with telescopes. **universal** involving all: One day mankind may speak a *universal* language.

university (u-ni-ver-si-ty) a place of higher education which grants degrees and where students carry on research in various subjects: The teachers in *universities* are known as professors, readers and lecturers.

unless (un-less) except on condition that, if not: I cannot go *unless* you pay my fare.

until (un-til) till, up to the time of: I will wait here *until* you come to fetch me.

up 1. in or to an erect position: He stood *up* and looked around. 2. in or to a higher place: Jack and Jill went *up* the hill. 3. towards: He came *up* to me. 4. completely: Who ate *up* all the pudding? 5. more loudly: Speak *up*, I can't hear you. 6. at an end: Time's *up*! 7. above or out of: Pull *up* the weeds. 8. busy with: He's *up* to his tricks again. 9. as far as: I have had no news *up* to now.

uphold (up-hold) *upheld* support, agree with, confirm: The judge's sentence was *upheld* by the court of appeal.

upholster (up-hol-ster) provide stools, armchairs, sofas etc. with springs, cushions and coverings: We are having the chair *upholstered*.

upkeep (up-keep) 1. keeping something in working order or in repair: I am in charge of the *upkeep* of this machine. 2. the cost of keeping up or maintaining: I can't afford the *upkeep* of this large house.

upon (up-on) on: 'Two little dicky birds sat *upon* a wall' (nursery rhyme).

upper (up-per) 1. higher or highest in place or rank: We reached the *upper* slopes of the mountain. 2. the *upper* part of a boot or shoe: The sole had come loose from the *upper* and the shoe was letting in water.

upright (up-right) 1. straight up; placed vertically: The flag flew from a tall *upright* post. 2. honest, just: 'O wise and *upright* judge!' (Shakespeare, *The Merchant of Venice*).

uprising (up-ris-ing) a revolt or rebellion: The new Prime Minister was faced with an *uprising* of the army.

uproar (up-roar) a noisy disturbance, a tumult: The meeting ended in *uproar*.

uproot (up-root) 1. pull up the roots: Before we could make a garden we had to *uproot* several trees. 2. take people from the place where they live: The building of the new road meant that several families had to be *uprooted*.

upset (up-set) 1. overturn: Don't stand up; you'll *upset* the boat. 2. cause trouble, disturbance: The bad news *upset* us all.– The rich food has *upset* him.

upside down 1. with the upper side underneath. 2. in confusion: The burglars had turned the room *upside down*.

upstairs (up-stairs) to or on a higher floor: The porter took our luggage *upstairs*.

upstream (up-stream) up the river, towards the source, against the current: We paddled slowly *upstream*.

up-to-date 1. extending to the present time: Show me an *up-to-date* record of the money received. 2. keeping up with the times in fashion, news, ideas etc.: He was completely *up-to-date* with the latest political events.

upward (up-ward) **upwards** 1. towards a higher point, a higher level: This year has seen an *upward* movement of prices. 2. more than; approximately: There were *upwards* of 200 people at the meeting.

urban (ur-ban) having to do with a town or towns: Traffic is increasing in *urban* areas.

urchin (ur-chin) 1. a small boy, especially one who is mischievous. 2. a ragged, shabbily dressed boy: In town we were amazed to see barefoot *urchins* at every street-corner.

urge 1. try to persuade a person: I must *urge* you to take more care. 2. press on: I have lost no time in *urging* this plan of action. 3. drive, push: He *urged* his tired horse to a gallop. **urgent** needing immediate action: The hospital sent out an *urgent* request for help.

urine (u-rine) waste liquid from the body which collects in the bladder and is discharged.

urn 1. a vase, usually having its own stem and base: An *urn* held hundreds of red roses. 2. a small vase in which the ashes of a dead person may be placed. 3. a metal container, often with its own heating apparatus, from which tea or coffee may be served hot.

use (pronounced *uze*) 1. employ for some purpose: Do you know how to *use* a sewing machine? 2. consume: This stove *uses* rather a lot of coal. **used** 1. second-hand: We went to a garage where *used* cars were sold. 2. accustomed: I am *used* to cold weather. 3. having been for a time in the habit of: I *used* to smoke a pipe.

use 1. the act of *using* or being *used*: This room is for the *use* of the staff. 2. a way of *using* or being *used*: This tool has many *uses*. 3. purpose: What's the *use* of worrying? 4. value: Worn out tyres are of no *use* to us. 5. the power to *use*: In the accident he lost the *use* of his right eye. **useful** of *use*: Let me give you a few *useful* hints. **useless** of no *use*: A car is *useless* if you can't drive.

usher (ush-er) 1. one who shows persons to their seats in a church, theatre etc. 2. lead or take one to a place: We were *ushered* to seats in the stalls. 3. be the beginning of, bring about: We hope the new reign will *usher* in an age of prosperity.

usual (u-su-al) such as generally happens: He behaved with his *usual* good manners. **usually** in the ordinary way: I *usually* get up at seven.

usurp (u-surp) take and hold without right a position, an office, power etc. belonging to another: The late king's cousin came with an army and *usurped* the throne. **usurper** a person who *usurps*: 'Down with the *usurper*!' howled the crowd.

utensil (u-ten-sil) a tool or instrument which is used especially in the house: All kinds of household *utensils* are sold here.

utility (u-til-i-ty) 1. usefulness: This cupboard is a thing both of beauty and *utility*. 2. something useful, usually supplied by a governing body: Public *utilities* such as water, electricity, gas and transport are largely in the hands of the government. **utilize** make use of: I think we could *utilize* this hut as a bicycle store.

utmost (ut-most) 1. greatest: This is a matter of the *utmost* importance. 2. the best of one's power: I will do my *utmost* to help you. 3. farthest: Marco Polo journeyed to the *utmost* ends of the earth.

utter (ut-ter) 1. give forth sounds or words: Not a word was *uttered* as the will was read. 2. circulate false money: He was arrested for *uttering* forged banknotes. 3. complete, total: The ship struck a rock and was an *utter* loss. **utterly** completely: The building was *utterly* destroyed.

V

vacant (va-cant) 1. empty, not occupied: There was one *vacant* room in the hotel. 2. not taken up with work etc.: I have two days *vacant* in the middle of March. 3. Not occupied with thoughts: He answered me with a *vacant* stare. **vacancy** 1. being *vacant*: A sign in the window of the boarding house read 'No *vacancies*'. 2. a *vacant* post: There is a *vacancy* in this office for a good typist.

vacation (va-ca-tion) a part of the year when schools, universities, law courts etc. are closed: I have found work in an office during the summer *vacation*.

vaccinate (vac-ci-nate) protect the body from certain diseases, especially smallpox, by injecting vaccine into it. **vaccine** a substance taken from the blood of a cow and prepared for injection into a human being. **vaccination** being *vaccinated*.

vacuum (vac-u-um) a space from which all air has been removed. **vacuum flask** a flask with a *vacuum* jacket which prevents a change in temperature of the contents. **vacuum cleaner** a cleaner which, by sucking air, picks up dust and dirt.

vague not clear or distinct, not definite in meaning: In the mist we saw the *vague* outline of a ship.

vain 1. without real value or result: We made a *vain* attempt to rescue the dog. 2. having too high an opinion of one's looks, abilities etc.: He is so *vain* as to imagine himself a genius. **in vain** 1. without success: We tried *in vain* to climb the cliff. 2. without the respect deserved: 'Thou shalt not take the name of the Lord thy God *in vain*' (the Third Commandment). **vanity** being *vain*: 'There is no need of such *vanity*' (Shakespeare, *Much Ado about Nothing*).

vale a valley: The *Vale* of Evesham is famous for its fertile soil and its splendid orchards.

valentine (val-en-tine) a letter or card sent to one's sweetheart on St *Valentine's* Day, February 14.

valet (val-et) a manservant employed to look after his master's clothing and attend to his needs: Jeeves is the most famous *valet* in English fiction.

valiant (val-iant) brave: 'Thy master is a wise and *valiant* Roman' (Shakespeare, *Julius Caesar*). **valour** bravery: The inscription on the Victoria Cross reads 'For *Valour*'.

valid (val-id) 1. sound: He has given a *valid* reason for leaving his post. 2. binding in law: My railway pass is *valid* for three months.

valley (val-ley) a stretch of low land between hills or mountains: Our path lay through a wooded *valley*.

value (val-ue) 1. worth or importance: Your help would be of great *value* to me. 2. estimate what something is worth in terms of money: I have had my house *valued*. 3. think highly of: I would *value* your opinion in this matter. **valuable** 1. having *value*: The shop was robbed of many *valuable* articles. 2. something of *value*: I have deposited most of my *valuables* in the bank. **valuation** the amount something is declared to be worth: The two surveyors arrived at different *valuations* of the property.

valve 1. a device for controlling the flow of liquid, air or gas through tubes or pipes: A *valve* prevents the air from leaking out of a tyre. 2. a structure in a blood vessel which allows the blood to flow in one direction only. 3. a tube in a radio or television set. 4. a device in certain wind instruments (trumpets, cornets, etc.) which, when certain keys are pressed, alters the length of the tubes and changes the pitch of notes.

van 1. a covered vehicle, used for carrying furniture and other goods: Every day the baker drives past our house in his *van*. 2. a closed railway wagon for carrying goods: We put our luggage in the guard's *van*. 3. the leading part of an army or a fleet in battle: The admiral's flagship led the *van*.

vandal (van-dal) a person who wilfully destroys or damages property and works of art: All the windows in the bus-shelter had been broken by *vandals*.

vane 1. a device with a pointer fixed on top of a spire or building to show the direction of the wind. 2. a device fixed on a windmill to turn the sails into the wind. 3. the blade of a propeller or other flat surface acted on by wind or water.

vanish (van-ish) disappear; go out of sight or existence: The thief ran off and *vanished* among the crowd.

vanquish (van-quish) defeat, conquer, overcome in battle or a contest: Our enemies were *vanquished* and sued for peace.

varnish (var-nish) 1. a transparent liquid that can be painted on to wood, metal, etc. to give a hard shiny surface: The door has been given a new coat of *varnish*. 2. paint on *varnish*: He was *varnishing* the door.

vary (va-ry) become or cause to become different: The weather *varies* from day to day. **variation** 1. *varying*, being *varied*: There have been great *variations* in the weather this summer. 2. in music, a melody repeated, changing its forms: The orchestra played a set of *variations* by Sir Edward Elgar. **variegated** marked in different colours: The vase held a bunch of *variegated* leaves. **variety** 1. a number of different kinds: We have a large *variety* of radio sets to choose from. 2. a kind of entertainment consisting of singing, dancing, acrobatics etc. given by performers appearing either singly or in small groups. 3. change in surroundings, occupations, pleasures etc.: *Variety*'s the very spice of life that gives it all its flavour (William Cowper). **various** different: The police tried *various* ways to get him to confess.

vase a vessel, used mainly for ornament or for holding cut flowers: On the table stood a *vase* of beautiful roses.

vaseline (vas-e-line) a yellowish greasy substance made from petroleum, used mainly as an ointment.

vast immense, very big, enormous: We found ourselves at the edge of a *vast* crater.– This building has cost *vast* sums of money.

vat a large tank for holding liquids: The beer was fermenting in a large *vat*.

vault 1. a large room or cellar: My valuables are stored in an underground *vault* at the bank. 2. an arched construction, part of the roof of a building or a sewer. 3. take a single leap: He *vaulted* over the fence. **vaulting-horse** an apparatus used in gymnastics for *vaulting*.

veal the flesh of a calf used as food.

vegetable (veg-e-ta-ble) 1. a plant, especially one used for food: What *vegetables* are we having for dinner? 2. having to do with plants: He lives on a *vegetable* diet.–All our cooking is done with *vegetable* oils. **vegetarian** a person who does not eat meat. **vegetation** plants, trees, bushes: All around us was sand with not a sign of *vegetation*. **vegetate** live as a plant does, doing little, thinking little: The old man *vegetates* in his small hut in the wood.

vehicle 1. anything used to convey people or things, usually on wheels: *Vehicles* are not allowed on this stretch of road. 2. a means of expressing thoughts or feelings: Language is a *vehicle* for expressing our thoughts.

veil 1. a piece of transparent material used as part of a headdress: The bride wore a white *veil*. 2. the headdress worn by a nun. 3. something that covers: The town was blotted out by a *veil* of smoke. 4. something pretended: Under the *veil* of friendship he persuaded me to lend him money. 5. hide: I could not *veil* my disgust at his conduct.

vein 1. one of the blood vessels that carries blood to the heart. 2. a *vein*-like marking on a leaf or in some kinds of stone: The marble was white with purple *veins*. 3. a crack in rock in which there are mineral deposits: He struck a rich *vein* of gold.

velocity (ve-loc-i-ty) speed, rate of speed: This aeroplane travels at twice the *velocity* of sound.

velvet (vel-vet) a soft cloth with a short raised pile: She wore a blue *velvet* jacket.

veneer (ve-neer) 1. a thin layer of better quality wood laid over cheaper wood in the making of furniture etc.: Because of the damp, the *veneer* has peeled off the wardrobe door. 2. a pleasing appearance concealing a person's true character: Don't be misled by his *veneer* of good manners. 3. put on a *veneer*: I have sent away the dressing-table to be *veneered*.

venerable (ven-er-a-ble) worthy of respect because of high character, office, or age: The vicar was a *venerable* old man.

vengeance (ven-geance) revenge, injury returned for injury: 'We will have *vengeance* for it' (Shakespeare, *Romeo and Juliet*).

venison (ven-i-son) the flesh of a deer: Isaac told his eldest son to go hunting and to bring back *venison*.

ventilate (ven-ti-late) 1. make air circulate freely in a building: We *ventilated* the room by opening the windows. 2. make an argument or an opinion known: The workers asked for a meeting with the manager to *ventilate* their grievances. **ventilation** *ventilating*, being *ventilated*: There are many faults in the *ventilation* of this building.

ventriloquist (ven-tril-o-quist) a person who produces sounds so that they seem to come from another person or place: Most *ventriloquists* use dolls which appear to speak.

venture (ven-ture) 1. take a risk: Don't *venture* too far from the shore. 2. put forward: I'd *venture* an opinion that he is not far away. 3. something *ventured*: The merchant had sent his captains on many *ventures*. **venturesome** willing to take risks: He is too *venturesome* in climbing the cliffs.

verandah (ve-ran-dah) an open space with roof and floor extending along one side or round the sides of a house, sports pavilion etc.: They sat on the *verandah* in the evening and watched the sun set.

verb a word which says what somebody or something does or is; a being or doing word: There are three *verbs* in this sentence: 'This man *is* a carpenter; he *has* many tools and he *makes* furniture.'

verbal (ver-bal) having to do with words, especially spoken words: He sent a *verbal* message by his little brother.

verdict (ver-dict) 1. the decision of a jury in a law case: The jury brought in a *verdict* of not guilty. 2. an opinion given after much thought and examination: What is your *verdict* on the quality of this cloth?

verge 1. a narrow strip of grass by the side of a road or a path: We picnicked on the grass *verge*. 2. limit; the extreme edge: She was on the *verge* of bursting into tears.

verger (ver-ger) 1. a church official who looks after the interior of the church and acts as an attendant. 2. an official who carries a staff before a bishop or a dean in a church.

verify (ver-i-fy) 1. prove something to be true: His statement was *verified* by three other witnesses. 2. test something to find if it is true: Please *verify* the dates on which these letters were received.

vermin (ver-min) animals or insects which are harmful, objectionable or which bring disease: Foxes, mice and fleas are considered to be *vermin*. **verminous** infested with *vermin*: The dog had been neglected and was *verminous*.

versatile (ver-sa-tile) clever at many different things: He is a *versatile* musician; he plays many instruments.

verse 1. poetry: The story is written in *verse*. 2. a small section of a poem: He recited a *verse* of Shelley's poem *To a Skylark*. 3. one of the numbered parts of a chapter in the Bible.

version (ver-sion) 1. an account of some matter from the point of view of one person: According to John's *version* there was no fighting at all. 2. a translation into another language: This is the English *version* of the Italian text.

vertebra (ver-te-bra) *vertebrae* one of the small bones or segments making up the backbone: The spinal cord, which is the chief nerve of the body, passes through the *vertebrae*.

vertical (ver-ti-cal) upright, at right angles to the earth's surface.

very 1. extremely: I feel *very* tired. 2. same: That's the *very* book I lent you. 3. mere: The *very* thought of it makes me feel ill. 4. actual: He was caught in the *very* act.

vessel (ves-sel) 1. a hollow article such as a cup, bowl, pot, pan or bottle made to hold things. 2. a ship.

vest 1. a short undergarment worn next to the body. 2. (of power) place: In Great Britain power is *vested* in the Prime Minister and the cabinet.

vestibule (ves-ti-bule) 1. a small hall between the outer door and rooms of a house or building: Ten people were waiting in the *vestibule*. 2. the porch of a church: The vicar greeted his congregation in the *vestibule*.

vestige (ves-tige) a trace or sign: There isn't a *vestige* of truth in his story.

vestry (ves-try) a small room attached to a church where the robes are kept, and which the minister sometimes uses as a study or private room.

veteran (vet-er-an) a former soldier, sailor or airman: The *veterans* of the Second World War attended the memorial service.

veterinary (vet-er-i-na-ry) having to do with the diseases of animals: The dog was ill and we took him to the *veterinary* surgeon (or, as we say, the *vet*).

veto (ve-to) the right to forbid or reject something: Every member of the United Nations Security Council has the right to exercise the *veto* against a motion with which his government does not agree.

vex irritate, annoy, make angry: I was *vexed* that you didn't ask my help.

viaduct (vi-a-duct) a bridge which carries a road or railway over a valley, a road, a built-up area etc.

vibrate (vi-brate) 1. move quickly backwards and forwards: The strings of a violin *vibrate* when the bow is drawn across them. 2. quiver or tremble: His voice *vibrated* with anger. **vibration** a *vibrating* movement: The *vibration* of the engines gave me a headache.

vicar (vic-ar) a clergyman in charge of a parish. **vicarage** the house in which the *vicar* lives.

vice 1. any kind of wrong-doing: Laziness, gluttony and greed are *vices*. 2. a device with two jaws which can be brought together by a screw to grip and hold a piece of work in position: He put the wood into the *vice* and began to saw it in half. **vicious** spiteful, evil; done with evil intention: This dog is *vicious*.

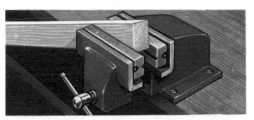

vice- a prefix meaning next below in rank: While the captain was ill the *vice*-captain took charge of the team.—The president could not attend, so the *vice*-president made the speech.

vicinity (vi-cin-i-ty) the region near a place, the neighbourhood: Somewhere in this *vicinity* there must be a post office.

victim (vic-tim) a person or animal suffering from misfortune, or any kind of evil: Money is being raised for the *victims* of the floods. **victimize** make a *victim* of: The tenant claimed that he had been *victimized* by his landlord when he was asked to leave the house.

victor (vic-tor) one who wins or conquers: The *victor* in this race will represent us at the Olympic Games. **victory** success in a contest: The *victory* of the Royal Air Force in the Battle of Britain saved England from invasion. **victorious** having won a *victory*: The *victorious* army returned home in triumph.

victual (pronounced *vittle*) 1. supply with provisions: The ship is being *victualled* for a long voyage. 2. take in provisions: The ship *victualled* at Newcastle. **victuals** provisions, food and drink: We took on board enough *victuals* to last us three weeks.

view 1. sight: He stood in full *view* of the crowd waving his arms. 2. that which is seen; a scene: There was a wonderful *view* from the top of the hill. 3. an opinion: I take a very poor *view* of your behaviour. 4. a purpose: I am doing this with a *view* to making less work for you. 5. examine, survey: Before deciding to build we need to *view* the site. 6. consider: I *view* this matter with grave concern. **viewer** 1. one who watches a television programme. 2. one appointed to inspect or examine.

vigil (vig-il) staying awake to keep watch: Nothing happened during our all-night *vigil*. **vigilant** watchful: You must be *vigilant* to see that the rules are not broken.

vigour (vig-our) 1. strength, energy: The *vigour* with which he worked amazed me. 2. force, activity: The thieves will be pursued with the utmost *vigour*. **vigorous** strong, energetic: The whole village joined in *vigorous* pursuit.

viking (vi-king) one of the sea-robbers from Norway and Denmark who raided the coasts of Britain and Europe over a thousand years ago: King Alfred fought many battles against the *vikings*.

vile 1. evil, wicked: I did not think him capable of such *vile* conduct. 2. bad: What *vile* weather we are having.

villa (vil-la) 1. a suburban house. 2. a country residence: My uncle has a town house and a *villa* in the south of France. 3. an ancient Roman farmhouse surrounded by its own estate: We have recently been excavating a Roman *villa* in Dorset.

village (vil-lage) a place smaller than a town with a main street, a few shops, one or two inns and a church: Is there a petrol station in this *village*? **villager** a person living in a *village*.

villain (vil-lain) a wicked man: In most plays the villain always comes to a bad end. **villainous** wicked: The rebels have been guilty of many *villainous* acts against innocent people.

vindictive (vin-dic-tive) wanting to take revenge: Because he was dropped from the first team he is in a *vindictive* mood.

vine a climbing plant which supports itself by means of tendrils: Hops, melons and grapes are produced on different kinds of of *vines*. **vineyard** a piece of ground on which grape-*vines* are grown. **vintage** 1. the grape harvest: The fine weather has brought an early *vintage*. 2. the year when the grapes for certain wines were grown: This is a 1948 *vintage* wine. **vinegar** an acid liquid made from wine, etc. used for preserving and flavouring in the preparation of foods.

violate (vi-o-late) 1. break rules or laws: The treaty was *violated* and war was declared once more. 2. disturb: The peace of the countryside was *violated* by the roar of aircraft engines. 3. pass by force: In 1940 the Germans *violated* the frontiers of Holland and Belgium. 4. behave badly in a sacred place: Vandals broke into the church and *violated* the altar. **violent** accompanied by force: He has a *violent* temper. **violence** the use of force: During the procession there were several acts of *violence* in the streets.

violin (vi-o-lin) a musical instrument with four strings, held under the chin and played with a bow. **viola** a *violin* of a rather larger size which plays lower notes. **violoncello** (or **cello**) a bass *violin* played with a bow and held between the player's knees. **violinist, violoncellist, cellist** musicians who play these instruments.

virgin (vir-gin) an unmarried girl, a maiden. **The Virgin Mary** the mother of Jesus Christ.

virile (vir-ile) manly, vigorous, showing strength: A group of *virile* young men overpowered the bull.

virtual (vir-tu-al) being a certain person or thing though not named as such: The chairman is ill and his son is *virtual* head of the firm.

virtue (vir-tue) goodness, any good quality: Patience is a *virtue*.–The *virtue* of this cooker is that it does not need frequent cleaning. **virtuous** possessing *virtue*: 'Your father was ever *virtuous*' (Shakespeare, *The Merchant of Venice*).

visa (vi-sa) a stamp on a passport made by an official of a foreign country giving the holder permission to visit it: Though our passports were in order we were turned back at the frontier because we had no *visas*.

viscount (vis-count) a nobleman next below an earl or count and next above a baron.

vision (vi-sion) 1. the power to see: My *vision* is not good and I have to wear spectacles. 2. the power to imagine: He has *visions* of great wealth. 3. the ability to see and deal with difficulties lying ahead: This business needs men of *vision*. 4. something seen in imagination or dreams: 'I have had a most rare *vision*' (Shakespeare, *A Midsummer Night's Dream*). **visible** that can be seen: The solar eclipse will be *visible* only in Africa. **visual** having to do with seeing: In our lessons we have *visual* aids such as films, maps, and charts.

visit (vis-it) 1. go to see a person because of friendship, duty, business etc.: How often do you *visit* your parents? 2. the act of *visiting*: During my *visit* to London I saw Buckingham Palace.

vital (vi-tal) 1. necessary to life: Food and drink are *vital* to our existence. 2. having much energy: He has a *vital* personality. 3. very important: Success in this examination is *vital* to me. **vitality** physical strength, vigour, power to endure: This firm requires a man of great *vitality* as its manager. **vitamin** one of the substances in food which is necessary for a person to live and be in good health: Oranges are a rich source of certain *vitamins*.

vivid (viv-id) 1. very bright and clear: She wore a *vivid* yellow scarf. 2. distinct: He gave a *vivid* account of his captivity.

vivisect (viv-i-sect) operate on the living bodies of animals for purposes of experiment. **vivisection** the practice of *vivisecting*: Many people in this country, called anti-*vivisectionists*, are violently opposed to *vivisection*.

vocabulary (vo-cab-u-la-ry) 1. a list of words used in a book; a book containing a list of words: I cannot read this French novel without a *vocabulary*. 2. the words known to a person: Shakespeare had an enormous *vocabulary*; he increased the *vocabulary* of the English language by hundreds of new words.

vocal (vo-cal) having to do with the voice: The tongue, the lips and the palate are some of the *vocal* organs of man. **vocalist** a singer: Caruso was one of the greatest tenor *vocalists* the world has known.

vocation (vo-ca-tion) 1. work one feels compelled to do: My *vocation* is to help the poor. 2. a special ability for: I do not feel I have a *vocation* to work with machines. 3. a person's profession. **vocational** having to do with a profession: After coming out of hospital he went for *vocational* training.

vogue fashion, popularity: Longer skirts are again in *vogue*.

voice 1. the sounds made when singing or speaking: He addressed me in a loud *voice*. 2. the power to speak or sing: She has a wonderful *voice*. 3. an opinion given, the right to give an opinion: I hope to have a *voice* in sharing out the money. 4. put into words: I have been asked to *voice* the feelings of the meeting.

volcano (vol-ca-no) an opening in the earth's crust, usually at the top of a mountain, through which molten lava is flung into the air: The Roman town of Pompeii was buried by a *volcano* from Mount Etna in AD 79.

volley (vol-ley) 1. a number of shells, bullets, arrows etc. discharged in the same direction at once: At Crécy in 1340 the advancing French were checked by *volley* upon *volley* of arrows. 2. in tennis, the return of a ball before it has touched the ground. 3. fly or be discharged together. 4. return a tennis ball before it touches the ground.

volume (vol-ume) 1. a book: In his bookshelf were all the *volumes* of an encyclopedia. 2. the amount of space occupied by something: What *volume* of wine will this cask hold? 3. a large amount: *Volumes* of smoke ascended from the fire at the factory. 4. sound: Please turn down the *volume* of your radio; it disturbs the neighbours.

voluntary (vol-un-ta-ry) 1. done without being compelled: The witness made a *voluntary* statement. 2. given of one's own free will: This hospital is supported by *voluntary* contributions. **volunteer** 1. a person who does something willingly and without being forced: We want help in building the new hut; are there any *volunteers*? 2. a soldier who enlists without being conscripted. 3. offer to do a thing; give information etc.: I have *volunteered* to act as an ambulance driver.

vomit 1. bring back the contents of the stomach through the mouth; be sick: The child was ill and began to *vomit*. 2. pour forth: All the chimneys were *vomiting* dense black smoke.

vote 1. the expression of a person's wish either by showing his hand or by the use of the ballot: My *vote* was given to the Conservative candidate. 2. the right to use the *vote*: All women have had the *vote* since 1927. 3. the number of *votes* given: The Labour *vote* in this election has increased. 4. an expression of feeling: Parliament has passed a *vote* of confidence in the government. 5. give a *vote*: I hope you *voted* for the right man. 6. propose: I *vote* that we give money to the fund for famine relief. **voter** one who *votes*.

voucher (vouch-er) 1. a ticket or document showing that money has been paid and received. 2. a ticket used in place of money: He was presented with a gift *voucher*. – This restaurant accepts luncheon *vouchers*.

vow 1. a solemn promise: He has broken his *vow* and should be punished. 2. make a *vow*: 'If I do *vow* a friendship I'll perform it' (Shakespeare, *Othello*).

vowel (vow-el) one of the letters a, e, i, o, u, and sometimes y, spoken through the open mouth without interference from tongue, teeth or lips.

voyage (voy-age) 1. a journey by water: How long did the *voyage* to Australia take? 2. journey by water. **voyager** a person who makes a *voyage* or *voyages*: The *voyagers* were relieved to see land after three weeks at sea.

vulgar (vul-gar) coarse, ill-mannered: He was expelled from the club for using *vulgar* language. **vulgarity** *vulgar* behaviour or appearance.

vulture (vul-ture) a large bird of prey whose head and neck are almost bare of feathers: *Vultures* feed on the flesh of dead animals.

wad 1. a small mass of soft material used for stuffing, padding or packing: I have plugged the hole with a *wad* of cotton wool. 2. a bundle or roll of banknotes: He drew a *wad* of notes out of his pocket.

wade 1. walk through a substance, such as water or snow, that hinders movement: To reach him I had to *wade* through the deep mud. 2. go through with difficulty: The book was very dull but I *waded* through it slowly. **wader** a bird, such as a stork or crane, that *wades*. **waders** high waterproof boots used for *wading*.

wafer (wa-fer) 1. a thin, flat, crisp biscuit, usually eaten with ice cream. 2. a thin disc of bread used in Holy Communion in Church. 3. a small thin piece of sticky paper, used for fastening larger pieces of paper together.

waffle (waf-fle) a small cake made of batter cooked on a special kind of iron made of two parts hinged together: The iron marks the *waffle* with small squares.

waft 1. carry lightly through the air or over the water: We heard the sound of voices *wafted* by the gentle breeze. 2. the sound or smell of something *wafted*; a light current of air: We heard the faint *waft* of church bells in the evening air.

wag 1. move or make move from side to side: The dog ran up to me, *wagging* his tail. 2. a merry person, full of wit and fond of playing jokes: 'How now, mad *wag*, what dost thou in Warwickshire?' (Shakespeare, *Henry IV, part 1*).

wage 1. that which is paid for work or services as at the end of each day or each week: We want a fair day's *wage* for a fair day's work. 2. carry on: The two countries had been *waging* war for many years.—We are *waging* a continual war against disease.

wager (wa-ger) 1. bet: He often *wagers* his money on horses. 2. a bet: I laid a *wager* that I could walk from London to Edinburgh.

wagon or **waggon** (wag-gon) 1. a four-wheeled vehicle for carrying heavy goods: The peasants brought in their harvest by ox-*wagon*. 2. a railway truck.

waif a person, especially a child, without home or friends. **waifs and strays** homeless children; cats and dogs without owners.

wail 1. cry or weep in a loud shrill voice: The child was *wailing* pitifully. 2. make a *wailing* sound: The wind *wailed* round the little cottage. 3. a loud mournful cry: In the distance we heard the *wails* of the funeral procession.

waist 1. the middle part of the human body between the ribs and the hips: He wore a red sash round his *waist*. 2. that part of a garment that goes round the *waist*: Your dress is too wide at the *waist*. **waistcoat** a close-fitting sleeveless garment that buttons in front, designed to be worn under a jacket.

wait 1. stay or remain until something expected happens: We are *waiting* until the rain stops. 2. be ready: Your breakfast is *waiting* on the table. 3. delay, postpone: Don't *wait* for me to come in. 4. serve, look after: I don't like being *waited* on. 5. a time spent in *waiting*: We had a long *wait* for the bus. **waiter** a man who *waits* at table as in a restaurant. **waitress** a woman who *waits* at table.

wake woke, woken, waking 1. stop sleeping: I *woke* at seven o'clock this morning. 2. stop another person sleeping: Don't make a noise or you may *wake* the baby. 3. the watch over a dead person before burial. 4. the track left by a ship as it moves through the water: We sat in the stern watching the *wake*. **wakeful** not able to sleep: I was *wakeful* for most of the night.

walk 1. travel on foot making steps in turn so that there is always one foot on the ground: I always *walk* to school. 2. make somebody or something *walk*: It is time to *walk* the dog. 3. pass over on foot: Ten years ago we *walked* the Yorkshire dales. 4. a journey on foot: Let's go for a *walk*. 5. a way of *walking*: I should recognize you anywhere by your *walk*. 6. a path or road along which one *walks*: My favourite *walk* is along the promenade. **walkie-talkie** a two-way radio telephone light enough to be carried about by one person.

wall 1. an upright structure of stone, brick, concrete etc. forming the side of a building or a room, or marking off one piece of land from another: London was once surrounded by a *wall*.–We hung the portrait on the dining room *wall*. 2. something reminding one of a *wall*: The wave rose in a high *wall* of water. 3. surround with a *wall*: I have *walled* in my piece of land. **wallflower** a plant with brown, red, yellow or orange flowers. **wallpaper** paper used for covering the *walls* of rooms as a decoration.

wallet (wal-let) a small, book-like folding case which holds money, papers etc. in the pocket: Remember to keep your driving licence in your *wallet*.

wallow (wal-low) roll about, usually in water, mud, dust etc.: Pigs enjoy *wallowing* in the mud.

walnut (wal-nut) 1. a nut with a hard shell, eaten especially at Christmas. 2. the wood of the *walnut* tree, used in making furniture.

walrus (wal-rus) a large sea animal with flippers, tusks and a very thick skin.

waltz 1. a dance in which couples move round and round. 2. the music, in three-time, for such a dance: The band played an old-time *waltz*. 3. make a person *waltz*: He *waltzed* me round and round until I was dizzy.

wan pale, looking ill, sad and anxious: 'Why so pale and *wan*, fond lover?' (Sir John Suckling)

wand 1. a slender stick carried supposedly by a magician or a fairy, in order to work magic: 'Abracadabra,' the fairy god-mother said, waving her magic *wand*. 2. a rod carried by an usher, a steward etc. in processions as a symbol of power.

wander (wan-der) 1. go from place to place without any set purpose: 'Goosey goosey gander, whither do you *wander*?' (nursery rhyme). 2. stray from the path: He *wandered* into the forest and was lost for days. 3. let the thoughts go their own way: My mind *wandered* back to the days of my youth. **wanderer** one who *wanders*. **wanderings** travels: Would you like to hear stories of my *wanderings*?

wane grow less and less: For fourteen days the moon waxes and for the same length of time it *wanes*.–As the days passed our hopes of rescue *waned*.

want 1. require, need: I *want* you to help paint the house. 2. desire; wish for: I *want* to go to the Isle of Man for my holidays.–He is *wanted* by the police. 3. a lack: My *wants* are few.–The door is in *want* of a coat of paint.

war 1. fighting between two or more countries: *War* broke out in September 1939.–Food was scarce during the *war*. 2. a struggle against some evil: We must carry on the *war* against disease. **war cry** a cry shouted in battle, a slogan used by a group in a contest or a campaign: Let Progress be our *war cry*. **warhead** the explosive head of a shell, a torpedo or a missile. **warpaint** paint put on the body and face by certain primitive tribes when they go to *war*. **warlike** ready for *war*, in the mood to make *war*: *Warlike* preparations had been going on for many years. **warrior** a soldier, a fighter.

warble (war-ble) 1. sing with trilling notes: The birds have been *warbling* since early morning. 2. the song of a bird: We heard the *warble* of the blackbird.

ward 1. a person left in the care of another: Since her parents died she has been a *ward* of her uncle. 2. a division of a city or area of local government: There are three councillors who represent this *ward*. 3. a separate room in a prison or hospital, usually for a particular class of patient: Our son is at present in the the children's *ward*. **ward off** avoid, keep away: He raised his arm to *ward off* the blow. **warden** a person who has authority to watch over or care for a place or thing: I was an air-raid *warden* during the war. **warder** a person who acts as a guard in a prison: The prisoners took exercise in the yard under the watchful eyes of the *warders*.

wardrobe (ward-robe) 1. a cupboard with hooks and shelves for holding clothes: I counted twelve suits hanging in the *wardrobe*. 2. the clothes one owns: My *wardrobe* is completely out of fashion.

ware 1. different kinds of goods: We stock glass*ware* and silver*ware* in our store. 2. things for sale: 'Said Simple Simon to the pieman, let me taste your *ware*' (nursery rhyme). **warehouse** a building in which goods for sale are stored: We bought a wardrobe at a large furniture *warehouse*.

warm 1. having a certain amount of heat; not cold: How *warm* your hands are! 2. sincere, enthusiastic: He received a *warm* welcome. 3. near to what is being sought: Keep searching; you're getting *warm*. 4. make or become *warm*: I'm *warming* up now. **warmth** the state of being *warm*: You can feel the *warmth* of the sun.

warn give notice to a person of some danger or of something that is going to happen: He was *warned* of the plot against his life. **warning** something that *warns*: Ships round the coasts have been given gale *warnings*.

warp 1. become bent or twisted: We could not close the door because the wood had *warped*. 2. the threads in a loom over and under which the crossthreads (weft or woof) are passed.

warrant (war-rant) 1. a right, an authority: You have no *warrant* for making such a statement. 2. a document giving a person a certain right: The police came to the house with a search *warrant*. 3. give a person the right to do a thing: Nothing could *warrant* such rude behaviour. 4. guarantee: We can *warrant* safe delivery of the goods.

warren (war-ren) a place where rabbits breed and live.

wart a small hard growth on the skin.

wary (wa-ry) watchful, on one's guard, cautious: When you talk to him, be *wary*, for he is easily offended.

wash 1. clean by using water or other liquids: You should *wash* your hands before a meal. 2. be easy or difficult to *wash*: These towels *wash* very easily. 3. flow over or against: The waves *washed* against the pier. 4. remove by *washing*: He *washed* the dirt off his face. 5. carry away by water: He was *washed* overboard. 6. *washing*: I've just had a *wash*. 7. articles that are *washed*: We took our *washing* to the laundry. 8. the movement of water: We heard the *washing* of the waves against the boat. **washer** 1. a machine for *washing* clothes or dishes. 2. a small flat ring put between a nut and bolt to tighten a joint. **washleather** a piece of chamois leather used for cleaning windows, cars etc.

wasp a flying insect with a black and yellow striped body and a sting in its tail.

wassail (was-sail) 1. a time of drinking and feasting, usually Christmas or the New Year. 2. wish health at such a time: 'Here we come a-*wassailing* among the leaves so green' (carol for Christmas and the New Year).

waste 1. thrown away because not wanted: The scouts are collecting *waste* paper. 2. use badly, throw away: We have been warned not to *waste* water. 3. lose weight and strength: He had *wasted* away to a mere shadow. 4. destroy, ravage: William the Conqueror *wasted* much of England with fire and sword. 5. being *wasted*: It's a *waste* of energy to try and advise him. 6. land on which little grows and which cannot be used: He was lost for six months in the *wastes* of the arctic. **wasteful** using more than is needed: He ruined his family through *wasteful* methods of living.

watch 1. look at: He *watched* me go down the road.—His favourite hobby is bird *watching*. 2. the act of *watching*: Two men were given orders to keep *watch*. 3. a period of duty *watching*: My *watch* begins at midnight. 4. a small timepiece or clock worn on a chain or on the wrist: When I looked at my *watch* I saw we had missed lunch. **watchman** a man em-

ployed to guard a building, especially during the night.

water (wat-er) 1. the liquid that forms rain, fills rivers, seas, lakes etc., which when pure has no colour, taste or smell: I should like a glass of *water*. 2. put *water* on; give *water*; add *water* to: He is *watering* the garden.—We stopped at the inn to *water* the horses. **watercolour** paint made by mixing with *water*; a picture painted in *watercolour*. **water-level** the height of the *water* in a reservoir or pond etc. **waterlogged** overflowing with *water*: No crops would grow in the *waterlogged* land. **water-power** *water* used to drive machinery. **waterproof** not letting *water* through; a coat which does not let *water* through. **watershed** high land on each side of which rivers and streams flow. **watertight** fastened so that *water* cannot leak through: Is this tank *watertight*? **waterway** a stream, river, canal etc. on which boats and ships can travel. **watery** containing too much *water*, running with *water*: This milk is *watery*.

wattle (wat-tle) 1. sticks and twigs woven together to make fences, walls etc.: The hut was made of *wattle* plastered over with clay. 2. the flesh hanging down from the chin or throat of a turkey or a chicken. 3. a shrub with yellow flowers growing mainly in Australia.

wave 1. move gently to and fro, or up and down: The flags *waved* in the breeze. 2. make something move in this way: The guard *waved* his flag. 3. a long moving ridge of water: The *waves* came rolling in to shore. 4. something resembling a *wave*: The first *wave* of infantry attacked at dawn. 5. a time of unusually hot or cold weather: How long is this heat-*wave* going to last? **wavy** in *waves*: He drew a *wavy* line across the page.

wax 1. a substance of plant or animal origin, used for making candles and polishes. 2. cover, polish, with *wax*: The floor had been *waxed*. 3. (of the moon) grow from new moon to full moon.

way 1. a path, road, street: There was a covered *way* between the shops. 2. a route: Which is the best *way* across the moor? 3. a method: Is there an easy *way* to learn to play the piano? 4. a distance: The Town Hall is a long *way* from here. 5. a direction: Which *way* did they go?– You're going the wrong *way*. 6. a space, room: Move on, you're getting in my *way*. 7. a manner of living or behaving: I don't like the *way* you treat your dog. 8. a state: The poor fellow is in a very bad *way*. **waylay** attack on the road: The coach was *waylaid* by a highwayman. **wayside** the side of the road.

we you and I; I with one or more others: *We* usually go on holiday in August.

weak 1. not strong; easy to break: He is too *weak* to walk long distances. 2. not good: I am *weak* in mathematics. 3. not having enough of a certain substance in it: He gave me a cup of *weak* coffee. **weaken** make *weak*: He was *weakened* by a long illness. **weakness** being *weak*: I cannot walk far because of the *weakness* in my legs. **weakling** a *weak* person or animal.

wealth 1. money and property: This man has acquired great *wealth*. 2. a great amount; a great number: I could give you a *wealth* of examples of brave actions. **wealthy** being rich: I have several *wealthy* friends.

weapon (weap-on) 1. any instrument used in attack or defence: My only *weapon* was a thick stick. 2. any means of getting one's own way: Her most powerful *weapon* is her good looks.

wear *wore*, *worn* 1. have on the body as covering, for use or for ornament: He *wore* a waistcoat, gold watch, and a bow tie. 2. make less useful by *wearing*: He *wore* a hole in his sleeve. 3. last: This cloth has *worn* very well. 4. pass slowly: As the day *wore* on we grew more and more tired. 5. gradual damage: This carpet is showing signs of *wear*. 6. use (of an article): I have had several years of hard *wear* from this suit. 7. things to

wear: In these shops you will find children's *wear*, men's *wear*, ladies' *wear*, foot*wear* and under*wear*.

weary (wea-ry) 1. tired: He was *weary* after the day's journey. 2. causing tiredness: We had a long, *weary* wait for the train. 3. make *weary*, become *weary*: You *weary* me with your excuses. **wearisome** tiring, boring, dull: We had to listen to a *wearisome* lecture.

weasel (wea-sel) a small animal with a long slender body and red-brown fur which feeds on rats, mice, birds' eggs etc.

weather (weath-er) 1. the state of the atmosphere, its heat, coldness, wetness, amount of wind etc.: What sort of *weather* did you have on your holidays? 2. expose to the *weather* to make it ready for use: This wood should not be used until it has been *weathered*. 3. last: The paint has *weathered* badly; it has peeled and lost its colour. 4. come through danger: This ship will *weather* any storm. **weathercock** a device, often shaped like a cock, put on top of a building to show the direction of the wind. **weatherproof** able to stand up to all kinds of *weather*: The traffic warden wears a long *weatherproof* coat.

weave *wove*, *woven* 1. make threads into cloth by crossing them over and under each other: She was *weaving* wool on a loom. 2. twist and turn: He *wove* in and out of the traffic. 3. the kind of *weaving* in a cloth: I prefer a loose *weave* for my suit. **weaver** a person who *weaves* cloth.

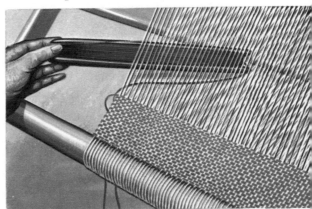

web 1. a thin silken network woven by spiders and other small creatures: A fly was caught in the spider's *web*. 2. the skin joining the toes of ducks and other birds that swim. **webbing** strong, woven material of various widths, used for upholstery, binding the edges of carpets etc.

wed marry: 'With this ring I thee *wed*' (from the wedding service). **wedding** the marriage ceremony: We have invited one hundred guests to the *wedding*.

wedge 1. an angled piece of wood or metal. 2. any substance of the same shape. 3. drive in a *wedge*: He *wedged* the door open. 4. force in like a *wedge*: He was *wedged* between two tall policemen.

Wednesday (Wednes-day) the fourth day of the week.

weed 1. a wild, unwanted plant growing in a garden: The lawn is full of *weeds*. 2. take out *weeds*: I have spent all morning *weeding*. **weeds** the black clothes and veil once worn by a widow. **weedy** having many *weeds*: This is a *weedy* patch of ground.

week a period of seven days beginning with Sunday: Tuesday is the third day of the *week*. **weekday** any day except Sunday: This museum is open on *weekdays*. **weekly** once a *week*, lasting a *week*: I draw my wages *weekly*. **weekend** the time from finishing work at the end of the *week*, usually Friday, to starting again, usually Monday morning.

weep *wept* cry, let tears fall from the eyes: I *wept* when my little dog died.

weigh 1. measure how heavy a thing is: Have you *weighed* yourself lately? 2. pull down through some cause: The tree is *weighed* down with fruit. 3. show a certain weight: How much does this sack of flour *weigh*?

weight 1. the amount a thing weighs: What is the *weight* of this sack of flour? 2. the force with which something is thrust down towards the earth: The roof gave way with the *weight* of the snow. 3. importance: I was convinced by the *weight* of his arguments. 4. a piece of metal used on a scale for measuring *weights*: On the counter stood a pile of metal *weights*. 5. something put on to make heavier or to keep in place: The pendulum of the clock had a heavy brass *weight* on the end. 6. put a *weight* on: The rope had been *weighted* with a heavy metal ring.

weir 1. a barrier, wall or dam put across a river to control its flow or direct it for running a mill, for supplying water to gardens, fields etc. 2. a fence or network put into a stream to catch fish.

weird strange, mysterious, ghost-like: Every night we hear *weird* sounds from the library.

welcome (wel-come) 1. a word of kindly greeting: *Welcome* home! 2. a joyful reception: They gave me a warm *welcome*. 3. receive with pleasure: They *welcomed* the hero with flags and banners. 4. permitted with pleasure: You are *welcome* to use my typewriter when you like. 5. gladly received: We had a *welcome* meal at the inn.

weld 1. join together pieces of metal by heat and pressure. 2. make more firm: Misfortune has served to *weld* our friendship. **welder** a person employed to *weld* metal.

welfare (wel-fare) 1. being healthy in body and mind: I am anxious for your *welfare*. 2. work devoted to helping people: I am engaged in work for old people's *welfare*.

well 1. in the right, satisfactory or desired way: Everything went *well* on holiday. 2. thoroughly: Shake the bottle *well* before using. 3. excellently: This job has been *well* done. 4. in good health: I hope you are keeping *well*. 5. satisfactory: All's *well* that ends *well*. 6. lucky: It was *well* for you that you were not there. 7. a hole or shaft in the ground usually lined with brick or stone, from which water is obtained: 'Ding, dong bell; pussy's in the *well*' (nursery rhyme). 8. a word used with other words whose meaning can be guessed: *well*-balanced; *well*-known; *well*-meant: meant with good intention; *well*-spoken: speaking politely or correctly; *well*-timed: said at just the right time etc.

wellingtons (wel-ling-tons) high waterproof boots made of rubber, reaching to the knees.

west The direction in which the sun sets: 'O young Lochinvar is come out of the *west*' (Sir Walter Scott).—Wales lies to the *west* of England. **westward** towards the *west*: We looked *westward* towards the setting sun. **westerly** 1. towards the *west*: We walked in a *westerly* direction. 2. (of winds) from the *west*: All day we faced a *westerly* (or *west*) wind. **western** 1. of, in, from the *west*: I live in the *western* part of the town. 2. a book or film dealing with life in the *west* of the United States particularly during the Indian wars: I have read three *westerns* this week.

wet 1. covered or soaked with water or other liquid: He washed the car with a *wet* sponge. 2. not hardened or dry: A notice on the door read '*Wet* paint'. 3. rainy: We have had a week of *wet* weather. 4. rain: Come in out of the *wet*. 5. soak, make *wet*: The wall should be well *wetted* before putting paper on.

whack 1. a hard blow: He gave the donkey a *whack* with his hand. 2. strike a hard blow. **whacking** a beating: 'You'll get a *whacking* for this,' he said.

whale a large sea animal, hunted for its oil and meat; the blue *whale* is the largest mammal on earth.

wharf a structure built on the shore or out into the water: A ship was being unloaded at the *wharf*.

what 1. a word which asks a question: *What* are you doing this evening?—*What* did it cost? 2. something that: I'll tell you *what* I'll do. 3. a word which exclaims: *What* a good idea! *What* a pity! **whatever** 1. *what*, anything that: He says *whatever* comes into his mind.—I'll do *whatever* I think best. 2. no matter *what*: He will fly the aeroplane *whatever* people say.

wheat grain from which white and brown flour is made and which is used for bread, cakes etc.: The *wheat* is ripening in the fields.

wheel 1. a circular object which turns on its centre: *Wheels* are used in all kinds of machinery and on vehicles such as carts, cars and bicycles. 2. push or pull a *wheeled* vehicle: Don't *wheel* your bicycle along the path. 3. turn in a curve or circle: Swallows were *wheeling* round the church steeple. **wheelbarrow** a small cart with one *wheel*, pulled or pushed by hand.

wheeze 1. breathe with a whistling sound: I had a cold last week and I'm still *wheezing*. 2. a bright idea, a cunning trick: I've thought of a good *wheeze* to make him hurry up.

whelk a small sea animal: with a spiral shell, like a snail. Some *whelks* are used as food.

when 1. a questioning word; at what time?: *When* are you coming to see me? 2. at the time, on the day: I'll see you on Thursday *when* I come to town. 3. although: Why do you catch a bus home *when* you can easily walk? **whenever** at whatever time: Come *whenever* you like.

where 1. in what place, at what place?: *Where* do you live? 2. to or from what place: *Where* are you going? 3. in, at, to a place: We can't find *where* the trouble lies. **wherever** in, at or to whatever place: *Wherever* did you get that hat?

whether (wheth-er) 1. if: I wonder *whether* we shall see him today. 2. a word introducing a single alternative: You never told me *whether* you preferred the photograph or the painting.

whey the liquid part of sour milk after the curds have been separated to make cheese.

which 1. what one? (of two or more): *Which* of these apples would you like? 2. that: The book *which* you need is on the top shelf. 3. from, to, behind, opposite, above, below a certain thing: The horse on *which* I rode has won the race.–The ground on *which* you stand was once a famous battlefield. **whichever** any one of a number: Take *whichever* book you like.

whiff a slight puff of wind, air, scent etc.: I caught a *whiff* of honeysuckle.

while 1. a certain time: I had to wait a *while* before I was served. 2. during the time that: He looked at the books *while* his uncle talked to the shopkeeper. 3. as long as: *While* there's life there's hope. 4. although: *While* I agree with you on some points, I still think you need to alter your plans. 5. pass (time) in an easy or pleasant manner: I *whiled* away a whole morning sitting in the park.

whim a sudden desire, often for something useless: He has enough money to satisfy every foolish *whim*.

whimper (whim-per) 1. cry with low, frightened or broken sounds: The puppy lay *whimpering* in a corner. 2. such a sound: The child gave a *whimper* of fright.

whine 1. utter a long, complaining cry or sound: We heard the dog *whining* in his kennel. 2. such a sound. **whinny** 1. the cry of a horse, usually to show pleasure. 2. utter such a cry: The pony *whinnied* when I entered his stall.

whip 1. a stick on which a cord or lash has been fastened, used for urging on a horse or for punishing: The jockey brought his *whip* down on the horse's side. 2. the member of a political party who is responsible for seeing that other members vote: The chief *whip* is in touch with absent members. 3. the order given by a political *whip*: A three-line *whip* (an urgent order to vote) demands the obedience of all members. 4. strike with a *whip*: 'She *whipped* them all soundly and put them to bed' (*The Old Woman Who Lived in a Shoe*). 5. beat eggwhites, cream etc. to make them stiff. 6. take, move or be moved quickly: He suddenly *whipped* out a revolver.

whippet (whip-pet) a small dog of an English breed, probably part greyhound, part terrier, used in racing and catching rabbits.

whirl 1. turn round or spin quickly: The dancers *whirled* round in a quick waltz. 2. go off; travel rapidly: Before we could refuse we were *whirled* off in his fast car. 3. (of the brain) be confused: His brain *whirled* at the thought of having so much money. 4. *whirling*: My mind is in a *whirl*. 5. things happening quickly one after another: I was suddenly flung into the *whirl* of city life. **whirlpool** water that goes round and round, sucking floating objects down when they reach the middle. **whirlwind** a violent wind that *whirls* round and round: Houses were destroyed in the recent *whirlwind*.

whirr or **whir** 1. make the buzzing sound of something moving fast: He pressed the button and the motor began to *whirr*. 2. such a sound: With a *whirr* of its wings, the pigeon flew away.

whisk 1. a small brush for removing dust from clothes etc.: She brushed his coat-collar with a *whisk*. 2. a small implement made of wire loops for whipping eggs, cream etc. 3. a quick sweeping movement: With a *whisk* of its tail the cow brushed off the flies. 4. move quickly through the air. 5. beat or whip eggs or cream. 6. take away, snatch quickly: She *whisked* the cloth off the table.

whiskers (whis-kers) 1. hair growing on the sides of a man's face: You will recognize my grandfather by his grey *whiskers*. 2. the hairs on the face which are shaved off each morning. 3. the long stiff hairs that grow about the mouth of a cat, mouse, rat and some other animals.

whisper (whis-per) 1. speak with soft, low sounds, using the breath: 'This is a secret,' she *whispered*. 2. talk secretly: It's *whispered* that they are going to get married. 3. make soft, low sounds; rustle: The leaves were *whispering* in the breeze. 4. something *whispered*, the act of *whispering*: I was forced to speak in a *whisper*.

whist a card game played by four players, two against two, with 52 cards.

whistle (whis-tle) 1. a sound produced by forcing air through a small space, by mouth, a pipe etc.: I heard a *whistle* behind me, and turned. 2. a device for producing such a sound: The referee blew his *whistle* for a free kick. 3. make the sound of a *whistle*: He walked down the street *whistling* gaily. 4. make a tune by *whistling*: He was *whistling* 'The British Grenadiers'. 5. pass quickly with a *whistling* sound: As we crossed the empty fields bullets *whistled* all round us.

white 1. the colour of snow: 'Your hair has become very *white*' (Lewis Carroll, *Alice's Adventures in Wonderland*). 2. the part of an egg between the yolk and the shell. 3. the *white* part of the eye. **whiten** make *white*: These walls need *whitening*. **white-wash** 1. a mixture of *white* materials in water used for *whitening* walls etc. 2. put on *whitewash*: I watched him *whitewashing* the cowshed.

whither (whith-er) where: 'Goosey, goosey gander, *whither* do you wander?' (nursery rhyme)

Whitsun (Whit-sun) the seventh Sunday after Easter. **Whitsuntide** the *Whitsun* weekend and the Monday following.

whiz make a humming or hissing sound as of something moving through the air: A stone *whizzed* past my head.

who 1. what person?: *Who* told you I was here?–*Who* is the man wearing the green jacket? 2. that: There was a man *who* had a dog. **whom, to whom,** from **whom,** with **whom**: to, from, with etc. a certain person: Is this the man to *whom* you gave the watch; the boy from *whom* you bought it; the girl with *whom* you went to the cinema?

whole 1. uninjured, undamaged or broken: There isn't a *whole* piece of furniture in the house. 2. complete: I have been here a *whole* day. 3. something that is complete: The *whole* of last year was spent in study.— This land is to be sold as a *whole* (not divided into parts). **wholesale** sold in large quantities, usually for sale again to the public: You can buy these articles at the *wholesale* price. **wholesome** good for the health, pure, sound: What you need is exercise and *wholesome* food.

whoop 1. a loud cry or shout, as made by children and warriors: The children received the news with *whoops* of joy.— We heard the savage *whoops* of the Indians as they attacked. 2. utter *whoops*. **whooping cough** a coughing disease of children in which they gasp, giving *whooping* sounds.

why 1. for what reason: *Why* have you come here? 2. for what purpose: *Why* do you want all this money?

wick 1. a length of thread running through the middle of a candle. 2. a strip of material in an oil lamp by which the oil is drawn up to be burnt: Before you light the lamp make sure that the *wick* is clean.

wicked (wick-ed) bad, evil: Little Red Riding Hood thought the *wicked* wolf was her grandmother.

wicker (wick-er) twigs or canes woven together, usually to make fences, furniture and baskets: The old lady sat in the garden in a *wicker* chair.

wicket (wick-et) 1. a small opening often closed by a sliding pane of glass at which tickets are sold or business is done. 2. in cricket, either of the two sets of sticks, each consisting of three stumps with two bails on top, before which the batsman stands. 3. the stretch of grass between the *wickets*. 4. the person who is batting: Four *wickets* fell for 24 runs. **wicket-keeper** the player who stands behind the *wicket* to stop balls, catch batsmen out etc. **wicket-gate** a small door or gate, usually made in or as part of a larger one.

wide 1. broad from side to side, not narrow: At the end of the day we came to a *wide* river. 2. open to the full extent: Open the window *wide*. 3. far from what was aimed at: The arrow went *wide* of the target. **widespread** spread over a large area: There is *widespread* famine in India. **widen** make *wide* or *wider*: This road is being *widened*. **width** 1. being *wide*: Do you know the *width* of this garden? 2. something of a certain *width*: We sell pieces of wood in various *widths*.

widow (wid-ow) a woman whose husband has died and who has not married again. **widower** a man whose wife has died and who has not married again.

wield hold and use something: The bricklayer *wields* a trowel; the author *wields* a pen; generals and statesmen *wield* power.

wife a married woman: 'Jack Sprat could eat no fat; his *wife* could eat no lean' (nursery rhyme).

wig a covering of hair for the head, worn to hide baldness, for disguise, theatricals etc.: *Wigs* were once worn in England by men as part of their ordinary dress.

wigwam (wig-wam) an American Indian hut or tent made with poles, on the top of which bark, mats and skins are laid.

wild 1. not tame: Lions, tigers and wolves are *wild* animals. 2. (of plants) not cultivated: We took the children into the field to pick *wild* flowers. 3. deserted, not settled by man, barren: We love the *wild* scenery of the Scottish highlands. 4. not in order, in confusion: The hall was in *wild* disorder after the crowd left. 5. uncultivated lands: He spent six months in the *wilds* of South America. **wildly** in a confused way: He talked *wildly* of running away to sea. **wilderness** a deserted expanse of land or water: For many years the Israelites wandered in the *wilderness*.

will *won't, would, wouldn't* 1. show something in the future: You *will* come with me to the circus, *won't* you? 2. something that cannot be helped or controlled: I pushed the door but it *wouldn't* open. 3. the statement written by a person concerning the future of his property after his death: All the relatives met in the library to hear the solicitor read the *will*. 4. leave property and money by making a written *will* or statement: He has *willed* his house and lands to his eldest son. 5. the power to affect one's actions and those of others: He had no *will* of his own. 6. determination: He has the *will* to succeed. **wilful** 1. obstinate, determined to have one's own way: She is a *wilful* child. 2. intended, thought out beforehand: The prisoner was accused of *wilful* murder. **willing** ready to do what is asked or needed: Are you *willing* to set him free?

willow (wil-low) a tree; the wood of a tree with tough branches which bend easily: *Willow* is used for making cricket bats, and *willow* twigs for making baskets.

wilt lose strength, droop: These flowers are *wilting* and need water.

wily (wi-ly) cunning: The *wily* fox crouched in his hole as the huntsmen galloped past.

win *won* 1. achieve by effort: He has *won* a scholarship to the university. 2. achieve by chance: He *won* a large sum of money on the pools. 3. be successful in a contest: We all cheered when our team *won*. 4. success in a contest: We have had five *wins* this season. **winner** a person or animal that *wins*: The champion jockey has ridden another *winner*.

wince flinch, start as in pain: The doctor inserted the needle but the boy did not even *wince*.

winch 1. a machine for pulling or lifting: A *winch* is used to draw the boats up on to the shore. 2. use a *winch*: The motorcar had to be *winched* out of the ditch.

wind 1. air which is moving: There's a strong *wind* today. 2. breath: I ran until I had no more *wind*. 3. gas formed inside the body making one feel uncomfortable: The baby had *wind* and her mother had to pat her back. 4. take away the breath: A punch on the chest *winded* him and he fell to the floor.

wind (rhymes with *mind*) *wound* 1. twist and turn: The river *winds* its way through the valley. 2. twist or wrap round: The climber *wound* the rope round his waist. 3. turn a handle to move weights or *wind* up springs: He took the key and *wound* up the church clock.

window (win-dow) an opening to let in light and air, usually filled by a movable sheet of glass: The *windows* were spattered with rain. **windowpane** the pane of glass which is set in a *window*.

wine 1. an intoxicating drink made from the fermented juice of the grape: The most famous *wines* in the world are French. 2. a fermented drink resembling *wine* but made from fruits, leaves, herbs etc.: Would you like a glass of my celery *wine*?

wing 1. that organ of a bird, insect or the part of a machine which keeps it in the air when flying: The eagle spread its *wings* and flew away. 2. part of a building situated to one side of the central part: The public is only admitted to the west *wing* of the house. 3. that part of an army situated to one side of the centre: In the battle of Crécy the Black Prince commanded the right *wing* of the English army. 4. places to the right and left of the stage in a theatre: The scene-shifters and the producer stood in the *wings*. 5. in football, hockey, etc. the person at the far right or left of the forward line: The left *wing* carried the ball forward and the centre forward scored. 6. fly: The summer is over and the swallows are *winging* their way south.

wink 1. close and open the eyes or one eye quickly: When he *winked* at me I knew it was time to go. 2. give a regular short flash of light: The light in the lighthouse began to *wink* shortly after sunset. 3. twinkle: Millions of stars *winked* in the sky. 4. a very short time: I haven't slept a *wink* all night.

winkle (win-kle) a peri*winkle*, a small sea-snail used as food.

winter (win-ter) the coldest season of the year beginning in December and ending in March in the northern hemisphere, and beginning in June and ending in September in the southern: We are going to Switzerland for the *winter* sports. **wintry** having to do with *winter*: What *wintry* weather we are having!

wipe make clean by rubbing: She *wiped* the table with a dishcloth. **wiper** something that *wipes*: I have had a pair of new windscreen *wipers* fitted to the car.

wire 1. a piece of flexible metal made into a cord or thread: The field was protected by a barbed *wire* fence. 2. a telegram: Send me a *wire* as soon as you reach home. 3. fasten with *wire*: The roses had to be *wired*. 4. supply electricity to a building: The electricians had to *wire* the house again. 5. send a telegram: He *wired* me to say when he would arrive. **wireworm** a common garden worm which eats the roots of plants. **wireless** radio: Marconi was the inventor of *wireless* telegraphy. **wiry** (of a person) lean with strong muscles: One has to be *wiry* to be a long-distance runner.

wise having the power to know and to judge what is true or right: The king called together all his *wise* men. **wisdom** being *wise*: He had the *wisdom* to say nothing.

wish 1. want, desire: I *wish* she would come. 2. hope for a person: I *wish* you a pleasant journey. 3. a desire: You don't pay any attention to my *wishes*. 4. that which is *wished*: At last I have got my *wish*. **wishbone** the forked bone in front of the breastbone in most birds.

wisp a handful, small bundle, a lock: He had a *wisp* of straw in his hair.

wistful (wist-ful) showing longing, desire: He cast a *wistful* glance at the plate of cakes.

wit 1. intelligence, quickness of mind: He hadn't the *wit* to see that he was being deceived. 2. humour: His conversation is full of *wit*. **wits** intelligence; mind: I'm driven out of my *wits* by all this noise. **witty** having a sense of humour; humorous: We all laughed at his *witty* speech.

witch a person, usually a woman, who supposedly practises magic: 'A *witch* drives back our troops' (Shakespeare, *Henry VI, part I*). **witchcraft** the use of magic. **witchdoctor** a man among primitive peoples, supposed to possess magic powers.

with 1. having: He is talking to the girl *with* blue eyes. 2. covering, filling: The cottage is thatched *with* straw. 3. by means of: He was digging *with* a spade. 4. accompanied by: Are you coming *with* me? 5. against: Great Britain was at war *with* France. 6. in a certain way or manner: His speech was received *with* applause. 7. in the same direction as: We were drifting *with* the stream. 8. from: I parted *with* him at the station. 9. in the care of, in the possession of: Leave it *with* me. 10. in agreement; in understanding: Jesus said, 'He that is not *with* me is against me.'

withdraw (with-draw) *withdrew, withdrawn* 1. take back: The charge against the prisoner was *withdrawn*. 2. draw or move back: After a fierce bombardment the enemy *withdrew* to stronger positions.

wither (with-er) fade, become dry or lifeless: The flowers have *withered* and must be thrown away.

withhold (with-hold) *withheld* keep or hold back: The information about the fire has been *withheld* until further enquiries have been made.

within (with-in) 1. inside: Not a single house *within* the walls of the town was left standing. 2. inside the bounds or limits of: You must try to live *within* your income.

without (with-out) 1. not having, lacking: We can't do the work *without* the tools. 2. (not used in conversation) outside. 'There is a green hill far away *without* a city wall' (hymn).

withstand (with-stand) *withstood* resist, hold out against: 'They have won the bridge, killing all those that *withstood* them' (Shakespeare, *Henry VI, part 2*).

witness (wit-ness) 1. a person who is present and sees an event and who, because of this, can give evidence in a court of law: There were no *witnesses* to the burglary. 2. evidence: I can bear *witness* to the truth of what he says. 3. a person signing a document to testify that another person's signature is genuine: I am a *witness* to my brother's will. 4. give evidence in court. 5. be present and see: I have *witnessed* many strange things in my life. 6. act as a *witness*: I have *witnessed* my brother's will.

wizard (wiz-ard) a person who supposedly practises magic: Merlin was a famous *wizard* in the days of King Arthur.

wobble (wob-ble) 1. move or make something move unsteadily, or from side to side: Don't *wobble* the table or you'll spill the tea. 2. an unsteady movement: This car has a bad wheel *wobble*; the wheels are not in line.

woe an old word meaning sorrow, distress: 'Heaven shield your grace from *woe*' (Shakespeare, *Measure for Measure*).

wolf *wolves* a wild animal related to the dog: We were followed through the snow by a pack of hungry *wolves*. **wolf cub** the young of the *wolf*. **wolfhound** a dog originally bred for hunting *wolves*.

woman (wo-man) *women* an adult female person: 'There was an old *woman* who lived in a shoe' (nursery rhyme).

wonder (won-der) 1. a feeling of awe, admiration or surprise: We gazed in *wonder* at the great waterfall. 2. something that causes the feeling of *wonder*: The pyramids of Egypt are among the *wonders* of the ancient world. 3. have a feeling of *wonder*: I *wonder* that you should ever have thought of trusting him. 4. be curious about something: 'Perchance you *wonder* at this show; but *wonder* on, till truth make all things plain' (Shakespeare, *A Midsummer Night's Dream*). **wonderful** causing *wonder* or admiration: The orchestra gave a *wonderful* performance.

wood 1. the hard part of a tree that is under the bark, used for making useful articles, for burning etc.: What kind of *wood* is this staircase made of?—Put some more *wood* on the fire. 2. land with trees growing on it: The children were lost in the *wood*. **woodwork** 1. things made of *wood*: The *woodwork* in this room is rotten. 2. carpentry: *Woodwork* is my favourite hobby. **woodland** land covered with *woods*. **wooden** made of *wood*: The Greeks dragged a *wooden* horse up to the walls of Troy.

wool 1. the fine, soft, curly hair of sheep, made into yarn, cloth and garments: The kitten was playing with a ball of *wool*. 2. material like *wool*, made from other substances: He plugged his ears with cotton *wool*. **woollen** made of *wool*: He wore a thick *woollen* jersey. **woolly** soft, like *wool*.

word 1. a sound or a group of sounds standing for a single idea: I could tell from her *words* that she was angry. 2. the sounds represented in printing or writing: I have read every *word* in this book. 3. a remark, something said: May I have a *word* with you? 4. news: Have you had *word* of your brother in Australia? 5. promise: 'Here lies our sovereign lord, the King, whose *word* no man relies on' (The Earl of Rochester's epitaph on Charles II). 6. command, order: The commander gave the *word* to fire.

work 1. the use of one's powers of body or mind to do or make something: It was hard *work* mending the damaged wheel. 2. what one does to make a living: He starts *work* at nine o'clock in the morning. 3. something to be done, not for a living: I have just done a day's *work* in the garden. 4. something to be *worked* on: I take my *work* with me on holiday. 5. do *work*: I *work* on the buses. 6. act or move as something should: The lift is not *working*. 7. get into a certain state: The doorknob has *worked* loose. 8. achieve something by *working*: He *worked* his passage to America. **worker** *work*man, a person who *works*: All the *workers* received an increase in wages. **works** 1. places to which people go to *work*, a factory: The brick*works* and the iron*works* are closed for the holidays. 2. the *working* parts of anything mechanical. **workshop** a room or building in which *work* is done.

world 1. the earth and mankind: Sir Francis Drake sailed round the *world*. 2. of all the *world*: Grandfather was wounded in the First *World* War. 3. part of the *world*: Great Britain is in the Old *World*, the United States is in the New *World* and both are in the English-speaking *world*. 4. people connected with special interests: This magazine will interest the *world* of sport. 5. one group of created things: There is nothing like it in the whole animal *world*. 6. a great deal: These pills will do you the *world* of good. **worldwide** spread through the *world*: He has gained *worldwide* fame as a singer.

worm 1. a small creature without limbs or spine that lives in the ground: The bird flew off with a *worm* in its beak. 2. go slowly and patiently through difficulties: He *wormed* his way through the dark cave. 3. get to know something by continual trying: She *wormed* the secret out of me.

worry (wor-ry) 1. feel uneasy and anxious: I'm *worried* in case something has happened to him. 2. cause trouble to others: He's always *worrying* me for money. 3. take with the teeth and shake: This dog has been *worrying* sheep. 4. uneasiness, anxious feelings: Business *worries* have made him ill.

worse the opposite of better: If my work is better than yours, your work is *worse* than mine. **worst** *worse* than any of the same kind: It is the *worst* weather we have had for a long time.

worship (wor-ship) 1. respect and revere God, a god or sacred person: The ancient Greeks *worshipped* many gods. 2. the title given to certain officers such as mayors and magistrates: 'Not guilty, Your *Worship*,' answered the prisoner.

worth 1. having a value equal to: How much do you think this watch is *worth*? 2. having property equal to a certain value: The old man died *worth* thousands of pounds. 3. good enough for: Westminster Abbey is well *worth* visiting.— This book is *worth* reading. **worthwhile** *worth* the time and trouble: I hope you will find the journey to London *worthwhile*. **worthless** of no value: I thought this was a diamond but it's *worthless*. **worthy** deserving: You will find him a *worthy* successor to the late headmaster.

wound 1. an injury to the body of a living being: He suffered severe scalp *wounds* in the accident. 2. inflict a *wound*: A number of soldiers were severely *wounded* in battle.

wrangle (wran-gle pronounced *rangel*) quarrel or argue noisily: They were *wrangling* as to who should have the largest share.

wrap (pronounced *rap*) 1. enclose, roll up in something: He *wrapped* himself in his blanket and fell asleep. 2. roll or fold in so as to cover or protect: He *wrapped* the book in paper and tied it with string. 3. be interested in: He's totally *wrapped* up in his hobby of model-making. **wrapper** a covering in which a newspaper or book is sent by post: He took the book out of its *wrapper*. **wrapping** material in which things are *wrapped*: This china is delicate and needs plenty of *wrapping*.

wreath (pronounced *reeth*) 1. flowers woven into a circle, used as a garland to put on the head or for placing on a grave: She wore a *wreath* of roses. 2. a curling line of smoke or mist: A *wreath* of smoke curled up from the chimney. **wreathe** cover, make a circle round, curl upwards: 'About his neck a green and gilded snake had *wreathed* itself' (Shakespeare, *As You Like It*).

wreck (pronounced *reck*) 1. ruin; destruction of a ship; something destroyed: Nothing was saved from the *wreck*. 2. a person who has been in some way damaged or hurt: The failure of his business left him a nervous *wreck*. 3. bring about a *wreck*: The lorry ran off the road and was *wrecked*. **wreckage** the fragments left after a *wreck*: The *wreckage* is being examined to find out the cause of the disaster

wren (pronounced *ren*) a small brown bird with a short tail and small wings, common in England: The *wren* eats small insects and lays its eggs among ferns, grass and leaves.

wrench (pronounced *rench*) 1. a sharp twist or pull: He gave the handle a *wrench* and it broke off. 2. a feeling of pain through separation: It was a great *wrench* to part with my children. 3. a tool for gripping, holding and turning. 4. twist or pull violently: He *wrenched* the stick out of the dog's mouth. 5. injure by twisting: I *wrenched* my ankle in a rabbit hole.

wrest (pronounced *rest*) 1. take away quickly by force: She *wrested* the pistol out of his hand. 2. achieve by great effort: He tried to *wrest* a living out of the barren soil.

wrestle (wres-tle pronounced *restle*) 1. take part in a contest in which two persons try to throw or force each other to the ground. 2. deal with a difficult task: I *wrestled* all evening with the problem but could not solve it.

wretch (pronounced *retch*) 1. an unfortunate person: The poor *wretch* was in rags. 2. a mean, wicked person: 'This *wretch* has partly confessed his villainy' (Shakespeare, *Othello*).

wretched (wretch-ed pronounced *retched*) 1. very unfortunate, miserable: This headache makes me feel *wretched*. 2. bad: What *wretched* weather we are having.

wriggle (wrig-gle pronounced *riggle*) 1. twist to and fro, squirm: The worm was *wriggling* along the garden path. 2. get out of trouble: He can *wriggle* out of any difficulty. 3. make something *wriggle*: Don't *wriggle* your toes when I'm putting on your socks. 4. a *wriggling* movement: One more *wriggle* and I was through the hole in the fence.

wring (pronounced *ring*) *wrung* 1. squeeze by twisting: I had to *wring* out my clothes after falling in the stream. 2. get something by hard effort: At last I *wrung* the truth from him. **wringer** a device with two rollers for taking the water out of anything wet; a mangle.

wrinkle (wrin-kle pronounced *rinkle*) 1. a small fold on a surface: The old man's face was full of *wrinkles*. 2. form *wrinkles* easily: This material *wrinkles* badly and needs frequent ironing.

wrist (pronounced *rist*) 1. the joint between the hand and the arm: He gripped my *wrist* to feel my pulse. 2. that part of the sleeve which goes round the *wrist*: My shirtsleeve is too tight at the *wrist*. **wristwatch** a watch worn on the *wrist*.

write (pronounced *rite*) wrote, written 1. make letters, words or other symbols which give a meaning: He hasn't learned to *write* yet. 2. produce from one's own mind a book, novel, play etc.: Shakespeare *wrote* plays and poetry. 3. *write* and send a message: I haven't *written* to my parents this week. **writer** a person who *writes*, an author: Dickens is my favourite *writer*. **writing** something *written*: I can't read your *writing*.

wrong (pronounced *rong*) 1. not right, not good, unjust: It was *wrong* of you to stay out so late. 2. not correct: We went the *wrong* way. 3. not in good order: There's something *wrong* with our television set. 4. that which is *wrong*: 'The king can do no *wrong*' (Sir William Blackstone). 5. treat unjustly: 'If you *wrong* us, shall we ...ot revenge?' (Shakespeare, *The Merchant of Venice*)

wry (pronounced *ry*) (of the face) twisted; the mouth pulled out of shape to show disappointment, displeasure etc.: He answered with a *wry* smile.

X

X-ray a ray that can penetrate solid substances and make it possible to see into or through them: The *X-ray* photograph showed that he had a broken wrist.

xylophone (xy-lo-phone pronounced *zylofone*) a musical instrument consisting of wooden bars of different lengths, each of which when struck produces a different note: A *xylophone* is played with small wooden hammers.

Y

yacht (rhymes with *dot*) 1. a boat with sails, used for pleasure and racing: We spent the day on my uncle's *yacht*. 2. a boat driven by an engine or motor: The princess is cruising in the royal *yacht*. 3. travel, sail or race in a *yacht*: We spent our holidays *yachting*.

yap 1. give short, sharp barks: The dog *yaps* every time there is a knock on the door. 2. a short, sharp bark.

yard 1. a space usually enclosed by a wall or fence: She was hanging out washing in the *yard*.—Children were playing in the school *yard*. 2. a measure equal to 36 inches or 3 feet: A *yard*, which is shorter than a metre, is a unit of measurement used in some English-speaking countries. **yardstick** a measuring-rod a *yard* in length. **the Yard** Scotland *Yard*, the branch of the police force engaged in criminal investigation.

yarn 1. thread which has been specially made for weaving or knitting: The weavers had to be sent home from the factory because of a shortage of *yarn*. 2. a story, a tale told by a sailor or traveller: 'All I ask is a merry *yarn* from a laughing fellow-rover' (John Masefield, *Sea-fever*).

yawn 1. open the mouth wide as one does when sleepy: The speech went on so long that people began to *yawn*. 2. stretch wide open: At our feet was the *yawning* crater of the volcano. 3. the act of *yawning*: He gave a *yawn*, stretched, and fell asleep.

year 1. the time it takes the earth to move once round the sun; $365\frac{1}{4}$ days. 2. the period divided into twelve months from January 1st to December 31st: In the *year* 1961 Major Yuri Gagarin made the first flight in space. 3. any period of 365 days: Today I shall have been in England a *year*. 4. age: He looks old for his *years*. **yearly** every *year*, once a *year*: The *yearly* profits of this firm are increasing.—Next week I shall pay you my usual *yearly* visit. **yearling** an animal between one and two *years* old. **leap year** a *year* of 366 days, coming once in four *years*.

yearn long for very much; want greatly: I *yearn* to see my son again.

yeast a yellowish substance used in baking to make dough rise and liquids such as beer and wine ferment.

yell 1. cry out with a loud, clear sound: A blow on the jaw made him *yell* with pain. 2. a loud, sharp cry: The speaker was greeted with *yells* of defiance.

yellow (yel-low) 1. a bright colour like that of butter, lemons and gold: The fields were full of *yellow* buttercups. 2. become *yellow*: The *yellowing* corn will soon be ready for reaping.

yeoman (yeo-man) *yeomen* in old England, a farmer who owned land: 'The freemen were the *yeomen*, the freemen of England' (Edward German, *Merrie England*). **Yeomen of the Guard** members of the royal bodyguard of the English sovereign.

yes a word expressing agreement: Can you help me? *Yes*, I can.

yesterday (yes-ter-day) the day before today: We arrived home from holiday *yesterday*.

yet 1. up to now: Has he finished the work *yet*? 2. at some time to come: 'You'll make a good farmer *yet*,' he said. 3. still: It's a hard job, *yet* it's worth while.

yield 1. produce: This field has *yielded* a good harvest. 2. give way, give in: Though defeated he refused to *yield* the fort. 3. the amount produced: There has been an excellent *yield* of fruit this season.

yoga (yo-ga) a system of meditation and self-control first practised in India. **yogi** one who practises *yoga*.

yoghourt, yoghurt, yogurt (yog-hourt) a food resembling custard prepared from milk that has been fermented.

yonder (yon-der) there, in that place: 'On *yonder* hill there stands a creature; who she is I do not know' (*Oh no, John*).

you the person or persons to whom one is speaking: I'll tell *you* a story. **your** belonging to *you*, having to do with *you*: Give me *your* promise. **yours** something belonging to you: Are these keys *yours*? **yourself** *you*: *you* must clean *your* shoes *yourself*. **yourselves** *you* (of more than one): come in and make *yourselves* comfortable.

young 1. being in the early stages of life, not old: This tree is too *young* to bear fruit. 2. near the beginning: The night is still *young*. 3. *young* people, *young* animals: We publish books for the *young*.—At the zoo we saw a lioness with her *young*.

youth 1. the state or time of being young: I was a good cricket player in my *youth*. 2. a young man: 'Thou art a gallant *youth*' (Shakespeare, *As You Like It*). 3. provided for young people: I will see you at the *youth* club. **youthful** young: She still looks extremely *youthful*.

yule, yuletide the Christmas season. **yule log** a log of wood traditionally burnt on Christmas Eve.

Z

zeal enthusiasm: He showed great *zeal* in studying for the examination. **zealous** full of enthusiasm.

zebra (ze-bra) a wild animal, resembling a horse, which lives in Africa: A *zebra* has black and white stripes on its body. **zebra crossing** a place on a road marked with black and white stripes where people may cross safely.

zenith (zen-ith) 1. the part of the sky directly overhead. 2. the highest point: At the age of forty he was at the *zenith* of his popularity.

zephyr (zeph-yr) a gentle breeze: 'Twin roses by the *zephyr* blown apart' (John Keats).

zero (ze-ro) 1. the figure 0. 2. the figure 0 on a thermometer or on other dials: Last night the temperature fell below *zero* and the pond froze.

zest great interest, glad enthusiasm: We started to produce the play with great *zest*.

zigzag (zig-zag) 1. darting here and there: He drew a *zigzag* line to represent lightning. 2. move here and there, making sharp turns: The ship had to *zigzag* to avoid being struck by torpedoes.

zinc a bluish-white metal used in coating iron sheets to protect them against rust.

zip a device in which metal teeth are made to lock together to unite (or separate) two edges: *Zip*-fasteners are put on bags and on articles of clothing to take the place of buttons.

zither (zith-er) a musical instrument consisting of a flat box with strings stretched over it: The *zither* is placed on a flat surface and played with the fingertips.

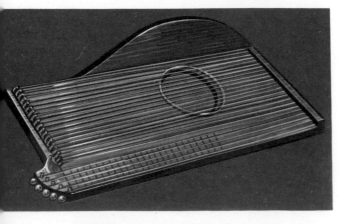

zodiac (zo-di-ac) an imaginary belt of the heavens in which lie the paths of the sun, the moon and the principal planets: The *zodiac* was divided by ancient peoples into twelve equal parts known as the signs of the *zodiac*. Each of these parts still has its own name.

zone 1. an area set aside for some special purpose: The parking *zone* extends along both sides of the street. 2. one of the five belts into which the earth's surface is divided: The torrid (or hot) *zone* is nearest the equator and the frigid (or cold) *zones* contain the north and south poles. 3. an area in which something is being carried on: During the floods people were evacuated from the danger *zone*.

zoo, zoological gardens a place where the public may go to see animals of all kinds. **zoology** (zo-ol-o-gy) the science that deals with animals or the animal kingdom.

zoom 1. a low, deep, humming sound: Overhead we heard the *zoom* of aeroplanes. 2. go at a high speed, making such a sound: The racing cars *zoomed* past us on the track. **zoom lens** a lens on a camera which can magnify distant objects, making them appear closer.